The Global Future

A Brief Introduction to World Politics

THIRD EDITION

CHARLES W. KEGLEY, JR.
Carnegie Council for Ethics in International Affairs

GREGORY A. RAYMOND
Boise State University

WADSWORTH
CENGAGE Learning™

Australia • Brazil • Japan • Korea • Mexico • Singapore • Spain • United Kingdom • United States

WADSWORTH
CENGAGE Learning™

The Global Future, Third Edition
Charles W. Kegley, Jr.,
Gregory A. Raymond

Executive Editor: Carolyn Merrill

Development Editor: Rebecca Green

Assistant Editor: Katherine Hayes

Marketing Manager: Amy Whitaker

Marketing Communications Manager:
Heather Baxley

Print Buyer: Judy Inouye

Permissions Editor: Roberta Broyer

Production Service: Lori Hazzard, Macmillan
Publishing Solutions

Photo Manager: Dean Dauphinais

Photo Researcher: Jaime Jankowski

Cover Designer: Blue Bungalow Design

Cover Image: ©Fotolia

Compositor: Macmillan Publishing
Solutions

For product information and technology assistance, contact us at
Cengage Learning Customer & Sales Support,
1-800-354-9706
For permission to use material from this text or product, submit all
requests online at
www.cengage.com/permissions.
Further permissions questions can be e-mailed to
permissionrequest@cengage.com.

Library of Congress Control Number: 2008938610

Student Edition:

ISBN-13: 978-0-495-56927-5

ISBN-10: 0-495-56927-5

Wadsworth
20 Channel Center Street
Boston, MA 02210
USA

Cengage Learning products are represented in Canada by Nelson Education,
Ltd.

For your course and learning solutions, visit **www.cengage.com.**
Purchase any of our products at your local college store or at our preferred
online store **www.ichapters.com.**

Printed in the United States of America
2 3 4 5 6 7 13 12 11 10 09

*To my wife Debbie, and to the Carnegie Council for
Ethics in International Affairs*
—Charles W. Kegley, Jr.

To Bethine Church and to the Frank Church Institute
—Gregory A. Raymond

Brief Contents

MAPS   xiv
PREFACE   xv
ABOUT THE AUTHORS   xxi

PART I   Trend and Transformation in World Politics   1

    1   Exploring Twenty-First-Century World Politics   3

    2   Theories of World Politics   27

PART II   The Actors in World Politics   55

    3   Foreign Policy Decision Making   56

    4   Great-Power Rivalry and the Lure of Hegemony: Cycles of War and Peace in Modern World History   80

    5   Rich and Poor in World Politics: The Plight of the Global South   106

    6   Nonstate Actors and the Challenge of Global Governance   139

PART III   The Politics of Global Security   175

    7   Armed Conflict in the Twenty-First Century   176

    8   Military Power and National Security in a Turbulent World   203

    9   Realist Paths to Peace: Alliances, Arms Control, and the Balance of Power   231

    10   Liberal and Constructivist Paths to Peace: International Norms, Institutions, and Integration   255

PART IV   The Politics of Global Welfare   285

    11   The Globalization of World Politics   286

    12   Trade and Monetary Relations in a Global Political Economy   310

    13   Human Rights and the Quest for Global Justice   340

    14   Population Dynamics and Global Environmental Politics   363

PART V   Alternative World Futures   391

    15   Prospects for a New World Order   392

GLOSSARY   407
REFERENCES   418
INDEX   439

Contents

MAPS   xiv
PREFACE   xv
ABOUT THE AUTHORS   xxi

PART I   Trend and Transformation in World Politics   1

1   Exploring Twenty-First-Century World Politics   3

Continuity and Change in World Politics   6

How Perceptions Influence Images of Reality   10

The Nature and Sources of Images   10

*CONTROVERSY: Should We Believe What We
See? The Organization of Observation and Projections
of Global Realities   11*

The Role of Images in World Politics   14

APPLICATION: Seeing the World through Foreign Eyes   15

A Framework for Examining World Politics   16

Levels of Analysis   16

Time Sequences   18

Applying the Framework to the Cold War's End   19

Facing the Future   20

The Investigative Challenge   22

The Plan of the Book   23

2   Theories of World Politics   27

Contending Theories of World Politics   29

Realist Theory   29

The Realist Worldview   29

The Evolution of Realist Thought   31

The Limitations of Realism   32

Liberal Theory   33

The Liberal Worldview   33

The Evolution of Liberal Thought   35

The Limitations of Liberalism   37

APPLICATION: Steel and Good Intentions   39

Constructivist Theory   40

The Constructivist Worldview   40

The Evolution of Constructivist Thought   40

The Limitations of Constructivism   43

What's Missing in Theories of World Politics?   44

The Radical Critique   44

The Feminist Critique   46

Forecasting the Global Future with Theories of
World Politics   47

*CONTROVERSY: Can Behavioral Science Advance the
Study of World Politics?   49*

PART II   The Actors in World Politics   55

3   Foreign Policy Decision Making   56

Explaining Foreign Policy   59

The Emergence of the Modern State System   59

The Determinants of States' Foreign Policy Behavior   60

International Sources of Foreign Policy   61

Polarity and Polarization   62

Geostrategic Position   62

Domestic Sources of Foreign Policy   63

Military Capabilities   64

Economic Conditions   64

Type of Government   65

Organizational Processes and Politics   68

APPLICATION: Bureaucratic Games   70

Individual Sources of Foreign Policy   70

Leaders as the Makers of the Global Future   71

Factors Affecting the Capacity to Lead   71

CONTROVERSY: Policy and Personality: Do Leaders Make a Difference?   72

Constraints on the Foreign Policy-Making Process   73

4   Great-Power Rivalry and the Lure of Hegemony: Cycles of War and Peace in Modern World History   80

Long Cycles of World Leadership   83

The First World War   83

The Causes of World War I   85

The Consequences of World War I   86

The Second World War   88

The Causes of World War II   89

The Consequences of World War II   92

The Cold War   93

The Causes and Evolutionary Course of the Cold War   93

CONTROVERSY: Was Ideology the Primary Source of East–West Conflict?   95

The Consequences of the Cold War   98

The Future of Great-Power Politics   99

America's Unipolar Moment   99

From Unipolarity to Multipolarity?   101

APPLICATION: Integrate, but Hedge   102

5   Rich and Poor in World Politics: The Plight of the Global South   106

Global Inequalities   109

The Colonial Experience of the Global South   111

The First Wave of European Imperialism   112

The Second Wave of European Imperialism   114

Self-Determination and Decolonization   116

North and South Today: Worlds Apart   117

Why Do North-South Disparities Persist?   119

Internal Factors: Classical Economic Development Theory's Interpretation   120

External Factors: Dependency Theory's Interpretation   120

Can the Economic Gap Be Closed?   122

The Global South's Foreign
Policy Response   123

In Search of Security   123

In Search of Prosperity   125

*CONTROVERSY: Multinational Corporations in the
Global South: Do They Help or Hurt?   131*

APPLICATION: Development, Democracy, and Debt   133

The Future of the Global South   135

**6   Nonstate Actors and the Challenge of Global
Governance   139**

Types of Nonstate Actors   141

Global Intergovernmental Organizations   144

The United Nations   144

Other Prominent Global IGOs   151

Regional Intergovernmental Organizations   154

The European Union   155

Other Regional IGOs   158

Nongovernmental Organizations   159

Ethnopolitical Movements   160

Religious Movements   161

*CONTROVERSY: Are Religious Movements Causes
of War or Sources of Transnational Harmony?   164*

Multinational Corporations and Transnational Banks   164

Issue-Advocacy Groups and Global Civil Society   168

Nonstate Actors and the Global Future   170

*APPLICATION: Mixed-Actor Approaches
to Global Diplomacy   170*

PART III   The Politics of Global Security   175

7   Armed Conflict in the Twenty-First Century   176

Trends in Armed Conflict   178

What Causes Armed Conflict?   181

The First Level of Analysis: Human Nature   181

APPLICATION: When Is It Worth Going To War?   183

The Second Level of Analysis: Internal Characteristics of States   *184*

CONTROVERSY: Does Nationalistic Love of Country Cause War with Foreign Nations?   *186*

The Third Level of Analysis: System Structure and Processes   *189*

The Future of Armed Conflict   192

The New Global Terrorism   *195*

Counterterrorism   *196*

8   Military Power and National Security in a Turbulent World   203

Power in World Politics   205

The Elements of State Power   *205*

Globalization and the Changing Nature of State Power   *206*

CONTROVERSY: Does High Military Spending Lower Human Security?   *207*

The Pursuit of Military Capability   208

Trends in Military Spending   *208*

Trends in the Weapons Trade   *210*

Trends in Weapons Technology   *211*

Military Strategy in the Nuclear Age   215

Compellence   *216*

Deterrence   *217*

Preemption   *218*

The Limits of Coercive Diplomacy   221

The Persuasive Use of Military Force   *221*

Economic Sanctions   *224*

APPLICATION: Who is Penalizing Whom?   *225*

Building World Security   227

9   Realist Paths to Peace: Alliances, Arms Control, and the Balance of Power   231

Realism and the Balancing of Power   234

Assumptions of Balance-of-Power Theory   *235*

Managing the Balance through a Concert of Great Powers   *239*

Stabilizing Power Balances through Arms Control   240

Arms Control versus Disarmament   *241*

Bilateral Arms Control and Disarmament   *241*

APPLICATION: Conflict Spirals and Self-Defeating Behavior 243

Multilateral Arms Control and Disarmament 243

The Problematic Future of Arms Control and Disarmament 244

Balancing Power in the Contemporary International System 245

The Cold War Pattern of Direct Opposition 246

A Future of Balance-of-Power Competition? 247

*CONTROVERSY: How Should the United States Respond
to China's Growing Power? 248*

**10 Liberal and Constructivist Paths to Peace: International
Norms, Institutions, and Integration 255**

International Legal Norms and World Order 259

Sovereignty and the Rules of International Law 259

The Limitations of International Law 261

International Law and the Preservation of Peace 263

CONTROVERSY: Was the War in Iraq Just? 265

APPLICATION: The Doctrine of International Community 269

International Institutions and World Order 272

The League of Nations and Collective Security 272

The United Nations and Peacekeeping 273

Regional Security Organizations and Collective Defense 275

International Integration and World Order 278

World Government 278

Regional Integration 279

PART IV   The Politics of Global Welfare 285

11 The Globalization of World Politics 286

What Is Globalization? 289

The Global Information Age 289

Globalization or Americanization? 291

The Economics of Globalization 294

The Globalization of Trade 295

The Globalization of Finance 299

APPLICATION: Markets and Economic Interdependence 301

The Challenges of a Borderless World 302

Global Ecopolitics 302

Global Health 302

Global Migration   303

Global Governance or Backlash?   305

*CONTROVERSY: Does Globalization Mean the End
of the Age of Nation-States?   306*

12   Trade and Monetary Relations in a Global Political Economy   310

Contending Economic Strategies for an Interdependent
World   312

The Shadow of the Great Depression   313

The Clash between Liberal and Mercantile Values   314

Hegemony and the Management of the Global Economy   317

The Hegemonic Pillars of Open Markets and Free Trade   318

A Liberal Economic Order without Hegemonic Leadership?   319

The Changing Free-Trade Regime   321

*CONTROVERSY: Is the World Trade Organization a Friend
or Foe?   322*

The Changing International Monetary Regime   323

The Elements of Monetary Policy   323

The Bretton Woods Monetary System   324

The End of Bretton Woods   327

Plans for Reforming the International Financial Architecture   329

Global Economic Concerns in the Twenty-First Century   330

The Fate of Free Trade   331

Emerging Regional Trade Policies   331

APPLICATION: NAFTA and the Politics of Trade   332

The Future of Global Economic Governance   334

13   Human Rights and the Quest for Global Justice   340

Evaluating the Human Condition   342

*Communitarian and Cosmopolitan Approaches to
Human Rights   344*

CONTROVERSY: What Is Security?   345

Human Development and Human Security   345

Human Rights and the Protection of People   348

The Subordinate Status of Women and Its Consequences   348

The Precarious Life of Indigenous Peoples   350

The Global Refugee Crisis   352

Responding to Human Rights Abuses   354

    Internationally Recognized Human Rights   *354*

    The Challenge of Enforcement   *356*

    APPLICATION: Human Rights Start in Small Places, Close to Home   *357*

14 Population Dynamics and Global Environmental Politics   363

Global Demographic Patterns   365

    The Demographic Divide between the Global North and South   *365*

    International Responses to Population Growth   *370*

    Prospects for a Global Population Implosion   *371*

Environmental Security and Sustainable Development   373

    The Ecopolitics of Energy   *374*

    APPLICATION: Cartels and Commodity Power   *375*

    The Ecopolitics of the Atmosphere   *377*

    The Ecopolitics of Land and Water   *382*

Future Environmental Policy Choices   386

    CONTROVERSY: How Should the World's Problems Be Prioritized?   *386*

PART V   Alternative World Futures   391

15 Prospects for a New World Order   392

The Global Predicament: Questions for a Turbulent World   394

    Will the State Remain the Primary Actor in World Politics?   *395*

    Is Economic Globalization Irreversible?   *396*

    Are Ecopolitical Challenges Reordering the Global Agenda?   *398*

    Will Technological Innovation Solve Pressing Global Problems?   *398*

    Are Cultural Differences the New Fault Lines on the Geostrategic Landscape?   *399*

    Is the World Preparing for the Wrong Kind of Security Threats?   *401*

    Should the World Brace for a New Cold War?   *402*

Human Choice and the Global Future   403

GLOSSARY   407

REFERENCES   418

INDEX   439

Maps

Map 1.1   Mercator Projection   12

Map 1.2   Peter's Projection   12

Map 1.3   Orthographic Projection   13

Map 3.1   The Location of Democratically Governed Countries   67

Map 4.1   Territorial Changes in Europe following World War I   87

Map 4.2   World War II Redraws the Map of Europe   90

Map 5.1   The Global North, Global South (and Global East)   110

Map 5.2   The Great North-South Divide in Wealth and Population   113

Map 5.3   Global Imperialism, 1914   114

Map 6.1   The UN's Headquarters and Global Network   146

Map 6.2   The Indigenous Cultures of the World   162

Map 7.1   Demographic Stress and the Likelihood of Civil War   185

Map 8.1   Does High Military Spending Lower Human Security?   207

Map 9.1   The Enlarged NATO in the New Geostrategic Balance of Power   251

Map 10.1   UN Peace Missions since 1948   276

Map 11.1   The World Trade Organization Goes Global   295

Map 12.1   Trade Blocs and the Regionalization of Global Trade   334

Map 13.1   The Percentage of People Living Below the Poverty Line   343

Map 13.2   The Map of Human Development   346

Map 14.1   Global Population Density   370

Preface

In all likelihood, you are enrolled in your first course on world politics (or international relations, as it is called in some college catalogues). Like most students in introductory courses, you probably have a few questions about the relevance of this subject for your education. In particular, you may be wondering why you should study world politics and when it became part of the typical college curriculum. Because we have written this textbook with students in mind, a good place to begin our exploration of world politics is by addressing these preliminary questions.

Why should I study world politics?

World politics is an endless source of mystery and surprise. As you will see throughout this book, common sense is not sufficient for understanding international events. All too often, our intuition is wrong about why certain things happened. Albert Einstein once hinted at the challenge of explaining world politics when he was asked, "Why is it that when the mind of man has stretched so far as to discover the structure of the atom we have been unable to devise the political means to keep the atom from destroying us?" He replied, "This is simple, my friend, it is because politics is more difficult than physics."

In recent years, the world has experienced many unsettling changes that have made world politics even more difficult than in Einstein's day. The destructive power of military force has increased, terrorism has become a serious global threat, the economic gap between rich and poor nations has widened, and the global environment has suffered from the combined pressures of population growth, resource scarcities, and pollution. Further complicating matters is the interconnectedness of nations. Pressing military, social, economic, and environmental problems now spill across national borders, affecting the security and personal well-being of all of us. In more ways than we realize, our lives are affected by world politics.

Because events in distant parts of the world touch our daily lives, we should not leave crucial decisions about international issues to others. In a democracy, every citizen has an opportunity to influence policies on these issues by voting in elections, lobbying government officials, writing letters to newspapers, or joining protest demonstrations. To make the most of these opportunities, we need to understand world politics. This text introduces a set of concepts and analytic tools that will help you better understand the nature of world politics. The effort that you make in learning these concepts and tools will strengthen your ability to think critically about international issues and enhance your capability to advocate effectively for policies you believe will improve the human condition.

When did world politics become an academic subject?

Although philosophers, theologians, historians, and statesmen have written about war and diplomacy since antiquity, the formal study of world politics began at the dawn of the twentieth century. Prior to the onset of World War I, many people believed that progress toward a more peaceful and prosperous world was inevitable. The great powers had not fought one another for decades, industrial development and international commerce were expanding at astonishing rates, and scientists seemed to be solving the deepest mysteries of the universe. By some accounts, it was the most optimistic period in history. Peace conferences held in The Hague during 1899 and 1907 inspired hope that future generations would settle their differences without resorting to arms. In 1910, the British writer Norman Angell declared that war had become obsolete because it was no longer profitable. Three years later, at the dedication of the building that would house the Permanent Court of Arbitration, the Scottish-American industrialist Andrew Carnegie wrote in his diary: "Looking back a hundred years, or less perchance, from today, the future historian is to pronounce the opening [of the Court] … the greatest one step forward ever taken by man, in his long and checkered march upward from barbarism."

In those tranquil, confident times, students of world politics surveyed current events to glean insight on the international issues of the day. The study of world politics consisted mainly of commentary about personalities and interesting incidents, past and present. Rarely did scholars seek to generalize about patterns of behavior that might account for international events.

The gruesome toll extracted by World War I destroyed the sense of security that made this approach popular. However interesting descriptions of current events might be, they were of doubtful use to a world in search of ways to prevent future wars. International relations as a field of academic study emerged as scholars began searching for the underlying causes of the First World War. Not long after the guns had fallen silent, the Royal Institute of International Affairs was established in London, the Council of Foreign Relations was set up in New York, and the first university chair in International Relations was created at the University College of Wales, Aberystwyth. Soon institutions of higher learning throughout Britain and the United States began offering courses on world politics. Since then, the academic study of international affairs has spread to virtually every region of the world.

OVERVIEW OF THE BOOK

Now that you have some idea about the relevance of studying world politics, let's briefly look at how *The Global Future* is organized and what you can do to take advantage of its features.

Organization and Content

To help you make sense of world politics, *The Global Future* is divided into five parts. Part I introduces the central issues and major theories in the study of international relations. Part II identifies the primary actors in the global arena and discusses the processes by which these actors make decisions. Part III looks at global security, focusing on the problems of war and terrorism as well as rival approaches to preserving peace. Part IV examines issues of global welfare. Following an analysis of the process of globalization, it addresses the topics of international economic relations, human rights, and the linkage between population dynamics and the environment. Finally, Part V explores alternative world futures by posing a set of questions that encourages you to consider what is possible in the decades ahead, what is probable, and what future you would most prefer.

Design and Pedagogy

The Global Future contains a variety of learning aids to help you understand the complexities of world politics.

- **Chapter outlines.** The first item in every chapter is an outline of the material that will be covered.
- **Introductory case studies.** To encourage you to think critically about the topics covered in the book, the narrative section of each chapter begins with a vignette that introduces its underlying theme.
- **Marginal glosses for all key terms.** Whenever we use a technical term for the first time, we highlight it in the text and define it in the margin. Pay close attention to these terms because they are part of the vocabulary scholars, journalists, and policymakers use when discussing world politics.
- **Controversy boxes presenting essential debates.** We use "controversy" boxes to portray ongoing debates within the field of international relations and to encourage you to weigh the arguments on each side as you develop your own opinion.
- **Application boxes highlighting the connection between theory and policy.** We also use box inserts to show how diplomats and world leaders applied the theoretical concepts covered in a particular chapter to policy problems that they faced.

Photographs. To amplify the main points in the text, we have included photographs with captions that explain each image's relationship to key concepts and themes.

Tables, figures, and maps. Visual aids are excellent tools for communicating complex material. When it would reinforce an explanation in the text, we have displayed important information in graphic form.

Chapter summaries, key terms, and critical thinking questions. Each chapter concludes with a summary of its main themes, a list of the key terms, and a set of questions designed to help you think theoretically about some of the issues that were covered.

CHANGES TO THE THIRD EDITION

Readers familiar with the previous edition of *The Global Future* will recognize that its underlying organizational structure remains intact, but the many changes that have taken place in world politics over the past few years have required us to revisit every chapter to integrate the latest international developments with the most current scholarship. The result is a text completely updated from beginning to end. Each chapter incorporates the most recent available data on global trends and the most recent research findings on their likely impact. In so doing, the third edition of *The Global Future* addresses the key issues on the world's agenda—ranging from terrorism and international hostilities to globalization and the world economy, and from the opportunities presented by the emergence of a global civil society to the challenges posed by global climate change. In addition, coverage has been expanded to take into account new departures in international relations theory that interpret these developments.

Beyond updating and refining each chapter, this edition contains the following new features:

- New chapter-opening case vignettes have been added on Venezuelan leader Hugo Chávez, civil strife in Sudan, India and the Nonproliferation Treaty, the Kosovo conflict, the collapse of the Doha Round of trade negotiations, and the political obstacles to providing humanitarian aid to Myanmar (Burma) following Cyclone Nargis.

- Application boxes have been added to demonstrate how diplomats and national leaders apply theory to policy problems. Included in these box inserts are statements by individuals from various countries and from different positions across the political spectrum. Among those people featured in application boxes are Madeleine Albright, James Baker, Benazir Bhutto, Tony Blair, Richard Holbrooke, Henry Kissinger, Colin Powell, Mary Robinson, and Margaret Thatcher.

- To help students analyze the complexities of world politics, a set of critical thinking questions has been placed at the end of each chapter. These questions engage students in a variety of activities, including game theoretical analyses of international bargaining, normative analyses of foreign policy behavior, and counterfactual analyses of major historical events.

- New maps, photos, and graphics have been included, all designed to enhance the clarity of the text and to reinforce the themes of the book.

- The treatment of human rights has been broadened to include a discussion of communitarian and cosmopolitan ethical theories. New material has been added on the responsibility to protect.

- The concluding chapter on alternative futures has been expanded to encourage students to think about what global futures are possible given current trends, what futures are probable, and what futures they would prefer. New material has been added on the impact of global ecopolitics, the worldwide economic recession, the election of Barack Obama to the presidency of the United States, and the reassertion of Russian military power in world politics.

SUPPLEMENTS

To enhance teaching and learning, *The Global Future* is accompanied by an extensive ancillary package:

Companion Web Site for *The Global Future*

The student companion website includes chapter outlines, chapter quizzing, Internet and InfoTrac exercises, web links, and glossary flash cards. The instructor's manual and PowerPoint lecture outlines are available for download on the instructor's site. You can access these resources at www.cengage.com/politicalscience/kegley/globalfuture3e.

Instructor's Manual and Test Bank through Ebank

The instructor's manual includes chapter outlines, learning objectives, suggested print and online resources, teaching aids, and ideas for class activities. The test bank includes a wide selection of multiple-choice and essay questions. These instructors resources are available exclusively in electronic format. Please contact your Cengage sales representative for access.

WebTutor Toolbox on WebCT or Blackboard

Rich with content for your International Relations course, this web-based teaching and learning tool includes course management, study/mastery, and communication tools. Use WebTutor™ to provide virtual office hours, post your syllabus, and track student progress with WebTutor's quizzing material. For students, WebTutor™ offers real-time access to interactive online tutorials and simulations, practice quizzes, and web links—all correlated to *The Global Future*.

ACKNOWLEDGMENTS

The list of those whom we are indebted for their contributions to the development of *The Global Future* continues to grow. We greatly appreciate the comments and suggestions offered by reviewers. In particular, we are grateful to the scholars who provided meticulous critiques of the manuscript at different stages in its evolution, including the reviewers of this edition:

Reggie Ecarma, North Greenville University

Richard Epps, San Diego State University

Craig Warkentin, SUNY-Oswego

Thomas Preston, Washington State University

Vaughn P. Shannon, University of Northern Iowa

John Shively, Longview Community College

And past reviewers:

Terrence Casey, Rose-Hulman Institute of Technology; Deborah Saunders Davenport, University of Buckingham; Richard Epps, San Diego State University; Damian Fernandez, Florida International University; Michael M. Gunter, Jr., Rollins College; William E. Hoehne, Jr., Georgia Institute of Technology; Ian Hurd, Northwestern University; George Kent, University of Hawaii; William W. Lamkin, Glendale Community College; John Mercurio, San Diego State University; Meike Mittelstadt, Spokane Falls Community College; John Thomas Preston, Washington State University; Bruce Sabin, Webber International University; David Schrupp, Montana State University Vaughn Shannon, University of Northern Iowa; John F. Shively, Longview Community College; and Craig Warkentin, SUNY-Oswego.

Deserving of special gratitude are Executive Editor Carolyn Merrill and Developmental Editor Rebecca Green. Other dedicated professionals at Wadsworth who contributed significantly to the production of the third edition of *The Global Future* include Joshua Allen, Content Project Manager; Katherine Hayes, Assistant Editor; Nathan Gamache, Editorial Assistant; and Amy Whitaker, Marketing Manager. In addition, we are grateful to Lori Hazzard from Macmillan Publishing Solutions for efficiently overseeing the book's production, as well as to Tricia Lawrence, our copyeditor, Susan Swanson, our proofreader, and Bernice Eisen, our indexer.

As in the previous editions, we have benefited greatly from the unwavering support and inspiration of our wives, Debbie and Christine.

Finally, we wish to acknowledge the encouragement that we have received from the Carnegie Council for Ethics in International Affairs and the Frank Church Institute. Through their educational missions, these exceptional institutions have raised awareness of important international issues and added immeasurably to the quality of public discussion about their policy implications.

Charles W. Kegley, Jr.
Gregory A. Raymond

About the Authors

Charles W. Kegley, Jr. is the Vice Chair of the Board of Trustees of the Carnegie Council for Ethics in International Affairs and the Distinguished Pearce Professor of International Relations Emeritus at the University of South Carolina. A graduate of American University and Syracuse University, and a Pew Faculty Fellow at Harvard University, Kegley served as a past president of the International Studies Association (1993–1994), and has held faculty appointments at Georgetown University, the University of Texas, the People's University of China, and the Graduate Institute of International Studies, Geneva. A recipient of the Distinguished Scholar Award in Foreign Policy from the International Studies Association, the most recent among Kegley's four dozen published books is *World Politics: Trend and Transformation* (twelfth edition, 2009).

Gregory A. Raymond is the Frank Church Distinguished Professor of International Relations at Boise State University. A graduate of Park College and the University of South Carolina, and a Pew Faculty Fellow at Harvard University, he currently serves as a Vice-President of the Comparative Interdisciplinary Section of the International Studies Association. Selected as the Idaho Professor of the Year (1994) by the Carnegie Foundation for the Advancement of Teaching, Raymond has also received nine teaching excellence awards from various faculty, student, and alumni organizations at Boise State University. The recipient of the university's outstanding researcher award, he has published over a dozen books on foreign policy and world politics, and has lectured on international issues at universities and research institutes in twenty-two countries.

Together, Kegley and Raymond have coauthored *The Multipolar Challenge* (2008), *After Iraq: The Imperiled American Imperium* (2007), *From War to Peace: Fateful Decisions in International Politics* (2002), *Exorcising the Ghost of Westphalia: Building International Peace in the New Millennium* (2002), *How Nations Make*

Peace (1999), *A Multipolar Peace? Great-Power Politics in the Twenty-First Century* (1994), and *When Trust Breaks Down: Alliance Norms and World Politics* (1990). They have also coedited *International Events and the Comparative Analysis of Foreign Policy* (1975) and coauthored over two dozen articles in such scholarly journals as the *International Studies Quarterly*, the *Journal of Conflict Resolution*, the *Journal of Politics*, the *Journal of Peace Research*, *International Interactions*, and the *Harvard International Review*.

Charles W. Kegley, Jr.   Gregory A. Raymond

PART I

Trend and Transformation in World Politics

Speaking to members of the United Nations in early 2008, UN Secretary-General Ban Ki-moon listed a set of grave challenges confronting "every nation and all people." In addition to highlighting the age-old scourges of war, poverty, and disease, he predicted that the world would face a host of new dangers arising from climate change. "Global threats in the twenty-first century will spare no one," he warned. Because many of these threats now regularly intrude on our daily lives, a gnawing sense of insecurity torments many of us, regardless of gender, ethnicity, or nationality. Anxious about what might happen next, we struggle to divine our collective fate. What lies ahead? Can we create a better world? How are we to think about the global future?

This book examines the impact of world politics on the global future. Of course, no one can foresee the future precisely. We can, however, identify emerging trends and imagine how they might coalesce in different ways to produce alternative global futures. According to engineer and social policy analyst Willis Harman (1976), thinking about trends is important because "our view of the future shapes the kind of decisions we make in the present." Almost every action we take "involves some view of the future—as we expect it to be, or as we desire it to be, or as we fear it may be." The objectives of Part I of this book are to encourage you to begin thinking about the integrative and disintegrative trends in world politics, and consider how the actions we take in response to our image of their impact will influence which alternative global future we will eventually inhabit.

A first step in thinking about the global future is to recognize that the events and trends we observe are not seen in all innocence. They are filtered through a lens of values and beliefs born from previous experiences. Chapter 1 shows how this lens can distort our perception of international affairs. It also demonstrates how viewing things from the individual, state, and systemic levels of analysis can help reduce distortions by providing an explicit, orderly way of examining world politics from multiple perspectives.

Chapter 2 introduces realism, liberalism, and constructivism, rival theories of world politics that emphasize causal factors operating at different levels of analysis. It also describes two powerful critiques of these mainstream theories: radicalism and feminism. As you will see in subsequent chapters, theories are important because they guide our search for answers to puzzling questions about the world. They help organize countless isolated observations into a coherent picture of reality. Yet no matter how compelling any particular theory may seem, its value hinges on whether it can provide us with a richer understanding of world politics than we would otherwise possess. In the remainder of the book, we will apply realism, liberalism, constructivism, radicalism and feminism to various international security, economic, and environmental issues in order to assess their strengths and weaknesses, and therein sharpen our ability to evaluate competing visions of the global future.

1

Exploring Twenty-First-Century World Politics

CHAPTER OUTLINE

Continuity and Change in World Politics

How Perceptions Influence Images of Reality

The Nature and Sources of Images

CONTROVERSY: Should We Believe What We See? The Organization of Observations and Projections of Global Realities

The Role of Images in World Politics

APPLICATION: Seeing the World through Foreign Eyes

A Framework for Examining World Politics

Levels of Analysis

Time Sequences

Applying the Framework to the Cold War's End

Facing the Future

The Investigative Challenge

The Plan of the Book

Today many things indicate that we are going through a transitional period, when it seems that something is on the way out and something else is painfully being born. It is as if something were crumbling, decaying, and exhausting itself, while something else, still indistinct, were arising from the rubble.

VÁCLAV HAVEL
DRAMATIST AND FORMER PRESIDENT OF THE CZECH REPUBLIC

state an organized political entity with a permanent population, a well-defined territory, and a government.

When people use the term *international relations,* they usually are referring to interactions among autonomous, territorial **states** that have no higher authority governing their behavior. Our earliest records of such states come from ancient Mesopotamia, where some two dozen rival city-states flourished on the flood plains between the Tigris and Euphrates Rivers. Archaeologists believe that civilization began in Sumeria, the region's southern edge, which borders the coastline of what we now call the Persian Gulf. Here they find evidence of the first wheel and plow, the first extensive use of writing and metallurgy, the first legal codes and business contracts, as well as the first production of beer, of which there were nineteen varieties (Fields, Barber, and Riggs 1998; Durant 1954).

By roughly 2500 BCE, the typical Sumerian city-state possessed several thousand inhabitants, with most living within the city's high mud-brick walls. Fortifications were necessary because the flat terrain of southern Mesopotamia left city-states vulnerable to attack, and frequent conflict over water rights, grazing lands, and trade routes made war an ever-present threat. Sumerian armies were composed of an infantry supported by archers and four-wheeled war carts. Soldiers wore copper helmets and rudimentary armored kilts, carried large rectangular shields, and were armed with spears, swords, and axes (Keegan 1993). Fighting occurred at close quarters. Victors in these brutal contests subjugated the defeated, plundering their land and enslaving their population.

The conflict between the city-states of Lagash and Umma exemplified the harsh nature of Sumerian warfare. After generations of sporadic hostilities, an army led by King Lugal-Zaggisi of Umma finally overwhelmed Lagash (circa 2350 BCE). He sacked the city, massacred many of its citizens, and, in a gesture of contempt, placed statues of their gods in bondage. In one of humanity's earliest works of literature, the poet Dingiraddamu mourned for the patron goddess of Lagash: "O Lady of my city, desolated, when wilt thou return?"

War continued to plague Mesopotamia long after the tragic clash between Lagash and Umma. Over the millennia, many armies marched into the region. When seen through the prism of history, the military campaign led by the United States during the spring of 2003 against Iraqi leader Saddam Hussein was simply the latest outbreak of war in this ancient land. Yet it was a war unlike any other. Touted as the world's first digital war, it used networked communications to merge data from multiple sources to coordinate precision air strikes with swarming ground attacks. Unlike the chaos that cloaked ancient battlefields, American commanders hundreds of miles from the fighting could monitor developments as they happened. Whereas scouts might relay sporadic reports on enemy defenses to Lugal-Zaggisi, Predator drones, Airborne Warning and Control System (AWACS) planes, and special operations units inserted behind enemy lines by helicopter fed General Tommy Franks a continual stream of intelligence. Whereas Sumerian warriors unleashed a volley of arrows and javelins

Werner Forman/Art Resource, NY

Photo Courtesy of Staff Sgt. Klaus Baesu/U.S. Army

War in Human History "The story of the human race is War," British Prime Minister Winston Churchill once lamented. As shown in the depiction of an ancient Sumerian war cart and the photograph of a modern American M1-A1 Abrams tank, although war has been a constant feature of international relations, the means by which it has been waged has changed over time. Rapid advances in military technology over the past century and a half have made armed forces more lethal than ever before. A single American B-52 bomber, for example, can carry more explosive power than that used in all of the wars fought throughout recorded history.

before closing with the enemy, U.S. troops could expect a devastating barrage of cruise missile, stealth fighter, and heavy bomber strikes to begin a campaign. In short, speed and mobility now substitute for mass; information and firepower, for sheer numbers.

The military clash between Lagash and Umma is separated from us by over four millennia. What can we learn about contemporary world politics by comparing warfare in ancient Mesopotamia and modern Iraq? Quite simply, it reminds us that **politics** among territorial states is a mixture of *continuity* and *change*. On the one hand, states have lived under what political scientist Kenneth Waltz (1979) calls the "brooding shadow of violence" since antiquity. On the other hand, the way armed forces wield violence has changed profoundly. In a time of rapid advances in science and technology, it is easy for us to focus on the latest innovations and dismiss the past as irrelevant. Change is riveting; it captures our attention and stimulates our imagination. Still, we must be mindful that some features of world politics are relatively permanent. When considering how world politics might affect the global future, we need to be attentive to these entrenched continuities as well as to the sources of dramatic change. If the future seems uncertain to us, a mysterious place of endless surprises, it is often because we overlook how much of what lies ahead will be

politics the exercise of influence by competing individuals and groups to affect the allocation of values and distribution of resources; to political scientist Harold Lasswell, the process that determines "who gets what, when, how and why."

what economic historian Robert Heilbroner (1960, 15) calls "the expected culmination of the past" and "the growing edge of the present."

Looking beyond the confines of our immediate time is difficult. It requires an appreciation of the impact of yesterday's events on today's realities and how current ideas and practices may shape tomorrow. As philosopher and mathematician Gottfried Wilhelm Leibniz once put it, "The present is big with the future, the future might be read in the past." Thus, to understand unfolding events and to forecast how they may shape the future, we will view them in the context of a long-term perspective that examines how some aspects of the international political **system**—the patterns of interaction among the world's political actors—have resisted change while other aspects have changed radically.

system a set of interconnected parts that function as a unitary whole. In world politics, the parts consist primarily of states, corporations, and other organizations that interact in the global arena.

CONTINUITY AND CHANGE IN WORLD POLITICS

Imagine yourself returning home from a two-week vacation on a tropical island where you had no access to the news. The trip gave you a well-deserved break from school and allowed you to relax with a few friends at the end of the term. But now you are curious about what has happened while you were away. As you glance at a newspaper someone is reading in the airport's baggage claim area, headlines catch your eye. They indicate that the insurgency in Iraq has taken the lives of more American soldiers, including a recent graduate from a local high school. While riding home from the airport you listen to a radio program on the growth in American demand for foreign oil and political instability in Nigeria and several other major oil-producing states. Glancing at service station signs along the highway you notice that gasoline prices have climbed sharply, which will make the daily commute to and from your part-time job more expensive. Shortly after arriving at home, you connect to the Internet and find that the value of the Euro has increased relative to that of the U.S. dollar, and you begin worrying about the rising cost of the study tour you had planned to take in Europe next semester. Finally, while listening to the news on television later that evening, you hear several other reports: local officials across the country have begun to complain that federal homeland security grants are so closely tied to countering potential Al Qaeda attacks that they ignore other serious threats; due to growing demand in China and India, burgeoning biofuels programs in Europe and North America, and export quotas by major producers, grain prices have risen throughout the world, leading the World Bank to estimate that thirty-three countries were at risk of civil strife because of food shortages; and, concerned about instability in global credit markets, several major American banks have indicated that they would temporarily suspend loans to students attending community colleges and many small schools.

Although we have taken some literary license, the scenario just described is not completely hypothetical; it draws from various events that actually occurred during May 2008. Thinking about this rather typical month, one cannot help but be reminded that we are all affected by events that occur far from home and that we can all benefit by having a better grasp of their causes and consequences. But how can we best understand the political convulsions that confront the world's 6.7 billion people almost daily? Are the episodic shock waves throughout the world clearing the way for a truly new twenty-first-century world order? Or will many of today's dramatic disruptions ultimately prove temporary, mere spikes on the seismograph of history?

At the beginning of a new century, people often speculate about the global future. What will the new world be like? Will humanity be better off in the years ahead? Or will it suffer? We invite you to explore these questions with us. To begin our search, let us examine how the differences between continuities and changes in world history can help us orient our effort.

Every historical period is marked to some extent by change. Now, however, the pace of change seems more rapid and its effects more far-reaching than ever. To many observers, the cascade of events at the start of the twenty-first century implies a revolutionary restructuring of world politics. Numerous *integrative* trends point to that possibility. The countries of the world are drawing closer together in communications and trade, producing a globalized market. Yet at the same time, *disintegrative* trends paint a less sanguine picture. Weapons proliferation, global environmental deterioration, and the resurgence of ethnic conflict all portend a restructuring fraught with disorder. To predict which forces will dominate the future, we must recognize that no trend stands alone. The future is influenced by many determinants, each connected to others in a complex web of linkages. Collectively, these trends may produce stability by limiting the impact of any single disruptive force. It is also possible for them to accelerate the pace of change, moving world politics in directions not possible otherwise.

As Václav Havel suggests in the epigraph of this chapter, we seem to be going through a transition period in world politics. The opposing forces of integration and disintegration point toward a transformation, but its long-term ramifications remain unclear. Distinguishing true historical watersheds from temporary changes is difficult. The moment of transformation from one system to another is not immediately obvious. Nevertheless, certain times are especially likely candidates. Major turning points in world politics usually have occurred at the conclusion of general wars, which typically disrupt or destroy preexisting international arrangements. In the twentieth century, World Wars I and II and the Cold War caused fundamental breaks with the past and set in motion major transformations, providing countries with incentives to rethink the premises underlying their interests, purposes, and priorities. Similarly, many people concluded that the terrorist attacks on September 11, 2001 (9/11) produced a fundamental transformation in world affairs. Indeed, 9/11 seemed to change

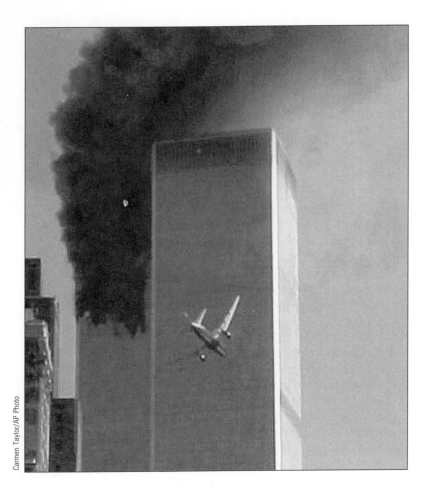

Carmen Taylor/AP Photo

Was September 11, 2001, a Transforming Event in World Politics? The terrorist attack on the World Trade Center's twin towers on 9/11 is regarded by many as a watershed event in world history. Columnist Anne Applebaum (2005, 14), for example, asserts that "overnight America's alliances changed, America's military objectives changed, [and] America's diplomatic priorities were transformed." Other observers, arguing that the attack did not affect other countries to the same degree, contend that 9/11 was not an event that truly changed the world.

everything: In U.S. president George W. Bush's words, "Night fell on a different world."

Despite all that appears radically different since the 9/11 terrorist attacks, much also remains the same in world politics. As William Dobson (2006, 23), managing editor of *Foreign Affairs*, observes: "What is remarkable is how little the world has changed." "The massive forces of international trade and globalization were largely unaffected by the attacks," adds historian Juan Cole (2006, 26). "China's emergence as an economic giant continues, with all its economic, diplomatic, and military implications." Decades-old flash points remain, including the conflicts between India and Pakistan, North Korea and the United States, and Israel and militants in south Lebanon and the Palestinian territories. "For all their visibility and drama," concludes Cole, "the 9/11 attacks left untouched many of the underlying forces and persistent tensions that shape international politics."

We often expect dramatic events to alter our lives forever and later are surprised to discover that certain patterns from the past have reappeared. Given the jolting changes that are occurring in the world alongside enduring continuities, these are uncertain times. Because some aspects of the future are likely to mirror the past, asserting that a major transformation in world politics is under way requires us to define what constitutes a new world order.

How can we determine when an existing pattern of relationships gives way to a completely new international system? Drawing upon the insights of various scholars who have wrestled with the criteria for identifying system transformation (Hoffmann 1961; Burns 1968; Gilpin 1981; Rosenau 1990), we will proceed by assuming that we have a new international system when we have a new answer to one of three questions: (1) *What are the system's basic units?* (e.g., empires, nation-states, or some other type of international actor); (2) *What are the predominant foreign policy goals that these units seek with respect to one another?* (e.g., territorial conquest, material gain through trade); and (3) *What can these units do to one another with their military and economic capabilities?*

Do these criteria lead us to conclude that a new system has now emerged? First, though states are still the primary actors on the world stage, they are not the sole actors. According to Richard Haass (2008, 45), a former senior staff member of the U.S. National Security Council, "states are being challenged from above, by regional and global organizations; from below, by militias; and from the side, by a variety of nongovernmental organizations." For example, the World Trade Organization and the International Monetary Fund now sometimes flex their political muscles in contests with individual states, as do groups ranging from Hezbollah and the Taliban to Greenpeace and Doctors Without Borders. Today's international system, in other words, includes more than sovereign, territorial states; it consists of a complex web of interactions among states, international institutions, and other **nonstate actors**.

Second, although competition over resources persists, as can be seen in the dispute between China and Japan over oil and natural gas fields in the East China Sea, territorial conquest is no longer the predominant goal of most states' foreign policies. Instead, their emphasis has shifted from traditional military methods of exercising influence to economic means. Meanwhile, the Cold War's ideological contest between capitalism and communism no longer comprises the primary cleavage in international politics, and a major new axis has yet to become clear.

Third, the proliferation of deadly weapons has altered the damage that states can inflict on one another. Great powers alone no longer control the world's most lethal armaments. Even more frightening, advanced weaponry is no longer necessary for a small, elusive group of fanatics to inflict catastrophic destruction. Ingenuity and box cutters allowed the 9/11 terrorists to kill thousands of people.

These changes in the types of units (actors), goals, and capabilities of recent years have dramatically altered the power rankings of state and nonstate actors on the world stage. Still, the hierarchies themselves endure. The economic hierarchy that divides the rich from the poor, the political hierarchy that separates the rulers from the ruled, the resource hierarchy that makes some suppliers and others dependents, and the military hierarchy that pits the strong against the weak all still shape the relations among states, as they have in the past.

nonstate actors all transnationally active groups other than states, such as international organizations whose members are states (IGOs) and nongovernmental organizations (NGOs) whose members are individuals and private groups from more than one state.

Similarly, the absence of institutions to govern the globe conspires with chronic national insecurity to encourage the use of force without international mandate. Thus change and continuity coexist, with both forces simultaneously shaping contemporary world politics.

The challenge, then, is to observe unfolding global realities carefully in order to describe and explain their character. This requires that we understand how our images of reality shape our expectations. It also requires a set of tools for analyzing the forces of constancy and change that affect our world. Hence, the remainder of this chapter will briefly examine the role that images of reality play in our understanding of world politics, and then will describe some of the tools we will use in this book to interpret trends and transformations in world politics.

HOW PERCEPTIONS INFLUENCE IMAGES OF REALITY

We all hold mental images of world politics—explicit or implicit, conscious or subconscious. But whatever our level of self-awareness, our images simplify "reality" by exaggerating some features of our environment while ignoring others. Thus we live in a world defined by our expectations and images.

These mental pictures, or perceptions, are inevitably distortions, as they cannot fully capture the complexity and configurations of even physical objects, such as the globe itself (see Controversy: Should We Believe What We See?).

Many of our images of the world politics are built on illusions and misconceptions. And even images that are now accurate can easily become outdated if we fail to recognize changes in the world. Indeed, the world's future will be determined not only by changes in the "objective" facts of world politics but also by the meaning that people ascribe to those facts, the assumptions on which they base their interpretations, and the actions that flow from these assumptions and interpretations—however accurate or inaccurate they might be.

The Nature and Sources of Images

The effort to simplify one's view of the world is inevitable and even necessary. Just as cartographers' projections simplify complex geophysical space so we can better understand the world, each of us inevitably creates a "mental map"—a habitual way of organizing information—to make sense of a confusing abundance of information. Although mental maps are neither inherently right nor wrong, they are important because we tend to react according to the way the world appears to us rather than the way it is. Political leaders, too, are captives of this tendency (Kirkpatrick 2007). As political psychologist Richard Ned Lebow (1981) warns, "Policymakers are prone to distort reality in accord with their needs even in situations that appear ... relatively unambiguous."

Most of us—policymakers included—look for information that reinforces our preexisting beliefs about the world, assimilate new data into familiar images, mistakenly equate what we believe with what we know, and deny information that contradicts our expectations. We also rely on our intuition and make snap judgments on many important issues (Gladwell 2005). Research in cognitive psychology suggests that human beings are "categorizers" who attempt to understand the world matching what they see with images in their memories of prototypical events and people—a process that psychologists refer to as **schematic reasoning** (Larson 1994). The absentminded professor, the shady lawyer, and the kindly

schematic reasoning
the process by which new information is interpreted by comparing it to generic concepts stored in memory about certain stereotypical situations, sequences of events, and characters.

| CONTROVERSY | Should We Believe What We See? The Organization of Observations and Projections of Global Realities |

Many people assume that "seeing is believing" without questioning whether their perceptions are accurate. But is there more to seeing than meets the eye? When looking at the world, do we perceive it in ways that produce distortions? Students of perceptual psychology think so. They maintain that seeing is not a strictly passive act: What we observe is partially influenced by our preexisting values and expectations. Two observers looking at the same object might easily perceive different realities. To illustrate this, perceptual psychologists are fond of displaying the drawing here, which, depending on how the viewer looks at it, can be seen as either a goblet or two faces opposing each other.

This principle has great importance for students of world politics. Depending on one's perspective, people can vary greatly on how they view international events, actors, and issues. To appreciate the disagreements that can result from the fact that different people can easily see different realities when they look at the same thing, consider something as basic as viewing objectively the location and size of the continents in the world. There exists a long-standing controversy among cartographers about the "right" way to map the globe, that is, how to make an accurate projection of the Earth's surface. All maps of the globe are distorted, because it is impossible to perfectly represent the three-dimensional globe on a two-dimensional piece of paper. The difficulty cartographers face can be appreciated by trying to flatten an orange peel. You can only flatten it by separating pieces of the peel that were joined when it was spherical. Cartographers who try to flatten the globe on paper, without "ripping it" into separate pieces, face the same problem. Although there are a variety of ways to represent the three-dimensional object on paper, all of them involve some kind of distortion. Thus cartographers must choose among the imperfect ways of representing the globe by selecting those aspects of the world's geography they consider most important to describe accurately, while making adjustments to other parts.

Cartographers' ideas of what is most important in world geography have varied according to their own global perspectives, or according to those of the person or organization for which a particular map was created (see Klinghoffer 2006). These three maps (Maps 1.1, 1.2, and 1.3) depict the distribution of the earth's land surfaces, but each portrays a different image. Each is a model of reality, an abstraction that highlights some features of the globe while ignoring others. What a map highlights is significant politically because it shapes how people view what is important. In examining these three ways of viewing and interpreting the globe, evaluate which projection you think is best. Which features of global reality are most worthy of emphasizing to capture an accurate picture? What does your answer reveal about your values and view of the world?

M A P 1.1 Mercator Projection

This Mercator projection, popular in sixteenth-century Europe, is a classic Eurocentric view of the world. It retained direction accurately, making it useful for navigators, but placed Europe at the center of the world and exaggerated the continent's importance relative to other landmasses. Europe appears larger than South America, which is twice Europe's size, and two-thirds of the map is used to represent the northern half of the world and only one-third the southern half. Because lines of longitude were represented as parallel rather than convergent, it also greatly exaggerates the size of Greenland and Antarctica.

M A P 1.2 Peter's Projection

In the Peter's projection, each landmass appears in correct proportion in relation to all others, but it distorts the shape and position of landmasses. In contrast with most geographic representations, it draws attention to the countries of Africa, Asia, and Latin America where more than three-quarters of the world's population live today.

MAP 1.3 Orthographic Projection

The orthographic projection, centering on the mid-Atlantic, conveys some sense of the curvature of the Earth by using rounded edges. The sizes and shapes of continents toward the outer edges of the circle are distorted to give a sense of spherical perspective.

grandmother are examples of "stock" images that many of us have of certain types of people. Although the professors, lawyers, and grandmothers that we meet may bear only a superficial resemblance to these stereotypical images, when we know little about someone our expectations will be shaped by presumed similarities to these characters.

Attribution biases also color the images we have of ourselves and others. When explaining our own actions, especially when questions may be raised about the propriety of what we have done, most of us emphasize the push and pull of external forces and constraints ("I did X because circumstances made it necessary; I had no choice."). However, when adversaries behave the same way, we generally attribute their actions to deficiencies in their character ("They did X because of their devious nature."). In other words, we highlight the importance of situational influences on what we do while accentuating the importance of dispositional influences on what others do (L. Ross 1977).

Many factors shape our images, including how we were socialized as children, traumatic events we may have experienced growing up, and exposure to the ideas of people whose expertise we respect (Jervis 1976). Once we have acquired an image, it seems self-evident. Accordingly, we try to keep it consistent with our other beliefs and, through a psychological process known as **cognitive dissonance** (Festinger 1957), reject information that contradicts how it portrays the world. In short, our mind selects, screens, and filters information; consequently, our perceptions depend not only on what happens in daily life but also on how we interpret and internalize those events.

attribution bias the tendency to emphasize situational factors when explaining one's own behavior while stressing dispositional factors when explaining the same behavior in others.

cognitive dissonance the psychological tendency to deny or rationalize away discrepancies between one's preexisting beliefs and new information.

Of course, tolerance of ambiguity and receptivity to new ways of thinking vary among individuals. Some people are better able than others to revise perceptual habits to accommodate new information. Nonetheless, to some extent, we are all prisoners of our perceptions.

The Role of Images in World Politics

We must be careful not to assume automatically that what applies to individuals applies to entire countries, and we should not equate the beliefs of national leaders with the beliefs of the people under their authority. Still, leaders have extraordinary influence, and leaders' images of historical circumstances often predispose them to behave in particular ways toward others, regardless of "objective" facts. For instance, the loss of 26 million Soviet lives in the "Great Patriotic War" (as the Russians refer to World War II) reinforced a longstanding fear of foreign invasion, which caused a generation of Soviet policymakers to perceive U.S. military moves with suspicion and often alarm.

mirror image the tendency of people in competitive interaction to perceive each other similarly—to see an adversary the same way as the adversary sees them.

Because leaders and citizens are prone to ignore or reinterpret information that runs counter to their beliefs, mutual misperceptions exacerbate disputes rooted in competing interests and values. Although the degree of misperception may not be the same on both sides of a dispute and one side may cling to its stereotypes with greater tenacity than the other, distrust and suspicion grow as conflicting parties view one another in a negative light. This so-called **mirror image** phenomenon occurred in Moscow and Washington during the Cold War. Each side saw its own actions as constructive but its adversary's responses as hostile, and both sides erroneously assumed that their counterparts would interpret policy initiatives as they were intended. When psychologist Urie Bronfenbenner (1961) traveled to Moscow, for example, he was amazed to hear Russians describing the United States in terms that were strikingly similar to the way Americans described the Soviet Union: Each side saw itself as virtuous and peace-loving while the other was seen as disingenuous and aggressive. Since then, researchers have found evidence of stark, black-and-white mirror images held by bitter rivals in other international disputes, including the India-Pakistan and Arab-Israeli conflicts (Stoessinger 1993, 111-135; R. White 1977). Under these circumstances conflict resolution is extraordinarily difficult. Not only do the opposing sides have different preferences for certain outcomes over others, but they do not see the underlying issues in the same light. Further complicating matters, the mirror images held by rivals tend to be self-confirming. When one side expects the other to be hostile, it may treat its opponent in a manner that leads the opponent to take counteractions that confirm the original expectation, therein creating a vicious circle of deepening hostilities that reduce the prospects for peace (M. Deutsch 1986; Sen 2006). Clearing up mutual misperceptions can facilitate negotiation between the parties, but eliminating the distorted views that rivals hold of each other will not automatically eradicate the truly incompatible aims and conflicts of interest that may divide them (see Application: Seeing the World through Foreign Eyes).

APPLICATION   Seeing the World through Foreign Eyes

A perennial issue within the field of international relations concerns the relationship between theory and practice. To what extent are theories of world politics relevant to the practice of statecraft? How can the theories produced by the academic community assist practitioners who formulate and conduct foreign policy?

In this chapter we have introduced you to some of the theoretical concepts that scholars use to describe the role of perceptions in world politics. Psychological research on human cognition reveals that our beliefs and expectations influence what we see, and that many people have difficulty imagining how others could perceive the world in different terms. Fixated on their own concerns and needs, they overestimate the accuracy of their worldview and misinterpret the character, intentions, and capabilities of others. According to Dennis Ross, former Middle East envoy and the chief peace negotiator in the administrations of George H. W. Bush and Bill Clinton, understanding the perceptions held by the other side is crucial for conducting successful international negotiations. It is important, he argues, to know what others value as well as what they fear, what pressures will harden their bargaining position as well as what may soften it. In the excerpt below, Ross describes how asking probing questions and carefully listening to the other side's responses helped him during arms control negotiations with the Soviet Union and the Russian Federation.

> With first the Soviets and then the Russians, I would have long conversations with Sergei Tarasenko and Yuri Mamedov, key aids to then foreign ministers Eduard Shevardnadze and Andrei Kosyrev. Conversations with them revealed a great deal about what was and wasn't possible on arms control—not necessarily because I was pumping them for information, but because I asked questions that conveyed an interest in

trying to understand the broader circumstances in which they had to operate.

For example, sometimes I would ask questions about how much reform was really possible. Frequently, this led to discussions about decline and malaise in the Soviet Union, the advocates and opponents of varying degrees of reform, their arguments, where arms-control agreements fit in, and their views about where we and others could either help or harm the reform process.

One essential attribute for any negotiator is to be a good listener. It's crucial to know when to talk but, more important, when to listen. You won't be learning when you are talking. You may be shaping or conditioning attitudes, but you will not be learning. You learn when you listen. Being a good listener conveys a level of interest and respect. It shows that you take seriously those with whom you are dealing. You are likely to elicit more when you convey such respect and listen actively (D. Ross 2007, 191–192).

Theory and research on the perceptual outlooks of political leaders indicates that each actor on the international stage sees the world somewhat differently. Policymakers who ignore these differences can easily overlook meaningful signals from their adversaries and fail to capitalize on fleeting opportunities for diplomatic breakthroughs. Empathy, seeing a situation from the other's point of view, is thus a valuable skill. "The more one can show an appreciation of why someone else believes what they do, and where that belief comes from," concludes Ross, "the more one has a chance to be successful."

As Ross's reflections on his experience in arms control negotiations reveals, the boundary between theory and statecraft is permeable. Not only does theoretical knowledge have policy relevance, but policymakers make use of it, whether consciously or not (George 1993, 135).

Although our images of world politics are resistant, change is possible. Overcoming old thinking habits sometimes occurs when we experience acute discomfort as a result of clinging to false assumptions. As Benjamin Franklin once observed, "The things that hurt, instruct." Dramatic events in particular can alter international images, sometimes drastically. The Vietnam War, for example, caused many Americans to change their ideas about the use of force in contemporary world politics. As we speculate about the global future, we need to think critically about the foundations on which our perceptions rest. Are they accurate? Are they informed? Might they be adjusted to gain a greater understanding of others?

Questioning our images is one of the most important challenges we face in analyzing world politics. A purpose of this book is to help you cultivate a critical perspective on your beliefs regarding international relations. To that end, we will ask you to evaluate rival perspectives on global issues, even if they differ from your standpoint. Indeed, we will expose you to schools of thought prevailing today that you may find unconvincing, and possibly repugnant. Why are they included? Because many other people make these views the bedrock of their outlooks on the world. Critical thinking within the field of international relations entails confronting one's own assumptions and biases, as well as recognizing that the perceptual predispositions held by others may lead them to see and interpret events in ways that may be at odds with our own point of view.

A FRAMEWORK FOR EXAMINING WORLD POLITICS

If people exaggerate the accuracy of their perceptions and seek information that confirms what they believe, how can we escape the biases created by our preconceptions? How can we avoid overlooking or dismissing evidence that runs counter to our intuition? There are no sure-fire solutions to the problem of making accurate observations, no way to guarantee that we possess an objective view of international relations. However, there are a number of tools available that can improve our ability to analyze world affairs. One approach is to use an analytical framework to discipline our observations. Analytic frameworks suggest where to look for information pertinent to some puzzling phenomenon, and how to organize it in an inventory of possible causes. Although no analytical framework can ensure that we will have an impartial view of world politics, social scientists frequently build *levels of analysis* and *time sequences* in the frameworks they use in an effort to illuminate causal factors that they might otherwise neglect.

Levels of Analysis

At the heart of almost every international event lies a puzzle. Someone is perplexed over why an event happened, or is curious about what would have happened if a different action had been taken by one of the participants. The first step in solving the puzzle is to ask: "Of what larger pattern is this event an instance?" (Rosenau and Durfee 1995; Lave and March 1975). Visualizing an event as part of a larger pattern invites us to imagine that the pattern is the end result of some unknown process, and encourages us to think about the causal mechanisms that might have produced the pattern.

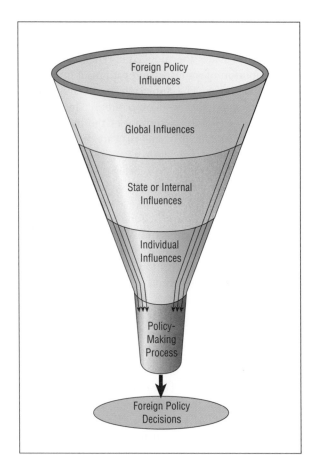

FIGURE 1.1 Explaining International Events: Influences at Three Levels

The factors that shape international events can be categorized at three levels. At the systemic level are those features of the global system such as the prevalence of alliances and the extent of trade interdependence. At the state level are domestic influences such as the type of government or the opinions of its citizens. At the individual level are the characteristics of the leader—his or her personal beliefs, values, and personality. Factors from all three levels may affect any given event, but their relative importance will vary depending upon prevailing circumstances and the issues involved.

Many scholars organize the list of possible causal mechanisms behind an event according to three levels of analysis: the individual, the state, and the entire global system (see Figure 1.1). The **individual level of analysis** refers to the distinctive personality traits, experiences, and behavior of those responsible for making important decisions on behalf of state and nonstate actors, as well as ordinary citizens whose behavior has important political consequences. Here, for example, we may properly locate the impact of a leader's political beliefs, attitudes, and opinions on his or her behavior, and explore questions such as why presidents Bill Clinton and George W. Bush dealt with Saddam Hussein in different ways.

The **state level of analysis** consists of the domestic attributes of nation-states, including their type of government, level of economic development, characteristics of their societies, and so on. The processes by which governments make decisions regarding war and peace, for instance, fall within the state level of analysis. A common example can be found in the argument that authoritarian governments are more bellicose than democracies because their leaders are not

individual level of analysis an analytical approach to the study of world politics that emphasizes the psychological factors motivating people who make foreign policy decisions on behalf of states and other global actors.

state level of analysis an analytical approach to the study of world politics that emphasizes how the internal attributes of states influence their foreign policy behavior.

constrained by competitive elections or political cultures grounded in norms of tolerance and compromise.

The **systemic level of analysis** provides the most comprehensive view of world politics, focusing on the distribution of resources and pattern of interaction among the political actors on the global stage. The dispersion of military capabilities, the density of alliance networks, and the level of economic interdependence among state and nonstate actors are all characteristics of the international system as a whole. Explanations of international events that are framed at the systemic level contend that the behavior of global actors stems from their placement within the international system. Different actors behave similarly when they have similar positions of power and wealth within the system.

To sum up, categorizing possible causes of an event according to levels of analysis is useful because it encourages us to look beyond our preconceived images. It helps guard against single-factor explanations that hinge on one decisive cause. Like a telescopic camera lens, it allows us to zoom in and examine fine-grained details at the individual level, and then move back to the state and systemic levels to see things from a broader perspective. Moving from one level to another, looking at parts as well as the whole, suggests different questions to ask and what kinds of evidence would be necessary to arrive at meaningful answers.

Time Sequences

Once we have identified factors from different levels of analysis that may combine to produce some outcome, it is useful to place them in a sequence that specifies the order in which they occurred. Anyone who owns a combination lock knows that the correct numbers must be entered in their proper order to open the lock. Similarly, to explain why something happened in world politics, we must determine how various individual, state, and systemic-level factors fit together in a process that unfolds over time.

One way to build time sequences into our analytic framework is to consider how close each individual, state, or systemic factor was to the occurrence of the event in question. We could do this in several different ways, but for illustrative purposes we will simply distinguish between remote and proximate causes. *Remote causes* are deep, underlying factors whose impact develops over a lengthy time span. *Proximate causes* are those with more immediate effects. Consider, for example, the outbreak of a forest fire following a brief thunderstorm over parched mountainous terrain. The remote cause was a prolonged draught that desiccated the region; the proximate cause, a lightening strike that ignited a dry pine tree.

In world politics, by searching for remote and proximate causes across multiple levels of analysis, we guard against having our perceptual biases unnecessarily constrict our frame of reference, which can lead us to hastily embrace enticing but incomplete explanations for the phenomena we hope to understand. To illustrate, let us apply our analytical framework to the puzzle of why the Cold War ended peacefully.

Applying the Framework to the Cold War's End

During the Second World War, the United States and the Soviet Union aligned against Nazi Germany. In the waning months of the conflict mutual suspicions in Moscow and Washington hardened into policy disagreements over the future of the postwar world. The day before his suicide, Adolph Hitler predicted that the "laws of both history and geography" would compel the Soviet Union and the United States to engage in "a trial of strength" (Bullock 1962). As Soviet–American relations plummeted in a downward spiral of charges and counter-charges, it seemed as if Hitler's ominous prediction would come to pass.

But fighting did not ensue. Despite over forty years of intense rivalry in what was called the Cold War, the Soviet Union and the United States avoided a trial of strength. Had they not, the results would have been catastrophic. By 1983, when President Ronald Reagan referred to the Soviet Union as an "evil empire," the two superpowers had amassed such enormous nuclear arsenals that if their combined explosive power was converted to an equivalent amount of TNT and loaded into boxcars on a freight train, the train would have stretched from the earth to the moon and back at least a half dozen times. Thus it came as a great relief when the Cold War ended without bloodshed following the collapse of the Soviet Union in 1991.

Some people argue that the American military buildup during the Reagan administration drove the Soviet Union into submission. The Cold War ended due to "the Reagan policy of firmness," insisted Richard Perle, one of the former president's military advisors. Our policy was "peace through strength," added George H. W. Bush, Reagan's vice president and immediate successor in the White House. "It worked."

This argument sounds persuasive because the disintegration of the Soviet Union occurred alongside a massive weapons-building program in the United States. Furthermore, the argument fit a set of preconceptions derived from America's experience with Nazi Germany: Dictators cannot be appeased; the language of military might is the only language they understand. Soviet leaders, many Americans believed, were demagogic and rapacious like Hitler. Whereas British and French vacillation in the 1930s emboldened Hitler, Reagan's steadfastness allegedly brought the Soviets to heel.

Vivid historical images are seductive. They frame how we see the present, often in ways that inhibit dissecting analogies to past events. Rather than patiently examining an issue from every angle, we draw parallels with a memorable incident and stop searching for additional information. For example, the assertion that "Ronald Reagan won the Cold War by being tough on the communists" (Glynn 1993) animates such powerful imagery that seeking other explanations might seem unnecessary. But by not evaluating plausible, rival explanations, we can be misled. The prominent Russian scholar Georgi Arbatov contends that rather than convincing Kremlin hardliners to give up, Reagan's "tough" policy actually stiffened their resolve, thereby prolonging the Cold War (see Kegley and Raymond 1994, 29).

Analytical frameworks help prevent us from giving easily recalled analogies more weight than they deserve by widening the search for additional insights and information. Table 1.1 shows how looking at different levels of analysis and time sequences can assist in identifying alternative explanations of why the Cold War ended peacefully. At the individual level, a case could be made that Mikhail Gorbachev's sweeping reforms, not Ronald Reagan's toughness, played the key role (Matlock 2004; Schneider, Windmer, and Ruloff 1993). Another possibility is that both leaders played important roles (Leffler 2007). Sill another possibility is that Pope John Paul II's visits to his native Poland had already begun eroding communism in Eastern Europe before Gorbachev came to power. At the state level of analysis, political inertia and economic mismanagement may have gradually weakened the Soviet Union, while social discontent, grassroots protest movements, and the explosive growth of **nationalism** among non-Russian ethnic groups in the Baltic republics and elsewhere accelerated the downfall of the communist regime. Finally, at the systemic level, the long-term U.S. policy of **containment**, the spread of human rights norms following the signing of the 1975 Helsinki Accords (Thomas 2001), and the eventual dissolution of the Soviet position in Eastern Europe may have been critical to ending the Cold War.

It is also useful to examine *chains of causation* that run between levels over time. For example, political inertia and economic deterioration within the Soviet Union (state level) may have been remote causes of Gorbachev's reforms (individual level), which became a proximate cause of the collapse of the network of Soviet military alliances (systemic level) by providing an opportunity for Eastern Europeans to chart a new course in the foreign affairs. Yet another possibility is that Gorbachev's political reforms gave non-Russian ethnic groups in various Soviet republics (state level) the opportunity to express nationalist sentiments and break away from the Soviet Union. We could hypothesize other chains of cause and effect. Determining which ones best account for the collapse of the Soviet Union and the end of the Cold War is a task for subsequent research. Our purpose here is merely to demonstrate how preconceived mental images limit a person's field of vision. We get a richer, more nuanced perspective by studying world politics from multiple levels of analysis across time.

nationalism the belief that political loyalty lies with a body of people who share ethnicity, linguistic, or cultural affinity, and perceive themselves to be members of the same group.

containment a term coined by U.S. policymaker George Kennan for deterring expansion by the Soviet Union, which has since been used to describe a strategy aimed at preventing a state from using force to increase its territory or sphere of influence.

FACING THE FUTURE

Throughout history people have tried to predict the future. To be sure, many of these efforts are more noteworthy today for their absurdity than for their accuracy. Early in the nineteenth century, for example, the *Quarterly Review* asserted that it would be foolish to expect locomotives to travel twice as fast as stage-coaches. High-speed rail travel was simply not possible, added British writer Dionysius Larder, "because passengers, unable to breathe, would die of asphyxia" (Lee 2000). Although these and other equally amusing examples of erroneous predictions remind us that we cannot know the distant future with certainty,

T A B L E 1.1   Contending Images of the Cold War's End

Level of Analysis	Time Sequence	
Individual		
	Remote Causes	**Proximate Causes**
	Leaders as moral exemplars "The pope [John Paul II] started this chain of events that led to the end of communism." —Lech Walesa	*Leaders as movers of history* "Ronald Reagan won the Cold War by being tough on the communists." —Patrick Glynn "[The end of the Cold War was possible] primarily because of one man—Mikhail Gorbachev. The transformations we are dealing with now would not have begun were it not for him." —James A. Baker III
State		
	Political inertia "Given communism's inherent unworkability ... the Soviet empire was doomed in the long run." —Arthur Schlesinger, Jr. *Economic mismanagement* "No other industrialized state [than the Soviet Union] in the world for so long spent so much of its national wealth on armaments and military forces. Soviet militarism, in harness with communism, destroyed the Soviet economy and thus hastened the self-destruction of the Soviet empire." —Fred Charles Iklé	*Media attention* "It was the moral reassessment of the seventy-odd years of this socialist experiment that shook the nation.... It was the flood of publications of the Soviet Union's human rights record and its tremendous distortions of moral and ethical principles that discredited the system, especially when introduced into the everyday lives of its individual citizens through the popular media." —Vladimir Benevolenski and Andrei Kortunov *Grassroots movements* "The changes wrought by thousands of people serving in the trenches [were] essential to events in recent years and at least partially responsible for [ending the Cold War]." —David Cortright *Ethnonationalism* "In less than two years, communism collapsed everywhere.... The causes [were] the national communities." —Hélèbe Carrère d'Encausse
Systemic		
	Containment "The U.S. and our allies deserve great credit for maintaining the military and economic power to resist and turn back the Soviet aggression." —Richard Nixon	*Imperial overstretch* "The acute phase of the fall of communism started outside of the Soviet Union and spread to the Soviet Union itself. By 1987, Gorbachev made it clear that he would not interfere with internal experiments in Soviet bloc countries ... Once communism fell in Eastern Europe, the alternative in the Soviet Union became civil war or dissolution." —Daniel Klenbort

SOURCES: Kegley (1994), Kegley and Raymond (1994, 42–44).

many theorists argue that events in the near future lie on a continuum of predictability, with some being foreseeable if a systematic effort is made to consider how social, economic, political, and technological trends may combine in different ways to yield alternative potential futures (see Bazerman and Watkins 2004). As you investigate various aspects of world politics in the chapters ahead, we encourage you to reflect on the global future. Think about what is possible, evaluate what is probable, and advocate for what is preferable. "We are not prisoners of fate," writes futurist Edward Cornish (2004, 210). Rather we have extraordinary power to assess past events and weigh current trends, responding to what we learn in ways that can improve the human prospect.

The Investigative Challenge

Because world politics is complex and our images of it are often discordant, scholars differ in their approaches to understanding world politics. Some take a *macropolitical* perspective that focuses on the global system as a totality and explains the behavior of the actors within it by emphasizing how they are positioned. Others scholars adopt a *micropolitical* perspective that focuses on the individual actors and extrapolates from their behavior to describe the global system as an aggregate whole. Both approaches make important contributions to understanding world politics: the former reveals how the external environment sets limits on political choice; the latter draws attention to how a state's preferences, capabilities, and strategic calculations account for the choices it makes from the options that are available. By looking at world politics from a macropolitical perspective, we can see why actors that are similarly situated within the system may behave alike, despite their internal differences. By taking a micropolitical perspective, we can appreciate why some actors behave differently, despite their similar placement within the global system (Waltz 1988, 43).

What happens in world politics thus depends on the constraining and enabling forces of the global system that establish the range of political choice (macropolitics), as well as on the perceptions and motives that influence the foreign policy decisions made by the individual actors (micropolitics). We get a richer, more comprehensive picture of world politics when we draw insights from both vantage points and explore how systemic structures influence the behavior of international actors, whose interactions in turn have an impact on the system's structure. Consequently, in the chapters that follow, we adopt an analytical approach that looks at (1) the key macro *trends* in world politics that set the parameters for action, (2) the preferences, capabilities, and strategic calculations of the individual *actors* affected by these trends, and (3) the *interactions* among actors on security and welfare issues that ultimately shape the trajectories of global trends.

Examining patterns of interaction among actors is important because many of the patterns that characterize world politics are the result of **contingent behavior**. According to political economist Thomas Schelling (1978, 13–17), sometimes the aggregate patterns we see can be easily projected from the individual actors. For example, if we know that every state increases its military

contingent behavior
actions that depend upon what others are doing.

budget annually by a certain amount due to internal bureaucratic demands for more funding, we can make a simple persistence forecast to project the trend in global military spending over time. But if some states increase their budgets when neighboring states have increased theirs, estimating the trend is more complicated. Here national leaders are *responding* to each other's behavior as well as *influencing* each other's behavior. Sometimes the resulting pattern may be sequential: If your expenditures induce me to increase my expenditures, mine may encourage someone else to spend more, and so on. Sometimes the pattern may be reciprocal: Apprehensive about your expenditures, I spend more, which prompts you to raise your expenditures even further. When, as in these two cases, state behavior is contingent on the behavior of other states, the results usually do not allow a simple summation to the aggregate. To forecast the global future under these circumstances we have to look at the dynamic interaction between actors and their environment, which includes other actors responding to each other's behavior.

The analytical approach outlined here is useful, not only because it takes into account the interplay of proximate and remote explanatory factors at the individual, state, and systemic levels of analysis, but also because it avoids dwelling on particular countries, individuals, or transitory events whose long-term significance is likely to diminish. Instead, we attempt to identify behaviors that cohere into general patterns that measurably affect global living conditions. Thus we explore the nature of world politics from a perspective that places historical and contemporary events into a larger, lasting theoretical context, providing the conceptual tools that will enable us to interpret subsequent developments.

The Plan of the Book

Our journey begins in Chapter 2 with an overview of the realist, liberal, and constructivist theoretical traditions that scholars and policymakers use most often to interpret world politics. Next we consider radicalism and feminism, which offer powerful critiques of these mainstream traditions. The comparison of these contending theories provides the intellectual background for the description and explanation of the issues and developments that are treated in the remaining chapters.

Chapter 3 begins the analysis of actors, issues, and their interactions with a close examination of foreign policy decision-making processes *within* nation-states, which remain the principal actors in world politics. It also considers the role of leaders in making foreign policy, and how various external and domestic forces can constrain the impact of political leaders.

We will then turn our attention to each of the types of actors in world politics and examine how their characteristics and capabilities affect their interests and influence in the world. Great powers (those wealthy countries with the most powerful militaries) are the focus of attention in Chapter 4. In Chapter 5, we turn our attention to the weaker, less economically developed countries, explaining how the fate of this group of states is shaped by their relations with great powers. Then, in Chapter 6, we cover two groups of nonstate actors, inter-governmental organizations (IGOs) and nongovernmental organizations (NGOs), and demonstrate how they interact with nation-states and increasingly challenge even the great powers.

The next group of chapters shifts attention to how the preferences, capabilities, and strategic calculations of the principal actors in world politics affect security and welfare issues on the global agenda. Security issues are addressed in Chapters 7 through 10. Finally, in Chapters 11 through 14, we examine problems relating to globalization, international political economy, human rights, and the environment.

In the concluding section, Chapter 15, we revisit the major trends in world politics surveyed throughout the book. It draws on the theories and evidence presented in earlier chapters, and presents alternative views of the global future by focusing on some of the most hotly debated questions most likely to dominate political discussion during the next decade.

Understanding today's world requires a willingness to confront complexity. The challenge is difficult but the payoff warrants the effort. Humankind's ability to chart a more rewarding future is contingent on its ability to entertain complex ideas, to free itself from the sometimes paralyzing grip of prevailing orthodoxies, and to develop a healthy, questioning attitude about rival perspectives on international realities. On that hopeful yet introspective note, we begin our exploration of world politics.

CHAPTER SUMMARY

- To understand the global future, one must examine the ways in which the contemporary international system has changed and the ways in which its fundamental characteristics have resisted change.

- Trends in world politics rarely unfold in a constant, linear direction. Moreover, no trend stands alone. The path to the future is influenced by multiple determinants, some integrative and others disintegrative.

- Everyone has some kind of "mental model" of world politics that simplifies reality by exaggerating some features of international affairs and ignoring others.

- The shape of the world's future will be determined not only by changes in the objective conditions of world politics, but also by the meanings that people ascribe to those conditions.

- Although most people are prone to look for information that reinforces their beliefs and give disproportionate weight to initial impressions and information they can easily recall, dramatic events can alter an individual's mental model of world politics.

- An adequate account of continuities and changes in world politics requires examining a variety of causal factors flowing from the individual, state, and systemic levels of analysis.

- Causal factors operating at the individual level of analysis explain international events by focusing on the personal characteristics of humans; those at the state level, by looking at the national attributes of states; and those at the systemic level, by concentrating on the structure and processes of the global system as a whole.

KEY TERMS

attribution bias

cognitive dissonance

containment

contingent behavior

individual level of
  analysis

mirror image

nationalism

nonstate actors

politics

schematic reasoning

state

state level of analysis

system

systemic level of analysis

SUGGESTED READINGS

Ferguson, Yale H., and Richard W. Mansbach. *Remapping Global Politics: History's Revenge and Future Shock.* New York: Columbia University Press, 2004.

Hughes, Barry B., and Evan E. Hillebrand. *Exploring and Shaping International Futures.* Boulder, CO: Paradigm Publishers, 2006.

Kegley, Charles W., Jr., and Gregory A. Raymond. *Exorcising the Ghost of Westphalia: Building World Order in the New Millennium.* Upper Saddle River, NJ: Prentice-Hall, 2002.

Kurki, Milja. *Causation in International Relations.* Cambridge: Cambridge University Press, 2008.

Tickner, Arlene B., and Ole Wæver. *Global Scholarship in International Relations.* London: Routledge, 2008.

CRITICAL THINKING QUESTIONS

Why did the United States invade Iraq in 2003? When weapons of mass destruction (WMD) were not found after Saddam Hussein was ousted, the most common argument was that the war was "largely about oil" (Greenspan 2007, 463). Facing rising energy demands and insecure supplies, the Bush administration sought access to Iraq's vast petroleum reserves (Hart 2004, 98–99). While seductive, this single-factor explanation overlooks other plausible causes of the Iraq War. Wars, according to most scholars, have multiple causes that can be found at different levels of analysis. What follows is a nonexhaustive inventory of other factors that may have caused the war to occur.

- Due to unipolarity, there was no countervailing power to deter an American attack (Keegan 2005, 98).

- The terrorist attacks of 9/11 shifted the Bush administration's attention to the problem of state-sponsored terrorism (Allawi 2007, 80; Aldonsi 2006, 408; Nuechterlein 2005, 39).

- The success in ousting the Taliban from power in Afghanistan boosted the confidence of the Bush administration, leading it to conclude that regime change in Iraq would be relatively easy (F. Kaplan 2008, 39-40; Steinberg 2008, 156).

- The decision-making process within the Bush administration was flawed; intelligence was "cherry picked," a wide range of policy options were not examined, and criticism of the favored course of action was not encouraged (McClelland 2008; Dobbins 2007, 64; Pillar 2006).

- Congress failed to provide sufficient oversight of administration actions (Ricks 2006, 4).

- Neoconservatives (e.g., Paul Wolfowitz, John Bolton, Douglas Feith) were a vocal pressure group insisting for years that Saddam Hussein was an evil leader who should have been removed from power during the 1991 Persian Gulf War; if his regime was replaced by a democratic government, they predicted that democracy would spread throughout the region (Galbraith 2006, 9; Stoessinger 2005, 279).

- Powerful, assertive members of the administration, such as Vice President Dick Cheney, believed in the importance of taking preventive military actions against perceived threats (Woodward 2004, 4).

- President Bush was an intuitive, risk-acceptant decision maker who saw the world as a moral struggle between the forces of good versus evil, with no neutral ground between them (Cashman and Robinson 2007, 336).

How would you classify these possible causes by level of analysis and time sequence? Which factors operated at the individual, state, and systemic levels? Which factors were remote and which might have been proximate causes of the war? How might certain specific factors from different levels of analysis interacted with one another over time in a chain of causation to increase the probability of the Iraq War?

2

Theories of World Politics

CHAPTER OUTLINE

Contending Theories of World Politics

Realist Theory

  The Realist Worldview

  The Evolution of Realist Thought

  The Limitations of Realism

Liberal Theory

  The Liberal Worldview

  The Evolution of Liberal Thought

  The Limitations of Liberalism

  APPLICATION: Steel and Good Intentions

Constructivist Theory

  The Constructivist Worldview

  The Evolution of Constructivist Thought

  The Limitations of Constructivism

What's Missing in Theories of World Politics?

  The Radical Critique

  The Feminist Critique

Forecasting the Global Future with Theories of World Politics

  CONTROVERSY: Can Behavioral Science Advance the Study of World Politics?

There is an inescapable link between the abstract world of theory and the real world of policy. We need theories to make sense of the blizzard of information that bombards us daily. Even policymakers who are contemptuous of "theory" must rely on their own (often unstated) ideas about how the world works in order to decide what to do ... Everyone uses theories—whether he or she knows it or not.

STEPHEN M. WALT
POLITICAL SCIENTIST

Although the academic study of international relations is relatively new, attempts to theorize about state behavior date back to antiquity. Perhaps the best example can be found in Thucydides, the Greek historian who analyzed the Peloponnesian War (431–404 BCE) between ancient Sparta and Athens. Thucydides believed "knowledge of the past" would be "an aid to the interpretation of the future" and therefore wrote a history of the war "not to win the applause of the moment, but as a possession for all time." Examining the hostilities like a physician diagnosing a patient, his detailed clinical observations were recorded as a case study that described the symptoms of war-prone periods and offered a prognosis of the probable consequences of different foreign policy actions.

Greece in Thucydides's day was not unified; it contained a welter of small, autonomous city-states scattered throughout the Balkan Peninsula, the Aegean Archipelago, and what is today western Turkey. Sparta and Athens were the strongest of these fiercely independent states. The former was a cautious, conservative land power; the latter, a bold, innovative sea power. Relations between them were contentious. When their rivalry eventually escalated to war in 431 BCE, they became trapped in a long, debilitating military stalemate.

Stung by mounting losses during a decade of fruitless combat, in 421 BCE Sparta and Athens agreed to a cessation of hostilities. Neither side expected it to last, however. The two rivals refrained from attacking one another over the next few years, but each side maneuvered to gain an advantage over the other in anticipation of the next round of fighting. A strong, reliable network of allies, the Athenians thought, might provide a decisive edge when the war resumed. To consolidate their position among Greeks living on islands throughout the Aegean Sea, in 416 BCE Athens sent an expedition of thirty-eight ships and approximately three thousand soldiers to Melos, a city-state that wished to remain nonaligned during the war. The Athenians declared that if Melos did not agree to become their ally, it would be obliterated. The Melians argued that such a brutal attack would be unjust since they had not harmed Athens. Moreover, it was in Athens's self-interest to show restraint: destroying Melos would drive other neutral city-states into the Spartan camp. Finally, the Melians pointed out that it would be unreasonable to surrender while there was still hope of being rescued by the Spartans. Scornful of these appeals to justice, expedience, and reasonableness, the Athenians proclaimed that in interstate relations "the strong do what they can and the weak suffer what they must." Regardless of the merits of the Melian argument, Athens had the strength to subjugate Melos if it so desired. Resistance was futile; nevertheless, the Melians refused to submit. The Athenian troops promptly besieged the city, forcing it to capitulate shortly thereafter. Following the city's surrender, they killed all adult men and sold the women and children into slavery.

The Athenian practice of raw power politics raises timeless questions about world affairs. How can states achieve security in an anarchic international system? In the absence of a central authority to resolve the disputes among states, are there limits to the use of military power? What role should ethical considerations play in the conduct of foreign policy? This chapter will focus on the three schools of thought that have most influenced how policymakers and scholars think about these kinds of questions: realism, liberalism, and constructivism.

CONTENDING THEORIES OF WORLD POLITICS

Imagine yourself the newly elected president of the United States. You are scheduled to deliver the State of the Union address on your views of the current world situation. Your task is to identify those international issues most worthy of attention and explain how you plan to deal with them. To convince citizens these issues are important, you must present them as part of a larger picture of the world, showing how the situation you face may be part of a pattern. You must, in short, think *theoretically*. The success of your effort to explain the causes of current problems, predict their long-term consequences, and persuade others that you have a viable policy to address them will hinge on how well you understand the way the world works.

When leaders face these kinds of intellectual challenges, they fortunately benefit from the existence of several theories of world politics from which they can draw guidance. A **theory** is a set of statements that purports to explain a particular phenomenon. In essence, it provides a map, or frame of reference, that makes the complex, puzzling world around us intelligible. Choosing which theory to heed is an important decision, because each rests on different assumptions about the nature of international politics, each advances different causal claims, and each offers a different set of foreign policy recommendations. Our aim in this chapter is to compare the assumptions, causal claims, and policy prescriptions of realism, liberalism, and constructivism, the most common theoretical perspectives policymakers and scholars use to interpret international relations. We begin with realism, the oldest of these contending schools of thought.

theory a set of interrelated propositions that explains an observed regularity.

REALIST THEORY

Political realism has a long, distinguished history that dates back to the writings of Thucydides about the Peloponnesian War. Other influential figures that contributed to realist thought include the sixteenth-century Italian philosopher Niccolò Machiavelli and the seventeenth-century English philosopher Thomas Hobbes. Realism deserves careful examination because its worldview continues to guide much thought about international politics.

The Realist Worldview

Realism, as applied to contemporary international politics, views the nation-state as the most important actor on the world stage since it answers to no higher political authority. States are sovereign: they have supreme power over their territory and populace, and no one stands above them wielding the legitimacy and coercive capability to govern the international system. Given the absence of a higher authority to which states can turn to for protection and to resolve disputes, realists depict world politics as a ceaseless, repetitive struggle for **power** where, like in the Melian episode described by Thucydides, the strong dominate the weak. Because each state is ultimately responsible for its own survival and feels uncertain about its neighbors' intentions, realism claims that prudent political leaders seek arms and allies to enhance national security. In other words, the anarchic structure of the international system leads even well-intentioned leaders to practice **self-help**, increasing military strength and aligning with others to deter potential threats. Realist theory does not preclude the possibility that rival powers will cooperate on arms control or on other security issues of common interest. Rather it asserts that cooperation will be rare because states worry about the distribution of **relative gains** emanating from cooperation and the possibility that the other side will cheat on agreements.

Realists, with their emphasis on the ruthless nature of international life, tend to be skeptical about the role of ethical considerations in foreign policy deliberations. As they see it, some policies are driven by strategic imperatives that may require national leaders to contravene moral norms. Embedded in this "philosophy

power the ability to make someone continue a course of action, change what he or she is doing, or refrain from acting.

self-help the principle that in anarchy actors must rely on themselves.

relative gains a measure of how much one side in an agreement benefits in comparison with the other's side.

Scala/ Art Resource, NY

Thomas Hobbes (oil on canvas), Fuller, Isaac (1606-72) (circle of)/Burghley House Collection, Lincolnshire, UK/The Bridgeman Art Library International

Realist Pioneers of Power Politics In *The Prince* (1532) and *The Leviathan* (1651) Niccolò Machiavelli and Thomas Hobbes, respectively, emphasized a political calculus based on interest, prudence, power, and expediency above all other considerations. This formed the foundation of what became a growing body of modern realist thinking that accepts the drive for power over others as necessary and wise statecraft.

of necessity" is a distinction between private morality, which guides the behavior of ordinary people in their daily lives, and reason of state *(raison d'état)*, which governs the conduct of leaders responsible for the security and survival of the state. Whatever actions that are in the interest of state security must be carried out no matter how repugnant they might seem in the light of private morality. "Ignoring one's interests, squandering one's resources in fits of altruism," so this line of argument goes, "is the fastest road to national disaster." For a national leader, "thinking with one's heart is a serious offense. Foreign policy is not social work" (Krauthammer 1993).

The Evolution of Realist Thought

We have seen how the intellectual roots of political realism reach back to ancient Greece. They also extend beyond the western world to India and China. Discussions of "power politics" abound in the *Arthashastra,* an Indian treatise on statecraft written during the fourth century BCE by Kautilya, as well as in works written by Han Fei and Shang Yang in ancient China.

Modern realism emerged on the eve of the Second World War, when the prevailing belief in a natural harmony of interests among nations came under attack. Just a decade earlier, this belief had led numerous countries to sign the 1928 Kellogg-Briand Pact, which renounced war as an instrument of national policy. Now, with Nazi Germany, Fascist Italy, and Imperial Japan all violating the treaty, British historian and diplomat E. H. Carr (1939) complained that the assumption of a universal interest in peace had allowed too many people to "evade the unpalatable fact of a fundamental divergence of interest between nations desirous of maintaining the *status quo* and nations desirous of changing it."

In an effort to counter what they saw as a utopian, legalistic approach to foreign affairs, Reinhold Niebuhr (1947), Hans J. Morgenthau (1948), and other realists articulated a pessimistic view of human nature. Echoing the seventeenth-century philosopher Baruch Spinoza, many of them pointed to an innate conflict between passion and reason; furthermore, in the tradition of St. Augustine, they stressed that material appetites enabled passion to overwhelm reason. For them, the human condition was such that the forces of light and darkness would perpetually vie for control.

The realists' picture of international life appeared particularly persuasive after World War II. The onset of rivalry between the United States and the Soviet Union, the expansion of the Cold War into a wider struggle between East and West, and the periodic crises that threatened to erupt into global violence all supported the realists' emphasis on the inevitability of conflict, the poor prospects for cooperation, and the divergence of national interests among incorrigibly selfish, power-seeking states.

Whereas these so-called "classical" realists sought to explain state behavior by drawing upon explanatory factors located at the individual level of analysis, *neorealism* (sometimes labeled structural realism), the next wave of realist theorizing, emphasized the systemic level of analysis. Kenneth Waltz (1979), the leading proponent of what has come to be called "defensive" realism, proposed that international anarchy—not some allegedly evil side of human nature—explained why states were locked in fierce competition with one another. The absence of a central arbiter was the defining structural feature of the international system. Vulnerable and insecure, states behaved defensively by forming alliances against looming threats. According to Waltz, balances of power form automatically in anarchic environments. Even when they are disrupted, they are soon restored.

The most recent variant of realist theory also resides at the systemic level of analysis, but asserts that the ultimate goal of states is to achieve military suprem-acy, not merely a balance of power. For John Mearsheimer (2001) and other exponents of "offensive" realism, the anarchic structure of the international sys-tem encourages states to maximize their share of world power in order to improve the odds of surviving the competition for relative advantage. A state with an edge over everyone else has insurance against the possibility that a pred-atory state might someday pose a grave threat. To quote the old cliché: The best defense is a good offense.

The Limitations of Realism

However persuasive the realists' image of the essential properties of international politics, their policy recommendations suffered from a lack of precision in the way they used such key terms as *power* and *national interest*. Thus, once analysis moved beyond the assertion that national leaders should acquire power to serve the national interest, important questions remained: What were the key elements of national power? What uses of power best served the national interest? Did arms furnish protection or provoke costly arms races? Did alliances enhance one's defenses or encourage threatening counteralliances? From the perspective of realism's critics, seeking security by amassing power was self-defeating. The quest for absolute security by one state would be perceived as creating absolute insecurity for other members of the system, with the result that everyone would become locked in an upward spiral of countermeasures that jeopardized the security of all (Vasquez 1998; 1993).

Because much of realist theorizing was vague, it began to be questioned. Realism offered no criteria for determining what historical data were significant in evaluating its claims and what epistemological rules to follow when interpret-ing relevant information (Vasquez and Elman 2003). Even the policy recom-mendations that purportedly flowed from its logic were often divergent. Realists themselves, for example, were sharply divided as to whether U.S. inter-vention in Vietnam served American national interests and whether nuclear weapons contributed to international security. Similarly, whereas some observers used realism to explain the 2003 U.S. invasion of Iraq (Gvosdev 2005), others drew upon realist arguments to criticize the invasion (Mansfield and Snyder 2005; Mearsheimer and Walt 2003).

A growing number of critics also pointed out that realism did not account for significant developments in world politics. For instance, it could not explain the creation of new commercial and political institutions in Western Europe in the 1950s and 1960s, where the cooperative pursuit of mutual advantage led

Europeans away from the unbridled power politics that brought them incessant warfare since the birth of the nation-state some three centuries earlier. Other critics began to worry about realism's tendency to disregard ethical principles and about the material and social costs that some of its policy prescriptions seemed to impose, such as retarded economic growth resulting from unrestrained military expenditures.

Despite realism's shortcomings, many people continue to think about world politics in the language constructed by realists, especially in times of global tension. A recent example can be found in the comments by former British adviser Michael Gerson (2006, 59–60) about how the United States should deal with Iran's nuclear ambitions. Arguing from the realist assumption that "peace is not a natural state," he has called for a robust American response based on a steely-eyed focus on the country's national security interest in preventing the proliferation of weapons of mass destruction in the Middle East. "There must be someone in the world capable of drawing a line—someone who says, 'This much and no further.'" Peace, he concludes, cannot be achieved by "a timid foreign policy that allows terrible threats to emerge." Unless those who threaten others pay a price, "aggression will be universal."

LIBERAL THEORY

Liberalism has been called the "strongest contemporary challenge to realism" (Caporaso 1993). Like realism, it has a distinguished pedigree, with philosophical roots extending back to the political thought of John Locke, Immanuel Kant, and Adam Smith. Liberalism warrants our attention because it speaks to issues realism disregards, including the impact of domestic politics on state behavior, the implications of economic interdependence, and the role of international norms and institutions in facilitating international cooperation.

The Liberal Worldview

There are several distinct schools of thought within the liberal tradition. Drawing broad conclusions from such a diverse body of theory risks misrepresenting the position of any given author. Nevertheless, there are sufficient commonalities to abstract some general themes.

Liberals differ from realists in several important ways. At the core of liberalism is a belief in reason and the possibility of progress. Liberals view the individual as the seat of moral value and assert that human beings should be treated as ends rather than means. Whereas realists counsel decision makers to seek the lesser evil rather than the absolute good, liberals emphasize ethical principle over the pursuit of power, and institutions over military capabilities (see Doyle 1997; Howard 1978; Zacher and Matthew 1995). Politics at the international level is more of a struggle for consensus and mutual gain than a struggle for power and prestige.

Pioneers in the Liberal Quest for World Order Immanuel Kant (left) in *Perpetual Peace* (1795) helped to redefine modern liberal theory by advocating global (not state) citizenship, free trade, and a federation of democracies as a means to peace. Richard Cobden (right) primarily foresaw the possibility of peace across borders; in his view, if contact and communication among people could expand through free trade, so too would international friendship and peace, secured by prosperity that would create interdependence and eliminate the need for military forces to pursue rivalries.

Instead of blaming international conflict on an inherent lust for power, liberals fault the conditions that people live under. Reforming those conditions, they argue, will enhance the prospects for peace. The first element common to various strands of liberal thought is an emphasis undertaking political reforms to establish stable democracies. Woodrow Wilson, for example, proclaimed that "democratic government will make wars less likely." Franklin Roosevelt later reflected this view when he asserted "the continued maintenance and improvement of democracy constitute the most important guarantee of international peace." Based on tolerance, accommodation, and procedural rights, democratic political cultures are said to shun lethal force as a means of settling disagreements. Politics is not seen as a **zero-sum game**, so that the use of persuasion rather than coercion, and a reliance on judicial avenues to settle rival claims are the primary means of dealing with conflict.

zero-sum game a situation in which what one side wins, the other side loses.

According to liberal theory, conflict resolution practices used at home are also employed when dealing with international disputes. Leaders socialized within democratic cultures share a common outlook. Viewing international politics as an extension of domestic politics, they externalize their norms of regulated competition. Disputes with kindred governments rarely escalate to war because each side accepts the other's legitimacy and expects it to rely on peaceful means of conflict resolution. These expectations are reinforced by the transparent nature of democracies. The inner workings of open polities can be scrutinized by anyone; hence, it is difficult to demonize them as scheming adversaries.

The second thrust common to liberal theorizing is an emphasis on free trade. The idea that commerce helps promote conflict resolution has roots in the work of Montesquieu, Adam Smith, and various Enlightenment thinkers. "Nothing is more favourable to the rise of politeness and learning," noted the philosopher David Hume (1817), "than a number of neighboring and independent states, connected by commerce." This view was later embraced by the Manchester School of political economy and formed the basis for Norman Angell's (1910) famous rebuttal of the assertion that military conquest yields economic prosperity.

The doctrine that unfettered trade helps prevent disputes from escalating to wars rests on several propositions. First, commercial intercourse creates a material incentive to resolve disputes peacefully: War reduces profits by interrupting vital economic exchanges. Second, cosmopolitan business elites who benefit most from these exchanges comprise a powerful transnational interest group with a stake in promoting amicable solutions to festering disagreements. Finally, the web of trade between nations increases communication, erodes parochialism, and encourages both sides to avoid ruinous clashes. In the words of Richard Cobden, an opponent of the protectionist Corn Laws that once regulated British international grain trade: "Free Trade! What is it? Why, breaking down the barriers that separate nations; those barriers, behind which nestle the feelings of pride, revenge, hatred, and jealousy, which every now and then burst their bounds, and deluge whole countries with blood" (cited in Wolfers and Martin 1956).

Finally, the third commonality in liberal theorizing is an advocacy of international institutions. Liberals recommend replacing cut-throat, balance-of-power politics with organizations based on the principle that a threat to peace anywhere is a common concern to everyone. They see foreign policy as unfolding in a nascent global society populated by actors who recognize the cost of conflict, share significant interests, and can realize those interests by using institutions to mediate disputes whenever misconceptions, wounded sensibilities, or aroused national passions threaten their relations.

The Evolution of Liberal Thought

Contemporary liberal theory rose to prominence in the wake of the First World War. Not only had the war involved more participants over a wider geographic area than any previous war, but modern science and technology made it a war of machinery: Old weapons were improved and produced in great quantities, new and far more deadly weapons were rapidly developed and deployed. By the time the carnage was over, nearly twenty million people were dead.

For liberals like U.S. President Woodrow Wilson, World War I was "the war to end all wars." Convinced that another horrific war would erupt if states resumed practicing power politics, liberals set out to reform the international system. These "idealists," as they were called by hard-boiled realists, generally fell into one of three groups (Herz 1951). The first group advocated creating international institutions to mitigate the raw struggle for power between egoistic,

collective security a security regime based on the principle that an act of aggression by any state will be met by a collective response from the rest.

mutually suspicious states. The League of Nations was the embodiment of this strain of liberal thought. Its founders hoped to prevent future wars by organizing a system of **collective security** that would mobilize the entire international community against would-be aggressors. The League's founders declared that peace was indivisible: An attack on one member of the League would be considered an attack on all. Since no state was more powerful than the combination of all other states, aggressors would be deterred and war averted.

A second group called for the use of legal procedures to adjudicate disputes before they escalated to armed conflict. Adjudication is a judicial procedure for resolving conflicts by referring them to a standing court for a binding decision. Immediately after the war, several governments drafted a statute to establish a Permanent Court of International Justice (PCIJ). Hailed by Bernard C. J. Loder, the court's first president, as the harbinger of a new era of civilization, the PCIJ held its inaugural public meeting in early 1922 and rendered its first judgment on a contentious case the following year. Liberal champions of the court insisted that the PCIJ would replace military retaliation with a judicial body capable of bringing the facts of a dispute to light and issuing a just verdict.

A third group of liberal thinkers followed the biblical injunction that states should beat their swords into plowshares and sought disarmament as a means of avoiding war. Their efforts were exemplified between 1921 and 1922 by the Washington naval conference, which tried to curtail maritime competition among the United States, Great Britain, Japan, France, and Italy by placing limits on battleships. The ultimate goal of this group was to reduce international tensions by promoting general disarmament, which led them to convene the Geneva Disarmament Conference in 1932.

Although a tone of idealism dominated policy rhetoric and academic discussions during the interwar period, little of the liberal reform program was ever seriously attempted, and even less of it was achieved. The League of Nations failed to prevent the Japanese invasion of Manchuria (1931) or the Italian invasion of Ethiopia (1935); major disputes were rarely submitted to the Permanent Court of International Justice; and the 1932 Geneva Disarmament Conference ended in failure. When the threat of war began gathering over Europe and Asia in the late 1930s, enthusiasm for liberal idealism receded.

transnational relations interactions across state boundaries that involve at least one actor that is not the agent of a government or intergovernmental organization.

complex interdependence a model of world politics based on the assumptions that states are not the only important actors, security is not the dominant national goal, and military force is not the only significant instrument of foreign policy.

The next surge in liberal theorizing arose decades later in response to realism's neglect of **transnational relations** (see Keohane and Nye 1971). Although realists continued to focus on the state, the events surrounding the 1973 oil crisis revealed that nonstate actors could affect the course of international events, and occasionally compete with states. This insight led to the realization that **complex interdependence** (Keohane and Nye 1977) sometimes offered a better description of world politics than realism, especially on international economic and environmental matters. Rather than contacts between countries being limited to high-level governmental officials, multiple communication channels connected societies. Rather than security dominating foreign policy considerations, issues on national agendas did not always have a fixed priority. Rather than military force serving as the primary instrument of statecraft, other means frequently were more effective when bargaining occurred between economically interconnected nations. In short, the realist preoccupation with government-to-government relations ignored the complex network of public and private exchanges crisscrossing national boundaries. States were becoming increasingly interdependent; that is, mutually dependent on, sensitive about, and vulnerable to one another in ways that were not captured by realist theory.

While interdependence was not new, its growth during the last quarter of the twentieth century led many liberal theorists to challenge the realist conception of anarchy. Although agreeing that the international system was anarchic, they suggested that it was more properly conceptualized as an "ordered" anarchy because most states followed commonly acknowledged normative standards, even in the absence of hierarchical enforcement. When a body of norms fosters shared expectations that guide a regularized pattern of cooperation on a specific issue, we call it an **international regime** (see Hansenclever, Mayer, and Rittberger 1996). Various types of regimes have been devised to govern behavior in trade and monetary affairs, as well as to manage access to common resources like fisheries and river water. By the turn of the century, as pressing economic and environmental issues crowded national agendas, a large body of liberal scholarship delved into how regimes developed and what led states to follow their injunctions.

international regime a set of principles, norms, and rules governing behavior within a specified issue area.

Fueled by a belief that increased interdependence can lead to higher levels of cooperation, this new wave of liberal theorizing, known as *neoliberalism* (also called neoliberal institutionalism), mounted a serious challenge to realism and neorealism during the last decade of the twentieth century. Neoliberals argued that states attempt to maximize **absolute gains** by cooperating to advance mutual interests, and that international institutions provide a mechanism for coordinating multilateral action and reducing the odds of anyone reneging on their commitments. On the one hand, institutions strengthen cooperative arrangements by providing information on the preferences of others; on the other, they dampen the incentive to cheat by monitoring compliance with agreements.

absolute gains conditions in which all participants in exchanges become better off.

More recently, neoliberals have explored **moral hazard** dilemmas that can arise when states behave in ways that exacerbate a pressing problem because they expect international institutions to bail them out. For example, a country that is unable to make payments on its outstanding debts may continue borrowing under the assumption that an institution such as the International Monetary Fund will provide it with financial backing (Martin 2007, 118–124). Research into dilemmas of this kind have led neoliberals to gain insights into how international institutions occasionally carve out enough autonomy to pursue their own agendas despite pressure to respond to the desires of their most powerful members.

moral hazard a situation in which international institutions create incentives for states to behave recklessly.

The Limitations of Liberalism

Liberal theorists share an interest in probing the conditions under which the convergent and overlapping interests among otherwise sovereign political actors may result in cooperation. Taking heart in the international prohibition, through community consensus, of such previously entrenched practices as slavery, piracy, dueling, and colonialism, they emphasize the prospects for progress through institutional reform. Studies of European integration during the 1950s and 1960s paved the way for the liberal institutionalist theories that emerged in the 1990s. The expansion of trade, communication, information, technology, and immigrant labor propelled Europeans to sacrifice portions of their sovereign independence to create a new political and economic union out of previously separate units. These developments were outside of realism's worldview, creating conditions that made the call for a theory grounded in the liberal tradition convincing to many who had previously questioned realism. In the words of former U.S. president Bill Clinton, "In a world where freedom, not tyranny, is on the march, the cynical calculus of pure power politics simply does not compute. It is ill-suited to the new era."

Yet as compelling as contemporary liberal institutionalism may seem at the onset of the twenty-first century, many realists complain that it has not transcended its idealist heritage (see Application: Steel and Good Intentions). They charge that just like the League of Nations and the Permanent Court of International Justice, institutions today exert minimal influence on state behavior. International organizations cannot stop states from behaving according to balance-of-power logic, calculating how each move they make affects their relative position in a world of relentless competition (Mearsheimer 1994/1995; 1995).

Critics of liberalism further contend that most studies supportive of international institutions appear in the **low politics** arena of commercial, financial, and environmental affairs, not in the **high politics** arena of national defense. While it may be difficult to draw a clear line between economic and security issues, some scholars note that different institutional arrangements exist in each realm, with the prospects for cooperation among self-interested states greater in the former than the latter (Lipson 1984). National survival hinges on the effective management of security issues, insist realists. Collective security organizations naively assume that all members perceive threats in the same way, and are willing to run the risks and pay the costs of countering those threats (Kissinger 1992). Because avaricious states are unlikely to see their vital interests in this light, international institutions cannot provide timely, muscular responses to aggression. On security issues, conclude realists, states will trust in their own power, not in the promises of international institutions.

A final realist complaint lodged against liberalism is an alleged tendency to turn foreign policy into a moral crusade. Whereas realists claim that heads of state are driven by strategic necessities, many liberals believe moral necessities impose categorical imperatives on leaders. Consider the 1999 war in Kosovo, which pitted the North Atlantic Treaty Organization (NATO) against the Federal Republic of Yugoslavia. Pointing to Yugoslav leader Slobodan Milosevic's repression of ethnic Albanians living in the province of Kosovo, NATO Secretary General Javier Solana, British Prime Minister Tony Blair, and U.S. President Bill Clinton all argued that humanitarian intervention was a moral imperative. Although nonintervention into the internal affairs of other states

low politics the category of global issues related to the economic, social, and environmental aspects of relations between governments and people.

high politics the category of global issues related to military and security aspects of relations between governments and people.

APPLICATION   **Steel and Good Intentions**

Political realists frequently refer to those who believe that international morality can contribute to fostering peaceful relations among states as "idealists" or "utopians." Asking us to look at the world with candor, they insist that politics is a struggle for power that cannot be eliminated from the international scene. In the words of Otto von Bismarck, German chancellor during the late nineteenth century and the foremost realist of his day, conducting foreign policy with moral principles would be like walking along a narrow forest path while carrying a long pole in one's mouth.

Although the prevailing caricature of realists depicts them as ruthless practitioners of guileful tactics, many policymakers who subscribe to realism aver that prudence requires raw power to be restrained by moral limitations. In the passage that follows, Margaret Thatcher, who served as prime minister of the United Kingdom from 1979 to 1990, discusses how realist prescriptions about the use of power as well as moral principles informed her foreign policy decisions.

> Above all, foreign and security policy is about the use of power in order to achieve a state's goals in its relations with other states. As a conservative, I have no squeamishness about stating this. I leave it to others to try to achieve the results they seek in international affairs without reference to power. They always fail. And their failures often lead to

outcomes more damaging than pursuit of national interest through the normal means of the balance of power and resolute defense would ever have done.

> It is sometimes suggested, or at least implied, that the only alternative ... [to idealism] is the total abandonment of moral standards. ...Yet I am not one of those who believe that statecraft should concern power without principle. For a start, pure *Realpolitik*—that is, foreign policy based on calculations of power and the national interest—is a concept which blurs at the edges the more closely it is examined. ...[T]he pursuit of statecraft without regard for moral principles is all but impossible, and it makes little sense for even the most hard-nosed statesman to ignore this fact.

> ...For my part, I favor an approach to statecraft that embraces principles, as long as it is not stifled by them; and I prefer such principles to be accompanied by steel along with good intentions (Thatcher 2002, xix–xxii).

For Thatcher, who dealt with issues ranging from confrontations with the Soviet Union to war with Argentina during her tenure in office, moral posturing was no substitute for a muscular foreign policy. However, effective policy required a moral vision.

---

had long been a cardinal principle of international law, they saw military action against Yugoslavia as a duty because human rights were an international entitlement and governments that violated them forfeited the protection of international law. Sovereignty, according to many liberal thinkers, is not sacrosanct. The international community has an obligation to use armed force to stop flagrant violations of human rights.

To sum up, realists remain skeptical about liberal claims of moral necessity. On the one hand, they deny the universal applicability of any single moral standard in a culturally pluralistic world. On the other hand, they worry that adopting such a standard will breed a self-righteous, messianic foreign policy. Realists embrace **consequentialism**. If there are no universal standards covering the many situations in which moral choice must occur, then policy decisions can only be judged in terms of their consequences in particular circumstances. Prudent leaders recognize that competing moral values may be at stake in any given situation, and they must weigh the trade-offs among these values, as well as how pursuing them might impinge on national security and other important interests. As the former U.S. diplomat and celebrated realist scholar George Kennan

consequentialism an approach to evaluating moral choices on the basis of the results of the action taken.

(1985) once put it, the primary obligation of government "is to the *interests* of the national society it represents, not to the moral impulses that individual elements of that society may experience."

CONSTRUCTIVIST THEORY

Since the end of the Cold War, many students of international relations have turned to social constructivism in order to understand world politics. In contrast to realism and liberalism, which emphasize how material factors such as military power and economic wealth affect the relations among states, constructivism focuses on the impact of ideas. As discussed in the previous chapter, international reality is defined by our images of the world. Constructivists emphasize the inter-subjective quality of these images. We are all influenced by collective concep-tions of world politics that are reinforced by social pressures from the reference groups to which we belong. Awareness of how our understandings of the world are socially constructed, and of how prevailing ideas mold our beliefs about what is immutable and what can be reformed, allow us to see world politics in a new, critical light.

The Constructivist Worldview

As shown in Table 2.1, constructivists differ from realists and liberals most fun-damentally by insisting that world politics is socially constructed. That is to say, material resources, such as those contributing to brute military and economic power, only acquire meaning for human action through the structure of shared knowledge in which they are embedded. The social structure of a system makes actions possible by constituting actors with certain identities and interests, and material capabilities with certain meanings (see Hopf 1998; S. Smith 1997; Onuf 1989). Hence the meaning of a concept such as "anarchy" depends on the underlying structure of shared knowledge. An anarchy among allies, for example, entails a different meaning for the states in question than an anarchy composed of bitter rivals. Thus, British nuclear weapons are less threatening to the United States than the same weapons in North Korean hands, because shared Anglo-American expectations about one another differ from those between Washington and Pyongyang. The nature of international life within an anarchy, in other words, is not a given. Anarchy, as well as other socially constructed concepts like "sovereignty" and "power," are simply what states make of them (Wendt 1995).

The Evolution of Constructivist Thought

The intellectual roots of constructivism extend from the work of the early twentieth-century Frankfurt School of critical social theory to more recent research by Peter Berger and Thomas Luckmann (1967) on the sociology of

TABLE 2.1   A Comparison of Realist, Liberal, and Constructivist Theories

Feature	Realism	Liberalism	Constructivism
Core concern	How vulnerable, self-interested states survive in an environment where they are uncertain about the intentions and capabilities of others	How rational egoists coordinate their behavior through rules and organizations in order to achieve collective gains	How ideas and identities shape world politics
Key actors	States	States, international institutions, global corporations	Individuals, nongovernmental organizations, transnational networks
Central concepts	Anarchy, self-help, national interest, relative gains, balance of power	Collective security, international regimes, complex interdependence, transnational relations	Ideas, shared knowledge, identities, discourses
Approach to peace	Protect sovereign autonomy and deter rivals through military preparedness	Democratization, open markets, and international law and organization	Activists who promote progressive ideas and encourage states to adhere to norms of appropriate behavior
Global outlook	Pessimistic: great powers locked in relentless security competition	Optimistic: cooperative view of human nature and a belief in progress	Agnostic: global prospect hinges on the content of prevailing ideas and values

knowledge and by Anthony Giddens (1984) on the relationship between agency and social structure. Sometimes described as more of a philosophically informed perspective than a fully fledged general theory (Ruggie 1998), contstructivism includes a diverse group of scholars who by and large agree that the international institutions most people take for granted as the natural and inevitable result of world politics need not exist (see Hacking 1999). Like the institution of slavery, they are social constructs that depend upon human agreement for their existence and are therefore changeable.

The unraveling of the Warsaw Pact and subsequent disintegration of the Soviet Union stimulated scholarly interest during the 1990s in constructivist interpretations of world politics. Neither realism nor liberalism foresaw the peaceful end to the Cold War and both theories had difficulty explaining why it occurred when it did. Constructivists pointed to the challenge that Mikhail Gorbechev's "new thinking" posed to traditional ideas about national security (Koslowski and Kratochwil 1994). New thinking, they suggested, led to the rise of new **norms** governing the relations between Moscow and Washington.

Norms can be the sources of action in three ways: they may be *constitutive* in the sense that they define what counts as a certain activity; they may be *constraining* in that they enjoin an actor from behaving in a particular way; or they may be *enabling* by allowing specific actions (Raymond 1997). In American football, for instance, there are constitutive rules that give meaning to action on the field

norms generalized standards of behavior that embody collective expectations about appropriate conduct.

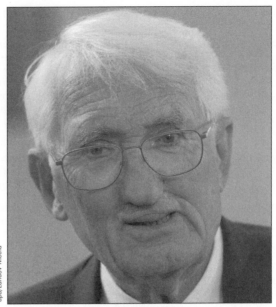

Pioneering Influences on Constructivist Thought Many constructivists have been influenced by critical theory, especially as it was developed by Max Horkheimer (1947) and Jürgen Habermas (1984). The roots of critical theory can be traced to the Institute for Social Research, which was founded in Frankfurt, Germany, during the 1920s. According to the so-called "Frankfurt School" of philosophical thought, the aims of critical theory were to critique and change society, not merely understand it. Rather than viewing the world as a set of neutral, objective "facts" that could be perceived apart from the situation in which observation occurred, critical theorists saw things as embedded within a specific socio-historical context (Price and Reus-Smit 1998; also see Cox 1996 and Hoffman 1987).

by defining what counts as a touchdown, a field goal, or a safety. There also are two kinds of regulative rules that guide play: constraining rules prohibit things like clipping and holding, while enabling rules permit players to throw laterals and forward passes. Similarly, in the modern world system, constitutive norms of sovereignty define what counts as statehood, while regulative norms that either constrain or enable specify how sovereign states ought to conduct themselves. Rather than simply following a *logic of consequences*, where the anticipatory costs and benefits of alternative actions are weighed to ascertain what will maximize one's interests, states take into account a *logic of appropriateness*, where the norms that define what consists of legitimate conduct guide behavior.

For constructivists, the game of power in international relations revolves around actors' abilities through debate about values to persuade others to accept their ideas. People and groups become powerful when their efforts to proselytize succeed in winning converts to those ideas and norms they advocate, and a culture of shared understandings emerges. The capacity of some activist transnational nongovernmental organizations, such as Human Rights Watch or Greenpeace, to promote global change by convincing many people to accept their ideas about political liberties and environmental protection are examples of how shared conceptions of moral and legal norms can change the world. Shared understandings of interests, identities, and images of the world—how people think of themselves, who they are, and what others in the world are like—demonstrably can alter the world when these social constructions of international realties change (Barnet 2005; Adler 2002; Onuf 2002).

The Limitations of Constructivism

The most common criticism of constructivism concerns its explanation of change. If changes in ideas and discourses lead to behavioral changes within the state system, what accounts for the rise and fall of different ideas and discourses over time? How, when, and why do social structures of shared knowledge emerge? "Constructivists are good at describing change," writes political scientist Jack Snyder (2004, 61), "but they are weak on the material and institutional circumstances necessary to support the emergence of consensus about new values and ideas." Moreover, even if new values and ideas are not reflections of developments in the material world, critics charge that constructivists remain unclear about what nonmaterial factors lead certain ideas and discourses to become dominant while others fall by the wayside (Mearsheimer 1994/95, 42–43). In particular, they "downplay the individual psychological needs" that "shape the social construction of identities" (Levy 2003b, 273). "What is crucial," asserts Robert Jervis (2005, 18), "is not people's thinking, but the factors that drive it." Constructivists, he continues, have excessive faith in the ability of ideas that seem self-evident today to replicate and sustain themselves; however, future generations who live under different circumstances and who may think differently could easily reject these ideas. For constructivists, socially accepted ideas, norms, and values are linked to collective identities—stable, role-specific understandings and expectations about self (Wendt 1994). Although constructivists recognize that shared identities are not pre-given and can change over time, critics submit that constructivists cannot explain why and when they dissolve.

A related concern about constructivism is that it overemphasizes the role of social structures at the expense of the purposeful agents whose practices help create and change these structures (Checkel 1998, 340–342). According to Cynthia Weber (2001, 76–78), constructivism as exemplified in the work of Alexander Wendt (1999) reifies states as the authors or producers of international life; that is, it treats them as objects that already exist and says little about the "practices that produce states as producers." Although Wendtian constructivism calls our attention to the importance of the intersubjectively constituted structure of identities and interests that influence how states see themselves and behave, it does not offer an account of the practices that construct states themselves as producers of international anarchy and other features of world politics.

Despite these criticisms, constructivism remains a popular approach to the study of world politics. By highlighting the influence that socially constructed images of the world have on our interpretations of international events, and by making us aware of their inherent subjectivity, constructivism reminds us of the contingent nature of all knowledge and the inability of any theory of world politics to fully capture global complexities.

WHAT'S MISSING IN THEORIES OF WORLD POLITICS?

Although realism, liberalism, and constructivism dominate thinking about international relations in today's academic and policy communities, these schools of thought have been challenged. Two of the most significant critiques have come from radicalism and feminism.

The Radical Critique

For much of the twentieth century, socialism was the primary radical alternative to mainstream international relations theorizing. Although there are many strands of socialist thought, most have been influenced by Karl Marx's (1818–1883) argument that explaining events in contemporary world affairs requires understanding capitalism as a global phenomenon. Whereas realists emphasize state security, liberals accentuate individual freedom, and constructivists highlight ideas and identities, socialists focus on class conflict and the material interests embodied by each class (Doyle 1997).

INTERFOTO Pressebildagentur/Alamy Limited

Marxism and Radical Political Thought
Pictured here is the German philosopher Karl Marx (1818–1883), who focused attention on the relationship between the means of economic production and political power.

"The history of all hitherto existing society," proclaim Marx and his coauthor Friedrich Engels (1820–1895) in the *Communist Manifesto,* "is the history of class struggles." Capitalism, they argue, has given rise to two antagonistic classes: a ruling class (bourgeoisie) that owns the means of production, and a subordinate class (proletariat) that sells its labor, but receives little compensation. According to Marx and Engels, "The need of a constantly expanding market for its products chases the bourgeoisie over the whole surface of the globe." By expanding worldwide, the bourgeoisie gives "a cosmopolitan character to production and consumption in every country."

Vladimir Ilyich Lenin (1870–1924) extended Marx's analysis to the study of imperialism, which he interpreted as a stage in the development of capitalism where monopolies supplant free-market competition. Drawing from the work of British economist John Hobson (1858–1940), Lenin maintained that advanced capitalist states eventually face the twin problems of overproduction and under-consumption. They respond by seeking foreign markets and investments for their surplus goods and capital, and by dividing the world into spheres of influence that they can exploit. While his assertions have been heavily criticized on conceptual and empirical grounds (see Dougherty and Pfaltzgraff 2001, 437–442), the attention given to social classes and uneven development engendered several new waves of theorizing about capitalism as a global phenomenon.

One prominent example is dependency theory. As expressed in the writings of André Gunder Frank (1969), Amir Samin (1976), and others (see Dos Santos 1970; Cardoso and Faletto 1979), dependency theorists claimed that much of the poverty in Asia, Africa, and Latin America stemmed from the exploitative structure of the capitalist world economy. As they saw it, the economies of less-developed countries had become dependent upon exporting inexpensive raw materials and agricultural commodities to advanced industrial states, while simultaneously importing expensive manufactured goods from them. Raúl Prebisch, an Argentinian economist who directed the United Nations Economic Commission for Latin America, feared that these producers of primary products would find it difficult to develop, because the price of their products would fall over time relative to the price of manufactured goods. Dependency theory was criticized for recommending withdrawal from the world economy (T. Shannon 1989; also Packenham 1992), and was eventually superseded by efforts to trace the economic ascent and decline of individual countries as part of long-run, system-wide change.

World-system theory, which was influenced by both Marxist and dependency theorists, represents the most recent effort to interpret world politics in terms of an integrated capitalist division of labor (see Wallerstein 2005 and 1988; Chase-Dunn and Anderson 2005; Chase-Dunn 1989). The capitalist world economy, which emerged in sixteenth-century Europe and ultimately expanded to encompass the entire globe, is viewed as containing three structural positions: a *core* (strong, well-integrated states whose economic activities are diversified and capital-intensive), a *periphery* (areas lacking strong state machinery and engaged in producing relatively few unfinished goods by unskilled, low-wage labor), and a *semi-periphery* (states embodying elements of both core and peripheral production). Within the core, a state may gain economic primacy by achieving productive, commercial, and financial superiority over its rivals. Primacy is difficult to sustain, however. The diffusion of technological innovations and the flow of capital to competitors, plus the massive costs of maintaining global order, all erode the dominant state's economic advantage. Thus in addition to underscoring the exploitation of the periphery by the core, world-system theory calls attention to the cyclical rise and fall of hegemonic core powers.

Whereas the various radical challenges to mainstream theorizing enhance our understanding of world politics by highlighting the roles played by corporations, transnational movements, and other nonstate actors, they overemphasize economic interpretations of international events and consequently omit other potentially important explanatory factors. According to feminist theorists, one such factor is gender.

The Feminist Critique

During the last quarter of the twentieth century, feminism began challenging conventional international relations theory. In particular, feminist theory attacked the exclusion of women in discussions about international affairs as well as the injustice and unequal treatment of women this prejudice caused. The mainstream literature on world politics dismissed the plight and contributions of women, treating differences in men's and women's status, beliefs, and behaviors as unimportant. As feminist theory evolved over time, it moved away from focusing on a history of discrimination and began to explore how gender identity shapes foreign policy decision making and how gendered hierarchies reinforced practices that perpetuated inequalities between men and women (see Tickner 2005 and 2002; Enloe 2004; Beckman and D'Amico 1994; Peterson and Runyan 1993).

Rather than conceiving of gender as the biological differences between men and women, feminists see gender as socially defined expectations regarding what it means to be masculine or feminine. Even though not all men and women fit these expectations, feminists assert that higher value is attributed in the political sphere to idealized masculine characteristics like domination, autonomy, and competition, which are then erroneously depicted as reflecting objective laws rooted in human nature (Tickner 1988). By treating this idealization as if it were grounded in universal laws of behavior, feminists insist that conventional international relations theories provide only a partial understanding of world politics.

Although all feminists stress the importance of gender in studying international relations, there are several contending schools of thought within feminist scholarship. Some feminists assert that on average there are no significant differences in the capabilities of men and women; others claim differences exist, with each gender being more capable than the other in certain endeavors; still others insist that the meaning ascribed to a person's gender is an arbitrary cultural construct that varies from one time or place to another (Goldstein 2002). Regardless of the position taken on the issue of gender differences, feminist scholars emphasize the relevance of women's experiences in international affairs and the contributions they have made. More than simply acknowledging the impact of female leaders such as Margaret Thatcher of Great Britain, Megawati Sukarnoputri of

Jorge Saenz/AP Photos

Franka Bruns/AP Photos

Women Leaders and World Politics Although world politics has been male dominated, some women have held important leadership positions. Their paths to power have varied. For example, Argentine President Christina Fernández de Kirchner (left) put gender at the forefront of her 2007 campaign, while German Chancellor Angela Merkel (right) chose to minimize the issue in her campaign.

Indonesia, Golda Meir of Israel, Corazón Aquino of the Philippines, Angela Merkel of Germany, Christina Fernández de Kirchner of Argentina, or Michelle Bachelet of Chile, they urge us to examine events from the personal perspectives of the countless women who have been involved in international affairs as caregivers, grassroots activists, and participants in the informal labor force. "Women have never been *absent* in world politics," writes Franke Wilmer (2000). They have, for the most part, remained "*invisible* within the discourse conducted by men" about world politics.

One result of the feminist critique of conventional international relations theorizing has been a surge in research that uses gender as an explanatory variable when analyzing world politics. For example, recent studies have found that high levels of gender equality within countries are associated with low levels of interstate and intrastate armed conflict (Caprioli 2005; Melander 2005; Regan and Pasevicute 2003; Caprioli and Boyer 2001). Pointing to the results from these and other studies, feminists recommend that everyone who studies international politics "ask gender questions and be more aware of the gendered implications of global politics" (Tickner and Sjoberg 2007, 199).

FORECASTING THE GLOBAL FUTURE WITH THEORIES OF WORLD POLITICS

As we seek to understand the global future, we must recognize the limitations of our knowledge of world politics. The world is complex, and our understanding of its workings remains incomplete (see Controversy: Can Behavioral Science

Advance the Study of World Politics?). As one scholar suggests, comprehending world politics is like trying to make sense of a disassembled jigsaw puzzle (Puchala 1994). Each piece shows a part of the whole picture, but it's unclear how they fit together. Some pieces depict a struggle for power among self-interested states; others reveal countries pooling their sovereignty to create a supranational union. Some pieces portray wrenching ethnonationalist conflicts; others reveal an absence of war between democracies. Some pieces show an upsurge in parochialism; others describe an emerging global civil society. As discussed in the pervious chapter, one of the difficulties of forecasting the global future is that disintegrative trends are splintering the political landscape at the very time that integrative trends are shrinking the planet. Whereas some countries seem mired in a dog-eat-dog world of international anarchy and self-help, others appear to live in a world of international institutions and interdependence.

Theories are like maps. They guide us in fitting the seemingly incompatible pieces of complex puzzles together to reveal the complete picture. But just as some maps are more accurate than others, some theories are more useful than others. "There is nothing so practical as a good theory," psychologist Kurt Lewin once remarked. But what makes a "good" theory? The following are some of the criteria that social scientists use when judging the quality of a theory (see Van Evera 1997):

- *Clarity*. A good theory is clearly framed: Its concepts are precisely defined, cause and effect relationships governing observed patterns are adequately specified, and the argument underpinning those hypothesized relationships is logically coherent.

- *Parsimony*. A good theory simplifies reality: It focuses on an important phenomenon and contains all of the factors relevant for explaining it without becoming excessively complex.

- *Explanatory power*. A good theory has empirical support: It deepens our understanding of a phenomenon, and explains things about it that are not accounted for by rival theories.

- *Prescriptive richness*. A good theory provides policy recommendations: It describes how problems can be avoided or mitigated through timely countermeasures.

- *Falsifiability*. A good theory can be proven wrong: It indicates what evidence would refute its claims.

Although realism, liberalism, and constructivism are the dominant ways of thinking about world politics today, none of these theories completely satisfies all of the criteria listed above. Recall that realism is frequently criticized for relying upon ambiguous concepts, liberalism is often derided for making naive policy recommendations based on idealistic assumptions, and constructivism is charged with an inability to explain change. Moreover, as the challenges mounted by radicalism and feminism suggest, these three mainstream theories overlook seemingly important aspects of world politics, which limits their explanatory power.

CONTROVERSY   Can Behavioral Science Advance the Study of World Politics?

How should scholars analyze world politics? Unfortunately, there is no simple answer to this question. The field of international relations is torn between differing conceptions of what the study of world politics should encompass and how its subject matter should be investigated. Traditionally, scholars tried to understand some unique political event or sequence of events by submerging themselves in archival records, legal documents, or field work related to the phenomenon under investigation. Relying on experience and wisdom to evaluate this material, they typically presented their insights in a narrative that asserted: "Based on *my judgment* of the information that I have examined, I conclude X, Y, and Z"

Dissatisfied with the reliability of a research methodology that depended so heavily on the personal judgment and intuitive information-gathering procedures of a single individual, various scholars in the 1960s promoted a movement known as **behavioralism**, which had as its goals the application of the scientific method and rigorous quantitative techniques to the study of world politics (see J. Singer 1968). In brief, behavioralists assumed that a world exists independent of our minds; this world has an order that is open to human understanding; recurring patterns within it can be discovered; and reproducible evidence about these patterns can be acquired by carefully formulating and stringently testing **hypotheses** inferred from theories devised to explain how the world works. What made behavioralism innovative was its systematic, empirical approach to the process of inquiry, replacing ad hoc, idiosyncratic procedures for information gathering with explicit, replicable procedures for data making, and supplanting the appeal to the "expert" opinion of authorities with a deliberate, controlled method of data analysis. Behavioralism attempted to overcome the tendency of many traditional researchers to select historical facts and cases to fit their preexisting conceptions about international behavior. Instead, all available data were examined. By being as clear and precise as possible, behavioralists asserted that other researchers could determine how a given study was conducted, evaluate the significance of its findings, and gradually build a cumulative body of intersubjectively transmissible knowledge.

A variety of criticisms have been leveled against behavioralism over the past few decades. One of the most common draws from the work of the German sociologist Max Weber (1864–1920), who believed that the mode of explanation used in the social sciences was different from that in the physical sciences. Many people influenced by Weber contend that unlike physicists who do not analyze sentient beings engaged in purposeful behavior, social

scientists face perplexing questions about why their subjects *chose* to act in a certain way and what meaning they ascribed to their actions. Not burdened with the need to consider how molecules may or may not choose to respond to external stimuli, physicists appeal to causal laws that hold true across time and space in order to explain such things as why gasses become liquids at certain temperatures. But to explain things like why a national leader chooses to respond in a particular way to some external stimulus, social scientists must understand the reasons behind the actions that were taken. This difference between the physical and social sciences, so the argument goes, makes it difficult for the student of world politics to emulate the physicist when conducting empirical research. Instead of using quantitative techniques to search for law-like regularities that span the universe of international phenomena, this school of thought urges the social scientist to employ qualitative, interpretative methods to figure out the intentions of particular actors at specific moments in time.

Another prominent criticism of applying the scientific method to world politics comes from postmodernism, a label commonly given to a diverse group of thinkers influenced by French philosophers Jean-Francois Lyotard (1924–1998), Michel Foucault (1926–1984), and Jacques Derrida (1930–2004), among others. Premised on the belief that knowledge is only true relative to some situation or historical condition, postmodernists contend that it is impossible to analyze world politics from an objective, value-free point of view. Because no one can discover transcendent truths, scholars are exhorted to unmask the hidden meanings in prevailing texts and discourses, question the adequacy of the worldviews they espouse, and examine how these accounts of world politics are able to dominate and silence others.

Most scholars today remain motivated by the quest to build theories of world politics that can be used to describe, explain, and predict occurrences in world politics. What do you think about how they should go about this task? Is the scientific analysis of international behavior a reasonable undertaking? If so, can the research techniques of the physical sciences be applied to the study of world politics? Or do the social sciences require a different approach to inquiry that gives more weight to the intentions of human agents? Alternatively, are both causal and interpretative explanations of world politics impossible? Do you concur with postmodernists who argue that any attempt to apply the scientific method to international behavior is misguided because there is no singular, objective reality to study?

behavioralism an approach to the study of world politics that emphasizes the application of the scientific method.

hypotheses conjectural statements that describe the relationship between an independent variable (the presumed cause) and a dependent variable (the effect).

Despite these drawbacks, each has strengths in highlighting certain kinds of international events and foreign policy behaviors. As international relations scholar and former U.S. policymaker Joseph Nye (2005, 8) notes, "When I was working in Washington and helping formulate American foreign policies as an assistant secretary in the State Department and the Pentagon, I found myself borrowing from all three types of thinking: realism, liberalism, and constructivism. I found them all helpful, though in different ways and in different circumstances." Because we lack a single overarching theory able to account for all facets of world politics, we will draw on realist, liberal, and constructivist thought in subsequent chapters. Moreover, we will supplement them with insights from radicalism and feminism, where these theoretical traditions can best help to interpret the topic covered.

CHAPTER SUMMARY

- A theory is a set of interrelated propositions that explains why certain events occurred. Three overarching theories have dominated the study of world politics: realism, liberalism, and constructivism.

- Several strains of realist theory exist. At the risk of oversimplification, the realist worldview can be summarized as follows:

  1. People are by nature selfish, competitive, and domineering. Changing human nature is a utopian aspiration.

  2. The international system is anarchic. Without the support and protection of a higher authority, states strive for autarchy and engage in self-help.

  3. Under such conditions, international politics is a struggle for power, "a war of all against all," as the sixteenth-century English philosopher Thomas Hobbes put it. The primary obligation of every state in this environment—the goal to which all other objectives should be subordinated—is to follow its "national interest" defined in terms of acquiring power.

  4. Security is a function of power, and power is a function of military capability. States should procure the military capability to deter or subdue any potential rival. They should not entrust their security to the good will of allies or to the promises of international law and organizations.

  5. International stability results from maintaining a balance of power among contending states.

- Various forms of liberal theory also exist. The liberal worldview can be summarized as follows:

  1. People are capable of collaboration and mutual aid. Malicious behavior is the product of an environment that encourages people to act selfishly.

Reason enables people to change the conditions they live under, and therefore makes progress possible.

2. The first important change needed to reduce the probability of war is to promote national self-determination and democratic governance. The domestic characteristics of states vary, and these variations affect state behavior. Democracies are more peaceful than autocratic governments.

3. The second important change is to promote international commerce. Economic interdependence leads states to develop mechanisms to resolve conflict, which reinforces the material incentive to avoid wars that inhibit business opportunities.

4. The third change is to replace secret diplomacy and the shifting, rival military alliances characteristic of balance-of-power politics with international institutions based on collective security. Competitive, self-interested behavior need not be arbitrary and disorderly. By encouraging reciprocity, reducing uncertainty, and shaping expectations, international institutions help states coordinate their behavior and achieve collective gains.

5. World politics is increasingly shaped by transnational networks, in which states are enmeshed in complex webs that include multinational corporations, international organizations, and nongovernmental organizations

- Constructivist theories of world politics are united by a common focus on the importance of ideas and discourse. Their worldview can be summarized as follows:

  1. The fundamental structures of world politics are social; they acquire meaning through shared human understandings and expectations, and are sustained by recurrent social practices.

  2. These collective, intersubjective structures define the identities of international actors.

  3. Social identities constitute actors' interests and shape their actions by stipulating what behavior is appropriate in a given situation

  4. International actors acquire agency through language; rules and other forms of discourse make the world what it is.

  5. Agents and structures are mutually constituted: Agents shape society, and society shapes agents through reciprocal interaction.

- The explanation of world politics cannot be reduced to any one simple yet compelling account. While realism, liberalism, and constructivism each explain certain types of international phenomena well, none of them adequately captures all facets of world politics. As a result, rival interpretations of world politics have periodically challenged these mainstream theories. In recent years, theorists belonging to the radical and feminist schools of thought have voiced some of the most prominent criticisms of conventional international relations theory.

KEY TERMS

absolute gains

behavioralism

collective security

complex
   interdependence

consequentialism

high politics

hypotheses

international regime

low politics

moral hazard

norms

power

relative gains

self-help

theory

transnational relations

zero-sum game

SUGGESTED READINGS

Baldwin, David A. *Theories of International Relations*. Burlington, VT: Ashgate, 2008.

Chernoff, Fred. *Theory and Metatheory in International Relations: Concepts and Contending Accounts*. New York: Palgrave-Macmillan, 2007.

Dougherty, James E., and Robert L. Pfaltzgraff, Jr., *Contending Theories of International Relations*, 5th ed. New York: Addison Wesley-Longman, 2001.

Dunne, Tim, Milja Kurki, and Steve Smith, eds. *International Relations Theories: Discipline and Diversity*. Oxford: Oxford University Press, 2007.

Elman, Colin, and Miriam Fendius Elman, eds., *Progress in International Relations Theory: Appraising the Field*. Cambridge, MA: MIT Press, 2003.

CRITICAL THINKING QUESTIONS

A vigorous debate between neorealists and neoliberals has dominated mainstream international relations scholarship for the past twenty-five years (Lamy 2008). The issues dividing the two camps center on the different assumptions they make about the following topics (Baldwin 1993, 4–8):

- *The Nature and Consequences of Anarchy.* Whereas everyone recognizes that the international system is anarchical because effective institutions for global governance are lacking, neorealists argue that anarchy may be preferable to the restraints of world government. Neoliberals see anarchy as a big problem that can be reformed through the creation of strong global institutions.

- *International Cooperation.* Although neorealists and neoliberals agree that cooperation is possible, neorealists think it is difficult to sustain while neoliberals believe it can be expected because collaboration yields rewards that reduce the temptation to compete.

- *Relative versus Absolute Gains.* Neorealists believe that the desire to get ahead of competitors by obtaining relative gains is the primary motive behind state behavior, whereas neoliberals believe states are motivated by the search for opportunities that will produce absolute gains for all parties.

- *Priority of State Goals.* Neorealists stress national security as the most important goal pursued by states. Neoliberals think states place a greater priority on economic welfare.

- *Intentions versus Capabilities.* Neorealists maintain that the distribution of states' capabilities is the primary determinant of their behavior and international outcomes. Neoliberals maintain that states' intentions, information, and ideals are more influential than the distribution of capabilities.

- *Institutions and Regimes.* Neorealists argue that institutions such as the United Nations are arenas where states carry out their competition for influence. Neoliberals believe that international institutions create norms that are binding on their members and that change patterns of international politics.

How significant are these differences between neorealists and neoliberals? Which assumptions do you think are the most accurate for interpreting twenty-first-century world politics? Are there any important issues that are left out of this debate?

The Actors in World Politics

In studying world politics we typically use the term *actor* to refer to the agents who participate in world politics. They include countries (for example, the United States and Japan), international organizations (the United Nations and the Nordic Council), multinational corporations (Wal-Mart and Sony), nongovernmental organizations (Greenpeace and the World Wildlife Federation), indigenous nationalities (the Kurds in Iran, Iraq, and Turkey), and terrorist networks (Al Qaeda).

Part II identifies the major actors in world politics today and describes the roles they perform and the policies they pursue. We begin in Chapter 3 with an analysis of nation-states. In Chapter 4 special attention is given to states with the greatest military and economic capabilities—the great powers. Next, in Chapter 5, we examine the weaker, economically less-developed countries known collectively as the Global South, because the majority of them are located along the equator or in the earth's southern hemisphere. Finally, Chapter 6 deals with the growing role of nonstate actors, which include intergovernmental organizations such as the European Union as well as nongovernmental organizations ranging from multinational corporations to transnational religious movements.

3

Foreign Policy Decision Making

CHAPTER OUTLINE

Explaining Foreign Policy

The Emergence of the Modern State System

The Determinants of States' Foreign Policy Behavior

International Sources of Foreign Policy

Polarity and Polarization

Geostrategic Position

Domestic Sources of Foreign Policy

Military Capabilities

Economic Conditions

Type of Government

Organizational Processes and Politics

APPLICATION: Bureaucratic Games

Individual Sources of Foreign Policy

Leaders as the Makers of the Global Future

Factors Affecting the Capacity to Lead

CONTROVERSY: Policy and Personality: Do Leaders Make a Difference?

Constraints on the Foreign Policy-Making Process

> Policy faces inward as much as outward, seeking to reconcile conflicting goals, to adjust aspirations to available means, and to accommodate the different advocates of these competing goals and aspirations to one another. It is here that the essence of policy making seems to lie, in a process that is in its deepest sense political.
>
> ROGER HILSMAN
> FORMER U.S. ASSISTANT SECRETARY OF STATE

Following the attacks of September 11, 2001 on the World Trade Center and the Pentagon, U.S. President George W. Bush and his national security advisers began formulating a new strategy for striking terrorist organizations and the states that harbor them. "We face a threat with no precedent," the president insisted during a commencement speech at West Point in June 2002. Imploring Americans to be forward-looking and resolute, he declared that the country's military "must take the battle to the enemy, disrupt his plans, and confront the worst threats before they emerge." Bush promised that his administration would be patient, focused, and methodical in choosing where and when to apply this strategy. As he explained in an interview with journalist Bob Woodward (2002), teamwork within his cabinet was necessary for the decision-making process to operate effectively.

By the fall of 2002, however, the national security decision-making process looked more messy than methodical, as serious divisions emerged within the Bush administration over whether to wage war against Saddam Hussein's regime in Iraq. On one side stood Vice President Dick Cheney; Secretary of Defense Donald Rumsfeld, and his Deputy Paul Wolfowitz; Chair of the Pentagon Defense Policy Board, Richard Perle; as well as House Majority Whip Tom Delay, a conservative Republican congressman. Arguing that Saddam Hussein possessed weapons of mass destruction that could be used against the United States, they urged the president to invade Iraq, even if America had little international support for launching a preventive war.

Mai/Time Life Pictures/Getty Images

Collective Decision Making During crises that threaten a country's national security, decisions usually are made by the head of state and a small group of advisers rather than by large-scale bureaucracies. George W. Bush and advisers in the White House Situation Room during October 2002 make plans for war against Iraq.

Opposing an invasion were Secretary of State Colin Powell and an unlikely coalition of officials from the first Bush administration, including trusted national security advisers Brent Scowcroft and James A. Baker III, as well as former secretary of state Larry Eagleburger. In one way or another, those questioning a military strike all reflected Powell's qualms about the costs of undertaking such a war with few allies and uncertain domestic support. Although they agreed that Saddam Hussein was a menace, they counseled against military action until it could be proved that the Iraqi dictator possessed weapons of mass destruction. A retired general and the only combat veteran among Bush's senior aides, Powell wrote in *My American Journey,* "Many of my generation, the career captains, majors, and lieutenant colonels seasoned in … [the Vietnam War], vowed that when our turn came to call the shots, we would not acquiesce in half-hearted warfare for half-baked reasons that the American people could not understand or support."

As rumors of war spread and the debate between these two groups intensified, the national security policy-making process fell into disarray. Treasury Secretary Paul O'Neill likened it to "June bugs hoping around on a lake" (quoted in Suskind 2004, 306). While the president had promised to craft a clear, coherent strategy for dealing with Iraq, discord among the members of his foreign policy team suggested otherwise. The fissures within the administration widened as key advisers quarreled over whether they should obtain United Nations backing for an American attack. Whereas one side stressed the immediate threat posed by Saddam Hussein and advocated acting unilaterally if necessary, the other side emphasized the long-term risks of removing him by force without UN Security Council approval and multilateral assistance. Disagreement over this issue so strained relations between Vice President Cheney and Secretary of State Powell that it "pulled apart the last fraying threads of what had connected them for so many years" (Woodward 2004).

The battle among Bush's advisers soon dominated Washington's headlines, leading many people to ask whether the administration was following a deliberate, methodical decision-making process as the president had promised. Republican Senator Chuck Hagel, for instance, worried that the White House had not explored all of the possible ramifications that might result from a military intervention. "If we invade Iraq," he asked, "what allies would we have? Who governs after Saddam? What is the objective? Have we calculated the consequences, particularly the unintended consequences? What does [a war with Iraq] mean for the unfinished work with Afghanistan? For the Israeli-Palestinian conflict?" (cited in Broder 2002). Looking askance at what he termed "the Babel in Babylon," Fareed Zakaria (2002a), former editor of the influential journal *Foreign Affairs*, criticized the way in which a major decision about war was unfolding when he claimed that "parlor politics" had trumped power politics in the Bush administration. Cheney, Rumsfeld, and their allies, he suggested, were as interested in marginalizing Powell's influence as they were in ousting Iraq's dictator.

What explains the disarray in the Bush policy-making process? National leaders often describe their foreign policies as the result of neat, orderly, and rational procedures. By their account, they carefully define emerging problems; specify the goals they wish to achieve; identify all the alternative ways of attaining these goals; weigh the costs, benefits, and risks associated with each alternative; and then select the option with the best chance of attaining the desired goals. Yet, promises to the contrary, the Bush policy-making process hardly followed these procedures. Despite the president's desire to have his administration function as a unified body, the process of deciding how to deal with Iraq was contentious and turbulent. Was this turmoil unique to the Bush administration's handling of the Iraq situation? Or, was it typical of how foreign policy is made generally? To put it another way, is **rational choice** more an idealized standard than an accurate description of real-world behavior?

> **rational choice** decision-making procedures guided by careful definition of problems, specification of goals, weighing the costs, risks, and benefits of all alternatives, and selection of the optimal alternative.

To answer these questions, this chapter will investigate how states make foreign policy. Drawing upon the levels of analysis framework introduced in Chapter 1, we will examine how the properties of the international system, various national attributes, and the personal characteristics of political leaders combine to shape foreign policy. After considering factors at the systemic, state, and individual levels of analysis that influence foreign policy, we will conclude by exploring how they create impediments to rational decision making.

EXPLAINING FOREIGN POLICY

When we speak about foreign policy and the decision-making processes that produce it, we mean the goals that officials heading nation-states (or other non-state actors) seek abroad, the values that underlie those goals, and the means or instruments used to pursue them. Although nation-states are not the only actors on the world stage, due to their preeminence we begin our examination of foreign policy making by looking back to the origins of the modern system of autonomous, territorial states.

The Emergence of the Modern State System

The modern state system was born with the Peace of Westphalia in 1648, which ended the Thirty Years' War. A complex, multidimensional conflict, the Thirty Years' War originated from a welter of intellectual, cultural, political, and economic crosscurrents that swept through Europe in the wake of the Reformation.

One dimension of the war was religious, involving a clash between Catholics and Protestants. Another dimension was governmental, consisting of a civil war over the issue of imperial authority within the Holy Roman Empire (a territory stretching from France to Poland, composed of numerous principalities united through marriages to the Hapsburg dynasty). A third dimension was geostrategic, pitting the Austrian and Spanish thrones of the House of Hapsburg against the Danish, Swedish, Dutch, and French thrones (see Kegley and Raymond 2002a).

By any measure, the Thirty Years' War was a tragedy of epic proportions. Much of central Europe lay desolate in its aftermath, stripped of resources and drained of population by massacre, pillage, famine, and disease. When the belligerents finally reached a peace agreement, they provided world politics with a new, decentralized structure. Throughout the Middle Ages, Europeans thought of themselves as part of an overarching Christian commonwealth, despite living in a galaxy of bishoprics, duchies, fiefdoms, and other principalities. Now the hierarchical medieval system of papal influence over political affairs was replaced with geographically and politically separate states that recognized no higher authority. Under the terms of the Peace of Westphalia (so named because it was negotiated at concurrent conferences in the German cities of Münster and Osnabrück in Westphalia), these newly autonomous states were all given the same legal rights: territory under their sole jurisdiction, unrestricted control of their domestic affairs, and the freedom to conduct foreign relations and negotiate treaties with other states. The concept of **sovereignty** embodies the exclusive rights of states to make, implement, enforce, and adjudicate laws within their territories. No duty could be imposed on them without their consent.

sovereignty under international law, the principle that no higher authority is above the state.

The Westphalian system still colors every dimension of world politics and provides the terminology used to describe the primary units in international affairs. Although the term *nation-state* is often used interchangeably with *state* and *nation,* technically the three are different. As noted in Chapter 1, a *state* is a legal entity that possesses a permanent population, a well-defined territory, and a government capable of exercising sovereignty. A *nation* is a collection of people who, on the basis of ethnic, linguistic, or cultural affinity, perceive themselves to be members of the same group. Thus the term *nation-state* implies a convergence between territorial states and the psychological identification of people within them. However, in employing this familiar terminology, we should exercise caution. As we shall explain in Chapter 5, most states are populated by many nations, and some nations are not states. These "nonstate nations" are ethnic groups (such as Native American tribes in the United States, Sikhs in India, or Basques in Spain) composed of people without sovereign power over the territory in which they live.

The Determinants of States' Foreign Policy Behavior

Many factors affect the opportunity, capacity, and willingness of states to make foreign policy choices. Due to the diversity of states, as well as their different positions within the contemporary global system, it is difficult to generalize about the influence of any one factor or combination of factors.

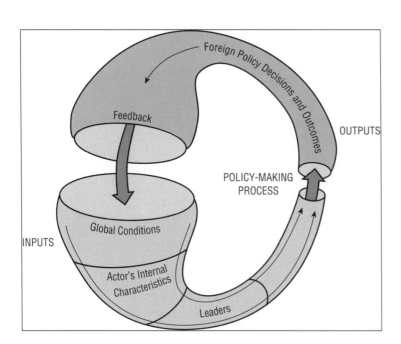

FIGURE 3.1 The Dynamics of Foreign Policy Making

The factors that influence foreign policy choices are depicted here as layers of a "causal funnel." Global conditions, characteristics of the state or nonstate actor in question, and the skills, personalities, and beliefs of the leaders who make key decisions can be thought of as *inputs* into a policy-making process that produces *outputs* in the form of actions. These actions yield results or *outcomes*, which eventually serve as *feedback* that has consequences for the input factors themselves at a later time.

To determine the relative impact of specific factors under different circumstances, we must first distinguish between different types of influences on policy choices. Figure 3.1 draws upon the levels-of-analysis framework introduced in Chapter 1 to describe the multiple influences on states' foreign policy-making processes. Recall that the systemic or global influences on foreign policy include all activities occurring beyond a state's borders that structure the choices its officials make. Such factors as the number of great powers and the pattern of alliances sometimes profoundly affect the choices of decision makers. State-level influences focus on the internal characteristics of states, including variations in military capabilities, level of economic development, type of government, and organizational processes. Finally, individual-level influences give attention to the personal characteristics of the leaders who govern different states. Let us examine each of these three types of foreign policy determinants in turn.

INTERNATIONAL SOURCES OF FOREIGN POLICY

The international environment within which states and nonstate actors operate shapes *opportunities* for action. It sets an ecological context that limits some foreign policy choices but facilitates others (Sprout and Sprout 1965; Starr 1978). Among the most significant facets of the international environment that make possible certain courses of action but not others are the distribution of power among states and the pattern of the alliances around the most powerful.

Polarity and Polarization

polarity the degree to
which military and eco-
nomic capabilities are concentrated among the
major powers in the state
system.

polarization the degree
to which states cluster in
alliances around the most
powerful members of the
state system.

Power can be distributed in many ways. It can be concentrated in the hands of one preponderant state, as in the ancient Mediterranean world at the zenith of the Roman Empire, or it may be diffused among several rival states, as it was during the Italian Renaissance when Venice, Florence, Milan, Naples, and the papal states possessed approximately equal strength. Scholars use the term **polarity** to describe the distribution of power among members of the state system. *Unipolar* systems have one dominant power center, *bipolar* systems contain two centers of power, and *multipolar* systems possess more than two such centers.

Closely related to the distribution of power is the pattern of alignments among states. The term **polarization** refers to the degree to which states cluster around the powerful. For instance, a highly bipolarized system is one in which small- and medium-sized states form alliances with one of the two dominant powers. The network of alliances around the United States and Soviet Union during the Cold War exemplified such a system.

Polarity and alliance polarization influence foreign policy by affecting the decision latitude possessed by states. To illustrate this point, let's consider two examples. Our first example pertains to polarity and great powers. When power is concentrated in the hands of a single state in a unipolar system, it has more latitude to use military force and intervene in the affairs of others than it would in a system characterized by a diffuse distribution of power, where rivals might obstruct its actions. Our second example focuses on polarization and smaller states. When alliances are tight military blocs, the members of each alliance will feel compelled to conform with the dictates of the alliance's leader. Conversely, when alliances are loosely structured and their membership is fluid, smaller states will have greater latitude to craft foreign policies that are independent of the wishes of the powerful. Of course, we could think of other examples to show how the structural properties of the international system affect decision latitude. What they would show is that the foreign policy impact of polarity and polarization hinges on the geostrategic position of a given state.

Geostrategic Position

Some of the most important influences on a state's foreign policy behavior are its location and physical terrain. The presence of natural frontiers, for example, may profoundly guide policy makers' choices. Consider the United States, which was secure throughout most of its early history because vast oceans separate it from potential threats in Europe and Asia. The advantage of having oceans as barriers to foreign intervention, combined with the absence of militarily powerful neighbors, permitted the United States to develop into an industrial giant and to practice safely an isolationist foreign policy for over 150 years. Consider also mountainous Switzerland, whose easily defended topography has made neutrality a viable foreign policy option.

Similarly, maintaining autonomy from continental politics has been an enduring theme in the foreign policy of Great Britain, an island country whose physical detachment from Europe long served as a buffer separating it from entanglement in major power disputes on the Continent. Preserving this protective shield has been a priority for Britain throughout its history, and helps to explain why London has been so hesitant to accept full integration into the European Union (EU).

Most countries are not insular, however. They have many states on their borders, denying them the option of noninvolvement in world affairs. Germany, which sits in the geographic center of Europe, historically has found its domestic political system and foreign policy preferences shaped by its geostrategic position. In the twentieth century, for example, Germany struggled through no less than six major radical changes in governing institutions, each of which pursued very different foreign policies: (1) the empire of Kaiser Wilhelm II; (2) the Weimar Republic; (3) Adolf Hitler's dictatorship; its two post–World War II successors, (4) the capitalist Federal Republic in West Germany, (5) the communist German Democratic Republic in East Germany; and, finally, (6) a reunited Germany after the end of the Cold War, now committed to liberal democracy and full integration in the European Union. Each of these governments was preoccupied with its relations with neighbors, but responded to the opportunities and challenges presented by Germany's position in the middle of the European continent with very different foreign policy goals. In no case, however, was isolationistic withdrawal from involvement in continental affairs a practical geostrategic option.

History is replete with other examples of geography's influence on states' foreign policy goals, which is why geopolitical theories have a venerable place in the field of international relations. **Geopolitics** stresses the influence of geographic factors on state power and international conduct. Illustrative of early geopolitical thinking is Alfred Thayer Mahan's (1890) *The Influence of Sea Power in History,* which maintained that control of the seas shaped national power. According to Mahan, states with extensive coastlines and ports enjoyed a competitive advantage. Later geopoliticians, such as Sir Halford Mackinder (1919) and Nicholas Spykman (1944), stressed that not only location but also topography, size (territory and population), climate, and distance between states are powerful determinants of the foreign policies of individual countries. The underlying principle behind the geopolitical perspective is self-evident: Leaders' perceptions of available foreign policy options are influenced by the geopolitical circumstances that define their states' places on the world stage.

geopolitics a school of thought claiming that states' foreign policies are determined by their location, natural resources, and physical environment.

System structure and geostrategic position are only two aspects of the global environment that may influence foreign policy. In other chapters we will discuss additional factors. But next, we comment briefly on the main internal attributes of states that influence their foreign policies.

DOMESTIC SOURCES OF FOREIGN POLICY

Whereas the structure of the international system and a state's geostrategic position within it influence the opportunities for state action, various domestic factors affect the *capacity* of states to act when opportunities arise (East 1978). While scholars have investigated many national attributes that determine the amount of resources available to states and the ability to use them, we will concentrate on four prominent factors: military capability, level of economic development, type of government, and organizational structures and processes.

Military Capabilities

The proposition that states' internal capabilities shape their foreign policy priorities is supported by the fact that states' preparations for war strongly influence their later use of force (Levy 2001). Thus, while most states may seek similar goals, their ability to realize them will vary according to their military capabilities.

Because military capabilities limit a state's range of prudent policy choices, they act as a mediating factor on leaders' national security decisions. For instance, in the 1980s, Libyan leader Muammar Qaddafi repeatedly provoked the United States through anti-American rhetoric and by supporting various terrorist activities. Qaddafi was able to act as he did largely because neither bureaucratic organizations nor a mobilized public existed in Libya to constrain his personal whims. However, Qaddafi was doubtlessly more highly constrained by the outside world than were the leaders in the more militarily capable countries toward whom his anger was directed. Limited military muscle compared with the United States precluded the kinds of belligerent behaviors he threatened to practice.

Conversely, Saddam Hussein made strenuous efforts to build Iraq's military might (partly with the help of U.S. arms sales) and by 1990 had built the fourth-largest army in the world. Thus, invading Kuwait to seize its oil fields became a feasible foreign policy option. In the end, however, even Iraq's impressive military power proved ineffective against a vastly superior coalition of military forces, headed by the United States. The 1991 Persian Gulf War forced Saddam Hussein to capitulate and withdraw from the conquered territory. Twelve years thereafter, the United States invaded Iraq and finally ousted Saddam Hussein from office.

Economic Conditions

The level of economic and industrial development a state enjoys also affects the foreign policy goals it can pursue. Generally, the more economically developed a state, the more likely it is to play an activist role in the global political economy. Rich states have interests that extend far beyond their borders and typically possess the means to pursue and protect them. Not coincidentally, states that enjoy industrial capabilities and extensive involvement in international trade also tend to be militarily powerful—in part because military might is a function of economic capabilities.

Although economically advanced states are more active globally, this does not mean that their privileged circumstances dictate adventuresome policies. Rich states are often "satisfied" ones that have much to lose from revolutionary change and global instability (Wolfers 1962). As a result, they usually perceive the status quo as serving their interests and often forge international economic policies to protect and expand their envied position at the pinnacle of the global hierarchy.

Levels of productivity and prosperity also affect the foreign policies of the poor states at the bottom of the hierarchy. Some economically weak states respond to their situation by complying subserviently with the wishes of the rich on whom they depend. Others rebel defiantly, sometimes succeeding (despite their disadvantaged bargaining position) in resisting the efforts by great powers and powerful international organizations to control their behavior.

Thus, generalizations about the economic foundations of states' international political behavior often prove inaccurate. Although levels of economic development vary widely among states in the global system, they alone do not determine foreign policies. Instead, leaders' perceptions of the opportunities and constraints that their states' economic resources provide may more powerfully influence their foreign policy choices.

Type of Government

A third important attribute affecting states' international behavior is their political system. Although realism predicts that all states will act similarly to protect their interests, a state's type of government demonstrably constrains important choices, including whether threats to use military force are carried out. Here the important distinction is between **constitutional democracy** (representative government) on one end of the spectrum and **autocratic rule** (authoritarian or totalitarian) on the other.

In neither democratic (sometimes called "open") nor autocratic ("closed") political systems can political leaders survive long without the support of organized domestic political interests, and sometimes the mass citizenry. But in democratic systems those interests are likely to spread beyond the government itself. Public opinion, interest groups, and the mass media are a more visible part of the policy-making process in democratic systems. Similarly, the electoral process in democratic societies more meaningfully frames choices and produces results about who will lead than the process used in authoritarian regimes, where the real choices are made by a few elites behind closed doors. In a democracy, public opinion and preferences may matter and, therefore, differences in who is allowed to participate and how much they exercise their right to participate are critical determinants of foreign policy choices.

The proposition that domestic stimuli, and not simply international events, are a source of foreign policy is not novel. In ancient Greece, for instance, the historian Thucydides observed that what happened within the Greek city-states often did more to shape their external behavior than what each did to the others. He added that Greek leaders frequently concentrated their efforts on influencing the political climate within their own polities. Similarly, leaders today sometimes make foreign policy decisions for domestic political purposes—as, for example, when bold or aggressive acts abroad are intended to influence election outcomes at home or to divert public attention from economic woes. This is sometimes called the "scapegoat" phenomenon or the **diversionary theory of war** (Levy 1989b).

Some see the intrusion of domestic politics into foreign policy making as a disadvantage of democratic political systems that undermines their ability to deal

constitutional democracy a governmental system in which political leaders' power is limited by a body of fundamental principles, and leaders are held accountable to citizens through regular, fair, and competitive elections.

autocratic rule a governmental system where unlimited power is concentrated in the hands of a single person.

diversionary theory of war the contention that leaders initiate conflict abroad as a way of steering public opinion at home away from controversial domestic issues.

decisively with crises or to bargain effectively with less democratic adversaries and allies. Democracies are subject to inertia. They move slowly on issues, because so many disparate elements are involved in decision making and because officials in democracies are accountable to public opinion and must respond to pressure from a variety of domestic interest groups. A crisis sufficient enough to arouse the attention and activity of a large proportion of the population may need to erupt in order for large changes in policy to come about. In contrast, authoritarian governments can make decisions more rapidly, and they have mechanisms to ensure domestic compliance with the policies they choose. But there is a cost: fear of retribution may lead advisers to avoid making policy proposals and to withhold criticism of ideas proposed by the leadership. Over time, these forms of self-censorship often make authoritarian governments less effective than democracies in developing foreign policy innovations.

The impact of government type on foreign policy choice has taken on great significance following the conversion of many dictatorships to democratic rule. These liberal government conversions have occurred in three successive "waves" since the 1800s (Huntington 1991). The first wave occurred between 1878 and 1926; the second between 1943 and 1962; and the third began in the 1970s and continued through 1998. According to Freedom House, the percentage of countries designated as free has not changed significantly since the turn of the century, but many countries that had been making progress toward democracy have regressed. Currently, 46 percent of the world's population lives in free countries and another 18 percent live in partially free countries (see Map 3.1).

The growth of democracy during the last decades of the twentieth century emboldened many liberals to predict that the twenty-first century will be safer than its predecessor. Their reasons for predicting the onset of a **democratic peace** vary, but rely on the logic that Immanuel Kant outlined in his 1795 treatise *Perpetual Peace*. Kant believed that because democratic leaders are accountable to the public, and that because ordinary citizens have to supply the soldiers and bear the human and financial cost of aggressive policies, they would constrain leaders from initiating foreign wars (especially against other liberal democracies similarly constrained by norms and institutions that respect compromise and civil liberties).

A considerable body of empirical evidence supports the proposition that democracies do not wage war against each other (Rasler and Thompson 2005; Russett 2001; Ray 1995). The type of government and, more specifically, whether leaders are accountable to opposition groups through multiparty elections, strongly influence foreign policy goals. Although liberals generally emphasize the pacifying effects of democracy, research findings on the democratic peace have led some political conservatives to advocate a policy called "democratic realism" (Yang 2005), which would promote democracy through targeted interventions into regions where the advance of freedom is deemed critical in the struggle against Al Qaeda and other radical groups that pose existential threats to the United States (Krauthammer 2004).

democratic peace the theory that although democratic states sometimes wage wars against other states, they do not fight each other.

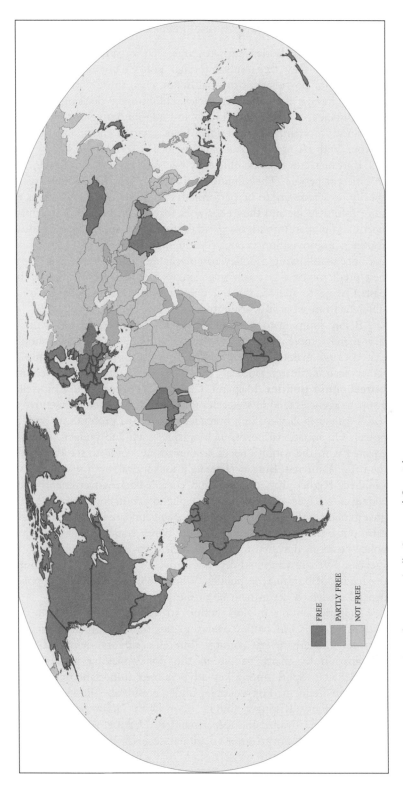

M A P 3.1 The Location of Democratically Governed Countries

This map shows the location in 2007 of (1) the ninety "free" countries whose governments provide their citizens with a high degree of political and economic freedom and safeguard basic civil liberties, (2) the sixty "partly free" electoral democracies, and (3) the forty-three "not free" states, where citizens' human rights and liberties are systematically abused or denied. Source: Adapted from Freedom House (2007, at http://www.freedomhouse.org).

FREE

PARTLY FREE

NOT FREE

Organizational Processes and Politics

In today's world, leaders turn to large-scale organizations for information and advice when they face critical foreign policy choices. Although this is more true of major powers than of small states, even those without large budgets and complex foreign policy bureaucracies seldom make decisions without the advice and assistance of many individuals and administrative agencies (Korany 1986). Bureaucratic organizations perform vital services, enhancing the state's capacity to cope with changing global circumstances.

Bureaucracies increase efficiency by assigning responsibility for different tasks to different people. They define **standard operating procedures (SOPs)** that specify how tasks are to be performed; they rely on record systems to gather and store information; and they engage in forward planning to anticipate long-term needs and prepare the means to attain them. Because they assiduously follow set routines, improvisation is rare. Although major shifts in organizational behavior may occur following a policy fiasco, change tends to occur incrementally. The best predictor of a government agency's behavior is what it did in the recent past. Owing to inertia, what it does tomorrow will likely be only marginally different from what it is doing today (Allison and Zelikow 1999).

Before jumping to the conclusion that bureaucracies are neutral instruments that merely implement what government leaders ordain, we should emphasize that decision making by and within large organizations sometimes compromises rather than facilitates rational choice. According to what is commonly called **bureaucratic politics** (Halperin, Clapp, and Kanter 2006; Caldwell 1977), government agencies tend to see each other as rivals. Every administrative unit within a state's foreign policy-making bureaucracy seeks to promote its own purposes and power. Organizational needs, such as larger staffs and budgets, sometimes become equated with the nation's needs, as bureaucrats come to see their own interests as the national interest. Bureaucracies fight for survival, even when their usefulness has vanished. Rather than thinning and cutting back, governments usually propose adding new layers of bureaucracy, a phenomenon known as the "thickening of government" (Shane 2005). Far from being impartial managers, desiring only to carry out orders from the head of state, bureaucratic organizations frequently take policy positions designed to increase their own influence relative to that of other agencies. "Where you stand depends on where you sit" is an aphorism that reflects the nature of bureaucratic politics. Where someone stands on a policy issue may depend on which department he or she sits within.

Fighting among insiders within an administration and the formation of factions to carry on battles over the direction of foreign policy decisions are chronic in nearly every country (but especially in democracies accepting of participation by many people in the policy-making process). Consider the United States. Splits among key advisers over important foreign policy choices have been frequent. For example, under presidents Nixon and Ford, Secretary of State Henry Kissinger fought often with James Schlesinger and Donald Rumsfeld, who headed the Department of Defense, over strategy regarding the Vietnam War; Jimmy Carter's national security adviser, Zbigniew Brzezinski,

standard operating procedures (SOPs) rules for reaching decisions about particular types of situations.

bureaucratic politics a description of decision making that sees foreign policy choices as based on bargaining and compromises among government agencies.

repeatedly engaged in conflicts with Secretary of State Cyrus Vance over the Iran hostage crisis; and under Ronald Reagan, Caspar Weinberger at Defense and George Shultz at State were famous for butting heads on most policy issues. Such conflicts are not necessarily bad because they force each side to better explain its viewpoint, and this allows heads of state the opportunity to weigh their competing advice before making decisions. However, battles among advisers can lead to paralysis and to rash decisions that produce poor results (see Application: Bureaucratic Games). As Morton Abramowitz (2002), a former assistant secretary of state in the Reagan administration, summarized the problem: Internal wars pervade the making of American foreign policy in every administration; however, when bureaucratic infighting becomes excessive, it can lead to policy inconsistencies and short-term concerns taking precedence over long-run goals.

The events of September 11, 2001 provide a telling example of what can go wrong when bureaucratic politics contaminate the policy-making process. The terrorist attacks on the World Trade Center and the Pentagon were regarded by many as the worst intelligence failure since Pearl Harbor. U.S. intelligence agencies, it was later discovered, received information before hand that terrorists were likely to attack the United States with hijacked airliners as weapons. Why weren't the warnings acted upon in time to prevent the disaster? Why weren't the dots connected? The answer accepted by most analysts was that America's system of intelligence was hampered by turf-protecting bureaucracies that did not share the vital information with each other. More than fifty units of government are involved with national security policy, and agencies like the CIA, the FBI, and the INS in the State Department are habitually loath to share information with each other for fear of compromising "sources and methods." As the bipartisan National Commission on Terrorist Attacks Upon the United States (2004, 353) concluded, these agencies "are like a set of specialists in a hospital, each ordering tests, looking for symptoms, and prescribing medications. What is missing is the attending physician who makes sure they work as a team." Moreover, as FBI Special Agent Coleen Rowley testified in June 2002, "There's a mutual-protection pact in bureaucracies. Mid-level managers avoid decisions out of fear a mistake will sidetrack their careers while a rigid hierarchy discourages agents from challenging superiors. There is a saying: 'Big cases, big problems; little cases, little problems; no cases, no problems.' The idea that inaction is the key to success manifests itself repeatedly" (Toner 2002). These types of problems are difficult to control, and few students of organizational behavior believe that they can automatically be overcome through massive reorganization and restructuring. Bureaucratic routines "favor continuity over change," notes political scientist Jean Garrison (2007), "because information is processed in certain ways and certain sources of information are privileged" (also see Neumann 2007). Indeed, as Ronald Reagan once commented, "a government bureau is the nearest thing to eternal life we'll ever see on this earth."

APPLICATION	Bureaucratic Games

When attempting to explain a foreign policy undertaking, most people assume that the agent was a national government engaged in purposeful, goal-directed behavior. It is in this sense that journalists report "Argentina decided to do X" or that scholars write "Chile responded to Argentina by doing Y." National governments are treated as if they were individuals with a single set of preferences that respond to strategic problems through deliberate choice.

In this chapter we have introduced another way of thinking about happenings in world politics. Rather than emanating from the carefully calibrated calculations of a single-minded entity, foreign policy may be the result of bargaining and infighting among a wide variety of organizations, each with competing preferences and unequal influence. An example of a statesman who understood how bureaucratic politics could affect his country's policies was Richard Holbrooke, who served as U.S. assistant secretary of state for European and Canadian affairs during the Clinton administration. Assigned the task in 1995 of bringing an end to a war in Bosnia that had been raging among Serbs, Croats, and Muslims for several years, Holbrooke was an experienced, pragmatic, and assertive negotiator, known by his peers as "the Muhammad Ali of diplomacy" because of his ability to wear down even the most difficult opponent (Traub 2000). In the excerpt below, he describes how various bureaucratic agencies began lobbying for roles in the peace process once his small negotiation team had begun to make headway.

> When we returned [to Washington], we found that interest in our activities had increased substantially. Agencies and individuals that had paid us little attention now wanted to be part of the process. For example, the Agency for International Development (AID), asserting that it would have to carry out the reconstruction program, sought a major role in the negotiations. Some agencies or bureaus wanted to place representatives on the

delegation; we fended them off on the grounds that our plane was too small.

...We were concerned that if the unprecedented degree of flexibility and autonomy we had been given by Washington were reduced, and we were subjected to the normal Washington decision-making process, the negotiations would become bogged down.

...Faced with similar challenges in earlier crises, some administrations had created secret bypass mechanisms that kept information and authority within a small group—but also deceived or cut out everyone else. Most famously, when [Henry] Kissinger was National Security Advisor, he had frequently ignored the entire State Department—once making a secret trip to Moscow without the knowledge of the American Ambassador, and regularly withholding almost all information about his secret discussions with China from the Secretary of State. We did not want to arouse the kind of distrust and intrigue that, as a result, had marred the Nixon-Kissinger period....

To avoid this classic bureaucratic dilemma, [Deputy Assistant Secretary of State] John Kornblum set up a small, informal team to support our efforts. As we envisioned it, the group would be, in effect, an extension of the negotiating team, but located in Washington.... [Its members] would have to agree *not* to process drafts through the regular interagency "clearance process" which... was too cumbersome and time-consuming for a fast-moving negotiation (Holbrooke 1998, 170–171).

Holbrooke's approach to sidestepping potential bureaucratic roadblocks was, in his words, "highly unusual." Rarely do foreign service officers have such free rein. But he maintained that it was crucial to minimize interference in his team's activities by holding off efforts by outsiders to get involved in the negotiation process.

INDIVIDUAL SOURCES OF FOREIGN POLICY

In addition to examining the opportunities for state action presented by the international environment and the capacity of states to act based on their national attributes, it is also necessary to consider the *willingness* of political leaders to act when they have the opportunity and capacity. Ultimately, leaders and the kind of leadership they exert shape the way in which foreign policies are made and the consequent behavior of states in world politics. "There is properly no history, only biography" is the way Ralph Waldo Emerson expressed the view that individual leaders move history.

Leaders as the Makers of the Global Future

We expect leaders to lead, and we assume new leaders will make a difference. Journalists and scholars reinforce this image when they attach the names of leaders to policies, such as the "Brezhnev Doctrine" used to justify the 1968 Soviet military intervention into Czechoslovakia. Moreover, leaders themselves seek to create impressions of their own self-importance while attributing extraordinary powers to other leaders. The assumptions they make about the personalities of their counterparts, consciously or unconsciously, in turn influence their own behavior (Wendzel 1980), as political psychologists who study the impact of leaders' perceptions and personalities on their foreign policy preferences demonstrate (Hermann and Hagan 2004).

Nevertheless, we must be wary of ascribing too much importance to individual leaders. Their influence is likely to be subtler, as U.S. president Bill Clinton suggested in 1998 when he observed, "Great presidents don't do great things. Great presidents get a lot of other people to do great things." Most leaders operate under a variety of pressures that limit what they can accomplish. The question at issue is not whether political elites lead or whether they can make a difference. They clearly do both. The relevant question is under what conditions leaders' personal characteristics are influential.

Factors Affecting the Capacity to Lead

The impact of leaders' personal characteristics on their state's foreign policy generally increases when their authority and legitimacy are widely accepted by citizens or, in authoritarian regimes, when leaders are protected from broad public criticism. Moreover, certain circumstances enhance individuals' potential influence. Among them are new situations that free leaders from conventional approaches to defining the situation; complex situations involving many different factors; and situations without social sanctions, which permit freedom of choice because norms defining the range of permissible options are unclear (Hermann 1988; DiRenzo 1974).

A leader's **political efficacy**, or self-image, combined with the citizenry's relative desire for leadership, will also influence the degree to which personal values and psychological needs govern decision making. For example, when public opinion strongly favors a powerful leader, and when the head of state has an exceptional need for admiration, foreign policy will more likely reflect that leader's inner needs. Thus, Kaiser Wilhelm II's narcissistic personality allegedly met the German people's desire for a symbolically powerful leader, and German public preferences in turn influenced the foreign policy that Germany pursued during Wilhelm's reign, ending in World War I (Baron and Pletsch 1985).

political efficacy the extent to which a policy maker believes in his or her ability to control events politically.

Other factors undoubtedly influence how much leaders can shape their states' choices. For instance, when leaders believe that their own political survival is at stake, they tend to respond by making decisions in a two-stage process (Mintz 2004). In the first phase, leaders reject policy options that appear too costly politically; in the second, they evaluate the remaining options analytically, gauging the costs and benefits of each in terms of its relation to their country's interests.

The amount of information available about a particular situation is also important. Without pertinent information, policy is likely to be based on leaders' personal likes or dislikes. Conversely, the more information leaders have about international affairs, the more likely they are to engage in rational decision making.

Similarly, the timing of a leader's assumption of power is significant. When an individual first assumes a leadership position, the formal requirements of that role are least likely to restrict what he or she can do. That is especially true throughout the "honeymoon" period routinely given to new heads of state, during which time they are relatively free of criticism and excessive pressure. Moreover, when a leader assumes office following a dramatic event (a landslide election, for example, or the assassination of a predecessor), he or she can institute policies almost with a free hand (Hermann 1976).

CONTROVERSY   Policy and Personality: Do Leaders Make a Difference?

Some theorists assume that any leader will respond to a choice in the same way, given the same costs and benefits. But does this assumption square with the facts? What do we know about the impact of people's perceptions and values on the way they view choices? Political psychology tells us that the same option is likely to have different value to different leaders. Does this mean that different leaders would respond differently to similar situations?

Consider the example of Richard Nixon. In 1971, Americans took to the streets outside the White House to protest Nixon's massive bombing of Vietnam. His reaction was to shield himself from the voice of the people, without success, as it happened. Nixon complained that "nobody can know what it means for a president to be sitting in that White House working late at night and to have hundreds of thousands of demonstrators charging through the streets. Not even earplugs could block the noise."

Earlier, on a rainy afternoon in 1962, John F. Kennedy faced a similar citizen protest. Americans had gathered in front of the White House for a Ban the Bomb demonstration. His response was to send out urns of coffee and doughnuts and invite the leaders of the protest to come inside to state their case, believing that a democracy should encourage dissent and debate.

Nixon saw protesters as a threat; Kennedy saw them as an opportunity. This comparison suggests that the type of leader can make a difference in determining the kinds of choices likely to be made in response to similar situations. More important than each president's treatment of the protesters, however, was whether he actually changed his policy decisions based on the protests. Although Kennedy was hospitable to protesters, he did not ban nuclear weapons; in fact, military spending under Kennedy grew to consume half of the federal budget. Many would insist that Kennedy alone could not be expected to eliminate nuclear weapons—that this period of history was dominated by fear of the Soviet Union and intense concern for national security. The protesters in 1971, however, were more in keeping with the spirit of the times. Although they alone may not have persuaded Nixon to alter his policies in Vietnam, widespread protest and discontentment with the war, as well as America's inability to win, eventually prompted Nixon to order the gradual withdrawal of U.S. troops, ending American participation in the Vietnam War. These outcomes suggest that leaders are captive to the larger forces that drive international relations in their times.

What do you think? Did Kennedy and Nixon choose courses of action that reflected who they were as individuals? Or would any president in their respective eras have made similar choices?

A national crisis is a potent circumstance that increases a leader's control over foreign policy making. Decision making during crises is typically centralized and handled exclusively by the top leadership. Crucial information is often unavailable, and leaders see themselves as responsible for outcomes. Not surprisingly, great leaders (e.g., Napoleon Bonaparte, Winston Churchill, and Franklin D. Roosevelt) customarily emerge during periods of extreme tumult. A crisis can liberate a leader from the constraints that normally would inhibit his or her capacity to control events or engineer foreign policy change.

History abounds with examples of the importance of political leaders who emerge in different times and places and under different circumstances to play critical roles in shaping world history. Mikhail Gorbachev dramatically illustrates an individual's capacity to change the course of history. As noted in Chapter 1, many scholars believe that the Cold War could not have been brought to an end had it not been for Gorbachev's vision, courage, and commitment to engineering revolutionary changes. Ironically, those reforms led to his loss of power when the Soviet Union imploded in 1991.

Having said that the influence of individual leaders can sometimes be significant, we must be cautious and remember that leaders are not all-powerful determinants of states' foreign policy behavior. Rather, their personal influence varies with the context, and often the context is more influential than the leader (see Controversy: Policy and Personality: Do Leaders Make a Difference?). Of course, this ultimately leaves us with the question of whether famous leaders would have an impact whenever and wherever they lived (see Greenstein 1987). That question may be unanswerable but it reminds us at least that multiple factors affect states' foreign policy decisions.

CONSTRAINTS ON THE FOREIGN POLICY-MAKING PROCESS

As we saw in the previous chapter, realists maintain that the primary goal of foreign policy is to ensure state survival. From their perspective, strategic calculations are the primary determinants of policy makers' choices; domestic politics and the process of policy making itself are of secondary concern.

Because realism assumes that leaders' goals and their corresponding approach to foreign policy choices are the same, realists tend to view states as if they were **unitary actors**—homogenous or monolithic units with few or no important internal differences that affect their choices. One way to picture this is to think of states as billiard balls and the table on which they interact as the state system. The balls (states) continuously clash and collide with one another, and the actions of each are determined by its interactions with the others, not by what occurs inside it. According to this view, the leaders who make foreign policy, the types of governments they head, and the characteristics of their societies are unimportant in explaining foreign policy behavior.

unitary actor an agent in world politics (usually a sovereign state) assumed to be internally united, so that changes in its internal circumstances do not influence its foreign policy as much as do the decisions that actor's leaders make to cope with changes in its global environment.

two-level games a concept that refers to the interaction between international bargaining and domestic politics.

In contrast to realism's tendency to concentrate on international interactions, Robert Putnam (1988) argues that national leaders actually play **two-level games**. Besides making moves on an international game board, they also maneuver on a domestic board to obtain support at home for their initiatives abroad. Because moves on one game board affect play on the other, neither level can be ignored. Indeed, astute players recognize that the right move on one level can affect the outcome on the other level. Foreign policies, in other words, have domestic consequences, and actions aimed at domestic constituencies frequently reverberate beyond national borders. As a result, it is often difficult to know where foreign policy ends and domestic policy begins.

Putnam's two-level game metaphor reminds us that foreign policy making occurs in an environment of multiple, competing international and domestic interests. On occasion, it also occurs in situations when national values are threatened, policy makers are caught by surprise, and a quick decision is needed. The stress produced by these factors impairs leaders' cognitive abilities and may cause them to rely on various psychological coping techniques. First, owing to the process of cognitive dissonance described in Chapter 1, policy makers may try to cope with stress by denying a problem exists, blocking out negative information, and looking instead for data that justifies their optimistic viewpoint. A second common coping technique is procrastination. Here they recognize that a problem exists, but hope that it will go away by itself. Finally, a third technique for dealing with stress is **satisficing** (Simon 1957). Because policy makers work in an environment of uncertainty, incomplete information, and short deadlines, their evaluation of alternative policy options is seldom exhaustive. Rather than finding the option with the best chance of success, they may end their evaluation as soon as an alternative appears that seems superior to those already considered. Moreover, according to **prospect theory**, the alternative that they perceive as superior will often be colored by a concern over relative losses. Experimental evidence suggests that policy makers tend to be risk averse in choices among gains but risk acceptant with respect to losses. Fearing potential losses more than they value potential gains, they frequently are willing to take risks in the hope of avoiding loss, even thought their actions may yield a far greater loss (Levy 2003a).

satisficing the tendency for decision makers to choose the first available alternative that meets minimally acceptable standards.

prospect theory a behavioral decision theory that contends decision makers assess policy options in comparison to a reference point and that they take greater risks to prevent losses than to achieve gains.

procedural rationality a method of decision making based on having perfect information with which all possible courses of action are carefully evaluated.

Thus, despite the image of **procedural rationality** that policy makers seek to project, the actual practice of foreign policy decision making contains many impediments to rational choice. Compounding the cognitive constraints just mentioned are emotional constraints. For example, when frustrated with a seemingly intractable problem and a looming deadline, impatient policy makers may "shoot from the hip" rather than carefully review a range of options, trusting that sheer boldness will yield good results. Furthermore, once they have invested resources in a particular course of action that is failing, powerful emotions involving self-esteem and guilt may lead them to try to rescue their ill-advised policy by allocating more resources to the enterprise, thus falling into what economists call the **sunk costs** trap. Reflecting on how these psychological constraints can cause leaders to commit *errors of commission* (selecting a perilous course of action when better options were available) and *errors of omission* (overlooking

sunk costs a concept that refers to costs that have already been incurred and cannot be recovered.

something important), Brent Scowcroft, President George H. W. Bush's national security adviser, lamented: "We continuously step on our best aspirations. We're humans. Given a chance to screw up, we will (quoted in George 2006, 63).

Finally, in addition to cognitive and emotional constraints on rational decision making, affiliative constraints also breed potential problems. During a crisis, national leaders typically bypass the standard operating procedures of their foreign affairs bureaucracies and rely on a small, ad hoc group of advisers. There is some evidence that when these groups contain people with similar backgrounds who are insulated from outside opinions and surmise their leader's preferred course of action, they may exhibit excessive concurrence-seeking, or what Irving Janis (1982) calls **groupthink**. In the interest of group cohesion, they place extraordinarily high values on conformity and consensus. In addition to stifling dissent, group members adopt stereotypes of their opponents, ignore the full range of possible options, suppress personal reservations about the moral consequences of their recommendations, and fail to develop contingency plans to deal with potential setbacks.

groupthink the propensity for members of small, cohesive groups to accept the group's prevailing attitudes in the interest of group harmony, rather than speak out for what they believe.

Studies of policy making suggest that groupthink is but one type of interaction pattern that may occur within small, high-level groups and therefore should not be thought of as a general propensity of their dynamics (Stern and Sundalius 1997; 't Hart 1990). Another pattern associated with excessive conformity is the **newgroup syndrome**. Rather than being triggered by crisis-induced stress, concurrence-seeking can arise in newly formed policy groups that lack well-developed decision-making procedures. Anxious and insecure about their roles, members may engage in self-censorship, avoid critiquing one another's ideas, and conform with the positions staked out by the most assertive individuals (Stern 1997), which leads to premature closure of the decision process.

newgroup syndrome the propensity of members of newly formed groups to conform with the opinions expressed by powerful, assertive peers or the group's leader due to a lack of well-developed procedural norms.

The quality of decisions made by small advisory groups is also affected by the leadership style of those in charge (Preston 2001; Garrison 1999). Personality, level of expertise in foreign affairs, and prior management experience all have a bearing upon leadership style, which varies according to the degree of control these individuals desire over the policy process, the extent to which they seek to manage the flow of information, their preferences regarding how interpersonal relations are conducted, their tolerance for conflict among advisers, and their openness to divergent viewpoints (Preston 1997, 201; Preston and Hermann 2004). The kinds of advisers a leader chooses and how they are organized are influenced by these variables. For example, leaders with a need for control and a desire to manage information gravitate toward formal, hierarchical advisory structures with clear chains of command. On the other hand, leaders comfortable with face-to-face interaction, vigorous argumentation, and political infighting generally favor structures based on competition and multiple channels of information. Each advisory system has its advantages and drawbacks. What matters most for the quality of decisions is having a system that fits the personal characteristics of the leader.

To sum up, although policy makers can sometimes absorb new information quickly under great pressure and launch creative policy initiatives based on careful planning, the cognitive, emotional, and affiliative impediments to procedural

TABLE 3.1   Foreign Policy Decision Making in Theory and Practice

Ideal Process	Actual Practice
Accurate, comprehensive information	Distorted, incomplete information
Clear definition of national interests and goals	Personal motivations and organizational interests bias national goals
Exhaustive analysis of all options	Limited number of options considered; none thoroughly analyzed
Selection of optimal course of action for producing desired results	Course of action selected by political bargaining and compromise
Effective statement of decision and its rationale to mobilize domestic support	Confusing and contradictory statements of decision, often framed for media consumption
Careful monitoring of the decision's implementation by foreign affairs bureaucracies	Neglect of the tedious task of managing the decision's implementation by foreign affairs bureaucracies
Instantaneous evaluation of consequences followed by correction of errors	Superficial policy evaluation, imperfect detection of errors, and delayed correction

rationality in foreign policy making are substantial (see Tetlock 2006; Janis 1989). An effective decision-making process, insists former U.S. Secretary of State Henry Kissinger (1999, 1067), must address the following questions: "What are we trying to achieve, or what are we trying to prevent? What consequences do we expect from this decision, and what steps do we have in mind for dealing with them? What is the cost of the proposed action? Are we willing to pay that price, and for what length of time?" Answering these questions is never easy, notes another former government official: "The facts may be in doubt or dispute. Several policies, all good, may conflict. Several means, all bad, may be all that are open … [and] there may be many interpretations of what is right, what is possible, and what is in the national interest" (Sorensen 1963, 19–20).

Table 3.1 compares how the decision process *should* work with how it usually works. Ideally, according to the tenets of procedural rationality, the process would be governed by the following sequential steps:

1. *Problem Recognition and Definition.* Policy makers identify the essential elements of an emerging problem as well as the severity and imminence of the risks they face. They have full information about the situation due to an exhaustive search for all the relevant facts.

2. *Goal Selection and Prioritization.* Next, those responsible for making foreign policy choices must determine what they want to accomplish. This requires clarifying the values that underpin one's interests, establishing feasible objectives that capture these interests, and ranking them from most to least preferred.

3. *Development and Assessment of Alternatives.* Once policy objectives have been specified and ranked, a broad range of options is created, each representing a different course of action for attaining desired objectives. In addition, the costs, benefits, uncertainties, and tradeoffs of each option are estimated.

4. *Choice and Evaluation.* Finally, following a rigorous means-ends, cost-benefit analysis, the option with the best prospects for success is selected. Implementation is monitored to determine whether adjustments are needed in the course of action that has been chosen.

Although policy makers often describe their deliberations in these terms, research suggests otherwise. Many policy makers just muddle through; rather than formulating policies with bold, innovative strokes, they make policy changes through trial-and-error adjustments (Lindblom 1979). As one former U.S. official put it, "Rather than through grand decisions or grand alternatives, policy changes seem to come through a series of slight modifications of existing policy, with new policy emerging slowly and haltingly by small and usually tentative steps, a process of trial and error in which policy zigs and zags, reverses itself, and then moves forward" (Hilsman 1967).

The trends currently unfolding in world politics are the products of countless decisions made daily throughout the world. Some decisions are more consequential than others, and some actors are more important than others. Throughout history, great powers such as the United States have at times stood at the center of the world political stage, possessing the combination of natural resources, military might, and the means to project power worldwide that earned them their lofty status. How great powers have responded to one another has had profound consequences throughout international history. To better understand this, we turn our attention next to the dynamics of great-power rivalry.

CHAPTER SUMMARY

- Actors on the world stage are many and varied. States demand special attention because they are the principal repositories of economic and military capabilities in world affairs, and they alone possess the legal right to use force.

- The modern system of sovereign territorial states dates back to the Peace of Westphalia (1648) that ended the Thirty Years' War in Europe.

- The foreign policies of states consist of purposeful acts aimed at achieving international goals. Foreign policy making is a complex process that occurs in an environment of multiple, competing international and domestic interests.

- Foreign policy behavior is shaped by a combination of factors operating at different levels of analysis. At the systemic level, polarity, alliance polarization, and geostrategic position influence the opportunity for states to act in certain ways. At the state level, military might, economic strength, the type of government and its organizational processes influence the capacity to act on available opportunities. At the individual level, a leader's personality and the situation surrounding his or her ascension to power influence the willingness or motivation to act.

- Scholars describe rationality as a sequence of decision-making activities involving the following intellectual steps: (1) problem recognition and definition; (2) goal specification; (3) identification and evaluation of alternatives for attaining the desired goals; and (4) selection of the option that maximizes benefits and minimizes costs and risks.

- Although national leaders often claim that they follow procedural rationality when formulating their foreign policies, rational choice is more of an idealized standard than an accurate description of real-world behavior. Many cognitive and organizational factors interfere with effective problem solving. Rather than choosing the course of action with the best chance of success, decision makers may end their analysis of policy options as soon as an alternative appears that seems better than those already considered.

KEY TERMS

autocratic rule

bureaucratic politics

constitutional democracy

democratic peace

diversionary theory of war

geopolitics

groupthink

newgroup syndrome

polarity

polarization

political efficacy

procedural rationality

prospect theory

rational choice

satisficing

sovereignty

standard operating procedures (SOPs)

sunk costs

two-level games

unitary actors

SUGGESTED READINGS

Breuning, Marijke. *Foreign Policy Analysis.* New York: Palgrave Macmillan, 2007.

Deibel, Terry L. *Foreign Affairs Strategy.* New York: Cambridge University Press, 2007.

Kegley, Charles W., Jr., and Gregory A. Raymond. *From War to Peace: Fateful Decisions in International Politics.* Boston: Bedford/St. Martin's, 2002.

Nye, Joseph S., Jr. *The Powers to Lead.* New York: Oxford University Press, 2008.

Smith, Steve, Amelia Hadfield, and Tim Dunne. *Foreign Policy: Theories, Actors, Cases.* Oxford: Oxford University Press, 2008.

CRITICAL THINKING QUESTIONS

Although research suggests that democracies lose fewer wars than nondemocracies (Reiter and Stam 2002), some analysts worry that they are slow to recognize emerging threats and mobilize the resources needed to counter them. The American diplomat George Kennan (1951, 59), likened democracy to "one of those prehistoric monsters with a body as long as this room and a brain the size of a pin." Because he pays little attention to his environment, said Kennan, "you practically have to whack off his tail to make him aware that his interests are being disturbed." Once aroused, however, he marshals the wherewithal to defeat his adversary.

A question that has intrigued some scholars is whether Kennan's observation is restricted to the American presidential system, or whether it also pertains to parliamentary systems, which place responsibility in a cabinet led by a prime minister, who obtains his or her position by being the leader of the party with the most seats in the legislature, not through a direct popular vote. A corollary question is whether the type of cabinet matters, since some have members from the same political party but others are coalitions composed of members from two or more parties (see Kaarbo 2008).

Do these institutional differences affect how different kinds of democracies formulate and conduct foreign policy? Are certain forms of democracy better at recognizing and responding to emerging foreign policy problems? Are presidential democracies, with their single dominant leaders who are directly elected by the public, able to respond more quickly and flexibly than parliamentary democracies? Among parliamentary systems, can we expect variation in the performance of single-party versus multiparty coalition cabinets that are attributable to differences in their structures?

4

Great-Power Rivalry and the Lure of Hegemony: Cycles of War and Peace in Modern World History

CHAPTER OUTLINE

Long Cycles of World Leadership

The First World War

   The Causes of World War I

   The Consequences of World War I

The Second World War

   The Causes of World War II

   The Consequences of World War II

The Cold War

The Causes and Evolutionary Course of the Cold War

CONTROVERSY: Was Ideology the Primary Source of East–West Conflict?

The Consequences of the Cold War

The Future of Great-Power Politics

   America's Unipolar Moment

   From Unipolarity to Multipolarity?

   APPLICATION: Integrate, but Hedge

Great powers fear each other. They regard each other with suspicion, and they worry that war may be in the offing. They anticipate danger. There is little room for trust…. From the perspective of any one great power, all other great powers are potential enemies…. The basis of this fear is that in a world where great powers have the capability to attack each other and might have the motive to do so, any state bent on survival must be at least suspicious of other states and reluctant to trust them.

JOHN MEARSHEIMER
REALIST POLITICAL THEORIST

On November 9, 1799, a young, ambitious general named Napoleon Bonaparte rose to power in France after leading a military coup against the ruling government. A man with remarkable persuasive and intellectual abilities, he described his mind as an ordered chest of drawers: Each drawer contained a vast amount of information on a particular topic, and he could open any of them whenever necessary to inspect their contents without missing a single detail. Napoleon was brilliant, but he was also coarse, temperamental, and unscrupulous. Claiming to be following a star of destiny, he gradually turned the French Republic into a personal dictatorship.

In foreign affairs, Napoleon's strategy was to win quick, decisive military victories in an incessant pursuit of territorial gain. Deftly maneuvering his formidable army against the weakest point in an opponent's lines, he won a series of triumphs that gave him dominion over most of Europe. Beyond France (which included Belgium and lands on the left bank of the Rhine) were rings of dependent states and political allies. The former encompassed what today is the Netherlands, Spain, Switzerland, western and southern Germany, most of Italy, and part of Poland. The latter included Austria, Prussia, Denmark, Sweden, and Russia. His ultimate objective was to establish a new, vertical international order, one that would replace the horizontal Westphalian system of sovereign autonomous states with a hierarchy of subservient territories presided over by the French emperor.

Napoleon's quest for hegemony stalled after 1811. British naval power thwarted his forays beyond the Continent, an interminable guerrilla war in Spain drained precious resources, and an invasion of Russia ended in disaster, with roughly two-thirds of his forces succumbing in the cold darkness of the Russian winter. Heartened by Napoleon's setbacks, a coalition consisting of Great Britain, Russia, Prussia, and Austria moved against France. Napoleon's dream of "universal monarchy" was finally crushed at Waterloo in 1815. His defeat concluded a period that had battered Europe for almost a quarter century and left 2.5 million combatants dead. When measured by battle deaths per population, the toll exceeded all previous wars fought during the preceding three centuries. The carnage galvanized a consensus among the victors who met at the Congress of Vienna to forge a peace settlement that would restore the decentralized Westphalian system of sovereign equals, and prevent any single great power from again becoming strong enough to threaten the others.

The Napoleonic Wars and the Congress of Vienna highlight a common pattern in world politics. The ascendancy of one great power relative to its principal rivals eventually prompts opposition from the rest. If this hegemonic struggle

Classic Image/Alamy Limited

Choosing Between Reconciliation and Retribution
A key part of the peace settlement crafted at the
Congress of Vienna (1814–1815) was its resuscitative
policy toward France. Although Napoleon was sent
into exile and France was divested of territories he
had conquered, the French were included within
the newly created Concert of Europe, a system of
great-power consultation and policy coordination.
The Vienna settlement suggests that the prospects
for a durable peace can be enhanced by giving
defeated states a stake in preserving the post-war
international order.

escalates to global war, the victors will try to design a security regime aimed at
preventing the recurrence of such a catastrophic conflict by staving off future
challenges to the new international order they have constructed.

This general pattern has colored twentieth-century world politics, with three
global wars breaking out. World Wars I and II were fought with fire and blood;
the Cold War was fought by less destructive means but with equal intensity. Like
the Napoleonic Wars, each of these wars triggered major transformations in
world politics. In this chapter we explore their causes and consequences in
order to uncover the dynamics of great-power rivalries. By understanding the
origins and impact of these struggles over world leadership, we will be in a better
position to anticipate whether in the twenty-first century the great powers will
be able to avoid yet another global war.

LONG CYCLES OF WORLD LEADERSHIP

"All history shows," political scientist Hans J. Morgenthau (1985) once remarked, "that nations active in international politics are continuously preparing for, actively involved in, or recovering from organized violence in the form of war." Recently, many scholars have become intrigued with the possibility that this process is cyclical and unfolds through a series of distinct phases. According to **long-cycle theory**, over the past five centuries periods of global war have been followed by periods of international rule-making and institution-building, with shifts in the cycle usually occurring in tandem with changes in the major states' relative power (Modelski and Thompson 1999). Each global war led to the emergence of a **hegemon**, a preponderant state capable of dominating the conduct of international political and economic relations (Nye 2001). With its unrivaled power, the hegemon reshapes the rules and institutions of the state system to preserve its preeminent position.

long-cycle theory a theory that focuses on the rise and fall of the leading global power as the central political process of the modern world system.

hegemon a single, overwhelmingly powerful state that exercises predominate influence over the global system.

Hegemony imposes an extraordinary burden on the world leader, which must bear the costs of maintaining political and economic order while protecting its position and upholding its dominion. Over time, as the weight of global engagement takes its toll: The hegemon overextends itself, challengers arise, and the security regime so carefully crafted after the last global war comes under attack. Historically, this struggle for power has set the stage for another global war, the demise of one hegemon and the ascent of another. Table 4.1 summarizes 500 years of the cyclical rise and fall of great powers, their global wars, and their subsequent efforts to restore order.

Critics note that long-cycle theorists disagree on whether economic, military, or domestic factors produce these cycles. They also express frustration with the deterministic tone of the theory, which to them implies that global destiny is beyond policy makers' control. Still, long-cycle theory invites us to consider how shifts in the relative strength of great powers affect world politics. It rivets our attention on hegemonic transitions, the rise and fall of leading states in the international system. To underscore the importance of struggles over world leadership in understanding world politics, this chapter inspects the three great-power wars of the twentieth century, as well as the lessons these clashes suggest for the twenty-first century.

THE FIRST WORLD WAR

World War I profoundly altered the world's geopolitical map. By the time it ended, nearly 10 million people had died, three empires had crumbled, and a generation of Europeans had become disillusioned with foreign policies grounded in political realism. How can such a catastrophic war be explained? Many scholars believe that World War I was inadvertent, not the result of anyone's master plan. It was a war bred by uncertainty and circumstances beyond the control of those involved, one that people neither wanted nor expected.

TABLE 4.1   The Evolution of Great-Power Rivalry for World Leadership, 1495–2025

Dates	Preponderant State(s) Seeking Hegemony	Other Powers Resisting Domination	Global War	New Order after Global War
1495–1540	Portugal	Spain, Valois, France, Burgundy, England, Venice	Wars of Italy and the Indian Ocean, 1494–1517	Treaty of Tordesillas, 1517
1560–1609	Spain	The Netherlands, France, England	Spanish-Dutch Wars, 1580–1608	Truce of 1609; Evangelical Union and the Catholic League formed
1610–1648	Holy Roman Empire (Hapsburg dynasty in Spain and Austria-Hungary)	Shifting ad hoc coalitions of mostly Protestant states (Sweden, Holland) and German principalities as well as Catholic France against remnants of papal rule	Thirty Years' War 1618–1648	Peace of Westphalia, 1648
1650–1713	France (Louis XIV)	The United Provinces, England, the Hapsburg Empire, Spain, major German states, Russia	Wars of the Grand Alliance, 1688–1713	Treaty of Utrecht, 1713
1792–1815	France (Napoleon)	Great Britain, Prussia, Austria, Russia	Napoleonic Wars, 1792–1815	Congress of Vienna and Concert of Europe, 1815
1871–1914	Germany, Austria-Hungary, Turkey	Great Britain, France, Russia, United States	World War I, 1914–1918	Treaty of Versailles creating League of Nations, 1919
1933–1945	Germany, Japan, Italy	Great Britain, France, Soviet Union, United States	World War II, 1939–1945	Bretton Woods, 1944; United Nations, 1945; Potsdam, 1945
1945–1991	United States, Soviet Union	Great Britain, France, China, Japan	Cold War, 1945–1991	NATO/Partnerships for Peace, 1995; World Trade Organization, 1995
1991–	United States	China, European Union, Japan, Russia, India	A cold peace or hegemonic war, 2015–2025?	A new security regime to preserve world order?

Other scholars regard the war as a product of calculated choices. It was "a tragic and unnecessary conflict . . . because the train of events that led to its outbreak might have been broken at any point during the five weeks of crisis that preceded the first clash of arms, had prudence or common goodwill found a voice" (Keegan 1999). As we shall see, each of these interpretations captures a different dimension of the war's origins. Although none of Europe's great powers deliberately sought a general war, prevailing conditions made such an outcome highly probable, though not inevitable.

To explain how this long, grueling war happened, let us return to the analytic framework introduced in Chapter 1. We can piece together an understanding about the war's origins by looking for causal mechanisms operating at different levels of analysis, and placing them in a time sequence. By examining World War I from multiple levels across time, we can inoculate ourselves against naive, single-factor explanations of this complex event.

The Causes of World War I

The proximate causes of World War I can be found at the individual level of analysis. A Serbian nationalist seeking to free Slavs in the Balkans from Austrian rule assassinated Archduke Franz Ferdinand, heir to the Hapsburg throne of the Austrian-Hungarian Empire, at Sarajevo on June 28, 1914. This incident sparked a series of moves and countermoves by political leaders in Austria, Germany, and Russia, who held virtuous images of themselves and diabolical images of their adversaries. Rather than take the time to carefully craft policies that did not risk war, they made reactive, fatalistic decisions that seized upon the first suitable option (Williamson 1988). Their impulsive behavior over the next few weeks turned what had been a local dispute between Austria and Serbia into a horrific conflagration.

The archduke's assassination offered Austria an opportunity to weaken Serbia, which Vienna perceived as the source of separatist agitation that was undermining Hapsburg authority within the empire's large Slavic population. On July 25, Serbia rejected an Austrian ultimatum demanding its officials be allowed to participate in Serbia's investigation of the assassination plot, as well as in the punishment of the perpetrators. Serbia's refusal prompted the Austrians to declare war and bombard Belgrade. Responding to Serbian pleas for help, Russia mobilized its forces along the Austrian and German frontiers. In turn, Germany declared war on Russia and its ally, France. When German troops swept into Belgium on August 4 in order to outflank France, Britain declared war on Germany. Eventually, 32 countries on six continents became enmeshed in the conflict.

As this rapid, almost mechanical sequence of moves suggests, a combination of deeper, more remote causes had created an explosive situation that the clumsy statesmen in Vienna, Berlin, and St. Petersburg ignited. At the state level of analysis, many historians view the growth of nationalism, especially in southeastern Europe, as having created a climate of opinion that made war likely. Groups that glorified the distinctiveness of their national heritage began championing their own country above all others. Long-suppressed ethnic prejudices soon emerged, even among political leaders. Russian foreign minister Sergei Sazonov, for example, claimed to "despise" Austria, and Kaiser Wilhelm II of Germany asserted: "I hate the Slavs" (Tuchman 1962).

Domestic unrest inflamed these passions, making it hard to see things from another point of view. Believing that they were upholding their national honor, the Austrians could not comprehend why Russians labeled them the aggressors. German insensitivity to others' feelings prevented them from understanding "the strength of the Russians' pride, their fear of humiliation if they allowed the Germans and Austrians to destroy their little protégé, Serbia, and the intensity of Russian anger" (White 1990). With each side denigrating the character of the other, diplomatic alternatives to war evaporated.

At the systemic level of analysis, a web of rigid alliances and interlocking war plans quickly spread the fighting from one end of the Continent to the other. During the decade before Franz Ferdinand's assassination, European military alignments had become polarized, pitting the Triple Alliance of Germany, Austria-Hungary, and the Ottoman Empire against the Triple Entente of France, Britain, and Russia. Once Russia mobilized in response to Austria's attack on Serbia, alliance commitments pulled one European great power after another into the war.

Another factor underlying the outbreak of the First World War was the rise of German power and the challenge it posed to the British. Although Germany did not become a unified country until 1871, it prospered and used its growing wealth to create an awesome military machine. As the leader of the Continent's foremost industrial and military power, Kaiser Wilhelm II proclaimed in 1898 that Germany had "great tasks outside the narrow boundaries of old Europe." Under the concept of *weltpolitik* (world policy), Germany began building a strong navy to command respect around the globe. Britain, alarmed by the threat this might present to its maritime interests, established formal ties with France and Russia. Convinced that the British, French, and Russians were trying to encircle Germany, Wilhelm sought more armaments and closer relations with Austria-Hungary.

Germany was not the only rising great power at the turn of the century. Russia was also expanding, and becoming a threat to Germany. The decline in power of the Austrian-Hungarian Empire, Germany's only ally, heightened Berlin's anxieties. Hence Germany reacted strongly to Archduke Ferdinand's assassination. Confident that a short, localized, and victorious Balkan war would shore up Austria-Hungary and weaken Russia's influence in Europe, Wilhelm gave the Austrians a "blank check" to crush Serbia.

Germany's unconditional support for Austria-Hungary proved to be a serious miscalculation, as it solidified the bonds between France and Russia, the two allied powers on Germany's western and eastern borders. Under the so-called Schlieffen Plan, Germany's generals had long based their military preparations on the premise that in the event of war with both France and Russia, German troops would first defeat the French and then turn against the larger but slower-moving Russian army. The quickest way to crush the French, they reasoned, was to swing through neutral Belgium in a vast arcing movement and attack France from the north, where its defenses were the weakest. But when the Germans stormed through Belgium, Britain entered the war on the side of France and Russia. Recognizing the magnitude of the unfolding catastrophe, British foreign secretary Sir Edward Grey lamented: "The lamps are going out all over Europe; we shall not see them lit again in our lifetime."

The Consequences of World War I

World War I transformed the face of Europe. In its wake, three empires—the Austrian-Hungarian, Russian, and Ottoman (Turkish)—collapsed, and in their place

MAP 4.1 Territorial Changes in Europe following World War I

World War I redrew the boundaries of Europe. The map on the left shows state boundaries on the eve of the war in 1914, as well as the members of the two major opposing coalitions that formed. The map on the right shows the new borders in 1920, with the nine new states that emerged from the war. Source: From *Strategic Atlas, Comparative Geopolitics of the World's Powers,* revised edition, by Gerard Chaliand and Jean-Pierre Ragau. Copyright © 1990 by Gerard Chaliand and Jean-Pierre Rageau. Reprinted by permission of HarperCollins Publishers, Inc.

the independent states of Poland, Czechoslovakia, and Yugoslavia emerged. In addition, the countries of Finland, Estonia, Latvia, and Lithuania were born (see Map 4.1). The war also contributed to the overthrow of the Russian czar in 1917 by the Bolsheviks, a change in government and ideology that would have consequences for another seventy years.

World War I evoked revulsion for war and theories of political realism that justified armaments, secret alliances, and power politics. The staggering human and material costs of the previous four years led many of the delegates to the 1919 peace conference convened at Versailles, outside Paris, to reevaluate their convictions about statecraft. The time was ripe for a new approach to building world order. Disillusioned with realism, many turned to liberalism for guidance on how to manage the global future.

The decade following World War I was the high point of liberal idealism. Woodrow Wilson's ideas about world order, as expressed in his January 1917 "Fourteen Points" speech, were anchored in a belief that by reordering the international system according to liberal principles, the Great War (as World War I was then called) would be "the war to end all wars." Wilson's chief proposal was to construct a League of Nations that allegedly would guarantee the independence and territorial integrity of all states. His other recommendations included strengthening international law, settling territorial claims on the basis of self-determination, and promoting democracy, disarmament, and free trade.

However, once the delegates to the peace conference began their work, the knives of parochial national interest began whittling away at the liberal philosophy underpinning Wilson's proposals. Many European leaders had been offended by the pontificating American president. "God was content with Ten Commandments," growled Georges Clemenceau, the cynical French prime minister. "Wilson must have fourteen."

As negotiations at the conference proceeded, hard-boiled power politics prevailed. Ultimately, the delegates were only willing to support those elements in the Fourteen Points that served their national interests. After considerable wrangling, Wilson's League of Nations was written into the peace treaty with Germany as the first of 440 articles. The rest of the treaty was punitive, aimed at stripping the country of its great-power status. Similar treaties were later forced upon Austria-Hungary and Germany's other wartime allies.

The Treaty of Versailles grew out of a desire for retribution. In brief, Germany's military was drastically cut; it was forbidden to possess heavy artillery, military aircraft, or submarines, and its forces were banned from the Rhineland. Germany also lost territory in the west to France and Belgium, in the south to the new state of Czechoslovakia, and in the east to the new states of Poland and Lithuania. Overseas, Germany lost all its colonies. Finally, in the most humiliating clause of the treaty, Germany was assigned responsibility for the war and charged with paying reparations for the damages. On learning of the treaty's harsh provisions, the exiled German Kaiser is said to have declared that "the war to end wars has resulted in a peace to end peace."

THE SECOND WORLD WAR

Germany's defeat in the First World War and its humiliation under the Treaty of Versailles did not extinguish its hegemonic aspirations. On the contrary, they intensified them. Thus conditions were ripe for the second great-power war of the twentieth century, which pitted the Axis trio of Germany, Japan, and Italy against an unlikely "grand alliance" of four great powers who united despite their incompatible ideologies—communism in the case of the Soviet Union and democratic capitalism in the case of Britain, France, and the United States.

The world's fate hinged on the outcome of this massive effort to defeat the Axis. The Allied powers achieved success, but at a terrible cost: 53 million people died during six years of fighting (see Murray and Millett 2000). To understand the origins of this devastating conflict, we will once again examine how causal factors operating at different levels of analysis fit into a time sequence.

The Causes of World War II

Following Germany's capitulation in 1918, a democratic constitution was drafted by a constituent assembly meeting in the city of Weimar. Many Germans had little enthusiasm for the Weimar Republic. Not only was the new government linked in their minds to the humiliating Versailles Treaty, but it also suffered from the 1923 French occupation of the industrial Ruhr district, various political rebellions, and the ruinous economic collapse of 1929. By the parliamentary elections of 1932, over half of the electorate supported extremist parties that disdained democratic governance. The largest of these was the Nazi, or National Socialist German Workers party.

On January 30, 1933, the Nazi leader, Adolf Hitler, was appointed chancellor of Germany. Less than a month later, the Reichstag (Parliament) building burned down under mysterious circumstances. Hitler used the fire to justify an emergency edict allowing him to suspend civil liberties and move against communists and other political adversaries. Once all meaningful parliamentary opposition had been eliminated, Nazi legislators passed an enabling act that suspended the constitution and granted Hitler dictatorial power.

In his 1924 book *Mein Kampf* ("My Struggle"), Hitler urged Germany to recover territories taken by the Treaty of Versailles, absorb Germans living in neighboring lands, and colonize Eastern Europe. During his first year in power, however, he cultivated a pacific image, signing a nonaggression pact with Poland in 1934. The following year, the goals originally outlined in *Mein Kampf* climbed to the top of Hitler's foreign policy agenda: In 1935, he repudiated the military clauses of the Versailles Treaty; in 1936, he ordered troops into the demilitarized Rhineland; in March 1938 he annexed Austria; and in September 1938, he demanded control over the Sudetenland, a region of Czechoslovakia containing ethnic Germans (see Map 4.2). To address the Sudeten German question, a conference was convened in Munich, attended by Hitler, British Prime Minister Neville Chamberlain, and leaders of France and Italy (ironically, Czechoslovakia was not invited). Convinced that **appeasement** would halt further German expansionism, Chamberlain and the others agreed to Hitler's demands.

Instead of satisfying Germany, appeasement encouraged Hitler to press for further revisions in the international status quo. He was joined in this effort by Japan and Italy. The former invaded Manchuria in 1931 and China proper in 1937; the latter attacked Ethiopia in 1935 and Albania in 1939. Furthermore, both Germany and Italy intervened in the Spanish civil war on the side of the fascists, headed by General Francisco Franco.

These acts of aggression paved the way for the century's second massive war. After Germany occupied the rest of Czechoslovakia in March 1939, Britain and

appeasement a strategy of making concessions to another state in the hope that, satisfied, it will not make additional claims.

M A P 4.2 World War II Redraws the Map of Europe

The map on the left shows the height of German expansion in 1943, when it occupied Europe from the Atlantic Ocean and Baltic Sea to the gates of Moscow in the Soviet Union. The map on the right shows the new configuration of Europe after the "Grand Coalition" of Allied forces—Great Britain, the United States, and the Soviet Union—defeated the Axis' bid for supremacy. Source: Europe in 1945 from *Strategic Atlas, Comparative Geopolitics of the World's Powers,* revised edition, by Gerard Chaliand and Jean-Pierre Rageau. Copyright © 1990 by Gerard Chaliand and Jean-Pierre Ragau. Reprinted by permission of HarperCollins Publishers, Inc.

France formed an alliance to protect the next likely victim, Poland. They also opened negotiations with Moscow in hopes of enticing the Soviet Union to join the alliance. Then, on August 23, 1939, Hitler and the Soviet leader Joseph Stalin stunned the world by signing a nonaggression pact. Certain that the Western democracies would not intervene without Soviet assistance, Hitler invaded Poland on September 1, 1939. Britain and France, honoring their pledge to defend the Poles, declared war on Germany two days later.

The war expanded rapidly. Hitler next turned his forces loose on the Balkans, North Africa, and westward. Powerful mechanized German units invaded Norway and marched through Denmark, Belgium, Luxembourg, and the Netherlands. They swept around France's defensive barrier, the Maginot line, and forced the British to evacuate an expeditionary force from the French beaches at Dunkirk. Paris itself fell in June 1940, and in the months that followed, the German air force pounded Britain in an attempt to force it into submission. Instead of invading Britain, in June 1941 Nazi troops attacked the Soviet Union, Hitler's former ally.

Germany's military successes provided an opportunity for Japan to move against British, French, and Dutch colonies in Asia, with the aim of replacing Western influence with a Greater East Asian Co-Prosperity Sphere under Tokyo's leadership. Japan followed its earlier conquests of Manchuria and eastern China with pressure on the Vichy French government to allow Japanese military bases in Indochina (now Vietnam, Laos, and Cambodia), from which the vital petroleum and mineral resources of Southeast Asia could be threatened. Concerned that the United States would try to thwart its ambitions, Japan launched a surprise attack on the U.S. naval base at Pearl Harbor, Hawaii, on December 7, 1941. Almost immediately, Germany declared war on the United States. Over the next six months, Japan occupied the Philippines, Malaya, Burma, and the Dutch East Indies (now Indonesia). The military challenges posed by the Japanese and Germans ended U.S. **isolationism**, enabling President Franklin Roosevelt to forge a coalition with Britain and the Soviet Union to oppose the Axis powers.

isolationism a policy of withdrawing from active participation with other actors in world affairs and instead concentrating state efforts on managing internal affairs.

The proximate cause of the war lies at the individual level of analysis. Adolf Hitler's truculent personality and aggressive schemes triggered the Second World War. Other more remote factors exerted significant impacts as well. At the state level of analysis, hypernationalism, domestic economic crises, and the demise of democratic governance in Germany provided an environment where Hitler could rise to power (Van Evera 1990–91). In addition, a belief in the dominance of defense over offense held by military establishments that had experienced the First World War made some states complacent in the face of German rearmament. Governments who remembered the rapid escalation of events during the summer of 1914 were also hesitant to respond to German actions in ways that might precipitate an upward spiral of conflict. Recalling the trauma produced by World War I, appeasement seemed preferable to confrontation.

Finally, at the systemic level of analysis, the vindictive peace settlement constructed at Versailles, U.S. isolationism, and the failure of the League of Nations were crucial factors in explaining the outbreak of the Second World War. Unlike in the aftermath of the Napoleonic Wars, when delegates to the Congress of Vienna gave France a stake in the new world order, the Versailles Treaty aggravated relations between victor and vanquished. With the United States retreating into isolationism and the League of Nations unable to deter aggression, France and Britain had difficulty coordinating their approaches to Germany. While France wanted to restrain Germany, it was unwilling to act without British support. Britain, in contrast, saw appeasement as the way to prevent a new round of bloodshed with Germany. Meanwhile, Japan saw in Germany's initial military victories an opportunity to expand its control over Chinese territory and move against British, French, and Dutch colonies in

Topham/Image Works

The Rise of Hitler and German Nationalism In the 1930s the ideologies of national socialism and fascism—belief systems that regarded the state as supreme, justified dictatorship, and mobilized society for aggression—took root in Germany and Italy. Adolf Hitler's propaganda experts staged dramatic political rallies to glorify the Führer (leader), condemn the Jews, and call for the acquisition of Lebensraum (living space) for the German race.

Southeast Asia. As the fighting gradually spread across the globe, liberal faith in the capacity of international law and organization to prevent great-power warfare seemed as naïve as political realists had suggested.

The Consequences of World War II

By May 1945, Germany lay in ruins. Three months later, the U.S. atomic bombing of Hiroshima and Nagasaki forced Japan to surrender. The Allied victory over the Axis redistributed power and reordered borders. The Soviet Union absorbed nearly 600,000 square kilometers of territory from the Baltic states of Estonia, Latvia, and Lithuania, and from Finland, Czechoslovakia, Poland, and Romania—recovering what Russia had lost in the 1918 Treaty of Brest-Litovsk. Poland, a victim of Soviet expansionism, was compensated with land taken from Germany. Meanwhile, Germany was divided into occupation zones that eventually provided the basis for its partition into East and West Germany. Finally, pro-Soviet regimes assumed power throughout Eastern Europe (see Map 4.2). In the Far East, the Soviet Union took the four Kurile Islands (or Northern Territories) from Japan, and Korea was divided into Soviet and U.S. occupation zones at the thirty-eighth parallel.

With the defeat of the Axis, one global system ended, but the defining characteristics of the new system had not yet become clear. Although the United Nations was created to replace the old, discredited League of Nations, the management of world affairs still rested in the hands of the victors. Yet victory only magnified their distrust of one another's intentions. The "Big Three" leaders—Winston Churchill, Franklin Roosevelt, and Joseph Stalin—had met at the Yalta Conference in February 1945 to design a new world order, but the vague compromises they reached concealed political differences percolating below the surface. Following Germany's unconditional surrender, the Big Three (with the United States now represented by Harry Truman) met again in July 1945 at Potsdam. The meeting ended without agreement, and the façade of Allied unity began to crumble.

Perhaps the most important change in the structure of the international system engendered by the war was the shift from a **multipolar** to a **bipolar** distribution of power. Whereas significant military capabilities previously were spread among several great powers, now they were concentrated in the hands of two superpowers, the United States and the Soviet Union. Great Britain and France, exhausted by the war, fell from the apex of world power. Germany, Italy, and Japan, defeated in war, also slipped from the ranks of the great powers. Thus, as the French political sociologist Alexis de Tocqueville had foreseen over a century earlier, the Americans and Russians would hold sway over the destinies of half of mankind. In what eventually became known as the Cold War, the two giants began the third and last hegemonic struggle of the twentieth century.

multipolar an international system with more than two dominant power centers.

bipolar an international system with two dominant power centers.

THE COLD WAR

Unparalleled in scope and unprecedented in destructiveness, the second great war of the twentieth century brought into being a system dominated by two superpowers, whose nuclear might far surpassed the military capabilities of the rest of the world. Out of these circumstances grew the conflict known as the Cold War, a competition between Washington and Moscow for hegemonic leadership.

The Causes and Evolutionary Course of the Cold War

The origins of the twentieth century's third struggle for world leadership are debated to this day because the historical evidence lends itself to different interpretations (see Gaddis 1997). Several possible causes stand out. The first is advanced by realism: The Cold War stemmed from discordant geostrategic interests. The preeminent status of the United States and the Soviet Union at the top of the international hierarchy made their rivalry inescapable. As direct competitors for global influence who presumed that gains by one side would yield losses for the other, they were mutually suspicious and relentlessly contentious.

A second interpretation holds that the Cold War was simply an extension of the superpowers' mutual disdain for each other's economic beliefs and political system. American animosity toward the Soviet Union arose during the 1917 Bolshevik revolution in Russia, which brought to power a government that embraced the radical ideas of Karl Marx. U.S. fears of Marxism led it to adopt an ideology of anticommunism and embark on a crusade to contain Soviet influence. Under what was popularly known as the **domino theory**, U.S. policy makers assumed that the fall of one country to communism would trigger the fall of its neighbors, and in turn still other countries, until the entire world came under Soviet domination.

Soviet leaders were equally hostile to the United States. Believing that communism could not coexist with capitalism, they tried to stoke revolutionary fires around the world in an effort to encourage communist insurgencies. Thus when viewed through the lens of ideology, diametrically opposed systems of belief precluded compromise between the superpowers, locking them into a long, bitter struggle (see Controversy: Was Ideology the Primary Source of East–West Conflict?).

A third explanation sees the Cold War rooted in psychological factors, particularly in the superpowers' misperceptions of each other's motives. Mistrustful actors are prone to see virtue in their own behavior and malice in those of their adversaries. When such mirror images exist, hostility is inevitable (Bronfenbrenner 1961). Moreover, as perceptions of an adversary's duplicity become accepted, **self-fulfilling prophecies** can arise. Suspicious of the other side, national leaders become fixated upon alleged intrigues, exaggerate the susceptibility of their opponent to coercion, and assume that decisive action will yield a **bandwagon** of support. From this perspective, the Cold War was not simply a product of divergent interests. Nor was it merely attributable to incompatible ideologies. Instead, it was a conflict steeped in reciprocal anxieties bred by the way policy makers on both sides misinterpreted each other's intentions.

Additional factors beyond those rooted in conflicting interests, ideologies, and images contributed to the Soviet-American rivalry. To sort out their relative causal influence, scholars have found it useful to trace how the Cold War changed over its forty-two-year history. We can highlight these changes by dividing the Cold War into the three chronological phases shown in Figure 4.1.

Confrontation, 1945–1962. A brief period of wary friendship preceded the mutual antagonism that developed between the United States and the Soviet Union. In February 1946, Stalin gave a speech in which he spoke of "the inevitability of conflict with the capitalist powers." Shortly thereafter, George F. Kennan, then a diplomat in the American embassy in Moscow, sent to Washington his famous "long telegram" assessing the sources of Soviet conduct. Kennan's ideas were circulated widely in 1947, when the journal *Foreign Affairs* published his views in an article signed simply "X." In it, Kennan argued that Soviet leaders forever would feel insecure about their political ability to maintain power against forces both within Soviet society and in the outside world. Their insecurity would lead to an activist—and perhaps aggressive—Soviet foreign

---

domino theory a metaphor popular during the Cold War which predicted that if one state fell to communism, its neighbors would also fall in a chain reaction, like a row of falling dominoes.

self-fulfilling prophecies the tendency for one's expectations to evoke behavior that helps to make the expectations become true.

bandwagon the tendency for weak states to seek alliance with the strongest power, irrespective of that power's ideology or form of government, in order to increase security.

CONTROVERSY   **Was Ideology the Primary Source of East–West Conflict?**

Cold War America was gripped by a "Great Fear" not simply of the Soviet Union but of communism. Senator Joseph McCarthy led an infamous hunt for communist sympathizers in government, Hollywood production companies blacklisted supposed communist sympathizers, and average American citizens were often required to take loyalty oaths at their offices. Everywhere communism became synonymous with treasonous, un-American activity. As the nuclear arms race escalated and the U.S. government took military action to contain the Soviet Union, its justification was almost always expressed in terms of ideology. The threat, it claimed, was that of an atheistic, inherently expansionistic communist system that challenged America's democratic freedoms. The Soviet Union also couched its Cold War rhetoric in terms of ideology, objecting to the imperialistic, capitalist system that Washington allegedly planned to impose on the whole world. Indeed, many Soviets echoed former leader Vladimir Lenin's prediction: "As long as capitalism and socialism exist, we cannot live in peace; in the end, either one or the other will triumph—a funeral dirge will be sung either over the Soviet Republic or over world capitalism."

Some would argue that fear of the other side's world dominance may have been more important in the Cold War than pure ideology. Both the American and the Soviet governments may have entered the Cold War to secure their relative power in the world order as much as to protect pure principles. After all, the United States and the Soviet Union had managed to transcend differing ideologies when they allied against the Axis powers in World War II. Following the war, a power vacuum created by the decline of Europe's traditional great powers drew them into conflict with each other, and as they competed, ideological justifications surfaced.

Ideologies fulfill a common human need to simplify and explain a complex and confusing world. But commitment to an ideology may at times cause hatred and hostility. Fervent believers in a particular ideology are prone to perceive other ideologies competitively— as challenges to the truth of their own core beliefs. Ideology can thus become an excuse for violence. Although scholars are still debating the causes of the Cold War, we need to ask whether it was, in fact, an ideological contest over ideas or a more general contest for power.

What do you think? Was the Cold War really an ideological contest between communism and democratic capitalism? Or was it an intense geostrategic rivalry that would have occurred even in the absence of contending ideologies?

---

policy. However, the United States had the power to increase the strains under which the Soviet leadership would have to operate, which could lead to a gradual mellowing or final end of Soviet power. Hence, Kennan concluded: "In these circumstances it is clear that the main element of any United States policy toward the Soviet Union must be that of a long-term, patient but firm and vigilant containment of Russian expansive tendencies" (Kennan 1947).

Soon thereafter, President Harry S. Truman made Kennan's assessment the cornerstone of American postwar foreign policy. Alarmed by domestic turmoil in Turkey and Greece, which he asserted was communist inspired, Truman declared, "I believe that it must be the policy of the United States to support free peoples who are resisting attempted subjugation by armed minorities or by outside pressures." Eventually known as the **Truman Doctrine**, this statement defined the grand strategy that the United States would pursue for the next 40 years, over Kennan's objections (1967, 361). The grand strategy of **containment** sought to prevent the expansion of Soviet influence by encircling the Soviet Union with military alliances backed with the threat of nuclear retaliation.

Truman Doctrine the declaration by President Harry S. Truman that U.S. foreign policy would use intervention to support peoples who allied with the United States against external subjugation.

containment a strategy to prevent another state from using force to expand its sphere of influence.

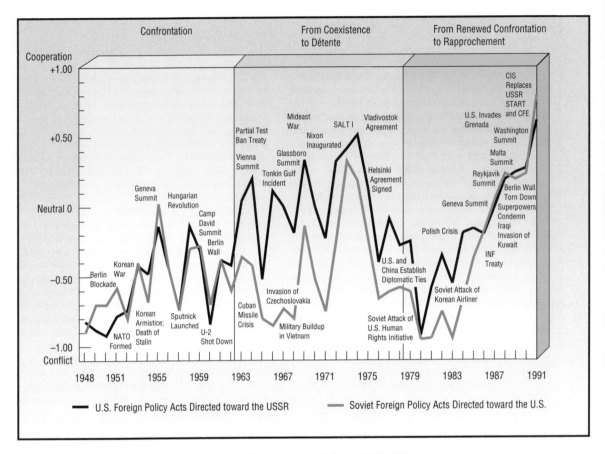

FIGURE 4.1 Key Events in the Evolution of U.S.–Soviet Relations, 1948–1991

The evolution of U.S.–Soviet relations during the Cold War displays a series of shifts between periods of conflict and cooperation. As this figure shows, each superpower's behavior toward the other tended to be reciprocal, and, for most periods prior to 1983, confrontation prevailed over cooperation.

peaceful coexistence
Soviet leader Nikita Khrushchev's 1956 doctrine that war between capitalist and communist states is not inevitable and that interbloc competition could be peaceful.

A seemingly endless series of Cold War crises soon followed. They included the communist coup d'état in Czechoslovakia in 1948; the Soviet blockade of West Berlin in June of that year; the communist acquisition of power on the Chinese mainland in 1949; the outbreak of the Korean War in 1950; the Chinese invasion of Tibet in 1950; and a series of on-again, off-again Taiwan Straits crises. The Soviets finally broke the U.S. atomic monopoly in 1949. Thereafter, the risks of massive destruction of each side necessitated restraint and changed the terms of their rivalry.

Because the Soviet Union remained strategically inferior to the United States, Nikita Khrushchev (who succeeded Stalin upon his death in 1953) pursued a policy of **peaceful coexistence** with capitalism. Nonetheless, the Soviet Union at times cautiously sought to increase its power in places where opportunities appeared to exist. As a result, the period following Stalin's death saw many Cold War confrontations, with Hungary, Cuba, Egypt, and Berlin becoming flash points.

In 1962, the surreptitious placement of Soviet missiles in Cuba set the stage for the greatest test of the superpowers' capacity to manage their disputes—the Cuban Missile Crisis. The superpowers stood eyeball to eyeball. Fortunately, one (the Soviet Union) blinked, and the crisis ended. This experience expanded both side's awareness of the suicidal consequences of a nuclear war, and transformed the way Washington and Moscow would henceforth think about how the Cold War should be waged.

From Coexistence to Détente, 1963–1978.   The looming threat of mutual destruction, in conjunction with the growing parity of American and Soviet military capabilities, made coexistence or nonexistence appear to be the only alternatives for political leaders in Washington and Moscow. At the American University commencement exercises in 1963, U.S. President John F. Kennedy warned that the superpowers were "caught up in a vicious and dangerous cycle in which suspicion on one side breeds suspicion of the other and new weapons beget counterweapons." He went on to signal a shift in how the United States hoped thereafter to interact with the Soviet Union, which elicited a positive response from the Kremlin.

Another step forward was taken following Richard Nixon's election in 1968. Coached by his national security adviser, Henry A. Kissinger, President Nixon initiated a new approach to dealing with the Soviet Union that he labeled **détente**. The Soviets also adopted this term to describe their policies toward the United States, and relations between the two countries moved in a more constructive direction. Arms control stood at the center of their activities. The Strategic Arms Limitation Talks (SALT), initiated in 1969, sought to restrain the threatening, expensive, and spiraling arms race by limiting the deployment of antiballistic missiles. As Figure 4.1 shows, cooperative interaction became more commonplace than hostile relations. Visits, cultural exchanges, trade agreements, and joint technological ventures replaced threats, warnings, and confrontations.

détente a strategy of relaxing tensions between adversaries to reduce the possibility of war.

From Renewed Confrontation to Rapprochement, 1979–1991.   Despite the careful nurturing of détente, it did not endure. When the Soviet Union invaded Afghanistan in 1979, President Jimmy Carter defined the situation as "the most serious strategic challenge since the Cold War began." He promptly declared America's willingness to use military force to protect its access to oil supplies from the Persian Gulf. In addition, he suspended grain exports to the Soviet Union, and attempted to organize a worldwide boycott of the 1980 Moscow Olympics.

Relations deteriorated dramatically thereafter. Carter's successor in the White House, Ronald Reagan, described the Soviet Union as "the focus of evil in the modern world." His counterparts in the Kremlin (first Yuri Andropov and then Konstantin Chernenko) responded with equally scathing criticisms of the United States. As the rhetorical salvos became increasingly harsh, the arms race resumed. Some American leaders hinted that a nuclear war could be "winnable," and advocated a military strategy that included the threat of a "first use" of nuclear weapons in the event of a conventional attack by the Soviets. Under the **Reagan Doctrine** the United States pledged support for anticommunist insurgents who sought to overthrow Soviet-supported governments in Afghanistan, Angola, and Nicaragua.

By 1985, superpower relations had deteriorated to the point that Mikhail Gorbachev, the new Soviet leader, characterized the situation as "explosive." Further complicating matters for the Soviet Union, its economy was buckling under the weight of exorbitant military expenditures, estimated at roughly a quarter of the country's gross domestic product. Faced with economic stagnation and declining civic morale, Gorbachev implemented a series of far-reaching domestic reforms to promote democratization and a market system. Meanwhile, in an effort to reduce the suffocating level of military expenditures, he sought a **rapprochement** or reconciliation with the West, and proclaimed his desire to end the Cold War. "We realize that we are divided by profound historical, ideological, socioeconomic, and cultural differences," he noted in 1987 during his first visit to the United States. "But the wisdom of politics today lies in not using those differences as a pretext for confrontation, enmity, and the arms race." Soviet spokesperson Georgi Arbatov elaborated, informing the United States that "we are going to do a terrible thing to you—we are going to deprive you of an enemy."

Surprisingly, the Soviets ended their aid to Cuba, withdrew from Afghanistan, and announced unilateral reductions in military spending. Gorbachev also agreed to two new disarmament agreements: the Strategic Arms Reduction Treaty (START) for deep cuts in strategic arsenals, and the Conventional Forces in Europe (CFE) Treaty to reduce the Soviet presence in Europe. Finally, to nearly everyone's astonishment, Moscow acquiesced to the disbanding of the Warsaw Pact and the reunification of Germany. In 1989, the Berlin Wall was dismantled. Long a stark, frightening symbol of the division between East and West, its removal heralded the end of the Cold War. Its peaceful conclusion suggested something quite different from the twentieth century's two world wars: Hegemonic struggles are not doomed to end in violence; sometimes great-power rivals can reconcile their differences without resorting to global war.

The Consequences of the Cold War

Though locked in a geostrategic rivalry exacerbated by antagonistic ideologies and mutual misperceptions, the United States and the Soviet Union avoided a fatal showdown. In accepting the devolution of their empire, Soviet leaders made the most dramatic peaceful retreat from power in history. The end of the Cold War altered the face of world affairs in profound and diverse ways. With the dissolution of the Soviet Union in 1991, no immediate great-power challenger confronted American hegemonic leadership. However, a host of new security threats

Reagan Doctrine a pledge of U.S. backing for anticommunist insurgents who sought to overthrow Soviet-supported governments.

rapprochement in diplomacy, a policy seeking to reestablish normal relations between enemies.

emerged, ranging from aspiring nuclear powers such as North Korea and Iran to terrorist networks such as Al Qaeda. As the turbulent twentieth century wound down, the simple Cold War world of clearly defined adversaries gave way to a shadowy world of elusive foes.

THE FUTURE OF GREAT-POWER POLITICS

Rapid, unanticipated changes in world politics often create uncertainty about the global future. To optimists, the tides of change that swept across the world following the collapse of communism signified "the end of mankind's ideological evolution and the universalization of Western liberal democracy as the final form of government" (Fukuyama 1989). To pessimists, these sea changes suggested not history's end, but its resumption (Kagan 2008). Both groups recognized that Cold War bipolarity had been superseded by a **unipolar** configuration of power that presented new and difficult challenges.

unipolar an international system with one dominant power center.

America's Unipolar Moment

Unipolarity refers to the concentration of power in a single preponderant state. Following the collapse of the Soviet Union, the United States stood alone at the summit of the international hierarchy. It was the only country with the military, economic, and cultural assets to be a decisive player in any part of the world it chose (Krauthammer 1991). Its military was not just stronger than anybody's—it was stronger than everybody's, with defense expenditures eventually exceeding all other countries combined.

Complementing America's military might was its economic strength. With less than 5 percent of global population, the United States accounted for almost a third of the global gross domestic product and two-fifths of the entire world's spending on research and development (Emmott 2002, 4). Furthermore, America wielded enormous **soft power** as a source of popular culture and the hub of global communications, through which its values spread all over the world (Nye 2004). In the words of former French Foreign Minister Hubart Vedrine, the United States was not simply a superpower; it was a hyperpower.

soft power the ability of a country to get what it wants in international affairs through the attractiveness of its culture, political ideals, and policies.

The United States began the new millennium with hopes of peace and prosperity. From Washington's perspective, a safe, prosperous world was emerging under its leadership. When Al Qaeda operatives crashed hijacked airliners into the World Trade Center and the Pentagon, they shattered widespread optimism about the prospects for the twenty-first century. Progress no longer seemed inevitable, a matter of steady, predictable advances toward a bright, promising future. Humanity, as United Nations Secretary-General Kofi Annan observed, had "entered the third millennium through a gate of fire."

The confluence of enormous military, economic, and cultural power on American soil after the Cold War gave the United States the ability to launch its so-called "global war on terror." Overwhelming power can easily tempt national leaders to act in a **unilateral** manner. Rather than working with others, independent

unilateral a strategy that relies on independent, self-help behavior in foreign policy.

action may seem attractive to a strong, self-confident nation worried about being hamstrung by quibbling lesser powers. Whereas others must address international problems through global organizations to be effective, some American policy makers believed that the United States had the capability to "go it alone," even in the face of strident criticism from abroad. Reflecting on the possibility that allied countries might withhold support for vigorous military action against Al Qaeda if it extended beyond the organization's mountain hideout in Afghanistan, President George W. Bush mused: "At some point, we may be the only ones left [in the war on terror]. That's okay with me. We are America" (Woodward 2002, 81).

Unilateralism has its costs, however. Acting alone may appear expedient, but it erodes international support on issues, such as combating global terrorism, where the United States needs cooperation from others. American power, writes political scientist Stephen Walt (2005, 229) "is most effective when it is seen as *legitimate*, and when other societies believe it is being used to serve their interests as well as those of the United States." But, as former Reagan administration official Clyde Prestowitz (2003) laments, Washington's neglect of the politics of consensus building when it expanded military operations from Afghanistan to Iraq in 2003 sullied America's status in the world, as many countries questioned the legitimacy of U.S. foreign policy.

With the unraveling of its financial system in the fall of 2008, many analysts have concluded that America's unipolar moment is ending. As Figure 4.2 shows, long-term economic trajectories based on differential national growth rates point to a world in which other great powers will challenge American economic preeminence within the next two decades. At the same time, the United States will find it costly to maintain military dominance. Aside from major deployments in Afghanistan and Iraq, U.S. forces are positioned in 737 military bases spread throughout 132 foreign countries reaching from the Korean Peninsula to the Gulf of Aden to Latin America (Freeland 2007, 18). As Richard Haass, in charge of policy planning for the U.S. Department of State from 2001 to 2003, warns: "America remains the world's preeminent actor, but it is also stretched militarily, in debt financially, divided domestically, and unpopular internationally" (*Economist*, November 4, 2004, 36). Historian Paul Kennedy (2006) agrees that there are limits to American power: The United States "possesses the world's single largest economy but faces huge trade and budget deficits and economic rivalries from an equally large European Union and a fast-growing China. Its armed forces look colossal, but its obligations look even larger."

imperial overstretch
the historical tendency of hegemons to weaken themselves through costly foreign pursuits that drain their resources.

Imperial overstretch, the gap between internal resources and external commitments, has bedeviled every leading great power (Kennedy 1987). Throughout history, hegemons repeatedly have defined their security interests more broadly than other states only to slip from the pinnacle of power by reaching beyond their grasp. "The problem in defense spending," former U.S. president Dwight Eisenhower concluded, "is to figure out how far you should go without destroying from within what you are trying to defend from without."

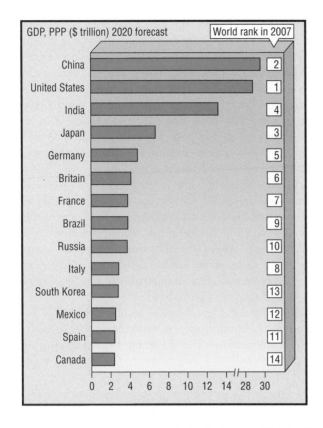

FIGURE 4.2 Emerging Centers of Power in the Twenty-First Century

Using purchasing power parities (PPP) to remove differences in countries' price levels, this figure presents a forecast of the largest economies in 2020.

SOURCE: *Economist*, April 1, 2006; WDR (2008, 334–335).

From Unipolarity to Multipolarity?

Many scholars and policy makers believe that the unipolar system of the past few years will be replaced by a multipolar one. The shift will be gradual; the world will not be unipolar one day and multipolar the next. Instead, new centers of meaningful power will arise over ensuing decades, making the United States one major power among many. Some of the rising powers frequently mentioned as potential members of this future multipolar system include China, the European Union, Japan, India, and Russia. The U.S. National Intelligence Council (2004), for example, forecasts that China's gross domestic product will equal Japan's in 2017 and the United States' in 2042. India, which by mid-century is projected to have 1.6 billion people with a larger, highly educated working-age population than China, is expected to surpass France's gross domestic product in 2020, Germany's a few years later, and Japan's shortly after 2030. Because multipolar systems include several comparatively equal great powers vying for influence and advantage, they are complex. When we take into account the interplay of military and economic factors, such systems are also fraught with uncertainty. Differentiating friend from foe becomes difficult when allies in military security may be rivals in trade relationships.

Predicting what cleavages and partnerships will develop among the great powers in a twenty-first-century multipolar system will be complicated. Conflict could emerge between any pair of great powers, but it may be restricted to one sphere of activity. For example, the United States and Japan exhibit conflict in their commercial relations but nevertheless also display continuing efforts to manage their security relations collaboratively. Such cross-cutting axes of conflict and cooperation will affect the stability of any future multipolar system. Throughout history different types of multipolar systems have existed, some of which have exhibited more stability than others. The most unstable have possessed rigid, polarized alignments, such as during the period prior to the outbreak of World War I (Kegley and Raymond 1994). Polarized systems are dangerous because they focus adversaries' attention on a single threat, thus making it more likely that minor disagreements will become magnified into larger tests of will. A system where great powers compete in one sphere of activity but cooperate elsewhere has the potential to prevent any given issue from polarizing the members of the state system. Great-power conflict would be frequent, but as long as security and economic disputes do not overlap, they would not necessarily divide the system into two antagonistic camps. Under these circumstances, the danger of polarization could be managed if the great powers developed international rules and institutions to manage their fluid, mixed-motive relationships.

Establishing rules to manage potential great-power conflicts will also be important because the transition to multipolarity is unlikely to be smooth. Scholars have found that the combination of a declining hegemon and an

---

APPLICATION   Integrate, but Hedge

One of the main foreign policy problems facing the United States today is how to reconcile itself to ascending powers that are becoming formidable competitors. Joseph S. Nye, Jr. served as U.S. assistant secretary of defense during the 1990s, with responsibility for developing an East Asian security strategy. In the following passage, he describes how he drew upon international relations theory to develop a strategy for responding to China's growing strength.

There was a great deal of concern [among policy makers] about the rise of Chinese power; indeed, some voices advocated a policy of containment before China became too strong. In my view, such an approach would guarantee Chinese enmity and unnecessarily discount possible benign futures. Yet treating China as a friend would not guarantee friendship. We designed a strategy that drew upon both realism and liberalism. From a realist perspective, the three key powers in East Asia were the United States, Japan, and China. We first reinforced the US-Japan security relationship which was then in disrepair because many analysts

regarded it as a Cold War relic and saw Japan as a "geo-economic" threat. By reestablishing the security relationship with Japan, we insured that China could not play a Japan card against us. The second part of the strategy relied on liberalism. We eschewed the language of containment, opened markets with China, and supported its accession to the World Trade Organization. I have termed the policy "integrate, but hedge." If China becomes aggressive as its strength increases, Japan will be a key partner in organizing a policy of containment, but if China mellows as it prospers and its ties of interdependence deepen, the world may see a more benign outcome. There are always uncertainties about the future, but the policy is robust against failure (Nye 2008, 159).

Nye uses this episode to point out that the theories produced in a university setting were valuable in making foreign policy in Washington. "Political science theory," he maintains, "was crucial to the way in which I framed and crafted solutions to practical policy issues."

unstable hierarchy among the major powers are related to increases in the occurrence of warfare (Geller and Singer 1998). Historically, interstate hostilities have tended to flare up when the principal defender of the status quo loses its relative advantage over other major powers.

Of course, we have no way of knowing whether the future will resemble the past history of multipolar systems. Patterns and practices can change, and it is possible for policy makers to learn from previous mistakes and avoid repeating them (see Application: Integrate, but Hedge). However, we can anticipate that the future will be largely in the hands of the great powers, because "powerful states make the rules" (Keohane and Nye 2001a). What kinds of rules and institutions will they create, and what impact will they have on other states? To explore these questions, in Chapter 5 we will turn our attention from the rich, powerful, and commercially active great powers at the center of the world system and examine the poorer, weaker, and economically dependent states that lie along its periphery.

CHAPTER SUMMARY

- Great powers possess enormous military and economic capabilities relative to other states. As a result, they play a leading role in world politics, particularly on international security issues.

- Change is endemic to world politics, but one constant stands out: great-power rivalry. World politics tends to be reordered following hegemonic wars among the great powers. In their aftermath, the victors tend to create new international rules and institutions in an effort to prevent a repetition of these horrific conflicts.

- Single-factor theories are inadequate for explaining great-power war. Such conflicts involve causal mechanisms operating on multiple levels of analysis, and a fusion of proximate causes with deeper, more remote structural causes.

- The twentieth century experienced three great-power struggles for world leadership: World Wars I and II, and the Cold War.

- The proximate causes of World War I were the assassination of Franz Ferdinand, and the series of reactive, fatalistic decisions made by political leaders of Austria, Germany, and Russia. Deeper underlying causes included the rise of nationalism in southeastern Europe, the growth of German power, the creation of rigid mobilization plans, and the development of a polarized system of military alliances.

- The proximate causes of World War II can be found in Adolf Hitler's voracious appetite for conquest and domination, and the failed efforts by the internally divided Western democracies to appease the Nazi dictator. The remote causes included German resentment over the Treaty of Versailles, the rise of hypernationalistic ideologies within the Axis countries, the collapse of the international economic system, and the U.S. foreign policy of isolationism.

- The advent of nuclear weapons transformed world politics by radically changing the role that threats of force would henceforth play in international bargaining.

- Scholars disagree about the causes of the Cold War. Some of them see it as the result of a conflict of interests between the United States and the Soviet Union, others point to ideological incompatibilities, and still others emphasize the superpowers' misperceptions of each other's motives.

- Several conspicuous patterns existed throughout the Cold War. While periods of intense conflict alternated with periods of relative cooperation, the United States and the Soviet Union consistently made avoidance of all-out war their highest priority. Reciprocal, action–reaction exchanges were also evident (friendly U.S. initiatives toward the Soviet Union were reciprocated in kind). Both rivals were also willing to disregard their respective ideologies whenever their perceived national interests rationalized such inconsistencies; for example, each backed allies with political systems antithetical to its own when the necessities of power politics seemed to justify doing so.

- Following the collapse of the Soviet Union in 1991, the United States emerged as the preponderant global power. However, many scholars believe that the current unipolar system will not persist. Factors such as uneven economic growth and imperial overstretch will alter the relative positions of the great powers and bring about a multipolar structure.

KEY TERMS

appeasement	imperial overstretch	self-fulfilling prophecies
bandwagon	isolationism	soft power
bipolar	long-cycle theory	Truman Doctrine
containment	multipolar	unilateral
détente	peaceful coexistence	unipolar
domino theory	rapprochement	
hegemon	Reagan Doctrine	

SUGGESTED READINGS

Chase-Dunn, Christopher, and E. N. Anderson, eds. *The Historical Evolution of World Systems.* London: Palgrave, 2005.

Hermann, Richard K., and Richard Ned Lebow, eds. *Ending the Cold War: Interpretations, Causation, and the Study of International Relations.* London: Palgrave MacMillan, 2004.

Kagan, Robert. *The Return of History and the End of Dreams*. New York: Alfred A. Knopf, 2008.

Kegley, Charles W., Jr., and Gregory A. Raymond. *After Iraq: The Imperiled American Imperium*. New York: Oxford University Press, 2007.

Zakaria, Fareed. *The Post-American World*. New York: Norton, 2008.

CRITICAL THINKING QUESTIONS

What are the root causes of great-power war? For some scholars, the question can be answered only if the effects of international anarchy are recognized. To illustrate their point, they ask us to consider the "parable of the tribes."

Imagine a remote island populated by several tribes living within reach of one another. If they all choose to behave peacefully, they all will enjoy security. But if all but one tribe choose peace, what will be the consequences for the others? What will happen if a single power-maximizing tribe embarks on a campaign of conquest?

Suppose their campaign begins with an attack on a peaceful neighboring tribe, which results in its inhabitants being exterminated and the territory seized. Shortly thereafter, another peaceful tribe is attacked, and its surviving members are forced to serve their conqueror. Fearing they will suffer a similar fate, a third peaceful tribe leaves the island, and its former homeland becomes part of the growing empire of the power-maximizing tribe. By this time, the remaining peaceful tribes learn of these alarming events and, wishing to preserve their independence and autonomy, arm and begin training for war. Ironically, defending themselves against a power-maximizing aggressor requires that they become more like their foe.

According to Andrew Schmookler (1984), the parable's author, the underlying lesson is that anarchy makes an intense competitive struggle for power inevitable. Given the existence of one ambitious, self-interested tribe, the peaceful tribes have few options: destruction, absorption, withdrawal (if physically possible), or imitation. In each case, he concludes, the ways of power spread. Power-maximizing behavior, once introduced, inexorably diffuses throughout a system of regularly interacting political entities.

Do you find this argument persuasive? Does anarchy constitute a sufficient cause of great-power war in the absence of any other? How would realists, liberals, and constructivists respond to the parable?

5

Rich and Poor in World Politics: The Plight of the Global South

CHAPTER OUTLINE

Global Inequalities

The Colonial Experience of the Global South

The First Wave of European Imperialism

The Second Wave of European Imperialism

Self-Determination and Decolonization

North and South Today: Worlds Apart

Why Do North-South Disparities Persist?

Internal Factors: Classical Economic Development Theory's Interpretation

External Factors: Dependency Theory's Interpretation

Can the Economic Gap Be Closed?

The Global South's Foreign Policy Response

In Search of Security

In Search of Prosperity

CONTROVERSY: Multinational Corporations in the Global South: Do They Help or Hurt?

APPLICATION: Development, Democracy, and Debt

The Future of the Global South

A global human society based on poverty for many and prosperity for a few, characterized by islands of wealth surrounded by a sea of poverty, is unsustainable.

THABO MBEKI
FORMER PRESIDENT OF SOUTH AFRICA

On February 4, 1992, Hugo Chávez Frías, a flamboyant and charismatic lieutenant colonel, led a military coup against the Venezuelan government. When his outnumbered forces failed to take control of Caracas and capture President Carlos Andrés Pérez, he surrendered and was taken into custody. In a televised statement, Chávez grudgingly admitted that the rebellion was over, but only *"por ahora"* (for now).

Three years earlier, the army had been used by President Pérez to suppress riots that erupted when he implemented economic austerity measures called for by the International Monetary Fund. Angered by what they saw as a weak government ceding control over the country's economy to foreign interests, Chávez and other junior officers began plotting their rebellion. Two figures provided inspiration. The first, Simón Bolívar, organized a movement to liberate much of South America from Spanish colonial rule and established a country that briefly included present-day Columbia, Panama, Venezuela, and Ecuador. The second, Fidel Castro, engineered a socialist revolution in Cuba and worked assiduously to undermine U.S. influence in Latin America. Animated by the dream of sparking a socialist revolution in Venezuela and constructing a large bloc of Latin American countries to challenge the United States, the officers launched their ill-fated coup.

During the next two years, while Chávez and his co-conspirators were incarcerated, President Pérez was impeached for corruption. Chávez subsequently received a pardon and, upon his release from prison, began campaigning for the presidency on a populist platform. Elected in 1998 (and reelected in 2000 and 2006), he promised to root out Venezuela's "predatory oligarchs" who served international capital. As he told his followers in a March 1, 2004 speech, he sought to end the oppressive system whereby rich countries kept poor countries in the role of "producers of wealth and recipients of leftovers." Capitalism, he reiterated in a speech to the World Social Forum the following year, "is savagery;" it causes misery and poverty.

Throughout his tenure in office, Chávez has unveiled numerous reforms, insisting that they would help Venezuela transcend capitalism. With great fanfare, socialist-inspired programs to reduce illiteracy, improve health care, and redistribute land have been initiated. The key to implementing them lay in the country's petroleum vast resources. Venezuela possesses the world's sixth largest proven oil reserves and ranks eighth worldwide in the number of barrels produced per day (*Economist* 2007, 55). To harness that potential wealth, Chávez exerted control over Petróleos de Venezuela (the state oil company), demanded an increase in royalty percentages on joint extraction contracts with foreign oil companies, and nationalized the pumping and refining facilities of those companies that refused to accept his terms. Whereas when Chávez came to power the price of oil was ten dollars a barrel and the government budget was seven billion dollars, by June 2008 oil had risen to over 140 dollars a barrel, which translated into a government budget exceeding 54 billion dollars (Anderson 2008, 48). As oil revenues soared, Chávez allocated larger amounts to his social-welfare programs, which buttressed his position among the country's impoverished masses.

Chávez's public policies are hotly debated. Observers disagree passionately over whether they have eroded or enhanced the country's quality of life. Venezuela's crime rate is high, its infrastructure remains in disrepair, unemployment stands at 16.8 percent, and inflation at 13.6 percent (*Economist* 2007, 236); nevertheless, Chávez has strong support in public opinion polls, with a majority of respondents reporting that their personal situation has improved under his leadership. Still, rumors of plots against him regularly swirl through the capital, fueled by memories of an unsuccessful coup that briefly removed him from power in April 2002. Although his current term ends in 2013, he has hinted that he would like to remain in office longer, although a referendum to amend the constitution to allow him to run again was defeated in 2007.

"I always think like a subversive," Chávez boasted in a March 2007 interview with journalist José Vicente Rangel. Perhaps nowhere is this more apparent than in his efforts to subvert U.S. foreign policy in Latin America, which he characterized in an address to the United Nations on September 20, 2006 as a "scheme of domination, exploitation and pillage." On the one hand, he has tried to forge strong bilateral relations with anti-U.S. leaders ranging from Iran's Mahmoud Ahmadinejad to the guerrillas heading the Colombian Revolutionary Armed Forces (FARC). On the other hand, he has attempted to cobble together multilateral organizations such as his Bolivian Alternative for the Americas (ALBA) to counter Washington's support for a regional trade agreement known as the Free Trade Area of the Americas (FTAA). In Chávez's mind, confrontation with imperial powers is inevitable. Venezuela, he vowed in a January 27, 2006 speech, will never be "a colony of the United States" or a pawn of international financial institutions run by wealthy industrialized countries.

Chávez's fiery rhetoric frustrates U.S. policy makers, who generally try to ignore what they see as his annoying provocations. Yet his depiction of a global capitalist system that benefits some states and limits others resonates elsewhere in the Western Hemisphere, especially among people who take a Marxist approach to understanding world poverty. Regardless of one's opinion about *Chavismo*, it is a political ideology that highlights the ways in which many people in developing countries interpret world politics differently than their counterparts in more powerful, prosperous countries.

In the previous chapter we examined the strongest states within the international system, those with the economic and military capabilities to dominate everyone else.

Leslie Mazoch/AP Photos

Hugo Chávez and Twenty-First-Century Socialism Criticizing what he calls the "siren song of capitalism," President Hugo Chávez of Venezuela campaigns against the privatization of state-owned enterprises and policies aimed at increasing the role of the market in Global South countries' economies.

The experience of Venezuela during the Chávez years raises important questions about those states that are not great powers. Does being a less wealthy and militarily mighty country place one's future in the hands of others? What accounts for the inequalities that currently divide humanity? Can anything be done to close the gap between the world's rich and poor?

GLOBAL INEQUALITIES

Earth is divided into two hemispheres, north and south, at the equator. This artificial line of demarcation is, of course, meaningless except for use by cartographers to chart distance and location on maps. However, this divide also represents a popular way of describing the inequalities that separate rich and poor states. By and large, these two groups are located on either side of the equator (see Map 5.1).

Life for most people in the Northern Hemisphere is very different from that in the Southern Hemisphere. The disparities are profound, and in many places appear to be growing. The division in power and wealth between the states comprising the **Global North** and **Global South** poses both moral and security

Global North a term used to refer to the world's wealthy, industrialized countries located primarily in the Northern Hemisphere.

Global South a term used to designate the less-developed countries located primarily in the Southern Hemisphere.

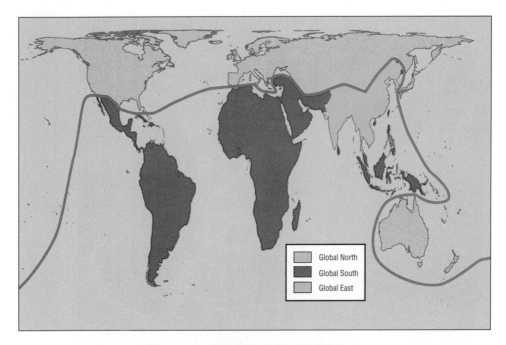

M A P 5 . 1 The Global North, Global South (and Global East)

The countries of the Global North are those that are wealthy, democratic, and technologically innovative, with declining birthrates and aging populations. In contrast, the countries in the Global South are poorer and have higher birthrates and younger populations. Some scholars also refer to a "Global East," countries that have arisen from the Global South and are now positioned to rival the levels of prosperity in the Global North.

problems. Poverty and inequality have existed throughout most periods of recorded history. But today the levels have reached unprecedented proportions. The states in the less-developed Global South find themselves marginalized, with even their very identities shaped by a subordinate position in the global hierarchy. The purpose of this chapter is to examine the causes and consequences of the inequality among the more than two hundred states in the global system. Why is it that the great powers experience abundance while many other countries seem trapped in poverty? What has bred such inequality?

Many analysts begin addressing these questions at the systemic level of analysis. They believe that the interstate system has properties built into it that account for the inability of most poor countries to close the gap with the wealthy countries. From their perspective, current inequalities are part of a much longer historical pattern. To understand the Global South today, they recommend we take into consideration the legacy of **colonialism**. Almost all the now-independent sovereign states in the Southern Hemisphere were at one time colonies, subjugated by far more powerful states.

colonialism the rule of a region by an external sovereign power.

THE COLONIAL EXPERIENCE OF
THE GLOBAL SOUTH

During the Cold War, the term **Third World** was used to describe the economically less-developed states that tended to share a colonial past. They were contrasted with the so-called **First World**, composed of the industrialized democracies in western Europe, North America, and Japan, and the **Second World**, which consisted of the Soviet Union and its allies. Today the communist countries comprising the former Second World have almost totally vanished, thus making the term *Third World* obsolete. Now the terms *Global North* (the wealthy countries previously known as the First World) and *Global South* (the less-developed countries along the equator and in the Southern Hemisphere) are popular.

Although journalists, policy makers, and scholars frequently generalize about the Global South, considerable diversity exists within this group of states. For example, it includes low-income countries such as Ghana and Haiti, where a majority of the population works in subsistence agriculture; middle-income countries like Brazil and Malaysia, who produce manufactured goods; and a few countries like Kuwait and Qatar, where petroleum exports have generated incomes rivaling those of Global North countries.

Global South countries are diverse in other ways as well. Included among their ranks is Indonesia, an archipelago of more than 17,000 islands scattered throughout an oceanic expanse larger than the United States, and Burundi, a landlocked state slightly smaller than Maryland. Also included are Nigeria, with some 150 million inhabitants, and Belize, with under 300,000 people. Aside from these geographic and demographic differences, Global South countries also vary politically and culturally, ranging from democratic Costa Rica to autocratic Myanmar (Burma).

Despite this diversity, most Global South countries in Africa, Asia, and Latin America share a set of common problems, which allow us to differentiate them from the countries in the Global North. Although the Global South is home to more than 85 percent of the world's people it commands less than 20 percent of its wealth. These countries are characterized by low productivity, high rates of population growth, and skewed patterns of income distribution, with large segments of their populations suffering from poverty, illiteracy, and ill health. Indeed, the world's three richest people—Microsoft co-founder Bill Gates, investor Warren Buffet, and Mexican businessman Carlos Slim Helú—possess more wealth than the poorest 48 Global South countries combined (see Map 5.2).

The emergence of the Global South as an identifiable group of states is a distinctly contemporary phenomenon. Although most Latin American countries were independent before World War II, not until then did other countries of the Global South gain that status. In 1947, Great Britain granted independence to India and Pakistan, after which **decolonization**—the freeing of colonial peoples from their dependent status—gathered speed. Since then, a profusion of new sovereign states has joined the global community, nearly all carved from the

Third World a Cold War term to describe the developing countries of Africa, Asia, and Latin America.

First World the relatively wealthy industrialized countries that share a commitment to varying forms of democratic political institutions and developed market economies.

Second World during the Cold War, the group of countries, including the Soviet Union and its then-Eastern European allies, that shared a commitment to centrally planned economies.

decolonization the achievement of independence by countries that were once colonies of other states.

British, Spanish, Portuguese, Dutch, and French empires built under colonialism 400 years ago.

Today, the decolonization process is almost complete. However, the effects persist. Many of the ethnic conflicts now so prevalent in the Global South have colonial roots, as the imperial powers drew borders with little regard for the identities of the indigenous peoples. In addition, the poverty facing most Global South countries is partly a product of their imperial pasts, when they were exploited by European powers. Given colonialism's impact, let us briefly examine how it evolved over the course of the past six centuries.

The First Wave of European Imperialism

The first wave of European empire building began in the late fifteenth century, as the Dutch, English, French, Portuguese, and Spanish used their military power to conquer territories for commercial gain. As scientific innovations made the European explorers' adventures possible, merchants followed in their wake, "quickly seizing upon opportunities to increase their business and profits. In turn, Europe's governments perceived the possibilities for increasing their own power and wealth. Commercial companies were chartered and financed, with military and naval expeditions frequently sent out after them to ensure political control of overseas territories" (B. Cohen 1973).

mercantilism an economic strategy for accumulating state wealth and power by using governmental regulation to encourage exports and curtail imports.

The economic strategy underlying the relationship between colonies and colonizers during this era is known as **mercantilism**: an economic philosophy advocating government regulation of economic life to increase state power and security. Early mercantilists believed acquiring gold and silver increased power. Later mercantilists shifted their emphasis to building strong, self-sufficient economies by using royal decrees to launch new industries, subsidize strategically targeted enterprises, protect domestic producers from foreign competition through tariff barriers, and maintain a "favorable" balance of trade by increasing exports and curbing imports.

To maximize national power and wealth, European leaders saw the conquest of foreign territory as a natural by-product of active government management of the economy. In addition to providing them with precious metals and other raw materials, colonies were untapped markets, which could be closed to commercial competition from other powers. By selling finished goods to their colonies under monopolistic conditions, it was thought that imperial powers could boost domestic employment and keep the profits from these sales at home.

By the end of the eighteenth century the European powers had spread themselves, although thinly, throughout virtually the entire world, but the colonial empires they had built now began to crumble. Britain's thirteen North American colonies declared their independence in 1776, and most of Spain's possessions in South America won their freedom in the early nineteenth century. Nearly 100 colonial relationships worldwide were terminated in the half-century ending in 1825 (Bergesen and Schoenberg 1980).

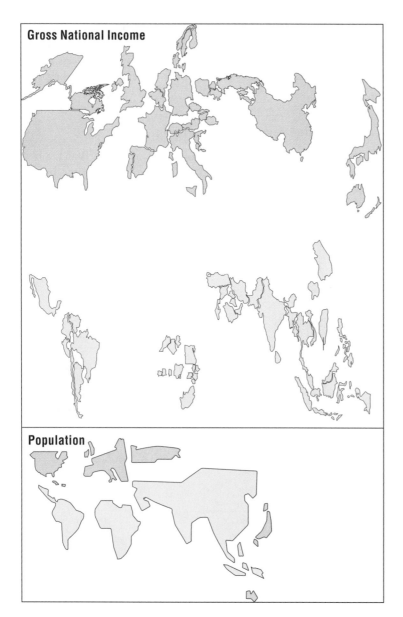

MAP 5.2 The Great North-South Divide in Wealth and Population

If the countries in the globe were redrawn to reflect the size of their economies and populations, as shown here, huge differences would be visible. Most of the wealth is in the Global North, and most of the people are in the Global South. If prevailing trends persist as expected, the disparities will continue to widen the existing division between rich and poor.

SOURCE: Adapted from data collected by the Wold Bank in its *World Development Report 2008,* 334–335.

As the first wave of European colonization waned, belief in the mercantilist philosophy also declined. In 1776, the Scottish political economist Adam Smith published *The Wealth of Nations,* a vigorous critique of mercantilism that called for free trade. While Smith acknowledged that the state should be involved in defending the nation against external aggression, enforcing property rights, upholding contracts, and the like, he denied that it could be more efficient or innovative than an unregulated market. His arguments laid much of the intellectual foundation for **laissez-faire economics**. Henceforth European powers would continue to seek colonies, but the rationale for their imperial policies began to change.

laissez-faire economics a body of thought emphasizing free markets with little governmental regulation.

The Second Wave of European Imperialism

Beginning in the 1870s and extending until the outbreak of World War I, a new wave of imperialism washed over the world as Europe, joined later by the United States and Japan, aggressively colonized new territories. The portion of the globe that Europeans controlled was one-third in 1800, two-thirds by 1878, and four-fifths by 1914 (Fieldhouse 1973, 3). As illustrated in Map 5.3, in the last 20 years of the nineteenth-century Africa fell under the control of seven

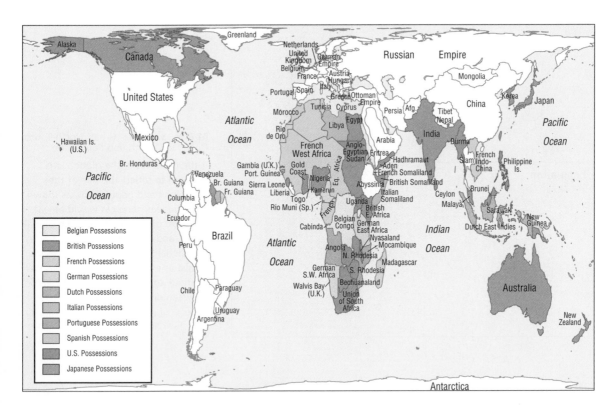

M A P 5.3 Global Imperialism, 1914

The ten major imperial powers competed for colonies throughout the globe in the present-day Global South, and on the eve of World War I their combined territories covered much of the world.

European powers (Belgium, Britain, France, Germany, Italy, Portugal, and Spain), and in all of the Far East and the Pacific, only China, Japan, and Siam (Thailand) were not conquered. China, however, was divided into **spheres of influence** by the foreign great powers, and Japan itself occupied Korea and Formosa (Taiwan). Elsewhere, the United States acquired Puerto Rico and the Philippines in the 1898 Spanish–American War, extended its colonial reach westward to Hawaii, leased the Panama Canal Zone "in perpetuity" from the new state of Panama (an American creation), and exercised considerable control over several Caribbean islands, notably Cuba. The preeminent imperial power, Great Britain, in a single generation expanded its empire to cover one-fifth of the earth's land area. As British imperialists were proud to proclaim, it was an empire on which the sun never set.

sphere of influence the area dominated by a great power.

Why did most of the great powers—and those that aspired to great-power status—engage in this expensive and often vicious competition to control other peoples and territories? What explains the second wave of imperialism? The answers are rooted in economics and politics.

Economic Explanations for the Second Wave of Imperialism. With the Industrial Revolution, capitalism grew, emphasizing the free market, private ownership of the means of production, and the accumulation of wealth. Theorists following Karl Marx, saw imperialism as the result of competition among capitalists for profitable overseas outlets for their surplus capital. One of them was the Soviet leader Vladimir Lenin. In his famous 1916 monograph *Imperialism, The Highest Stage of Capitalism,* Lenin argued that military expansion abroad was produced by the "monopoly stage of capitalism." He concluded that the only way to end imperialism was to abolish capitalism. Liberal economists, on the other hand, regarded the new imperialism not as a product of capitalism as such but rather as a result of maladjustments within the capitalist system, which could be corrected. What the two perspectives shared was the belief that economics explained the new wave of imperialism: "The fundamental problem was the presumed material needs of advanced capitalist societies—the need for cheap raw materials to feed their growing industrial complexes, for additional markets to consume their rising levels of production, and for investment outlets to absorb their rapidly accumulating capital" (Cohen 1973). Thus, from both the Marxist and classical liberal perspectives, the material needs of capitalist societies explained their imperial drive.

Political Explanations for the Second Wave of Imperialism. Not everyone agreed that economic motives underpinned the second wave of imperial expansion. Political factors were also identified. For example, in his influential 1902 book, *Imperialism,* J. A. Hobson argued that the jockeying for power and prestige between competitive empires had always characterized the great powers' behavior in the European balance-of-power system, and that imperialism through overseas expansion was simply a global extension of this inter-European competition for dominance.

Self-Determination and Decolonization

self-determination the doctrine that people should be able to determine the government that will manage their affairs.

Regardless of the causes underlying the second wave of imperialism, world opinion took an anti-imperial turn when the Versailles peace settlement that ended World War I embraced the principle of national **self-determination** advocated by U.S. president Woodrow Wilson. Self-determination meant that each distinct people would have the right to decide which authority would represent and rule them. Wilson and others who shared his liberal convictions believed that freedom of choice would lead to the creation of states and governments content with their territorial boundaries and therefore less inclined to make war. In practice, however, the attempt to redraw states' borders to separate nationality groups was applied almost exclusively to war-torn Europe, where six new states were created from the territory of the former Austrian-Hungarian Empire (Austria, Czechoslovakia, Hungary, Poland, Romania, and the ethnically divided Yugoslavia). Other territorial adjustments were also made in Europe, but the proposition that self-determination should be extended to Europe's overseas empires did not receive serious support.

Still, the colonial territories of the powers defeated in World War I were not simply parceled out among the victorious allies, as had typically happened in the past. Instead, the territories controlled by Germany and the Ottoman Empire were transferred under League of Nations auspices to countries that would govern them as "mandates" pending their eventual self-rule. The principle implicit in the mandate system was that colonies were a trust, not something to be exploited. This set an important precedent for the negotiations after World War II, when territories of the defeated powers placed under the United Nations trusteeship system were not absorbed by others but were promised eventual self-rule, and support for self-determination gained momentum. The decolonization process accelerated in 1947, when the British relinquished political control of India and Pakistan. War eventually erupted between these newly independent states as each sought to gain control over disputed territory in Kashmir. Violence also broke out in Indochina and Algeria in the 1950s and early 1960s as the French sought to regain control over colonial territories they had held before World War II. Similarly, bloodshed followed closely on the heels of independence in the Congo when the Belgians granted their African colony independence in 1960, and it dogged the unsuccessful efforts of Portugal to battle the winds of decolonization that swept over Africa as the 1960s wore on.

With colonialism in retreat, in 1960, Global South states took advantage of their growing numbers in the UN General Assembly to secure passage of the historic Declaration on the Granting of Independence to Colonial Countries and Peoples. "The General Assembly proclaimed that the subjection of any people to alien domination was a denial of fundamental human rights, contrary to the UN Charter, and an impediment to world peace and that all subject peoples had a right to immediate and complete independence. No country cast a vote against this anticolonial manifesto. . . . It was an ideological triumph" (Riggs and Plano 1994).

As the old order crumbled—and as the leaders in the newly emancipated territories discovered that freedom did not translate automatically into autonomy, economic independence, and domestic prosperity—the conflict between the rich Global North and the emerging states of the Global South began.

NORTH AND SOUTH TODAY: WORLDS APART

The Global South is sometimes described today as a "zone of turmoil" in large measure because, in contrast with the democratic and peaceful Global North, many of the people in the Global South face poverty, war, and tyranny (Collier 2005). Although democracy has spread to much of the Global South since the 1980s, the commitments of some of these governments to regular elections and human rights are fragile (Gershman 2005). Furthermore, many Global South countries lack well-developed domestic market economies based on entrepreneurship and private enterprise. Differences in technological capabilities also separate North and South. Typically, Global South countries have been unable to evolve an indigenous technology appropriate to their own resources and have been dependent on powerful Global North **multinational corporations (MNCs)** to transfer technical know how. This means that research and development expenditures are directed toward solutions of the Global North's problems, with technological advances seldom meeting the needs of the Global South. And in the information age, technology has not been distributed equally geographically: The highest density of computer connections to the Internet is in the Global North.

The fact that 85 percent of the world's population is poor is a reflection of these unequally distributed resources. As Table 5.1 shows, the data on the division between Global North and Global South point to brutal disparities and inequalities. This picture darkens even more when focus is shifted to the plight of the poorest in the low-income developing countries. According to criteria used by the UN Economic and Social Council, 53 countries currently comprise the **least developed countries (LDCs)** of the Global South. They have gross national incomes (GNI) per capita of under $905 per year and frequently rely on **barter** in many of their economic exchanges. These low-income countries are not significant participants in the global market. Their meager exports are largely confined to inexpensive primary products, including food stuffs (cocoa, coffee, and tea), minerals, hides, and timber. Because they consume most of what they produce, theirs is typically a subsistence economy, and the prospects for change are dim, because most of these countries have been bypassed by direct foreign investment and ignored by foreign aid donors (WDR 2008, 335; WDI 2007).

High rates of population growth have compounded the problems faced by the LDCs. It will take only 25 years for the LDCs' total population to double, compared with two and a half centuries for that in the Global North. LDCs' economic growth rates in the recent past have averaged less than 0.1 percent each year. Growth rates elsewhere have almost uniformly been higher. This is a

multinational corporations (MNCs) business enterprises headquartered in one state that invest and operate extensively in other states.

least-developed countries (LDCs) the most impoverished states in the Global South.

barter the exchange of one good for another rather than the use of currency to buy and sell items.

T A B L E   5.1   Two Worlds of Development: An International Class Divide

Characteristic	Developing Global South	Developed Global North
Number of countries	152	56
Population (millions)	5,489	1,029
Land area (thousands of sq. km)	99,346	34,595
GNI ($ billions)	$10,978	$37,529
Gross national income for each person	$2,000	$36,487
Net Foreign direct investment ($ millions)	$280,795	$693,488
Imports ($ billions)	$2,869	$7,816
Exports ($ billions)	$3,057	$7,377
Women in policy positions (%)	16%	24%
Primary pupil/teacher ratio	31	16
Life expectancy at birth	64	76
Percent of population living in cities	44%	78%
Access to improved sanitation (% of population)	52%	100%
Number of motor vehicles for each 1,000 people	47	636
Personal computers for each 10,000 people	113	579
Internet users for each 1,000 people	84	527
Households with television (%)	48%	97%
Daily newspapers for each 1,000 people	49	263
Electric power consumption for each person (kwh)	1,243	9,609

Where people live on the earth influences how they live. As this information shows, the quality of life is quite different in the developed countries of the Global North than it is in the developing countries of the Global South. The World Bank predicts that the discrepancy between the rich and the poor will grow considerably by the year 2050.

SOURCES: WDR (2008); WDI (2007).

powerful reason why the rich minority gets richer while the poorest of the poor will likely become even poorer.

Geographic location also hampers the economic development in Global South countries. Landlocked developing countries that lack navigable rivers or efficient road and rail networks are highly disadvantaged due to the expenses they face in accessing world markets. The "median landlocked country pays up to 50 percent more in transportation costs than the median coastal nation," points out Ricardo Hausmann (2001, 47), former chief economist of the Inter-American Development Bank. Some small island developing states are burdened with high transportation costs as well, largely due to their remoteness from major global markets. Moreover, because many of these landlocked and island countries are located in tropical areas, their economies are further strained by the ravages of diseases such as malaria. According to recent statistical estimates, when controlling for other factors, the per capita economic growth in countries with malaria is more than 1 percent lower than in countries without malaria (Sachs 2002).

For many people living in the Global South, the future is bleak. The aggregate pattern underlying global trends in the last 20 years shows that more than sixty countries today are worse off than they were and are falling ever further behind the levels achieved by the countries in the Global North. This tragic situation raises a basic theoretical question: Why does so much of the Global South suffer from such destitution?

Why Do North-South Disparities Persist?

Why has the Global South lagged so far behind the Global North in its comparative level of well-being and **development**? And why, as shown in Table 5.2, have the development experiences even within the Global South differed so widely? A generation ago, for example, Nigeria's gross national product (GNP) per capita exceeded those of Thailand, Malaysia, and Indonesia. By the 1990s, however, Nigeria lagged far behind its Asian counterparts. Nor was Nigeria's experience atypical. The economic fortunes of various other African countries declined precipitously as the twentieth century drew to a close, just as several

development the processes through which a country increases its capacity to meet its citizens' basic human needs and raise their standard of living.

T A B L E 5.2   **Global South Progress in Attaining Development Goals**

	North Africa	Sub-Saharan Africa	Western Asia	South Asia	South-eastern Asia	Latin America & Caribbean
Reduce extreme poverty by half	+	– –	– –	+	++	– –
Reduce hunger by half	+	-	--	-	+	+
Improve the lives of slum-dwellers	+	– –	--	-	+	-
Reduce mortality of under five year olds by two-thirds	+	– –	-	-	+	+
Measles immunization	++	– –	+	-	+	++
Halt and reverse spread of HIV/AIDS	N/A	– –	N/A	– –	-	-
Halt and reverse spread of malaria	+	– –	+	-	-	-
Halve proportion without improved drinking water	+	-	+	+	+	+
Halve proportion without sanitation	+	– –	+	-	– –	-
Universal primary schooling	+	-	-	-	-	+
Equal girl's enrollment in primary schools	+	-	-	-	-	++

– – No progress or a deterioration or reversal

- Target not expected to be met by 2015 if current trends persist

+ Target expected to be met by 2015 if current trends persist

++ Target already met or very close to being met

N/A Insufficient data

While meeting at the United Nations in 2000, 189 countries signed the Millennium Declaration, which outlined a set of developmental goals to be attained by 2015. This chart shows the progress as of 2006 that different regions within the Global South have made toward reaching the some of the key targets for the health, education, and economic welfare goals.

SOURCES: The Millennium Development Goals Report (2006).

East Asian countries enjoyed significant economic growth (Richburg 1992; Landes 1998). What accounts for these stark differences, and will they continue during the twenty-first century?

The diversity evident in the Global South invites the conclusion that underdevelopment is explained by a combination of factors. Some theorists explain underdevelopment by looking primarily at internal causes. Other theorists focus on the position of developing countries in the global political economy. We shall briefly discuss each of these schools of thought, beginning with the interpretation proposed by classical economic development theory.

Internal Factors: Classical Economic Development Theory's Interpretation

modernization a view of development that argues that self-sustaining economic growth is created through technological innovation, efficient production, and investments from capital accumulation.

Liberal economic development theories of **modernization** emerged in the early post–World War II era. They argued that the major barriers to development were posed by the Global South countries' own internal characteristics. Productivity remained low due to managerial inefficiency, a lack of modern technology, and inadequate transportation and communication infrastructures. To overcome these barriers, most classical theorists recommended that the wealthy countries supply various "missing components" of development, such as investment capital through foreign aid or private foreign direct investment.

Once sufficient capital was accumulated to promote economic growth, these theorists predicted that its benefits would eventually "trickle down" to broad segments of society. In this way, everyone, not just a privileged few, would enjoy the benefits of rising affluence. Walt W. Rostow, an economic historian and U.S. policy maker, formalized this theory in his influential book *The Stages of Economic Growth* (1960). He predicted that traditional societies beginning the path to development would inevitably pass through various stages by means of the free market and would eventually "take off" to become similar to the mass-consumption societies of the capitalist Global North. Even though the rich are likely to get richer, it was argued, as incomes in the world as a whole grow, the odds increase that a preindustrialized economy will grow faster and eventually reduce the gap between it and richer countries.

That prognosis and the policies on which it was based were ultimately rejected by the Global South. Leaders there did not accept the classical liberal argument that Global North countries became prosperous because they concentrated on work, invention, and skill (see Thurow 1999). Instead, they were persuaded by a rival theory that attributed the Global South's plight to the structure of the global political economy.

dependency theory a view of development asserting that the leading capitalist states dominate and exploit the poorer countries on the periphery of the world economy.

External Factors: Dependency Theory's Interpretation

Whereas classical developmental theory pointed to internal factors to explain the plight of the Global South, **dependency theory** emphasized external factors. Although the dependency literature is large and diverse (see Caporaso and Levine 1992; Packenham

1992), all dependency theorists reject Rostow's stages-of-growth thesis, arguing that underdevelopment "is not a stalled stage of linear development, a question of precapitalism, retarded or backward development" (Shannon 1989). As noted in Chapter 2, dependency theory builds on Lenin's critique of imperialism, but goes beyond it to account for changes that have occurred in recent decades. Its central proposition is that the structure of the capitalist world economy is based on a division of labor between a dominant core and a subordinate periphery. As a result of colonialism, the Global South countries that make up the periphery have been forced into an economic role whereby they export raw materials and import finished goods. While classical liberal theorists submit that specialization according to comparative advantage will increase income in an unfettered market and therein help close the gap between the world's haves and have-nots, dependency theorists maintain that global inequalities cannot be reduced so long as developing countries continue to specialize in primary products for which there are often numerous competing suppliers and limited demand.

Dependency theorists also argue that countries in the Global South are vulnerable to cultural penetration by MNCs and other outside forces, which saturate them with values alien to their societies. Once such penetration has occurred, the inherently unequal exchanges that bind the exploiters and the exploited are sustained by elites within the penetrated societies, who sacrifice their country's welfare for personal gain.

The argument that a privileged few benefit from dependency at the expense of their societies underscores the dual nature of many developing countries. **Dualism** refers to the existence of two separate economic and social sectors operating side by side. Dual societies typically have a rural, impoverished, and neglected sector operating alongside an urban, developing, or advanced sector—but with little interaction between the two. Thus whatever growth occurs in the industrial sector in dual societies "neither initiates a corresponding growth process in the rural sector nor generates sufficient employment to prevent a growing population in the stagnant sectors" (Singer and Ansari 1988). MNCs contribute to dualism by promoting "the interests of the small number of well-paid modern-sector workers against the interests of the rest by widening wage differentials . . . and worsen the imbalance between rural and urban economic opportunities by locating primarily in urban areas and contributing to the flow of rural-urban migration" (Todaro 2000).

Although dependency theory has great appeal within the Global South, it cannot easily explain the emergence of what many people call **newly industrialized countries (NICs)**, members of the Global South that have begun exporting manufactured goods to the Global North. To explain this phenomenon, they sometimes use the term **dependent development** to describe the industrialization of peripheral areas in a system otherwise dominated by the Global North. The term suggests the possibility of either growing or declining prosperity, but not outside the confines of a continuing dominance–dependence relationship between North and South.

dualism the existence of a rural, impoverished, and neglected sector of society alongside an urban, developing, or modernizing sector, with little interaction between the two.

newly industrialized countries (NICs) prosperous members of the Global South, which have become important exporters of manufactured goods.

dependent development the industrialization of areas outside of the leading capitalist states within confines set by the dominant capitalist states, which enables the poor to become wealthier without ever catching up to the core Global North countries.

Can the Economic Gap Be Closed?

Is it possible for the Global South to escape the vicious cycle of poverty? When we look at the situation from the perspective of the poorest of the poor countries, the prospects appear dismal. However, there is a basis for optimism that can be found if you broaden the picture and see the conspicuous exceptions to the general pattern of persistent poverty. Although many Global South countries appear to be mired in inexorable poverty, some have managed to break the chains of underdevelopment. By pursuing bold paths for growth, they have seen their fortunes rise and are poised to enter the ranks of the advanced industrial economies. The ability for some developing countries to escape the syndrome that still affects the rest of the Global South suggests that others can succeed as well.

Consider the example of the newly industrialized countries, which have moved beyond the export of primary products to the export of manufactured goods. Today the NICs are among the largest exporters of manufactured goods. Because of the economic success of several NICs located in East and South Asia, they sometimes are distinguished from the rest of the Global South and referred to as the **Global East** (recall Map 5.1). In particular, the so-called "Asian Tigers" (South Korea, Singapore, Taiwan, and Hong Kong) have taken advantage of comparatively low wage rates to promote export-led economic growth through "neomercantilist" practices such as protecting infant industries from foreign competition with tariff and non-tariff barriers and providing financial incentives for manufacturing industries. Spectacular economic growth has followed. With their population growth generally in check, the Asian Tigers have joined the ranks of the world's wealthiest states, and still other "new tigers" such as India have emerged as exports and foreign investment have stimulated a booming economy.

Global East the rapidly growing economies of East and South Asia that have made their countries competitors with the traditionally dominant members of the Global North.

Neither geography nor current levels of economic performance identify well the emerging markets with the greatest potential. What most distinguishes these countries engineering an economic revolution is that their governments have stabilized the value of their currencies, brought inflation under control, and privatized the businesses once owned by the government. In addition, many opened themselves to foreign investment. This change in philosophy about the causes of and cures for underdevelopment formerly prevalent throughout the Global South was a concession in Global South thinking, stimulated in part by pressure for reforms by such powerful global IGOs as the World Bank and the International Monetary Fund.

The success of the free-market practices of the Asian NICs in elevating themselves from the rest of the Global South encouraged others to emulate their strategies and heightened cries for additional reforms in the Global South countries in order to remove still other obstacles standing in the way of economic growth. Nevertheless, as the example of Hugo Chávez in Venezuela illustrates, not everyone is convinced by this model of economic development.

The achievements of the Asian NICs alongside the plummeting financial fate of the poorest Global South countries provoke policy questions: Despite these differences and the inequalities between Global South states, is there a commonality, a consensus, that unites them as a group? What strategies have they forged to deal with their position of weakness in a world of powers?

THE GLOBAL SOUTH'S FOREIGN POLICY RESPONSE

The vast political, economic, and social differences separating the Global North (and East) from the Global South indicate that the remaining countries in the South are vulnerable and insecure, and that these conditions are products of both domestic and international factors. Coping with this insecurity has long been a primary foreign policy goal of Global South states, and efforts to overcome it have often brought the Global South into contention with the Global North. Ironically, the end of the Cold War reduced the great powers' security interest in providing economic aid to Global South countries. However, with the Global South now experiencing a burst of new armed conflicts, aid from the advanced industrialized countries has recently begun to increase.

Given the myriad problems confronting the Global South, crafting foreign policy strategies to maximize security and prosperity preoccupy its leaders. Different states have taken different approaches. Let us examine how the Global South countries are pursuing their objectives, particularly in their relationships with the Global North.

In Search of Security

The Global South countries emerging after World War II struggled on separate tracks to find a foreign policy approach that could provide them with the security they lacked. Some states aligned themselves with either the United States or Soviet Union; others avoided taking sides in the Cold War. The latter approach gathered momentum in 1955, when twenty-nine Asian and African countries met in Bandung, Indonesia, to devise a strategy to combat colonialism. Six years later, leaders from twenty-five countries, mostly former colonies, met in Belgrade, Yugoslavia, where they created the Nonaligned Movement (NAM), a political coalition whose membership would later grow to more than 100 countries.

Nonalignment.   Because many Global South countries feared becoming entrapped in the Cold War, they adopted foreign policies based on **nonalignment**. The strategy energized both the United States and the Soviet Union to renew their efforts to woo the uncommitted Global South countries to their own network of allies, often offering economic and military aid as an inducement. The Cold War's end eroded the bargaining leverage nonalignment had provided the Global South. As a strategy, nonalignment "died" with the Cold War. But the passion of Global South leaders to eradicate global inequalities lives on, as can be

nonalignment a foreign policy posture that rejects participating in military alliances with rival blocs for fear that formal alignment will entangle the state in an unnecessary war.

seen in the 2003 *Non-Aligned Kuala Lumpur Summit Declaration*, which raised questions about the inability of many Global South countries to benefit from globalization.

The challenge facing the nonaligned states today is how to promote their interests in a world where few listen to their voices. The nonaligned Global South can complain, but its bargaining power to engineer institutional reforms is limited. This weakness is displayed in the UN, where the most influence the Global South has mustered has symbolically been to delay serious proposals to make Germany and Japan permanent members of the Security Council by insisting that one of the larger developing countries (such as Brazil, Indonesia, Mexico, or South Africa) also be given a seat among the mighty. Weak states have some vocal power in numbers, but no clout or control. Thus, the Global South worries that in the future even newer forms of imperialism might continue to erode any Global South hopes for progress.

Arms Acquisitions. During the Cold War, many developing countries became battlegrounds on which the superpowers conducted covert activities, paramilitary operations, and proxy wars. More than 90 percent of the inter- and intrastate conflicts and 90 percent of the casualties in the past half-century occurred within the Global South (Gleditsch et al. 2002). Today, the danger of anarchy and violence has reached epidemic proportions, as the Global South contains numerous **failed states** that do not have governments strong enough to preserve domestic order.

failed states countries whose governments have little or no control over their territory and population.

Faced with seemingly endless conflict at home or abroad, it is not surprising that the Global South has joined the rest of the world's quest to acquire modern weapons of war—including in some cases (China, India, North Korea, Pakistan) nuclear weapons. As a result, the burden of military spending (measured by the ratio of military expenditures to GNP) is highest among those least able to bear it. In the Global South military spending typically exceeds expenditures on health and education; impoverished states enmeshed in ethnic or religious strife at home are quite prepared to sacrifice expenditures for economic development in order to acquire weapons.

Few Global South states produce their own weapons. Weak governments, anxious over the possibility of separatist revolts and other forms of civil strife, have invested large proportions of their country's modest national budgets in arms rather than allocating these scarce revenues to social and economic programs aimed at reducing poverty. Ironically, many Global South countries have raised their military spending to purchase arms produced in the Global North at higher rates than their wealthy Global North counterparts do (Grimmett 2005). Thus in responding to its security concerns, the Global South appears to be increasing its dependence for arms purchases on the very same rich states whose military and economic domination they historically have most feared and resented.

Reducing Vulnerability to Natural Disasters. Adding to the Global South's problems is still another source of turmoil. The widespread death and disease that resulted from the 2005 tsunami in the Indian Ocean and the 2008 cyclone that devastated Myanmar (Burma) underscore the magnitude of the threat posed by recurring natural disasters. Although the scale of tragedies such as these can be reduced with effective warning and response systems, the economic struggle for survival within the world's poorest countries leaves few resources for investing in the technology needed for disaster preparedness. As a result, the Global South is petitioning the Global North for help, to expand its global network of seismometer and tidal monitoring instruments, and to share data from weather satellites that can be used to chart dangerous storms and reduce their risks.

In Search of Prosperity

Breaking out of their dependent status and pursuing their own industrial development remains their greatest foreign policy priority for countries in the Global South. To this end, some of them (particularly those in Latin America) have pursued development through an **import–substitution industrialization** strategy designed to encourage domestic entrepreneurs to manufacture products traditionally imported from abroad. Governments (often dictatorships) have been heavily involved in managing their economies and in some cases became the owners and operators of industry.

import–substitution industrialization a strategy for economic development that involves encouraging domestic entrepreneurs to manufacture products traditionally imported from abroad.

Import-substitution industrialization eventually fell from favor, in part because manufacturers often found that they still had to rely on Global North technology to produce goods for their domestic markets. The preference now is for **export-led industrialization**, based on the realization that "what had enriched the rich was not their insulation from imports (rich countries do, in fact, import massively all sorts of goods) but their success in manufactured exports, where higher prices could be commanded than for [Global South] raw materials" (Sklair 1991).

export-led industrialization a growth strategy that concentrates on developing domestic export industries capable of competing in overseas markets.

As exemplified by the NICs, the shift toward export-led growth strategies (often buttressed by neomercantilist protectionist practices) has transformed some Global South countries from being suppliers of raw materials into manufacturers of products already available in the Global North. Thus a new international division of labor is emerging as production, capital, labor, and technology are increasingly integrated worldwide and decision making has become transnational. "The old ideas of national autonomy, economic independence, self-reliance, and self-sufficiency have become obsolete as the national economies [have] become increasingly integrated" (Dorraj 1995).

Not all Global South economies are positioned to survive in this highly competitive globalized market. Many of the least-developed countries remain heavily dependent on raw materials and other primary products for their export earnings. While some benefit from such integration and prosper, others remain immune from the alleged benefits of globalization, and are especially vulnerable to recessions in the global economy.

How to cope with dominance and dependence thus remains a key Global South concern. As they search for status and economic security, let us next evaluate the Global South's key strategies in their relations with the Global North.

A New International Economic Order? The emerging Global South countries were born into an international economic order with rules they had no voice in creating. In order to gain control over their economic futures, they began coordinating their efforts within the United Nations where their growing numbers and voting power gave them greater influence than they could otherwise command. In the 1960s, they formed a coalition of the world's poor, the **Group of 77** (known in diplomatic circles simply as the **G-77**) and used their voting power to convene the UN Conference on Trade and Development (UNCTAD). UNCTAD later became a permanent UN organization through which the Global South would express its interests concerning development issues.

A decade later, the G-77 (then numbering more than 120 countries) again used its UN numerical majority to push for a **New International Economic Order (NIEO)** to replace the international economic regime championed by the United States and the other capitalist powers since World War II. Motivated by the oil-exporting countries' rising bargaining power, the Global South sought to compel the Global North to abandon practices perceived as perpetuating their dependence. More specifically, the proposals advanced under the banner of the NIEO included:

- Giving preferential, nonreciprocal treatment to Global South exports to industrialized countries;

- Establishing commodity agreements to regulate and stabilize the world market for primary commodities;

- Linking the price of Global South exports to the price of imports from industrialized states;

- Increasing financial resource transfers to Global South countries;

- Reducing the burden of Global South debt through rescheduling, interest subsidization, or cancellation;

- Increasing the participation and voting power of Global South countries in international financial institutions;

- Regulating the activities of multinational corporations in the Global South to promote the reinvestment of profits earned by MNCs in host country economies; and

- Expanding technical assistance programs and reducing the cost of transferring technology to the Global South.

Not surprisingly, the Global North rebuffed many of the South's proposals, although some of the issues that were raised (such as debt relief) remain on the global agenda. At the 2003 World Trade Organization meeting in Cancún, Mexico, for example, the poor countries united to demand major concessions from the wealthy countries, especially with regard to foreign subsidies. In 2008 another step was taken when *Banco del Sur* (Bank of the South) was launched in Latin America to go around financial institutions dominated by

Group of 77 (G-77) the coalition of Third World countries that sponsored the 1963 Joint Declaration of Developing Countries calling for reforms to allow greater equity in North–South trade.

New International Economic Order (NIEO) the 1974 policy resolution in the UN that called for a North–South dialogue to open the way for the less-developed countries of the Global South to participate more fully in the making of international economic policy.

Global North countries and fund large infrastructure projects with the region's oil wealth.

Regional Trade Regimes. With the failure of reform envisioned by the NIEO, the integration of Global South countries into the globalization process will occur according to the rules dictated by the Global North. Are there alternatives? Can regional arrangements enable Global South states to take advantage of growing economic interdependence to achieve their development goals?

To promote growth through regional economic agreements, in the 1990s the global economy began to subdivide into three "trade blocs"—one in Europe, with the European Union (EU) as its hub; a second in the Americas, with the United States at the center; and a third in the Global East, with Japan and China dominant. Consider some recent developments:

- *In the Americas:* The North American Free Trade Agreement (NAFTA), formalized in 1994, brought Canada, Mexico, and the United States into a single free-trade area, in which tariffs among member countries are eliminated. In addition, the Mercosur agreement, which links Argentina, Brazil, Paraguay, and Uruguay (Latin America's largest trade bloc), hopes to incorporate the Andean Group (Bolivia, Colombia, Ecuador, Peru, and Venezuela) in its free-trade union. In addition, the 2005 Central American Free Trade Agreement (CAFTA) to reduce trade barriers between the United States and Costa Rica, El Salvador, Guatemala, Honduras, Nicaragua, and the Dominican Republic has been ratified.

- *In Asia:* The association of Asia-Pacific Economic Cooperation (APEC), an informal forum created in 1989 that has committed itself to creating a free-trade zone during the next 25 years. In addition, the members of the Association of Southeast Asian Nations (ASEAN), first established in 1967 by Brunei, Indonesia, Malaysia, the Philippines, Singapore, and Thailand and now including Vietnam, agreed to set up a free-trade area.

- *In Africa:* The Southern African Development Community (SADC) formed in 1980 is the largest of 12 free-trade areas in the region.

Will the lofty expectations of these regional politico-economic groups be realized? In the past, political will and shared visions have proven to be indispensable elements in successful regional trade regimes. Economic complementarity is another essential component, as the goal is to stimulate greater trade among the members of the free-trade area, not simply between it and others. If one or more members export products that each of the others wants, the chances of the regime's success are greater; if, on the other hand, they all tend to export the same products or to have virtually no trade with one another (typically the case in Africa), failure is more likely.

Prospects for the success of regional trade regimes seem greatest when Global South countries cobble their futures to Global North states—but, complain Global South leaders, on terms that the North dictates. That conclusion hardly bodes well for regional economic agreements as an effective method for balancing the North–South relationship.

Foreign Aid, Investment, and Debt Relief.   The developing countries have long pleaded for greater access to the Global North's markets in order to fuel their economic growth. These pleas have meet with success in recent years, with the number of free-trade agreements between Global South and Global North countries increasing to 109, from only 23 in 1990 (*Harper's*, February 2005, 13). But many Global South countries have not improved their lot, often for two major reasons. First, market access has become increasingly difficult because domestic pressure groups in Global North countries have lobbied their governments to reduce the imports of other countries' products that compete with their own industries. Trade may be desired by the Global South, but political barriers often interfere with free trade. Second, the character and distribution of foreign aid have changed as criticism of its effectiveness and effects has risen. Consequently, levels of aid have remained moderate.

Foreign aid comes in a variety of forms and is used for a variety of purposes. Some aid consists of outright grants of money, some of loans at concessional rates, and some of shared technical expertise. Although most foreign aid is bilateral and is termed **official development assistance (ODA)**—meaning the money flows directly from one country to another—an increasing portion is now channeled through global institutions such as the World Bank, and hence is known as "multilateral aid." Moreover, the purposes of aid are as varied as its forms. Commonly stated foreign aid goals include not only the reduction of poverty through economic development, but also human development, environmental protection, the development of private enterprise, increased power for women, the promotion of democratic governance and human rights, humanitarian disaster relief, and assistance to refugees. However, security objectives traditionally have figured prominently as motives of donors in the allocation of both economic aid and military assistance, and still do. For example, the United States continues to target Israel and Egypt as major recipients to symbolize friendship, maintain a balance of power, and tilt the scales toward peace in the Middle East. Also, security was the primary motive behind the doubling of the U.S. foreign assistance budget following 9/11, to provide funds for allies' use in the war on global terrorism.

Overall global official development assistance has in fact declined since peaking in 1991 (see Figure 5.1). In 2006, for example, Global North donors gave $104 billion to poor countries (five percent less than 2005), though at the 2007 G-8 Summit in Gleneagles, Scotland the donors promised to increase aid to $130 billion by 2010.

Many aid donors have become frustrated with the slow growth rates of many of the Global South recipients and have grown doubtful of the effectiveness of their aid programs, despite strong evidence that foreign aid has made a positive difference (Easterbrook 2002). Critics particularly resent what they perceive to be a state of mind in many Global South cultures that stands in the way of development, which—while bemoaning poverty—at the same time

official development assistance (ODA) grants or loans to countries from other countries, usually channeled through multilateral aid organizations, for the primary purpose of promoting economic development and welfare.

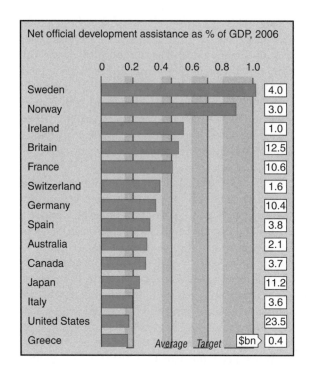

FIGURE 5.1 Global North Foreign Aid to the Global South

Official Developmental Assistance (ODA) from the top Global North donors totaled $104 billion in 2006. The United States, with the world's largest economy, pledged to give the most ($23.5 billion), but as a share of GDP, its aid budget was one of the smallest of the group. Few donors gave the 0.7 percent of their national incomes set by UN resolutions as an international target.

SOURCES: ODA data from the Organization for Economic Cooperation and Development, presented in the *Economist*, February 23, 2008, 120.

condemns competition, the profit motive, and individual entrepreneurial activity. Most bothersome to these critics are the failures caused by corrupt, autocratic Global South leaders. Former U.S. Secretary of State Colin L. Powell summarized this point of view in 2005 when he argued the case for assistance as a provider of market incentives: "Economic systems work best when access to opportunity is fair, when free people can use their talents to help themselves and others prosper. Aid can be a catalyst for development, but the real engines of growth are entrepreneurship, investment, and trade. They are what produce jobs, and a job is the most important social safety net for any family. If economic aid to developing countries is to succeed, it must be part of an incentive system for good governance. Foreign aid that succeeds is foreign aid that makes itself obsolete."

The shift to market-oriented models has led some donors to conclude that long-term foreign aid may be detrimental. Roughly a dozen African countries depend on aid for a fifth or more of their national incomes. This climate of opinion has spawned more "conditionality," or demands that recipient countries must meet to receive aid. Almost one-fourth of official development assistance is tied to purchasing goods and services from the donor country. It has been estimated that tying aid reduces its value by 15 to 30 percent.

On top of this practice of tying aid, donors are highly selective in choosing the countries they target for assistance, especially when they treat foreign aid as a subsidy for their domestic corporations producing exports. Although most donors distribute aid to the poorer countries, 38 percent of aid goes to middle- and high-income countries (WDI 2007, 362). The result is that the poorest of the poor Global South countries are receiving the least assistance and are suffering the most from the recent declines in foreign aid. In fact, far more money is funneled into Global South economies through the **remittances** that migrant laborers working in the Global North send home to their families. Global remittances have steadily climbed since the 1970s to teach $318 billion in 2007—more than three times the amount of all ODA. To cite one example, nearly ten percent of the population of the Philippines lives abroad, sending home $15 billion a year, a seventh of the country's gross domestic product (*International Herald Tribune*, April 21-22, 2007, 2).

Another indicator of the modest level of Global North support for Global South development assistance is seen in charitable contributions from private citizens to humanitarian aid agencies such as CARE. Although some $11.1 billion a year is funneled to Global South countries through charities, official developmental assistance dwarfs private giving, even though in most donor countries charitable gifts are income tax write-offs (*Economist*, March 4, 2006, 96).

Recently, some Global South leaders have criticized the various conditions that donors attach to foreign aid, calling the practice an instrument of neocolonialism imposed by the International Monetary Fund and other multilateral economic institutions. They have joined the chorus of developmental economists advocating increases in **foreign direct investment (FDI)**. Of course, this strategy for economic growth has always been the target of critics who question whether the investment of capital by multinational corporations (and, to a lesser extent, private investors) into local or domestic business ventures is really a financial remedy. The strategy has always been controversial, because there are many hidden costs, or **externalities**, associated with permitting corporations controlled from abroad to set up business within the host state for the purpose of making a profit. What share of the benefits will foreign investors and host countries get from the investments that are made? Considerable risks are entailed, as are a number of trade-offs among competing values (see Controversy: Multinational Corporations in the Global South: Do They Help or Hurt?).

The primary danger with this strategy is the potential for foreign investments to lead to foreign control, the erosion of sovereign governments' capacities to regulate the economy within their borders, and the probability that the multinational foreign investors will not invest their profits locally but channel them abroad for new investments or disburse them as dividends for their wealthy Global North shareholders. However, despite the risks, many developing countries have relaxed restrictions in order to attract foreign investors, with emphasis placed less on liberalizing investment restrictions and encouraging open domestic economic competition than on offering tax and cash enticements and opportunities for joint ventures. This has stimulated a recent surge in the flow of capital investments to the Global South (see Figure 5.2). However, keep in mind that 71 percent of all FDI is channeled to the Global North, and the poorest Global South countries benefit from only 0.2 percent of investments from abroad (WDI 2007, 342).

remittances the money earned by immigrants working in wealthy countries that they send to family members still living in their home country.

foreign direct investment (FDI) an investment in a country involving a long-term relationship and control of an enterprise by nonresidents and including equity capital, reinvestment of earnings, other long-term capital, and short-term capital as shown in balance of payments accounts.

externalities the unintended side effects of choices that reduce the true value of the original decision.

CONTROVERSY   Multinational Corporations in the Global South: Do They Help or Hurt?

Within the Global South, there is widespread concern about the impact of multinational corporations (MNCs) on the economies and societies of the countries in which they operate. Because their record can be evaluated on different criteria, MNCs are praised by some people and condemned by others. The following is a "balance sheet" summarizing the major arguments for and against MNCs. Using this summary of contending interpretations, you can easily see why the role of MNCs is so controversial. What do you think? On balance, do MNCs help or harm the Global South's ability to close the gap in wealth with the Global North? How do you assess their relative benefits and costs for Global South countries?

Positive

- Increase the volume of trade.
- Assist the aggregation of investment capital that can fund development.
- Finance loans and service international debt.
- Lobby for free trade and the removal of barriers to trade, such as tariffs.
- Underwrite research and development that allows technological innovation.
- Introduce and dispense advanced technology to less-developed countries.
- Reduce the costs of goods by encouraging their production according to the principle of comparative advantage.
- Generate employment.
- Encourage the training of workers.
- Produce new goods and expand opportunities for their purchase through the internationalization of production.
- Disseminate marketing expertise and mass advertising methods worldwide.
- Provide investment income to facilitate the modernization of less-developed countries.
- Generate income and wealth.
- Advocate peaceful relations between and among states in order to preserve an orderly environment conducive to trade and profits.
- Break down national barriers and accelerate the globalization of the international economy and culture and the rules that govern international commerce.

Negative

- Give rise to huge conglomerations that reduce competition and free enterprise.
- Raise capital in host countries (thereby depriving local industries of investment capital) but export profits to home countries.
- Breed debtors and make the poor dependent on those providing loans.
- Limit the availability of commodities by monopolizing their production and controlling their distribution in the world marketplace.
- Create "sanctuary markets" that restrict and channel other investments to give MNCs an unfair advantage.
- Export technology ill-suited to underdeveloped economies.
- Inhibit the growth of infant industries and local technological expertise in less-developed countries while making Global South countries dependent on Global North technology.
- Conspire to create cartels that contribute to inflation.
- Curtail employment by driving labor competition from the market.
- Limit workers' wages.
- Limit the supply of raw materials available in international markets.
- Erode traditional cultures and national differences, leaving in their place a homogenized world culture dominated by consumer-oriented values.
- Widen the gap between rich and poor countries.
- Increase the wealth of local elites at the expense of the poor.
- Support and rationalize repressive regimes in the name of stability and order.
- Challenge national sovereignty and jeopardize the autonomy of the states.
- Create cartels with other MNCs that share markets in order to cut competition.

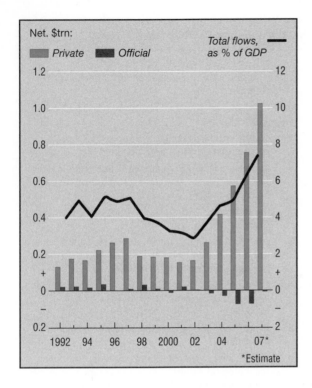

FIGURE 5.2 Trends in Capital Investments in the Global South

The Global South's developing countries are beginning to receive increasing capital in the form of direct foreign investments and commercial bank loans. In 2006, net capital flows climbed to $647 billion, the highest level on record. The Asia/Pacific region now accounts for two-fifths of worldwide capital investments.

SOURCE: : World Bank as reported in the *Economist*, June 14, 2008, 113.

The impact of this new infusion of foreign investments in the developing countries has been substantial, given the relatively small economies of the Global South. It has paved the way for emerging markets in the Global South to expand their rates of economic development despite the resistance of local industries in the Global South threatened by the competition and critics who have complained about the income inequalities that the investments are causing. Such fears and consequences notwithstanding, an intensified push among Global South developing countries to compete for foreign investment capital in order to liberate themselves from dependence and destitution seems likely.

The prospects for either foreign aid or for foreign direct investments to contribute to the future development of, and relief of poverty in, the Global South will depend on a number of other factors. Foremost is the extent to which the staggering level of debt facing many Global South countries can be managed (see Application: Development, Democracy, and Debt).

The International Monetary Fund estimates that Global South debt in 2006 exceeded $3,207 billion for 146 countries and that their debt-service payments were $495.3 billion. Because this accounts for 14 percent of the value of their combined export of goods, services, and income, most developmental economists see this situation as unsustainable (WDI 2007, 256). Worse off are the 28 **Heavily Indebted Poor Countries (HIPCs)**, with arrears of $782 billion, seeking relief through debt rescheduling or cancellation. The financial dilemmas

Heavily Indebted Poor Countries (HIPCs) the subset of countries identified by the World Bank's Debtor Reporting System whose ratios of government debt to gross national product are so substantial that they cannot meet their payment obligations without experiencing political instability and economic collapse.

APPLICATION   Development, Democracy, and Debt

What determines whether a country is able to make the transition from authoritarian to democratic government? Benazir Bhutto, who twice served as the prime minister of Pakistan (1988–1990; 1993–1996) before her assassination in December 2007, gave considerable thought to this question. She wrote fondly in her autobiography about the time that she devoted to studying Locke, Mill, and other democratic theorists during her university years (Bhutto 1988). As the passage below describes, once in office she tried to apply what she studied, but found herself constrained by the country's debt and pressures from international financial institutions to cut spending on programs that she saw as the foundation for building democracy in Pakistan.

> Democracy cannot be sustained around the world in the absence of a stable and growing middle class. Huge economic disparities between social classes in a society strain national unity, creating a gap between the rich and the poor.
>
> ...But how can a nation build a middle class? The first step is to build an education system that allows children to rise to a higher social and economic status than their parents—in other words, an educational system that delivers hope and real opportunity is a prerequisite for democracy. Good public educational opportunity is the key to the economic and political progress of nations....
>
> As prime minister, I attempted to put as much funding into the social sector and education as I could. Overburdened with the debts run up by [the

previous] dictatorship, my government still built almost fifty thousand elementary and secondary schools around the country, and especially in the rural areas. I wish our debts had been rescheduled so we could have done more. The fundamental constraint upon my government in prioritizing our budget was the enormous percent of our GNP that was directed to debt repayment and defense.

> ...I was under enormous pressure—from the public, the military, and key international players—all of whom expected a chunk of the federal budget, which was already burdened by debt. All this occurred while international financial institutions, including the International Monetary Fund, were pressing me to cut national expenditure to reduce the budget deficit. This undermined my ability to govern effectively (Bhutto 2008, 284–286).

Making the transition from authoritarian to democratic rule is difficult. Since Aristotle, political philosophers have linked democracy to the presence of a vibrant, influential middle class. Experts disagree about what factors are necessary for democracy-building, but many concur that when a country's middle class is "small, weak, or politically dependent on authoritarian elements in society..., democratic development is less likely" (Handelman 2009, 41). However, finding the funds for programs that can promote democratic development in a country saddled with debt can frustrate even the most energetic political leader.

faced by Zambia illustrate the problem. According to the World Bank, Zambia began the new millennium with $5.2 billion in public external debt (net present value), which was roughly equivalent to 60 percent of its GDP and 500 percent of Zambia's exports of goods and nonfactor services. Merely servicing this debt (paying the interest and principal) amounted to 24.5 percent of the central government's revenues. Obviously, such a staggering amount of debt poses an enormous constraint on the government's ability to improve the quality of life of the 70 percent of its citizens that live in poverty.

Debt relief—slashing the amount owed by Zambia and the other heavily indebted poor countries—is reflective of the changing attitudes toward the Global South by the great powers and multilateral institutions, such as the World Bank. In October 2005, the IMF Steering Committee, with the support of the Group of Eight, agreed to forgive $40 billion worth of debt for the 18 poorest countries and to consider debt cancellation of another $15 billion for as many as 20 other countries. Partly this was done out of compassion but also due to the economic self-interest of the Global North, which sees in debt relief a pragmatic method for preventing an economic collapse that could threaten the entire world economy in the age of interdependent globalization. The World Bank's "Enhanced HIPC Initiative" and the International Monetary Fund's "Enhanced **Structural Adjustment** Facility," are the primary products of this attempt to reduce the widening disparities between the Global North and Global South. Whether these programs will succeed, argue their sponsors, will depend on the degree to which developing countries can undertake, with minimal corruption, the often painful liberalizing political and economic reforms that are required for sustained economic growth (see Kim and Wolfensohn 1999). This argument reflects what is known as the "**Washington consensus**," the view held by numerous U.S. government, World Bank, and IMF officials (all headquartered in Washington, D.C.) that balanced government budgets, the privatization of state-owned enterprises, the reduction of barriers to trade and foreign investment, and the elimination of subsidies to domestic producers are prerequisites for economic growth.

Yet these reforms may not be as successful as their advocates claim. On the one hand, China and Singapore have enjoyed rapid economic growth without undertaking significant political liberalization. On the other hand, many Global South countries that have implemented economic liberalizing reforms have not experienced growth (Vreeland 2003). Joseph Stiglitz (2003), a Nobel Laureate in economics and former chief economist of the World Bank, complains that the policies emanating from the Washington consensus produce disappointing results because they are anchored in a free-market dogma that ignores the unique sociocultural contexts of the countries where they are applied. Indeed, some of the most successful programs have taken a local, grassroots approach to development. **Microfinance**, pioneered by Bangladeshi economist Muhammad Yunus through his Grameen Bank, has help many people climb out of poverty. It entails loaning as little as a hundred dollars to poor, budding entrepreneurs that lack the incomes or collateral typically required of borrowers. Rural women, who tend to be ignored by lending institutions when they seek credit to start small businesses, have been major beneficiaries of these community-based programs.

In summary, an unqualified free-market approach to development that minimizes the role of the state may not be sufficient by itself to create rapid economic growth. Other factors, such as fair, effective systems of property and regulatory law, and honest, responsive political institutions, need to augment trade openness. Moreover, under certain circumstances, a stronger role for the state is advantageous, especially in providing a safety net for the most vulnerable members of society and in addressing distributional inequities related to ethnicity, gender, or geographic region. Given the diversity of the Global South, development strategies for the future should avoid grandiose claims of universality and one-size-fits-all policies. What works in one country may be impractical or undesirable in another (Cohn 2005, 399, 427–429).

structural adjustment reforms aimed at reducing the role of the state while increasing the role of the market in Global South countries' economies.

Washington consensus the view that Global South countries can best achieve sustained economic growth through democratic governance, fiscal discipline, free markets, a reliance on private enterprise, and trade liberalization.

microfinance providing small loans to poor entrepreneurs, usually to help start or expand a small business.

THE FUTURE OF THE GLOBAL SOUTH

It is useful to remember the historic trends underlying the problems faced by the countries of the Global South. Most were colonized by people of another race, experienced varying degrees of poverty, and felt powerless in a world system dominated by the affluent countries that once controlled them and perhaps still do. Considerable change occurred as post–World War II decolonization proceeded, but much also remained the same.

According to economist Paul Collier (2007), today poverty is declining for many people living in developing countries. An annual average growth of 3.9 percent in GDP per person since 2000 has cut poverty rates across the Global South. In Latin America, for example, the Bank of Santander estimates that some 15 million households arose from poverty between 2002 and 2006, and, if the trend continues, by 2010 a significant number will approach lower middle-class incomes. Nevertheless, almost half of the Global South's population lives on less than two dollars a day at purchasing-power parity, which equalizes prices of goods in different countries (*Economist*, April 21, 2007, 110; August 18, 2007, 22). Yet from Collier's perspective, the real problem for the Global South lies in the extreme poverty suffered by the bottom billion of the world's population, 70 percent of whom live in Sub-Sahara Africa. Data from the World Bank reveal that roughly 41 percent of the people in that region live on less than one dollar a day, measured at purchasing-power parity. Nigeria, Zambia, and Madagascar, for instance, all have extreme poverty rates exceeding 60 percent (*Economist*, November 24, 2007, 106).

As poverty rates change, the relationships between the world's developed and developing countries will no doubt continue to change, but exactly how remains uncertain. A turn inward, toward isolationist foreign policies, in the Global North could lead to a posture of "benign neglect" of the Global South. Conversely, a new era of North–South cooperation could commence, dedicated to finding solutions to common problems ranging from commercial to environmental and security concerns. Elements of both approaches are already evident.

Although the fate of the Global South remains to be determined, it is clear that, for the time being, the choices of the great powers will strongly influence its future. That influence is often funneled through international organizations like the United Nations and the World Bank, which the great powers have created. To fully understand world politics, we need to inspect the roles played by these intergovernmental organizations, or IGOs, as actors in the global arena. And to complete the picture, we also need to examine nongovernmental organizations, or NGOs, whose roles are important as well. We turn to these nonstate actors in Chapter 6.

CHAPTER SUMMARY

- The term *Global South* refers to the world's poorer, economically less-developed countries, most of which lie along the equator or in the Southern Hemisphere and were once colonies of other states. Significant inequalities exist between these countries and those industrialized states that comprise the Global North. Whereas the Global South contains more than 85 percent of the world's population, it commands less than 20 percent of its wealth.

- Considerable diversity exists among Global South countries: some are big, others are small; some possess vast quantities of oil and natural gas; others lack significant natural resources; some have subsistence economies, others export manufactured goods; some are democracies, others are autocracies. Despite these and other differences, most Global South countries share a set of common problems related to their poverty and vulnerability.

- Between the fifteenth and twentieth centuries, two waves of European imperialism resulted in the colonization of the Global South. Decolonization began in earnest after World War II and is now complete. For the most part, it was not only extraordinarily rapid but also remarkably peaceful. Still, the vestiges of colonialism remain, and they have important consequences for the shape of the global future.

- Although the debate over how to eliminate the disparities between the Global North and South focuses on the economic development of impoverished countries, these issues are intensely political. They derive from the struggle by those at the bottom of the international hierarchy to improve their position in the global pecking order.

- The development process is complex because the problems faced by the Global South are characterized by a series of intertwined vicious circles, none of which seems capable of being broken without addressing the others.

- Classical economic development theory claims that the causes of underdevelopment are internal. Among the factors it identifies are low rates of productivity, a lack of sufficient investment capital, and inadequate communication and transportation systems.

- Dependency theory holds that the causes of underdevelopment are external. Less-developed countries are vulnerable to penetration by outside forces. According to dependency theory, the Global South has been exploited by wealthier, more powerful members of the world capitalist system.

- Global South states have tried various strategies to overcome their weakness and insecurity. To cope with the threat of separatist movements, many of them have sought to acquire modern weaponry, even if that meant sacrificing funds for health, education, and welfare programs. To promote economic growth, many have tried to forge regional free-trade groups, encourage foreign direct investment, and seek relief from staggering levels of debt.

KEY TERMS

barter

colonialism

decolonization

dependency theory

dependent development

development

dualism

export-led
industrialization

externalities

failed states

First World

foreign direct
investment (FDI)

Global East

Global North

Global South

Group of 77 (G–77)

Heavily Indebted Poor
Countries (HIPCs)

import-substitution
industrialization

laissez-faire economics

least developed
countries (LDCs)

mercantilism

microfinance

modernization

multinational
corporations
(MNCs)

New International
Economic Order
(NIEO)

newly industrialized
countries (NICs)

nonalignment

official development
assistance (ODA)

remittances

Second World

self-determination

spheres of influence

structural adjustment

Third World

Washington consensus

SUGGESTED READINGS

Collier, Paul. *The Bottom Billion*. New York: Oxford University Press, 2007.

Goldin, Ian, and Kenneth Reinert. *Globalization for Development*. London: Palgrave Macmillan, 2006.

Kapstein, Ethan B. *Economic Justice in an Unfair World*. Princeton: Princeton University Press, 2006.

Sachs, Jeffrey. *The End of Poverty*. New York: Penguin Press, 2005.

Satler, David. *Geopolitics and the Post-Colonial: Rethinking North-South Relations*. Malden, MA: Blackwell, 2005.

CRITICAL THINKING QUESTIONS

Are large endowments of petroleum, natural gas, gold, diamonds, or other valuable natural resources a blessing or a potential source of trouble? According to what has been called the "resource curse," resource-abundant countries often grow more slowly than less well-endowed countries. Although the harmful effects of export booms in oil and minerals can be counteracted in various ways, such as setting aside some revenue in a "rainy day" fund for future use, sharp increases in the returns from the sale of these commodities can breed inflation and an appreciation in the domestic currency. With a stronger currency, imported goods now become cheaper and possibly less expensive than products produced domestically, which makes the agricultural and manufacturing sectors of the economy less competitive on the world market and thus less profitable. Under these conditions, foreign investment tends to go into oilfields and mines, which employ few unskilled people and yield cash windfalls that are concentrated in the hands of a few powerful individuals who can use these revenues to ease social pressures that might otherwise lead to demands for economic diversification, political accountability, and higher levels of education (M. Ross 2001; Friedman 2006).

Beyond the economic impacts of windfall profits from natural resources, are there significant political impacts? If a country lacks well-established, transparent governmental institutions and it suddenly becomes flush with cash due to skyrocketing prices for its resources (or the discovery of valuable resources within its borders), will the political system be skewed in an authoritarian direction? Can civil liberties and political freedoms be jeopardized by a sudden influx of wealth from oil or mineral exports? If so, what causal processes do you think impede democracy?

6

Nonstate Actors and the Challenge of Global Governance

CHAPTER OUTLINE

Types of Nonstate Actors

Global Intergovernmental Organizations

The United Nations

Other Prominent Global IGOs

Regional Intergovernmental Organizations

The European Union

Other Regional IGOs

Nongovernmental Organizations

Ethnopolitical Movements

Religious Movements

CONTROVERSY: Are Religious Movements Causes of War or Sources of Transnational Harmony?

Multinational Corporations and Transnational Banks

Issue-Advocacy Groups and Global Civil Society

Nonstate Actors and the Global Future

APPLICATION: Mixed-Actor Approaches to Global Diplomacy

A novel redistribution of power among states, markets, and civil society is underway, ending the steady accumulation of power in the hands of states that began with the Peace of Westphalia in 1648.

JESSICA T. MATHEWS
PRESIDENT OF THE CARNEGIE ENDOWMENT FOR INTERNATIONAL PEACE

On July 12, 2006, guerrillas from Lebanon's Islamist movement, Hezbollah, ambushed an Israeli army patrol along the border, killing several soldiers and taking two hostages. When the Israelis pursued them in an unsuccessful rescue attempt, they lost several more soldiers. Coming on the heels of the abduction of an Israeli corporal by Hamas, the primary Islamist group in the Palestinian territories, the incident prompted Israeli Prime Minister Ehud Olmert to order ferocious artillery and air assaults against suspected Hezbollah strongholds in Beirut and southern Lebanon, an action some of his military advisors had been long advocating. According to Israeli Defense Minister Amir Peretz, the goal was for this to end with Hezbollah "so badly beaten that not a man in it does not regret having launched the incident" (*Time*, July 24, 2006, p. 28).

As the Israelis blockaded Lebanon and pummeled its transportation infrastructure in hopes of isolating Hezbollah militants, Hezbollah retaliated by firing salvos of Katyusha rockets into northern Israel, paralyzing Haifa, the country's third-largest city and one of its busiest ports. "Our homes will not be the only one's destroyed," declared Hezbollah leader Sheikh Hassan Nasrallah. "You don't know who you're fighting" (*Newsweek*, July 24, 2006, p. 24).

Hezbollah (or, the "Party of God') was formed in 1982 after Israel invaded Lebanon to drive out the Palestinian Liberation Organization (PLO), which had been using Lebanon as a base for harassing northern Israeli settlements with small arms and mortar fire. An extremist Shiite Muslim organization with close ties to Iran, Hezbollah's members have been blamed for the 1983 bombing of the U.S. Marine barracks in Beirut, the 1985 hijacking of TWA Flight 847, and numerous kidnappings. Operating within a weak and fractious nation-state, Hezbollah has had virtually free reign over parts of Lebanon.

During the 1990s, Hezbollah evolved beyond a simple paramilitary organization, developing extensive social welfare programs, which included operating several schools and health clinics within the Shiite parts of Lebanon. It also began participating in Lebanese elections, winning 14 seats of 128 parliamentary seats in 2005. Despite these changes, Hezbollah continued to view Israel as an illegal entity and vowed to pressure the Israelis into releasing imprisoned Lebanese and withdrawing from the disputed Shebaa region.

Israel's foremost concern about Hezbollah centers on its growing arsenal of Iranian-supplied weaponry. While the inaccurate Katyusha rocket has a range of between 10 and 20 miles, the Israelis worry that Iran has provided Hezbollah with an unknown quantity of more sophisticated missiles, which could target all of Israel's population centers with warheads capable of carrying chemical or biological agents. Their anxiety increased a few days into the conflict when a

C-802 radar-guided missile disabled an Israeli warship off the coast of Lebanon. Fearing that Hezbollah might also possess the longer-range Zelzal-2 missile, the Israelis continued pounding Lebanon despite calls from UN Secretary-General Kofi Annan for a cease-fire. Hezbollah, in turn, maintained its constant barrage against northern Israel. As the grim toll of civilian casualties mounted on both sides, Lebanese Prime Minister Fouad Siniora lamented that his country was being torn to shreds.

Over the ensuing weeks, three contending explanations for why Hezbollah initiated hostilities circulated among journalists, diplomats, and world leaders. The first claimed that the July 12 attack was a miscalculation: Hezbollah had undertaken similar cross-border raids in recent years without triggering a major Israeli response, so its commanders presumably thought they could do it again with impunity. The second argued that it was a diversion: Iran, which had trained and supplied Hezbollah, allegedly encouraged the attack to draw international attention away from its budding nuclear weapons program. Finally, the third explanation proposed that the attack was a provocation: After Israel ended its occupation of southern Lebanon in 2000, Hezbollah fortified the area and acquired thousands of short and medium-range rockets. With the United States bogged down in Iraq and the Israelis preoccupied with unrest in the Palestinian territories, Hezbollah's leadership may have concluded that Israel was vulnerable; bold action would allow Hezbollah to demonstrate its military prowess to the Arab world while dealing Israel a crippling blow.

Although long-time observers of the Middle East disagree over what weight to give any of these explanations, they concur that the political dynamics of the region involve more than the interactions of nation-states. Any analysis that concentrated on Israel, Lebanon, Iran, and other states to the neglect of Hezbollah, Hamas, the PLO, and other nonstate actors would be woefully incomplete. Nonstate entities ranging from global and regional intergovernmental organizations (IGOs) to ethnic and religious nongovernmental organizations (NGOs) are important actors that must be taken into account when examining world politics. Indeed, as the Lebanese conflict demonstrates, it would be impossible to make sense of contemporary international affairs without devoting attention to them. In view of their importance, the aims of this chapter are to describe the various types of nonstate actors and to explain when and how they exert their influence.

TYPES OF NONSTATE ACTORS

The history of world politics for the past 350 years has largely been a chronicle of interactions among sovereign, territorial states. Today, however, world affairs

intergovernmental organizations (IGOs) institutions created and joined by states' governments, which give them authority to make collective decisions to manage particular problem(s) on the global agenda.

nongovernmental organizations (NGOs) transnational organizations of private citizens that include foundations, professional associations, multinational corporations, or groups in different countries joined together to work toward common interests.

are also being shaped by organizations that transcend national boundaries. In addition to the United Nations and regional bodies such as the European Union, the course of world affairs is affected by groups of people who band together for ethnic, religious, or other reasons. Diverse in scope and purpose, these nonstate actors push their own agendas and increasingly exert international influence.

There are two principal types of nonstate actors: **intergovernmental organizations (IGOs)**, whose members are states, and **nongovernmental organizations (NGOs)**, whose members are private individuals and groups. The Union of International Organizations, which maintains comprehensive, up-to-date information on these organizations, records that their numbers increased sharply during the nineteenth century, as international commerce and communications grew alongside industrialization. In 1909, there were 37 IGOs and 176 NGOs. By 1960, there were 154 IGOs and 1,255 NGOs, and by 2007, these numbers had risen to 246 and 27,723, respectively (see Figure 6.1).

IGOs are created by states to solve shared problems. As shown in Table 6.1, they vary widely in size and purpose. The North Atlantic Treaty Organization (NATO), for example, is primarily a military alliance, while others, such as the Organization of American States (OAS), promote economic

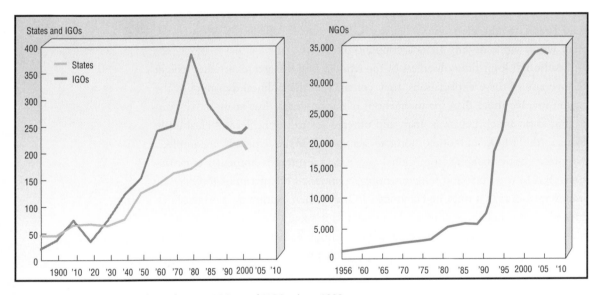

FIGURE 6.1 The Number of States, IGOs, and NGOs since 1900

The number of independent states increased greatly in the twentieth century, especially since the decolonization movement began after World War II. The number of intergovernmental organizations (IGOs) and nongovernmental organizations (NGOs) has grown even more rapidly.

SOURCES: Figures for states are based on the Correlates of War (COW) project (http://www.correlatesofwar.org); IGOs and NGOs from *Yearbook of International Organizations 2005/2006,* edition 42, vol. 5 (2006, 33), and moving averages from selected prior volumes.

TABLE 6.1   A Simple Classification of Intergovernmental Organizations (IGOs)

Geographic Scope of Membership	Range of Stated Purpose	
	Multiple Purposes	Single Purpose
Global	United Nations	World Health Organization
	World Trade Organization	International Labor Organization
	UNESCO	International Monetary Fund
	Organization of the Islamic Conference	Universal Postal Union
Interregional, regional, subregional	European Union	European Space Agency
	Organization for Security and Cooperation in Europe	Nordic Council
	Organization of American States	North Atlantic Treaty Organization
	Organization of African Unity	International Olive Oil Council
	League of Arab States	International North Pacific Coffee Organization
	Association of Southeast Asian Nations	African Groundnut Council

development. Most IGOs concentrate their activities on specific economic or social issues of special concern to them, such as the management of trade, or of transportation.

NGOs also differ widely. They span virtually every facet of political, social, and economic activity, including science, health care, culture, theology, law, security, and defense. As organizations that are independent of governments, NGOs link people from different societies in transnational networks in order to advocate specific policies. For this purpose, many NGOs interact formally with IGOs. More than 1,000 NGOs actively consult with various agencies of the extensive UN system, maintain offices in hundreds of cities, and hold parallel conferences with IGO meetings to which states send representatives. Such partnerships between NGOs and IGOs enable both types of organizations to work (and lobby) together in pursuit of common policies and programs.

In this chapter, we will begin our analysis of nonstate actors by discussing some prominent and representative IGOs, including the United Nations (UN) and the European Union (EU). Next, we will turn our attention to NGOs, examining the impact of ethnopolitical groups, religious movements, multinational corporations and transnational banks, and issue-advocacy groups. Finally, we will ask whether the activities of nonstate actors are undermining the position of the nation-state in world politics.

GLOBAL INTERGOVERNMENTAL ORGANIZATIONS

The United Nations

The United Nations is the best-known global organization. What distinguishes it from most other IGOs is its nearly universal membership, including today 192 independent states from every region of the world (see Figure 6.2). The UN's nearly fourfold growth from the fifty-one states that joined it in 1945 has been spectacular, but the admission process has from the start been governed by political conflicts that show the extent to which the organization reflects the relationships of the five great powers that shape its direction through their veto authority in the Security Council.

Purposes and Agenda.   In addition to possessing nearly universal membership, the UN is also a multipurpose organization. As Article 1 of the UN Charter states, its objectives are to:

- Maintain international peace and security
- Develop friendly relations among nations based on respect for the principle of equal rights and self determination of peoples

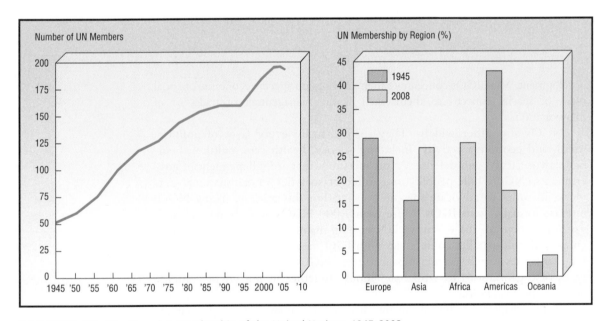

F I G U R E 6.2 The Changing Membership of the United Nations, 1945–2008

As the figure on the left shows, the UN's membership has seen episodic bursts of growth from fifty-one states in 1945 to 192 in 2008 with the admission of newly independent Montenegro (the world's 212th sovereign state). Over nearly six decades of expansion, the United Nations has increasingly included Global South countries (see figure on right). This shift has influenced the kinds of issues the UN has confronted, expanding the global agenda from the priorities of the great powers in the Global North to include those important to the developing states in the Global South.

SOURCES: United Nations.

Achieve international cooperation in solving international problems of an economic, social, cultural, or humanitarian character and in promoting and encouraging respect for human rights and for fundamental freedoms for all

- Function as a center for harmonizing the actions of nations in the attainment of these common ends

Peace and security figured prominently in the thinking of those responsible for creating the United Nations at the end of the Second World War to replace the League of Nations. However, the ambitions that the UN's founders had in the security realm were soon frustrated by the Cold War between the United States and the Soviet Union. Although unable to make headway on security issues, work toward the goal of improving the quality of life for humanity carried the UN into nearly every corner of the world.

The history of the UN reflects the fact that both rich countries and developing countries have successfully used the organization to promote their own foreign policy objectives, and this record has bred hopes throughout the world that the UN will be able to manage an ever changing and growing agenda. However, ambitions for the UN may exceed its meager resources. Since the end of the Cold War, the organization has been asked to address an expanding set of global problems, including AIDS, economic development, climate change, energy shortages, dwindling fresh water supplies, human rights abuses, and internationally organized crime. In response to the demands that have been placed upon it, the United Nations has developed an administrative structure with offices not only in the UN Headquarters in New York but also in centers spread throughout the world (see Map 6.1). To evaluate the capacity of the United Nations to shoulder the huge burdens that it has been asked to carry, let us examine how it is organized.

Organizational Structure.   The UN's limitations are perhaps rooted in the ways it is organized for its wide-ranging purposes. According to the Charter, the UN structure contains the following six principal organs:

- *General Assembly.* Established as the main deliberative body of the United Nations, all members are equally represented according to a one-state/one-vote formula. Decisions are reached by a simple majority vote, except on so-called "important questions," which require a two-thirds majority. The resolutions it passes, however, are only recommendations.

- *Security Council.* Given primary responsibility by the Charter for dealing with threats to international peace and security, the Security Council consists of five permanent members with the power to veto substantive decisions (the United States, the United Kingdom, France, Russia, and the People's Republic of China), and ten nonpermanent members elected by the General Assembly for staggered two-year terms.

- *Economic and Social Council.* Responsible for coordinating the UN's social and economic programs, functional commissions, and specialized agencies, its fifty-four members are elected by the General Assembly for staggered

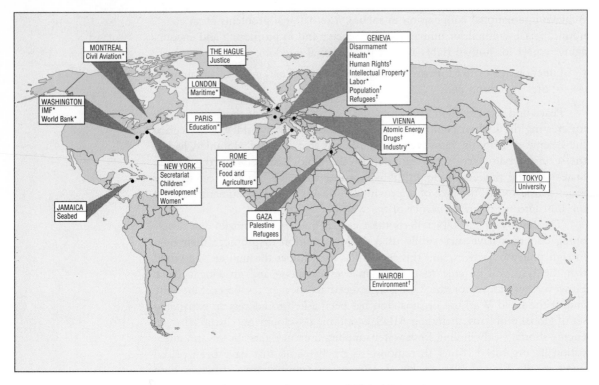

MAP 6.1 The UN's Headquarters and Global Network

The United Nations has sought, since its creation, to address the continuously expanding problems on the global agenda. As shown on this map, the United Nations has spread its administrative arm to every corner of the globe in order to fulfill its primary purpose of spearheading international cooperation.

*Specialized agencies.

† Funds and programs.

SOURCE: *The UN Handbook.*

three-year terms. This body has been particularly active addressing economic development and human rights issues.

- *Trusteeship Council.* Charged with supervising the administration of territories that had not achieved self-rule, the Trusteeship Council suspended operation in 1994, when the last remaining trust territory gained independence.

- *International Court of Justice.* The principal judicial organ of the United Nations, the International Court of Justice is composed of 15 independent judges who are elected for nine-year terms by the General Assembly and Security Council. The competence of the Court is restricted to disputes between states, and its jurisdiction is based on the consent of the disputants. The Court may also give nonbinding advisory opinions on legal questions raised by the General Assembly, Security Council, or other UN agencies.

- *Secretariat.* Led by the secretary-general (currently, Ban Kai-moon of South Korea), the Secretariat contains the international civil servants who perform the administrative and secretarial functions of the UN. The staff numbers over 8,000 under the core budget, and almost as many people working under special funding.

The founders of the UN expected the Security Council to become the organization's primary body, since it was designed to maintain peace and its permanent members were the victorious great powers who had been allied during the Second World War. With the onset of the Cold War, however, frequent use of the veto power—initially by the Soviet Union and later by the United States—prevented the Council from acting on many security problems, with the result that the General Assembly gradually assumed wider responsibilities.

Beyond the six principal organs, the UN system also contains numerous programs and funds, research and training institutes, and functional and regional commissions (see Figure 6.3). In addition, it is affiliated with a host of autonomous specialized agencies that have their own charters, budgets, and staffs. They include the World Health Organization (WHO), the International Labor Organization (ILO), and the UN Educational, Scientific, and Cultural Organization (UNESCO).

The United Nations has changed in many ways not envisioned by its founders, evolving into an extraordinarily complex network of overlapping institutions, some of which (the UN Children's Fund or the United Nations University, for example) fulfill their mission in part through NGOs. The UN has also increasingly come to rely on the many NGOs that are not under its formal authority. This collaboration blurs the line between governmental and nongovernmental functions, but UN-NGO cooperation helps the UN's mission. In the process, the UN has become not one organization but a decentralized conglomerate of countless committees, bureaus, boards, commissions, centers, institutes, offices, and agencies scattered around the globe, with each of its many specialized activities managed from offices in various cities.

Many of the UN's changes have come in response to concerns voiced by Global South countries, who seized the advantage of their growing numbers under the one-state/one-vote rules of the General Assembly to push the UN in new directions. Today, a coalition of 132 Global South countries comprising three-fourths of the UN and led by the **Group of 77**, attempt to steer the organization's programs toward the needs of its poorer members.

Group of 77 (G-77)
a coalition of the world's poor countries formed in 1964 to press for concessions from wealthy Global North states.

North-South differences over perceived priorities are most clearly exhibited in the heated debate over the UN's budget. This controversy centers on how members should interpret the organization's charter, which states that "expenses of the Organization shall be borne by the members as apportioned by the General Assembly."

The UN budget consists of three distinct elements: the core budget, the peacekeeping budget, and the budget for voluntary programs. The core budget is roughly $1.9 billion per year, with the total spending by all UN agencies, peacekeeping operations, and programs and funds totaling approximately $15 billion.

FIGURE 6.3 The Organization of the United Nations

NOTES: Solid lines from principal organs indicate direct reporting relationship; – – – indicate a non-subsidiary relationship. *Specialized agencies are autonomous organizations working with the UN through the coordination of the Economic and Social Council.

SOURCES: Abridged organizational chart from United Nations Department of Public Information, December 2007.

States contribute to the voluntary programs and some of the peacekeeping activities as they see fit. The core budget and other peacekeeping activities are subject to assessments.

The precise mechanism by which assessments have been determined is complicated, but, historically, assessments were allocated according to states' capacity to pay. Although this formula is under attack in many wealthy states, it still governs. Thus the United States, which has the greatest resources, contributes 22 percent of the core UN budget (and is also the primary contributor to UN peacekeeping and voluntary programs), whereas the poorest 70 percent of the UN's members pay the minimum (0.01 percent) and contribute only $13,000 annually. By this agreement, the richest states paid more than four-fifths toward the UN's 2006–2007 budget.

Resistance to this budgetary formula for funding UN activities has always existed. But it has grown progressively worse, in large part because when the General Assembly apportions expenses, it does so according to majority rule. The problem is that those with the most votes (the Global South countries) do not have the money, and the most prosperous (the Global North countries) do not have the votes. Wide disparities have grown so that the ten largest contributors to the UN command only ten votes, but pay 82 percent of the cost. At the other end of the spectrum, the poorest members paid only 18 percent of the UN budget but commanded 182 votes. This deep imbalance has led to many fierce disputes over the kinds of issues on which the UN's attention and resources should be focused. The wealthy members charge that the existing budget procedures institutionalize a system of taxation without fair representation. The critics counter with the argument that the great-power members should bear financial responsibilities commensurate with their wealth and influence.

At issue, of course, is not simply money. Differences in images of what is important and which states should have political influence are the real issues. Poor states argue that needs should determine expenditure levels. Major contributors, sensitive to the amounts asked of them and the purposes to which the funds are put, do not want to pay for programs they oppose. The United States in particular was historically the most vocal about its dissatisfaction, and since 2000 has been in arrears an average of $1.35 billion each year.

In response to persisting cash flow problems and rising complaints about the UN's inefficient administration, bold "Millennium+5" reforms were undertaken in 2005 to consolidate programs, reduce costs, eliminate waste, and reassign administrative responsibilities in order to make the UN more efficient. These massive reforms cut the Secretariat's administrative costs by one-third, from 38 percent of the core budget to 25 percent, and put the savings into a development fund for poor countries. The assessments of some Global North members were also adjusted: The United States in 2008 was paying 22 percent of the core budget, and the four other permanent members of the Security Council were scheduled to pay proportionally less (Britain and France, 6.1 percent; China, 2.1 percent; and Russia, 1.1 percent). This formula understandably upsets the other major contributors who pay large sums but are still excluded from Security Council participation as permanent members. Consider Japan, which pays 19.5 percent of the core budget (second only to the United States) while holding fewer key posts in the organization than states paying far less. Frustrated by what it considers an unreasonably high assessment and over a decade of unsuccessful efforts to obtain a permanent seat on the Security Council, Japan is considering cutting its annual contributions to voluntary programs.

Japan's interest in joining the Security Council as a permanent member are shared by several other states, most notably Germany, India, and Brazil. They contend that the current makeup of the council does not reflect the political and economic changes that have occurred in the world since 1945. Opponents of adding new permanent members assert that enlargement would make the council unwieldy. The United States has resisted proposals to expand the Security Council because they would dilute the American influence within the UN, adding that those states campaigning for permanent seats would only be supported by Washington if they agreed not to request the veto power. For now, the great-power victors in World War II hold privileged positions within the organization; however, the debate over enlargement continues as South Africa, Nigeria, and various Middle Eastern states have also called for reforms that would make the Security Council more representative culturally and geographically.

The future of shape and direction of the UN is uncertain. Concerns about the organization have been compounded by a string of scandals, including charges of mismanagement in the 1990s Iraqi "Oil-for-Food" program, sexual abuse of women in the Congo by UN peacekeepers, and inaction in the face of genocide in the Darfur region of Sudan. John Bolton, a former U.S. ambassador to the UN, exemplified those who are frustrated with the organization when he once quipped that if the top ten floors of the UN headquarters building were eliminated it wouldn't make a difference. Nevertheless, many of the UN's supporters feel optimistic about the organization's long-term prospects, because past crises have been overcome and the UN's many previous contributions to world peace and development have given most countries a stake in its survival. In 2005, the UN undertook a series of reforms to strengthen accountability and management performance. These reforms include protection for "whistle-blowers," an anti-fraud and corruption policy, a unified standard of conduct for peacekeepers, and expanded financial disclosure requirements for senior officials. Still, with less money than the annual budget for New York City's police department, the UN will be challenged to serve the needs of the world's 6.7 billion people.

In the final analysis, the UN can be no more than the mandates and power that the member states give to it. The English poet Alfred Tennyson "dreamed of a parliament of man" and through the United Nations "we have now lived it," observes essayist Charles Krauthammer (2006, 39). Because of what realists would describe as the diverging interests and priorities of the great powers, he adds that the UN "has not worked. It never will." As one high-level UN civil servant, Brian Urquhart, described the organization's dilemma, "Either the UN is vital to a more stable and equitable world and should be given the means to do the job, or peoples and governments should be encouraged to look elsewhere. But is there really an alternative?" The United Nations may be much maligned, but according to liberals it is much needed. The organization may be "everybody's whipping boy," concludes Jonathan Power (2004), "but it is revealing how in a crisis the big powers can run to it . . . [when they] have talked or fought themselves into a corner."

Other Prominent Global IGOs

Beyond the UN, literally hundreds of other IGOs are active internationally. Less than 14 percent are truly global, including as members every independent state. To round out our examples of global IGOs, we look briefly at three of the most significant: the World Trade Organization, the World Bank, and the International Monetary Fund.

The World Trade Organization.   Remembering the hardships caused by the Great Depression of 1929, the United States sought to create international economic institutions after World War II that would prevent another depression by facilitating the expansion of world trade. One proposed institution was the International Trade Organization (ITO), first conceived as a specialized agency within the overall framework of the UN. While negotiations for the anticipated ITO were dragging on, many people urged immediate action. Meeting in Geneva in 1947, 23 states agreed to a number of **bilateral** tariff concessions that were written into a final act called the General Agreement on Tariffs and Trade (GATT), which originally was thought of as a temporary arrangement until the ITO came into operation.

bilateral relationships or agreements between two states.

When a final agreement on the ITO proved elusive, GATT provided a mechanism for continued multilateral negotiations on reducing tariffs and other barriers to trade. Over the next several decades, eight rounds of negotiations were held to liberalize trade. Under the principle of nondiscrimination, GATT members were to give the same treatment to each other as they gave to their "most favored" trading partner.

On January 1, 1995, GATT was superseded by the World Trade Organization (WTO). Although not exactly the ITO envisaged immediately following World War II, it nevertheless represented the most ambitious undertaking yet launched to regulate world trade. Unlike GATT, which functioned more as a coordinating secretariat, the World Trade Organization is a full-fledged intergovernmental organization with a formal decision-making structure at the ministerial level. Mandated to manage trade conflicts among members, the WTO was given authority for enforcing trading rules and adjudicating trade disputes among its 152 members. As of 2007, an average of almost thirty disputes per year have been brought to the WTO for resolution.

The present goal of the WTO is to transcend the existing matrix of free-trade agreements between pairs of countries and within particular regions or free-trade blocs, and replace them with an integrated and comprehensive worldwide system of liberal or free trade. This liberal agenda poses a threat to some states. At the heart of their complaint is the charge that the WTO undermines the traditional rule of law prohibiting interference in sovereign states' domestic

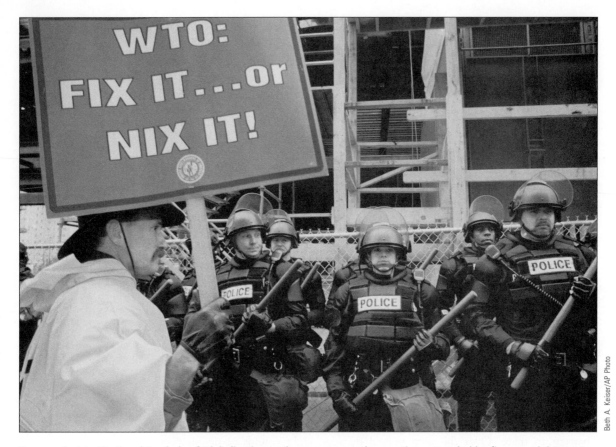

Beth A. Keiser/AP Photo

Rage against Institutional Symbols of Globalization In the recent past, the meetings attended by finance ministers at such powerful IGOs as the World Bank or the International Monetary Fund drew little interest or publicity. Now, with increasing criticism of the globalization of national economies, these meetings are convenient targets for protesters. Seen here is one recent outburst, when the meeting of the World Trade Organization mobilized a broad-based coalition of NGOs to criticize the impact of economic globalization.

affairs, including management of economic practices *within* the states' territorial jurisdiction. However, the WTO, it should be kept in mind, developed as a result of agreements states reached to voluntarily surrender some of their sovereign decision-making freedom, under the conviction that this pooling of sovereignty would produce greater gains than losses. Nonetheless, the WTO seems destined to remain a target for criticism because "there is little evidence of democracy within the WTO operations" (Smith and Moran 2001). Many of its policies are orchestrated by its most powerful members during informal meetings that do not include the full WTO membership.

The World Bank.   Created in July 1944 at the United Nations Monetary and Financial Conference held in Bretton Woods, New Hampshire, attended by forty-four countries, the World Bank (or International Bank for Reconstruction and Development) was originally established to support reconstruction efforts in Europe after the Second World War. Over the next decade, the Bank shifted its attention from reconstruction to developmental assistance. Because Global South countries often have difficulty borrowing money to finance projects aimed at promoting economic growth, the Bank offers them loans with lower interest rates and longer repayment plans than they could typically obtain from commercial banks. By 2008, the Bank had provided loans of more than $600 billion, making it "the largest and most influential antipoverty institution operating in developing countries" (Pound and Knight 2006, 41).

Administratively, ultimate decision-making authority in the World Bank is vested in a board of governors, consisting of a governor and an alternate appointed by each of the Bank's 185 member countries. A governor customarily is a member country's minister of finance, or an equivalent official. The board meets annually in the Bank's Washington, DC headquarters to set policy directions, and delegates responsibility for the routine operations of the Bank to the twenty-four directors of its executive board. The five countries with the largest number of shares in the World Bank's capital stock (the United States, Germany, Japan, France, and the United Kingdom) appoint their own executive directors, and the remaining executive directors are either appointed (Saudi Arabia), elected by their states (China, Russia, and Switzerland), or elected by groups of countries. Votes are tallied according to a weighted system that is intended to protect the interests of the great powers that make the most substantial contributions to the World Bank's resources. As a result, the president of the Bank has always been an American, and the United States together with Western Europe possesses majority control over the board of governors.

Over the years, both the self-image and operations of the World Bank have changed—from a strictly financial IGO passing judgment on loan applications to that of a development agency assisting states with planning and training. The World Bank also has promoted democratic governance, by its recent insistence on political reforms as a condition for economic assistance. Additionally, with charges of bribery, kickbacks, and embezzlement being leveled against World Bank projects from road building in Kenya to dam construction in Lesotho, the Bank has insisted on anticorruption reforms as well.

The Bank's president, Robert Zoellick, has set a goal of raising $33 billion to support development projects through mid-2011. However, the Bank has been criticized for focusing on middle-income countries, with just 7 percent of its lending going to states without investment-grade credit ratings and no access to private capital (*Economist*, September 8, 2007, 61; October 20, 2007, 97). Critics have called upon the Bank to focus its attention on the world's poorest countries, providing them with grants rather than loans.

Despite its increased pace of activity, the World Bank has never been able to meet all the needs for financial assistance of the developing states. The repayment of loans in hard currencies has imposed serious burdens on impoverished and indebted borrowing states from the Global South. The deficiencies of the World Bank, however, have been partly offset by the establishment of another lending IGO, the International Monetary Fund.

The International Monetary Fund.   Prior to World War II, the international community lacked institutional mechanisms to manage the exchange of money across borders. At the 1944 Bretton Woods Conference, the United States was a prime mover in creating the International Monetary Fund (IMF), a global institution designed to maintain currency-exchange stability by promoting international monetary cooperation and orderly exchange arrangements, and by functioning as a lender of last resort for countries experiencing financial crises.

The IMF is now one of the sixteen specialized agencies within the UN system. Each IMF member is represented on its governing board, which meets annually to fix general policy. Day-to-day business is conducted by a twenty-four-member executive board chaired by a managing director, who is also the administrative head of a staff of approximately 2,000 employees.

The IMF derives its operating funds from its 185 member states. Contributions are based on a quota system set according to a state's national income, monetary reserves, and other factors affecting each member's ability to contribute. In this way, the IMF operates like a credit union that requires each participant to contribute to a common pool of funds from which it can borrow when the need arises. The IMF's voting is weighted according to a state's monetary contribution, giving a larger voice to the wealthier states. Responding to criticism of this system, the organization's new director, Dominique Strauss-Kahn, has begun renegotiating the formula that allocates quotas for contributions and votes.

The IMF attaches strict conditions to its loans, which has led to considerable criticism. Some people charge that the IMF imposes austerity measures on countries in financial crises, forcing them to cut government spending on social programs when they are most needed. Others complain that the IMF makes political demands regarding democratization and privatization that exceed the institution's original mandate. Many theorists from radical branches of the socialist tradition argue that IMF conditions are tools for weakening domestic groups opposing the spread of international capitalism. IMF officials retort that they are simply trying to ensure that the problems that produced the crisis are remedied, so foreign investment can flow into the country.

REGIONAL INTERGOVERNMENTAL ORGANIZATIONS

The tug-of-war between states within global IGOs is a reminder that these organizations are run by the states that join them. This severely inhibits the IGOs' ability to rise above interstate competition and pursue their own purposes. Because they cannot act autonomously, universal IGOs are often viewed more as instruments of their state members' foreign policies and arenas for debate than as independent nonstate actors.

When certain states dominate universal international organizations like the UN, the prospects for international cooperation decline because, as realist theorists emphasize, national leaders fear multilateral organizations that may compromise their country's vital interests. Yet, as liberal theorists argue, *regional* cooperation among powerful states is possible, as evidenced by the evolution of the European Union (EU). In many respects the EU is unique, if for no other reason than that it stands as the world's greatest example of peaceful international cooperation producing an integrated **security community** with a single economy and a common currency.

security community
a group of states whose high level of noninstitutionalized collaboration results in the settlement of disputes by compromise rather than by force.

The European Union

Europe emerged from the Second World War a devastated continent with a demoralized population. Over 35 million Europeans perished during the fighting. Much of the urban landscape was reduced to bomb craters and rubble. Countless buildings were uninhabitable, the transportation infrastructure lay in ruins, and food was scarce. Some Europeans felt that the only way to prevent their countries from squaring off on the battlefield in a generation was through political and economic unification.

The process of European unification began with the creation of the European Coal and Steel Community (ECSC) in 1951. A year earlier, French Foreign Minister Robert Schuman had proposed placing all French and German coal and steel resources under a joint authority, and allowing other European states to take part in the new organization. As part of the ECSC, Germany could revive its heavy industry after the war without alarming its neighbors, who would now possess some degree of control over key German resources by virtue of their representation in the joint authority. Ultimately, France and Germany were joined in the ECSC by Belgium, Luxembourg, The Netherlands, and Italy.

The drive toward further European unity gathered momentum in 1957 with the creation of the European Atomic Energy Community (Euratom), patterned after the ECSC, and the European Economic Community (EEC), a fledgling common market providing for the free movement of goods, people, and capital among member states. These three communities were collectively recognized in the 1992 Maastricht Treaty as the first "pillar" of the EU structure. Two additional pillars have since been under construction: a Common Foreign and Security Policy pillar and a Justice and Homeland Affairs pillar. The former is an attempt to create a single European foreign and defense policy; the latter, common policies on immigration and criminal justice.

During this process of regional institution-building, membership grew in a series of waves to encompass twenty-seven countries: Belgium, France, Germany, Italy, Luxembourg, and the Netherlands (the original "six"); Denmark, Ireland, and the United Kingdom (which joined in 1973); Greece (1981); Portugal and Spain (1986); Austria, Finland, and Sweden (1995); Poland, the Czech Republic, Slovakia, Hungary, Slovenia, Latvia, Lithuania, Estonia, Malta, and Cyprus (2004); and Bulgaria and Romania (2007). These sequential enlargements have created the world's biggest free-trade bloc, with nearly half a billion citizens and an economy exceeding $13 trillion.

Further expansion is also conceivable, with the procedures for possible membership currently underway for Croatia and Turkey, and with various political leaders from countries in the western Balkans expressing interest in future membership. Expansion remains controversial, however. In particular, the prospect of a populous Muslim Turkey joining the EU raises fundamental questions about Europe's identity. As constructivists point out, identities shape how agents envision their interests and, in turn, how they act. The possible entry of Turkey and perhaps countries even farther afield would have major implications for the way many people, especially within the six western founders of the EU, conceive of Europe. Nevertheless, the idea of a single, integrated Europe is compelling for those who are haunted by the specter of European nationalities and states that have been fighting each other ever since the Pax Romana collapsed 1,800 years ago.

The enlargement of the European Union through eastward expansion has thus presented the organization with a host of troublesome questions, compounded by the fact that citizens in the members added since 2004 earn far less than people living elsewhere in the EU. These new members have different needs and interests that can make reaching agreement on policy decisions difficult. Some of the EU's original members, suffering from unemployment and sluggish economic growth, worry about competition from cheaper labor from the east and chafe over paying subsidies to these poorer but faster growing countries. Furthermore, because the new eastern members tended to support the American war in Iraq while the older western members, with the exception of Great Britain, generally opposed the invasion, some observers fear that the EU could fracture into two opposed coalitions, which would immeasurably complicate collective policy making.

The principal institutions for EU governance and policy making include the Council of the European Union, the European Commission, a European Parliament, a Court of Justice, and the European Central Bank. The EU's key policy making unit, the Council of the European Union (formerly, the Council of Ministers), consists of cabinet ministers drawn from the EU's member states, whose participation depends on the specific issue being considered. For example, agriculture ministers attend when farm policies are discussed; environmental ministers, when pollution control is on the agenda. Most decisions are made by a complex weighted system called "qualified majority voting," designed to give more votes to larger countries while simultaneously preventing them from dominating smaller ones. Highly sensitive issues, such as tax or security policy, require unanimity, however.

The council also sets general guidelines for the European Commission, which consists of twenty-seven commissioners, nominated by EU member governments and approved by the European Parliament. Headquartered in Brussels, the primary functions of the European Commission are to propose new laws for the EU, oversee EU treaties, and execute the decrees of the European Council. A professional staff of over 18,000 civil-service "Eurocrats" assist the commission in proposing legislation and implementing EU policies. It also manages the EU's budget, which, in contrast with most international organizations, derives part of its revenues from sources not under the control of member states.

The European Parliament represents the political parties and public opinion within Europe. It has existed from the beginning of Europe's journey toward political unification, although at its creation this legislative body was appointed rather than elected and had very little power. That is no longer the case. The European Parliament is now chosen in a direct election by the citizens of the EU's member states. Its 785 deputies debate issues at the monumental glass headquarters in Brussels and at a lavish Strasbourg palace in the same way that democratic national legislative bodies do. The European Parliament shares authority with the Council of the European Union, but the Parliament's influence has increased over time. The deputies elected through universal suffrage pass laws with the council, approve the EU's budget, oversee the European Commission, and can overturn its acts.

The European Court of Justice in Luxembourg has also grown in prominence and power as European integration has gathered depth and breadth. From the start, the court was given responsibility for adjudicating claims and conflicts among EU governments as well as between those governments and the new institutions the EU created. Comprising twenty-seven judges, the court interprets EU law for national courts, rules on legal questions that arise within the EU's institutions, and hears and rules on cases concerning individual citizens. The fact that its decisions are binding distinguishes the European Court of Justice from most other international tribunals.

Finally, the European Central Bank was established to manage the common monetary policy that emerged when the euro replaced the national currencies of twelve member states in 2002 (Slovenia joined the Euro zone in 2007, bringing the total to thirteen). Its responsibilities include setting interest rates and controlling the money supply. Having a common currency facilitates commerce by eliminating the transaction costs involved when one currency is converted to another. It also makes it easier to compare commodity prices in different countries. On the other hand, eliminating German marks, French francs, and other national currencies entails a loss of sovereignty to a supranational authority.

The political unification of Europe has been built step-by-step as the EU has marched toward ever greater unity. Moving beyond the nation-state toward a single integrated European federation has not been smooth, and disagreement persists over the extent to which the EU should become a single, truly united superstate, a "United States of Europe." Some people complain that the only democratically elected institution in the EU is the European Parliament. Debate continues also over how far and how fast such a process of **pooled sovereignty** should proceed, and about the natural geographical limits of the EU's membership and boundaries. These concerns are reflected in the difficulty implementing a European Constitutional Treaty. Following a set of general principles sketched out at a December 2001 leadership summit in Laeken, Belgium, representatives from EU countries drafted a document, which was approved in modified form by an Intergovernmental Conference in 2004, but required ratification by all member countries in order to go into effect. During the following year,

pooled sovereignty
legal authority granted to an IGO by its members to make collective decisions regarding specified aspects of public policy heretofore made exclusively by each sovereign government.

however, French and Dutch voters rejected the draft constitution. By 2007, EU leaders agreed on a new treaty but were dismayed when Irish voters rejected it in a June 2008 referendum.

Following the Irish referendum, pessimists groused that the EU's future was in limbo. Optimists proclaimed that the EU represented a remarkable success story in the history of international relations, one whose final chapter had yet to be written. A solution to the impasse, they predicted, would be found. Who, after all, would have expected competitive states, which have spent most of their national experiences waging war against one another, to put their clashing ambitions aside, and construct a new European identity built on confederated decision making?

Other Regional IGOs

Since Europe's move toward economic and political integration, more than a dozen regional IGOs have been created in various other parts of the world, notably among states in the Global South. Most seek to stimulate regional economic growth, but many have drifted from that original purpose to pursue multiple political and military purposes as well. The major regional IGOs include:

- The North Atlantic Treaty Organization (NATO), a military alliance created in 1949 primarily to deter the Soviet Union in Western Europe, has expanded its membership to twenty-six countries and broadened its mission to promote democratization and combat terrorism outside its traditional territory within Europe.

- The Council of Arab Economic Unity (CAEU), established in 1964 to promote trade and economic integration among its 10 members.

- The Association of Southeast Asian Nations (ASEAN), established in 1967 to promote regional economic, social, and cultural cooperation, created a free-trade zone among its ten members in 1999 and focuses today on political, economic, and environmental problems that beset the region.

- The Caribbean Community (CARICOM), established in 1973 as a common market to promote economic development among its fifteen country and territory members.

- The Economic Community of West African States (ECOWAS), established in 1975 to promote regional trade and economic cooperation among its fifteen members.

- The Latin American Integration Association (LAIA), established in 1980 to promote and regulate free trade among its twelve members.

- The South Asian Association for Regional Cooperation (SAARC), established in 1985 to promote economic, social, and cultural cooperation among its seven members.

- The Asia Pacific Economic Cooperation (APEC) forum, established in 1989 and with a current membership of twenty-one countries, plans to establish free and open trade in the region for developed countries by 2010 and for developing countries by 2020.

- The Southern African Development Community (SADC), established in 1992 to promote regional economic development among its fourteen members.

As these examples illustrate, most IGOs are organized on a regional rather than global basis. The governments creating them usually concentrate on one or two major goals instead of attempting to address at once the complete range of issues that they face in common. Africa illustrates this tendency, possessing a complex network of regional IGOs with multiple cross-cutting memberships. Some are large multipurpose groups such as the Economic Community of Western African States (ECOWAS) and the Southern African Development Community (SADC). Alongside these are many smaller organizations such as the Economic Community of the Great Lakes Countries, the Mano River Union, and the East African Community (EAC).

While it is hazardous to generalize about organizations so widely divergent in membership and purpose, we can say that none of the regional IGOs outside of Europe have managed to collaborate at a level that begins to match the institutionalized collective decision making achieved by the EU. The reasons vary, but in general these regional IGOs are limited by national leaders' reluctance to make politically costly choices that would undermine their personal popularity at home and their governments' sovereignty. The obstacles to creating new political communities out of previously divided ones are enormous; nonetheless, these attempts at regional cooperation demonstrate many states' acceptance of the fact that they cannot individually resolve many of the problems that confront them collectively.

IGOs are not the only nonstate actors on the world stage. Another set of agents are nongovernmental organizations (NGOs), such as ethnopolitical groups, religious movements, multinational corporations, transnational banks, and issue-advocacy groups. NGOs are growing in number and voice, making them increasingly influential in world politics. We now turn our attention to their behavior and impact.

NONGOVERNMENTAL ORGANIZATIONS

If you are like most people, there is at least one problem of concern to you that crosses national borders. You would like to see it resolved, but you probably realize that you cannot engineer global changes all by yourself. Recognizing that collective voices are more likely to be heard, many people have found that by joining nongovernmental organizations (NGOs) they can lobby more effectively for causes they support. NGOs are international actors whose members are not states, but instead are people drawn from the populations of two or more societies who have come together to promote their shared interests. There are almost 30,000 NGOs in existence worldwide, and they tackle global issues ranging from environmental protection to human rights. Most of them pursue objectives that are highly respected and constructive, and therefore do not arouse much opposition. For example, NGOs such as the International Chamber of Commerce, the Red Cross, Save the Children, and the World Wildlife Federation enjoy widespread popular support. Others, like Hezbollah, are more controversial.

What makes NGOs increasingly prominent on the world stage is that their activities are now shaping responses to issues that once were determined exclusively by governments. Greenpeace, Amnesty International, and other global issue-advocacy groups have used their technical expertise, organizational flexibility, and grassroots connections to affect every stage of the development of **international regimes**, from problem recognition through policy implementation. As constructivists point out, NGOs matter because of the power of ideas: They help set political agendas, promote normative change, and energize constituencies to support the policies they back. Their influence demonstrates that world politics is not merely the interaction of sovereign, territorial states. It also involves complex networks of people, who coalesce in myriad combinations at different times for various purposes.

As NGOs rise in numbers and influence, it is important to consider how they may transform world politics. Although NGOs comprise a large, heterogeneous group of nonstate actors, a small subset of them receive the most attention. Within this subset, NGOs based on ethnic identity are particularly noteworthy.

international regimes sets of principles, norms, rules, and decision-making procedures agreed to by a group of states to guide their behavior in particular issue-areas.

Ethnopolitical Movements

Although the state remains the most visible actor in world affairs, some people pledge their primary allegiance not to the government that rules them, but rather to an **ethnopolitical group**, whose members share a common nationality, language, cultural tradition, and kinship ties. They view themselves as members of their ethnic group first and of their state only secondarily. Many states are divided, multiethnic societies made up of a variety of politically active groups that seek, if not outright independence, a greater level of regional autonomy and a greater voice in the domestic and foreign policies of the state. "Nearly three quarters of the world's larger countries have politically significant minorities," and 284 minority groups comprising one-sixth of the world's population are at risk from persecution worldwide (Gurr 2001, 175). Some of these minorities, such as the Kurds in Iraq, Turkey, and Iran, spill across several countries. Thus, images of the state as a unitary actor and of governments as autonomous rulers of integrated nations are not very accurate. These ethnic divisions and the NGOs that often develop around them make thinking of international relations as exclusively interactions between homogeneous states with impermeable, hard-shell boundaries—the realist "billiard ball model"—dubious.

Indigenous peoples are the ethnic and cultural groups that were native to a geographic location now controlled by another state or political group. The world is populated by an estimated 6,800 separate indigenous nations, each of

ethnopolitical group people whose identity is primarily defined by their sense of sharing a common ancestral nationality, language, cultural heritage, and kinship ties.

indigenous peoples the native ethnic and cultural inhabitant populations within countries ruled by a government controlled by others, referred to as the "Fourth World."

which has a unique language and culture and strong, often spiritual, ties to an ancestral homeland. In most cases indigenous people were at one time politically sovereign and economically self-sufficient. As shown in Map 6.2, today an estimated 650 million indigenous people, or about one-tenth of the world's population, are scattered in more than seventy countries (Center for World Indigenous Studies, http://www.cwis.org, January 17, 2008).

Religious Movements

Religion is another force that can create identities and loyalties that transcend national boundaries. In theory, religion would seem a natural force for global harmony. Yet millions have died in the name of religion. The Crusades between the eleventh and fourteenth centuries left countless Christians and Muslims dead. Similarly, the religious conflicts during the Thirty Years' War (1618–1648) between Catholics and Protestants killed nearly one-fourth of all Europeans.

Many of the world's more than 6.7 billion people are affiliated in some form with a religious movement—a politically active organization based on strong religious convictions. At the most abstract level, a religion is a system of thought shared by a group that provides its members an object of devotion and a code of behavior by which they can ethically judge their actions. This definition points to commonalities across the great diversity of organized religions in the world, but it fails to capture that diversity. The world's principal religions vary greatly in the theological doctrines they embrace. They also differ widely in the size of their followings, in the geographical locations where they are most prevalent, and in the extent to which they engage in political efforts to influence international affairs.

These differences make it risky to generalize about the impact of religious movements on world affairs. Those who study religious movements comparatively note that a system of beliefs provides followers with their main source of identity, and that this identification with and devotion to their religion springs from the natural human need to find a set of values with which to evaluate the meaning of life. Unfortunately, this need sometimes leads believers to perceive the values of their own creed as superior to those of others. Members of many religious movements believe that their religion should be universal, and actively proselytize to convert nonbelievers to their faith. Although conversion is usually sought through persuasion, at times it has been achieved by the sword (see Controversy: Are Religious Movements Causes of War or Sources of Transnational Harmony?).

In evaluating the impact of religious movements, it is important to distinguish carefully the high ideals of doctrines from the activities of the people who head these religious bodies. The two realms are not the same, and each can be judged fairly only against the standards they set for themselves. To condemn what large-scale religious movements sometimes do when they abuse the principles of the religions they manage does not mean that the principles themselves deserve condemnation. Still, many observers maintain that otherwise humanitarian religions sometimes oppose each other violently, despite their professed doctrines of tolerance. When they do, religious movements become sources of international tension.

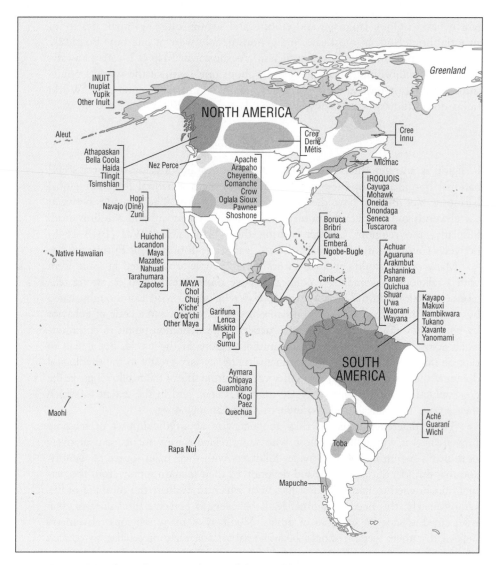

M A P 6.2 The Indigenous Cultures of the World

Indigenous peoples live in many countries. As the UN's Office of the High Commissioner for Human Rights has noted, "All over the world indigenous peoples are asserting their cultural identity, claiming their right to control their futures, and struggling to regain their ancestral lands." To protect their human rights, they have begun to organize, as can be seen in the 1992 World Conference of Indigenous Peoples held in Rio de Janeiro, Brazil. As a result of their lobbying, the UN named 1993 the International Year of the World's Indigenous Peoples.

NOTE: Colors indicate regional concentrations of indigenous peoples.

SOURCES: Julian Burger, United Nations. Adapted from "Vanishing Cultures" by Wade Davis, *National Geographic*, August 1999, pp. 66–67. NG Maps/NGS Image Collection.

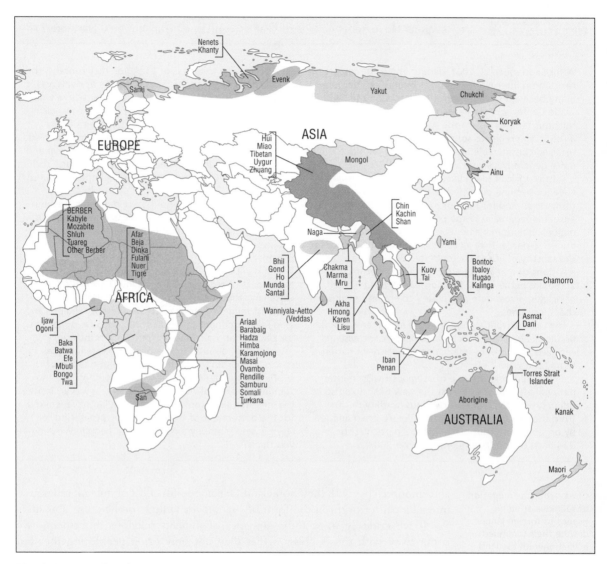

M A P 6.2 Continued

Along with ethnopolitical groups, militant religious movements may contribute to five types of transnational activities. The first is **irredentism**—the attempt by a dominant religion or ethnic group to reclaim previously possessed territory in an adjacent region from a foreign state that now controls it. The second is **secession**—the attempt by a religious (or ethnic) minority to break away from an internationally recognized state in a separatist revolt. Third, militant religions tend to incite migration, the departure of religious minorities from their countries of origin to escape persecution. Whether they move by force or by choice, the result—a fourth consequence of militant religion—is the same: The emigrants create **diasporas**, or communities that live abroad in host countries but maintain economic, political,

irredentism efforts by an ethnonational or religious group to regain control of territory by force so that existing state boundaries will no longer separate the group.

secession the attempt by a religious or ethnic minority to break away from an internationally recognized state.

CONTROVERSY Are Religious Movements Causes of War or Sources of Transnational Harmony?

After September 11, 2001, debate about the impact of religion on international conflict intensified, because many believed that the terrorist attacks on the World Trade Center and the Pentagon were motivated by religious fanatics within the Al Qaeda organization. As a result, the religious sources of political violence have received considerable attention, as have religious NGOs more generally (Haynes 2004).

It is difficult to understand the religious origins of violence because most people equate religion with compassion and forgiveness, not hatred and intolerance. Indeed, many of the principles that the world's major religious movements espouse would seem conducive to peace. They all voice respect and reverence for the sanctity of life and acceptance of all people as equal creations of a deity, regardless of race or ethnicity. These are noble ideals. Religions speak to universal principles, across time and place—to enduring values in changing times.

If all the world's great religious movements espouse pacific ideals, why are those same religions increasingly criticized as sources of international conflict—of hatred, terror, and war?

In evaluating the role of religious NGOs in international affairs, consider first the view of sociologists of religion who contend that religious hostility results from the fact that universalistic religions are managed by organizations that often adopt a particularistic and dogmatic outlook (see Juergensmeyer 2003).

Fundamentalist followers of a religion may conceive the world through a lens that sees outsiders as rivals and other creeds as challenges to their own faith. In a word, religious movements often practice intolerance—disrespect for diversity and the right of people to freely embrace another religion's beliefs. Sometimes the next step is for fanatics to portray these outsiders as evil and call for violence against them. "If you want war," sociologist William Graham Sumner once quipped, "nourish a doctrine."

Does this argument hold up under careful examination? Those who think it doesn't point out that societies recognizing no higher deity also have waged war against others. Meanwhile, many religions perform ably the mission of peace making.

It is important for you to weigh the evidence about the impact of religious NGOs on international affairs. Observing that many wars have been fought in the name of religion, some people argue that religion can be a serious danger to world order, because it may foster zealotry and a crusading spirit that transforms international disputes into prolonged wars for total stakes. Compromise, the mutual accommodation of conflicting claims, is difficult when disputants are the standard-bearers of rival faiths. Others, however, insist that the moral precepts in religious belief have worked for the betterment of world affairs by promoting fellowship and harmony among diverse people. What do you think?

---

diasporas the migration of religious or ethnic groups to foreign lands despite their continued affiliation with the land and customs of their origin.

and emotional ties with their homelands. Finally, a fifth effect of militant religions is international terrorism in the form of support for radical coreligionists abroad.

If we critically inspect the activities of militant religious movements, we come away with the impression that they not only bring people together but also divide them. Religious movements often challenge state authority, and religious-driven strife can tear countries apart.

Multinational Corporations and Transnational Banks

In an age of porous borders and growing interdependence, we need to look beyond ethnopolitical groups and religious movements to consider the roles of multinational corporations and transnational banks as nonstate actors, even though some people only apply the designation "NGO" to nonprofit organizations. **Multinational corporations (MNCs)** have grown dramatically in scope and influence since World War II. By one count, some 77,175 parent firms together own a total of 773,019 foreign affiliates and employ more than

multinational corporations (MNCs) business enterprises headquartered in one state that invest and operate extensively in other states.

95 million people (OECD 2007, 260–261). Wal-Mart exemplifies the impact that these giants have over global trade. With annual sales of more than $360 billion and 2 million employees, Wal-Mart attracts 100 million customers every week to its stores worldwide. According to recent statistics, the combined sales of the top 200 MNCs were the equivalent of 28 percent of the world's gross domestic product (Piasecki 2007, 9). The UN estimates that MNCs account for approximately two-thirds of the world's exports and one-third of the stock of all **foreign direct investment (FDI)**.

foreign direct investment (FDI) ownership of assets in a country by nonresidents in order to control the use of those assets.

In the past, MNCs were headquartered almost exclusively in the United States, Europe, and Japan, and their common practice was to make short-term investments in the Global South's plants, sales corporations, and mining operations. At the end of the twentieth century, about 80 percent of all MNCs' employees worked in developing countries, where wages were lower, to bolster corporate profits at the parent headquarters where key business functions remained. But no longer, aided by the spread of digital information technology, a growing number of companies are now shifting many of these headquarter functions away from their home offices, with nearly a quarter of them being relocated to the Global South (Hindle 2004, 97–98). For example, Thomson, a Canadian media company, has 97.8 percent of its assets, 96.6 percent of its sales, and 97.3 percent of its jobs outside of Canada. Other MNCs that rank almost as high include Roche and Nestlé, based in Switzerland, and Phillips, based in the Netherlands (*Economist*, October 20, 2007, 131).

Another new trend is the rise of MNCs from the Global South, which are investing in Global North countries as well as in the developing world. In 2006, 100 companies from Global South countries had total assets of $520 billion. Whereas in 1990 foreign direct investment from companies in these countries accounted for 5 percent of the world's total, by 2006 it had reached 14 percent. Brazil's Embraer, which specializes in regional jets, has become the world's third-largest aircraft company, with over 95 percent of its sales outside Brazil. Four-fifths of the revenues earned by Mexico's Cemex, one of the world's largest producers of ready-mixed concrete, comes from outside Mexico. Similarly, China's Hisense Electronic, and India's Tata Motors, have fanned out across the world (*Economist*, January 12, 2008, 62–64).

MNC expansion has been facilitated by **transnational banks (TNBs)**, another type of global NGO whose revenues and assets are primarily generated by financial transactions in the international economy. In 2006 the world's ten largest banks held a staggering $12.8 trillion in assets. Although the financial services industry was rocked the following year by the crisis in the sub-prime mortgage market, which resulted in losses and write-downs that reached $335 billion by early 2008 (*Economist*, May 17, 2008, 17), TNBs continue to funnel trade and help to reduce the meaning of political borders by making each state's economy dependent on other states' economies by transferring capital through international loans and investments. One feared consequence in the Global South is that the TNBs advance the rich Global North at the South's expense, because 87 percent of foreign direct investment flows into the richest countries with the poorest countries typically receiving very little (WDR 2007, 342). Like

transnational banks (TNBs) the world's top banking firms, whose financial activities are concentrated in transactions that cross state borders.

MNCs, TNBs spread the rewards of globalization unequally, increasing wealth for a select group of countries and marginalizing the others.

Through their loans to the private sector, TNBs have made capital highly mobile and expanded the capacity of MNCs to function as the primary agents in the globalization of production. MNCs have expanded in scope and size, fueled by a growing number of mergers and acquisitions that reached 465 deals totaling $2.7 trillion in the first half of 2007 (*Economist*, July 7, 2007, 94). Table 6.2 captures the importance of MNCs in world politics, ranking firms by annual sales and states by GNI. The profile shows that of the world's top 100 economic entities, multinationals account for only fourteen of the top fifty, but in the next fifty, they account for thirty-five. MNCs' financial clout thus rivals or exceeds that of most countries, with the result that many people worry that these corporate giants are undermining the ability of national governments to control their own economies and therefore their own fates.

Because of their financial strength and global reach, it is tempting to conclude that MNCs are a threat to state power. Their ability to make decisions on many issues over which national political leaders have little control appears to be eroding state sovereignty, the international system's major organizing principle. However, this interpretation overlooks the fact that at the same time MNCs have grown in size, the regulatory power of states has increased. Corporations must deal with governments on a host of matters, ranging from opening banks to establishing aviation routes.

Still, controlling intricate webs of corporate interrelationships, joint ventures, and shared ownership for any particular national purpose is nearly impossible. Part of the reason is that about 30 to 40 percent of world trade in goods and services occurs *within* multinationals, from one branch to another (Oatley 2008, 170). Joint production and **strategic corporate alliances** to create temporary phantom "virtual corporations" undermine states' ability to identify the MNCs they seek to control. "There is widespread concern that MNCs are becoming truly 'stateless' [as] the explosion of strategic alliances is transforming the corporate landscape" with more than 10,000 strategic alliances estimated to be forged each year recently (Stopford 2001, 74-75). This changing business environment is so dramatic, argues IBM CEO Samuel Palmisano, that the very term "multinational" no longer adequately describes the major companies of the twenty-first century. He prefers to call them "globally integrated enterprises" to reflect how "their many components, from back office to manufacturing to product development, . . . [are] dispersed around the planet in a vast network" (Pethokoukis 2006, 42). Roughly half of Xerox's employees, for example, "work on foreign soil, and less than half of Sony's employees are Japanese. More than 50 percent of IBM's revenues originate overseas; the same is true for Citigroup, ExxonMobil, DuPont, Procter & Gamble, and many other corporate giants" (Weidenbaum 2004, 26). The question raised by this blurring of the boundaries between foreign and domestic enterprise is how can any single state manage MNCs when no country can claim that any of them is "one of ours."

strategic corporate alliances cooperation between multinational corporations and foreign companies in the same industry, driven by the movement of MNC manufacturing overseas.

T A B L E 6.2   Countries and Corporations: A Ranking by Size of Economy and Revenues

Rank	County/Corporation	GNI/Revenues (Billions of Dollars)	Rank	County/Corporation	GNI/Revenues (Billions of Dollars)
1	United States	12,912.9	36	CHEVRON	200.6
2	Japan	4,976.5	37	Finland	196.9
3	Germany	2,835.6	38	Hong Kong	192.1
4	United Kingdom	2,272.7	39	DAIMLER-CHRYSLER	190.2
5	China	2,269.7	40	Portugal	181.3
6	France	2,169.2	41	Iran	177.3
7	Italy	1,772.9	42	Thailand	175.0
8	Spain	1,095.9	43	Argentina	173.1
9	Canada	1,052.6	44	CONOCO PHILLIPS	172.5
10	India	804.1	45	Ireland	171.1
11	South Korea	765.0	46	TOTAL	168.4
12	Mexico	753.4	47	GENERAL ELECTRIC	168.3
13	Australia	673.2	48	FORD MOTOR	160.1
14	Brazil	662.0	49	ING GROUP	158.3
15	Netherlands	642.0	50	CITIGROUP	146.8
16	Russia	638.1	51	AXA	139.7
17	Switzerland	411.4	52	VOLKSWAGEN	132.3
18	Belgium	378.7	53	SINOPEC	131.6
19	Sweden	369.1	54	Israel	128.7
20	WAL-MART STORES	351.2	55	CRÉDIT AGRICOLE	128.5
21	EXXON MOBIL	347.3	56	Venezuela	128.1
22	Turkey	342.0	57	Malaysia	125.9
23	ROYAL DUTCH/SHELL	318.8	58	ALLIANZ	125.5
24	Austria	306.2	59	FORTIS	121.2
25	Saudi Arabia	289.2	60	Singapore	119.8
26	Indonesia	282.2	61	BANK OF AMERICA	117.0
27	Norway	281.5	62	HSBC HOLDINGS	115.4
28	BRITISH PETROLEUM	274.4	63	Czech Republic	114.8
29	Poland	273.1	64	AMERICAN INTERNATIONAL GROUP	113.2
30	Denmark	261.8	65	CHINA NATIONAL PETROLEUM	110.5
31	South Africa	223.5	66	BNP PARIBAS	109.2
32	Philippines	223.1	67	ENI	109.0
33	Greece	220.3	68	UBS	107.3
34	GENERAL MOTORS	207.4	69	Pakistan	107.3
35	TOYOTA MOTOR	204.8	70	SIEMENS	107.3

TABLE 1.2   Countries and Corporations: A Ranking by Size of Economy and Revenues (Continued)

Rank	County/Corporation	GNI/Revenues (Billions of Dollars)	Rank	County/Corporation	GNI/Revenues (Billions of Dollars)
71	STATE GRID	107.2	86	VERIZON COMMUNICATIONS	93.2
72	New Zealand	106.3	87	NIPPON TELEGRAPH & TELEPHONE	92.0
73	Colombia	104.5	88	HEWLETT-PACKARD	91.7
74	United Arab Emirates	103.5	89	IBM	91.4
75	ASSICURAZIONI GENERALI	101.8	90	VALERO ENERGY	91.1
76	Hungary	101.6	91	HOME DEPOT	90.8
77	J.P. MORGAN CHASE	100.0	92	Egypt	90.1
78	CARREFOUR	99.0	93	Algeria	89.6
79	BERKSHIRE HATHAWAY	98.6	94	NISSAN MOTOR	89.5
80	PEMEX	97.5	95	SAMSUNG ELECTRONICS	89.5
81	DEUTSCHE BANK	96.2	96	CREDIT SUISSE	89.4
82	DEXIA GROUP	95.8	97	HITACHI	87.6
83	Chile	95.7	98	Romania	84.6
84	HONDA MOTOR	94.8	99	SOCIÉTÉ GÉNÉRALE	84.5
85	MCKESSON	93.6	100	AVIVA	83.5

By integrating production and marketing their products worldwide, MNCs are dominating the global economy. As a result, MNCs rival many countries in wealth, which they are translating into political influence.

SOURCES: MNC revenues, *Fortune* (July 23, 2007), pp. 133–140; countries' gross national income (GNI), WDI (2007, 14–16).

Issue-Advocacy Groups and Global Civil Society

A final type of NGO that we will examine is composed of associational interest groups organized around special policy interests, such as environmental protection or upholding human rights. Greenpeace, for example, focuses much of its attention on preventing pollution and maintaining biodiversity through education programs, lobbying, and nonviolent protest demonstrations. Boasting a worldwide membership of 2.8 million and offices in forty countries, Greenpeace has a total income of over $200 million, derived largely from individual donations and foundation grants. Included among what it claims as its successes are international prohibitions on large-scale driftnet fishing, dumping of radioactive wastes at sea, and mining in Antarctica.

Issue-oriented NGOs like Greenpeace flourish when governments permit freedom of expression and association, and thus have increased exponentially as the number of democracies worldwide has risen over the past two decades. Their increase has led some scholars to observe that NGOs are empowering ordinary people, giving them a voice and a means of political leverage. In effect, the proliferation of NGOs is "creating an incipient, albeit imperfect, civil society at the global level" (Keohane and Nye 2001a).

However, not everyone believes that we are witnessing the formation of a global civil society. Skeptics claim that "NGOs have tended to reinforce rather than counter existing power structures, having members and headquarters that are primarily in the rich Global North countries. Some also believe that NGO decision making does not provide for responsible, democratic representation or accountability" (Stephenson 2000). According to this account, world politics is still controlled by states—especially the great powers.

How influential and effective are grassroots NGOs? Research on this question suggests the following conclusions, which reduce confidence in the expectation that pressure from NGOs can lead to far-reaching reforms in the conduct of international relations:

- Interest group activity operates as an ever-present, if limited, constraint on global policy making, but the impact varies with the issue.

- As a general rule, NGOs are relatively weak in the high politics of international security, because states remain in control of defense policy. Conversely, the NGOs' clout is highest with respect to issues in low politics, such as protecting endangered species or combating climate change.

- The influence between states and NGOs is reciprocal, but it is more probable that government officials exercise somewhat greater influence over transnational interest groups. When NGO interests parallel those of states, government officials often channel funds through NGOs in order to allow them to bring their expertise to bear on a given policy problem.

- Single-issue NGO interest groups have more influence than large general-purpose organizations.

- NGOs sometimes seek inaction from governments and maintenance of the status quo; such efforts are generally more successful than efforts to bring about major changes in international relations.

To sum up, the mere presence of NGOs, and the mere fact they are organized with the intent of persuasion, does not guarantee their penetration of the global policy-making process. On the whole, NGOs have participation without real power and involvement without real influence, given that most have limited economic resources and the ability of any *one* to exert influence is offset by the tendency for countervailing powers to materialize over the disposition of major issues. That is, as any particular coalition of NGOs combine in a caucus to work together on a common cause, other groups threatened by the changes advocated spring up to balance it. When an interest group seeks vigorously to push policy in one direction, other NGOs—aroused that their interests are being disturbed—are stimulated to push policy in the opposite direction. Global policy making consequently resembles a taffy pull: Every NGO attempts to yank policy in its own direction, with the result that movement on many global problems fails to proceed consistently in any single direction.

This balance between opposing actors helps to account for the reason why so few global issues are resolved. Competition stands in the way of consensus, and contests of will over international issues are seldom settled. No side can ever claim permanent victory, for each decision that takes international policy in one direction merely sets the stage for the next round of the contest, with the possibility that the losers of the moment will be winners tomorrow. The struggle between those wishing to make protection of the environment a global priority and those placing economic growth ahead of environmental preservation provides one among many examples.

NONSTATE ACTORS AND THE GLOBAL FUTURE

Political realists generally discount IGOs and NGOs as important actors on the global stage. From their perspective, some of these organizations simply serve the interests of states, whereas others are marginal players in the drama of world politics. Liberals and constructivists disagree. They believe that as people, products, and information increasingly move across the planet, IGOs and NGOs will play ever-larger roles in the world, multiplying channels of access to international affairs for concerned citizens everywhere. More than at any time since the Peace of Westphalia in 1648, nonstate actors are challenging sovereign, territorial states in the management of international affairs (Keck and Sikkink 2004; Alesina and Spolaore 2003). Not only are they challenged from above by multinational corporations, transnational banks, and global economic IGOs, but they are also being challenged from below by the grassroots NGOs of an emerging global civil society (see Application: Mixed-Actor Approaches to Global Diplomacy).

APPLICATION   **Mixed-Actor Approaches to Global Diplomacy**

World politics is increasingly shaped by advocacy groups whose influence transcends national boundaries. Many of these NGOs interact with IGOs and attend conferences to which states send representatives (Tarrow 2006). A prominent example can be seen in the diplomatic process that led to a 1997 treaty banning antipersonnel landmines, which was signed by 155 countries. Lloyd Axworthy, Canada's foreign minister from 1996 to 2000, sees that process as an alternative to the traditional "top down," great power approach to diplomacy. Called the "Ottowa Process" because the key meetings occurred in the Canadian capital, it involved a close working relationship among officials from like-minded middle powers, IGOs, and NGOs. Below Axworthy describes its origins at a 1996 meeting attended by representatives from over seventy countries, UN officials, and a large delegation of NGOs. Many attendees were frustrated by the insistence of the great powers that future discussions of landmines be confined to established channels, which would allow

them to control the pace of negotiations and exclude NGOs.

> As the conference began to wind down, I assembled a group of senior officials and staff . . . . The next afternoon was to be the wrap-up to the meeting and I was scheduled to give the benediction. What should I say?
>
> It was then that a senior official—Paul Heinbecker, then the new Canadian Assistant Deputy Minister for Global Affairs—mentioned . . . the possibility of short-circuiting the conventional process and setting up a separate track leading to a treaty banning landmines.
>
> . . . There was no one else to pass the decision to. I said, "It's the right thing. Let's do it." As the Saturday session drew to a close, with delegates voting on a declaration and an action plan, I waited in the wings to deliver the closing remarks with more than a twinge of nervousness. I knew I

would be committing Canada to a course of action that defied diplomatic niceties and procedures and challenged the positions of the permanent members of the Security Council.

...[At the podium] I went through the normal list of thank-yous and words of appreciation, and then concluded: "The challenge is to see a treaty signed no later than the end of 1997 . . . . I then issued an invitation for all the delegates (and their friends) to come to Ottawa a year hence to sign the treaty.

The reaction in the hall was a mixture of surprise, applause, and incredulity. The NGO contingents rose to their feet, the representatives of many governments sat in their seats, too stunned to react, several barely suppressing their anger and opposition.

...[We] had just stepped out of the accustomed protocol of diplomatic deference to the powerful, and launched forth on an uncharted course of action (Axworthy 2008, 237–238).

Established diplomatic channels, argues Axworthy, were a recipe for stalemate, because some of the great powers were reluctant to forego controlling the negotiations. The "bottom up" mixed-actor approach pioneered through the Ottawa Process enabled a coordinated network of NGOs and sympathetic officials from IGOs and middle-power countries to create an alternative to the state-centric way of conducting diplomacy.

After three and a half centuries, it is sometimes difficult to think about world politics as involving anything beyond the interaction of sovereign, territorial nation-states. Yet in a world characterized by ever-increasing ties among individuals and organizations who see territorial boundaries as anachronisms, nation-states are not the Leviathans described by the seventeenth-century philosopher Thomas Hobbes. Rather than being autonomous entities, they are enmeshed with nonstate actors in complex webs that obscure the distinction between foreign and domestic affairs. If the traditional Westphalian worldview could be symbolized by a static two-dimensional map depicting discrete territorial states on a grid of longitude and latitude, then a post-Westphalian worldview might be represented by a dynamic holographic projection of a vast, multilayered network linking states with many other types of actors.

To sum up, IGOs and NGOs are changing the face of international affairs as they seek to reshape the global agenda. The question for the twenty-first century is whether the nation-state system as we know it will survive. States cannot insulate their populations from "the flow of images and ideas that shape human tastes and values. The globalized 'presence' of Madonna, McDonald's, and Mickey Mouse make a mockery of sovereignty as exclusive territorial control" (Falk 2001). Of course, this does not mean that the era of state dominance is over. States retain a (near) monopoly on the use of coercive force in the world, and they mold the activities of nonstate actors more than their behavior is molded by them. It is also true that increases in political influence by nonstate actors do not necessarily translate into reductions in state power (see Paul, Ikenberry, and Hall 2003; Slaughter 1997). Nevertheless, we must conclude that whereas it would be premature to abandon the focus on the state in world politics, it would be equally mistaken to exaggerate the state's power as a determinant of the world's fate and dismiss the expanding role of nonstate actors in shaping the global future.

CHAPTER SUMMARY

- Despite states having an enormous capacity to influence national and global welfare, the state is ill-suited for managing many transnational policy problems; consequently no analysis of world politics would be complete without a treatment of the role played by nonstate actors.

- There are two principle types of nonstate actors in world politics, intergovernmental organizations (IGOs) and nongovernmental organizations (NGOs). Even though the vast majority of nonstate actors are NGOs, IGOs generally wield more influence because their members are states.

- Most IGOs engage in a comparatively narrow range of activities. Given its global membership and purposes, the United Nations (UN) differs from other IGOs. Because the UN is a mirror of world politics, not an alternative to it, the UN reflects the forces outside the organization that have animated world politics since the end of World War II.

- Although the European Union (EU) has some supranational elements, the term *pooled sovereignty* captures its essence, because states remain paramount in its institutional structures and decision-making processes. Regional IGOs outside of Europe have not approached the same level of institution building because of the reluctance of national leaders to make political choices that would undermine their state's sovereignty.

- Many people do not pledge their primary allegiance to the state. Rather, they think of themselves primarily as members of an ethnic nation group and the cultural values it represents. Ethnopolitical groups based on these feelings are among the most important NGOs in contemporary world politics.

- As a force in world politics, religious movements not only bring people together but also divide them. While not all extremist religious NGOs are alike, many of them incite irredentist claims, separatist revolts, migration, and political violence.

- Since World War II, MNCs have grown dramatically in scope and power. To some observers, this growth has undermined the ability of sovereign states to control their own economies; to others, this growth is helping to create a more prosperous world.

- Issue-advocacy NGOs have become influential in the fields of economic development, human rights, and the environment. Although some people see these groups as rabble-rousers, others contend that they provide an avenue for citizens of different countries who have shared interests to associate with one another, lobby collectively, and exert leverage over state policies. Moreover, they believe that these kinds of interactions are creating a rudimentary global civil society.

- The dramatic growth of nonstate actors challenges the traditional state-centric view of world politics. Although some nonstate actors are capable of advancing their interests largely outside the direct control of states, the state still molds the activities of nonstate actors more than its behavior is molded by them.

KEY TERMS

bilateral

diasporas

ethnopolitical group

foreign direct
    investment (FDI)

Group of 77 (G-77)

indigenous peoples

intergovernmental
    organizations (IGOs)

international regimes

irredentism

multinational
    corporations (MNCs)

nongovernmental
    organizations (NGOs)

pooled sovereignty

secession

security community

strategic corporate
    alliances

transnational banks
    (TNBs)

SUGGESTED READINGS

Hurd, Ian. *After Anarchy: Legitimacy and Power in the United Nations Security Council.* Princeton: Princeton University Press, 2007.

Joachim, Jutta M. *Agenda Setting, the UN and NGOs.* Washington, DC: Georgetown University Press, 2007.

Kennedy, Paul. *The Parliament of Man: The Past, Present, and Future of the United Nations.* New York: Random House, 2006.

Puchala, Donald J., Katie Verlin Laatikainen, and Roger A. Coate. *United Nations Politics: International Organizations in a Divided World.* Upper Saddle River, NJ: Prentice-Hall, 2006.

Woods, Ngaire. *The Globalizers: The IMF, the World Bank and Their Borrowers.* Ithaca: Cornell University Press, 2006.

CRITICAL THINKING QUESTIONS

Is it time to replace the global intergovernmental organizations that were established at the end of World War II? Are they too old to meet the challenges of a rapidly changing world? Recently, several people have called for the creation of a "League of Democracies" (see Carothers 2008). By most accounts, it would be an exclusive club, composed of countries with democratic political systems. One school of thought proposes that such an organization would focus on security, leaving issues of health, development, and the like to a truncated United Nations. A second school would eliminate the UN and have the democratic league absorb its main features. What do you think? Is a League of Democracies a viable alternative to the UN? Would its smaller size, shared values, and political commonalities make it more effective than the UN in addressing global security problems? How would it fare in dealing with global health, economic development, or environmental problems? What organizational difficulties might arise when designing its charter?

PART III

The Politics of Global Security

The threat of violence casts a dark cloud over much of the world. Many people live in fear of terrorist attacks, invasion by neighboring states, or repression by their own government, bent on persecuting its citizens because of their ethnicity or religion. Even though the Cold War is long over, global security remains precarious. Millions of people are the victims of aggression, and millions more have had to flee their homelands to seek sanctuary from the ravages of war.

Part III of *The Global Future* examines the quest for security in the twenty-first century. Chapter 7 begins our examination by looking at trends in the incidence of armed conflict since the birth of the modern world system. In addition to analyzing what scholars and policy makers believe are the major causes of interstate and intrastate war, it traces the evolution of political terrorism into a worldwide threat. Chapter 8 addresses the national security strategies national leaders use to cope with the dangers posed by rival states and global terrorists. Finally, in the last two chapters of Part III, we consider the alternative paths to peace prescribed by the realist theoretical tradition and its liberal and constructivist critics. Whereas Chapter 9 assesses the use of military alliances to prevent war by creating a balance of power among rival states, Chapter 10 evaluates the use of international law, organization, and integration.

7

Armed Conflict in the Twenty-First Century

CHAPTER OUTLINE

Trends in Armed Conflict

What Causes Armed Conflict?

The First Level of Analysis: Human Nature

APPLICATION: When Is It Worth Going To War?

The Second Level of Analysis: Internal Characteristics of States

CONTROVERSY: Does Nationalistic Love of Country Cause War with Foreign Nations?

The Third Level of Analysis: System Structure and Processes

The Future of Armed Conflict

The New Global Terrorism

Counterterrorism

> War is a matter of vital importance to the state: the province of life or death; the road to survival or ruin.
>
> SUN TZU
>
> ANCIENT CHINESE MILITARY STRATEGIST

On July 8, 2008, a combined United Nations and African Union peacekeeping force was ambushed while on patrol sixty miles east of Al Fāshir in the Sudanese province of Darfur. Approximately 200 heavily armed men in trucks and on horseback attacked the peacekeepers, killing seven and wounding twenty-two in a battle that raged for over two hours.

The peacekeeping force had been deployed to protect civilians from a series of complex, overlapping armed conflicts involving the central government in

Khartoum, neighboring countries, and a galaxy of rival militias. In the words of a Western aid official, Sudan "is just a free-for-all. Security simply doesn't exist" (*International Herald Tribune*, July 10, 2008, http://www.iht.com). The UN estimates that between 2003 and 2008, roughly 300,000 people have died in Darfur due to political violence, starvation, and disease, and another 2.7 million have fled to refugee camps. According to one respected African diplomat, if the fighting in Sudan escalates, "it will unlock the gates of hell" (cited in Natsios 2008, 81).

Preventing Sudan from collapsing into chaos is complicated by the multidimensional nature of the conflict. One dimension is a long-standing dispute between the politically dominant Arab Muslims living in the northern Nile River valley and the more numerous non-Arab Christians and animists residing in the south. Hostilities between the two sides were temporarily extinguished by a 1972 peace agreement but reignited eleven years later, resulting in bitter fighting that claimed the lives of 2.5 million southerners and displaced 4.6 million people. After slow, painstaking negotiations, a new peace agreement was reached in 2005, based on a political power-sharing arrangement between the Arab National Congress Party (NCP) and the southern rebel group, the Sudan People's Liberation Movement (SPLM). Additionally, a semi-autonomous Government of Southern Sudan was established for six years, after which a referendum would be held to determine whether the south would secede. Despite this agreement, relations between the NCP and SPLM remain strained over the status of Abyei, an area rich in petroleum resources that each side covets.

A second dimension of the political violence plaguing Sudan is an armed conflict between the Arab-dominated central government and black, non–Arab Muslim rebels in the western region of Darfur, who seek a power-sharing agreement with Khartoum similar to the one obtained by the SPLM. In 2003, against the backdrop of growing tensions over water and grazing rights between the region's Arab herdsmen and black African subsistence farmers, two rebel groups, the Sudanese Liberation Army (SLA) and the Justice and Equality Movement (JEM), began attacking government offices and military outposts. Khartoum responded with a brutal campaign against the African population, orchestrated by the Sudanese military and the pro-government Janjaweed militia. Over the next five years, some 2,700 villages were destroyed, leading to charges of genocide being brought against President Omar al-Bashir by the chief prosecutor of the International Criminal Court. Meanwhile, Darfur's rebel groups have splintered into over twenty competing factions, further complicating efforts to bring the fighting to a halt.

The third dimension of the ongoing violence is a proxy war pitting Sudan against Chad. Friction between these neighboring countries has increased in recent years as refugees from Darfur began pouring across the border into

Chad, with the Janjaweed militia on their heels. Relations deteriorated rapidly in early 2008 when the Sudanese government backed Chadian guerrillas who assaulted N'Djamena, Chad's capital, in the hope of toppling President Idriss Déby, whose Zaghawa tribe has links to leaders of some Darfur rebel groups. Chad retaliated three months later by supporting a JEM offensive that reached the outskirts of Khartoum. Sudanese troops, in turn, attacked a Chadian border garrison at Ade, raising fears that the cold war between the two countries could escalate to a military showdown.

Finally, the last dimension of political violence in Sudan concerns the possible erosion of a 2006 peace accord between the central government and the Beja and Rashida peoples in the east. Backed by the neighboring country of Eritrea, a rebel group known as the Eastern Front has engaged in sporadic skirmishing with government troops. Concerned by the multifaceted problems facing Khartoum, British diplomat Mark Malloch-Brown cautioned that Sudan could be on the verge of "a dangerous tipping point where the country goes into a freefall" (*International Herald Tribune*, June 30, 2008, http://www.iht.com). Indeed, by one estimate, Sudan ranks second worldwide in vulnerability to state collapse ("Failed State Index" 2008, 67).

In international relations, conflict regularly occurs when actors on the world stage have disputes that arise out of incompatible interests. However, the costs can become staggering when disputants take up arms to settle their differences. Most people conceive of armed conflict as conventional war—sustained fighting between the regular military units of sovereign states undertaken to coerce adversaries into submission. But as the fighting in Sudan illustrates, this conception is too narrow. The belligerents may include a kaleidoscope of state and non-state actors that wage war through both conventional and unconventional means. This chapter explores the challenge these multidimensional armed conflicts pose in world politics, examining their trends, causes, and changing form since the end of the Second World War.

TRENDS IN ARMED CONFLICT

Throughout history, war has caused untold human misery. By one account, in the past 3,400 years, "humans have been entirely at peace for 268 of them, or just eight percent of recorded history" (Hedges 2003). Social scientists have attempted to measure the frequency of military conflict in an effort to ascertain if the level of international violence has been increasing, decreasing, or holding steady over time. Figure 7.1 charts the number of armed conflicts globally from two perspectives: The first looks at changes by decade since 1400; the second takes a closer look at the years since 1950 by examining the annual number of

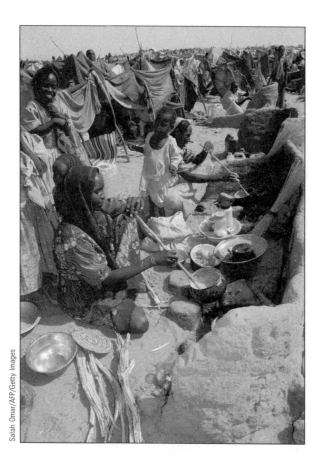

Salah Omar/AFP/Getty Images

Refugees in Search of Sanctuary Since 2003, the Janjaweed, a paramilitary group supported by the Sudanese government, has attacked the country's non-Arab population in the Darfur region. Shown here is the Kalma refugee camp filled with 150,000 people from Darfur.

armed conflicts underway. These trends reveal that the frequency of military conflict has risen significantly during the last 300 years, with the twentieth century being extraordinarily violent.

Several patterns in the incidence of armed conflict have emerged since the end of World War II with implications for the global future. A total of 231 armed conflicts occurred between 1946 and 2005. Although the average death-tolls have declined over the past twenty years, the proportion of states involved is larger now than in any other time during the past six decades (Hewitt, Wilkenfeld, and Gurr 2008). As 2007 began, there were thirty-two armed conflicts underway in twenty-three locations throughout the world (Harbom and Wallensteen 2007, 632). Behind these frequency counts are the following general trends:

- The proportion of countries throughout the world engaged in **interstate wars** has declined in recent years.

- In particular, wars between the great powers have decreased; since 1945 the world has experienced a long peace—the most prolonged period in modern history in which no wars occurred between the most powerful countries.

interstate war sustained armed conflict between two or more sovereign states.

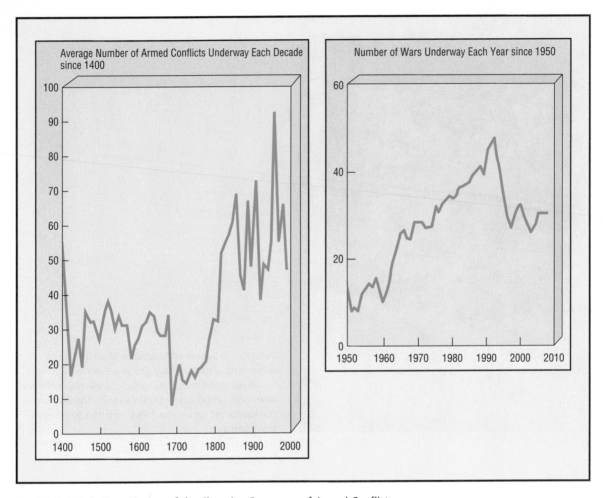

FIGURE 7.1 Two Pictures of the Changing Frequency of Armed Conflicts

Armed conflict between states has been around for as long as sovereign states have existed, as the trend on the left inventorying 2,566 individual wars for each decade since the year 1400 indicates. The figure on the right captures the ebb and flow of active armed conflicts each year since 1950. Most of these conflicts have occurred in the Global South, with three-fourths being civil wars.

SOURCES: Left: Adapted from "The Characteristics of Violent Conflict since 1400 A.D." by Peter Brecke. Used with permission. Right: University of Hamburg, presented in *Vital Signs 2006–2007*, p. 83; Harbom and Wallensteen (2007, 62).

> **civil war** armed conflict within a country between the central government and one or more insurgent groups, sometimes referred to as internal war.

- Most armed conflicts now occur in the Global South, which is home to the highest number of states, with the largest populations, the least income, and the least stable governments.

- The majority of these armed conflicts are **civil wars** within countries.

These trends, together with the wars in Afghanistan and Iraq, hint that the character of armed conflict is changing. In the past, when people thought about armed conflicts, they focused on wars between states and only secondarily on civil wars within states. Now military planners expect to face a more complex security environment that includes **internationalized civil wars**. Between 1989 and 2008, 94 percent of all 122 active armed conflicts world wide were civil wars, with almost a third involving military intervention by outside powers (Harbom and Wallersteen 2007, 624; SIPRI 2007, 79).

internationalized civil war an armed conflict between the central government of a country and insurgents with outside intervention by at least one other state in support of the insurgents.

Further complicating matters, old security threats have reappeared in new form. Pirates armed with assault rifles and rocket-propelled grenades have used high-speed motorboats to attack commercial vessels in some of the world's major shipping lanes. With insufficient resources to patrol their coastal waters, African countries such as Somalia, Tanzania, and Nigeria have been unable to stop pirates from hijacking ships and kidnapping the crews for ransom. According to the International Maritime Bureau, over the past decade 3,200 seafarers have been kidnapped, 500 injured, and 160 killed worldwide in pirate attacks (*New York Times*, April 20, 2008, 12). Worried about these kinds of unconventional security threats, some countries and companies have turned for help to mercenaries and private contractors to conduct operations that regular military units would have carried out in the past (Kibbe 2004).

Trends such as these raise several questions about the nature of contemporary war. Why do certain states and nonstate actors resort to violence? What causal factors increase the probability of armed conflict? Do they interact with one another in a dynamic sequence of steps that unfold over time? To seek answers, let's examine a few of the most common theories about the sources from which wars originate.

WHAT CAUSES ARMED CONFLICT?

Throughout history, efforts have been made to explain why people engage in organized violence. Inventories of war's origins (see Cashman 2000; Midlarsky 2000; Vasquez 2000; Geller and Singer 1998) generally agree that hostilities are rooted in multiple sources found at various levels of analysis. Some are proximate causes that directly influence the odds of war; others are remote and indirect, creating explosive background conditions that enable any one of a number of more immediate factors to trigger violence. The most commonly cited sources of war can be classified into three broad categories: (1) aggressive traits found in the human species; (2) pernicious national attributes that beget conflict-prone states; and (3) unstable structures and volatile processes within the international system that encourage disputes to become militarized.

The First Level of Analysis: Human Nature

In a sense, all wars between states originate from the decisions of national leaders, whose choices ultimately determine whether armed conflict will occur (see Chapter 3). We must therefore begin looking for the causes of war at the individual level of analysis, where questions about human nature are central.

The repeated outbreak of war has led some, such as psychologist Sigmund Freud (1968), to conclude that aggression is an instinctive part of human nature that stems from humans' genetic programming and psychological makeup. Identifying *Homo sapiens* as the deadliest species, ethologists (those who study animal behavior in order to understand human behavior) such as Konrad Lorenz (1963) similarly argue that humankind is one of the few species practicing intraspecific aggression (routine killing of its own kind), in comparison with most other species, which practice interspecific aggression (killing only other species, except in the most unusual circumstances—cannibalism in certain tropical fishes being one exception). Robert Ardrey (1966) proposes a "territorial imperative" to account for intraspecific violence: Like most animals, humans instinctively defend territory they believe belongs to them. Ethologists are joined in their interpretation by those political realists who assume that the drive for power is innate and cannot be eliminated. Some of them even apply Charles Darwin's ideas about evolution to world politics. For these so-called "social" Darwinists, international life is a struggle for survival of the fittest, where natural selection eliminates traits that interfere with successful competition.

Many scholars question these views on both empirical and logical grounds. If aggression is a deep-seated drive emanating from human nature, then shouldn't all people exhibit this behavior? Most people, of course, do not; they reject killing as evil and neither murder nor excuse homicide committed by others. At some fundamental level, argues Francis Fukuyama (1999; see also Gazzaniga 2005), human beings are built for consensus, not for conflict: "People feel intensely uncomfortable if they live in a society that doesn't have moral rules." Even accepting natural selection as an explanation of human evolution need not lead to the conclusion that aggression is ordained by hereditary. As James Q. Wilson (1993) argues, "the moral sense must have adaptive value; if it did not, natural selection would have worked against people who had such useless traits as sympathy, self-control, or a desire for fairness in favor of those with the opposite tendencies."

Most social scientists now strongly disagree with the premise that humans fight wars because of innate genetic drives. Although conflict among humans is ubiquitous, a compelling body of anthropological evidence indicates that various societies have avoided outright warfare. Some, like the Semi of the Central Malay Peninsula have accomplished this through internalized psychological restraints; others, like the Mehinaku of the Xingu River in Brazil, have done it through external sociocultural constraints (Gregor and Robarcheck 1996). For these reasons, the 1986 *Seville Statement,* endorsed by more than a dozen professional scholarly associations, maintains that "it is scientifically incorrect" to say that "we have inherited a tendency to make war from our animal ancestors," or that war is "genetically programmed into our human nature."

If the origins of war do not lie in elemental instincts, are there other factors at the individual level of analysis that may increase the probability of disputes escalating to war? In Chapter 3, we saw how the idiosyncrasies, perceptions, and beliefs of political leaders can, on occasion, impair rational decision making, which may lead to hard-line behavior even when political differences between rivals are bridgeable. To be sure, some military conflicts are consciously sought by their initiators. But this does not mean that war is a product of violent instincts deeply engrained within the human species. On the contrary, the origins of many wars are traceable to certain psychological processes experienced by specific leaders at certain points in time. Under stress, for example, leaders are more sensitive to the hostile acts they perceive. In a crisis atmosphere they tend to draw superficial lessons from the immediate past, inflating the meaning of recent successes and ignoring information that contradicts their convictions. Believing that their adversaries have more options than they have themselves, force may be seen as a simple way of resolving problems (Vasquez 1993, 205). Yet, as the eighteenth-century Prussian general Karl von Clausewitz stressed, "war is a continuation of policy by other means." As an instrument of statecraft, it should not be wielded without a thorough analysis of political aims, possible side effects, and long-term repercussions. In an early expression of this admonition, the Athenians told the Spartans on the eve of the Peloponnesian War that it is a common mistake to go into war the wrong way around, starting with action and only later turning to a discussion of the costs, risks, and trade-offs. (see Application: When Is It Worth Going To War?).

| **APPLICATION** | When Is It Worth Going To War? |

Early on the morning of August 2, 1990, columns of T-72 tanks from Iraq's elite Republican Guard crossed the country's southern border with Kuwait and raced down a six-lane highway toward its capital city. Within hours, resistance to the invasion collapsed. Saddam Hussein, the Iraqi leader who ordered the attack announced that the tiny, oil-rich emirate would be annexed. If he followed up his conquest of Kuwait by overrunning Saudi Arabia, Hussein would control almost half of the world's proven petroleum reserves.

In the following passage, General Colin Powell, then-chairman of the Joint Chiefs of Staff, describes a meeting of the National Security Council convened by President George H.W. Bush to discuss what posture the United States should take regarding the potential Iraqi threat to Saudi Arabia. Echoing Clausewitz, he asked the group to weigh the strategic value of a war with Iraq before concentrating on logistics and tactics.

> [Secretary of Defense] Cheney turned to me to review military options. Again, I went over the . . . plan for defending Saudi Arabia. I described the units we could put into the Gulf region in a hurry. I was reasonably sure that the Iraqis had not yet decided to invade Saudi Arabia. I was also confident that they did not relish a war with the United States. "But it's important," I said, "to plant the

American flag in the Saudi desert as soon as possible, assuming we can get their okay." We did not want our inaction to embolden Saddam further.

> . . .I then asked if it was worth going to war to liberate Kuwait. It was a Clausewitzian question which I posed so that the military would know what preparations it might have to make. I detected a chill in the room. The question . . . should not have come from me. I had overstepped. I was not the National Security Advisor now; I was only supposed to give *military* advice. Nevertheless, . . . as a midlevel career officer, I had been appalled at the docility of the Joint Chiefs of Staff, fighting the war in Vietnam without ever pressing the political leaders to lay out clear objectives for them. Before we started talking about how may divisions, carriers, and fighter wings we need, I said we have to ask, to achieve what end?

> . . .[Later] Cheney brought up our earlier meeting with the President. "Colin," he said. "you're Chairman of the Joint Chiefs. You're not Secretary of State. You're not the National Security Advisor any more. And you're not Secretary of Defense. So stick to military matters." . . .I was not sorry, however, that I had spoken out in the White House. What I had said

about giving the military clear objectives had to be said (Powell 1995, 464–466).

On August 7, Saudi Arabia requested American help in deterring a possible Iraqi attack and the next day President Bush ordered the deployment of U.S. troops to the Persian Gulf. In November, UN Resolution 678 authorized member states to use all necessary means to evict Iraq from Kuwait. On January 17, 1991, the United States began a relentless air assault on Iraqi positions, followed a few weeks later by a devastating ground attack. Kuwait was liberated on February 26. Two days later, the president ended offensive military operations. It was an impressive military victory. However, little thought had gone into analyzing the long-term strategic consequences of a postwar Iraq still ruled by Saddam Hussein.

The Second Level of Analysis: Internal Characteristics of States

Do different types of states exhibit different amounts of war involvement? Conventional wisdom holds that variations in the geography, culture, society, economy, and government of states influence whether their leaders will initiate war. To evaluate this claim, we need to examine research findings on how the internal characteristics of states affect leaders' choices regarding the use of force.

Geographic Location.   Natural resources, transportation routes, strategic borders, and other factors related to a country's territory have long been recognized as important sources of international friction. Following the end of the Cold War, competitions over access to valuable commodities ranging from oil to water "have produced a new geography of conflict, a reconfigured cartography in which resource flows rather than political and ideological divisions constitute the major fault lines" (Klare 2001; also Flint 2004)). Territorial issues can be thought of as remote, underlying causes of war. That is to say, depending on how they are handled, they can set off a chain of events that increases the probability of war. Researchers have found that contiguous states are more likely than geographically distant states to have their disputes escalate to full-scale war (Gibler 2007), especially when they involve territorial issues. Furthermore, states involved in territorial disputes tend to experience recurrent conflict (Hensel 2000).

Geographic factors affect the prospects for civil war as well. Mountainous countries with a lightly populated hinterland, for example, have been found to face an enhanced risk of rebellion when valuable natural resources are discovered because the people living in such localities suddenly have an enormous incentive to secede. Additionally, rebels can extort funds from the trade in these resources to finance their operations (Collier 2005).

Finally, geography influences civil war through a neighborhood effect. The likelihood of domestic political instability increases when a neighboring state is experiencing armed conflict, especially when there are ethnic ties to groups in that conflict (Buhaug and Gleditsch 2008).

Demographic Stress.   A number of demographic factors contribute to the onset of armed conflict. Map 7.1 shows that the risk of civil war is the greatest in those countries where population dynamics impact heavily on living conditions.

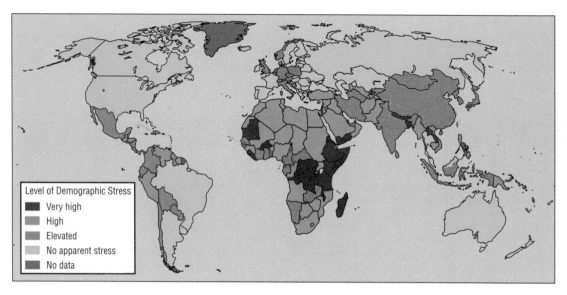

M A P 7.1 Demographic Stress and the Likelihood of Civil War

The odds of civil war increase dramatically when large numbers of unemployed youth are concentrated in cities. Shown here are those countries where such demographic stress is expected to raise the probability of civil war over the next few years.

SOURCE: *The Security Demographic* (Washington, DC: Population Action International, 2003), p. 71.

Particularly influential is the presence of a large proportion of young, unemployed males in the population (Urdal 2006). "Countries with a high proportion of adults under thirty have two and a half times the probability of experiencing a new outbreak of civil conflict as do those more mature age structures relative to population size" (Cincotta and Engleman 2004, 18).

Cultural Values.   Human behavior is strongly influenced by culture. Some governments promote political cultures that encourage citizens to accept whatever their leaders declare is necessary for national security, including using military force to resolve international disagreements. The risk of war increases whenever values that sustain **xenophobia** and blind obedience gain wide acceptance. **xenophobia** a fear of foreigners.

Nationalism can become a caldron within which these self-glorifying and other-maligning values simmer (Van Evera 1994). "The tendency of the vast majority of people to center their supreme loyalties on the nation-state," Jack Levy (1989a) explains, is a powerful catalyst to war. When people "acquire an intense commitment to the power and prosperity of the state [and] this commitment is strengthened by national myths emphasizing the moral, physical, and political strength of the state and by individuals' feelings of powerlessness and their consequent tendency to seek their identity and fulfillment through the state . . . nationalism contributes to war."

The connection between nationalism and war has a long history and provokes much debate (see Controversy: Does Nationalistic Love of Country Cause

War with Foreign Nations?). Critiques of nationalism were especially pronounced in the last century. The English essayist Aldous Huxley once termed nationalism "the religion of the twentieth century." Today nationalist feelings remain intense in many parts of the world, and continue to arouse violence among stateless nations seeking their own independent states.

CONTROVERSY   Does Nationalistic Love of Country Cause War with Foreign Nations?

What does *patriotism* mean? The most familiar definition is popularly expressed as "love for one's country." Often, it involves "love for the nation or nationality of the people living in a particular state," especially when the population of that state primarily comprises a single ethnonational racial or linguistic group.

Because "love" for valued objects of affection, such as a person's homeland, is widely seen as a virtue, it is understandable why governments everywhere teach young citizens that love for country is a moral duty. Nationalism fosters a sense of political community, and thereby contributes to civic solidarity. On these grounds, nationalism is not controversial.

However, critics of nationalism find patriotism to be potentially dangerous in its extreme form. Superpatriots, these critics warn, are hypernationalists who measure their patriotism by the degree of hatred and opposition exhibited toward foreign nations and by the blind approval of every policy and practice of the "patriot's" own nation. In this sense, nationalistic patriotism can ignore transcendent moral principles such as the love for all humanity (Etzioni 2005). It is skeptical about cosmopolitan values that put the interests of all above those of a specific national group (O'Sullivan 2005; Grosby 2006). Furthermore, it runs counter to the admonition that love should be extended even toward one's enemies, as preached by Jesus Christ in the Sermon on the Mount and other religious leaders such as Muhammad, the founder of Islam, and the legendary King Solomon in Judaism. Given these criticisms, is nationalism sometimes a cause of war between nations? What do you think?

In thinking about this controversial issue—about whether nationalism and internationalism are mutually exclusive—consider the view of Karl Deutsch, a German-born immigrant and famous scholar who taught for many years at Harvard University. Deutsch, an authority on nationalism, described nationalism's linkage to armed conflict in these moving words:

Nationalism is an attitude of mind, a pattern of attention and desires. It arises in response to a

condition of society and to a particular stage in its development. It is a predisposition to pay far more attention to messages about one's own people, or to messages from its members, than to messages from or about any other people. At the same time, it is a desire to have one's own people get any and all values that are available. The extreme nationalist wants his people to have all the power, all the wealth, and all the well-being for which there is any competition. He wants his people to command all the respect and deference from others; he tends to claim all rectitude and virtue for it, as well as all enlightenment and skill; and he gives it a monopoly of his affection. In short, he totally identifies himself with his nation. Though he may be willing to sacrifice himself for it, his nationalism is a form of egotism written large. . . .

Even if most people are not extreme nationalists, nationalism has altered the world in many ways. Nationalism has not only increased the number of countries on the face of the earth, it has helped to diminish the number of its inhabitants. All major wars in the twentieth century have been fought in its name. . . .

Nationalism is in potential conflict with all philosophies or religions—such as Christianity—which teach universal standards of truth and of right and wrong, regardless of nation, race, or tribe. Early in the nineteenth century a gallant American naval officer, Stephen Decatur, proposed the toast, "Our country! In her intercourse with foreign nations, may she be always in the right, but our country, right or wrong." Nearly 150 years later the United States Third Army, marching into Germany following the collapse of the Nazi regime, liberated the huge concentration camp at Buchenwald. Over the main entrance to that place of torture and death, the Nazi elite guard had thoughtfully written, "My Country, Right or Wrong." (Deutsch 1974, 124–125)

While not denying the power of nationalism, feminist theory points to another set of cultural values that may lead to war. As pointed out in Chapter 2, some feminists believe that aggression is rooted in the masculine ethos that prepares people to accept war and to respect the warrior as a hero (see especially Enloe 2000 and Tickner 2002). Celebrating certain gender roles and marginalizing others contributes to society's militarization, they argue. The penchant for warfare does not breed in a vacuum; it is produced by **socialization**. When powerful social institutions promote values that condone organized violence, disputes within and between states are more likely to be resolved through force than amicable procedures (Lind 1993). Furthermore, as feminist scholars maintain, civil strife is more common when cultural norms condone gender repression (Caprioli 2005; Melander 2005).

socialization the processes by which people learn the beliefs, values, and behaviors that are acceptable in a given society.

Economic Conditions.   Does a state's economic system affect the probability that it will initiate a war or suffer from civil strife? The question has provoked controversy for centuries. Marxists, for example, claim that capitalism is the primary cause of war. Recall from Chapter 5 that according to Vladimir Lenin's theory of imperialism, the need for capitalist states to export surplus capital spurs military efforts to capture and protect foreign markets. For Marxists, the only way to end war is to end capitalism.

Contrary to Marxist theory is liberalism's conviction that free-market systems promote peace, not war. The reasons are multiple, but they center on the premise that commercial enterprises are natural lobbyists for world peace because their profits depend on it. War interferes with trade, destroys property, causes inflation, consumes scarce resources, and encourages big government and counterproductive controls over business activity. By extension, this reasoning continues, as government regulation of internal markets declines, prosperity will increase and fewer wars will occur.

The debate between Marxists and liberals was at the heart of the ideological contest between East and West during the Cold War, when the relative virtues and vices of socialism and capitalism were uppermost in people's minds. At the time, Marxists cited the record of European colonial wars to support their claim that capitalist states were war-prone. However, they generally omitted references to communist uses of military force, including the Soviet invasion of Finland in 1939, North Korea's attack on South Korea in 1950, and the People's Republic of China's occupation of Tibet in 1959. Nor did they explain the repeated military clashes between communist states, such the Soviet Union with Hungary (1956), Czechoslovakia (1968), and China (1969), and China with Vietnam (1979 and 1987). Simply put, the proposition that communist states were inherently peaceful failed to stand up to empirical evidence.

The end of the Cold War did not end the debate about the relationship between economics and war. It simply moved the discussion away from a preoccupation with capitalism versus communism and riveted people's attention on whether economic interdependence promoted peace. The widening and deepening economic connections among wealthy countries in the Global North led scholars to ask whether openness to the global economy, high amounts of bilateral trade, and economic development reduce the probability of war. The evidence to date supports the liberals' belief that economic openness and high levels of economically important trade are significant constraints on the use of force (Russett and Oneal 2001). In addition, states with highly advanced economies appear less likely to fight one another than pairs of states with less developed economies, or pairs with one advanced and one less developed economy (Bremer 1992; Lemke 2003).

Aside from affecting the probability of interstate war, a country's level of economic development is related to the incidence of intrastate violence. Poor countries experiencing newly imposed economic liberalization policies can experience violent protests and civil strife (Bussmann and Schneider 2007). The probability of a country undergoing civil strife also is affected by a feeling of **relative deprivation**. When people perceive they are unfairly deprived of the wealth, status, or opportunities that they deserve in comparison with advantaged others, their frustration and anger often explodes into violence (Gurr 1970). These feelings can be particularly pronounced in countries experiencing rapid, unequal economic growth (Murdoch and Sandler 2004).

relative deprivation
people's perception that they are unfairly deprived of wealth and status in comparison to others who are advantaged but not more deserving.

Many analysts believe that internal economic strife is linked to interstate war because leaders who experience acute opposition at home provoke crises abroad to divert attention from their domestic failures. As mentioned in Chapter 3, this diversionary theory of war stems from sociological research that shows in-group bonds tighten when faced with an out-group threat. War, according to this theory, gives a leader the opportunity to introduce ruthless forms of domestic political control while simultaneously being hailed as a protector. The evidence does not point to a clear, direct connection between civil strife and interstate war initiation, however. Perhaps the most compelling reason for these results is that when domestic conflict becomes severe there is a greater likelihood that a state will reduce its foreign engagements in order to handle the situation at home.

Before drawing any final conclusions about the impact of poverty on war, we must note that the *most* impoverished countries have been the least prone to start wars with their neighbors. The poorest countries cannot vent their frustrations aggressively because they lack the military or economic resources to do so. This does not mean that the poorest countries will always remain peaceful. If the past is a guide to the future, then the impoverished countries that develop economically will be those most likely to acquire arms and eventually go to war. In particular, many studies suggest that states are likely to initiate foreign wars *after* sustained periods of economic growth—that is, during periods of rising prosperity, when they can most afford them (Cashman 2000). This signals danger if rapidly developing countries in the Global South direct their new resources toward armament rather than invest in sustained development.

Political Institutions.   As discussed in Chapter 2, liberal theory assigns great weight to the kinds of political institutions that states possess. Furthermore, as pointed out in Chapter 3, researchers have found that although democratic governments use force against nondemocracies, they rarely make war on other democracies. In fact, they hardly ever skirmish. "Pairs of democratic states have been only one-eighth as likely as other kinds of states to threaten to use force against each other, and only one-tenth as likely actually to do so" (Russett 2001, 235; see also Sobek 2005).

The capacity of democracies to manage conflict with one another has led scholars to speculate about the consequences of having democratic institutions diffuse around the world. As the proportion of democracies grows, will norms and practices of nonviolent conflict resolution cascade throughout the state system? Some scholars imagine that once a critical mass of democratic states is reached, many other states would be persuaded to adopt democratic institutions, which would prompt another round of adoptions, and so on. A world populated by stable democracies, they predict, would be freed from the curse of war.

Although the community of liberal democracies has grown over the past two centuries, the euphoria surrounding democraticization has given way to the realization that there is no certainty that liberal democracy will become universal. Nor will halting, erratic moves toward liberalization by the world's remaining autocracies automatically produce a more peaceful global order. Democratizing countries pass through an unstable transition period (Bremmer 2007), and unlike their older, constitutionally secure brethren, fledgling democracies occasionally resort to force (Mansfield and Snyder 2005). Finally, the fact that leaders in established democracies are accountable to electoral approval does not guarantee that they will moderate the use of force when it is applied. The sensitivity of democratic leaders to casualties "sometimes leads to profligate uses of firepower or violent efforts to end wars quickly" (E. Cohen 1998).

The preceding discussion of the characteristics of states that influence their proclivity for armed conflict does not exhaust the subject. Many other state-level causes have been hypothesized. But, however important domestic influences might be, many believe that the nature of the international system is even more critical.

The Third Level of Analysis: System Structure and Processes

As we saw in Chapter 2, some political realists see war as a product of the decentralized character of the international system that encourages self-help rather than teamwork. To illustrate how the absence of a central authority affects behavior, the philosopher Jean-Jacques Rousseau suggests we imagine a group of primitive hunters tracking a stag (male deer). The hunters are hungry, and must all cooperate in order to have a chance of trapping an animal large enough to feed the entire group. While stalking the creature, one hunter spots a hare. If he leaves the group to pursue the hare, he would almost certainly bag it and feed himself. But without his help, the remaining hunters could not catch the stag and would go hungry. Rousseau uses this allegory to show how egoistic actors in an anarchic environment are tempted to follow their own short-term interests, which undercuts the opportunity to attain larger goals that benefit everyone. Applying this reasoning to the outbreak of the First World War, the British scholar G. Lowes Dickinson (1926) claimed "whenever and wherever the anarchy of armed states exists, war does become inevitable."

International anarchy may make war likely, but as a constant condition of modern international life it doesn't explain why some periods erupt in violence, while others remain tranquil. As discussed in Chapter 2, constructivists point out that international anarchy is what states make of it: Anarchies of distrustful actors are different from anarchies of friends. To account for variation in the amount of interstate war and internationalized civil war over time, we need to look at changes in the structure and processes operating within the anarchic international system. More specifically, we need to consider how the distribution of power among the members of the state system, as well as shifts in that distribution, may affect the outbreak of armed conflict.

Power Distributions. Theories of world politics are abstract, conjectural representations of the world. Thus far we have examined theories that attempt to explain the outbreak of armed conflict by concentrating on human nature and the internal makeup of states. An alternative approach focuses on the structure of the state system; that is, how states are positioned or arranged according to the distribution of power among the system's members (Waltz 1979). In Chapter 3 we introduced the concept of polarity to describe the distribution of material capabilities. Unipolar systems contain a structure with one dominant power center, bipolar systems have two centers of power, and multipolar systems possess more than two such centers. Although civil wars have become internationalized under each type of structure, preliminary research indicates that unipolar periods characterized by the concentration of power in the hands of a single preponderant state are highly intervention-prone (Raymond and Kegley 1987). When it comes to predicting interstate war, however, the evidence is less clear, with scholars debating whether bipolar or multipolar systems are more likely to experience war.

Advocates of bipolarity assert that a world containing two centers of power that are significantly stronger than the next tier of states will be stable because the dire consequences of war between these giants encourages them to exercise caution when dealing with one another, and to prevent conflicts among their allies from engulfing them in a military maelstrom. Conversely, those favoring multipolarity believe that situations of rough parity among several great powers will be peaceful because a rise in interaction opportunities and a diminution in the share of attention that can be allocated among many potential adversaries reduce the rigidity of conflicts. In rebuttal, the former submit that because of its ambiguous nature, multipolarity will promote war through miscalculation. The latter retort that bipolarity, lacking flexibility and suppleness, will deteriorate into a struggle for supremacy (see Christensen and Snyder 1990; Midlarsky 1988; Deutsch and Singer 1964).

Research into the relative merits of bipolar versus multipolar structures suggests that the distribution of material capabilities within the state system is not related to the onset of war (Kegley and Raymond 1994; Bueno de Mesquita 1981; Ostrom and Aldrich 1978); nevertheless it affects the *amount* of war should armed conflict occur (Levy 1985; Wayman 1985). Wars occur in both bipolar and multipolar systems, but multipolar systems experience larger, more severe wars (Vasquez 2000; 1986).

Although different polarity configurations do not raise or lower the probability of war, alliance polarization makes war more likely. Recall that polarity differs from polarization. As discussed in Chapter 3, polarity concerns the distribution of power; alliance polarization refers to the propensity of lesser powers to cluster around the strongest states. The interstate system can be said to be moving toward greater polarization if its members align in two hostile blocs.

Alliance polarization is hazardous because the structural rigidity it fosters reduces the opportunities for a wide array of multifaceted interactions among states, therein decreasing the chances for **crosscutting cleavages** to emerge. Crosscutting reduces the odds of war, because opponents on one issue may be partners on another. They are not implacable enemies confined to an endless zero-sum struggle. In an international environment of **overlapping cleavages**, adversaries have few interests in common, and thus become fixated on the things that divide them. Under these circumstances, minor disagreements are magnified into bigger tests of will where reputations are thought to be at stake. Tight, polarized blocs of states are thus war-prone; peace is best preserved when there is a moderate amount of flexibility in the structure of alliances (Kim 1989; Kegley and Raymond 1982; Wallace 1973).

Power Trajectories and Transitions. Although the international system is anarchic, possessing no higher authority above the sovereign state, it is nonetheless stratified due to variations in the relative power of its members. If the international pecking order is clear, with the dominant state holding a substantial advantage over its nearest potential rival, then efforts to alter the rank order of states by force are unlikely. Conversely, if the capability advantage of the dominant state is minimal or eroding due to the growth of a challenger, the probability of war increases (Geller 2000).

According to what has been dubbed **power transition theory**, "peace is preserved best when there is an imbalance of national capabilities between disadvantaged and advantaged nations" (Kugler 1993; Organski and Kugler 1980). War, it is argued, often involves "rear-end" collisions between a rapidly rising dissatisfied state and the dominant state, which wishes to preserve the status quo. When the relative strength of the revisionist challenger and the dominant state converge toward rough parity, armed conflict can erupt in two different ways. First, the dominant state may initiate a preventive war so as not to be overtaken by the challenger. Second, and more commonly, the challenger may strike first, confident that it can accelerate its climb to the apex of international power. Research suggests that these patterns also hold within regional subsystems, where the confluence of parity among small state rivals and dissatisfaction with the status quo increase the probability of minor-power wars (Lemke 2002).

Some scholars believe that the trajectory of state power follows a cycle of ascendance, maturation, and decline, based on the ratio of its strength relative to others within the system (Doran 2000; Doran and Parsons 1980). According

crosscutting cleavages
a situation where politically relevant divisions between international actors are contradictory, with their interests pulling them together on some issues and separating them on others.

overlapping cleavages
a situation where politically relevant divisions between international actors are complementary; interests pulling them apart on one issue are reinforced by interests that also separate them on other issues.

power transition theory
the contention that war is likely when a dominant great power is threatened by the rapid growth of a rival's capabilities, which reduces the difference in their relative power.

power cycle theory the contention that armed conflict is probable when a state passes through certain critical points along a generalized curve of relative power, and wars of enormous magnitude are likely when several great powers pass through critical points at approximately the same time.

to **power cycle theory**, war is most likely at certain critical points along this cycle; namely when shifts in the rate of growth or decline in a state's relative power creates discontinuities between prior foreign policy expectations and future realities. Whenever "these states encounter an unexpected reversal in the direction or rate of change in their power trajectories, they are subject to various psychological impulses or judgmental challenges that increase the danger of extensive wars" (Tessman and Chan 2004, 131). Preliminary research indicates that when numerous great powers pass through these critical points at the same time, massive wars ensue (Doran 1989).

Cyclical theories have always provoked discussion. Years ago, for example, Italian historian Luigi da Porto received considerable attention by asserting: "Peace brings riches; riches bring pride; pride brings anger; anger brings war; war brings poverty; poverty brings humanity; humanity brings peace; peace, as I have said, brings riches, and so the world's affairs go round." For many people, assertions like this make it seem plausible that certain rhythms characterize the tides of history.

As discussed in Chapter 4, various scholars have looked for long cycles in the rise and fall of hegemonic leaders over the past five centuries (see Hopkins and Wallerstein 1996; Modelski and Thompson 1996; Goldstein 1988). However, they have failed to reach a consensus about the existence of periodicities in global war. Their findings diverge, because different definitions of hegemonic leadership and different measures of global war lead to different estimates of the duration of periods of peace and war. Hence the debate continues as to whether the onset of global warfare follows a repeating sequence.

THE FUTURE OF ARMED CONFLICT

Since the birth of the modern world system some three and a half centuries ago, national leaders have prepared for wars against other countries. Throughout this period, war has been conceived as large-scale organized violence between the regular armies of sovereign states. Although leaders today still ready their nations for such clashes, increasingly they are faced with the prospect of **asymmetric warfare**—armed conflict between terrorist networks and conventional military forces.

asymmetric warfare armed conflict between belligerents of vastly unequal military strength, in which the weaker side is often a nonstate actor that relies on unconventional tactics.

terrorism the premeditated use or threat of violence perpetrated against noncombatants, usually intended to induce fear in a wider audience.

Terrorism was well known even in ancient times, as evident in the campaign of assassinations conducted by the Sicarii (named after a short dagger, or *sica*) in Judea during the first century CE. Today it is practiced by a diverse group of movements, as seen by the fact that in 2008 the U.S. National Counter-Terrorism Center identified dozens of different organizations as worldwide terrorist groups. Political terrorism is the deliberate use or threat of violence against noncombatants, calculated to instill fear, alarm, and ultimately a feeling of helplessness in an audience beyond the immediate victims. Because perpetrators of terrorism often strike symbolic targets in a horrific manner, the psychological impact of an attack can exceed the physical damage. A mixture of drama and dread, political terrorism is not senseless violence; it is a premeditated strategy of extortion that presents people with a danger that seems ubiquitous, unavoidable, and unpredictable.

Terrorism can be employed to support or change the political status quo. Repressive terror, which is wielded to sustain an existing political order, has been utilized by governments as well as by vigilantes. From the Gestapo (secret state police) in Nazi Germany to the "death squads" in various countries, establishment violence attempts to defend the prevailing political order by eliminating opposition leaders and by intimidating virtually everyone else.

Dissidents who use terrorism to change the political status quo vary considerably. Some groups, like the MPLA (Popular Movement for the Liberation of Angola), used terrorism to expel colonial rulers; others, such as ETA (Basque Homeland and Liberty), adopted terrorism as part of an ethnonational separatist struggle; still others, including the Islamic Jihad, the Christian Identity Movement, the Sikh group Babbar Khalsa, and Jewish militants belonging to Kach, placed terror in the service of what they saw as religious imperatives; finally, groups such as the Japanese Red Army and Italian Black Order, turned to terrorism for left- or right-wing ideological reasons. In short, dissident terror may be grounded in anticolonialism, separatism, religion, or secular ideology.

Although the ultimate goals of individuals and groups that employ terrorism differ, they seek similar intermediate objectives as a means of attaining their goals. The following objectives are the most common:

- The *agitational* objectives of terrorism include promoting the dissident group, advertising its agenda, and discrediting rivals. Shocking behavior makes people take heed, especially when performed at a time and place imbued with symbolism. Nineteenth-century anarchists were among the first to emphasize the propaganda value of terrorism. One stunning act, they believed, would draw more attention than a thousand leaflets.

- The *coercive* objectives of terrorism include disorienting a target population, inflating the perceived power of the dissident group, wringing concessions from authorities, and provoking a heavy-handed overreaction from the police and military. Launching vicious, indiscriminate attacks at markets, cafes, and other normally tranquil locations can create a paralyzing sense of foreboding within the general public and goad political leaders into adopting repressive policies, which terrorists hope will drive the population to their side of the struggle.

- The *organizational* objectives of terrorism include acquiring resources, forging group cohesion, and maintaining an underground network of supporters. Robbing banks, obtaining ransom for hostages, and collecting protection money from businesses can finance training and logistical support for field operations. Moreover, since high initiation costs tend to lower group defections, these activities can increase allegiance when recruits are required to participate in violent acts.

To accomplish these objectives, terrorists use a variety of tactics, including bombing, assault, hijacking, and taking hostages. Hijacking and hostage-taking generally involve more complex operations than planting a bomb in a crowded department store or gunning down travelers in an airport lounge. An example of such careful planning can be seen in the coordinated hijacking of five airliners by Palestinians during September 1970, which eventually led to one airliner being blown up in Cairo and three others at Dawson Field in Jordan. To be successful, these kinds of seizures require detailed preparation, vigorous bargaining, and the capacity to guard captives for long periods of time. Among the payoffs of such efforts is the opportunity to articulate the group's grievances. The Lebanese group behind the 1985 hijacking of TWA flight 847, for instance, excelled at using U.S. television networks to articulate their grievances to the American public, which had the effect of circumscribing the options that the Reagan administration entertained while searching for a solution to the crisis.

Beyond the conventional tactics of bombings, assaults, hijacking, and hostage-taking, two other threats could become part of the terrorist repertoire. First, dissidents may acquire weapons of mass destruction to deliver a mortal blow against detested enemies. Nuclear armaments are the ultimate terror weapons, but radiological, chemical, and biological weapons also pose extraordinary dangers. Crude radiological weapons can be fabricated by combining ordinary explosives with nuclear waste or radioactive isotopes, which could be stolen from hospitals, industrial facilities, or research laboratories. Rudimentary chemical weapons can be made from herbicides, pesticides, and other toxic substances that are available commercially. Biological weapons based on viral agents are more difficult to produce, though the dispersal of anthrax spores through the mail during the fall of 2001 illustrated that low-technology attacks with bacterial agents in powder form are a frightening possibility.

The second tactical innovation on the horizon is cyberterrorism. Not only can the Internet be used by extremists as a recruiting tool and a means of coordinating their activities with like-minded groups, but it allows them to case potential targets by hacking into a foe's computer system. Viruses and other weapons of **information warfare** could cause havoc if they disabled financial institutions, power grids, air traffic control systems, and other key elements in country's communication infrastructure.

information warfare
attacks on an adversary's telecommunications and computer networks to degrade the technological systems vital to its defense and economic well-being.

Efforts to measure the frequency and severity of terrorism began in earnest during the 1960s. According to the U.S. Department of State's Office of Counterterrorism, global terrorist activity increased nearly threefold between 1968 and 1987, after which the number of incidents gradually but erratically declined—until 2004 when the new National Counter-Terrorism Center (NCTC) took over responsibility for counting the number of terrorist incidents and broadened the definitional criteria to include civilian casualties from the war in Iraq. Figure 7.2 shows that as measured by these new criteria, 14,499 terrorist attacks occurred in 2007, claiming 22,685 lives (60 percent in Iraq). In a May 2008 poll of terrorist experts, 70 percent said that the world was growing more dangerous due to the mounting wave of global terrorism (http://www.foreignpolicy.com/story/cms.php?story_id=4431).

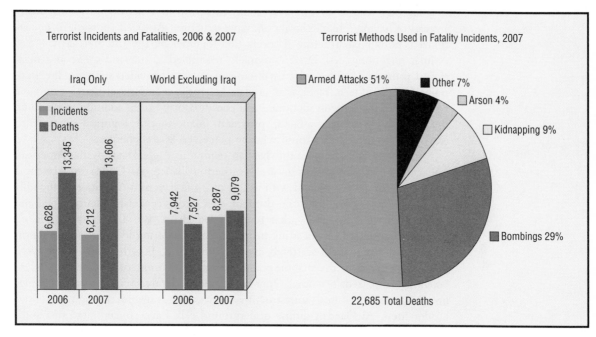

FIGURE 7.2   The Threat of Global Terrorism

The figure on the left shows the number of terrorist incidents and fatalities during 2006 and 2007, both in Iraq and throughout the rest of the world. The figure on the right records the share of deaths that were caused by the major methods used by terrorists in 2007.

SOURCES: NCTC (2008, 30 and 36).

The New Global Terrorism

The conventional view of terrorism as a rare and relatively remote threat was challenged by the events of September 11, 2001. The horrors visited upon the World Trade Center and the Pentagon forced the world to confront a grim new reality: Terrorists were capable of executing catastrophic attacks almost anywhere, even without an arsenal of sophisticated weapons. Not only did groups like Al Qaeda have global reach, but stealth, ingenuity, and meticulous planning could compensate for their lack of firepower. "America is full of fear," proclaimed a jubilant Osama bin Laden. "Nobody in the United States will feel safe."

What arguably made September 11 a symbolic watershed was that it epitomized a deadly new strain of terrorism. Previously, terrorism was regarded as political theater, a frightening drama where the perpetrators wanted a lot of people watching, not a lot of people dead. Now there seemed to be a desire to kill as many people as possible. Driven by searing hatred, annihilating enemies appeared more important to these global terrorists than winning sympathy for their cause.

Another feature of this new strain of terrorism is its organizational form. Instead of having a hierarchical command structure, Al Qaeda possesses a decentralized, horizontal structure. Loosely tied together by the Internet, e-mail, and cellular telephones, Al Qaeda originally resembled a hub-and-spoke organization: Osama bin Laden and a small core of loyalists provided strategic direction, training, and aid to a franchise of affiliated terrorist cells. Rather than serving as a commander, bin Laden functioned as a coordinator who, in addition to planning dramatic, high-casualty attacks, provided financial and logistical support to extremist groups fighting those who he perceived as archenemies.

Following the ouster of the Taliban regime in Afghanistan by the American military and its partners from the Northern Alliance, Al Qaeda underwent a structural change. Combined with its loss of a safe haven in Afghanistan, the killing or capture of roughly one-third of Al Qaeda's leadership transformed the organization into an entity that resembled a chain. Bin Laden and his close associates continued broadcasting propaganda and offering ideological inspiration to small, disparate cells scattered around the world, but they no longer were directly involved in the planning and execution of most of the attacks undertaken in Al Qaeda's name. Operating independently, without the training, financing, and logistical infrastructure previously available through a central headquarters, Al Qaeda's diffuse underground cells have concentrated on "soft" targets, sometimes attacking in conjunction with sympathetic local forces. The July 2005 resort bombings in Sharm el Sheikh, Egypt and the November 2005 hotel bombings in Amman, Jordan, illustrate this pattern of activity. Although Al Qaeda has been regrouping in Pakistan's mountainous tribal areas along the frontier with Afghanistan, the group is experiencing a backlash from former supporters for its wanton violence.

What makes the new breed of terrorists who belong to organizations such as Al Qaeda more lethal than previous terrorists is their religious fanaticism, which allows them to envision acts of terror on two levels. At one level, terrorism is a means to change the political status quo by punishing those culpable for felt wrongs. At another level, terrorism is an end in itself, a sacrament performed for its own sake in an eschatological confrontation between good and evil (Juergensmeyer 2003). Functioning only on the first level, most secular terrorist groups rarely employ suicide missions. Operating on both levels, religious terrorist groups see worldly gain as well as transcendent importance in a martyr's death (Bloom 2005; Pape 2005). Ramadan Shalah of the Palestinian Jihad is reported to have explained the military logic of suicide tactics within asymmetric warfare in the following way: "Our enemy possesses the most sophisticated weapons in the world. . . . We have nothing . . . except the weapon of martyrdom. It is easy and costs us only our lives."

Counterterrorism

The threat facing civilization after September 11, 2001 was described by U.S. president George W. Bush as a network of terrorist groups and rogue states that harbored them. Efforts to combat this threat, he insisted, "will not end until every terrorist group of global reach has been found, stopped, and defeated." In what was subsequently called the **Bush Doctrine**, the president declared that each nation had a choice to make: "Either you are with us, or you are with the terrorists."

Terrorist groups are a type of nonstate actor (or global NGO), distinguished by the fact that they use violence as their primary method of exercising influence. States have often financed, trained, equipped, and provided sanctuary for terrorists whose activities serve their foreign policy goals. The practice of such **state-sponsored terrorism** is among the charges that the United States leveled against Iraq prior to toppling Saddam Hussein in 2003, and continues to apply to countries like Iran, Sudan, and Syria. However, disagreement about the character and causes of global terrorism remain pronounced, and, without agreement on these preliminaries, a consensus on the best response is unlikely. Much like a disease that cannot be treated until it is accurately diagnosed, so the plague of the new global terrorism cannot be eradicated until its sources are understood. Those persuaded by one image of terrorism are drawn to certain counterterrorism policies, while those holding a different image recommend contrary policies. As constructivist theorists remind us, what we see depends on what we expect, what we look at, and what we wish to see.

Consider the diametrically opposed views of whether repression or conciliation is the most effective counterterrorist policy. Those advocating repression see terrorism springing from the cold calculations of extremists who should be neutralized by preemptive surgical strikes. As expressed by former U.S. secretary of defense Donald Rumsfeld: "If the [United States] learned a single lesson from September 11, it should be that the only way to defeat terrorists is to attack them. There is no choice. You simply cannot defend in every place at every time against every technique."

In contrast to this coercive approach to counterterrorism, those who see terrorism rooted in frustrations with political oppression and relative deprivation urge negotiation and compromise (Krueger 2007). Rather than condoning military strikes aimed at exterminating the perpetrators of terrorism, they endorse conciliatory policies designed to reduce terrorism's appeal.

The debate about how to deal with the new global terrorism thus revolves around a series of interconnected issues: Are repressive counterterrorist policies ethical? Are they compatible with democratic procedures? Do they require multilateral (international) backing to be legal, or can they be initiated unilaterally? Is conciliation more effective than military coercion? What are its relative costs, risks, and benefits?

Although most experts would agree that whereas it is not possible to eradicate terrorism, they share faith in the more modest goal of containing it (Shapiro 2007). Accomplishing this goal while maintaining a proper balance between undertaking resolute action and upholding civil liberties will be difficult for several reasons. First, today's relatively open, borderless world makes terrorism easy to practice. Second, many **failing states** in the Global South offer out-of-the-way places for terrorist groups to locate and train (see Figure 7.3). Third, the growing possibility that terrorists will obtain weapons of mass destruction will

Bush Doctrine a policy that singles out states that support terrorist groups and advocates military strikes against them to prevent a future attack on the United States.

state-sponsored terrorism formal assistance, training, and arming of foreign terrorists by a state in order to achieve foreign policy goals.

failing states states in danger of political collapse due to overwhelming internal strife.

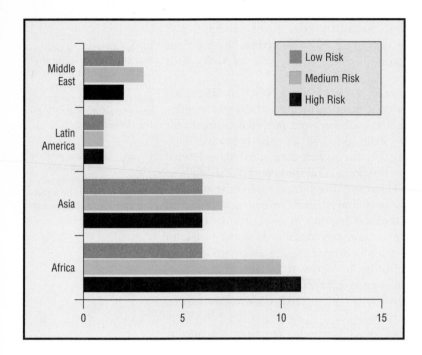

FIGURE 7.3 Global South States on the Brink of Failure

This figure shows the number of countries in different regions of the Global South where there is a high, medium, or low risk of state failure. The index of vulnerability to failure is based on a composite of twelve social, economic, political, and military indicators. Currently, Africa contains the most at-risk states.

SOURCES: "The Failed States Index," *Foreign Policy* 167 (July/August 2008): 67.

create unprecedented opportunities for them to commit unspeakable atrocities. Finally, contemporary terrorists have become extremely violent, holding few reservations about inflicting heavy casualties and causing enormous physical destruction (Laqueur 2001).

The history of terrorism indicates that there is no terrorist orthodoxy on strategic questions, no canon with strict precepts running from ultimate political goals to intermediate objectives to specific tactics. Strategic thinking about the use of terrorism in asymmetric warfare has evolved in response to new technologies, new targets of opportunity, and new counterterrorist policies. The perpetrators of political terrorism are not mindless; they have long-term aims and they carefully consider how different operations may facilitate accomplishing their purposes. Indeed, it is their ability to plan, execute, and learn from these operations that makes them so dangerous.

Armed conflict in all its forms extracts a terrible toll on human life. In this chapter we have briefly examined trends in its frequency and changing character, as well as several prominent theories about its causes. We have seen that inter-state and civil wars are not the legacy of what Sigmund Freud once called a "death instinct" embedded within human nature. Neither are they the product of a single cause, such as capitalism or communism. Wars can be brought on by several different causal sequences, each involving a complex combination of factors. In the next chapter, we will explore the national security policies states use to advance their interests in a world where the threat of war abounds.

CHAPTER SUMMARY

- Force is an instrument that states often use to resolve their conflicts. However, war is not inevitable: some societies have never known the outbreak of war, and some historical periods have not experienced warfare.

- Since the end of World War II, all wars have been between countries in the Global South or have entailed military action by great powers against them. None have occurred between the great powers. Civil wars have become more common than interstate wars.

- War is best explained by multiple factors operating at various levels of analysis.

- There is little evidence that human nature is a direct cause of war.

- Evidence pertaining to state-level explanations of interstate war suggests that the probability of militarized conflict is increased by hypernationalism and territorial disputes among contiguous countries. Its probability declines significantly when both parties to a dispute are stable democracies, and they possess open, advanced economies linked by commerce. The likelihood of civil wars increases when countries experience demographic stress, relative deprivation, and border other states undergoing civil strife.

- Evidence pertaining to system-level explanations of war suggest that the following conditions increase the probability of militarized conflict: polarized alliances, an unstable hierarchy of states, and the existence of several great powers simultaneously passing through critical points in their cycle of relative power. Whether a system is bipolar or multipolar in structure does not affect the occurrence of war; however, it influences the magnitude and severity of any wars that break out, with multipolarity suffering from larger wars involving more casualties.

- The global future is likely to experience an increasing amount of asymmetric warfare between sovereign states and terrorist networks.

- Political terrorism is the purposeful use or threat of violence against noncombatants, undertaken to intimidate a wider audience. The ultimate goals of those who employ terrorism vary: Some groups employ it to support the political status quo; others, to overthrow the status quo. For both types of groups, terror is used to accomplish agitational, coercive, and organizational objectives.

- Traditionally, terrorist groups have relied on bombing, assault, hijacking, and hostage-taking to intimidate their target audience. Two emerging threats are the use of weapons of mass destruction (nuclear, radiological, chemical, and biological weapons) and cyberterrorism—attacks on an opponent's computer systems.

- Some contemporary terrorist groups have acquired the means to strike targets almost anywhere in the world. Their fanaticism has led to a vigorous debate over counterterrorist policies. Those who see the roots of the new global terrorism in an inextinguishable hatred by extremists generally call for aggressive efforts at military preemption. In contrast, those who would attribute terrorism to frustration over oppression and deprivation tend to advocate more conciliatory policies.

KEY TERMS

asymmetric warfare

Bush Doctrine

civil war

crosscutting cleavages

failing states

information warfare

internationalized civil war

interstate war

overlapping cleavages

power cycle theory

power transition theory

relative deprivation

socialization

state-sponsored terrorism

terrorism

xenophobia

SUGGESTED READINGS

Russett, Bruce, ed. *International Security and Conflict*. Burlington, VT: Ashgate, 2008.

Cashman, Greg, and Leonard C. Robinson. *An Introduction to the Causes of War*. Landham, MD: Rowman & Littlefield, 2007.

Colaresi, Michael P., Karen Rasler, and William R. Thompson. *Strategic Rivalries in World Politics*. New York: Cambridge University Press, 2007.

Goertz, Gary, and Jack S. Levy (eds.). *Explaining War and Peace*. New York: Routledge, 2007.

Gray, Colin. *War, Peace, and International Relations*. New York: Routledge, 2007.

CRITICAL THINKING QUESTIONS

Game theory is a branch of mathematics used to analyze the strategic interaction of two or more actors. One of the most widely known game theoretic approaches to the study of conflict dynamics is the Prisoner's Dilemma game. Imagine two suspects following an armed robbery are taken into police custody and placed in separate cells by the district attorney, who is certain that they are guilty but only has sufficient evidence to convict them on an illegal weapons charge. The district attorney tells prisoner A and prisoner B that there are two choices: confess to the robbery, or remain silent. If one prisoner confesses and the other doesn't, he will be given immunity from prosecution for turning state's evidence while his accomplice will get a sentence of ten years in the state penitentiary. If both confess, they will be given a reduced sentence of five years in the penitentiary. If neither confesses, they will be convicted on the weapons charge and serve only six months in the county jail. Because both prisoners want to spend as little time incarcerated as possible, their preferences are rank-ordered from the best to the worst outcomes as follows: (1) immunity from prosecution; (2) six months in the county jail; (3) five years in the state penitentiary; and (4) ten years in the penitentiary. The matrix below depicts the results that will occur depending upon whether each prisoner chooses to cooperate with his accomplice by remaining silent or defect by confessing to the district attorney.

	B	
	Cooperate	Defect
Cooperate	2, 2	4, 1
Defect	1, 4	3, 3

A

Note: The first number in each cell of the matrix is A's payoff, the second number is B's payoff. The number 1 represents the most preferred outcome, whereas 4 represents the least preferred outcome.

Faced with this situation, what should each prisoner do? Remember that they both want as little time behind bars as possible, and they are being interrogated separately so they cannot communicate. Furthermore, neither prisoner is sure that he can trust the other.

Although the optimal strategy for both prisoners would be to tacitly cooperate with each other and keep quiet so each receives only a six-month sentence (the payoff of 2,2 in the matrix), the structural properties of this situation are such that there are powerful incentives to defect from your partner and give state's evidence to the district attorney. First, there is an offensive incentive to defect based on the prospect of getting immunity by confessing. Second, there is a defensive incentive to defect grounded in the fear of being double-crossed by an accomplice who squeals. If one prisoner refuses to talk but the other confesses, the one who tried to cooperate with his accomplice to get a mutually beneficial result would receive the worst possible payoff (4, or ten years in the penitentiary), while the prisoner who defected to the district attorney would receive the best payoff (1, or immunity). Not wanting be a "sucker" who spends a decade incarcerated while his partner in crime goes free, both prisoners conclude that it is in their self-interest to defect and testify against one another; consequently, they both receive a worse result (the payoff 3, 3 in the matrix, or five years in prison) than if they had tacitly cooperated by remaining silent. The dilemma is that seemingly rational calculations by each individual actor can yield collectively worse results for both than had they chosen other strategies.

Many theorists liken various aspects of world politics to the Prisoner's Dilemma game. Consider two countries (A and B) that are approximately equal in military capability, uncertain of whether they can trust one another, and currently face two choices: cooperate in lowering arms spending or defect by increasing arms spending. Suppose that each country prefers to have a military advantage over the other and fears being at a serious disadvantage, which would happen if one increased arms spending while the other reduced expenditures (the payoffs 1, 4 and 4, 1 in the matrix above). By cooperating to lower arms spending they could devote more resources to other national needs such as education and health care (the payoff 2, 2), but given offensive and defensive incentives that are similar to those tempting the two prisoners in our earlier example, they both conclude that it is in their individual self-interest to play it safe and arm. As a result of their joint defection (payoff 3, 3), they end up worse off by locking themselves into an expensive arms race that may destabilize the prevailing balance of power.

The Prisoner's Dilemma game highlights some of the difficulties in reaching mutually beneficial agreements among self-interested actors who distrust their peers. Beyond the study of arms races, do you see any other possible applications of this game in world politics? What strategies might help the players escape the dilemma they portrayed in the game?

8

Military Power and National Security in a Turbulent World

CHAPTER OUTLINE

Power in World Politics

The Elements of State Power

Globalization and the Changing Nature of State Power

CONTROVERSY: Does High Military Spending Lower Human Security?

The Pursuit of Military Capability

Trends in Military Spending

Trends in the Weapons Trade

Trends in Weapons Technology

Military Strategy in the Nuclear Age

Compellence

Deterrence

Preemption

The Limits of Coercive Diplomacy

The Persuasive Use of Military Force

Economic Sanctions

APPLICATION: Who is Penalizing Whom?

Building World Security

> If you want peace, prepare for war.
> FLAVIUS VEGETIUS RENATUS
> ROMAN GENERAL

On September 30, 1862, Count Otto von Bismarck, the chief minister of Prussia, addressed a legislative budget committee on the need to expand the country's military. It was a difficult task for the tall, broad-shouldered, and often abrasive minister. Many members of parliament had been resisting tax increases for some time, even to fund reforms of the armed forces.

Prussia was one of thirty-eight Germanic states scattered across central Europe in the mid-nineteenth century. According to German nationalists, the division of the German people into numerous small and medium-sized states kept them at the mercy of larger neighbors. Many Germans supported unification, but were leery of Prussian ambitions to lead a united Germany. Austria and France were worried as well. A united Germany under Prussian leadership would pose an enormous security threat. With skilled labor, and educated population, and unparalleled electrical, chemical, and steel industries, German unification would create an economic and military powerhouse. Consequently, political leaders in Vienna and Paris preferred to leave the Germans divided among several dozen innocuous states.

Bismarck recognized these barriers to Prussian aspirations, and feared they might not be overcome without a modern military. "The position of Prussia in Germany," he told the legislative budget committee, "will be determined not by its liberalism but by its power." Prussia must strengthen its military. "Not through speeches and majority decisions are the great questions of the day decided," he thundered, "but through iron and blood."

During the next decade, Bismarck's policy of iron and blood led to wars against Denmark (1864), Austria (1866), and France (1870–1871). Collectively known as the Wars of German Unification, they were won by a combination of Bismarck's uncanny ability to isolate his international opponents, and the training, firepower, and mobility of Prussia's modernized military. Together, they transformed the fragmented German lands into a strong centralized state. Before these wars, Prussia was the smallest of Europe's great powers; afterward, it had a near-hegemony over the continent.

Bismarck's genius resided in his ability to entertain multiple courses of action, explore all of their permutations, and move on several fronts simultaneously. No single move was an end in itself; each positioned him to advance in another direction. "One cannot play chess," he insisted," if from the outset sixteen of the sixty-four squares are out of bounds." A tenacious advocate of Prussian interests and a master of intrigue, he could see opportunities presented by different diplomatic configurations on the diplomatic chessboard. To exploit them, he was willing to be disingenuous and, at times, even ruthless. "If it hadn't been for me, there wouldn't have been three great wars, 80,000 men would not have died, and parents, brothers, sisters, and widows would not be in mourning," he once admitted. "But that I have to settle with God."

Like Karl von Clausewitz, the Prussian general who had fought against Napoleon half a century earlier, Bismarck saw war as an extension of foreign policy by other means, a political instrument for attaining one's goals when diplomacy fails to resolve a stalemate. To Bismarck, conflict was normal, and war was a way to resolve it by compelling an adversary to do one's will. Success hinged on military power. As Frederick the Great, king of Prussia during the eighteenth century put it: "Diplomacy without an army is like music without instruments."

This chapter examines the role of power in world politics. It begins by analyzing the ambiguous concept of "power." After reviewing the difficulties in measuring a country's power potential, it evaluates states' efforts to amass military capabilities by exploring trends in military spending, the arms trade, and weapons technology. Finally, the chapter concludes by discussing how states use their military and economic resources to exercise influence over other international actors.

POWER IN WORLD POLITICS

Throughout history, many leaders have seen the acquisition of power as their primary objective. In their eyes, security is a function of power; therefore increasing power is in the national interest. Yet the meaning of "power" is not self-evident. It is used in different ways by different people. Most scholars define power in relational terms, as the ability of one state to make another continue a course of action, change what it is doing, or refrain from acting. A powerful state, in other words, has the capacity to control others. By exercising power, it can reduce the probability of something it does not want to happen and increase the probability of a preferred outcome.

The Elements of State Power

Having defined power in terms of control, the question remains as to how we might measure the potential of one international actor to make another do what it otherwise would not. As David Baldwin (1989) points out, "the problem of measuring political power is like the problem of measuring purchasing power in an economy without money." In the absence of a standard unit of account, it is difficult to create a precise ranking of states that would predict who would prevail in a political conflict. Our intuition may suggest that larger countries are more powerful than smaller ones, but size alone does not always determine the outcome of political conflicts. France and, later, the United States were unable to exercise control over Vietnam. Similarly, the Soviet Union could not control Afghanistan. Indeed, history is replete with examples of small countries that won wars or defended their independence against much larger states.

Since we lack a single measuring rod for assessing **power potential**, scholars and policy makers alike try to rank order states according to a combination of capabilities or resources presumed necessary to influence others. Like chefs at a chili cook-off, everyone has his or her own list of ingredients. Normally, some combination of geographic, demographic, economic, and other tangible factors are mixed with intangible factors like leadership and public morale. Though the

power potential the relative capabilities or resources held by a state that are considered necessary to its asserting influence over others.

recipes may differ, the results are the usually the same: Power is equated with those capabilities that enhance a country's war-making ability.

The importance customarily accorded to military prowess arises from the tendency to regard force as the ultimate arbiter of serious international disputes. Recall from earlier chapters that the anarchical environment of world politics requires states to rely on self-help for protection. No higher authority safeguards their interests. Under such conditions, military strength is seen as the primary source of national security and international influence.

While military strength may be effective in controlling the behavior of friends and foes in some contexts, it is ineffective in others. Power is situationally specific: The capabilities that allow an actor to influence one set of countries on a certain issue may be useless in influencing other countries on a different matter. A state's overall power, therefore, is defined in terms of the kinds of actors that it can control and the types of issues over which it has influence. As discussed in Chapter 4, a great power is a state that is able to exercise control over a wide domain of targets and an extensive scope of issues, usually by having a broad range of rewards and punishments at its disposal.

Globalization and the Changing Nature of State Power

Although military capability is central to most realist conceptions of power and security, some liberal theorists argue that the sources of state power today depend less on military strength than on factors such as information, technology, and trade competitiveness (Nye 1990). Since the end of World War II, a handful of states have increased their relative power by investing their resources in civilian rather than military technology. Whereas the United States spends most of its research and development budget on military programs, Japan and many European countries invest heavily in developing new technologies related to consumer goods. If we are entering a world based on education and human capital, one where creative ideas, product design, financing, and marketing will increasingly become major sources of wealth and power as political scientist Richard Rosecrance (1999) suggests, then the United States is not keeping up with its competitors, even though it accounts for almost half of the world's military expenditures.

opportunity costs the concept in decision-making theories that when the occasion arises to use resources, what is gained for one purpose is lost for other purposes, so that every choice entails the cost of some lost opportunity.

Critics of the realist emphasis on continually preparing for war also claim that military expenditures extract high **opportunity costs** (see Controversy: Does High Military Spending Lower Human Security?). Military spending, they assert, crowds out private and public investment. Had U.S. military outlays remained at the 1990 level, the peace dividend from the end of the Cold War would have exceeded $700 billion in the next fifteen years and potentially could have been made available for other purposes. In addition to sacrificing other economic opportunities, this argument continues, military spending has direct costs, because expensive equipment quickly becomes outdated in the face of rapid technological innovations. This creates the need for even more sophisticated new weapons, the costs of which are staggering.

Finally, critics of realism submit that less-tangible sources of national power now figure more prominently in calculations regarding national defense. Sometimes it is possible for political leaders to get what they want by setting

CONTROVERSY   Does High Military Spending Lower Human Security?

Politics requires making hard choices about how public funds should be spent. One such choice is between "guns versus butter"—how much of a country's budget should be allocated to military preparedness as opposed to social welfare programs. The former emphasizes *state security*; the latter, *human security*. Neither goal can be pursued without making some sacrifice for the realization of the other.

The guns-versus-butter trade-off is a significant in every country, and different leaders deal with it in different ways. One way to picture these differences is to group states according to how much of their gross domestic product (GDP) they devote to the military. As the map below shows, there exist wide variations, with many countries allocating high proportions of their GDP to defense and other countries choosing to spend their wealth on enhancing human security. Indeed, some comparatively wealthy states (Kuwait, Israel, and Brunei) bear a heavy defense burden, whereas other states that provide a high average income for their citizens (Japan, Austria, and Luxembourg) have a low defense burden. Likewise, the citizens of some very poor countries (Sierra Leone, Mozambique, and Chad) are heavily burdened, whereas those of others (Bhutan and Zaire) are not. Thus, it is difficult to generalize about the precise relationship between a country's

defense burden and its citizens' standard of living, human development, or stage of development.

"The problem in defense spending," as former U.S. President Dwight D. Eisenhower once observed, "is to figure out how far you should go without destroying from within what you are trying to defend from without." How much should a country spend on national security? To some, the price is never too high. However, others argue that high levels of military spending reduce a state's ability to provide for its citizens. This view was expressed by Oscar Arias, the 1987 Nobel Peace laureate and former president of Costa Rica, who argued that "World leaders must stop viewing militaristic investment as a measure of national well-being. The sad fact is that half the world's governments invest more in defense than in health programs. If we channeled just $40 billion each year away from armies and into antipoverty programs, in ten years all of the world's population would enjoy basic social services—education, health care and nutrition, potable water and sanitation. Another $40 billion each year over ten years would provide each person on this planet with an income level above the poverty line for his or her country."

The case of the United States, the world's biggest spender on defense, speaks to Dr. Arias's contention that high military spending reduces what can be spent on social

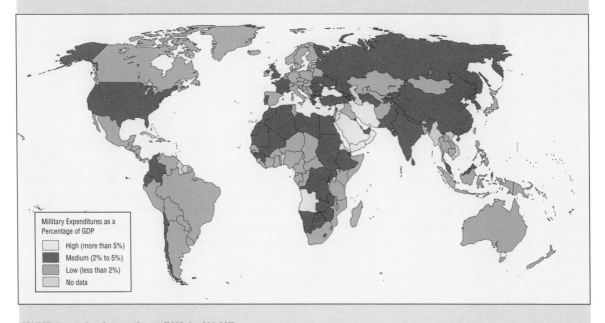

Military Expenditures as a Percentage of GDP

- High (more than 5%)
- Medium (2% to 5%)
- Low (less than 2%)
- No data

SOURCE: Human Development Report (2008, Pp. 294–297)

and health programs. Consider how the United States ranks on various nonmilitary indicators of human security:

How the United States Ranks in the World

Social Indicators

Public education expenditures per person: 14

Human development index: 10

Child material well-being: 17

Environmental performance: 28

Total incarcerated population for every 100,000 people: 1

Health Indicators

Public health expenditures (% of GDP): 35

Life expectancy: 40

Index of child health and safety: 21

Under-five mortality rate: 15

Number of physicians per person: 27

These rankings (*HDR* 2008, 294-297; *Economist* 2007) raise serious questions about the true costs of national security. Who really pays for defense? If you were a head of state, what budget priorities would you propose for your country's national security and your citizens' human security? How would you reconcile the need for defense with the need to provide for the common welfare? The choices you would make would be difficult, because they entail trade-offs between competing values.

the agenda and determining the framework of a debate, instead of relying upon inducements and threats to coerce people. The ability to get others to embrace your values, to see your objectives as legitimate, tends to be associated with intangible power resources such as the attractiveness of your country's ideals and the seductiveness of its culture. These intangible resources constitute *soft power,* in contrast with the *hard power* usually associated with tangible resources like military and economic strength (Nye 2004). Soft power is "the ability to achieve goals through attraction rather than coercion . . . by convincing others to follow or getting them to agree to norms and institutions that produce the desired behavior" (Keohane and Nye 2001b). If soft power grows in relative importance in today's so-called information age, military force ratios will no longer translate into power potential in the way they once did. Of course, military capability will remain important. While "it could be a mistake to assume that political influence is proportional to military strength, it would be an even bigger mistake to deny any connection between the two" (Majeed 1991).

THE PURSUIT OF MILITARY CAPABILITY

How people spend their money reveals their values. Similarly, how governments allocate their revenues reveals their priorities. An examination of national budgets discloses an unmistakable pattern: Although the sources of global political power may be changing, many states continue to seek security by spending substantial portions of their national treasures on arms.

Trends in Military Spending

The weapons that governments believe they require for national security are costly. World military expenditures by the beginning of 2007, for example, reached $1,204 billion, exceeding more than $1.9 million each minute (WDI 2007, 267). When measured in constant dollars adjusted for inflation, this level of military spending shows an increase over past levels: three times that spent in 1960, twice that of the 1970 total, and above the 1980 Cold War peak. Compared to the mid-1930s, world military spending has increased seventeen-fold, a growth rate exceeding that of world population, the rate of expansion of global economic output, and expenditures for public health.

These aggregate figures do not tell the entire story, because the global total spent for arms conceals widely varying trends for particular groups of countries. Historically, the rich countries have spent the most money on arms acquisitions, a pattern that has continued. In 2007 the Global North spent $1,000 billion for defense, in contrast with the Global South's $204 billion. Thus the developed countries' share of the world total was about 85 percent. However, when measured against other factors, the differences are not so great. The Global North spent an average of 2.0 percent of their GNPs for defense, whereas the Global South spent an average of 2.5 percent. While these two groups' military spending levels were different, over time they have been converging. As Figure 8.1 reveals, the Global South's military expenditure in 1961 was about 7 percent of the world total, but by 2005 it had more than doubled (SIPRI 2006, 326–327). In short, poor states are copying the costly, military budgetary habits of the wealthiest states.

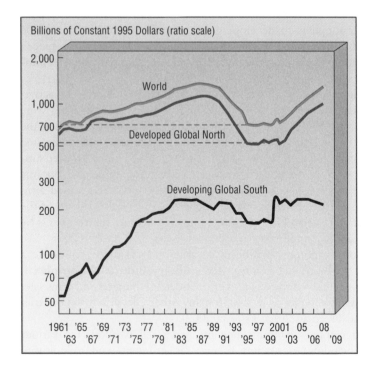

FIGURE 8.1 Changes in the Levels of Military Expenditures since 1960, Global North and Global South

Global military spending has fluctuated since 1960, with total expenditures worldwide peaking in 1987, after which they fell until the terrorist attacks on New York and Washington in 2001. As the trend lines show, the Global South's defense spending peaked during a 1982–1986 plateau, then declined before rising again since 1993 to about 15 percent of the world's total.

SOURCES: 1961–1995, U.S. ACDA (1998); 1996–2008 SIPRI Yearbooks.

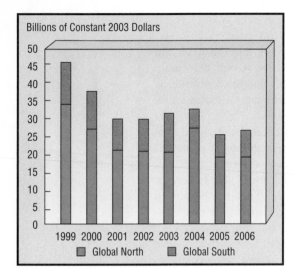

FIGURE 8.2 Arms Deliveries to the Global North and Global South, 1999–2006

The global arms trade has led to the diffusion of military capabilities from the Global North to the Global South. In 2004, arms deliveries to developing countries accounted for three-fourths of all arms deliveries worldwide.

SOURCE: Grimmett (2007, 38).

Trends in the Weapons Trade

During the Cold War, many states sought to increase their security by purchasing weapons. The Cold War's end did not slow the arms trade, however. The total value of all international arms deliveries between 1991 and 2006 exceeded $485 billion (Grimmett 2007, 4) of which the majority were exported to developing countries, primarily in Asia and the Middle East (see Figure 8.2). The weapons delivered by major suppliers to developing countries between 2003 and 2006 alone included 2,612 tanks and self-propelled cannons, 2,854 artillery pieces, 774 supersonic combat aircraft, 4,565 surface-to-air missiles, and other technologically advanced weapons systems (Grimmett 2007, 72).

Besides looking at arms importers, it is also important to observe the activities of arms suppliers. By the end of the Cold War, more than sixty states were selling weapons abroad (Sivard 1991, 11), with the United States dominating the arms export market. Since the turn of the century, the United States accounted for a higher proportion of worldwide contracts to sell arms than any other supplier, agreeing to weapons-export contracts exceeding $61 billion. Economic gain was an important rationale for these sales, as the United States used arms exports to offset its chronic balance-of-trade deficits. To cement its share of the arms trade, one quarter "of all U.S. foreign aid goes to helping the recipients by U.S.-produced weapons, equipment, or services (*Harper's,* October 2005, 11). Because the sale of weapons is big business, arms manufacturers constitute a powerful domestic lobby. A highly organized **military–industrial complex** is widely believed to exercise enormous power over defense budgets and arms sales agreements in the United States as well as in many other Global North countries (Mount, Maier, and Freeman 2003; Fallows 2002).

In addition to reaping economic benefits, states sell weapons for various political reasons, including to support friendly governments and to cultivate

military-industrial complex a term coined by U.S. president Eisenhower to describe the coalition among arms manufacturers, military bureaucracies, and top government officials that promotes defense expenditures for its own profit and power.

new allies. This was illustrated by U.S. arms export policy prior to and in the aftermath of the 1990 Persian Gulf War. The United States delivered 56 percent of the $101 billion in arms sold to the strife-torn Middle East between 1994 and 2001 (Grimmett 2002, 53, 5), allegedly for the purpose of anchoring allies and preserving the military balance of power in that explosive region. Whether arming other countries has accomplished all of its intended political goals is open to question, however. During the Cold War, for example, the United States and the Soviet Union thought they could maintain peace by spreading arms to politically pivotal recipients. Between 1983 and 1987 the United States provided arms to 59 less-developed countries while the Soviet Union supplied 42 (Klare 1990, 12). Yet many of the recipients engaged in war with their neighbors or experienced internal rebellion. Of the top twenty arms importers in 1988, more than half "had governments noted for the frequent use of violence" (Sivard 1991, 17). When seen in this light, it appears to some observers that the U.S. arms export program undermines the current U.S. policy of promoting democracy, because roughly one-third of the recipients of U.S. arms exports in recent years have not been democracies (Blanton and Kegley 1997, 94–95).

The inability of arms suppliers to control the uses to which their military hardware will be put is troubling. Friends can become foes, and supplying weapons to other states can backfire, as the United States discovered when the weapons it sold to Iraq were used against U.S. forces by Saddam Hussein in the Persian Gulf War (Timmerman 1991), and when the Stinger missiles the United States supplied to mujahideen forces resisting the Soviet Union's 1979 invasion in Afghanistan fell into the hands of terrorists later opposing the United States. Likewise, in 1982, Great Britain found itself shipping military equipment to Argentina just eight days before Argentina's attack on the British-controlled Falkland Islands (Sivard 1982). Nevertheless, suppliers seem eager to sell to any purchaser, and they continue to sell weapons to both sides of a number of international disputes.

Trends in Weapons Technology

The widespread quest for armaments has created a potentially "explosive" global environment. This description is especially apt when we consider not only trends in defense expenditures and the arms trade but also the destructiveness of modern weapons.

Nuclear Weapons. Technological research and development has radically expanded the destructiveness of national arsenals. The largest "blockbuster" bombs of World War II delivered a power of ten tons of TNT. The atomic bomb that leveled Hiroshima had the power of over fifteen thousand tons of TNT. Less than twenty years later, the former Soviet Union built a nuclear bomb with the explosive force of fifty-seven megatons (million tons) of TNT. Since 1945, more than 130,000 nuclear warheads had been built, all but 2 percent by the United States (55 percent) and the Soviet Union (43 percent). Most have been dismantled since the 1986 peak, but more than 11,530 worldwide remained operational in 2007—a collective explosive force of over 1.3 million Hiroshima bombs (SIPRI 2007, 515).

At the start of 2008, there were nine "official" members of the nuclear club—the United States, Russia, Great Britain, France, China, India, Pakistan, Israel, and North Korea. In addition, Iran, and as many as twenty other states or terrorist organizations were believed seeking nuclear capability. Obstacles to nuclear **proliferation** are weak. First, the expertise necessary for weapons development has spread with the globalization of advanced scientific training. Second, export controls designed to stop technology transfer for military purposes are ineffectual. Finally, the materials needed to make a nuclear weapon are widely available, primarily due to the widespread use of nuclear technology for generating electricity. As of 2006, 443 nuclear power reactors were in operation in thirty-eight countries throughout the world, with twenty-six new reactors under construction and another thirty-five planned (SIPRI 2006, 690). States could reprocess the uranium and plutonium that power plants produce as waste for clandestine nuclear weapons production. Current estimates suggest that commercial reprocessing reactors are producing enough plutonium to make as many as 40,000 nuclear weapons.

Nuclear weapons serve as a symbol of status and power. Because of the widespread conviction rooted in realism that military might confers political stature, some countries regard the **Nuclear Nonproliferation Treaty (NPT)** as

proliferation the spread of weapon capabilities throughout the state system.

Nuclear Nonproliferation Treaty (NPT) an international agreement that seeks to prevent the spread of nuclear weapons by prohibiting the further nuclear weapons sales, acquisitions, or production.

STOCKFOLIO/Alamy Limited

Nuclear Testing Since the dawn of the nuclear age in 1945, nine known nuclear powers have conducted 2,057 documented tests of their weapons. Pictured here is a 1995 French nuclear test in the South Pacific.

hypocrisy because it provides a seal of approval to those who first acquired nuclear weapons while denying it to all others. The underlying belief that it is acceptable to develop a nuclear capacity for deterrence, influence, and prestige was expressed in 1999 by Brajesh Mishra, India's national security adviser, when he justified his country's acquisition of nuclear weapons by asserting that "India should be granted as much respect and deference by the United States and others as is China today."

Ironically, the same kinds of arguments were once voiced by some of the first members to join the nuclear club. Half a century ago, for instance, former French President Charles de Gaulle insisted that without an independent nuclear capability France could not "command its own destiny." Britain's Aneurin Bevan echoed his concern, stating that without the bomb the British would go "naked into the council chambers of the world." Given these attitudes, "There's not a snowball's chance in hell we'll eliminate all nuclear weapons from the face of the earth," explains Matthew Bunn, editor of *Arms Control Today*. "That genie is long since out of the bottle and there's no chance of ever getting him back in" (cited in Kegley and Wittkopf 2004, 471).

Biological and Chemical Weapons. Despite the 1972 Biological Weapons Convention prohibiting the development, production, and stockpiling of biological weapons, many people fear that some states and terrorist organizations are trying to "weaponize" bacteria, viruses, and toxins. Similarly, although the 1925 Geneva Protocol banned the use of chemical weapons in warfare, and the Chemical Weapons Convention (CWC), now signed by four-fifths of the world's countries, required the destruction of existing stocks of nerve, blood, blister, and choking agents, roughly a dozen states are suspected of producing chemical weapons. As realists note, Iran's and Iraq's use of gas in their war against one another in the 1980s, and Iraq's use of chemical weapons in 1989 against its own Kurdish people demonstrate the weakness of these legal barriers.

Because biological and chemical weapons are lethal, can be produced at comparatively low cost, and are easy to manufacture, transport, and deliver, their acquisition by state and nonstate actors may be unavoidable. On the one hand, weak states that acquire such weapons may see in them a way to deter great powers by threatening to inflict significant damage on anyone who dares attack them. On the other hand, extremist groups, often operating beyond the control of failing states, may find these weapons of mass destruction to be an effective means of promoting global terror.

From the perspective of the user, biological weapons have fewer disadvantages than chemical weapons, whose effectiveness is limited by wind, temperature, and other environmental conditions. For example, many pathogens are highly contagious and have a substantial incubation period. Consequently, an attack would not have to target a large number of people to produce mass casualties, and the perpetrators would have time to go into hiding before authorities realized that an attack had occurred. Although the dangers of nuclear proliferation are widely recognized, less attention has been given to the strategic consequences emanating from the development and diffusion of modern biological weaponry (Preston 2007).

Weapons Delivery Systems. Advances in weapons technology have been rapid and extraordinary. Particularly deadly have been the technological refinements in ballistic missiles that enable states to deliver weapons from as far away as 11,000 miles to within 100 feet of their targets in less than thirty minutes. During the Cold War, the United States and Soviet Union equipped their ballistic missiles with **multiple independently targetable reentry vehicles (MIRVs)**, which enable a single missile to launch several warheads toward different targets simultaneously. One U.S. MX (Peacekeeper) missile equipped with MIRV could carry ten nuclear warheads—enough to wipe out a city and everything else within a fifty-mile radius.

Other technological improvements have led to steady increases in the speed, accuracy, range, and effectiveness of weapons. As the recent wars in Kosovo, Afghanistan, and Iraq have shown, **smart bombs** have become a part of the weapons inventory. Furthermore, remote-controlled aircraft like the Predator drone are being used for surveillance, force protection, and close air support. Linked by satellites to pilots thousands of miles away from the war zone, Predators are armed with two Hellfire missiles that can be launched at targets on the ground. Newer drones, such as the Reaper, carry more ordinance, and Northrop-Grumman is developing an unmanned bomber that would operate from an aircraft carrier. The main drawback of these systems resides in the vulnerability of the military reconnaissance and communication satellites upon which they rely. On January 11, 2007, China used a medium-range ballistic missile to destroy one of its own weather satellites orbiting about 530 miles above Earth, therein demonstrating that control of space cannot be taken for granted by the United States.

Military strategists expect future wars to include even more innovative weapons technologies. They foresee the development of beamed energy and acoustic weapons that can take down enemies without necessarily killing them;

multiple independently targetable reentry vehicles (MIRVs) a technological innovation permitting many nuclear warheads to be delivered from a single missile.

smart bombs precision-guided military technology that enables a bomb to search for its target and detonate at the precise time it can do the most damage.

Remote Control Warfare Unmanned aerial vehicles (UAVs) are playing a major role in counterinsurgency operations. Shown here is the Predator. With a wingspan of almost fifty feet and weighing only 1,130 pounds, it can loiter over a target area for hours at an altitude where it cannot be seen or heard.

electromagnetic pulse bombs, which can be hand delivered in a suitcase and can immobilize an entire city's computer and communications systems; and logic bombs that can confuse and redirect traffic on the target country's air and rail system. Finally, within the next decade or so, robots, which already are used in bomb disposal, may begin replacing soldiers for certain missions. Many of these technological advances in warfare are likely to make orthodox ways of classifying weapons systems as well as prior equations for measuring power ratios obsolete.

For decades, a **firebreak** has separated conventional wars from nuclear wars. The term comes from the barriers of cleared land that firefighters use to keep forest fires from racing out of control. In the context of modern weaponry, it is a psychological barrier whose purpose is to prevent even the most intensive forms of conventional combat from escalating into nuclear war. As both nuclear and conventional weapons technologies advance, there is danger that the firebreak is being crossed from both directions—by a new generation of "near-nuclear" conventional weapons capable of levels of violence approximating those of a limited nuclear strike, and by a new generation of "near-conventional" nuclear weapons capable of causing destruction similar to that of the most powerful conventional weapons. Once the firebreak has been crossed, many people fear that a major restraint on the conduct of modern warfare will disappear.

In sum, a pervasive sense of insecurity haunts much of the world. The danger of nuclear annihilation has not disappeared with the end of the Cold War. Nor are there effective controls over the proliferation of biological and chemical weapons. The twenty-first century has not become the peaceful and prosperous period many people expected. In response, many national leaders today echo the recommendation of the Roman general, Flavius Vegetius Renatus: "If you want peace, prepare for war." Security, as realists insist, requires military capability. But since the possession of military capability does not automatically result in its wise use, we turn now to look at how it is employed as an instrument of statecraft. We begin with an examination of nuclear weapons.

firebreak the psychological barrier between conventional and nuclear war.

MILITARY STRATEGY IN THE NUCLEAR AGE

The dropping of the atomic bomb on Japan on August 6, 1945 is the most important event distinguishing pre– from post–World War II international politics. In a blinding flash, the world was transformed from a "balance-of-power" to a "balance-of-terror" system. In the following decades, policy makers in nuclear-armed states had to grapple with two central policy issues: (1) whether they should use nuclear weapons; and (2) how to prevent others from using them. The search for solutions has been critical, for the immediate and delayed effects of an all-out nuclear war are terrifying to contemplate. Simply put, life as we know it would cease. The planet would be uninhabitable, because a **nuclear winter** would result, with devastating consequences: "Fires ignited in such a war could generate enough smoke to obscure the sun and perturb the

nuclear winter the expected freeze that would occur in the earth's climate from the fallout of smoke and dust in the event nuclear weapons were used, blocking out sunlight and destroying plant and animal life that survived the original blast.

atmosphere over large areas . . . [lowering] average planetary temperatures . . . [and darkening] the skies sufficiently to compromise green plant photosynthesis" (Sagan and Turco 1993, 369). It has been estimated that the twenty-four Trident II missiles on board a single U.S. submarine, each carrying an average of six 455 kiloton W88 warheads, may be enough to initiate nuclear winter—enough to end human existence.

Although weapons of mass destruction have existed since World War II, the postures of the nuclear-armed powers toward them evolved as technologies, defense needs, capabilities, and global conditions changed. For analytical convenience, we can treat those postures in terms of three periods: compellence, deterrence, and preemption. The first began at the end of World War II and lasted until the Cuban missile crisis. U.S. nuclear superiority was the dominant characteristic of this period. The second began in 1962 and lasted until the breakup of the Soviet Union in 1991. Growing Soviet military capability was the dominant characteristic of this period, which meant that the United States no longer stood alone in its ability to annihilate another country without fear of its own destruction. The third phase began after the end of the Cold War, taking shape as the great powers began revising their strategic doctrines in the light of new global threats.

compellence a threat of force aimed at making an adversary grant concessions against its will.

brinkmanship intentionally taking enormous risks in bargaining with an adversary in order to compel submission.

massive retaliation a policy of responding to any act of aggression with the most destructive capabilities available, including nuclear weapons.

countervalue targeting strategy targeting strategic nuclear weapons against an enemy's most valued non-military resources, such as the people and industries located in its cities (sometimes known as countercity targeting).

counterforce targeting strategy targeting nuclear weapons on the military capabilities of an opponent.

Compellence

Countries that possess military preeminence often think of weapons as instruments in diplomatic bargaining. The United States, the world's first and, for many years, unchallenged nuclear power, adopted the strategic doctrine of **compellence** (Schelling 1966) when it enjoyed a clear-cut superiority over the Soviet Union. Military capabilities do not have to be used for them to be useful; a state may exercise influence over others simply by "demonstrating the quantity of force and highlighting the capability of, and intention to, use force" (Majeed 1991). The U.S. doctrine of compellence made nuclear weapons tools of political influence, used not for fighting but to convince others to do what they might not otherwise do.

The United States sought to gain bargaining leverage by conveying the impression that it would actually use nuclear weapons. This posture was especially evident during the Eisenhower administration, when Secretary of State John Foster Dulles practiced **brinkmanship**, deliberately threatening U.S. adversaries with nuclear destruction so that, at the brink of war, they would concede to U.S. demands. Brinkmanship was part of the overall U.S. strategic doctrine known as **massive retaliation**. To contain communism and Soviet expansionism, it called for a **countervalue targeting strategy**, that is, aiming U.S. nuclear weapons at what the Soviets valued most—their population and industrial centers. Some strategists, however, argued that it would be sufficient to adopt a **counterforce targeting strategy**, which would aim at military installations, thus presumably sparing civilian lives.

Massive retaliation heightened fears in the Kremlin that a nuclear exchange would destroy the Soviet Union but permit the survival of the United States.

Thus in addition to augmenting their nuclear capabilities, Soviet leaders accelerated their space program and successfully launched the world's first satellite (*Sputnik*), therein demonstrating Moscow's ability to deliver nuclear weapons beyond the Eurasian landmass. As Soviet leader Nikita Khrushchev put it in a July 1957 interview: "If you live among dogs, keep a stick." The superpowers' strategic competition now took a new turn, as the United States for the first time faced a nuclear threat to its homeland.

Deterrence

As U.S. strategic superiority eroded, American policy makers began to question the usefulness of weapons of mass destruction as tools in political bargaining. They were horrified by the destruction that could result if compellence provoked a nuclear exchange. The nearly suicidal Cuban missile crisis of 1962 brought about a major change in American strategic thought, shifting strategic policy from compellence to **deterrence**.

deterrence a strategy designed to dissuade an adversary from doing what it would otherwise do.

Whereas compellence contains an offensive coercive threat aimed at persuading an adversary to relinquish something without resistance, deterrence seeks to dissuade an adversary from undertaking some future action against one's homeland (direct deterrence) or against an ally (extended deterrence). Strategists often distinguish between two variants of deterrence. The first, *deterrence by denial*, is based on the assumption that opponents can be convinced to forego an attack if they are shown that their efforts would be futile. The second, *deterrence by punishment*, rests on the assumption that the deterrer has the ability to punish an adversary with unacceptably high costs if an attack is launched. This latter variant informed most of the theorizing about how the United States and Soviet Union would deter one another. The key elements of a deterrence strategy based on punitive threats are: (1) *capabilities*—the possession of military resources that can make threats of military retaliation plausible; (2) *credibility*—the belief that the target of an attack will actually follow through on its threats; and (3) *communication*—the facility to send a potential aggressor the clear message that the deterrer has both the ability and willingness to strike back. Advocates of deterrence by punishment argue that it "will succeed if threatened costs can be communicated to the challenger, assessed by the challenger, and believed by the challenger" (Harknett 1994).

Ironically, the shift from compellence to deterrence stimulated rather than inhibited the U.S.-Soviet arms race. A deterrent strategy that depends on the unquestionable ability to inflict intolerable damage on an opponent requires a **second-strike capability**, which would enable a country to withstand an adversary's first strike and still retain the ability to retaliate with a devastating counterattack. To ensure a second-strike capability and an adversary's awareness of it, deterrence rationalized an unrestrained search for sophisticated retaliatory capabilities. Any system that could be built was built because, as President Kennedy explained in 1961, "only when arms are sufficient beyond doubt can we be certain without doubt that they will never be employed." Both superpowers ultimately deployed a **triad** of land-based intercontinental ballistic

second-strike capability a state's capacity to retaliate after absorbing a first-strike attack with weapons of mass destruction.

triad the combination of ICBMs, SLBMs, and long-range bombers in a second-strike nuclear force.

missiles (ICBMs), submarine-launched ballistic missiles (SLBMs), and long-range bombers, believing that all three could not be destroyed simultaneously in a first-strike attack.

mutual assured destruction (MAD) a system of deterrence in which both sides possess the ability to survive a first strike and launch a devastating retaliatory attack.

Policy makers coined the phrase **mutual assured destruction (MAD)** to describe the strategic balance that emerged between the United States and the Soviet Union after the Cuban missile crisis. Regardless of who struck first, the other side could destroy the attacker. Under these circumstances, initiating a nuclear war was irrational; the frightening costs outweighed any conceivable benefits. As Soviet Premier Nikita Khrushchev warned: "If you reach for the push button, you reach for suicide." Safety, in former British prime minister Winston Churchill's words, was "the sturdy child of terror and survival the twin brother of annihilation."

nuclear utilization theory (NUTs) a body of strategic thought that claimed deterrent treats would be more credible if nuclear weapons were made more usable.

As U.S.-Soviet relations evolved, strategic thinking in the United States split into rival positions. Although MAD continued to dominate the policy recommendations of some, others in the 1980s called for what became known as **nuclear utilization theory (NUTS)**, an approach whereby nuclear weapons would not simply play a deterrent role but also could be used in war. Advocates of this position argued that the use of nuclear weapons would not necessarily escalate to an all-out exchange; instead, they reasoned, it was possible to fight a "limited" nuclear war. By making nuclear weapons more usable, the United States allegedly could make its threats more credible. Proponents of MAD, on the other hand, held that deterrence remained the only sane purpose for nuclear weapons. They contended that any use of nuclear weapons, however limited initially, would surely escalate to an unrestrained exchange.

Strategic Defense Initiative (SDI) a plan conceived by the Reagan administration to deploy an antiballistic missile system using space-based lasers that would destroy enemy nuclear missiles. However, the United States was unable to build a reliable ballistic missile defense during the remaining years of the Cold War.

Yet another shift in strategic thinking occurred in 1983, when U.S. president Reagan proposed building a space-based defensive shield against ballistic missiles. The **Strategic Defense Initiative (SDI)**, or "Star Wars" as critics labeled it, called for the development of a defense against Soviet ballistic missiles, using orbiting laser-based weapons to destroy missiles launched in fear, anger, or by accident. The goal, as President Reagan defined it, was to make nuclear weapons "impotent and obsolete." Thus SDI sought to shift U.S. nuclear strategy away from mutual assured destruction, which President Reagan deemed "morally unacceptable." However, despite spending over $150 billion by 2008, the United States still remains far away from a reliable ballistic missile defense. But with North Korea and Iran testing ballistic missiles, the American effort to construct such a system, now with ground-based interceptors rather than space-based lasers, continues.

Preemption

The end of the Cold War has not brought strategic planning to a conclusion. New dangers are on the horizon, dangers that some strategists believe can only be addressed through a new strategy of **preemption**. "We face a threat with no precedent," President George W. Bush insisted during his commencement address at West Point on June 1, 2002. On the one hand, modern technology allows shadowy terrorist networks to launch catastrophic attacks against the

preemption a quick first-strike attack that seeks to defeat an adversary before it can organize a retaliatory response.

United States. On the other hand, these networks cannot be dissuaded by the threat of punishment because they have no fixed territory or populace to protect. "We must take the battle to the enemy," he exhorted, "and confront the worst threats before they emerge."

Bush's call for acting preemptively against terrorists and the states that harbored them was reiterated in his September 17, 2002 report, *The National Security Strategy of the United States of America* (NSS), and reaffirmed in a subsequent document published in March 2006. Building on the proposition that "nations need not suffer an attack before they can lawfully take action to defend themselves against forces that present an imminent danger," the report argued that the acquisition of weapons of mass destruction by terrorists and rogue states provided the United States with a compelling case for engaging in anticipatory self-defense. Preemption rather than deterrence was required for national security.

Although under international law states have a legal right to defend themselves against imminent attacks, critics charge that beneath the language of military preemption lies a more radical policy of **preventive war**. In brief, a *preemptive* military attack entails the use of force to quell or mitigate an impending strike by an adversary. A *preventive* attack entails the use of force to eliminate any possible future strike, even if there is no reason to believe that the capacity to launch an attack is operational. Whereas the grounds for preemption lie in evidence of a credible, imminent threat, the basis for prevention rests on the suspicion of an incipient, contingent threat (Kegley and Raymond 2007).

preventive war a war undertaken to preclude an adversary from acquiring the capability to attack sometime in the future.

To illustrate the differences between military actions grounded in preemptive versus preventive motivations, let us briefly compare two historical cases. The Six Day War between Israel and an alliance of Egypt, Syria, Jordan, and Iraq was an example of preemption. Tensions between Israel and its Arab neighbors had been growing throughout the spring of 1967 and reached their zenith in May, when Egyptian President Gamal Abdel Nasser undertook a series of steps that raised fears in Tel Aviv of an imminent attack. Besides mobilizing his troops and cementing military ties with Syria, Jordan, and Iraq, Nasser ordered the UN Emergency Force to leave the Sinai, where they had been deployed since the 1956 Suez War as a buffer between Egypt and Israel. Furthermore, he announced a blockade of the Straits of Tiran, Israel's vital waterway to the Red Sea and Indian Ocean, and proclaimed that his goal in any future war with Israel would be the destruction of the Jewish state. Assuming that an invasion was forthcoming and survival was doubtful if Egypt landed the first blow, the Israelis launched a surprise attack on June 5, which enabled them to win a decisive victory.

Whereas the Six Day War exemplifies preemption, Israel's June 1981 raid on Iraq's Osiraq nuclear reactor illustrates preventive military action. From the Israeli perspective, the type of reactor Baghdad had acquired, its purchase of fuel that could be used in weapons manufacturing, and the termination of inspections by the International Atomic Energy Agency provided circumstantial evidence that Iraq was seeking a military nuclear capability. Given the vehement hostility expressed by Iraqi leaders toward Israel, as well as the vulnerability of Israel's population centers and nuclear arsenal to a first strike, Israeli leaders concluded that Saddam Hussein could not be deterred; Iraq's reactor had to be destroyed before it became operational. In contrast to 1967, when Israeli leaders saw an immediate threat from Egypt, they attacked in 1981 on the chance that someday Iraq might become a nuclear threat. It was better, they reasoned, to take preventive action straightaway in order to avoid the risk of fighting under less favorable circumstances later.

It is tempting for national leaders to order a swift, decisive attack against a budding threat, especially when they believe that the cost of inaction today may be devastation tomorrow. Throughout history, many advocates of "power politics" have accepted preventive warfare as a strategic necessity in the rough and tumble environment of world politics. In a classic statement of this opinion, the sixteenth-century Florentine political philosopher Niccolò Machiavelli (1950, 10-11) insisted that political leaders must always guard against looming dangers: "foreseen they can easily be remedied, but if one waits till they are at hand, the medicine is no longer in time as the malady has become incurable." Similarly, Cardinal Richelieu (1961, 80), the prime minister of France under King Louis XIII, maintained that "Just as a doctor who knows how to prevent illness is more esteemed than one who works cures, so too . . . it is more important to anticipate the future than to dwell upon the present, since with enemies of the state, as with diseases, it is better to advance to the attack than to wait."

Yet critics maintain that the preventive use of military force sets a dangerous precedent. Pointing to America's failure to accurately assess Iraq's weapons programs, they argue that preventive wars may be triggered by unreliable intelligence about an adversary's aims and capabilities. Predicting another state's future behavior is difficult because leadership intentions are hard to discern, information on long-term goals may be shrouded in secrecy, and signals of its policy direction may be distorted by background noise. If mere suspicions about an adversary become a justifiable cause for military action, critics continue, every truculent leader will have a rough-and-ready pretext for ordering first strikes against prospective foes. But such strikes entail a high risk of "false positives" (incorrect predictions about future aggression by other states). A major policy dilemma facing political leaders who make preventive decisions concerns the ratio of false positives to false negatives. How can leaders avoid launching preventive wars against states that are wrongly believed to be planning aggression without foregoing action against states that are indeed planning aggression?

The strategy of anticipatory self-defense thus raises anew timeless questions about the conditions under which, and the purposes for which, military force is justifiable. What does precaution warrant when nameless, faceless enemies are willing to engage in indiscriminate, suicidal attacks against noncombatants? How can force be used to influence an adversary's decision-making calculus? What are the conditions that affect the success of coercive diplomacy?

THE LIMITS OF COERCIVE DIPLOMACY

Since the end of the Second World War, strategists have debated the relative merits of two approaches to the use of military force (Gacek 1994). The first would apply force decisively, employing every possible means to win a swift, unequivocal victory whenever vital interests are at stake. Operation Desert Storm, the U.S. plan for liberating Kuwait from Iraqi control in 1991, exemplified this approach. It centered on what then-Chairman of the Joint Chiefs of Staff Colin Powell called the "doctrine of invincible force." Powell advocated using all of the resources available to overwhelm the Iraqis in a massive, fast and furious campaign. In his words, it was the mindset of a New York street fighter: "Here's my bat, here's my gun, here's my knife, I'm wearing armor. I'm going to kick your ass."

The second approach contends that limits on the use of force may be necessary depending on one's political objectives. Rather than going all out or doing nothing, members of this school of thought recommend widening the array of policy options by applying military force in a flexible, discriminating manner calibrated to the type of threat one faces. Power and diplomacy, they maintain, must work in tandem when dealing with security challenges that are significant but do not demand full-scale war.

The strategy of **coercive diplomacy** exemplifies this latter approach to the use of force. It employs threats or limited force to persuade an opponent to change its behavior. The goal is to alter the target state's calculation of costs and benefits, so it is convinced that acceding to one's demands will be better than defying them. This may be accomplished by delivering an **ultimatum** that promises an immediate and significant escalation in the conflict, or by issuing a warning and gradually increasing pressure on the target (Craig and George 1990).

Coercive diplomacy's reliance on threats and exemplary uses of force is designed to avoid the bloodshed and expenses associated with all-out military campaigns. Nevertheless, these attempts at forceful persuasion carry some risk of war. Figure 8.3 shows the annual frequency of international crises between 1918 and 2008 involving coercive efforts. Most of these crises were initiated by the great powers, and about one of every three led to war (www.CIDCM. umd.edu/ICB).

coercive diplomacy the use of threats or limited armed force to persuade an adversary to alter its foreign and/or domestic policies.

ultimatum a demand that contains a time limit for compliance and a threat of punishment for resistance.

The Persuasive Use of Military Force

Orchestrating the mix of threats and armed force can be done in various ways. One method involves military intimidation, which can range from traditional "gunboat diplomacy" (threatening an adversary with a show of naval force) to "tomahawk diplomacy" (striking it with cruise missiles). Another method entails **military intervention**. States can intervene physically through direct entry into another country or indirectly with propaganda. They can act alone or in league with other states. Military intervention involves "operations undertaken openly by a state's regular military forces within a specific foreign land in such a manner

military intervention overt or covert use of force by one or more countries that cross the border of another country in order to affect the target country's government and policies.

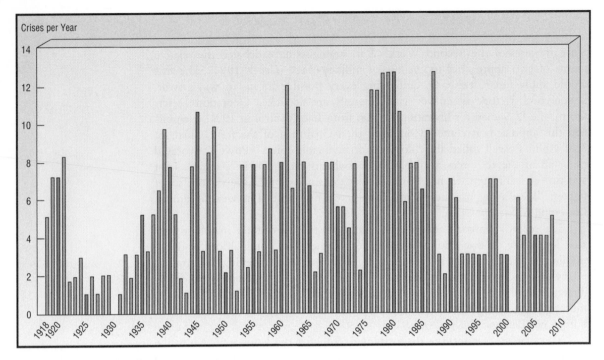

FIGURE 8.3 The Annual Frequency of International Crises

A crisis in international affairs is a situation that (1) threatens a state's high-priority goals; (2) surprises its political leaders; and (3) restricts the amount of time available for making a response (Hermann 1972). On 451 occasions between 1918 and 2008, crises developed because states confronted each other militarily, in the hopes of forcing concessions. One of the problems with such efforts at coercive diplomacy is that crises can easily escalate to war because of the time pressures, inadequate information, heightened anxieties, and impulsive behavior that normally accompany decision-making procedures during threatening situations.

SOURCE: Based on International Crisis Behavior (ICB) data, provided courtesy of Jonathan Wilkenfeld. Frequencies after 2006 are preliminary estimates.

covert operations
secret activities undertaken by a state outside its borders through clandestine means to achieve specific political or military goals.

as to risk immediate combat" (Tillema 1994). Altogether, nearly 1,000 individual acts of military intervention were initiated between 1945 and 2001, involving 2.4 million fatalities (Tilleman 2006). Excluded from this estimate are an unknown number of **covert operations**.

Military interventions have often heightened international tension and led to war. As mentioned in the previous chapter, between 1816 and 2008, forty-nine cases of third-party military intervention into 213 civil wars occurred, with the result that 23 percent were "internationalized." These statistics raise important questions about the use of military intervention for coercive diplomacy. Do interventions yield positive results or do they make matters worse? Are they able to solve security problems quickly or are they more likely to trap their initiators in a quagmire?

Policy makers today disagree about the appropriate use of military coercion. Research on coercive diplomacy suggests that its success depends upon the context of each specific situation. The following conditions are thought to favor the effective use of coercive diplomacy (Art 2005; Pape 1996; George 1991):

- *Clarity of user objectives.* The coercing power's demands must be clearly understood by the target state. Having the target refrain from taking an action is considered less difficult than demanding the target do something it otherwise would not do.

- *Asymmetry of motivation favoring the user.* Military superiority does not guarantee success. The coercing power must be more highly motivated than the target by what is at stake. Timing is critical. Military coercion tends to be effective when it occurs prior to the target making a firm commitment on the issue at hand, and when factions exist within the target state's government. It is far more difficult for a coercing power to undo something that has already been accomplished by the target state.

- *Opponent's fear of escalation and belief in the urgency for compliance.* The coercing power must create in the adversary's mind a sense of urgency for compliance with its demand. Two factors are important in affecting an adversary's perceptions: (1) the coercing power's reputation for successfully using armed force in the past, and (2) its capability to increase pressure to a level that the target would find intolerable. Coercion generally fails when the target has the ability to absorb the punishment delivered by the coercing state.

- *Adequate domestic and international support for the user.* In addition to having political support at home, the coercing power is helped when it also can count on support from key states and international organizations.

- *Clarity on the precise terms of settlement.* The coercing power must be able to articulate the specific conditions for ending the crisis, as well as give assurances that it will not formulate new demands for greater concessions once the target capitulates. Offering positive inducements to the target state can lower its cost of acquiescence. Rewards improve the chances of success when made after a threat of demonstrative use of force, not before. Coercive diplomacy is more potent when the target state understands that you are seeking policy change rather than regime change.

Although these conditions improve the odds of coercive diplomacy being effective, they do not guarantee a favorable outcome. Historically, coercive diplomacy has a success rate of 32 percent (Art 2003, 387). National leaders who resort to forceful persuasion start a process over which they have imperfect control.

Given the uncertainties surrounding the use of armed force, states often employ nonmilitary methods to alter an opponent's behavior. Recalling an ambassador and terminating cultural or scientific exchanges are some of the ways states signal their displeasure. Economic sanctions also figure prominently in this regard, being widely thought of as a proportional response to threats to interests that are less than vital (Haass 1997).

Economic Sanctions

economic sanctions the punitive use of trade or monetary measures, such as an embargo, to harm the economy of an enemy state in order to exercise influence over its policies.

When the Arab members of the Organization of Petroleum Exporting Countries (OPEC) placed an embargo on the shipment of oil to the United States and the Netherlands in 1973, their purpose was to alter these countries' policies toward the Arab-Israeli conflict. When the UN Security Council decided in August 1990 that the world organization should cease trade with Iraq, its purpose was to accomplish the immediate and unconditional withdrawal of Iraqi forces from Kuwait. Both are examples of the use of **economic sanctions**—deliberate actions to penalize a target state by imposing trade or financial restrictions on normal economic relations.

Economic sanctions are an increasingly popular approach to convincing another state to desist from some unacceptable behavior. They include a broad array of instruments: withholding foreign aid, placing tariffs and quotas on imports from a targeted state, boycotting its products, declaring an embargo on the sale of goods to the target, and freezing assets it may have in local banks. Between World War I and 1990, 120 episodes of economic sanctions were undertaken, 104 of which have been enacted since World War II (Hufbauer, Schott, and Elliott 1990). Since the mid-1990s, "more sanctions of more types were employed by more different states and international organizations than ever before" (Allen 2005), leading one prominent journalist to call them the Energizer Bunny of foreign policy.

The rationale for employing sanctions as instruments of influence stems largely from the fact that they avoid the dangers of using armed force. Military coercion can easily backfire, draining government budgets, producing undue casualties, and provoking widespread criticism at home and abroad. In comparison, economic sanctions appear less risky and far less costly.

Another reason for the rising use of economic sanctions is that today national economies are increasingly integrated through trade, which increases the dependence on others for their own prosperity. This circumstance makes sanctions that threaten targets with the loss of an export market more effective than in the past, when countries could better withstand a foreign embargo on the purchase of their products. Likewise, countries dependent on imports from abroad for their energy needs are highly vulnerable to sanctions, since supply disruptions could bring their economies to a standstill.

inelastic demand a condition under which the quantity demanded of a good does not decrease as its price increases.

Research on the effectiveness of economic sanctions indicates that financial restrictions on assets and investment have a higher success rate than trade restrictions (Cortwright and Lopez 1995). The latter, which generally attempt to pressure a country by depriving it of certain imports tend to be more effective when there is (1) an **inelastic demand** for the commodity in the target country, (2) inadequate supply of the commodity in the target country, (3) no inexpensive substitutes for the commodity; and (4) multilateral support for the restrictions. However, the more trade sanctions cost domestic economic interests in the country applying the sanctions (for example, due to lost sales), the less likely they will be imposed decisively and kept in place long enough for them to succeed (see Application: Who is Penalizing Whom?).

APPLICATION   Who is Penalizing Whom?

Economic sanctions often promise more than they produce because the target state's government can take countermeasures to blunt their impact. Madeleine Albright served as the U.S. secretary of state from 1997 to 2001. In the following excerpt, she describes the domestic repercussions in the coercing country that can weaken the effectiveness of sanctions on a target country.

> When I was secretary of state, President Clinton issued an executive order imposing sanctions on Sudan, whose government was violating human rights, bombing school children, and giving aid and comfort to terrorists. This seemed a simple step, and I supported it; and yet it was not simple—the reason was sap. Gum Arabic, which is derived from the acacia tree, is a natural emulsifier used in such products as candy bars, colas, cosmetics, and fireworks. The two leading American processors are located in New Jersey, while 80 percent of the world's supply comes from Sudan. I soon received a phone call from New Jersey congressman Robert Menendez demanding that we exempt gum Arabic from the sanctions. I asked him, "How can you ask for an exemption to sanctions for Sudan while you

oppose so vehemently any exceptions to our embargo of Cuba" His answer: "jobs." Over my objections, Menendez won his exemption for gum Arabic, which remains the law. In 2007, the Bush administration announced plans to seek UN sanctions against Sudan in connection with the genocide in Darfur. Sudan's ambassador to Washington responded by calling a press conference. Standing surrounded by a display of soft drink products, he warned that his country would retaliate against UN sanctions by halting shipments of gum Arabic to the United States—thereby threatening to hit us with the same club we had intended to use against Sudan. That's the problem with sanctions: it is often unclear who is penalizing whom (Albright 2008, 96–97).

Foreign policy, observes Albright, is "not like tennis practice, where you bang the ball against a concrete barrier and the ball bounces back straight and true. It's more like Wimbledon, where your opponent has his own tricks." As such, she concludes, "the use of economic sanctions is no more amenable to a rigid set of rules than the use of military force. Each situation has unique aspects."

Five major policy goals are customarily pursued by states when they adopt economic sanctions to pressure a foreign target:

- *Compliance* ("to force the target to alter its behavior to conform with the initiator's preferences"), as in the case of the 1982 U.S. trade embargo on Libya, designed to force it to end its support of terrorism.

- *Subversion* ("to remove the target's leaders . . . or overthrow the regime"), as in the cases of the 1993–1994 U.S. trade embargo on Haiti and the 2002 U.S. efforts to topple Saddam Hussein in Iraq.

- *Deterrence* ("to dissuade the target from repeating the disputed action in the future"), as in the case of the Soviet grain embargo by the United States.

- *International symbolism* ("to send messages to other members of the world community"), as in the case of the British sanctions against Rhodesia after its unilateral declaration of independence in 1965.

- *Domestic symbolism* ("to increase its domestic support or thwart international criticism of its foreign policies by acting decisively"), as in the case of U.S. sanctions against Iran following its seizure of U.S. diplomats in 1979 (Lindsay 1986).

These multiple uses notwithstanding, it is rare for policy makers to advocate the use of economic sanctions without generating criticism. Critics invariably argue that they do not work because they easily can be circumvented. Even worse, they can be counterproductive, triggering rally-around-the-flag support for the target state's government while hurting disenfranchised groups rather than ruling elites (Pape 1997). To be sure, sanctions have a checkered history. At times they have succeeded, such as in the case of Libya, where after a decade of international pressure, Libyan dictator Muammar Qaddafi finally turned over to Western powers for trial two Libyans alleged to have blown up the Pan Am flight 103 over Scotland in 1988 that killed all of its 280 passengers. Despite this and a few other successes, the historical record casts great doubt on the capacity of sanctions to work, even when used by the world's foremost powerful economic power, the United States. Between 1970 and 1990, "just 5 of 39 unilateral U.S. sanctions [achieved] any success at all" (Elliott 1998, 58). Conspicuous in the many cases where U.S. economic coercion failed is the experience with Cuba. The United States placed sanctions on the Castro regime shortly after it came to power in 1959 and forged an alliance with the Soviet Union. In response, Washington banned all trade with Cuba and pressured other countries to do the same, hoping to overthrow the Castro regime. This goal was not realized, as the regime has survived even after Fidel Castro stepped down due to illness almost a half century after his rise to power.

Cuba is often cited as perhaps the best example of the inherent obstacles to successful sanctions. Other such U.S. failures include the inability of the United States to impose a partial embargo on the sale of grain to the Soviet Union after its 1979 intervention in Afghanistan as well as the inability of the Reagan administration in 1981 to use sanctions to stop Poland and the Soviet Union from building the trans-Siberian gas pipeline designed to bring Soviet energy into western European markets. These examples suggest that sanctions are seldom effective in bringing about major changes in the policies of a target country. According to one statistical survey, they only work about a third of the time and require an almost 2.5 percent impact on the target's GNP for three years (Hufbauer, Schott, and Elliott 1990). Furthermore, sanctions are rarely successful in preventing war. A study of 200 cases found that when economic sanctions were used to punish a government, military conflict actually became "as much as six times more likely to occur between two countries than if sanctions had not been imposed" (*Foreign Policy*, July/August 2007, 19). Rather than efficiently achieving the foreign policy goals of compliance, subversion, or deterrence, economic sanctions mainly serve an important symbolic function by publicizing unacceptable behavior by other states.

The limitations of economic sanctions as a tool of coercive diplomacy can be seen in the unsuccessful efforts to topple the Iraqi dictator Saddam Hussein after the Persian Gulf War ended in 1991. Despite a UN embargo, Hussein was able to continue exporting oil on the black market through dummy corporations and purchase weapons from foreign manufacturers. Meanwhile, ordinary Iraqis suffered, leading the UN to begin experimenting with so-called "smart" sanctions (Cortright and Lopez 2002), which would target governmental elites, not innocent citizens.

The choice between the options of military force and economic sanctions is always a difficult one when national leaders face situations that seem to demand coercive measures. Reliance on economic sanctions is likely to remain high because they enable leaders to take action without bearing the costs and risks of military coercion. Sanctions appear, therefore, destined to remain a major tool of statecraft in the global future.

BUILDING WORLD SECURITY

Since antiquity, preparation for war has often been seen as a prerequisite for security.

Calls for a policy of "peace through strength" are understandable in a world where states alone remain responsible for their own self-defense. As former U.S. president Dwight Eisenhower once noted, "until war is eliminated from international relations, unpreparedness for it is well nigh as criminal as war itself."

Fear of national vulnerability in an anarchic, self-help environment induces defense planners to assume the worst about other states' capabilities and intentions. Even if the military capabilities accumulated by a neighbor are defensively motivated, they may trigger a strong reaction. The state "always feels itself weak if there is another that is stronger," observed the eighteenth-century political philosopher Jean-Jacques Rousseau. "Its security and preservation demand that it make itself more powerful than its neighbors. It can increase, nourish, and exercise its power only at their expense. . . . It becomes small or great, weak or strong, according to whether its neighbor expands or contracts, becomes stronger or declines."

State power, Rousseau reminds us, is relative. Efforts to obtain absolute security by one state tend to be perceived as creating absolute insecurity for others, with the result that everyone becomes locked into an upward spiral of counter-measures that diminishes the security of all. Scholars refer to this as a **security dilemma**, a condition that results when each state's increase in military capabilities is matched by the others, and all wind up with no more security than when they began arming (Snyder 1984; Jervis 1976). "Security based on strength is a mirage," concluded French theorist Raymond Aron (1965, 212) as he observed the United States and Soviet Union during the Cold War. "If one side feels safe from attack, the other will feel at the mercy of the enemy."

Asking whether preparing for war endangers, rather than ensures, national security raises an uncomfortable question that challenges the prevailing approach to national security throughout much of the world's history. Yet many experts believe such questioning is justified. To their way of thinking, security in the twenty-first century must be defined more broadly so as to include nonmilitary, transnational threats, including environmental, economic, and epidemiological hazards that can jeopardize the global future. At issue is whether this new way of thinking about security will gain wider acceptance, or whether traditional realist approaches to national security will continue to resonate in the world's

security dilemma the propensity of armaments undertaken by one state for ostensibly defensive purposes to threaten other states, which arm in reaction, with the result that their national security declines as their arms increase.

capitals. The next chapter examines the ways in which arms, alliances, the balance of power are pursued by national leaders who believe that political realism provides the safest path to peace.

CHAPTER SUMMARY

- In world politics, power refers to the ability of one international actor to control the behavior of another actor, making it continue some course of action, change what it is doing, or refrain from acting.

- Although most scholars agree that states are not equal in their ability to influence one another, there is little consensus on how to best weigh the various factors that contribute to state power. Their impact depends on the circumstances in a bargaining situation between states, and especially on how leaders perceive them.

- National leaders tend to assume that security is a function of power, and power is a function of military capabilities.

- As states spend increasing amounts of national wealth on arms, war-making capabilities have become more widespread than ever. Those countries least able to afford the broad spectrum of available weapons have made the greatest sacrifices to get them, often reducing the quality of their citizens' lives by retarding social welfare programs and economic development.

- Advances in military technology have increased the destructive capacity of weapons and improved their range and precision.

- Although states ostensibly arm for defensive purposes, neighboring countries frequently perceive their military acquisitions as threatening. When one state's armaments increases are matched by others, everyone winds up paying higher costs with no more security than they had before this vicious cycle began.

- States that enjoy military superiority over their adversaries often think of their weapons as instruments for coercive bargaining. Threats of military force are used for both compellence and deterrence. Deterrence requires three ingredients: (1) capabilities—the possession of military resources to make threats of retaliation plausible; (2) credibility—the belief by others that a state is willing to carry out its threats; and (3) communication—the ability to send an opponent a clear message about one's capabilities and intentions.

- Preemptive military attacks entail the use of force against imminent threats; preventive attacks are aimed at threats that might possibly emerge in the future.

- International interdependence multiplies the opportunities to use economic instruments for coercive purposes, though they often fall short of their objectives. Nonetheless, economic sanctions serve an important symbolic function, providing a policy alternative to the use of military force and a way to publicize unacceptable behavior by other states.

- Although security policies in the twenty-first century will continue to focus on military threats, some scholars contend that many nontraditional security threats will demand greater attention, including global climate change, the depletion of the earth's finite resources, and pandemic diseases.

KEY TERMS

brinkmanship

coercive diplomacy

compellence

counterforce targeting strategy

countervalue targeting strategy

covert operations

deterrence

economic sanctions

firebreak

inelastic demand

massive retaliation

military-industrial complex

military intervention

multiple independently targetable reentry vehicles (MIRVs)

mutual assured destruction (MAD)

Nuclear Nonproliferation Treaty (NPT)

nuclear utilization theory (NUTs)

nuclear winter

opportunity costs

power potential

preemption

preventive war

proliferation

second-strike capability

security dilemma

smart bombs

Strategic Defense Initiative (SDI)

triad

ultimatum

SUGGESTED READINGS

Arreguín-Toft, Ivan. *How the Weak Win Wars: A Theory of Asymmetric Conflict*. Cambridge: Cambridge University Press, 2005.

Caldwell, Dan, and Robert E. Williams. *Seeking Security in an Insecure World*. Lanham, MD.: Rowman & Littlefield, 2006.

Mandel, Robert. *The Meaning of Military Victory*. Boulder, CO: Lynne Rienner, 2006.

Morgan, Patrick. *International Security: Problems and Solutions*. Washington, D.C.: CQ Press, 2006.

Preston, Thomas. *From Lambs to Lions: Future Security Relationships in a World of Biological and Nuclear Weapons*. Landham, MD: Rowman & Littlefield, 2007.

CRITICAL THINKING QUESTIONS

As the discussion of compellence in this chapter notes, brinkmanship is a bargaining strategy in which rival states threaten mutual disaster in an effort to make the other side capitulate. The game of Chicken often is used to analyze crises where brinkmanship may be attempted. The game originates from the 1950s story of rival teenagers (A and B) who want to demonstrate their fortitude to peers by racing their cars toward one another on a narrow road. If one driver doesn't swerve and the other does, the former gains a reputation for courage while the latter is disgraced. If both swerve, each loses some prestige. If neither swerves, they both die in a head-on collision. Because both drivers want to live and earn as much status as possible, their preferences can be rank ordered from best to worst as follows: (1) win a reputation for fearlessness; (2) suffer a slight loss in prestige; (3) suffer a significant loss in prestige; and (4) die in a collision. The matrix below depicts the results that will occur depending on whether each driver swerves or doesn't.

		B	
		Swerve	Not Swerve
A	Swerve	2, 2	3, 1
	Not Swerve	1, 3	4, 4

Note: The first number in each cell of this matrix is A's payoff, the second number is B's payoff. The number 1 represents the most preferred outcome, whereas 4 represents the least preferred outcome.

Now imagine that players A and B in the matrix are heavily armed states, not teenage drivers; furthermore, assume that swerving represents backing down in a confrontation and not swerving represents standing firm. In this representation, the lower right cell shows the outcome when neither side gives way (collision/war, or payoff 4, 4), the upper left cell displays the outcome when both sides flinch (de-escalation, or payoff 2, 2), and the remaining cells (payoffs 3,1 and 1, 3) signify one side's victory and the other's capitulation.

Given the payoff structure of this game, what would you expect a player to do when he or she must act without knowing what the other player will do? Is it "irrational" to commit to a strategy of standing firm in a crisis regardless of the costs? What incentives are there to manipulate shared risk, acting provocatively to induce the other side to accommodate? How important is credibility to the outcome of this game? Beyond armed confrontations such as the Cuban missile crisis, is the game of Chicken a good analogue for other bargaining situations in world politics where mutual intransigence would be catastrophic for both sides?

Realist Paths to Peace: Alliances, Arms Control, and the Balance of Power

CHAPTER OUTLINE

Realism and the Balancing of Power

Assumptions of Balance-of-Power Theory

Managing the Balance through a Concert of Great Powers

Stabilizing Power Balances through Arms Control

Arms Control versus Disarmament

Bilateral Arms Control and Disarmament

APPLICATION: Conflict Spirals and Self-Defeating Behavior

Multilateral Arms Control and Disarmament

The Problematic Future of Arms Control and Disarmament

Balancing Power in the Contemporary International System

The Cold War Pattern of Direct Opposition

A Future of Balance-of-Power Competition?

CONTROVERSY: How Should the United States Respond to China's Growing Power

As nature abhors a vacuum, so international politics abhors unbalanced power. Faced by unbalanced power, states try to increase their own strength or they ally with others to bring the international distribution of power into balance.

KENNETH N. WALTZ

POLITICAL SCIENTIST

The specter of a world teeming with nuclear-armed states has haunted many people for decades. Although some scholars contend that the spread of nuclear weapons would make war more dangerous and therefore less likely, most people fear that an increase in the number of fingers on nuclear triggers would raise the probability of one being pulled, whether by accident or by design.

As mentioned in the previous chapter, the 1968 Nuclear Nonproliferation Treaty (NPT) sought to control the diffusion of nuclear weapons by requiring those who possessed them to pledge not to share the technology with others, and by stipulating that those without these weapons promise not to acquire them. Under the terms of the treaty, which eventually was ratified by 189 countries (North Korea withdrew in 2003, however), all parties could develop civilian nuclear power for peaceful purposes, although nonnuclear weapons states were required to accept safeguards over their activities as set forth in an agreement negotiated with the UN's International Atomic Energy Agency (IAEA).

India, which had not signed the NPT, possessed an active program for developing nuclear power to meet its enormous energy needs. On May 18, 1974, India exploded a nuclear device made from its reactor in Trombay, demonstrating that given sufficient scientific expertise and technological skill, nations seeking to join the nuclear club could use fuel from civilian power plants to fabricate weapons.

In response, Pakistan, which had fought bitter wars against India in 1947–1948, 1965, and 1971, began working covertly to build nuclear weapons. Concerned that Chinese military assistance to the Pakistanis might embolden them, the Indians decided to demonstrate their strength by conducting a series of nuclear weapons tests in 1998. Pakistan, however, followed suit with its own tests. The United Nations condemned both sides, and the United States underscored the UN reprimand by imposing sanctions against New Delhi and Islamabad.

India strongly objected to the criticism. In the aftermath of the tests, it accelerated the modernization of its air and naval power-projection capabilities, announcing that it expected to deploy at least three aircraft carriers by 2020. From roughly $11 billion for 1999–2000, India's defense budget climbed to over $21 billion by 2007–2008 (Yuan 2007, 136). With its economy growing at 7 percent a year, India also embarked on an ambitious space program, launching eleven satellites between 1998 and 2007 and a lunar mission in 2008. Like other up-and-coming powers, India's continued economic growth is not assured. Widespread poverty, water shortages, and a problematic infrastructure could stall the country's drive to be accepted on an equal footing with other great powers.

Nevertheless, projections by many analysts suggest that India's percentage share of the world's gross domestic product will rank third by mid-century, behind only the United States and China.

Despite international pressure on India to halt its weapons program and become a party to the NPT, it has continued to complain that the nonproliferation regime arbitrarily defines the possession of nuclear weapons by the United States, Russia, Britain, France, and China as legitimate while outlawing them to everyone else. Given the history of friction between New Delhi and Washington over nuclear weapons, many observers were shocked when Prime Minister Manmohan Singh and President George W. Bush announced at a 2006 meeting that they had reached an agreement that would treat India as an exception to the rules of the nonproliferation regime. In exchange for obtaining nuclear fuel and technology from the United States, India would open its nonmilitary reactors to IAEA inspectors. If approved by the Indian Parliament, U.S. Congress, and the IAEA, critics grumble that the agreement would undermine the NPT.

Why did the United States abruptly change its position regarding India and the NPT? Democratic India, the Bush administration professed, had been a responsible custodian of its nuclear facilities; New Delhi had not transferred nuclear weapons or technology to others. Although there would be no surveillance over India's military reactors and no limits would be placed on the number of nuclear weapons that India could produce, supporters of the agreement maintained that placing the country's civil nuclear programs under permanent inspections was a significant step forward.

Political realists expressed skepticism over this explanation. They believed that America's policy shift was a product of balance-of-power politics, not India's probity. With China emerging as a near-peer competitor, the United States wanted to augment its longstanding ties to Japan with new ties to India, which it viewed as a "swing state" in the Asian balance of power (Mohan 2006). By making a deal favorable to New Delhi, America would have an opportunity to build a strategic partnership with India, adding its weight to Japan's in counterbalancing China. Joint naval exercises held in the Bay of Bengal during the summer of 2007 by the United States, Japan, and India accentuated the converging security policies.

From Beijing's perspective, this triangular arrangement is aimed at containing China's influence, denying the country its rightful status in the world. Leery of American motives, Japanese ambitions, and Indian assertiveness, China has looked for countervailing alliances. In addition to its

Manish Swarup/AP Photos

Wary Neighbors Despite the meeting in 2005 between Prime Ministers Wen Jiabao of China and Manmohan Singh of India, colliding interests, mutual suspicions, and unresolved territorial disputes have complicated the relations between these rising Asian powers.

traditional ties with Pakistan on India's western border, China has worked to build relationships with several of India's eastern neighbors, including Bangladesh and Myanmar. More importantly, it has established the Shanghai Cooperation Organization (SCO). Although not a collective defense pact like NATO, the SCO has brought together China, Russia, Kazakhstan, Kyrgyzstan, Tajikistan, and Uzbekistan for joint military exercises, such as those conducted in 2007 near the Ural Mountains. In March 2008, Iran indicated that it wished to join the organization.

Realists submit that this geopolitical maneuvering reflects an age-old process of balancing against potential threats. The United States may support the principle of nonproliferation, but it was willing to carve out an exception to the NPT for India to enlist New Delhi's help in balancing against an ascending China. New Delhi may have been frustrated with America's nuclear policies, but the Indians also had apprehensions about China. Although the United States and India were at loggerheads for years, they shared a common interest in preserving a balance of power in Asia.

REALISM AND THE BALANCING OF POWER

Our discussion of conflict and its management in Part III of *The Global Future* has followed a logical progression. Chapter 7 began by exploring why the frequency of war makes preparations for it so necessary. Chapter 8 examined the search for national security through the acquisition of military capabilities. We now take up the question of how to sustain peace in a world populated by armed, egoistic states that frequently practice coercive diplomacy.

Realists, liberals, and constructivists offer different answers to this question. In this chapter, we will concentrate on the realist response: maintaining a **balance of power** by forming alliances with other countries to offset the military might of an adversary, and negotiating arms control agreements to maintain strategic parity.

balance of power the theory that national survival in an anarchic world is most likely when military power is distributed to prevent a single hegemon or bloc from dominating the state system.

Assumptions of Balance-of-Power Theory

The concept of a balance of power has a long and controversial history. Although the practice of balance-of-power politics can be traced back to antiquity, its modern usage in theorizing about state behavior begins in 1561 with Francesco Guicciardini's history of the Renaissance Italian city-state system. Early in the fifteenth century, when Milan was growing in power, Florence aligned with Venice to restrain Milan. Later, as Venice grew in strength, Florence joined with Milan to counterbalance the Venetians. For the next five centuries in Europe, great powers tended to balance against hegemonic threats. According to one statistical study of this period, when the leading state possessed a disproportionate and growing share of power, counterbalancing alliances formed against it nearly two-thirds of the time (Levy and Thompson 2005, 28).

Proponents envision balancing as an equilibrating process that maintains peace by offsetting the military might of any state that seeks preponderance. They also believe that by checking hegemonic ambitions and promoting restraint, a balance of power fosters conditions conducive to the development of international law. However, critics scoff at these claims, arguing that balance-of-power politics breeds jealousy, intrigue, and antagonism. Part of the difficulty in evaluating these rival claims lies in the different meanings attributed to the concept (Claude 1962; Haas 1953). Although "balance of power" may be widely used in everyday discourse, there is confusion over precisely what it entails.

At the core of nearly all of the various meanings of "balance of power" is the idea that national security is enhanced when military capabilities are distributed so that no one state is strong enough to dominate everyone else. If one state gains inordinate power, balance-of-power theory predicts that it will take advantage of its strength and attack weaker neighbors; therefore compelling incentives exist for those threatened to unite in a defensive coalition. According to the theory, their combined military might would deter (or, if need be, defeat) the state harboring expansionist aims. Thus for realists, laissez-faire competition among states striving to maximize their national power yields an international equilibrium, which ensures everyone's survival by checking hegemonic ambitions.

The Balancing Process.   Although balancing is occasionally described as an automatic, self-adjusting process, most realists see it as the result of deliberate actions undertaken by national leaders to maintain an equilibrium among contending states. Some actions, like augmenting military capabilities through armaments and alliances, attempt to add weight to the lighter side of the international balance. Others, such as negotiating limits on weaponry and spheres of influence, attempt to decrease the weight of the heavier side. Only by constantly monitoring shifts in relative strength can leaders calibrate their policies to rectify imbalances of power.

Various theorists have attempted to specify a set of rules that must be heeded in order for the balancing process to function effectively. What follows is a brief synthesis of these rules:

1. *Stay vigilant.* Constantly watch foreign developments in order to identify emerging threats and opportunities. Because international anarchy makes each state responsible for its own security, and states can never be sure of one another's intentions, self-interest encourages them to maximize their relative power. As Morton Kaplan (1957) writes: "Act to increase capabilities but negotiate rather than fight … " [however] "Fight rather than pass up an opportunity to increase capabilities."

2. *Seek allies whenever you cannot match the armaments of your adversaries.* States align with each other when they adopt a common stance toward some shared security problem. An **alliance** is produced when they formally agree to coordinate their behavior under certain specified circumstances. The degree of coordination may range from a detailed list of military forces that will be furnished by each party in the event of war to the more modest requirement that they will consult with one another should hostilities erupt. According to balance-of-power theory, alliances are the primary means of compensating for an inability to keep up with a rival's arms acquisitions.

3. *Alliances should remain flexible.* Formed and dissolved according to the strategic needs of the moment, alliances must be made without regard to cultural or ideological affinities (Owen 2005). Because alliances are instrumental, short-term adjustments aimed at rectifying imbalances in the distribution of military capabilities, past experiences should not predispose states to accept or reject any potential partner. Nowhere is this better seen than in the **balancer** role Great Britain once played in European diplomacy. From the seventeenth through the early twentieth centuries, the British shifted their weight from one side of the Continental balance to the other, arguing that they had no permanent friends and no permanent enemies, just a permanent interest in preventing the balance from tipping either way (Dehio 1962). As described by Winston Churchill, Britain's goal was "to oppose the strongest, most aggressive, most dominating Power on the Continent. … [It] joined with the less strong Powers, made a combination among them, and thus defeated and frustrated the Continental military tyrant whoever he was, whatever nation he led." Indeed, when Churchill faced Nazi Germany in the early days of World War II, he indicated that Britain would be flexible enough to make common cause with anyone, regardless of their political ideology. "If Hitler invaded Hell," he once quipped, "I would at least make a favorable reference to the Devil in the House of Commons."

alliance a formal agreement among sovereign states for the purpose of coordinating their behavior to increase mutual security.

balancer an influential global or regional state that throws its support in decisive fashion to the weaker side of the balance of power.

4. *Oppose any state that seeks hegemony.* The purpose of engaging in balance-of-power politics is to survive in a world of potentially dangerous neighbors. If any state achieves absolute mastery over everyone else, it will be able to act with impunity. Under such circumstances, the territorial integrity and political autonomy of other states will be in jeopardy. By joining forces with the weaker side to prevent the stronger side from reaching preponderance, states can preserve their independence. As Joseph Nye (2005) has put it: "Balance of power is a policy of helping the underdog because if you help the top dog, it may eventually turn around and eat you."

5. *Be moderate in victory.* "An equilibrium," argues Edward Gulick (1955), "cannot perpetuate itself unless the major components of that equilibrium are preserved." In the event of war, the winning side should not eliminate the defeated. Looking forward rather than backward, it should do as little damage as possible to those it has vanquished because yesterday's enemy may be needed as tomorrow's ally. Victors who couple firmness regarding their own interests with fairness toward the interests of others encourage defeated powers to work within the postwar balance of power. Similarly, states who win at the bargaining table can stabilize the balance of power by granting the other side compensation in return for their concessions.

To sum up, political realists urge states to check the ambitions of anyone who threatens to amass overwhelming power, because aspiring hegemons are a potential threat to everyone. Human beings, they argue, are by nature selfish and shortsighted, but balancing rival interests stabilizes their interactions. Weakness, insist realists, invites aggression. Thus when faced with unbalanced power, national leaders should mobilize their domestic resources or ally with others to bring the international distribution of power back into equilibrium (Schweller 2004; Vasquez and Elman 2003). As expressed in the 1713 Treaty of Utrecht, which spelled out the terms of the peace settlement after a coalition of European countries defeated French King Louis XIV's bid for hegemony over the continent, the balance of power is "the best and most solid foundation of ... a lasting general concord" among states.

Difficulties with Balance-of-Power Systems.   Can balancing power further international order, as most realists believe? Critics of balance-of-power theory raise several objections about the proposition that balancing promotes peace. First, some scholars argue that the theory's rules for behavior are contradictory (Riker 1962). On the one hand, states are urged to increase their power. On the other hand, they are told to oppose anyone seeking preponderance. Yet sometimes **bandwagoning** with (rather than balancing against) the dominant state can increase a weaker country's capabilities by allowing it to share in the spoils of a future victory. Preliminary research on this issue suggests that states that are content with the status quo tend to balance against rising powers more than states that are dissatisfied.

A second objection to balance-of-power theory is that it assumes policy makers possess accurate, timely information about other states. As we have

bandwagoning the strategy of seeking national security by aligning with the strongest state, irrespective of its ideology or form of government.

Paul Popper/Popperfoto/Getty Images

Anti-hegemonic Alliance Balance-of-power theory counsels national leaders to put aside their ideological differences and align together against common threats. Shown here are the "Big Three" (Joseph Stalin, Franklin Roosevelt, and Winston Churchill), who fought together against Nazi Germany despite having significant political differences among themselves.

discussed in the previous chapter, "power" is an ambiguous concept. Tangible factors, such as the performance capabilities of the different types of weapons found in an adversary's inventory, are hard to compare. Intangible factors, such as leadership skills and troop morale, are even more difficult to gauge. Without a precise measure of relative strength, how can policy makers know when power is becoming unbalanced? Moreover, in an environment of secret alliances, how can they be sure who is really in league with whom? An ally who is being counted on to balance the power of an opponent may have secretly agreed to remain neutral in the event of a showdown; consequently the actual distribution of power may not resemble the distribution one side or the other imagines.

Problems in determining the strength of adversaries and the trustworthiness of allies lead to a third objection to balance-of-power theory: The uncertainty of power balances frequently causes defense planners to engage in worst-case analysis, which can spark an **arms race**. The intense, reciprocal anxiety that shrouds balance-of-power politics fuels exaggerated estimates of an adversary's strength, which prompts one side, and then the other, to expand the quantity and enhance the quality of their weaponry. Critics of realism warn that if a serious

arms race an action-reaction process in which rival states rapidly increase their military capabilities in response to one another.

dispute occurs between states locked in relentless arms competition, the probability of war increases.

A fourth objection is that balance-of-power theory assumes that decision makers are risk averse. When confronted with countervailing power, they refrain from fighting because the dangers of taking on an equal are too great. Yet national leaders assess risk differently. Some are risk acceptant and believe that with a little luck they can prevail. After all, the historical record from 1800 to 2003 of armed conflict between actors with wide disparities in power reveals that the weaker side was victorious 28.5 percent of the time (Arreguín-Toft 2005, 3). Thus rather than being deterred by equivalent power, they prefer gambling on the chance of winning, even if the odds are long. Marshaling comparable power against adversaries with a high tolerance for risk will not have the same effect as it would on those who avoid risks.

Although states with awesome military capabilities can pose potential security dangers, a fifth objection to balance-of-power theory is that perceptions of intent are more important when determining whom to balance against. "Even states with rather modest capabilities may prompt others to balance if they are perceived as especially aggressive," writes political scientist Stephen Walt (1987, 264). He theorizes that national leaders form counterbalancing alliances against the most threatening state on the horizon, not necessarily against the most powerful.

Finally, many people object to the balance-of-power theory because it has not been effective. If the theory's assumptions are correct, historical periods during which its rules were followed should also have been periods in which war was less frequent. Yet a striking feature of those periods is their record of warfare. Researchers have found that a balance of capabilities between opposing alliances increases the probability of war (Kim 1989). From the Thirty Years' War through World War II, the great powers participated in a series of increasingly destructive general wars that threatened to engulf and destroy the multistate system. As Inis L. Claude (1989, 78) soberly concludes, it is difficult to consider these wars "as anything other than catastrophic failures, total collapses, of the balance-of-power system. They are hardly to be classed as stabilizing maneuvers or equilibrating processes, and one cannot take seriously any claim of maintaining international stability that does not entail the prevention of such disasters...." Indeed, the historical record has led some theorists to offer **hegemonic stability theory** as an alternative to the balance of power, which postulates that a single, dominant state can guarantee peace better than military parity among contending great powers (Ferguson 2004; Wohlforth 1999; Organski 1968).

hegemonic stability theory the argument that a single dominant state is necessary to enforce international cooperation, maintain international rules and regimes, and keep the peace.

Managing the Balance through a Concert of Great Powers

A significant problem with the balance-of-power system is its haphazard character. To bring order to the system, occasionally the great powers have tried to institutionalize channels of communication. The Concert of Europe that commenced with the Congress of Vienna in 1815 exemplified this strategy. In essence, it was "an exclusive club for the great powers" (Claude 1971).

concert a cooperative agreement among great powers to jointly manage international relations.

The idea behind a **concert** is "rule by a central coalition" of great powers (Rosecrance 1992). It is predicated on the belief that the leading centers of power will see their interests advanced by collaborating to contain conflict from escalating to war in those regions under their mutual jurisdiction. Although it is assumed that the great powers share a common outlook, concerts still allow "for subtle jockeying and competition to take place among them. Power politics is not completely eliminated; members may turn to internal mobilization and coalition formation to pursue divergent interests. But the cooperative framework of a concert, and its members' concern about preserving peace, prevent such balancing from escalating to overt hostility and conflict" (Kupchan and Kupchan 1992).

A common sense of duty is the glue that holds great-power concerts together. When a belief in mutual self-restraint dissipates, concerts unravel. "Friction tends to build as each state believes that it is sacrificing more for unity than are others," notes Robert Jervis (1985). "Each will remember the cases in which it has been restrained, and ignore or interpret differently cases in which others believe they acted for the common good." Overcoming this friction requires continuous consultation in order to reinforce expectations of joint responsibilities. Concert members should not be challenged over their vital interests, nor should they suffer an affront to their prestige and self-esteem (Elrod 1976). A "just" equilibrium among contending great powers bound together in a concert means more than an equal distribution of military capabilities; it includes recognition of national honor, rights, and dignity (Schroeder 1989).

While a concert framework can help manage relations among counterpoised great powers, the normative consensus underpinning this arrangement is fragile and easily eroded. As a result, realists have looked beyond concerts for other ways to steady vacillating power balances. One approach is to limit everyone's arsenals, especially with regard to those weapons that are seen as provocative and thus destabilizing.

STABILIZING POWER BALANCES THROUGH ARMS CONTROL

Liberal reformers have often questioned the theory that power can be balanced to preserve world order. They have advocated instead the biblical prescription that states should beat their swords into plowshares. The destructiveness of today's weapons has inspired many people once again to take this tenet of liberal theory seriously. But this approach is not solely a liberal preserve. Many realists also see utility in arms limitation, primarily as a way of stabilizing the balance of power by dampening arms races. In fact, most policy makers who have negotiated such agreements have been realists who perceived these treaties as a prudent tool to promote their countries' security.

Despite renewed interest in arms control, military competition is difficult to curb because states acting in what they perceive as their rational self-interest can become trapped in self-defeating behavior, rejecting efforts to restrain arms buildups despite the fact that all parties could benefit by cooperating. As a first step toward determining why it is hard to rein in arms races, let us draw a distinction between arms control and disarmament.

Arms Control versus Disarmament

Although the terms *arms control* and *disarmament* are often used interchangeably, they are not synonymous. **Arms control** refers to agreements designed to regulate arms levels either by limiting their growth or by restricting how they may be used. This is a far more common and less ambitious endeavor than **disarmament**, which is the reduction or elimination of weapons. Controlling war by reducing weapons inventories is hardly a novel idea. Yet until very recently, states have generally failed to negotiate disarmament agreements. True, some countries in the past did reduce their armaments. For example, the Chinese states in 600 BCE formed a disarmament league that produced a peaceful century for the league's members, and Canada and the United States disarmed the Great Lakes through the 1817 Rush-Bagot Agreement. Nonetheless, these kinds of achievements have been relatively rare in history. Most disarmament has been involuntary, the product of reductions imposed by the victors in the immediate aftermath of a war, as when the Allied powers attempted to disarm a defeated Germany after World War I.

> **arms control** bilateral or multilateral agreements to contain arms buildups by setting limits on the number and types of weapons that states are permitted.

> **disarmament** agreements to reduce or eliminate weapons or other means of attack.

In addition to differentiating between arms control and disarmament, we should also distinguish between bilateral and multilateral approaches to limiting weaponry. Because the former involve only two countries, they are often easier to negotiate and to enforce than are the latter, which are agreements among three or more countries. As a result, bilateral arms agreements tend to be more successful than multilateral agreements. By far the most revealing examples are the superpower agreements to control nuclear weapons. Let us briefly look at the record of Soviet-American negotiations before examining the checkered history of multilateral arms control and disarmament.

Bilateral Arms Control and Disarmament

The Cold War between the Soviet Union and the United States never degenerated into open warfare. One of the reasons was the series of more than twenty-five arms control agreements Moscow and Washington negotiated in the wake of the Cuban missile crisis. Prior to their nuclear face-off in October 1962, the superpowers seemed trapped in a self-reinforcing cycle of hostilities and armaments (see Application: Conflict Spirals and Self-Defeating Behavior). Beginning with the 1963 Hot Line Agreement, which established a direct radio and telegraph communication system between the two governments, Soviet and American leaders reached a series of modest agreements aimed at stabilizing the military balance and reducing the risk of war. Each of these bilateral treaties lowered tensions and helped build a climate of trust that encouraged efforts to negotiate further agreements.

Perhaps the most important agreements were the Strategic Arms Limitation Talks (SALT) of 1972 and 1979; the Strategic Arms Reduction Treaties (START)

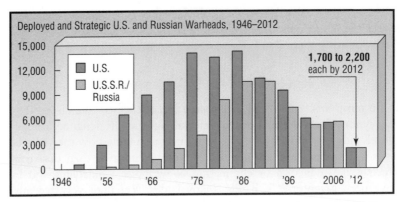

FIGURE 9.1 Countdown to Strategic Parity

After decades of adding weapons to their arsenals, the United States and
Russia, through a series of arms control agreements, have cut the number of
nuclear warheads in their stockpiles. Shown here are trends in their nuclear
arsenals between 1946 and 2012, as projected under the 2002 Strategic
Offensive Reductions Treaty (SORT).

SOURCE: Based on data from the U.S. Arms Control Association and Stockholm International Peace
Research Institute.

of 1991, 1993, and 1997; and the Strategic Offensive Reductions Treaty (SORT)
of 2002. The first two agreements stabilized the nuclear arms race, while the
remaining ones reduced the weapons in each side's inventory (see Figure 9.1).
When the Cold War ended in 1991, the United States had more than 9,500
nuclear warheads and Russia had about 8,000. However, the 1993 START
agreement pledged to cut their combined arsenals to about 6,500 by the year
2003. Even more dramatically, this agreement also affected the kinds of weapons
each country could possess. Under its terms, Russia and the United States gave
up all the multiple independently targetable reentry vehicles (MIRVs) on their
land-based intercontinental ballistic missiles (ICBMs) and reduced submarine-
launched ballistic missile (SLBM) warheads to no more than 1,750.

The next major step occurred in May 2002 when presidents George W.
Bush and Vladimir Putin signed the Strategic Offensive Reductions Treaty
(SORT). This brief document calls for the two countries to cut their combined
number of strategic nuclear warheads by two-thirds over the next ten years. Still,
both parties were left with enough firepower to retain the deterrent threat of
mutual assured destruction (see Chapter 8). In addition, the treaty contained no
requirement to destroy warheads taken out of service, and permitted either side
to withdraw from the agreement with three months' notice by citing "a supreme
national interest." Hence, while this treaty signaled a step toward nuclear disarmament, it was regarded as mostly symbolic in importance (Mendelsohn 2002).
That said, the success recently enjoyed by Moscow and Washington over the
past two decades inspires some hope that negotiations can be expanded to
include other states. The history of multilateral arms control and disarmament
speaks to this aspiration.

APPLICATION   Conflict Spirals and Self-Defeating Behavior

Many scholars have described the dynamics of arms competition between states as a conflict spiral (Jervis 1976, 62–113). The imagery highlights the tendency of military preparations by one state to exacerbate the insecurities its rival, engendering confrontational policies that raise tensions, the perceived stakes of the conflict, and the level of preparations by both sides to new heights. In a speech to the editors of United Press International in San Francisco on September 18, 1967, U.S. Secretary of Defense Robert S. McNamara drew upon the spiral model when reflecting on the irony that decisions made by the United States and Soviet Union for the sake of security actually resulted in greater insecurity.

> In 1961, when I became Secretary of Defense, the Soviet Union possessed a very small operational arsenal of intercontinental missiles. However, they did possess the technological and industrial capacity to enlarge that arsenal very substantially over succeeding years.
>
> Now we had no evidence that the Soviets did in fact plan to fully use that capacity. But ... a strategic planner must be "conservative" in his calculations; that is, he must prepare for the worst plausible case and not be content to hope and prepare merely for the most probable.
>
> Since we could not be certain of Soviet intentions—since we could not be sure that they would not undertake a massive buildup—we had to insure against such an eventuality by undertaking ourselves a major buildup....

> Clearly, the Soviet buildup [was] in part a reaction to our buildup since the beginning of the decade. Soviet strategic planners undoubtedly reasoned that if our buildup were to continue at its accelerated pace, we might conceivably reach, in time, a credible first-strike capability against the Soviet Union.
>
> This was not in fact our intention. Our intention was to assure that they—with their theoretical capacity to reach such a first-strike capability—would not in fact outdistance us.
>
> But they could not read our intentions with any greater accuracy than we could read theirs. And thus the result has been that we both built up our forces to a point that far exceeds a credible second-strike capability against the forces we each started with....
>
> It is futile for each of us ... at the end of all the spending, and at the end of all the deployment, and at the end of all that effort, to be relatively at the same point of balance on the security scale (cited in G. Snyder 1971, 72–73).

Whereas McNamara and others use the spiral model to draw attention to self-amplifying and destabilizing pressures, the model also offers a policy recommendation: "If you seek security, cut your arms and make your adversary more secure" (Jervis 1997, 287n). Realists who subscribe to balance-of-power theory caution that any cuts should be mutual, verifiable, and result in parity.

Multilateral Arms Control and Disarmament

There are many historical examples of multilateral arms control and disarmament efforts. As early as the eleventh century, the Second Lateran Council prohibited the use of crossbows in fighting. The 1868 St. Petersburg Declaration prohibited the use of explosive bullets. In 1899 and 1907, International Peace Conferences at the Hague restricted the use of some weapons and prohibited others. The leaders of the United States, Britain, Japan, France, and Italy signed treaties at the Washington Naval Conferences (1921–1922) agreeing to adjust the relative tonnage of their fleets.

Nearly thirty major multilateral agreements have been signed since the Second World War. Of these, the 1968 Nuclear Nonproliferation Treaty (NPT), which prohibited the transfer of nuclear weapons and production technologies to nonnuclear-weapons states, stands out as the most symbolic multilateral agreement with 189 signatory parties. While adherence to the treaty has been widespread, India, Pakistan, and North Korea have broken the NPT's barriers to become nuclear-weapons states. In addition, Israel is believed to have clandestinely produced nuclear weapons, and Iran remains outside the NPT and is seeking to become a nuclear-weapon state. The forty-six countries that launched the International Nuclear Fuel Cycle Evaluation negotiations in 2005 to sever the link between nuclear energy and nuclear proliferation was a step forward; however, some of the signatory parties complain that the pledge by the original nuclear powers to disarm has gone unheeded.

Similar problems plague other multilateral agreements. The 1993 Chemical Weapons Convention (CWC), for example, required all stockpiles of chemical weapons to be destroyed within ten years. However, the agreement lost some of its authority in 2001 when the Bush administration refused to accept the enforcement measures. This erosion of support for arms control caused then-UN secretary-general Kofi Annan to warn that "much of the established multilateral disarmament machinery has started to rust."

The Problematic Future of Arms Control and Disarmament

The obstacles to arms control and disarmament treaties are formidable. Critics complain that these agreements frequently regulate obsolete armaments or ones that the parties to the agreement have little incentive for developing in the first place. Even when agreements are reached on modern, sophisticated weapons, the parties often set ceilings higher than the number of weapons currently deployed, so they do not have to slash their inventories.

A second pitfall is the propensity of limits on one type of weapon system to prompt developments in another system. Like a balloon that is squeezed at one end but expands at the other, constraints on certain parts of a country's arsenal can lead to enhancements elsewhere. An example can be seen in the 1972 SALT I agreement, which limited the number of intercontinental ballistic missiles possessed by the United States and the Soviet Union. Although the number of missiles was restricted, no limits were placed on the number of nuclear warheads that could be placed on each missile; consequently both sides began developing multiple independently targetable reentry vehicles (MIRVs). In short, the quantitative freeze on launchers led to qualitative improvements in their warhead delivery systems.

Also reducing faith in the future of meaningful arms control is the slow, weak, and ineffective ability of the international community to ban some of the most dangerous and counterproductive weapons. Consider the case of antipersonnel landmines (APLs). These are weapons that cannot discriminate between soldiers and civilians. Between 100 and 300 million landmines are believed to be scattered on the territory of more than seventy countries (with another 100 million in stockpiles). In the mid-1990s there was about one mine for every fifty humans on earth, and each year they killed or maimed more than 26,000 people—almost all of them civilians. Yet not a single state would endorse a prohibition on these deadly weapons. It took a peace activist, Jody Williams, to organize the International Campaign to Ban Landmines that produced the Convention on the Prohibition of the Use, Stockpiling, Production, and Transfer of Antipersonnel Mines and Their Destruction, which was opened for signature in December 1997. For her efforts, she was awarded the Nobel Peace Prize. Still, the challenge of enforcing the ban now signed by 155 states, and the task of removing APLs, remains staggering.

A final problem facing those advocating arms control and disarmament is continuous innovation. By the time limits are negotiated on one type of weapon, a new generation of weapons has emerged. Further complicating matters, modern technology is creating an ever-widening range of novel weapons— increasingly smaller, deadlier, and easier to conceal.

Why do states often make decisions to arm that apparently imprison them in the grip of insecurity? On the surface, the incentives for meaningful arms control seem numerous. Significant controls would save money, reduce tension, reduce the environmental hazards, and diminish the potential destructiveness of war. However, most countries are reluctant to limit their armaments in a self-help system that requires each state to protect itself. Thus states find themselves caught in a vicious cycle summarized by two basic principles: "(1) Don't negotiate when you are behind. Why accept a permanent position of number two?" and (2) "Don't negotiate when you are ahead. Why accept a freeze in an area of military competition when the other side has not kept up with you?" (Barnet 1977).

The tendency of states to make improving their weapons a priority over controlling them is illustrated by the example of nuclear testing. The nine known nuclear states conducted a total of 2,056 nuclear explosions in twenty-four different locations since 1945—an average of one test every ten days. The Partial Test Ban Treaty of 1963, which prohibited atmospheric and underwater testing but not underground explosions, did not slow the pace of testing. Three-fourths of all nuclear tests took place after the ban went into effect in 1963. Today both China and the United States regularly conduct so-called zero-yield nuclear experiments and are suspected of conducting explosive tests so small that they can't be detected.

To sum up, arms control remains a murky policy area, and the past record suggests that we should not exaggerate its potential. As long as aggressive national leaders exist, it would be imprudent to disarm. Limits on weapons may confine the rivalry between states, but they do not remove the underlying source of the conflict. Arms, after all, are less the causes of war than the symptoms of political tension: People do not fight because they have weapons; they have weapons because they fear that they must fight to preserve their security.

BALANCING POWER IN THE CONTEMPORARY INTERNATIONAL SYSTEM

The use of alliances and arms control to balance power typically follows one of two distinct patterns (Morgenthau 1985). In the pattern of "direct opposition," one powerful state tries to prevail over another powerful state, which raises arms or seeks allies to offset its adversary's strength. Over time, each increase in military capabilities by one side calls forth an increase by the other. If neither side yields, they may negotiate arms control agreements to stabilize their competition and avoid waging war.

In the more fluid pattern of "competition," encroachment by one state against another also precipitates a quest for arms and allies. But rather than resulting in the formation of rigid, counterbalanced blocs, it triggers shifts in a kaleidoscope of overlapping alliances. The diplomatic checkerboard of eighteenth-century Europe illustrates this second pattern of balance-of-power politics. As described by Michael Doyle (1997, 177), France was sandwiched between its rivals, Britain and Austria (who possessed what today is Belgium); consequently France established ties with Prussia, an enemy of the British and Austrians. Simultaneously, Holland balanced against France with British support, Saxony balanced against Prussia with Austrian support, and Bavaria leaned toward France and Prussia in an effort to balance against Austria. Owing to a desire to offset what he saw as an alarming increase in Prussian power ever since it seized the province of Silesia from his country in 1740, Austrian foreign minister Wenzel Kaunitz forged an alliance with France, Austria's longstanding foe and heretofore Prussia's ally. Britain, Austria's former ally, responded by concluding an alliance with Prussia. In what is known as the "Diplomatic Revolution of 1756," the configuration of great-power alliances was completely reversed in response to growing Prussian power.

According to the eminent realist Hans J. Morgenthau (1985), if no state possesses overwhelming military superiority, world politics follows either the pattern of direct opposition or the more complex pattern of ever-shifting competition. Having examined the theory of how the balance of power is supposed to operate, let us consider how it actually functioned in world politics since the end of the Second World War.

The Cold War Pattern of Direct Opposition

Most countries were devastated by World War II. The United States, however, was left in a clearly dominant position, its economy accounting for about half the world's combined gross national product (GNP). The United States was also the only country with the atomic bomb, and had demonstrated its willingness to use the new weapon. American hegemony was short-lived, however, as the recovery of the Soviet economy and the growth of its military capabilities eroded U.S. supremacy and gave rise to a new distribution of world power. The Soviets broke the U.S. monopoly on atomic weapons in 1949 and exploded a thermonuclear device in 1953, less than a year after the United States. This achievement symbolized the creation of a bipolar system of direct opposition. Military capabilities were now concentrated in the hands of two rival "superpowers," each heading its own bloc of allies.

The formation of the North Atlantic Treaty Organization (NATO), linking the United States to the defense of Western Europe, and the Warsaw Pact, linking the former Soviet Union in an alliance with its Eastern European clients, reinforced this bipolar structure. The opposing blocs formed in part because the superpowers competed for allies and in part because the less-powerful states looked to one superpower or the other for protection. Correspondingly, each superpower's allies gave it forward bases from which to carry on the competition.

By grouping the system's states into two blocs, each led by a superpower, the Cold War's bipolar structure bred insecurity among all. The balance was constantly at stake. Each bloc leader, worrying that its adversary would attain primacy, viewed every move, however defensive, as the first step toward world conquest. Both superpowers attached great importance to recruiting new allies. Fear that an old ally might desert the fold was ever-present. Nonalignment was viewed with suspicion. Bipolarity left little room for compromise or maneuver and worked against the normalization of superpower relations.

The major Cold War coalitions associated with bipolarity began to disintegrate in the 1960s and early 1970s. As their internal cohesion eroded, new centers of power emerged. At the same time, weaker alliance partners were afforded more room for maneuvering. Diverse relationships among the states subordinate to the superpowers developed, such as the friendly relations between the United States and Romania, and between France and the Soviet Union. The superpowers remained dominant militarily, but this less-rigid system allowed other states to perform more independent foreign policy roles.

Rapid technological innovation in the superpowers' major weapons systems was a catalyst in the dissolving of the Cold War blocs. Intercontinental ballistic missiles, capable of delivering nuclear weapons from one continent to another, lessened the importance of forward bases on allies' territory. Furthermore, the narrowed differences in the superpowers' arsenals loosened the ties that had previously bound allies to one another. The European members of NATO in particular began to question whether the United States would, as it had pledged, protect Paris or Bonn by sacrificing New York. Under what conditions might Washington or Moscow be willing to risk a nuclear holocaust? The uncertainty became pronounced while the pledge to protect allies through **extended deterrence** seemed increasingly insincere.

The movement toward democracy and market economies by some communist states in the late 1980s further eroded the bonds of ideology that had formerly helped these countries face their security problems from a common posture. The 1989 dismantling of the Berlin Wall tore apart the Cold War architecture of competing blocs. With the end of this division, and without a Soviet threat, the consistency of outlook and singularity of purpose that once bound NATO members together disappeared. Many perceived the need to replace NATO and the defunct Warsaw Pact with a new security arrangement. However, most leaders maintained that some configuration of a European defense architecture was still necessary to cement relationships and stabilize the rush of cascading events.

extended deterrence
the use of military threats by a great power to deter an attack on its allies.

A Future of Balance-of-Power Competition?

Following the dissolution of the Soviet Union in 1991, most analysts concluded that a new era of unipolarity had arisen, with the United States emerging as the world's only superpower. Columnist Charles Krauthammer proclaimed that "no country has been as dominant culturally, economically, technologically, and militarily in the history of the world since the Roman Empire." For hegemonic stability theorists, this was beneficial. As they see it, a unipolar concentration of power allows the global leader to police chaos and maintain international peace.

Against this optimistic view runs a strong suspicion about the future stability of a unipolar world under U.S. management. Warns one critic, "It is virtually universal in history that when countries become hegemons … they tend to want everything their own way, and it never works" (Mathews 2000). Others condemn the shortsightedness of U.S. leadership, guided, as they see it, more by self-interests than by ideals, and motivated primarily by a desire to preserve America's position as top dog and less toward multilateral cooperation to promote peace and prosperity.

Regardless of whether the optimists or pessimists are correct, many scholars believe that U.S. preponderance will not last far into the twenty-first century. Other "countries will obstruct American purposes whenever and in whatever way they can, and the pursuit of American interests will have to be undertaken through coercion rather than consensus. Anti-Americanism will become the global language of political protest—the default ideology of opposition—unifying the world's discontents and malcontents, some of whom, as we have discovered, can be very dangerous" (Zakaria 2002b). Unipolarity, many analysts argue, is giving way to a new configuration of power whose probable consequences are not clear. Some forecast the return of a bipolar pattern of direct opposition, with the United States facing off against China (see Controversy: How Should the United States Respond to China's Growing Power?). Others see the emergence of a more complex pattern of balance-of-power competition, where the United States, China, Japan, India, Russia, the European Union, and possibly Brazil would constitute multiple centers of global power. According to this image of the future, as power becomes more equally distributed, each player will be increasingly assertive, independent, and competitive, leading to confusion about the identity of friends and foes. Finally, still others speculate that the erosion of unipolarity will begin a descent into apolarity—a fragmented world characterized by dozens of regional power centers, with no one exercising global leadership (Ferguson 2004, 296).

CONTROVERSY   How Should the United States Respond to China's Growing Power?

In explaining the origins of the twenty-seven-year Peloponnesian War between Athens and Sparta, the historian Thucydides pointed the growth of Athenian power and the alarm that it caused in Sparta, the dominant state in Greece during the fifth century BCE. As noted in the discussion of power transition theory in

Chapter 7 and depicted in the figure on the next page, we can categorize states according to where they stand on the international hierarchy of power and how satisfied they are with the status quo. The likelihood of war increases, argue some theorists, when the power of states lower on the hierarchy that are dissatisfied with the international status quo grows to the point of overtaking the dominant state, which supports the status quo (Kugler, Tammen, and Efired 2004, 164). Just as Sparta faced the challenge of an ascending Athens, throughout history states at the apex of power have wrestled with the question of how to respond to rising competitors.

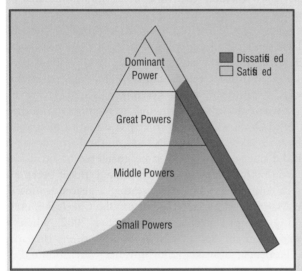

One of the principal foreign policy challenges for contemporary American foreign policy, suggests historian John Lewis Gaddis (2005, 9), is not to make the Middle East the single lens through which the United States views the world. Iraq is a serious problem today and a nuclear-armed Iran may be the "wild card" of the next decade or so, but what happens in China "may well be as important for the future of the international system as what transpires in the Middle East." The question is no longer whether China will become strong, but how the United States will respond to the growth of Chinese power.

When China began its market reforms in 1978, it accounted for less than 1 percent of the world's economy, and its foreign trade totaled $20.6 billion. Since then, China has averaged 9.4 percent annual GDP growth and by 2005 accounted for over 4 percent of the world economy, with foreign trade increasing to $851 billion. Today, China is the world's largest producer of steel, the largest exporter of information technology goods, the second largest consumer of energy, and its GDP is projected by the U.S. National Intelligence Council to equal the United States' in 2042. These resources position China, formerly regarded as a sleeping giant, to awaken and play an active role on the world stage commensurate with its power.

Still, China has far to go in order to become a military superpower. Its annual defense spending has been growing at a double-digit rate for the past decade, but most estimates place total expenditures somewhere between 14 and 19 percent of those of the United States. Over the next several decades, however, China's defense budget could triple as the country upgrades its antiquated ground, air, and maritime forces, and deploys a credible, second-strike nuclear arsenal.

A future U.S. confrontation with a more muscular China is, of course, not preordained. Yet some people in the United States are alarmed about China's growing economic power, which they worry will be translated into a robust military capability. They recommend that America craft a foreign policy that contains China, just as the country did when addressing the challenge posed by the Soviet Union after World War II. Others are concerned that a new containment policy will eventually lead Washington and Beijing to square off against one another. From their perspective, the United States will have to accommodate itself to peer competitors. Rather than attempt to block China's rise, they recommend making room for an ascending China, giving it a stake in the existing international order, and enmeshing it in a web of international institutions that smooth any future power transitions.

The United States and China are at a crossroads. America's bombing of the Chinese embassy during the war with Serbia in 1999, the collision of an American spy plane with a Chinese interceptor in 2001, and continued friction over human rights, intellectual property rights, and the attempt by the Chinese National Offshore Oil Corporation to acquire Unocal, a California-based oil company, have sparked lively discussions across the United States over what policy Washington should adopt toward China. What do you think? How should the United States respond to China's growing power?

Although those who see a gradual passing of America's unipolar moment disagree on what will come next, they concur that U.S. security commitments have stretched the country's military capabilities thin. Further complicating matters, the United States is suffering under a staggering debt burden and the worst financial crisis since the Great Depression. America may still be the home of astonishing creativity and a vibrant entrepreneurial spirit, and it will continue to be a formidable power, but these analysts conclude that the combination of military overreaching abroad, domestic economic problems, and the rise of fast-growing challengers will shape the contours of global future. "The international landscape of a few decades hence," writes one scholar, "may resemble that of Easter Island: dominated by giants, and battered by tempestuous winds of change" (Bell 2005, 21).

The evolution of the North Atlantic Treaty Organization (NATO) since the end of the Cold War reflects this shifting geopolitical landscape. At first, many observers felt that NATO would disappear along with the rival Warsaw Pact. The purpose for which NATO was first created—containing Soviet expansionism—no longer was relevant, because the threat no longer existed. However, NATO did not dissolve. It reinvented itself, changing its membership and its mission. In January 1994, NATO allowed four formerly communist bloc states (Poland, the Czech Republic, Slovakia, and Hungary) to join the Partnership for Peace (PfP) plan. The PfP did not give them the same guarantee of aid in the event of an attack that the existing full members were promised. But it became a pivotal step in the process of enlargement aimed at creating a peaceful, united, and democratic Europe. As Map 9.1 shows, after admitting the Czech Republic and Poland in 1999, NATO enlarged further in November 2002, when it undertook the biggest expansion in its fifty-three-year history. Bulgaria, Estonia, Latvia, Lithuania, Romania, Slovakia, and Slovenia were admitted as full members along with the nineteen existing countries under NATO's security umbrella. In addition, some people have proposed that Georgia and Ukraine become members, much to the dismay of Russian leaders who insist they had been promised at the end of the Cold War that former Soviet Republics and Warsaw Pact members would not be brought into NATO.

Enlargement of both NATO's membership and its mission opens a new chapter in that organization's history. Following the 2001 terrorist attacks on the World Trade Center and the Pentagon, NATO invoked its mutual defense principle for the first time, declaring that the attack on the United States was an attack on all members. This helped dispel doubts about NATO's usefulness in addressing twenty-first-century security challenges. Revitalized with a larger membership and territorial reach, in 2006 NATO took command of security and reconstruction work throughout most of southern Afghanistan.

Yet critics complain that the advantages of NATO enlargement are offset by the risk that expansion will reduce the alliance to a mere conference association for discussing security issues. They also complain that the alliance undermines the security of the states it excludes. The presence of a solidified military alliance in Europe without other strong military alliances to balance it, they argue, poses a threat to outsiders. NATO asserts that this charge is unjustified because its new decision rules, giving every full member a veto over decisions regarding military

MAP 9.1 The Enlarged NATO in the New Geostrategic Balance of Power

The geostrategic landscape has been transformed by NATO's expansion. As shown in this map, NATO now casts its security umbrella across Europe to include states that once were its enemies.

SOURCE: Past European alliances from *U.S. News & World Report,* July 14, 1997. Copyright © 1997, U.S. News & World Report, L.P. Reprinted with permission.

operations, remove the threat of a NATO preemptive strike. Other proponents of NATO enlargement claim that the maze of overlapping European security organizations (including the OSCE and the Council of Europe) are too cumbersome to permit any of them to take decisive military action outside their sphere of influence.

Despite its innovative redesign and new decision rules, NATO cohesion has been affected by American military intervention into Iraq as part of its proclaimed war on global terrorism. NATO today is being pulled in two directions. Led by the British and U.S. governments, some members favor a broad interpretation of NATO's strategic role, which would authorize it to operate in areas like Afghanistan. Led by France, other members prefer a narrow interpretation, therein allowing the European Union to take on more military responsibilities.

Adding to the transatlantic debate over collective defense was the decision by the European Union to create its own rapid deployment force so it could undertake military actions on its own without the approval of the United States. As the European reaction to America's use of its military might demonstrates, the quest for national security in an anarchical world springs from states' uncertainties of the intentions of others. Because the unchecked growth in one country's power makes others insecure, nearly all states continually look for ways to defend themselves. In this sense the realists' military paths to peace discussed in this chapter are intimately related to the widespread quest for armaments described in Chapter 8. Convinced that a more peaceful world is not on the diplomatic horizon, realists insist that the tragic struggle for security among great-powers will continue (Mearsheimer 2001).

The validity of this interpretation of the global future is still at issue, however. In the next chapter we will turn our attention away from the balance-of-power politics of realism and examine proposals by liberal and constructivist theorists for using international norms and institutions to create a more peaceful world.

CHAPTER SUMMARY

- The term *balance of power* is used in many ways. At the core of its many meanings is the idea that state security and survival is most likely when there is a rough military parity among rivals.

- In order to function effectively, balance-of-power theory prescribes that national leaders follow certain rules of statecraft. They should be vigilant, forge alliances when they cannot keep pace with the arms increases of competitors, choose alliance partners on the basis of strategic needs rather than cultural or ideological affinity, always oppose those who seek hegemony, and act with moderation toward those who are defeated in battle.

- Balance-of-power theory is criticized for its logical inconsistencies, the lack of a reliable way for national leaders to gauge accurately the distribution of military capabilities, the propensity to foster rapid arms buildups, the assumption that leaders are risk averse, and its inability to prevent destructive wars.

- Great-power concerts attempt to stabilize power balances by creating regular channels of communication among latent rivals. Concerts are fragile, however. Friction often develops when some members come to believe that they have sacrificed more for the common good than others.

- Some realists argue that military parity can be preserved through arms limitation agreements. Whereas arms control refers to restrictions on the growth of weapons inventories, disarmament pertains to the reduction or elimination of weapons. Arms control agreements have tended to be more effective than disarmament agreements, especially when they involve bilateral negotiations.

- Various obstacles stand in the way of reaching effective arms control agreements. Negotiations are generally slow, they rarely cover new weapons systems, and those agreements that are reached pose difficult verification problems and are hard to enforce.

- Throughout the Cold War, the balance of power between the United States and the Soviet Union followed a pattern of direct bipolar opposition, with two counterbalanced blocs facing off against one another.

- After the collapse of the Soviet Union, the structure of the state system moved toward unipolarity, with the United States standing as the world's sole superpower. Unipolarity has never lasted long in modern history. As described in balance-of-power theory, states eventually combine forces to check the power of the dominate state. Currently, many scholars are debating how long the United States will remain in its dominant position. Some scholars predict that American unipolarity will be followed by a return to the pattern of direct bipolar opposition, with a rising China and perhaps several additional states counterbalancing the United States. Other scholars disagree. They foresee a return to the classical balance-of-power pattern of fluid competition, involving the United States, China, Russia, Japan, and a united Europe.

KEY TERMS

alliance	balancer	extended deterrence
arms control	bandwagoning	hegemonic stability theory
arms race	concert	
balance of power	disarmament	

SUGGESTED READINGS

Kegley, Charles W., Jr., and Gregory A. Raymond. *After Iraq: The Imperiled American Imperium.* New York: Oxford University Press, 2007.

Lieber, Robert J., ed. *Foreign Policy.* Burlington, VT: Ashgate, 2008.

Little, Richard. *The Balance of Power in International Relations: Metaphors, Myths, and Models.* Cambridge: Cambridge University Press, 2007.

Mandelbaum, Michael. *The Case for Goliath: How America Acts as the World's Government in the Twenty-First Century.* New York: Public Affairs, 2006.

Walt, Stephen M. *Taming American Power: The Global Response to U.S. Primacy.* New York: Norton, 2005.

CRITICAL THINKING QUESTIONS

Metaphorical expressions are routinely used by national leaders to explain certain aspects of world politics. For example, they may assert that others should not interfere with geographic areas in their country's "backyard," or that military forces should be engaged somewhere to fill a power "vacuum" but not elsewhere because intervention would be a "slippery slope" (see Shimko 1995). Balance-of-power theory contains metaphors as well. The most common is an intricate weighing scale (Little 2007). Statecraft, according to this imagery, is similar to mechanical engineering.

Strategist Terry Deibel (2007, 54–56) proposes two other ways of conceptualizing international political processes. First, rather than seeing these processes as machine-like, he suggests imagining them as being akin to those of a living organism that goes through cycles of growth and decay. A second metaphor comes from chaos theory, where seemingly minor random events can cause dramatic, system-wide changes in a network of interacting entities, as in the flow of information traffic on the Internet. How does adopting a mechanical metaphor to describe international processes shape the way one thinks about world politics? Are organic metaphors or metaphors based on complex networks better suited for making sense out of world politics? Do they provide useful insights that are not apparent from a mechanistic worldview?

10

Liberal and Constructivist Paths to Peace: International Norms, Institutions, and Integration

CHAPTER OUTLINE

International Legal Norms and World Order

Sovereignty and the Rules of International Law

The Limitations of International Law

International Law and the Preservation of Peace

CONTROVERSY: Was the War in Iraq Just?

APPLICATION: The Doctrine of International Community

International Institutions and World Order

The League of Nations and Collective Security

The United Nations and Peacekeeping

Regional Security Organizations and Collective Defense

International Integration and World Order

World Government

Regional Integration

I refuse to accept the cynical notion that nation after nation must spiral down a militaristic stairway . . . .

MARTIN LUTHER KING, JR.
AMERICAN CIVIL RIGHTS LEADER

Some people left in a caravan of tractors and rusty old cars. Others jammed into trains and cattle trucks. Many more hobbled along on foot. An estimated 740,000 ethnic Albanian refugees streamed out of Kosovo during March 1999. Not since World War II had Europe witnessed such an exodus.

On the eve of this exodus, Kosovo was a province within Serbia, one of the republics that formed Yugoslavia. Roughly 90 percent of Kosovo's 2 million inhabitants were ethnic Albanians. They had the highest birthrate on the Continent and a population largely under the age of thirty, demographic trends that disturbed many Serbs, angered by what they believed were Albanian efforts to gain independence by pressuring the Serb minority into leaving. Slobodan Milosevic, who had risen to the presidency of Yugoslavia in 1997 under a banner of Serb nationalism, insisted that Kosovo, the location of many important cultural and religious sites for Serbs, would never become an independent Albanian state. "Yugoslavia would disintegrate without Kosovo," he told a crowd of supporters on a field near Prestina, where Serbs had fought an epic battle against the Ottoman Empire centuries earlier.

Milosevic proposed to retain control over Kosovo by ridding the province of ethnic Albanians by brute force, a policy known euphemistically as "ethnic cleansing." Friction between Serbs and Kosovo's Albanians had existed long before Milosevic's rise to power. Claiming that discrimination against Albanians had led the per capita income in Kosovo to fall to less than one-third of the national average, some Kosovars had called for the province to be decoupled from Serbia and elevated to the legal status of a full republic within Yugoslavia. Others within Kosovo's Albanian population made more radical demands, insisting on secession from Yugoslavia. The conflict escalated to violence in May 1993, when an ethnic Albanian organization called the Kosovo Liberation Army (KLA) gunned down a group of Serb police officers in Glogovac. Over the next few years, KLA guerrillas launched sporadic raids against Serbs, which prompted harsh reprisals against villages suspected of supporting the KLA. Each KLA attack triggered stronger Serbian retaliation, which radicalized even more ethnic Albanians.

Beginning in the late spring of 1998, intermittent skirmishing gave way to protracted fighting. After weeks of KLA gains, a Serb counteroffensive in mid-July drove the guerrillas into hiding but brutally displaced some 200,000 ethnic Albanians. The violence worsened a year later, unleashing a tidal wave of refugees and prompting the United States and several European countries to summon the Serbs and Kosovar Albanians to peace talks in Rambouillet, a small town about thirty miles from Paris. When efforts to persuade the Serbs to accept a cease-fire, remove their military units from Kosovo, and allow the deployment of a NATO peacekeeping force failed, many observers feared that the situation would deteriorate into a humanitarian catastrophe. In a last-minute attempt to stop further ethnic cleansing, U.S. envoy Richard Holbrooke told Milosevic that NATO would bomb Yugoslavia unless he accepted the Rambouillet proposal.

NATO's air attack began on March 24, 1999 at 8:00 pm local time. By the end of the seventy-eight-day war, NATO aircraft had flown more than 37,000 sorties, causing an estimated $60 billion in damage to Serbia's industry and infrastructure. Within days after Milosevic accepted defeat, hundreds of thousands of ethnic Albanians began returning to Kosovo. By late November, 808,913 refugees had returned and 247,391 people, primarily Serbs intimidated by KLA members bent on revenge, had departed (Judah 2000, 286–287).

Although Milosevic remained in power when the war ended, he was indicted by the International Criminal Tribunal for the former Yugoslavia (ICTY), a court in The Hague, Netherlands created by the UN Security Council to prosecute those who committed war crimes, crimes against humanity, and acts of genocide during the armed conflicts that led to the breakup of Yugoslavia. Milosevic, the first sitting head of state to be indicted by an international court for war crimes, had no intention of surrendering to the ICTY. Moreover, his government did not buckle under diplomatic and economic pressure from the Clinton administration. However, his tenure in office came to an end when Vojislav Kostunica, a constitutional lawyer backed by a coalition of eighteen opposition parties, defeated him in the fall 2000 presidential election.

In January 2001, Carla del Ponte, the ICTY chief prosecutor, delivered an arrest warrant for Milosevic to the Kostunica government. Arguing that the ICTY was biased because it had not vigorously prosecuted Kosovar Albanians or NATO members for war crimes, Kostunica hesitated to comply. But when Milosevic was subsequently linked to the theft of state funds, Prime Minister Zoran Djindzic and Justice Minister Vladan Batic pushed for his arrest. After being taken into custody by Yugoslav authorities, he was transferred to The Hague to stand trial.

Milosevic's trial began on February 12, 2002 but ended without a verdict when he died of a heart attack on March 11, 2006. Chief Prosecutor del Ponte expressed regret that his death during the proceedings had deprived the victims of ethnic cleansing the justice they deserved; nonetheless, she noted that the indictment of an incumbent head of state for war crimes set an important precedent. No longer could national leaders evade legal accountability for their actions by invoking state sovereignty.

Slobodan Milosevic's indictment and trial draws attention to the role of international law and organization in world politics. Whereas liberal theorists place great stock in these approaches to the control of armed conflict, hard-boiled realists have long scoffed that without compulsory jurisdiction and a mechanism to ensure compliance with judicial verdicts, these procedures will remain a blind alley rather than a path to peace. The purpose of this chapter is to examine the contributions that international legal norms and institutions make to world order. We will begin by analyzing the nature and functions of international law.

Boris Grdanoski/AP Photo

NATO's Expanded Mission NATO's 1999 humanitarian intervention in Kosovo marked the first time that alliance used force "out of area." Here a British tank is greeted by ethnic Albanians, thankful that NATO's KFOR (Kosovo Force) peacekeepers have ended Slobodan Milosevic's use of brute force to drive them out of Kosovo.

INTERNATIONAL LEGAL NORMS AND
WORLD ORDER

Throughout recorded history, all autonomous, independent political entities engaged in sustained interaction have developed rules defining appropriate behavior for certain situations. Although the rules of modern international law may not be backed by a formal, unified system of sanctions, both state and non-state actors rely on them to coordinate their behavior and redress grievances. Most of this activity falls within the realm of **private international law**—the regulation of routine transnational activities in such areas as commerce, communications, and travel. This is where the majority of international disputes are regularly settled and where the record of compliance compares favorably with that achieved in domestic legal systems.

private international law law pertaining to routinized transnational intercourse between or among states as well as nonstate actors.

In contrast, **public international law** covers relations between governments as well as the interactions of governments with intergovernmental organizations (IGOs) and nongovernmental organizations (NGOs). Most critics of international law focus their attention here rather than on private international law. Their complaints generally emphasize instances where bystanders overlooked the transgressions of aggressive states engaged in illegal activities. As Israeli diplomat Abba Eban once lamented, public international law "is that law which the wicked do not obey and the righteous do not enforce."

public international law law pertaining to government-to-government relations.

Although public international law has deficiencies, that should not lead to the conclusion that it is irrelevant or useless. No legal system can prevent all of its members from breaking laws. There are miscreants who ignore domestic law just as there are states who flagrantly violate international law. In spite of its shortcomings, states themselves find international law useful and expend considerable effort attempting to shape its development. Because this chapter examines the capacity of public international law to control war, our discussion will address only the laws and institutional machinery created to manage armed conflict between states. That is, it will explore that segment of international law popularly regarded as the most deficient.

Sovereignty and the Rules of International Law

Public international law is the body of general normative principles and specific legal rules that govern the behavior of states in their relations with one another. Rather than being a static code of conduct, it has evolved significantly over the past four centuries, changing in response to transformations in world politics.

No principle of international law is more important than state sovereignty. As discussed in previous chapters, sovereignty means that no authority is legally above the state, except that which the state voluntarily confers on the international organizations it joins. Nearly every legal doctrine supports and extends the principle that states are the primary subjects of international law. As outlined in the Montevideo Convention of 1933 on the Rights and Duties of States, a state must possess a permanent population, a well-defined territory, and a government capable of ruling its citizens and of managing formal diplomatic relations with other states. This last criterion is particularly important because the acquisition of statehood ultimately depends on a political entity's acceptance as such by other states, which are entitled to give or withhold **diplomatic recognition**. In other words, recognition is a political tool, through which approval of a government can be expressed and certain rights granted.

diplomatic recognition the formal legal acceptance of a state's official status as an independent country. *De facto* recognition acknowledges the factual existence of another state or government short of full recognition. *De jure* recognition gives a government formal, legal recognition.

The Rights of States.   Under international law, political entities that meet the criteria of statehood hold certain rights. First, states possess the right of continued national existence, which means the prerogative to use force in self-defense. Second, they have the right of independence, which allows them to manage their domestic affairs without external interference and act as free agents in foreign affairs, negotiating commercial treaties, forming military alliances, and entering into other types of agreements without the supervision of another state. Finally, states also have the right of legal equality. Although unequal in size and strength, states are equal before the law in the sense that they all (1) possess the same privileges and responsibilities, (2) can appeal to the same rules of conduct when defending themselves, and (3) can expect to have these rules applied impartially whenever they consent to have a third party help settle their quarrels. The most common third-party procedures used in international dispute resolution include:

- *Good offices:* A third party offers a location for discussions among disputants but does not participate in the actual negotiations.

- *Conciliation:* A third party assists both sides but does not offer any solution.

- *Mediation:* A third party proposes a nonbinding solution to a conflict between states.

- *Arbitration:* A third party gives a binding decision through an ad hoc forum.

- *Adjudication:* A third party gives a binding decision through a standing court.

By defining states' rights in this manner, international law traditionally held that no state could claim jurisdiction over another, nor could it sit in judgment over the validity of the public acts other states initiated under their own laws. Furthermore, heads of state and diplomatic representatives were immune from prosecution in foreign courts.

The Duties of States.   Besides recognizing the rights of existence, independence, and equality, international law acknowledges certain corresponding duties. A sovereign state has the right to maintain its corporate personality as a state, but it also possesses a corollary duty of **nonintervention**—not meddling in the internal matters of other states. Another duty is carrying out promissory obligations in good faith. A sovereign state possesses the right to act as a free agent when dealing with others, but it also has a duty to honor agreements not signed under duress. As expressed in the norm *pacta sunt servanda* (treaties are binding), promises made voluntarily by parties to international treaties must be upheld.

nonintervention the legal principle prohibiting one state from interfering in another state's internal affairs.

However, some legal scholars claim that a radical change in the circumstances that existed when a commitment was made can be invoked under the norm *rebus sic stantibus* (as matters stand) as a ground for unilaterally terminating an agreement.

The Limitations of International Law

Sovereignty and the legal principles derived from it provide the foundation upon which the international legal order rests. But because the international legal order is premised upon the voluntary consent of sovereign states, many people question whether international law is *really* law. From their perspective, international law suffers from the following limitations:

- *The international system lacks a legislative body capable of making binding legal rules.* Whereas in most national legal systems a legislature makes domestic laws, there is no global legislature empowered to make international laws. The UN General Assembly makes recommendations, not statutes. According to Article 38 of the Statute of the International Court of Justice, the sources of legal rules are: (1) custom; (2) international treaties and agreements; (3) national and international court decisions; (4) the writings of legal authorities and specialists; and (5) the "general principles" of law recognized since antiquity as part of "natural law" and "right reason." Of these, custom and multilateral treaties signed by a substantial number of states are considered the most important. Critics question the efficacy of these sources, however, retorting that there can never be an "authentic rule of law among nations" until everyone is "under a common sovereignty" (Bork 1989/1990).

- *The international system lacks a judicial body with compulsory jurisdiction that can identify breaches of legal rules and impose remedies for violations.* The International Court of Justice differs from national courts primarily in that its jurisdiction is based on the consent of the disputants. Sovereign states cannot be forced to appear before the ICJ when charged with breaking legal rules, and they are hesitant to give unconditional consent given the risk of receiving an unfavorable verdict on an issue of vital importance. John Bolton, a former U.S. ambassador to the United Nations, reflected this hesitancy when he claimed it would be "a big mistake" for anyone "to grant validity to international law." In his opinion, "those who think that international law really means anything are those who want to constrict the United States" (*New Yorker*, March 21, 2005, 23).

- *The international system lacks an executive body capable of enforcing legal rules.* Unlike in national legal systems, no centralized mechanism exists to apprehend and punish those who violate legal rules. Although the UN Security Council has the power to act when there is a "threat of breach of international peace and security" (Article 39 of UN Charter), it is often paralyzed by vetoes in cases involving serious militarized disputes, and it is not designed to operate like a municipal police force investigating and bringing to justice those who commit other violations of the law. As one skeptic quipped, without meaningful enforcement capability international law will be "to law as professional wrestling is to wrestling" (*U.S. News & World Report*, September 29, 1993, 8).

- *In the absence of robust global institutions that can make, interpret, and enforce legal rules, international law serves as an instrument of the powerful, justifying the competitive pursuit of national advantage without regard to morality or justice.* By accepting unbridled sovereign autonomy, the international legal system is essentially a "horizontal" normative order composed of laws of coordination, not a "vertical" order based on laws of subordination. Within horizontal orders, the behavior of the powerful has a significant impact in establishing how others should behave. As Stanley Hoffmann (1971) has put it, rules *of* behavior tend to become rules *for* behavior. The legal rules to which the powerful willingly agree are those that serve their interest, legitimizing self-help under the precept that moral considerations must yield to national interest. The outcome of any legal dispute is thus left "to the vicissitudes of the distribution of power between the violator of the law and the victim of the violation." Therefore, Hans J. Morgenthau (1985) concedes, "it makes it easy for the strong both to violate the law and to enforce it, and consequently puts the rights of the weak in jeopardy" (also see Goldsmith and Posner 2005).

Despite the limitations listed here, most states comply with international law because it communicates the "rules of the game" through which virtually everyone within the international system conducts their relations. By shaping expectations, legal rules reduce uncertainty about the behavior of others and increase predictability in world affairs. Those who consistently play by recognized rules enhance their reputations for trustworthiness; those who opportunistically break them undermine their credibility, which weakens their bargaining positions in future interactions as other states become suspicious about their intentions. National leaders who value their reputations are likely to violate an international legal norm only if it or the situation they face is ambiguous enough to plausibly claim an exemption (Shannon 2000). Leaders with high levels of distrust, a belief that they can control events, and a tendency to see the world in "us versus them" terms are less likely to be constrained by legal norms (Shannon and Keller 2007).

In summary, compliance with law does not necessarily derive from commands backed by punishment from some central authority. States voluntarily observe international legal rules because their long-term self-interests are served by the order that comes from shared expectations (Joyner 2005). Legal scholar William Slomanson (2003) likens this process to the behavior of motorists at intersections. Most drivers stop when the traffic light is red and go when it turns green, even when no police officer is present to enforce traffic laws. They comply with the law because of a common interest to proceed safely, knowing that collisions would occur if people ignored the signals at intersections. Similarly, "almost all nations observe almost all principles of international law and almost all of their obligations almost all of the time," writes Louis Henkin (1979), because everyone benefits from avoiding the chaos that would otherwise exist.

International Law and the Preservation of Peace

Although rudimentary when compared to national legal systems, international law nonetheless mitigates the most pernicious aspects of an anarchic state system. Among the most important international legal rules prescribing limits on state behavior are those that pertain to the use of armed force. They delineate when it is legitimate for states to employ force, how it should be used, and against whom it may be applied. Because the content of these rules has been heavily influenced by **just war doctrine**, we begin our analysis of the role of international law in preserving peace by examining this ethical tradition.

Just War Doctrine. The term *just war* originated with Aristotle. Attempts to enumerate criteria for determining whether a particular war was just were subsequently undertaken by the Roman writer Cicero, as well as by early Christian thinkers such as Ambrose, Augustine, and Aquinas. Over the intervening centuries, philosophers and theologians continued to advance contending theories regarding when it would be morally justifiable to use military force as a tool of foreign policy.

just war doctrine a set of criteria that indicate when it is morally justifiable to wage war and how it should be fought once it begins.

The roots of modern just war doctrine lie in the effort of Hugo Grotius to transform these earlier moral theories into a body of international law that would specify those circumstances under which war might be legally initiated and how it should be waged upon its commencement. An eminent Dutch scholar who was outraged by the brutality of the Thirty Years' War (1618–1648), Grotius complained that states "rush to arms" for "trifling pretexts," and then behave "as though by some edict a fury had been let loose to commit every crime." To counteract this deplorable pattern, he drew upon ancient and medieval writers to develop two bodies of rules about warfare, *jus ad bellum* (the justice of a war) and *jus in bello* (justice in a war). The former set the standards by which a political leader could determine whether a war was just. The latter described the military actions that were permissible in fighting a just war.

The rules proposed by Grotius have inspired international lawyers since their publication in 1625 (see Controversy: Was the War in Iraq Just?). Rather than condemning all warfare as intrinsically evil, just-war theorists submit that recourse to war is permissible when the following conditions are met:

1. *Just cause:* The state contemplating the use of military force must have a morally good objective.

2. *Right intention:* War must be waged for the purpose of correcting a wrong and establishing peace and justice, not for revenge or some other malicious reason.

3. *Last resort:* War should not be undertaken until all other reasonable means of resolving the conflict have been exhausted.

4. *Political proportionality:* The harm caused by the fighting must not outweigh the good toward which the war aims.

RUIT HORA

Erich Lessing/Art Resource, NY

War and the Birth of Modern International Law Revolted by the international violence he witnessed during his lifetime, Dutch reformer Hugo Grotius (1583–1645) wrote *On the Law of War and Peace* in the midst of the Thirty Years' War. His treatise called on the great powers to resolve their conflicts by pacific means rather than on the battlefield, and specified the legal principles he felt could encourage cooperation, peace, and more humane treatment of people. Grotius consequently became known as the "father of international law."

5. *Declaration by legitimate authority:* Duly constituted rulers must publicly declare a state of war.

6. *Reasonable chance of success:* States must not engage in futile uses of force.

In addition to elucidating *when* it is morally permissible to fight, just war theory also stipulates *how* wars should be fought. While numerous rules have been proposed on the right and wrong ways to conduct war, most revolve around the following two principles:

1. *Discrimination:* Noncombatants must be immune from attack; civilians not engaged in their state's war efforts cannot be targeted.

2. *Military proportionality:* Combatants must cause no more destruction than is required to achieve their military objectives.

These *jus ad bellum* and *jus in bello* standards continue to color thinking about the laws of war. However, the advent of weapons of mass destruction raised new

CONTROVERSY Was the War in Iraq Just?

On February 5, 2003, U.S. Secretary of State Colin Powell delivered a lengthy address to the United Nations Security Council, charging Iraq with a breach of its disarmament obligations under UN Security Council Resolution 1441. American intelligence agencies, Powell asserted, had evidence that Saddam Hussein's regime possessed weapons of mass destruction. After emphasizing the gravity of the threat these weapons posed, Powell reminded his audience of the Iraqi leader's ruthlessness and warned that he would "stop at nothing until something stops him."

Over the next few weeks, U.S. President George W. Bush and other members of his administration reiterated these accusations. On March 17, Bush claimed that Iraq "continued to possess and conceal some of the most lethal weapons ever devised," and threatened military action if Saddam Hussein did not leave the country within forty-eight hours. When Hussein failed to comply, the United States and its allies launched a series of precision air strikes and swarming ground attacks that quickly overwhelmed Iraqi defenses.

The Bush administration gave three primary justifications for its war against Iraq: (1) Saddam Hussein had weapons of mass destruction; (2) he had close ties with the al Qaeda terrorist network; and (3) his removal from power would provide an opportunity to transform Iraq into a democratic regime, which would change the political atmosphere throughout the entire Middle East.

Yet more than three years after the president declared victory on May 1, 2003 from the flight deck of the USS *Abraham Lincoln,* American and allied troops were locked in fierce fighting with Iraqi insurgents. Though expected to be welcomed with rice and rose petals, the coalition forces came to be seen as occupiers rather than liberators. Iraqi public opinion polls spon-

sored by the U.S. Coalition Provisional Authority, showed over 80 percent of those interviewed indicated that they had no confidence in the United States after the Abu Ghraib prison abuse scandal, and wanted Washington to withdraw its troops as soon as possible. Meanwhile, the much-touted Iraqi weapons of mass destruction had not been found, and the commission investigating the September 11 terror attacks on the United States indicated that they failed to discover any collaborative relationship between Saddam Hussein and Al Qaeda.

In response, the Bush administration continued to insist that the war had been just. Vice President Dick Cheney maintained that even if there was just a 1 percent chance of terrorists getting weapons of mass destruction, the United States had to act as if it were a certainty (Suskind 2006, 62). According to Cheney, absolute proof of an adversary's capabilities and intentions should not be a precondition for American military action; it's too high a threshold in a world where warnings of a catastrophic attack would be limited and confirmation of the perpetrator's identity unattainable in operational time. "Absence of evidence," as Secretary of Defense Donald Rumsfeld put it, "is not evidence of absence."

What do you think? Drawing upon the criteria proposed by just war theorists, would you evaluate the 2003 war against Iraq as a just war? Was it initiated for a just cause and with the right intentions? Was it undertaken as a last resort with the appropriate authorization? Did the good toward which the war aimed outweigh the harm caused by the fighting? Do you agree with Vice President Dick Cheney's claim that the risks of American inaction were far greater than the risks of action?

---

questions about the ethics of war and peace, since their use would violate many of the traditional principles of just war doctrine. A high-yield nuclear device, for example, would not only obliterate the target area, but it would also produce enough radioactive fallout to kill vast numbers of people in countries that had no part in the conflict, thereby violating the standards of military proportionality and discrimination. Scholars and policy makers alike are now struggling to rethink just war doctrine in the light of the new strategic realities of contemporary warfare.

Problems in the Legal Control of Warfare. As Figure 10.1 shows, the international legal community has increasingly rejected the realist contention that states can use military force to achieve their foreign policy objectives.

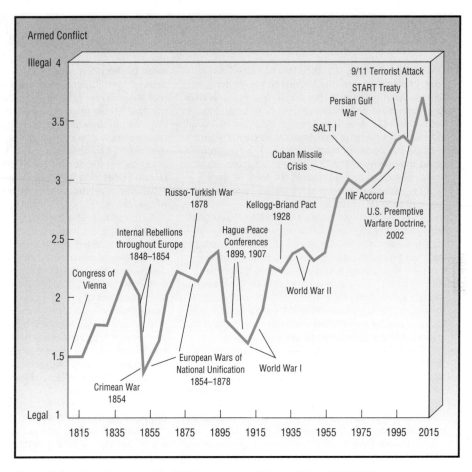

FIGURE 10.1   The Legal Prohibition against Initiating Wars, 1815–2008

Legal restraints on the historic right of states to use war as a tool of foreign policy have grown steadily since World War I. After the attacks of September 11, 2001, these legal prohibitions were questioned by U.S. policy makers who favored military preemption against states that support terrorist movements.

SOURCE: Adapted from Transnational Rules Indicators Project, as described in *When Trust Breaks Down: Alliance Norms and World Politics* by Charles W. Kegley, Jr. and Gregory A. Raymond. Copyright © 1990 Charles W. Kegley, Jr. and Gregory A. Raymond. Reprinted with the permission of the University of South Carolina.

reprisal   a hostile but legal retaliatory act aimed at punishing another state's prior illegal actions.

Influenced by many of the standards contained in just war doctrine, the laws of war have sought to prohibit all uses of force by individual states except in self-defense. Traditionally, the right of self-defense has been understood as allowing states recourse to force when repelling armed attacks and when facing imminent security threats. As articulated by U.S. Secretary of State Daniel Webster in 1837, to exercise this right a state must face an "instant, overwhelming necessity . . . leaving no choice of means, and no moment for deliberation." In addition, the defensive actions taken must be proportionate to the danger, should not endanger noncombatants to minimize one's own risk, and cannot serve as a **reprisal**.

Self-defense is thus restricted to protection, not excessive or punitive measures aimed at redressing injuries.

Following the promulgation of the UN Charter, appeals to this customary right of self-defense became more problematic. The charter addresses self-defense in two places. First, Article 2 (4) declares that "all members shall refrain in their international relations from the threat or use of force against the territorial integrity or political independence of any State, or in any other manner inconsistent with the purposes of the United Nations." Second, Article 51 proclaims that "Nothing in the present Charter shall impair the inherent right of individual or collective self-defense if an armed attack occurs against a Member of the United Nations, until the Security Council has taken the measures necessary to maintain international peace and security." One school of thought about the Charter interprets Articles 2 (4) and 51 as superseding customary international law, and thus limiting forcible self-defense to cases where the Security Council has not yet responded to an armed attack. A second school of thought disagrees. Highlighting the concept of "inherent right" in Article 51, it argues that pre-charter, customary rules of self-defense continue in place. States, in other words, have a right to use military force so long as the traditional criteria of necessity, proportionality, and protection are met.

The difficulty with the second interpretation of self-defense lies in defining what constitutes an "overwhelming necessity." Appeals to the exigencies of **military necessity** challenge the wrongfulness of an act on the basis that it was the only means of safeguarding an essential interest against a grave peril (Raymond 1999). According to those who invoke the necessity defense, a state may be absolved from taking military actions that violate the rules of warfare when it faces an absolute strategic imperative that makes it practically impossible to do anything else. Those responsible for national security, they insist, must often make tragic choices among lesser evils. As the former British Secretary of State for War Lord Kitchener once put it: "We must make war as we must; not as we should like."

In addition to the problems that claims of military necessity create for international laws governing the use of force, recent suggestions that the international community has a moral imperative to stop brutal governments from violating the human rights of their citizens raises another set of problems. Allowing the use of coercion by one state to change the political regime in another would significantly change the normative climate of world affairs. As we have seen, the twin principles of sovereignty and nonintervention underpin international law. Traditionally, the only widely accepted exception to the prohibition against interfering in the domestic affairs of other nation-states was military intervention to liberate one's own nationals when they are being held hostage. Yet recently, some states have asserted the right, and even a moral obligation, to use military intervention for humanitarian purposes. As shown in Figure 10.2, the nonintervention principle has begun to erode as a growing proportion of countries has sought a way to stop human rights abuses in a globalized, interconnected world.

The argument claiming it is legally permissible to intervene with armed force in order to end egregious violations of human rights rests on three

military necessity a legal doctrine asserting that violation of the rules of war may be excused during periods of extreme emergency.

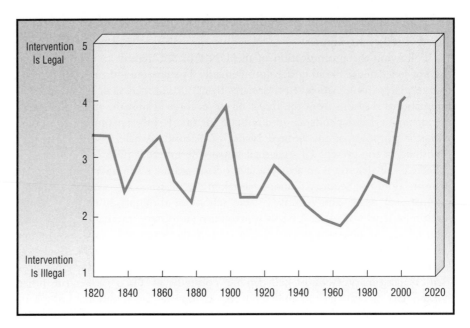

FIGURE 10.2 The Changing Status of the Nonintervention Rule in International Law since 1820

Over time, the illegality of intervening into the domestic affairs of sovereign states has changed. Since 1960, international law has adopted an increasingly permissive posture toward this form of coercive diplomacy for a variety of purposes, including preventing genocide, promoting democracy, and combating global terrorism.

SOURCE: From Transnational Rules Indicators Project, as originally measured in "The Rise and Fall of the Nonintervention Norm: Some Correlates and Potential Consequences" by Charles W. Kegley, Jr., Gregory A. Raymond, and Margaret G. Hermann from the *Fletcher Forum of International Affairs* (Winter 1998).

propositions. The first proposition asserts that human rights are an international entitlement. Article 55 (c) of the UN Charter requires member states to promote "universal respect for, and observance of, human rights." Over the past 50 years, the UN has developed a detailed list of inherent, inalienable rights of all human beings. The most important legal formulation of those rights is expressed in the so-called International Bill of Human Rights, the informal name given to the Universal Declaration of Human Rights (which was passed by a vote of the UN General Assembly in 1948), the International Covenant on Civil and Political Rights, and the International Covenant on Economic, Social, and Cultural Rights (which were both opened for signature in 1966 and entered into force a decade later). For advocates of humanitarian intervention, the legal rules governing these rights are regarded as *jus cogens*—peremptory legal norms that override all other considerations.

The second proposition maintains that governments committing grave violations of human rights lose their legitimacy. Although Article 2 (7) of the UN Charter prevents member states from interfering in one another's domestic affairs, the Charter's legal protection does not extend to genocide, torture, or other horrific acts shocking to the conscience of the international community. Those favoring humanitarian intervention argue that governments involved in these abuses forfeit their protection under international law.

The third proposition asserts that the international community has a responsibility to halt human rights violations. According to the International Court of Justice, there are some obligations that a state has "towards the international community as a whole," and all members of that community "have a legal interest in their protection." The entitlement for protection against genocide, slavery, and the like gives legal standing to any member of the international community to impose sanctions if these wrongful acts continue. When massive human rights violations occur, "intervention from the outside is not only legally justified but morally required" (D'Amato 1995).

The advent of these new justifications for military intervention into the domestic affairs of sovereign states reflects a growing sentiment that sovereignty is no longer sacrosanct. Shocked by the carnage in the civil war that broke out in Bosnia during 1992, former British prime minister Margaret Thatcher captured this mood when she lamented, "We cannot just let things go on like this" (*Time,* April 26, 1993, 35). "Something, anything, must be done," implored Nobel laureate Elie Wiesel (*Time,* May 3, 1993, 35). Sovereignty, they and others argued, cannot shield the perpetrators of grievous crimes against humanity from punishment. "There are common norms and standards of conduct and countries must be answerable for failing to observe these" (de Wijk 1998). Heads of state and military commanders who have been involved in **war crimes** must be held accountable. The international community has a responsibility to protect vulnerable populations from human rights violations [See Application: The Doctrine of International Community].

war crimes acts performed during war that the international community defines as illegal, such as atrocities committed against enemy civilians and prisoners of war.

APPLICATION   **The Doctrine of International Community**

Ever since the Peace of Westphalia ended the Thirty Years' War in 1648, the principles of sovereignty and nonintervention have governed international politics. As the twentieth century drew to a close, however, many legal scholars and human rights activists began arguing that these principles did not apply to national leaders who violated the human rights of their citizens. According to Tony Blair, who served as the prime minister of the United Kingdom from May 1997 to June 2007, the old "rule book of international politics has been torn up." The world is "witnessing the beginnings of a new doctrine of international community." In the passage below, Blair describes the policy implications of this new theoretical doctrine.

The most pressing foreign policy problem we face is to identify the circumstances in which we should

get actively involved in other people's conflicts. Non-interference has long been considered an important principle of international order. And it is not one we would want to jettison too readily. One state should not feel it has the right to change the political system of another . . . . But the principle of non-interference must be qualified in important respects. Acts of genocide can never be a purely internal matter.

...So how do we decide when and whether to intervene? I think we need to bear in mind five major considerations.

First, are we sure of our case? War is an imperfect instrument for righting humanitarian distress; but armed force is sometimes the only means of dealing with dictators. Second, have we exhausted all diplomatic options? We should always give peace every chance . . . . Third, on the basis of a practical assessment of the situation, are there military operations we can sensibly and prudently undertake? Fourth, are we prepared for the long term? In the past we talked too much of exit strategies. But having made a commitment we cannot simply walk away once the fight is over; better to stay with moderate numbers of troops than return for repeat performances with large numbers. And finally, do we have national interests involved (Blair 1999).

National interests, Blair would later go on to say, cannot be divorced from national values. Speaking at Georgetown University on May 26, 2006, he noted that in his years as prime minister he had "become more persuaded that the distinction between a foreign policy driven by values and one driven by interests, is obviously wrong." In his opinion, "our values are our guide."

To deal with the rising concern about serious violations of international humanitarian law, the UN Security Council set up two *ad hoc* criminal tribunals between 1993 and 1994: the International Criminal Tribunal for the former Yugoslavia, and the International Criminal Tribunal for Rwanda. In 1998, 120 countries meeting in Rome voted to establish a *permanent* International Criminal Court (ICC), so future acts of genocide, crimes against humanity, and war crimes would not go unpunished.

The new International Criminal Court differs from the older International Court of Justice (or "World Court"). Whereas the ICC has criminal jurisdiction to prosecute individuals charged with heinous violations of human rights, the ICJ

Jacques Collet/AFP/Getty Images

Prosecuting War Criminals In 1999, Swiss criminal lawyer Carla del Ponte was appointed chief prosecutor of the International Criminal Tribunals for Rwanda (ICTR) and the former Yugoslavia (ICTY). As of 2007, the ICTR had rendered judgments on twenty-eight people and had trials involving twenty-seven more in progress. The ICTY had closed proceedings against 106 of 161 indicted people. In July 2008, Radovan Karadzic, the former Bosnian Serb leader, was arrested after being wanted by the ICTY for thirteen years.

deals with disputes between sovereign states. Founded in the hope that international adjudication would help resolve disputes before they escalated to war, the ICJ languished through much of the Cold War. Powerful countries hesitated to relinquish their military advantage and put issues of importance in the hands of foreign judges that might rule against them. Political realists, depicting the world as a place where states perpetually jockey for relative gains, urge leaders to act in terms of national self-interest, trusting in their own power rather than in international courts. "A statesman who has any other motive," proclaimed one exponent of realism, "would be deserved to be hung" (Johannes Haller cited in Niebuhr 1947).

Despite realist predictions that the World Court would always have more judges than cases, in recent years it has begun to play the kind of role envisioned by its liberal founders. Between 1946 and 1991, the World Court heard only sixty-four contentious cases between states, rendered judgments on less than half of these, and handed down only nineteen advisory opinions. Since then, it has expanded its workload and considered cases dealing with many new issues (Raymond 2004). Between 1992 and 1995, the ICJ heard twenty-four cases, and the judicial activity jumped to an average of sixteen cases each year between 1996 and 2002. By 2006, the court was managing eleven pending cases and was increasingly active in responding to requests for advisory opinions.

Critics assert that the World Court remains ineffective despite its increased caseload, with many states still refusing to submit their most serious disputes. It is instructive, they note, that two-thirds of today's states have never appeared before the ICJ, and those who agree to litigate comply with ICJ judgments only 60 percent of the time. Supporters, however, point to recent high-profile cases that were successfully resolved. For example, in 1992 Honduras and El Salvador accepted the Court's verdict on a border dispute that had been festering for decades. Unconvinced, the ICJ's critics aver that the Court's successes tend to involve litigants who wish to preserve their overall relationship, not bitter foes locked in high-stakes confrontations. They argue that the outcome of Nicaragua's 1984 suit against the United States was more representative of the Court's impact on serious disputes than the case between Honduras and Nicaragua.

In 1979, Nicaraguan dictator Anastasio Somoza was overthrown by a broad-based movement known as the Sandinista National Liberation Front. After ousting Somoza, a Marxist faction within the movement gained power and established ties with Cuba and the Soviet Union. Disturbed by the leftist tilt of the new regime and its support for revolutionary groups elsewhere in Central America, the United States trained antigovernment insurgents, mined three of Nicaragua's harbors, and attacked the country's petroleum facilities in an effort to undermine the Sandinistas. Nicaragua responded by filing suit against the United States on April 9, 1984 in the International Court of Justice.

Nicaragua's suit accused the U.S. Central Intelligence Agency of illegally attempting to destabilize and topple the elected Sandinista government. The Reagan administration replied by refusing to recognize the World Court's jurisdiction and withdrawing from further judicial proceedings. Nevertheless, the ICJ heard Nicaragua's arguments, and on June 27, 1986, ruled against the United States. The verdict had little effect on Washington, however. Neither the World Court nor Nicaragua had any means to enforce the judgment.

As the Nicaragua case demonstrates, international judicial institutions remain a far cry from most domestic courts. Because the ICJ lacks teeth, detractors liken its rulings to sermons, providing gallant rhetoric to encourage the pursuit of wistful ideals (Wedgwood 2002, 45). For some people, one way to dismantle some of the barriers impeding the development of international law is to strengthen international organizations; hence we next consider their role in building and maintaining world peace.

INTERNATIONAL INSTITUTIONS AND WORLD ORDER

Critics of realism often recommend creating international institutions as a second political path to peace. To understand this recommendation, we must delve into their beliefs about **collective security** as an alternative to balance-of-power politics.

collective security a security regime guided by the principle that an act of aggression by any state will be met with a unified response from the rest.

The League of Nations and Collective Security

The outbreak of World War I, perhaps more than any other event, discredited the argument that peace was a byproduct of international equilibrium. Citing arms races, secret treaties, and competing alliances as sources of acute tension, many liberals viewed power balancing as a *cause* of war instead of an instrument for its prevention. U.S. president Woodrow Wilson voiced the strongest opposition to balance-of-power politics. He hoped to replace it with a League of Nations, based on a system of world order in which aggression by any state would be met by a united international response.

The Logic of Collective Security.   Long before Wilson and other liberal reformers called for the establishment of a League of Nations, the idea of collective security had been expressed in various peace plans. Between the eleventh and thirteenth centuries, for example, French ecclesiastic councils held in Poitiers (1000), Limoges (1031), and Toulouse (1210) discussed rudimentary versions of collective security. Similar proposals surfaced in the writings of Pierre Dubois (1306), King George Podebrad of Bohemia (1462), the Duc de Sully (1617–1638), and the Abbé de Saint-Pierre (1713). Underlying these plans was the belief that an organized "community" of power would be more effective in preserving peace than shifting alliances aimed at balancing power.

Collective security is based on the creed voiced by Alexandre Dumas' d'Artagnan and his fellow Musketeers: "One for all and all for one!" In order for collective security to function in the rough-and-tumble environment of international politics, its advocates usually translate the Musketeer creed into the following rules of statecraft:

1. *All threats to peace must be a common concern to everyone.* Peace, collective security theory assumes, is indivisible. If aggression anywhere is ignored, it will eventually spread to other countries and become more difficult to stop; hence an attack on any one state must be regarded as an attack on all states.

2. *Every member of the state system should join the collective security organization.* Instead of maneuvering against one another in rival alliances, states should link up in a single "uniting" alliance. Such a universal collectivity, it is assumed, would possess the international legitimacy and strength to keep the peace.

3. *Members of the organization would pledge to settle their disputes through pacific means.* Collective security is not wedded to the status quo. It assumes that peaceful change is possible when institutions are available to resolve conflicts of interest. In addition to providing a mechanism for mediating disagreements, the collective security organization would also contain a judicial organ authorized to issue binding judgments on contentious disputes.

4. *If a breach of the peace occurs, the organization will apply timely, robust sanctions to punish the aggressor.* A final assumption underpinning the theory holds that members of the collective security organization would be willing and able to give mutual assistance to any state suffering an attack. Sanctions could range from public condemnation to an economic boycott to military retaliation.

In summary, this approach to world order tries to inhibit national self-help by guaranteeing the territorial integrity and political independence of states through "collective self-regulation." The key to its success is universal participation: To deter war, a potential aggressor would need to be faced by the united opposition of the entire international community (Downs 1994; Claude 1962; K. Thompson 1953).

Difficulties with Collective Security.   As discussed in Chapters 2 and 3, the League of Nations was constructed according to the blueprint of collective security. To the disappointment of its advocates, the League was not endorsed by the United States, the very power that had most championed it in the waning months of the First World War. Other problems for the League arose when its members disagreed over how to define "aggression," and how to share the costs and risks of mounting an organized response to aggressors. In the final analysis, collective security theory's central fallacy was that it expected states to be as anxious to see others protected as they were to protect themselves. That assumption did not prove true in the years preceding World War II; consequently the League of Nations never became an effective collective security system.

The United Nations and Peacekeeping

Like the League, the United Nations was established to promote international peace and security after a gruesome world war. Article 1 (1) of its Charter directed the organization to take "effective collective measures for the prevention and removal of threats to the peace." In Article 2, all members were called upon to "refrain in their international relations from the threat or use of force" (paragraph 4) and "settle their international disputes by peaceful means" (paragraph 3).

The architects of the United Nations were painfully aware of the League's disappointing experience with collective security. They hoped a new structure would make the United Nations more effective than the defunct League. Recall from Chapter 6 that the UN Charter established a Security Council of fifteen members, a General Assembly composed of representatives from all member states, and an administrative apparatus (or Secretariat) under the leadership of a secretary-general. While the UN's founders voiced support for collective security, the structure they designed was heavily influenced by the idea of a great-power concert. The UN Charter permitted any of the Security Council's five permanent members (the United States, the Soviet Union, Great Britain, France, and China) to veto and thereby block proposed military actions. Because the Security Council could approve military actions only when the permanent members fully agreed, the United Nations was hamstrung by great-power rivalries, especially between the United States and the Soviet Union.

To further enhance the great powers' authority relative to the UN, the Charter severely restricted the capacity of the General Assembly to mount collective action, authorizing it only to initiate studies of conflict situations, bring perceived hostilities to the attention of the Security Council, and make recommendations for initiatives to keep the peace. Moreover, it restricted the role of the secretary-general to that of chief administrative officer. Article 99 confined the secretary-general to alerting the Security Council to peace-threatening situations and to providing administrative support for the operations that the Security Council approved.

Because the UN's structure limited its ability to function as a collective security organization, the United Nations fell short during the Cold War of many of the ideals its more ambitious founders envisioned, principally because its two most powerful members in the Security Council, the United States and the Soviet Union, did not cooperate. Over 230 Security Council vetoes were cast, stopping action of any type on about one-third of the UN's resolutions. Nevertheless, the United Nations found other ways to contribute to world order. Under Secretary-General Dag Hammarskjöld, **preventive diplomacy** replaced collective security as the organization's primary approach to promoting international peace and security. Recognizing that the United Nations had little leverage in areas where the superpowers were heavily engaged, Hammarskjöld sought to involve the UN in other regions and thus prevent Washington and Moscow from intruding into local disputes. His approach was based on the UN experience in the Middle East crises of 1956 and 1958, the Laos crisis of 1959, and Congo crisis of 1960. In essence, it involved establishing a cease-fire and inserting UN troops as a buffer to separate the belligerents. Ideally, an impartial UN presence would keep the conflict localized, although it did little to resolve the dispute.

preventive diplomacy actions taken in advance of a predictable crisis to prevent superpower involvement and limit violence.

The next major innovation in UN peacekeeping efforts began during the 1980s when the organization moved beyond supervising truces and turned its attention to **peacemaking** and **peace-building**. The former involved the UN in actively working to resolve the underlying dispute between the belligerents; the latter involved it in activities such as monitoring arms control agreements and providing developmental assistance to create the conditions that would make a renewal of the fighting less likely.

The end of the Cold War removed many impediments to the UN's ability to preserve international security by means that the founders of the UN originally envisioned. The potential to play an active security role was demonstrated in 1990 when Iraq invaded Kuwait. The Security Council promptly passed Resolution 678, authorizing member states "to use all necessary means" to dislodge Iraqi forces from Kuwait. Under the authority of this resolution, on January 17, 1991, a U.S.-led coalition launched military actions against Iraq's armed forces, the fourth largest in the world. Forty-three days later, Iraq agreed to a cease-fire and withdrawal from Kuwait.

Bolstered by this success at collective security, optimism about the UN role in promoting peace started to grow. After 1990, the UN launched five times as many peacekeeping missions as it had in its forty previous years of existence. Since then, it has managed on average seventeen operations each year (see Map 10.1). Despite this upsurge in the aftermath of the Cold War, peacekeeping missions have shown mixed results, failing in roughly half of the time and straining the UN's budget (Brooks and Laroia 2005, 121–122.). For the UN's peacekeeping operations since 1948, expenditures have totaled more than $53 billion, and for the period between July 2007 and June 2008, the cost of supporting 82,868 UN peacekeeping personnel was $5.3 billion. In view of the costs, the UN has sought to deploy its missions alongside non-UN forces and at other times has requested regional organizations or multi-party state alliances to act as a substitute for the UN. This has raised questions about in whose interest these forces are acting and whether they can be held accountable by the UN.

peacemaking peaceful settlement processes such as good offices, conciliation, and mediation, designed to resolve the issues that led to armed conflict.

peace-building post-conflict actions, predominantly diplomatic and economic, that strengthen and rebuild governmental infrastructure and institutions in order to avoid recourse to armed conflict.

Regional Security Organizations and Collective Defense

If the UN remains hampered by a lack of resources, perhaps regional organizations, whose members already share many common interests and cultural traditions, offer better prospects for maintaining peace and security. Indeed, some would argue that the kinds of wars raging today do not lend themselves to control by a worldwide body, because these conflicts are now almost entirely civil wars. The UN was designed to manage interstate wars; it was not conceived as an instrument for dealing with battles inside sovereign borders. This, however, is not the case for regional institutions, who see their security interests vitally affected by armed conflicts within countries in their geographic areas. In 2008, no less than fifty-nine peace missions with a total of 167,630 military and civilian personnel were carried out by regional organizations and UN-sanctioned coalitions of states (SIPRI 2008). Given the rising number of peacekeeping operations

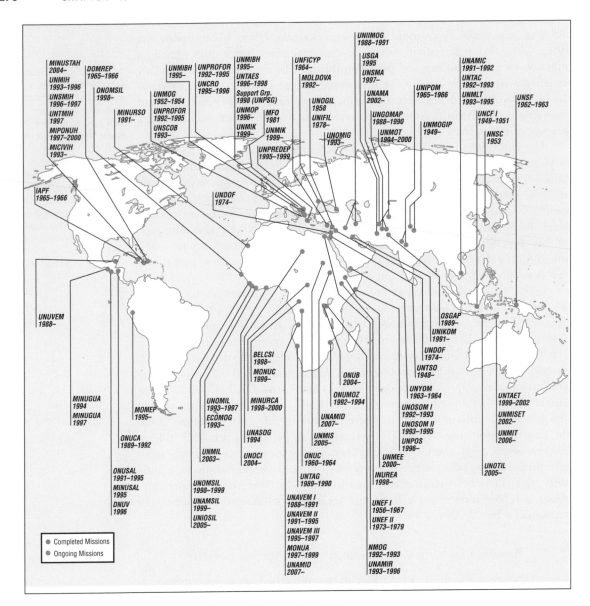

M A P 10.1 UN Peace Missions since 1948

In its first forty years, only thirteen UN peacekeeping missions were undertaken. But since 1986 the UN has been much more active, sending peacekeepers to forty-eight additional flash points. Most of the sixty-one missions between 1948 and 2008 have been in operation for at least a decade. *Source:* Based on data from the United Nations Department of Public Information.

in recent years that involve regional security organizations, most observers expect them to play an increasingly larger role in the future.

The North Atlantic Treaty Organization (NATO) is the best-known regional security organization. Others include the Organization for Security and Cooperation in Europe (OSCE), the ANZUS pact (Australia, New Zealand, and the United States), and the Southeast Asia Treaty Organization (SEATO). Regional organizations with somewhat broader political mandates beyond defense include the Organization of American States (OAS), the League of Arab States, the Organization of African Unity (OAU), the Nordic Council, the Association of Southeast Asian Nations (ASEAN), and the Gulf Cooperation Council.

Although Article 51 of the UN Charter encourages the creation of regional organizations for collective self-defense, it would be misleading to describe NATO and the other regional organizations as a substitute collective security instrument for the UN. They are not. More accurately, regional **collective defense** systems are designed to deter a potential common threat to the region's peace, one typically identified in advance.

Many of today's regional security organizations face the challenge of preserving consensus and solidarity without a clearly identifiable external enemy or common threat. Cohesion is hard to maintain in the absence of a clear sense of mission. Consider NATO, which faces a European security setting marked by ethnopolitical conflicts. NATO's original charter envisioned only one purpose—mutual self-protection from external attack by the Soviet Union; it never defined policing civil wars as a goal. Consequently, until 1995, when NATO took charge of all military operations in Bosnia-Herzegovina from the UN, it was uncertain whether the alliance would survive long beyond the demise of the Soviet Union. Since then, NATO has taken on a peacemaking assignment in Kosovo (1999) and a combat role in Afghanistan (2007). NATO has transformed itself to become both a *military* alliance for enhancing the security of its members and a *political* alliance for encouraging the spread of democracy.

From the philosopher Immanuel Kant onward, liberal theorists have argued that democratization enhances the prospects for peace between states. As discussed in earlier chapters, a growing body of research supports their argument. Constitutionally secure democracies rarely (if ever) make war on one another, and they form the most durable, peaceful leagues (Weart 1994; see also Huth and Allee 2003 and Mandelbaum 2002). This lesson is not lost on the leaders of today's democratic states searching for a principle on which to ground their security policies. NATO and the European Union have insisted on democracy as a condition for membership. Major international organizations from the World Bank to the International Monetary Fund have also made the promotion of democracy a policy priority. Since democratic states have a greater propensity than other types of states to employ amicable, legally binding methods of conflict resolution (Dixon 1994; Raymond 1994), liberals contend that enlarging the community of democracies will exert a pacifying effect on world politics.

collective defense
a military organization within a specific region created to protect its members from external attack.

INTERNATIONAL INTEGRATION AND
WORLD ORDER

Since antiquity, the world has pursued two primary paths to peace: one road emphasizes military solutions; the other, political solutions. Thus far in this chapter we have examined international law and organization as political approaches to the control of armed conflict. We turn now to consider an approach based on changing the way international actors think about themselves; that is, changing what constructivists would characterize as their identities.

Many theorists who focus on international law and organization see armed conflict as deriving from deeply rooted institutional deficiencies. They believe weak international institutions make humankind's security subservient to the parochial interests of competing, egoistic states. For them, the major security problems of our day simultaneously affect almost everyone. Terrorists with global reach, refugees fleeing horrific civil wars, and the proliferation of weapons of mass destruction exemplify these problems. National borders cannot insulate people from security threats lurking over the horizon. Nor can states manage them unilaterally. According to some theorists, the dangers facing humanity are so grave that they require solutions beyond the nation-state.

World Government

If the anarchic state system is a major obstacle to peace, then one possible solution to the problem of war is a world government. The idea is not new. During the early fourteenth century, for example, the Italian poet Dante responded to incessant fighting among the states of his day by proposing that power be centralized in the hands of a universal monarch. While proposals for a world monarchy are rare today, it is not unusual to hear calls for **world federalism**; that is, incorporating previously sovereign states into a single union, therein reducing the likelihood that the actors on the world stage will have antagonistic identities.

world federalism
a reform movement proposing to combine sovereign states into a single unified federal state.

Federalists reason that if people value humanity's survival in an era of weapons of mass destruction, they will willingly transfer their loyalty to a supranational authority and dismantle the anarchic system of competitive territorial states. Agreeing with Albert Einstein, they argue that "there is no salvation for civilization, or even the human race, other than the creation of a world government." Scholars disagree over whether a single state or a looser form of global governance by a combination of supranational institutions would be sufficient (Baratta 2005). Alexander Wendt (2003), a leading constructivist, says that a formal world state is inevitable. Just as city-states were superseded by nation-states when advances in military technology undermined their ability to provide their citizens with security, nation-states will someday be amalgamated into a world-state (Ferencz and Keyes 1991), although some wonder whether a practical first step would be for the world's democracies to combine in a federal union (Yunker 2007).

The thesis that world government is inevitable remains controversial (see Shannon 2005). In addition to those who believe it is unfeasible, many complain that it is undesirable. For example, ardent nationalists have vehemently attacked the federalist "top-down" peace plan. Because it seeks to abate the national identities associated with the current system of sovereign states, the plan threatens many entrenched interests. Other critics reject the notion that eliminating nation-states will end warfare. Civil wars can erupt under a world government. Still other critics fear that such a global political entity would be unresponsive to the local needs of the diverse indigenous cultures that comprise humanity. A world government need not be a leviathan, respond supporters. Because the threat of external invasion would be nonexistent, it could function as a small, decentralized federal authority without a massive defense establishment (Deudney 2006).

Although the idea of world government has received increased attention in recent years (see Craig 2008), aversion to war and concern about climate change and other transnational problems has not mobilized widespread grassroots enthusiasm for creating a universal state. Regional approaches to reforming the world politics have attracted far more adherents.

Regional Integration

While the merging of sovereign states into a world government is unlikely in the foreseeable future, integration is occurring in certain regions of the world. **Political integration** refers to the process of building new political communities and identities that transcend the nation-state. Advocates of political integration seek reform programs that transform international institutions from instruments *of* states to structures *over* them.

The Functionalist Approach to Integration.   In contrast to federalism, **functionalism** is not directed toward creating a world federal government with all its constitutional paraphernalia. Instead, it calls for a "bottom-up," evolutionary strategy based on using specialized technical agencies that solve problems that cross national borders. The Rhine River Commission (1804), the Danube River Commission (1857), the International Telegraphic Union (1865), and the Universal Post Union (1874), were forerunners of these agencies. They were early attempts at crafting administrative units that conformed to the geography of a transnational problem rather than the boundaries of a particular state.

According to functionalists, technical experts, rather than professional diplomats, are the best agents for building collaborative links among people living in separate states. They see diplomats as being overly protective of their country's national interests at the expense of collective human interests. Rather than addressing the immediate sources of national insecurity, the functionalists' peace plan calls for transnational cooperation in technical areas as a first step. Habits of cooperation learned in one technical area (such as transportation), they suggest, will **spill over** into others (such as communication)—especially if the experience

political integration the processes and activities by which the populations of two or more states transfer their loyalties to a merged political and economic unit.

functionalism a theory of political integration based on the assumption that technical cooperation among different nationalities in economic and social fields will build communities that transcend sovereign states.

spill over the propensity for successful integration across one area of cooperation between states to propel further integration in other areas.

is mutually beneficial and demonstrates the potential advantages of further cooperation.

To enhance the probability that cooperative endeavors will prove rewarding, the functionalist plan recommends that less-difficult tasks be tackled first. It assumes that successful mastering of a relatively simple problem will encourage working on other more demanding problems collaboratively. If the process continues unabated, the bonds among people living in different countries will multiply, because no government would oppose a web of functional organizations that provide such clear-cut benefits to its citizens (Mitrany 1966).

Critics charge that as a theory of peace and world order, functionalism does not take into account some important political realities. First, they question its underlying assumption about the causes of war. Functionalism argues that poverty and other socioeconomic woes create frustration, anger, and ultimately war. Critics counter that war may instead cause poverty and other miseries. Addressing issues of poverty may not alleviate war, they also argue, especially if the rapid acquisition of wealth enables dissatisfied states to build armies for war.

Second, functionalism assumes that political differences among countries will be dissolved through the habits of cooperation learned by experts organized transnationally to cope with technical problems such as transportation or telecommunication. The reality, say critics, is that technical cooperation is often more strongly influenced by politics than the other way around. The U.S. withdrawal in the 1980s from the International Labor Organization (ILO) and the UN Educational, Scientific, and Cultural Organization (UNESCO) because Washington felt that those IGOs were too politicized illustrate this charge.

As skeptics conclude, functionalists are naïve to argue that technical (functional) undertakings and political affairs can be separated. If technical cooperation becomes as important to state welfare as the functionalists argue, states will assume an active role in technical developments. Welfare and power cannot be separated, because the solution of economic and social problems cannot be divorced from political considerations. The expansion of transnational institutions' authority and competency at the expense of national governments and state sovereignty is, therefore, unlikely.

neofunctionalism a revised functionalist theory asserting that the IGOs states create to manage common problems provide benefits that exert pressures for further political integration.

These criticisms led to the emergence of a second wave of functionalist theorizing, known as **neofunctionalism**. It argues that growing economic interdependence among states requires closer political coordination, which ultimately will lead to greater political integration. In other words, political integration occurs not simply because of pressures to address common technical problems more efficiently; it comes about when the interests of different pressure groups, political parties, and government officials converge on creating a greater role for supranational institutions.

The Neofunctional Approach to Integration.   Europe provides the best example of how a group of independent nation-states can become an integrated political community along the lines suggested by neofunctional thinking. Today, the European Union (EU) is the world's biggest free-trade area, bringing together under a single administrative umbrella some 500 million people in twenty-seven countries (recall Chapter 6).

In order to speak with one voice and act in unison on security issues, the EU adopted a Common Foreign and Security Policy (CFSP), which defined as the EU's objectives safeguarding "the common values, fundamental interests, and independence of the Union," strengthening the EU's security, preserving "world peace and international security [as well as promoting] international cooperation to develop and consolidate democracy and the rule of law, and respect for human rights and fundamental freedoms." To fulfill these goals, at the 2001 Nice Summit, the EU established the European Rapid Reaction Force, seen by its founders as a preliminary step toward becoming a military presence on the world stage capable of unilateral action. According to the officials assembled at Nice, this 60,000-strong military force would enable the EU to reduce its dependence on the United States and NATO.

The political unification of Europe represents an enormous achievement, overturning a past of chronic suspicion and warfare. Constructing a new European identity reinforced by collateral institutions has served as a model for integration in other regions, including Africa, Asia, the Caribbean, and South America. However, current evidence suggests that the factors promoting successful integration efforts are many and their mixture complex. It is not enough that two or more countries choose to interact cooperatively. Research indicates that chances of political integration wane without geographical proximity, similar political systems, supportive public opinion led by enthusiastic leaders, internal political stability, similar experiences in historical and internal social development, compatible economic systems with supportive business interests, a shared perception of a common external threat, and previous collaborative efforts. While not all of these conditions must be present for integration to occur, the absence of more than a few considerably reduces the chances of success. The integration of two or more societies—let alone entire world regions—is, in short, not easily accomplished. Europe's experience indicates that even when conditions are favorable there is no guarantee that integration will proceed automatically.

The substantial difficulty that most regions have experienced in achieving a level of institution building similar to that of the EU suggests the enormity of the obstacles to creating new political communities out of previously divided ones. Even parts of Europe have splintered rather than integrated. In 1991, for example, the Soviet Union shattered into fifteen countries. Since then, six additional states have been created from the former Yugoslavia. Disintegration of many of the world's states could continue. With fewer than twenty-five countries ethnically homogeneous and with 3,000–5,000 indigenous peoples interested in securing sovereign homelands, the prospects are high that the number of independent states will increase in the years ahead.

The division of the globe into more and more smaller states could be slowed if existing states accepted **devolution** (the granting of greater political power to quasi-autonomous regions), as some central governments have done for the purpose of containing separatist revolts. However, in many states where governmental

devolution granting political power to ethno-political groups within a state under the expectation that greater autonomy for them in particular regions will curtail their quest for independence.

institutions are fragile, the leadership has repressed the minority peoples seeking to share power. About a third of the world's countries contain restless, politically repressed minorities struggling at various levels for human rights and independence (see Allen and Leppman 2004, 37; Gurr, 2001). Within such countries, uneven growth rates and vast income inequalities between different groups could easily destabilize the political landscape.

In conclusion, contemporary global affairs are being shaped by centripetal and centrifugal pressures. At the same time that unifying forces are pulling some of the planet's inhabitants together, fragmenting forces are pushing others apart. The paradox of twenty-first-century world politics is that political integration and disintegration are occurring simultaneously. Given this turbulence, many theorists continue to raise concerns about the capacity of independent sovereign states to solve the many shared problems humanity faces. For them, the major issues on the global agenda are ones that cannot be meaningfully managed unilaterally. In the next four chapters, we shall examine these global welfare issues, which transcend political boundaries and resist national solutions.

CHAPTER SUMMARY

- The field of international law is composed of private and public international law. The former pertains to the regulation of transnational activities among individuals and other nongovernmental actors; the latter, to the relations among sovereign states.

- Nearly every legal tenet of public international law supports the principle that sovereign states are the primary actors in world politics. The major rights of states include self-defense, independence and legal equality. The major duties are nonintervention and upholding the commitments that they voluntarily make.

- Although public international law lacks a central authority for punishing violators, states value international law because it performs an important communication function. By communicating the "rules of the game" in world politics, international law helps shape expectations, reduce uncertainty, and enhance predictability.

- For centuries, philosophers, religious leaders, and legal scholars have debated over when it is morally justifiable to go to war and how wars should be conducted. Just war doctrine emphasizes the need for the cause to be just; for the fighting to be undertaken for the right intention, exhausting all other means of resolving the conflict before issuing a public declaration of war; and for using force in a way that discriminates between legitimate and illegitimate targets, causes no more destruction than necessary, and is not undertaken in a futile effort.

- Collective security is often viewed as an alternative to the balance of power as a method for preserving peace. It calls for all states to join a universal organization, pledge to punish aggressors, and resolve their disagreements through pacific means.

- While the architects of the United Nations voiced support for the ideal of collective security, conflict in the Security Council between the United States and the Soviet Union during the Cold War prevented the UN from attaining many of the ideals envisioned by its founders. As a result, the UN has employed a variety of other means to help promote peace, including preventive diplomacy, peacemaking, and peace-building.

- Because many people see the anarchic structure of the state system as one of the most important causes of war, various theorists have proposed that the political integration of previously sovereign states might dampen the prospects for war. Whereas some have advocated world federalism as a solution to war, most place greater emphasis on regional integration, though they disagree on how to incorporate independent nation-states into a greater political whole. The European Union is the foremost example of regional integration.

KEY TERMS

collective defense

collective security

devolution

diplomatic recognition

functionalism

just war doctrine

military necessity

neofunctionalism

nonintervention

peace-building

peacemaking

political integration

preventive diplomacy

private international law

public international law

reprisal

spill over

war crimes

world federalism

SUGGESTED READINGS

Guzman, Andrew T. *How International Law Works: A Rational Choice Theory*. New York: Oxford University Press, 2008.

Joyner, Christopher C. *International Law in the 21ˢᵗ Century: Rules for Global Governance*. Lanham, MD: Rowman & Littlefield, 2005.

Kegley, Charles W., Jr., and Gregory A. Raymond. *Exorcising the Ghost of Westphalia: Building World Order in the New Millennium*. Upper Saddle River, NJ: Prentice-Hall, 2002.

Puchala, Donald, Katie Verlin Laatikainen, and Roger A. Coate. *United Nations Politics: International Organization in a Divided World*. Upper Saddle River, NJ: Prentice-Hall, 2006.

Rochester, J. Martin. *Between Peril and Promise: The Politics of International Law*. Washington, DC: CQ Press, 2006.

CRITICAL THINKING QUESTIONS

Journalists, scholars, and policy makers frequently use the concepts international "system," "society," and "community" when discussing world politics, sometimes without realizing how each concept frames their discussions in a different way. An international system refers to a set of regularly interacting political actors that are sufficiently interdependent to make the behavior of each influential on the others. When these actors are conscious of common interests and share certain fundamental values, they can be considered members of an international society (Bull 1977). As pointed out by the so-called "English School" of international relations (see Watson 1992; Bull and Watson 1984), the identity of these members is reinforced by criteria of inclusion/exclusion that enumerate what constitutes appropriate behavior for insiders and how it differs from the behavior of outsiders. Finally, if those actors also possess collective feelings of loyalty and solidarity that transcend self-regarding, instrumental interests, they can be thought of as belonging to an international community. As articulated by the ancient Athenian sage Solon, in a community "any wrongs that are done to individuals are resented and redressed by the other members of the community as promptly and as vigorously as if they themselves were personal sufferers."

A number of puzzling questions arise once distinctions are drawn among these concepts. Under what circumstances might states within the international system develop into an international society? What engenders the emergence of an international community? How would norms of behavior and diplomatic practices differ among states belonging to an international system versus an international society or international community? Does an international community exist today? If so, who are its members and what are their moral responsibilities to each other and to outsiders? What are the implications for world politics if an international community cannot be said to exist?

PART IV

The Politics of Global Welfare

What factors most affect the welfare of humanity? World politics may be played out on a large stage, but with the expansion of international communication and commerce, a new era of globalization has arisen, knitting the world into a tight web of interdependence. Money, goods, and people travel across national borders at an accelerating pace. To an increasing extent, what happens in one part of the globe influences what happens elsewhere.

The chapters that follow draw attention to "human security"—the welfare of peoples of the world—and the ways that state-to-state relations have combined with the activities of nonstate actors to transform humanity's living standards and future prospects. Part IV of *The Global Future* begins by looking at the ways globalization is transforming everyday life (Chapter 11), and then analyzes how changes in international trade and monetary affairs affect world politics (Chapter 12). After exploring the international political economy, the topics of human rights (Chapter 13) and the relationship between population demographics and the earth's ecological system (Chapter 14) are examined.

11

The Globalization of World Politics

CHAPTER OUTLINE

What Is Globalization?

The Global Information Age

Globalization or Americanization?

The Economics of Globalization

The Globalization of Trade

The Globalization of Finance

APPLICATION: Markets and Economic Interdependence

The Challenges of a Borderless World

Global Ecopolitics

Global Health

Global Migration

Global Governance or Backlash?

CONTROVERSY: Does Globalization Mean the End of the Age of Nation-States?

> The twenty-first century has revealed a world more intertwined than at any time in human history.
> BARACK OBAMA
> PRESIDENT OF THE UNITED STATES

In the early summer of 2004, Zilog Incorporated closed its manufacturing facilities in southwestern Idaho after a quarter century of operations. Headquartered in San Jose, California, Zilog concentrates on the micro-logic device segment of the semiconductor market, designing and producing devices used in embedded control. Although the firm had design centers in several locations, the Idaho facilities were the firm's only manufacturing plants. With their closure, 150 workers became unemployed. According to company executives, the intention was to convert Zilog into a "fabless" semiconductor company; that is to say, Zilog would continue to design microcontrollers, but would contract with firms in Asia to fabricate them (*Idaho Statesman*, June 20, 2004, B2).

Zilog's actions were mirrored over the next few years by several other companies in southwestern Idaho. In the fall of 2007, Micron Technology Inc., which makes dynamic random access memory (DRAM) for computers and flash memory for small digital devices, laid off more than 1,100 workers from various facilities in the Boise Valley. According to its chief executive officer, the company was moving some of its production to China in an effort to lower operating expenses (*Idaho Statesman*, October 20, 2007, B1). A year later, SuperValu, a Minneapolis-based leader in the grocery retailing industry, announced that eighty employees in its Boise finance office would be laid off because the firm's asset management operations were being moved to India (*Idaho Statesman*, June 11, 2008, B1).

The decisions made by Zilog, Micron, and SuperValu are examples of offshore outsourcing—subcontracting a business function to a foreign supplier (Drezner 2004). More than 3.3 million U.S. jobs are projected to be lost to outsourcing by 2015, and 14 million (11 percent of the U.S. total) have been identified as at risk of being sent overseas (*Time*, March 1, 2004, 33). In addition to affecting manufacturing, offshore outsourcing also has an impact on jobs in the fields of information technology, document management, and customer service. The educational field has recently been affected as well. India, for example, now has a $10 million e-tutoring industry, where companies such as Educomp Solutions (New Delhi), TutorVista (Bangalore), and Growing Stars (Cochin) provide inexpensive online assistance to American college and high school students, primarily in mathematics and science. With a vast pool of English-speaking chemists and engineers, and costs estimated by investment bank Goldman Sachs to be one-eighth of western levels (*Economist*, February 4, 2006, 58), India is also poised to play a larger role in offshore research and development, a market that is expected to grow to $12 billion.

Nor is India alone in benefiting from jobs that have moved offshore from high-wage countries. CompuPacific International in Xian, China processes medical claims, loan applications, and similar documents for American firms. Seagate Technology, which operates a research laboratory in Pittsburgh, uses scientists in Singapore to conduct some of its studies (*New York Times*, April 20, 2008, 5). Furthermore, in what has been called "nearshoring," Estonia, Bulgaria, and other post-communist states, where wages may be half of those paid elsewhere in Europe, provide data processing services and call-centers for companies in neighboring countries.

Although American consumers may enjoy lower prices and investors may see increases in the value of the stock they hold in companies that outsource business functions to foreign suppliers, some people worry that globalization is causing a "race to the bottom" as corporations move more and more operations to countries with lower wages, less benefits, and fewer government regulations. Fearing a growth in unemployment (even in high-tech industries once thought immune to competition from low-cost foreign labor), critics of outsourcing vehemently condemn corporate executives for "exporting" American jobs.

Yet at the same time that American jobs are moving abroad, new jobs are arriving as foreign firms outsource some of their jobs to the United States. According to the Bureau of Labor Statistics, the number of these jobs increased from 2.5 million in 1983 to 6.5 million in 2000. As the worldwide demand for services increases, the wages of service workers in some Global East countries are expected to rise, thereby making offshoring less cost competitive for companies in the United States and making foreign firms more likely to consider shifting some jobs to America. In 2007, for example, Wipro, an Indian firm, was negotiating agreements with several U.S. cities to establish software-development centers.

globalization   a set of processes that are widening, deepening, and accelerating the interconnectedness among societies.

What in the world is going on? The answer: **globalization**. Money, goods, people, and information are moving across national borders at an accelerating pace, linking societies in ways that are transforming world politics. This interconnectedness creates both possibilities and problems. On the one hand, globalization is generating unprecedented levels of wealth as many firms streamline their operations and discover new overseas markets for their products. On the other hand, it is producing enormous social strain as displaced workers often cannot replace their lost incomes, even when they retrain in a different industry or move to another location. It is understandable, therefore, that the effects of globalization are controversial.

"We were born into a world that will soon cease to exist," predicts German journalist Gabor Steingart (2008, 4). Due to globalization, the old world of our childhood "is disappearing into the fog of history, while the new one is only beginning to take shape." In this chapter we will examine the diverse forces driving the process of globalization. In particular, we will look at the growth of worldwide telecommunication, the increased mobility of capital, labor, goods, and services, and the burgeoning number of new problems that cross national borders. As we consider these issues, it is important to think about the prospects for the continuation of states as sovereign and independent actors. But before inspecting globalization's consequences, we must first examine its causes.

Richard Vogel/AP Photo

Offshoring Jobs One of the foremost complaints about globalization is that it has led to a shift in labor-intensive jobs from Global North countries to lower-wage countries in the Global East and South. Shown here is one example: workers in Vietnam making sport clothing for sale in European and U.S. markets.

WHAT IS GLOBALIZATION?

Until the fifteenth century, most civilizations remained relatively isolated from one another. Circumscribed by slow, costly, and often dangerous transportation routes, international intercourse tended to occur within self-contained regions of the world. Except for intermittent trade, occasional waves of migrants, and periodic clashes with invaders, contact with distant peoples was rare.

What distinguishes contemporary world politics from earlier eras is its global scope. Various processes are the widening, deepening, and accelerating worldwide interconnectedness. Rapid, unrestrained communication is perhaps the most significant of these processes. Indeed, many see it as the foundation of an emerging **global village**—a metaphor used by futurologists to portray a world in which borders vanish and people become a single community.

global village a popular image used to describe the growth of awareness that all people share a common fate, stemming from a view that the world is an integrated and interdependent whole.

The Global Information Age

The decline in the importance of geographic distance as a determinant of the cost of communication has been described as perhaps the single most important economic force shaping societies in the first half of the twenty-first century. It is not only affecting where people live and work, but, as constructivists point out, it has the potential to change the images people have of their own identity and the meaning they attribute to "community."

The wireless technology of cellular phones is spreading across the planet, enabling even isolated individuals, who have never before made a phone call, to communicate instantly with others. Text messaging, for example, has empowered political movements, allowing people to organize resistance to policies they oppose and bolster those they support. The rallies that led to the ouster of Philippine President Joseph Estrada in 2001 exemplify what some analysts have called "cellular people power."

Computers are another potent agent of global communication, with ever more people going online to get news, be entertained, or conduct business. In particular, the growth of Internet blogs has created an elaborate transnational network with agenda-setting power on issues ranging from human rights in China to the U.S. war in Iraq. Furthermore, with the rapid diffusion of iPods and the enormous popularity of podcasting, a growing number of people are creating their own website channels and sharing audio and visual information with anyone throughout the world who signs on. Anyone with access to this technology can bypass traditional news organizations and give their personal perspective on current events to a global audience. Muslim outrage in 2006 over Danish political cartoons that belittled the prophet Muhammad demonstrated how rapidly people throughout the world can be mobilized by these new forms of global communication.

Although the entire world is becoming connected, it is happening at different rates: Only one in five Internet users lives in the Global South. Moreover, the Internet has not liberated most people from their technological dependence on the places in the Global North where the management of most websites is located. Therefore, even if the Internet has made for the worldwide hypermobility of ideas and information, it has contributed to the "soft power" resources of Global North countries. This is especially evident with respect to global e-commerce. Roughly three-quarters of all e-commerce currently takes place in the United States, the home of 90 percent of commercial websites. Given central position of the United States in cyberspace, a question raised by the rest of the world is whether America's technological and information edge will enable it to dominate the global future.

Although some people see the communications revolution as a leveling factor that empowers nongovernmental organizations (NGOs) to organize previously unheard voices into a new lobbying force, critics warn that it is widening the gap between rich and poor. As shown in Figure 11.1, use of the Internet is heavily concentrated in the Global North. Thus its effects remain uneven, benefiting some countries while putting the rest at a great disadvantage. The result is a vast **digital divide**, where one-third of the world's inhabitants lack access to modern information and communications technology.

Nevertheless, the communications revolution holds great promise for the Global South, since modern information technology may allow poorer countries to "leap frog" technologies in which the Global North invested heavily as it

digital divide the division between those states that have a high proportion of Internet users and hosts, and those that do not.

Visions of America, LLC/Alamy Limited

The World at One's Fingertips The revolution in telecommunications has contributed to "the death of distance," as virtually instantaneous communications are possible nearly everywhere. Here, in a remote and desolate region of northern Kenya, a Samburu warrior makes a call on his cellular telephone.

developed economically. Inexpensive wireless phones, for example, enjoy both popularity and promise in many Global South countries, where the cost of stringing line from pole to pole for traditional wired phones is often prohibitive. As programming makes each generation of new software easier to use, the digital divide may gradually close. But because the social, economic, and geographic factors that created the digital divide are complex, narrowing it will prove difficult. Many cutting-edge technologies require infrastructures based on older technologies, which are not widespread throughout the Global South. In countries without reliable electrical grids, for example, computer technology tends not to achieve mass-market scale. Three-quarters of low-income countries have less than 15 personal computers per 1,000 people, compared to 862 in Switzerland and 761 in Sweden (*Economist*, February 9, 2008, 75). Thus the Global North remains at present the primary beneficiary of the communications revolution.

Globalization or Americanization?

Ours is often described as the information age, but a remarkably large portion of the information we receive is controlled by a few huge corporations: AOL Time

Communications in the Globalized World

FIGURE 11.1 **The Digital Divide**

This figure, which shows the density of international communications flows throughout the world, reveals the striking division between the technological "haves" in the Global North and the technological "have-nots" in the Global South. Despite the recent growth in Internet usage in parts of the Global South, some regions still lag far behind others. For example, in 2007 only 4 percent of Africans had access to the Internet, and they paid the highest amount in the world for the slowest connection speeds.

SOURCE: Communication flows worldwide, Flanagan, Frost, and Kugler, (2001, 24).

Warner, Disney, General Electric, News Corporation, and Viacom in the United States, and, Viendi (France), Sony (Japan), and Berstelsmann (Germany) in other Global North countries. Some people worry that as the world's media sources are merged into ever larger units, fewer and fewer corporate executives will control what people hear and see about the world around them. Although thousands of potential sources of information about politics, society, and culture are available, the influence of such media midgets is negligible compared to that of the giants.

The type of power the media wields over international affairs is, in fact, a specific and limited type of power. Scholarship shows that the media influence what people *think about* more than what they *think*. In this way, the media primarily functions to set the agenda of public discussion about current affairs instead of determining public opinion. In the process of **agenda setting** the media shapes international public policy. For example, many national leaders have grumbled about a "CNN-effect," the alleged capacity of round-the-clock news services to highlight certain issues by immediately televising heart-wrenching

agenda setting the ability to influence which issues receive attention from governments and international organizations by giving them publicity.

Richard Vogel/AP Photo

The Making of a Global Culture? Some people regard globalization as little more than the spread of American values and beliefs. Shown here is one example that fuels these images—a Santa Claus attempting to attract customers in downtown Hanoi, Vietnam, a predominantly Buddhist country still subscribing to communist principles.

scenes of famine, atrocities, and other human tragedies to millions of viewers throughout the world. When combined with the use of electronic mail by grassroots activists to mobilize people around the world quickly on a particular issue, governments may find that these issues cannot be ignored.

Control of television and other media sources by the United States and a small number of other Global North countries became the focus of a hot dispute with the Global South during the 1980s. Dissatisfied with the media coverage it received from western news agencies, leaders in developing countries demanded a New World Information and Communication Order (NWICO). The flow of images and information from North to South, they insisted, fostered Northern values of consumerism and conspicuous consumption that perpetuated the South's dependence on the North. As the North-South conflict brewed, the United States angrily withdrew from the United Nations Educational, Scientific, and Cultural Organization (UNESCO), in part as a rejection of its role in promoting the new communications order. (However, in September 2002, in an effort to galvanize multilateral support for a preventive war against Iraq, the United States announced that it would rejoin UNESCO.)

The NWICO has since receded on the global agenda, but the issue of "cultural imperialism" remains alive as numerous people continue to express concern about the concentration of so much media power in so few hands. The ability to shape the preferences of others is easier in an Information Age. Those who control information, as well as those who control access to information, have clear-cut advantages in international bargaining over those whose major source of influence is confined to threatening sanctions. The popularity of the Al Jazeera network in the Middle East illustrates the interest in the Global South for alternatives to the western media, which is often seen as giving a biased, inaccurate portrayal of Southern concerns.

Contrary to the claim that globalization imposes an American uniformity on the world is that argument that cultural influence runs in more than one direction. Not only do various ideas and practices flow from the Global South to the North, but many of the products from the Global North are modified to suit indigenous tastes and needs. Approximately 25 percent of Costco's warehouses operate outside of the United States, where the product mix is tailored to fit foreign markets. Similarly, after committing cultural gaffs in Paris and Hong Kong, Disney theme parks adapted to local conditions. Native cultures, writes William Marling (2006), even put their imprint on McDonald's, arguably one of the most visible symbols of Americanization around the world. Its recipe for chicken, for instance, is far spicier in Indonesia than in the United States. McDonald's franchises outside the United States also sell items that are not on the typical American fast food menu, including beer in Germany, wine in France, salsa in Mexico, and soy flavors in Japan. Local cultures, Marling suggests, are more resilient than most people imagine. Despite worries about the homogenization of the planet, adds British analyst Philippe Legrain (2003), globalization has triggered "an explosion of cultural exchange" and a "rich feast of cultural mixing."

THE ECONOMICS OF GLOBALIZATION

When the nation-state emerged in seventeenth-century Europe as the primary actor on the world stage, many national leaders sought to increase their power by acquiring territory. Aside from land that held precious metals or offered access to navigable waterways, the most valuable territory in an age without refrigeration contained cereal grains, an easily transported and stored source of food with sufficient nutrition to sustain farmers as well as people not engaged in agriculture.

With the onset of the Industrial Revolution, physical capital (machinery, equipment, buildings, etc.) increased in value as a factor of production, although the demand for coal, iron ore, and later oil continued to underscore the importance of land. Only after World War II did some states shift their emphasis from territorial expansion through military conquest to international commerce. These "trading states" recognized that exporting manufactured goods could fuel economic growth (Rosecrance 1986). Soon they realized that exporting was only one path to prosperity; products could be designed at home but made abroad for both foreign and domestic markets. Rather than goods and services being produced by and for people living within a single territorial state, they are now increasingly produced by people working in different regions of the world for a global marketplace. We are entering an era where traditional territorial distinctions will be less important than the financial and managerial skills to create products, provide services, and control assets globally (Rosecrance 1999).

The Globalization of Trade

After World War II, the victors in that long, debilitating struggle believed that they could stimulate economic growth by removing barriers to international trade. As we have seen in Chapter 6, under the auspices of the General Agreement on Tariffs and Trade (GATT), the so-called "Geneva Round" of negotiations in 1947 reduced **tariffs** by 35 percent. Successive rounds of negotiations in the 1950s, 1960s (the Kennedy Round), 1970s (Tokyo Round), and the 1980s and 1990s (Uruguay Round) virtually eliminated tariffs on manufactured goods. The World Trade Organization (WTO), which succeeded GATT in 1994 and enlarged its membership (see Map 11.1), is currently engaged in reducing **nontariff barriers** to international trade.

tariffs taxes imposed by governments on imported goods.

nontariff barrier governmental restrictions not involving a tax or duty that increase the cost of importing goods into a country.

The reduction of tariff rates has permitted international trade and world economic output to grow hand in hand. Since the founding of GATT, the world economy has grown six-fold, in part because trade has expanded twenty-fold (Samuelson

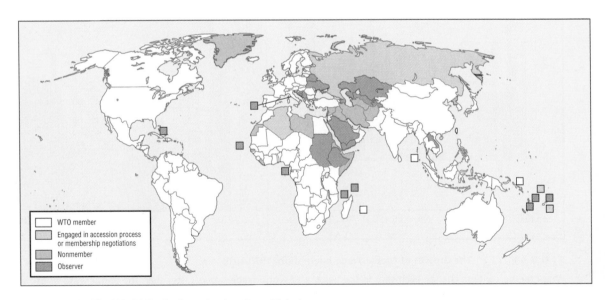

M A P 11.1 The World Trade Organization Goes Global

At the start of 2008, 151 countries, or 70 percent of the world's states, were members of the World Trade Organization. In addition, thirty "observers" are in the process of negotiating to become formal members. If and when these states join, the volume of international trade is expected to climb, contributing further to the integration of the world marketplace.

SOURCE: World Trade Organization.

2006). The impact of the rising volume of goods shipped from one country to another has been enormous, making trade increasingly important to all states.

trade integration
economic globalization measured by the extent to which world trade volume grows faster than the world's combined gross domestic product.

Trade integration is the measure of the extent to which the growth rate in world trade increases faster than does the growth rate of world gross domestic product. As trade integration grows, so does globalization, because states' interdependence grows when countries' exports account for an increasing percentage of their gross domestic product (GDP). As Michael Mazarr (1999) explains, "Measuring global trade as a percentage of GDP is perhaps the simplest and most straightforward measure of globalization. If trade in goods and merchandise is growing faster than the world economy as a whole, then it is becoming more integrated."

Figure 11.2 documents the remarkable speed at which trade integration has progressed since 1970. Countries have become more interdependent, and the

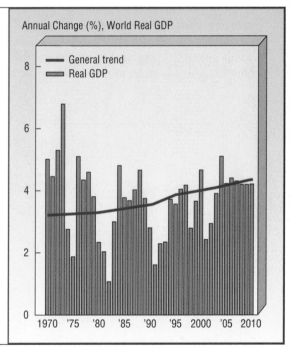

F I G U R E   11.2 **The Growth of Global Trade Integration, 1970-2010**

When the percentage change each year in the volume of world trade grows faster than the annual rate of growth of the combined world economy, "trade integration" increases. The growth of world trade has far outpaced the growth of real world gross product (WGP), and the trend toward trade interdependence has been accelerating since 1970. Compare the two trends. On the left we observe that the annual percentage change of world trade has been growing on average almost 7 percent each year. On the right we see that the annual percentage change in world economic output has grown in close association with the growth in world trade, but at about half the same average rate. Trade integration has globalized economic interdependence by making countries increasingly dependent on the expansion of trade with others for economic growth.

SOURCE: International Monetary Fund, trend lines from 2008 to 2010 are IMF projections.

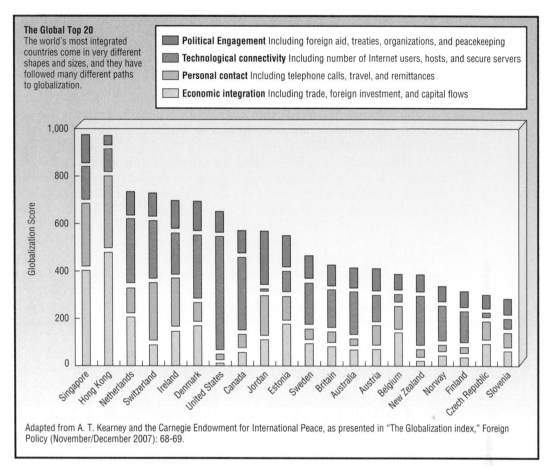

The Global Top 20
The world's most integrated countries come in very different shapes and sizes, and they have followed many different paths to globalization.

- **Political Engagement** Including foreign aid, treaties, organizations, and peacekeeping
- **Technological connectivity** Including number of Internet users, hosts, and secure servers
- **Personal contact** Including telephone calls, travel, and remittances
- **Economic integration** Including trade, foreign investment, and capital flows

Adapted from A. T. Kearney and the Carnegie Endowment for International Peace, as presented in "The Globalization index," Foreign Policy (November/December 2007): 68–69.

F I G U R E 11.3 Levels of Globalization

There are various ways to measure the extent to which countries are integrated in the globalization of the world. This chart scales and ranks the twenty most globalized countries, based on an index that combines the following four factors: political engagement (number of memberships in international organizations, foreign embassies hosted, and UN Security Council missions in which the country participates); technology (number of Internet users, Internet hosts, and secure servers); personal contact (international travel and tourism, international telephone traffic, and cross-border transfers); and economic integration (trade, foreign investment and portfolio capital flows, and income payments and receipts).

world increasingly globalized, because international trade has far outpaced growth in the world economy (and in world population as well). Of course, countries differ in the degree to which their economies have become integrated through trade in the global political economy (see Figure 11.3). The pace of trade integration has been higher in the Global South than in the Global North, reflecting the less-developed Global South's rising contribution to world trade and its mounting importance to economic prosperity in the Global North. Not only has the Global South's share of global trade grown (from 23 percent in 1985 to 28 percent in 2005), but its share of global exports in manufactured products has also grown (increasing from 10 percent in 1980 to 27 percent in 2005). In this context the Global South's growth in the share of *new* products for exports is especially impressive, although it is important to bear in mind that South Korea, Singapore, Taiwan, Malaysia, Thailand, and India account for almost two-thirds of this new export trade (WDI 2007, 314; WDR 2006, 261–263; HDI 2005, 277).

A similar pattern may be emerging with regard to trade in services. Because the United States enjoys comparative advantages in this area, it has been a strong advocate of bringing services under the liberalizing rules of the WTO. Trade in services has already expanded more than threefold since 1980, with the Global North reaping most of the benefits. However, the spread of information technology, the ease with which new business software can be used, and the comparatively lower wage costs in developing economies are among the reasons why the World Bank predicts that developing countries will capture a greater share of world trade in services during the first two decades of the twenty-first century. Global South countries such as India, with significant numbers of educated, English-speaking citizens, are already operating call centers and consumer assistance hotlines for companies based in the Global North.

Selling products to another country often requires companies to establish a presence abroad, where they can produce goods and offer services. Traditionally the overseas operations of multinational corporations (MNCs) were "appendages" of a centralized hub. The pattern nowadays is to dismantle the hub by dispersing production facilities worldwide, which was made economically feasible by the revolutions in communication and transportation (including use of the standardized international shipping container). The sales of most large companies are now geared to the global market and a large proportion of their revenues are generated from sales outside the countries where they are headquartered. This globalization of production is transforming the international political economy. It once made sense to count trade in terms of flows between countries, and that practice continues because national account statistics are still gathered with states as the unit of analysis. But that picture increasingly fails to portray current realities. Countries do not really trade with each other, corporations do. The world's 68,549 multinational corporations and their 582,579 foreign affiliates sell an estimated $10 trillion in goods and services across borders every year (Oatley 2008, 173). Together they are now responsible for about one-fourth of the world's production and two-thirds of the world's exports.

MNCs have discovered that to export to another country it is helpful to locate there. Placing production and management in an MNC's regional foreign affiliate avoids tariffs and taxes. Today roughly 40 percent of what we call foreign trade actually involves transactions between MNCs' cross-border affiliates; that is, between a firm and its overseas subsidiaries (Oatley 2008, 170).

By forming **strategic corporate alliances** with companies in the same industry, and by merging with one another, many MNCs now rival nation-states in financial resources. These corporate networks pursue truly global strategies for financial gain, often through long-term supplier agreements and licensing and franchising contracts. As they funnel large financial flows across national borders, these global corporate conglomerates are integrating national economies into a worldwide market. Since 1970, flows of foreign direct investment have increased almost one hundred-fold, with Global East and South countries increasingly becoming recipients.

Among some of the most ardent advocates of globalization, the progressive integration of national economies into a single world marketplace is seen as a panacea for poverty. Such a view is inaccurate, however. Despite evidence that widening and deepening of international trade flows have been associated with economic growth, the distribution of these gains has not been uniform. Globalizing forces have reduced poverty in Global East and South countries that have been able to take advantage of their low labor costs to attract jobs fabricating standardized goods and assembling finished goods from components. But critics of globalization claim that more benefits have accrued to Global North producers of innovative, human-capital-intensive products. Consider the Apple iPod. The 30-gigabyte video model was manufactured in China by Inventec and sold in 2005 for $224 wholesale. According to one study, Apple claimed about $80 in gross profit. The Chinese, who tested and assembled the iPod's 424 parts, accounted for only $3.70 because the research, development, and design, as well as the components, originated elsewhere (*Economist*, November 10, 2007, 8). As the *Human Development Report* of the UN Development Program once put it: "A rising tide of wealth is supposed to lift all boats. But some are more seaworthy than others. The yachts and ocean liners are indeed rising in response to new opportunities, but the rafts and rowboats are taking on water—and some are sinking fast." Trade globalization, in other words, is creating winners and losers, both between and within countries. As a result, a backlash against these inequalities is developing among those groups that see themselves as victims of an integrated trade world (Broad 2002; Aaronson 2002).

strategic corporate alliances cooperation between MNCs and foreign companies in the same industry, driven by the movement of MNC manufacturing overseas.

The Globalization of Finance

Finance represents another important aspect of economic globalization. It encompasses "all types of cross-border portfolio-type transactions—borrowing and lending, trading of currencies or other monetary claims, and the provision of commercial banking or other financial services. It also includes capital flows associated with foreign direct investment—transactions involving significant control of producing enterprises" (B. Cohen 1996). Evidence of financial globalization abounds. Since World War II, the volume of cross-border capital flows has increased dramatically, and now greatly exceeds the volume of trade. Similarly, cross-border transactions in bonds and equities have increased at an astonishing rate over the past twenty years. In the mid-1990s, another indicator of the expansion of the global capital market is captured by the fact that it has increased at twice the rate of global GDP, fueled in part by the explosion of hedge-fund trading worldwide that reached $69.8 trillion in 2007 (*Economist*, May 26, 2007, 75).

Further evidence of financial globalization can be seen in recent increases in the daily turnover on the foreign exchange market. On many days, private currency traders may exchange as much as $2 trillion to make profits through **arbitrage** on the basis of minute shifts in the value of states' currencies. Such interconnected markets require more than ever a reliable system of money to conduct business across borders while coping with an array of fluctuating national currencies. The daily turnover on currency markets often is greater now than the global stock of official foreign exchange reserves, and has practically eliminated the capacity of government central banks to influence exchange rates by buying and selling currency in those markets. Globalization has cost states a huge measure of the control that they formerly could exercise over the value of their currencies internationally. The powerlessness of the U.S. government to raise the price of the Chinese yuan against the dollar between 2005 and 2008 (to reduce the enormous U.S. balance-of-trade deficit), speaks volumes to the breakdown of governments' ability to modify the rates at which their currencies are exchanged.

As the market value of stock transactions increased five-fold between 1980 and 2008, the rise or fall in the security market of any one state began to immediately cause similar changes in other countries' stock indexes (see Application: Markets and Economic Interdependence). "Derivatives" are one tool for managing risk by combining speculation in "options" and "futures" to hedge against volatility in financial markets. They are complex financial contracts whose value is determined from the prices or rates of other securities, but they require no actual purchase of stocks or bonds. In the years leading up to the 2008 world financial crisis, derivatives accounted for trillions of dollars in cross-border transactions and were estimated to be the most globalized financial market. Automated online trading for equity sales on the Internet in the emerging digital world economy had lowered the costs and increased the volume of such cross-border exchanges.

The computerization of financial transactions and contracts occurred at the same time that state deregulation of global investments and capital movements gained acceptance. States reduced their authority by relaxing legal control over their economies and by opening their markets to foreign capital. The result was an upsurge in international financial transactions. According to the **capital mobility hypothesis**, the free or unregulated flow of money across borders has produced the globalization of finance. However, one result of the economic turmoil that rocked the world during the fall of 2008 has been a call for greater regulation of financial markets.

Because the accelerating mobility of capital means that financial markets are no longer centered within states, the globalized financial system is not subject to regulation by any one state in particular. Most states are losing the capacity to control the flow and level of finance in their national economies. The globalization of finance has expanded the power of private markets and corporations no

arbitrage the selling of one currency (or product) and purchase of another to make a profit on the changing exchange rates; traders ("arbitragers") help to keep states' currencies in balance through their speculative efforts to buy large quantities of devalued currencies and sell them in countries where they are valued more highly.

capital mobility hypothesis the contention that MNCs' movement of investment capital has led to the globalization of finance.

| APPLICATION | Markets and Economic Interdependence |

Anthony Lake served as the national security advisor in the Clinton administration from 1993 to 1996. Whereas early in his tenure policy makers at high-level meetings tended to think along traditional state-centric lines, by the time that he stepped down from his position he noticed that they had come to grips with how globalization was transforming world politics. In the following episode, which refers to an economic crisis in Brazil during 1998, he illustrates how the thinking in Washington had changed.

> During the crisis ... I ran into Treasury Secretary Robert Rubin. As we chatted about old times, I recalled how, at our morning senior staff meeting in the White House, we would sometimes ask him what the effect of one event or another might be on the stock market.
>
> As he smiled . . . at the recollection, an aide rushed up to his side. Secretary Rubin turned to him and, and with real concern asked, "How is the market doing?" As the aide replied and they discussed the implication of the news, I realized that he was asking not about the Dow Jones, but about the Brazilian stock market. This is the reality of life in the era of globalization. Secretary Rubin . . . understood that a strong Brazilian economy is in America's national security interest . . . [The] clear

corollary is that a weak Brazil could hurt our people at home. How? It could curb American exports, crimping prosperity and chipping at jobs. As Latin America's largest market, with more than half of its people, Brazil is the engine of regional growth. If its economy started to sink, it could pull down its neighbors as well. Not only would we lose our eleventh-largest export market . . . we would see demand dry up throughout a region that buys 20 percent of American exports. And that could put a lot of our people out of work. A Brazilian setback could also have devastating effects on U.S. private lenders. Both Citibank and BankBoston, for example, have loaned billions of dollars each to Brazil; American enterprises have invested billions more. It could rattle American businesses, some two thousand of which operate in Brazil. Globally, a major panic in Brazil could spark a new contagion . . . risking a global recession (Lake 2000, 213–214).

Increasingly, observes Lake, U.S. policy makers realized that globalization complicated their ability to manage America's foreign and domestic affairs. It did so, in his opinion, because national autonomy and state sovereignty gradually were being eroded.

---

longer tied to any one country thereby undermining states' regulatory power. As the globalization of finance has accelerated, the increasing mobility of capital has challenged the traditional realist assumption that states are autonomous, unitary actors capable of governing their economic affairs.

The lightning speed of capital mobility has made national markets extremely volatile and vulnerable to sudden reversals caused by their dependence on foreign capital, which may flee at the first sign of economic trouble. By 2008, capital mobility had reached historically high levels, having tripled since 1990 as a share of world GDP. But when foreign capital began fleeing from the emerging economies of ex-communist and Global South states as the global credit market seized up that fall, stock markets in these countries plunged and the value of their currencies dropped.

True, all countries are mutually vulnerable to rapid transfers of capital in an interdependent, globalized financial world. But the emerging economies are the most dependent and vulnerable. This circumstance suggests why bankers and economists have called for the creation of more reliable multilateral mechanisms for policy coordination to manage the massive cross-border flows of capital.

THE CHALLENGES OF A BORDERLESS WORLD

Thus far we have seen how technological advances in communication and transportation over the past few decades have fueled a series of far-reaching economic changes. The torrent of cross-border trade and financial flows that have swept across the world raises the question of whether it is still meaningful to think of the nation-state as a basis for organizing economic activities. As globalization has ruptured one national frontier after the next, questions have also been asked as to whether the nation-state is the most effective problem-solving unit for addressing other challenges that face humanity. Three of the most important involve the impact of globalization on the environment, public health, and migration. In each instance, problems in one part of the world have had consequences for people living elsewhere.

Global Ecopolitics

Ever since the rise of the nation-state, political leaders have claimed sovereign rights over their territorial domain, viewing the use of land, water, and airspace as domestic matters. Although some environmental issues are purely local and can be addressed unilaterally, many span national boundaries and require multilateral action. For example, sulfur oxide emissions from industries in one country may fall as acid rain on a neighboring country. Greenhouse gas emissions (carbon dioxide, chlorofluorocarbons, methane, and nitrous oxide) from numerous countries contribute to global climate warming, which could disrupt weather patterns across the planet and expose coastal lowlands everywhere to the threat of rising seas. The political world may be a checkerboard of sovereign states, but the natural world is a seamless web. Damage to the ecosystem often transcends national jurisdictions. Yet, as we shall see in Chapter 14, many states remain unwilling to relinquish or pool their sovereignty to forge new global institutions that could offer a more effective response to global environmental problems.

Global Health

Humankind and the threat of infectious disease have always coexisted uneasily. Population growth in the Global South has led many people to move into previously uninhabited regions, exposing them to new sources of disease. Moreover, their ability to travel from one continent to another makes it difficult to contain outbreaks to a single locale. Millions of airline travelers, for example, share cabin-sealed environments with passengers who might be infected with potentially fatal diseases. As the 2003 outbreak of Severe Acute Respiratory Syndrome (SARS) showed, a mobile world population has made the spread of disease across borders rapid, frequent, and hard to control. SARS was initially discovered in Hong Kong, China in early 2003 but was soon spread by air travelers to Toronto, Canada, where forty people subsequently died from the disease. As a result of fears causes by the SARS epidemic, the Women's World Cup in soccer was moved out of China, Air Canada lost some 400 million Canadian dollars in the second quarter of 2003, and Hong Kong's second quarter economic output dropped 3.7 percent (Kelleher and Klein 2006, 142).

The AIDS (acquired immune deficiency syndrome) epidemic has become a symbol for the spread of disease in a shrinking world. It is a global problem, with the number of people infected with HIV—the virus that causes AIDS—climbing to an estimated 70 million people by 2008. AIDS strikes most virulently in the impoverished Global South among youthful wage earners who are the foundation of the labor force, but it undermines economic growth everywhere on the planet. The human toll from AIDS-related disease has been most severe in sub-Saharan Africa, where the disease accounts for three-quarters of the world's HIV infections and is the leading cause of death, cutting life expectancy almost in half. The virus is not confined to any one region, however; it travels throughout the world alongside the more than 2 million people who cross international borders daily.

Adding to the challenge of preventing infectious diseases is another problem brought on by rising globalization: as a result of underuse of antibiotics in the developing world and overuse in the developed world, viruses are developing stronger strains that are able to overcome standard antibiotics. The World Health Organization reports that almost all infectious diseases are slowly becoming resistant to existing medicines. And humans are not the only victims, as was made evident in 2001 when the contagious hoof-and-mouth disease swept through Europe killing livestock. As national leaders desperately tried to seal their frontiers to a virus that spread with frightening speed, many noted that such epidemics in the European Union were increasingly difficult to contain because borders between countries had all but dissolved and it had been years since anybody needed a passport to travel between most European countries.

Another unfortunate byproduct of globalization has been the spread of alien animal, plant, and insect species throughout the globe that are causing massive ecological destruction. As the World Conservation Union (an NGO that includes more than seventy-eight states and over 10,000 scientists) warns, alien species that cross national borders aboard aircraft, ships, or other means of conveyance are doing irreparable damage to thousands of native species and, in the process, creating an enormous problem for the planet's environment and public health. In May 2001 the Union used World Biodiversity Day to heighten awareness of the threat posed by this invasion, which it labeled "among the costliest and least understood aspects of globalization," proclaiming "If this were an invasion from space, governments would be alarmed. But these are not extraterrestrials. They are ordinary animals, plants, and insects that have escaped from their normal environment to wreak havoc someplace else" (James 2001).

Global Migration

The movement of populations across frontiers has reached unprecedented proportions. Each year since 1998 on average more than 12 million people

Patrick Lin/Agence France-Presse/Getty Images

Globalization and the Fear of Pandemics In addition to diffusing commodities and capital throughout the world, globalization has increased the danger that infectious diseases will spread far and wide. Shown here are commuters in Taipei who are alarmed by warnings of an influenza pandemic.

qualified for and received refugee assistance. Porous borders, combined with the ease of modern travel, have made it possible for streams of people to leave their homelands for other countries. Emigration has become routine in the global age, raising a host of political, economic, and social issues. The meaning of citizenship, the composition of the labor force, and the protection of minority rights are just a few of the issues large flows of migrants raise for host countries. Particularly troubling is the moral inconsistency between liberal democracies that simultaneously defend the fundamental right of refugees to emigrate and the absolute right of sovereign states to control their borders.

Far more troubling are the 800,000 to 900,000 people each year that are estimated to be victims of forced migration, which includes the victims of "ethnic cleansing" as well as the trade in humans sold into servitude. The UN estimates that 80 percent of today's slaves are women, with roughly half under the age of eighteen. This criminal activity grosses between $12 and $17 billion annually, ranking as the third largest illicit global business after trafficking in drugs and the arms trade (Obduah 2006, 241).

National governments are losing their grip on regulating the movement of foreigners across their borders. From American efforts to barricade the southern border of the United States to European attempts to interdict migrants from Africa who are crossing the Mediterranean Sea on make-shift vessels, Global North countries have wrestled with the question of how to cope with people who cross porous borders furtively to flee discrimination and repression, or to find jobs that will allow them to support family members in their home countries. Every day, the combination of legal and illegal migrants living in the Global North send "remittances" (money they have earned while working abroad) back home to their families. By one account, these remittances totaled some $318 billion in 2007—more than double the amount of foreign aid given to the Global South (*Economist*, December 15, 2007, 106). Thus the worldwide movement of people across national boundaries, like many other aspects of globalization, cannot be understood in isolation from other factors; global migration is intimately linked to global economic as well as humanitarian issues.

These environmental, health, and migration problems are representative of the kinds of challenges presented by globalization. Whether nation-states will be able to cope with them remains uncertain. Globalization is eroding state sovereignty, but it is not necessarily creating a global community.

GLOBAL GOVERNANCE OR BACKLASH?

Globalization, driven in large measure by technological revolutions, is likely to continue. Analysts differ over its consequences, depending in part on the political perspectives that inform their worldviews. Some analysts focus on the economic benefits of globalization; others, on its unevenness and the prospects for marginalizing large numbers of people. Some focus on the challenge globalization poses to an international system founded on the sovereign territorial state; others hope cooperation among state and nonstate actors will usher in a new era of global governance (see Controversy: Does Globalization Mean the End of the Age of Nation-States?). We can expect the controversies about globalization's alleged virtues and vices, benefits and costs, to heighten as finance, population, trade, labor, and culture continue to converge globally. While the revolutions in communication and transportation have overcome many of the physical barriers separating the world's people, some have gained and others have lost ground. The global village is not proving to be an equally hospitable home for everyone, and the losers are mounting a backlash.

The key question raised by this chapter concerns the role of the nation-state in the global future. A world of permeable borders challenges all territorial states, rich and poor alike. Globalization reduces the capacity of states to exercise political power over the territory in which private-sector actors operate. Although some analysts believe this loss of control probably means that the nation-state as

CONTROVERSY   Does Globalization Mean the End of the Age of Nation-States?

Is globalization an unprecedented, inexorable process that is driving an epochal transformation in world politics? What does it mean for the survival of the nation-state? To some thinkers globalization spells the end of sovereignty as the world's organizing principle. According to this interpretation of the global future, states are being "overwhelmed by globalization, and have lost control of their economies" (Boli, Elliot, and Bier 2004). Other thinkers remain skeptical. Not only do they question whether globalization is unprecedented historically, they doubt that the term accurately describes the current pattern of international economic interactions. They see a resurrection of the idea of national power (Saul 2004).

According to the skeptics, globalization is a new word for an old process. Although the contemporary world economy differs in many ways from that of the late nineteenth and early twentieth centuries, the current level of trade integration is similar to that which existed on the eve of World War I. Aside from not being a novel phenomenon, skeptics add that globalization is less significant today than regionalization. The degree of trade integration within the world's geographic

regions exceeds the amount of integration between them, although the North American, European, and East Asian regional economies are becoming more interconnected. Contrary to the argument that economic globalization is diminishing the influence of nation-states, the most powerful states have become the "backbone" of world trade: Over three-fourths of total production is traded inside national borders; most corporations are national companies whose assets and ownership are within their own nation-states; and the state is consuming an ever-larger share of the global GDP (Malešević 2008, 98).

Globalists admit that a homogeneous McWorld (Barber 1995) doesn't exist, but they contend that the extraordinary advances in telecommunication and transportation technologies have unleashed globalizing forces that are eroding the power of nation-states. Do you agree? Will globalization undermine the Westphalian state system? Is state sovereignty destined to be replaced by some new organizing principles? If so, what principles would guide world politics in a post-Westphalian world order?

a sovereign actor on the world stage will become a thing of the past, most agree that it is not about to disappear. Although an erosion of sovereignty is underway, territorial states will still lay claim as the principal source of security and identity in most people's lives. Nevertheless, they will increasingly find themselves sharing the world stage with powerful nonstate actors. As discussed in Chapter 6, we are moving away from a world dominated by a single type of actor and toward one composed of many qualitatively different types of actors.

What does this mean for humanity's ability to address the environmental, health, and other challenges raised by globalization? International regimes such as those that evolved after World War II to promote global governance in trade and monetary affairs may also prove effective in coping with borderless crises. Everyone is now more closely connected than ever before, but the architecture for multilateral cooperation and coordination remains shaky. Because stubborn problems continue to seep through the world's porous borders, many scholars contend that it is time to think seriously about sharing sovereignty. "To agree to share one's sovereignty is difficult," cautions Peter Sutherland, former director-general of the World Trade Organization; consequently "a genuine enhanced institutional sharing, or pooling of sovereignties is today the structural issue which has yet to be settled."

Can states and nonstate actors find a focal point, a norm, around which multilateral cooperation could coalesce? Liberal theorists, who emphasize mutual gains, are optimistic. Realists, who are more concerned with relative gains, remain pessimistic. Constructivists aver that globalization will be what state and nonstate actors make of it. Regardless of who is correct, technological innovations will continue to facilitate the flow of trade and finance across national boundaries, creating mutual vulnerabilities and blurring the distinction between foreign and domestic economic policy. Globalization presents opportunities as well as risks, and some people are better positioned than others to take advantage of its potential benefits. Moreover, as the earlier example of job loss to overseas outsourcing illustrates, globalization can be a disruptive process.

This chapter began by asking whether globalization will create a global village—one free of conflict and intent only on improving everyone's welfare. Global *pillage* is an alternative description of what can happen. Instead of worldwide prosperity emanating from the free movement of commodities, services, and capital across national borders, will globalization exacerbate existing economic inequities? The next chapter investigates possible answers to this question.

CHAPTER SUMMARY

- Globalization is a set of processes that are fostering worldwide interconnectedness. Because it is uneven—benefitting some, disadvantaging others—globalization threatens to widen the gulf between the world's rich and poor states.

- Recent advances in telecommunication technology are a major driving force behind globalization. These technologies are changing our conceptions of time and space. With the emergence of a digitized global economy, the boundary between domestic and international transactions is becoming less distinct.

- Technology is reshaping patterns of production, trade, and finance. Markets no longer correspond with national boundaries. Rather than goods and services being produced by and for people living within a particular territorial state, they are now increasingly produced by people from several different states who are aiming at a world market. Similarly, a system of financial arrangements is emerging that is not centered on a single state. As a result, international economic flows are not subject to regulation by any single country.

- Globalization has shrunk geographic distances and linked people together in ways that create new challenges for solving environmental, health, and other problems that do not respect territorial boundaries. Owing to their transnational nature, many of these problems cannot be solved unilaterally. However, states are often hesitant to relinquish or pool their sovereignty in order to strengthen global institutions that can better address borderless crises.

■ Globalization is a process unlikely to be forestalled, but the consequences are not easily agreed upon. Regardless of whether globalization is desirable or despicable, state power will retain its relevance in shaping the global future. Nevertheless, the sovereign, territorial state will not be the only important player on the world stage. What the process of globalization has done in recent years is to disaggregate sovereignty, creating multiple layers of authority which are interlaced in ways that blur distinctions between foreign and domestic, and public and private, entities.

KEY TERMS

agenda setting

arbitrage

capital mobility
   hypothesis

digital divide

globalization

global village

nontariff barriers

strategic corporate
   alliances

tariffs

trade integration

SUGGESTED READINGS

Chanda, Nayan. *Bound Together: How Traders, Preachers, Adventurers and Warriors Shaped Globalization*. New Haven: Yale University Press, 2007.

Friedman, Thomas L. *The World Is Flat: A Brief History of the Twenty-first Century*. New York: Farrar, Straus, and Giroux, 2005.

Martin, Lisa, ed. *Global Governance*. Burlington, VT: Ashgate, 2008.

Sachs, Jeffrey. *Common Wealth: Economics for a Crowded Planet*. New York: Penguin, 2008.

Scholte, Jan Aart. *Globalization: A Critical Introduction*, 2nd ed. London: Palgrave, 2005.

CRITICAL THINKING QUESTIONS

As the pace of economic globalization has increased, the ethics of deepening market relations across borders has become a heated topic of debate. The philosopher Peter Singer (2004) sees great benefits to the retreat of the doctrine of state sovereignty with its emphasis on crafting policies that try to advance narrow self interests. Global interdependence, he argues, encourages acting from a moral awareness that there is only "one humanity" and "one economy." In an interdependent world, someone else's problems soon become our own; thus altruism and a concern for others pays dividends under globalization. The economist Jagdish Bhagwati (2004) submits that this concern should extend to allowing people to move freely, just as under globalization capital moves from country to country in search of higher returns. Until restrictions on migration are lifted, large national differences in pay for similar work will persist. Financial journalist Martin Wolf (2004) disagrees. While condemning restrictions on capital mobility, he accepts them on labor mobility, even if they perpetuate wage differences. Governments, in his opinion, are responsible for the welfare of their citizens; they can rightly limit immigration when it is in their national interest.

What do you think? Does globalization encourage a moral outlook that promotes a worldwide definition of ethical responsibilities? If so, do these responsibilities include liberalizing immigration policies in order to foster a convergence of wage levels among different countries? Or are the responsibilities of national leaders anchored to the interests of the states that they govern, regardless of the impact of their policies on living standards elsewhere?

12

Trade and Monetary Relations in a Global Political Economy

CHAPTER OUTLINE

Contending Economic Strategies for an Interdependent World

The Shadow of the Great Depression

The Clash between Liberal and Mercantile Values

Hegemony and the Management of the Global Economy

The Hegemonic Pillars of Open Markets and Free Trade

A Liberal Economic Order without Hegemonic Leadership?

The Changing Free-Trade Regime

Controversy: Is the World Trade Organization a Friend or Foe?

The Changing International Monetary Regime

The Elements of Monetary Policy

The Bretton Woods Monetary System

The End of Bretton Woods

Plans for Reforming the International Financial Architecture

Global Economic Concerns in the Twenty-First Century

The Fate of Free Trade

Emerging Regional Trade Policies

Application: NAFTA and the Politics of Trade

The Future of Global Economic Governance

> Much of politics is economics, and most of economics is politics.
> CHARLES E. LINDBOLM
> POLICY ANALYST

In November 2001, Qatar, a sheikdom on a small peninsula jutting from Saudi Arabia into the Persian Gulf, hosted the Fourth Ministerial Conference of the World Trade Organization (WTO) in Doha, its capital city. The aim of the conference was to launch a round of negotiations that would result in lower tariffs among WTO members. Although the "Doha Round" of trade negotiations was scheduled to conclude in four years, it dragged on far past the original deadline, finally stalling in July 2008.

The collapse of the Doha Round puzzled observers on two counts. First, the World Bank had estimated that an agreement would yield significant economic gains by 2015: 32 million people raised from poverty; $125 billion less in tariffs paid by consumers; and $50 to $100 billion in growth for the world economy. Second, the negotiations unfolded in an atmosphere that seemed conducive to liberalizing trade: the world GDP had been averaging roughly 3 percent annual growth since 2001; the volume of global merchandise exports had increased over twice as much; and many governments had already reduced import duties unilaterally (Naím 2007). Given the anticipated benefits of a successful Doha Round and the apparent momentum behind the negotiations, what went wrong? Why did the negotiators fail to seal an agreement at their July 2008 summit in Geneva?

For many analysts, the answer could be found in the politics of international economic relations. Frequently political complications lurk beneath economic phenomena, as Charles Lindbolm suggests in the epigraph of this chapter. The first such complication in the Doha Round pertained to agricultural trade. Led by China and India, a coalition of developing countries within the WTO (the G-20, or Group of 20) pushed for the European Union and the United States to cut farm subsidies, and for Japan and several other advanced industrial countries to phase out agricultural import barriers. They also wanted "special safeguard" duties to protect their own framers from unexpected surges in agricultural imports.

A second complication revolved around demands by Global North countries for Global South and East countries to lower their barriers to nonagricultural imports, strengthen agreements on intellectual property rights, and address a host of issues originally raised during the WTO's 1996 Singapore meetings, including government procurement, competition policy, trade facilitation, and investment. Whereas the European Union desired prompt attention on the Singapore issues, the G-20 was reluctant to proceed until progress occurred on agricultural matters.

Ultimately, the negotiators were unable to resolve their disagreement over safeguards for protecting farmers in the Global South. China and India favored a low threshold for triggering special duties when agricultural imports surged; the United States and various other developed countries backed a higher threshold. Because under WTO procedures nothing is finalized until an agreement is reached on everything comprising the agenda, the negotiators were unable to conclude the Doha Round. In the wake of their failure, many observers feared that the global trade regime would unravel as countries began to question the WTO's usefulness and turned their energies toward creating regional trade agreements (RTAs). The danger, they warned, would be the possible division of the world into rival trade blocs.

A week after the political gridlock in Geneva, Pascal Lamy, the WTO's director-general, urgently called upon all parties to resume negotiations. The stakes were too high to allow things to drift. In view of their importance, this chapter will examine how trade and currency exchanges affect world affairs. The quest for wealth is an ageless pursuit. Because it provides the means by which many other values can be realized, the successful management of economics lies at the center of how governments define their national interests. What practices should they embrace to regulate commercial and monetary activities within their borders? What should they do to influence economic exchanges with other states? These are among the most important issues we face in an era of accelerating globalization. They form the principal concerns within the field of **international political economy**. To introduce this topic, we will first examine the ways in which the world economic system has evolved. This will allow us to then investigate how trade and monetary activities today are creating new issues in the twenty-first century.

international political economy the study of the intersection of politics and economics that illuminates the reasons why changes occur in the distribution of states' wealth and power.

CONTENDING ECONOMIC STRATEGIES FOR AN INTERDEPENDENT WORLD

international monetary system the financial procedures governing the exchange and conversion of national currencies so that they can be bought and sold for one another to calculate the value of currencies and credits when capital is transferred across borders through trade, investment, and loans.

In today's world, politics and economics are merging. The relentless march in the volume of international commerce has made trade increasingly important to countries' economies and is expected to increase at an even faster rate through the year 2015 (*Global Trends 2015*). World trade now accounts for 41.5 percent of global domestic product, up from 20 percent in 1990 (WDR 2006, 297, 299). While trade is the most visible symbol of globalization, the dynamics of the **international monetary system** are equally important. To comprehend the debates that are currently raging over trade and monetary issues, we first need to understand the contending economic philosophies of liberalism and mercantilism, which underpin the strategies different states have adopted in their pursuit of power and wealth.

The Shadow of the Great Depression

In July 1944, forty-four states allied in the Second World War against the Axis powers met in the New Hampshire resort community of Bretton Woods. Their purpose was to devise new rules and institutions to govern international trade and monetary relations after the fighting ended. As the world's preeminent economic and military power, the United States played the leading role. Its proposals were shaped by the perception that the Great Depression of the 1930s created the conditions that gave rise to political extremists in Germany, Italy, and Japan. Operating under the philosophy of **commercial liberalism**, the United States sought free trade, open markets, and monetary stability in the hope that they would foster economic growth. Worldwide prosperity, U.S. leaders believed, was the best antidote to political extremism.

commercial liberalism
an economic theory advocating free markets and the removal of barriers to the flow of trade and capital.

The rules established at Bretton Woods, which governed international economic relations for the next twenty-five years, rested on three political bases. First, power was concentrated in the rich Western European and North American countries, which reduced the number of states whose agreement was necessary for effective management of economic relations. Second, the system's operation was facilitated by the dominant states' shared preference for an open international economy with limited government intervention. Third, Bretton Woods worked because the United States assumed the burdens of leadership and others willingly accepted that leadership. The onset of the Cold War helped cement Western unity, because a common external enemy led America's allies to perceive economic cooperation as necessary for both prosperity and military security.

The political bases of the Bretton Woods system crumbled in 1972 when the United States suspended the convertibility of the dollar into gold and abandoned the system of fixed currency exchange rates. Since then, as floating exchange rates and growing capital mobility have made monetary mechanisms unstable, more chaotic processes of international economic relations have materialized. Still, commercial liberalism's preference for market mechanisms over government intervention and the urge to privatize and otherwise reduce government regulation of markets has spread worldwide. Thus it is still useful to characterize the contemporary international economic system as a **Liberal International Economic Order (LIEO)**—one based on such free-market principles as openness and nondiscriminatory trade.

Liberal International Economic Order (LIEO)
the set of regimes created after World War II, designed to promote monetary stability and reduce barriers to the free flow of trade and capital.

Not all states consistently support the liberal tenet that governments should refrain from interfering with trade flows. Commercial liberalism is under attack where political pressure to protect local industries and jobs is growing. States' trade policies are naturally influenced by the desire to increase the domestic benefits of international economic transactions and to lessen their adverse consequences, even if this undermines the expansion of a global capitalist economy propelled by free trade.

The Clash between Liberal and Mercantile Values

How should states behave in the global economy to maximize their gains and minimize their vulnerability? Most controversies in the international political economy are ultimately reducible to the competing ideologies of liberalism and **mercantilism**, which represent fundamentally different conceptions of the relationships among society, state, and market (Gilpin 2001). A comparison of the logic behind the two theoretical traditions can help us to appreciate why different national leaders often pursue disparate policies in their international economic relations, with some advocating free trade and others devising ways to protect their countries from foreign competition.

mercantilism the seventeenth-century theory preaching that trading states should increase their wealth and power by expanding exports and protecting their domestic economy from imports.

Commercial Liberalism.   As described in Chapter 2, liberalism begins with the presumption that humankind's natural inclination is to cooperate in order to increase prosperity and enlarge individual liberty under law. Commercial liberal theory has many variations, but all liberal thinkers agree that everyone benefits from unfettered exchanges. Open markets and free trade are seen as engines of progress, capable of lifting the poor from poverty and expanding political liberties.

Adam Smith, the eighteenth-century political economist who helped define the precepts of classical liberalism, used the metaphor of the unregulated market's "invisible hand" to show how the collective or public interest can be served by humans' natural tendency to "truck, barter, and exchange" in pursuit of private gain. David Ricardo, a nineteenth-century British political economist, added an important corollary to liberal thought by demonstrating that when all states specialize in the production of those goods in which they enjoy a **comparative advantage** and trade them for goods in which others enjoy an advantage, a net gain in welfare for both states, in the form of higher living standards, will result. The principle of comparative advantage underpins commercial liberalism's advocacy of free trade as a method for capital accumulation. Material progress is realized and mutual gains are achieved, according to this principle, when countries specialize in the production of what they can produce least expensively; are willing to purchase, from other countries, goods that are costly for them to produce; and, in addition, do not restrict the flow of trade across borders.

comparative advantage the concept in liberal economic theory that a state will benefit if it specializes in those goods it can produce comparatively cheaply and acquires through trade goods that it can only produce at a higher cost.

Liberals such as Smith and Ricardo believed that economic processes governing the production, distribution, and consumption of goods and services operate according to certain natural laws; consequently markets work best when free of government interference. Transferring the logic of **laissez-faire economics** to the international level, commercial liberals suggest that removing trade restrictions among nations promotes more equal access to scarce resources, attracts foreign capital and expertise, and fosters competition—which generates pressure for increasing efficiency to lower production costs (Todaro 2000). These economic benefits are thought to have positive political consequences. Because war reduces profits by interrupting commerce, high levels of international trade create a material incentive for states to resolve their disputes peacefully. Besides encouraging states to find amicable solutions to their disagreements, trade also makes conflict resolution easier by increasing international communication and eroding parochialism.

laissez-faire economics from a French phrase (meaning literally "let do") that Adam Smith and other commercial liberals in the eighteenth century used to describe the advantages of freewheeling capitalism without government interference in economic affairs.

T A B L E   12.1   Comparative Advantage and the Gains from Free Trade

Country	Worker Productivity per Hour		Before Specialization		Specialisation, No Trade		Specialization, with Trade	
	Cameras	Computers	Cameras	Computers	Cameras	Computers	Cameras	Computers
Japan	9	3	900	300	990	270	910	300
United States	4	2	400	200	320	240	400	210

Why does free trade produce benefits for trade partners who specialize in the production of goods for which they have comparative advantage? Consider a hypothetical illustration of Japan and the United States, each of which produces cameras and computers but with different worker productivity (output per hour) for each country, as shown in the first column above.

Clearly Japan has an absolute advantage in both products, as Japanese workers are more productive in turning out cameras and computers than American workers are. Does this mean that the two countries cannot benefit by trading with each other? If trade does occur, should each country continue to allocate its resources as in the past? The answer to both questions is no.

Each country should specialize in producing the item for which it has the greatest cost advantage or least cost disadvantage, and trade for others. Because Japan is three times more productive in cameras than computers, it should direct more of its resources into manufacturing cameras. One cost of doing so is lost computer output, but Japan can turn out three additional cameras for every computer given up. The United States, on the other hand, can obtain only two computers. Like their Japanese counterparts, American workers are also more productive in making cameras than computers. Still, U.S. resources should be directed to computers because the United States is at a smaller disadvantage compared with Japan in this area. If the United States specializes in computers and Japan in cameras and they trade with one another, each will benefit. The following scenario shows why.

Begin with 100 workers in each industry without specialization or trade (second column). Next specialize production by shifting ten Japanese workers from computer to camera production and shifting twenty American workers from camera production to computers (third column). Then permit free trade so that eighty Japanese-manufactured cameras are exported to the United States and thirty U.S. computers are exported to Japan. With specialization *and* free trade, the benefits to both countries improve.

By shifting Japanese resources into the production of cameras and U.S. resources into computers and allowing trade, the same total allocations will cause camera and computer output to rise ten units each (fourth column). Resources are now being used more efficiently. Both countries realize benefits when each trades some of its additional output for the other's. Japan ends up with more cameras than before specialization and trade and with the same number of computers. The United States finds itself with more computers and the same number of cameras. More output in both countries means higher living standards.

There is a fly in this liberal ointment, however. Although commercial liberal theory promises that the "invisible hand" will maximize efficiency so that everyone will gain, it does not promise that everyone will gain equally. Productivity varies among individuals. "Under free exchange, society as a whole will be more wealthy, but individuals will be rewarded in terms of their marginal productivity and relative contribution to the overall social product" (Gilpin 2001). This applies at the global level as well: The gains from international trade may be distributed quite unequally, even if the principle of comparative advantage governs. Commercial liberal theory ignores these differences, as it is concerned with *absolute* rather than relative gains. Other theorists, however, are more concerned with the relative distribution of economic rewards.

Mercantilism.   In contrast to liberalism, mercantilism advocates government regulation of economic life to increase state power and security. It emerged in Europe as the leading political economy philosophy after the decline of feudalism and helped to stimulate the first wave of Europe's imperialist expansion, which began in the fifteenth century. Accumulating gold and silver was seen by early mercantilists as the route to state power and wealth. Later mercantilists focused on building strong, self-sufficient economies by curbing imports, subsidizing strategically targeted enterprises, and protecting domestic companies from foreign competition.

Today's so-called **neomercantilists** support policies aimed at maintaining a balance-of-trade surplus by reducing imports, stimulating domestic production,

neomercantilism a contemporary version of classical mercantilism which advocates promoting domestic production and a balance-of-payment surplus by subsidizing exports and using tariffs and nontariff barriers to reduce imports.

and promoting exports. These "new" mercantilists are sometimes called "economic nationalists." In their view, states must compete for position and power, and economic resources are the source of state power. From this it follows that "economic activities are and should be subordinate to the goal of state building and the interests of the state" (Gilpin 2001).

Mercantilism shares much in common with political realism: Realists and mercantilists both see the state as the principal world actor; both view the international system as anarchical; and both dwell on the aggressively competitive drive of people and states for advantage. While commercial liberals emphasize the mutual benefits of cooperative trade agreements, mercantilists are more concerned that the gains realized by one side of the bargain will come at the expense of the other. For mercantilists, relative gains are more important than both parties' absolute gains. An American economic nationalist, for instance, would complain about a trade agreement that promised the United States a 5 percent growth in income and the Chinese 6 percent. Although the bargain would ensure an eventual increase in U.S. living standards, its position compared with China's would slip. Calculations such as these explain why trade agreements that promise mutual gains often encounter stiff resistance. It also explains why those who fear the loss of domestic manufacturing and high-skilled service jobs to foreign competitors also lobby for mercantilist measures, and why they sometimes succeed against the unorganized interests of consumers who benefit from free trade.

Protectionism is the generic term used to describe a number of mercantilist policies designed to keep foreign goods out of a country and to support the export of domestically produced goods to other countries. These policies include:

protectionism a policy of creating barriers to foreign trade, such as tariffs and quotas, that protect local industries from competition.

import quotas limits on the quantity of particular products that can be imported.

export quotas barriers to commerce agreed to by two trading states to protect their domestic producers.

orderly market arrangements (OMAs) voluntary export restrictions that involve a government-to-government agreement and often specific rules of management.

- *Quotas.* Two types of quotas are common. **Import quotas** unilaterally specify the quantity of a particular product that can be imported from abroad. **Export quotas** result from negotiated agreements between producers and consumers and restrict the flow of products (e.g., shoes or sugar) from the former to the latter. An **orderly market arrangement (OMA)** is a formal agreement in which a country agrees to limit the export of products that might impair workers in the importing country, often under specific rules designed to monitor and manage trade flows. Exporting countries are willing to accept such restrictions in exchange for concessions on other fronts from the importing countries. The Multi-Fiber Arrangement (MFA) is an example of an elaborate OMA that restricts exports of textiles and apparel. It originated in the early 1960s, when the United States formalized earlier, informal **voluntary export restrictions (VERs)** negotiated with Japan and Hong Kong to protect domestic producers from cheap cotton imports. The quota system was later extended to other importing and exporting countries and then, in the 1970s, to other fibers, when it became the MFA. Under both import and export quotas, governments rather than the marketplace regulate the flow of goods between countries.

voluntary export restrictions (VERs) a protectionist measure popular in the 1980s and early 1990s, in which exporting countries agree to restrict shipments of a particular product to a country to deter it from imposing an even more onerous import quota.

- *Tariffs.* Instead of using quotas, governments can limit imports by placing a tax on foreign goods. The tax may be a fixed amount imposed on each unit of an item being imported, or it may be based on some percentage of the value of each unit. Under what is known as "strategic trade policy," governments sometimes provide subsidies to a particular industry in order to make its goods more competitive abroad. Two protectionist responses to this practice are **countervailing duties**, the imposition of tariffs to offset alleged subsidies by foreign producers, and **antidumping duties** imposed to counter the alleged sale of products at below the cost of production.

- *Nontariff barriers.* Governments may limit imports without resorting to direct tax levies. Nontariff barriers cover a wide range of creative government regulations designed to shelter particular domestic industries from foreign competition, including health and safety regulations, as well as arcane government purchasing procedures.

Realist theory helps to account for states' impulse to engage in protectionism. Recall that realism argues that states in an anarchic, self-help environment often shun cooperation because they are suspicious of one another's motives. Uncertainty encourages each state to spend "a portion of its effort, not forwarding its own good, but in providing the means of protecting itself against others" (Waltz 1979). Among developing countries whose domestic industrialization goals may be hindered by the absence of protection from the Global North's more efficient firms, the **infant industry** argument is often used to justify mercantilist trade policies. According to this argument, tariffs or other forms of protection are necessary to nurture young industries until they eventually mature and lower production costs to compete effectively in the global marketplace.

In sum, the insecurity that breeds political competition frequently occurs in international economic relations. Those who see states' power and wealth as inextricably linked conclude that "even if nation-states do not fear for their physical survival, they worry that a decrease in their power capabilities relative to those of other states will compromise their political autonomy, expose them to the influence attempts of others, or lessen their ability to prevail in political disputes with allies and adversaries" (Mastanduno 1991). Thus many states are "defensively positional actors" that seek not only to promote their domestic well-being but also to defend their rank (position) in comparison with others (Grieco 1995).

countervailing duties tariffs imposed by a government to offset suspected subsidies provided by foreign governments to their producers.

antidumping duties tariffs imposed to offset another state's alleged selling of a product at below the cost to produce it.

infant industry a newly established industry that is not yet strong enough to compete effectively in the global marketplace.

HEGEMONY AND THE MANAGEMENT OF THE GLOBAL ECONOMY

The relative gains issue speaks to the difficulties of achieving international cooperation under anarchical conditions and explains why some domestic producers vigorously oppose liberal (open) international economies despite the evidence that free trade promotes economic growth. Thus while some people see an unregulated market as the best method for providing the greatest good for the greatest number, others prefer protectionism over the liberalization of trade. According to many scholars, the key to bringing order to this competitive environment lies in the emergence of an all-powerful hegemon.

Hegemony is the ability to shape the rules under which international political and economic relations are conducted. In the world economy it occurs when a single great power garners a sufficient amount of material resources to channel the international flow of raw materials, capital, and trade.

Charles Kindleberger (1973), an international economist, first theorized about the need for a liberal hegemon to open and manage the global economy. In his explanation of the 1930s Great Depression, Kindleberger concluded that "the international economic and monetary system needs leadership, a country which is prepared, consciously or unconsciously, . . . to set standards of conduct for other countries; and to seek to get others to follow them, to take on an undue share of the burdens of the system, and in particular to take on its support in adversity." Britain played this role from 1815 until the outbreak of World War I in 1914, and the United States assumed the British mantle in the decades immediately following World War II. In the interwar years, however, Britain was unable to play its previous leadership role, and the United States, although capable of leadership, was unwilling to exercise it. The void, Kindleberger concluded, was a principal cause of the "width and depth" of the Great Depression throughout the world in the 1930s.

hegemonic stability theory a school of thought that argues free trade and economic order depend on the existence of an overwhelmingly powerful state willing and able to use its strength to open and organize world markets.

According to what has become known as **hegemonic stability theory**, a preponderant state is able to design and promote rules for the whole global system that protect its own long-term interests. Hegemons such as the United States (and Britain before it), whose domestic economies are based on capitalist principles, have championed liberal international economic systems, because their comparatively greater control of technology, capital, and raw materials has given them more opportunities to profit from a system free of protectionist restraints. When they have enforced such free-trade rules, the hegemon's economies typically have served as "engines of growth" for others in the "liberal train."

Hegemons have also had special responsibilities. They have had to manage the international monetary system to enable one state's money to be exchanged for other states' money, make sure that countries facing balance-of-payments deficits (imbalances in their financial inflows and outflows) could find the credits necessary to finance their deficits, and serve as lenders of last resort during financial crises. When the most powerful liberal states could not perform these tasks, they have often backtracked toward more closed (protected or regulated) domestic economies, and in doing so have undermined the open international system that was previously advantageous to them. This kind of departure historically has made quotas, tariffs, and nontariff barriers to trade more widespread. In short, hegemonic states not only have had the greatest capacity to make a free-trade regime succeed but in the past they also have had the greatest responsibility for its effective operation and preservation. To interpret whether hegemonic stability theory is likely to hold in the future, a closer look at the theory's logic is useful.

The Hegemonic Pillars of Open Markets and Free Trade

collective goods goods from which everyone benefits regardless of their individual contributions.

Much of the discussion about the free movement of commodities across national borders centers on the concept of public or **collective goods**—benefits that everyone shares and from which no one can be excluded selectively. National security is one such collective good that governments try to provide for all of their citizens, regardless of the resources that individuals contribute through taxation. In the realm of economic analysis, an open international economy permitting the relatively free movement of commodities is similarly seen as a desirable collective good, inasmuch as it permits economic benefits for all states that would not be available if the global economy were closed to free trade.

According to hegemonic stability theory, the collective good of an open global economy needs a single, dominant power—a hegemon—to remain open and liberal. A major way in which the hegemon can exercise leadership is to open its own market to less-expensive imported goods even if other countries **free ride** by not opening their own markets. However, if too many states refuse to forego the short-term gains of free riding and capitulate to domestic protectionist pressures, the entire liberal international economy may collapse.

The analogy of a public park helps us to illustrate this dilemma. If there were no central government to provide for the maintenance of the park, individuals themselves would have to cooperate to keep the park in order (the trees trimmed, the lawn mowed, and so on). But some may try to come and enjoy the benefits of the park without pitching in. If enough people realize that they can get away with this—that they can enjoy a beautiful park without helping with its upkeep—it will not be long before the once beautiful park looks shabby. Cooperation to provide a public good is thus difficult. This is also the case with the collective good of a liberal international economy, because many states that enjoy the collective good of an orderly, open, free-market economy pay little or nothing for it. A hegemon typically tolerates some free riders, partly because the benefits that the hegemon provides, such as a stable global currency, encourage other states to accept its rules. But if the costs of leadership multiply and everyone's benefits seem to come at the expense of the hegemon, it will become less tolerant of free riding and may gravitate toward more coercive policies. In such a situation, the open global economy could crumble amidst a competitive race for individual gain at others' expense.

free riders those who enjoy the benefits of collective goods but pay little or nothing for them.

A Liberal Economic Order without Hegemonic Leadership?

Although hegemonic powers benefit from the liberal economic systems that their power promotes, the very success of liberalism eventually erodes the pillars that support it.

Competition fostered by open markets and free trade encourages productive efficiency and economic growth, which affects the international distribution of industrial power. As economic strength shifts from the hegemon to other states, the capacity of the hegemon to maintain the system decreases. The leading economic power's ability to adapt is critical to maintaining its dominant position. Britain was unable to adapt and fell from its top-ranked position. Many wonder if the United States is destined to suffer the same fate, not because of economic failure but because of the lack of political will to exercise leadership through concerted multilateral action. At the twenty-first century's dawn, the United

States stood as an economic superpower; however, the circumstances confronting the United States today are eroding its capacity to continue exercising hegemonic leadership.

At present, the United States has the world's largest economy, but few predict that position of dominance will remain indefinitely. The U.S. share of world output has fallen steadily since World War II. In 1947, the United States accounted for nearly 50 percent of the combined gross world product (largely because the war ravaged the territory of its industrial competitors). By 1960, its share had slipped to 28 percent, by 1970 to 25 percent, and by the 1990s to 20 percent—less than what it had been during the Spanish-American War, when the country first emerged as a world power (D. White 1998, 42). Another symptom of economic stress is that the U.S. share of world financial reserves has declined. The United States went from being the globe's greatest creditor country in 1980 to the world's largest debtor by 1990, and, with a projected budget deficit for fiscal 2009 of $482 billion, the debt continues to mount. A third symptom lies in the growth of the U.S. trade deficit, which has risen from $31 billion in 1991 to $818 billion in 2007. Finally, alongside these debt burdens and trade imbalances, U.S. investment in public infrastructure to stimulate future growth is lower than that of all the other major industrialized nations. The American Society of Civil Engineers estimates that $1.6 trillion will be needed to rebuild the nation's infrastructure (*Time*, August 11, 2008, 35).

These trends suggest that American economic primacy will not continue. The United States possesses the world's largest economy, but it is straining under the cost of the wars in Afghanistan and Iraq, the fallout from the subprime-mortgage fiasco, high oil prices, and entitlement commitments exceeding $43 trillion in unfunded liabilities (Brooks 2007, A7). For many Americans, the purchase of Anheuser-Bush by Belgium-based InBev symbolized the changing economic environment. In 2007 alone, there were more then 2,000 foreign-led acquisitions of U.S. companies in deals valued at $405.4 billion, up from $60.8 billion just four years earlier. Overseas buyers also spent $52.2 billion in U.S. commercial real estate, double the 2006 total. As Joseph Stiglitz, a Nobel Prize-winning economist, summarized the situation, "an increasing proportion of the country is owned abroad" (*Time*, August 25, 2008, 45–46).

What will happen if the willingness and capability of the United States to lead declines? Have the institutions and rules put into place to govern the liberal economic order in the post–World War II era now taken on a life of their own? Commercial liberals think so, arguing that trade liberalization may be too deeply entrenched for it to collapse. Significant institutional and normative restraints now exist on imposing new trade barriers. By establishing mechanisms for creating and monitoring shared expectations about open markets and free trade, some theorists believe that "institutions can create an environment in which interstate cooperation is possible even without a single dominant leader" (Krasner 1993). The free-trade regime may no longer depend on the existence of an all-powerful hegemon.

To better evaluate this argument and probe the likely future of global economics, let us now inspect how those international trade and monetary rules have evolved since the Second World War.

THE CHANGING FREE-TRADE REGIME

In the period immediately following World War II, when the United States became the world's dominant political power, it simultaneously became the preeminent voice in international trade affairs. The liberal trading system the United States chose to promote rejected the **beggar-thy-neighbor policies** widely seen as a major cause of the economic depression of the 1930s. Removing barriers to trade became a priority and led to the recurrent rounds of trade negotiations that produced remarkable reductions in tariff rates. As the large U.S. market was opened to foreign producers, other countries' economies grew, and rising trade contributed to a climate that encouraged others to open their markets as well.

beggar-thy-neighbor policies the attempt to promote trade surpluses through policies that cause other states to suffer trade deficits.

The General Agreement on Tariffs and Trade (GATT) became the principal international organization designed to promote and protect free trade in the aftermath of World War II. GATT was never intended to be a formal institution with enforcement powers. Instead, a premium was placed on negotiations and reaching consensus to settle disputes among parties to the agreement, which was first and foremost a commercial treaty. As trade disputes multiplied, GATT increasingly became involved in legalistic wrangling. In 1995, GATT was superseded by the World Trade Organization (WTO), a new free-trade IGO with "teeth." The WTO represents a breathtaking step in free-trade management, although it has also provoked violent disagreements over the nature of global capitalism (see Controversy: Is the World Trade Organization a Friend or Foe?). The WTO extended GATT's coverage to products, sectors, and conditions of trade not previously covered adequately. It also enhanced previous dispute-settlement procedures by making the findings of its arbitration panels binding on the domestic laws of participating states (GATT's findings were not binding). Finally, the WTO deals with the problem of free riding by being available only to states that belong to GATT, subscribe to all of the Uruguay Round agreements, and make market access commitments (under the old GATT system, free riding was possible when some small states were permitted to benefit from trade liberalization without having to make contributions of their own).

The creation of the WTO signaled a victory for multilateralism, because it "reduced the powers of all governments to regulate behavior and set independent economic policies" (Thurow 1998). Trade squabbles will nonetheless continue despite overwhelming profits from trade liberalization. Free trade generates wealth, but it also brings risks. As Joseph Grieco and John Ikenberry (2003) explain: Open markets stimulate economic growth, but they can also create dependencies. "So a state contemplating expanding its exposure to the world economy must calculate the trade-offs between the absolute economic gains from trade and the losses it produces in terms of autonomy."

In late November 1999, the then 135-member countries of the World Trade Organization (WTO) and thirty additional observer states made final preparations to stage in Seattle what was billed as the Millennium Round on trade negotiations—the follow-up to the Uruguay Round of trade talks completed in 1993. The mood was optimistic. Everyone expected to celebrate the contributions that lower trade barriers arguably had made to the growth of international exports and, for many members (particularly the United States), their longest and largest peacetime economic expansion in the twentieth century. There appeared to be widespread recognition that a world without walls promotes prosperity and welfare.

A half-century of generally rising prosperity had generated a climate of enthusiasm for the power of free trade. Fears of imports tend to recede in good economic times, and, with the best decade ever, most leaders in the twilight of the twentieth century emphasized the sunnier side of free trade. The delegates to the Seattle meetings shared the liberal conviction that countries, companies, and consumers had much to gain by a globalized economy freed from restraints on the exchange of goods across borders. They expected added benefits from a new trade round that could slash tariffs and other trade barriers in agriculture, manufactured goods, and services.

That mood and the seeming consensus on which it was based was shattered when the Seattle trade talks opened. An estimated 50,000 to 100,000 protesters and grassroots anti-WTO activists, who differed widely in their special interests (the poor, environment, labor, women, indigenous people), joined hands to shout their common opposition to the general idea of globalization and free trade. A plane trailed a banner proclaiming "People Over Profits: Stop WTO" as part of what became known as "The Battle in Seattle." A tirade against open trade ensued, fueled by citizen backlash.

The Seattle conference will be remembered as the moment when the debate over the benefits and costs of the globalized economy rose to the pinnacle of the global agenda. The immediate target of the demonstrations was the WTO; however, the organization itself was simply a convenient symbol of a much larger sea of discontent. The WTO protests (and the failure of the

WTO conference attendees to compromise on tightly held positions and agree on even a minimal accord) exposed the deep divisions about the best ways to open global commerce and adopt new rules at a time of rapid change.

Controversies about globalization, free trade, and global governance are multiple. At the core is the question of whether a globalized economy is inevitable and, if so, is it an antidote to human suffering or a source of new inequities. The debates are explosive, because everyone is affected, but in quite different ways. Many people enjoyed the boom years under liberalized trade engineered by the WTO's trade agreements, but the celebration was confined largely to the privileged, powerful, and prosperous. Many others saw themselves as victims of an open global economy, as when a company outsources some of its business functions overseas and workers lose their jobs. Those discontented with globalized free trade include a diverse coalition of protestors, many of whom harbor very specific concerns about wages, the environment, and human rights issues. Labor leaders contend that the WTO is sacrificing worker rights; environmental groups complain that when green values collide with world commerce, environmental standards are left out of trade negotiations; and human rights activists accuse the WTO of serving the preferences of multinational corporations for erasing trade barriers in ways that fail to protect human rights. In addition, enraged trade ministers from the Global South's developing countries see a Global North conspiracy in the WTO's efforts to adopt core labor standards, because the less-developed Global South views such high-sounding rules as a method to take away the comparative advantages Global South developing nations enjoy with lower wage scales.

These, and other issues, are certain to continue as major controversies. What do you think? Is the WTO a valuable tool for improving global governance or a threat to human welfare? Is the WTO and the free trade practices it promotes too strong or too weak? Does the WTO put corporate profits above human rights and environmental protection, as critics charge? Or do you agree with the WTO's claim that "Trade is the ally of working people, not their enemy."

THE CHANGING INTERNATIONAL
MONETARY REGIME

States cannot always trade as they wish. Their exports and imports depend on many factors, especially on changes in global demand and prices for the goods and services that countries' producers sell in the global marketplace. The mechanisms for setting the currency exchange rates by which the value of traded goods are priced heavily influence international trade. Indeed, the monetary system is crucial for international trade, for without a stable and predictable method of calculating the value of sales and foreign investments, those transactions become too risky, causing trade and investment activities to fall. Simply put, the success of international trade depends on the health of the monetary system.

The Elements of Monetary Policy

Monetary and financial policies are woven into a complex set of relationships between states and the international system, and, because monetary and currency issues have their own specialized technical terminology, they are difficult to understand. However, the essentials are rather basic. "Monetary policy works on two principal economic variables: the aggregate supply of money in circulation and the level of interest rates." Monetarist economic theory assumes that the **money supply** (currency plus commercial bank demand deposits) is related to economic activity. Increases in the supply facilitate economic growth by enabling people to purchase more goods and services, but a supply that grows too fast may lead to inflation. Through controlling the level of the money supply, some monetarists contend, "governments can regulate their nations' economic activity and control inflation" (Todaro 2000, 657), although others worry that its effects are too unpredictable in the short run to guide policy.

To understand the importance of monetary policies as a determinant of states' trade, growth rates, and wealth consider both why **exchange rates** fluctuate and the impact of these currency fluctuations. Money works in several ways and serves different purposes. First, money must be widely accepted, so that people earning it can use it to buy goods and services from others. Second, money must serve to store value, so that people will be willing to keep some of their wealth in the form of money. Third, money must act as a standard of deferred payment, so that people will be willing to lend money knowing that when the money is repaid in the future, it will still have purchasing power.

Governments attempt to manage their currencies to prevent inflation. Inflation occurs when the government creates too much money in relation to the goods and services produced in the economy. As money becomes more plentiful and thus less acceptable, it cannot serve effectively to store value or to satisfy debts or as a medium of exchange.

Movements in a state's exchange rate occur in part when changes develop in peoples' assessment of the national currency's underlying economic strength or

money supply the total amount of currency in circulation in a state, calculated to include demand deposits—such as checking accounts—in commercial banks and time deposits—such as savings accounts and bonds—in savings banks.

exchange rate the rate at which one state's currency is exchanged for another state's currency in the global marketplace.

balance of payments
a calculation summarizing
a country's financial transactions with the external
world, determined by the
level of credits (export
earnings, profits from foreign investment, receipts
of foreign aid) minus the
country's total interna-
tional debts (imports,
interest payments on
international debts, for-
eign direct investments,
and the like).

the ability of its government to maintain the value of its money. A deficit in a country's **balance of payments**, for example, would likely cause a decline in the value of its currency relative to that of others. This happens when the supply of the currency is greater than the demand for it. Similarly, when those engaged in international economic transactions change their expectations about a currency's future value, they might reschedule their lending and borrowing. Fluctuations in the exchange rate could follow.

Speculators—those who buy and sell money in an effort to make a profit—may also affect the international stability of a country's currency. Speculators make money by guessing the future. If, for instance, they believe that the Japanese yen will be worth more in three months than it is now, they can buy yen today and sell them for a profit three months later. Conversely, if they believe that the yen will be worth less in three months, they can sell yen today for a certain number of dollars and then buy back the same yen in three months for fewer dollars, making a profit. The globalization of finance now also encourages managers of investment portfolios to move funds from one currency to another in order to realize gains from differences in states' interest rates and the declining value of other currencies in the global network of exchange rates. Short-term financial flows are now the norm: The International Monetary Fund estimates that more than 80 percent of transactions relate to round-trip operations of a week or less.

In the same way that governments try to protect the value of their currencies at home, they try to protect them internationally by intervening in currency markets. Their willingness to do so is important to importers and exporters, who depend on orderliness and predictability in the value of the currencies they deal in to carry out transnational exchanges. Governments intervene when countries' central banks buy or sell currencies to change the value of their own currencies in relation to those of others. Unlike speculators, however, governments are pledged not to manipulate exchange rates so as to gain unfair advantages, for states' reputations as custodians of monetary stability are valuable. Whether governments can affect their currencies' values in the face of large transnational movements of capital is, however, increasingly questionable. So is the value of any country's currency in relation to any other's (see Figure 12.1).

The Bretton Woods Monetary System

When the leaders of the capitalist West met in Bretton Woods, New Hampshire in 1944, they were acutely aware of the need to create a reliable mechanism for determining the value of countries' currencies in relation to one another, and agreed to a set of concepts to define monetary and currency policy for conducting international trade and finance. Recognizing that a shared system and vocabulary was a necessary precondition for trade, and from it post–World War II economic recovery and prosperity, the negotiating parties agreed that the post-war monetary regime should be based on **fixed exchange rates** and assigned governments primary responsibility for enforcing its rules. In addition, they foresaw the need to create what later became the International Monetary Fund

fixed exchange rates
a system under which
states establish the parity
of their currencies and
commit to keeping fluc-
tuations in their exchange
rates within narrow limits.

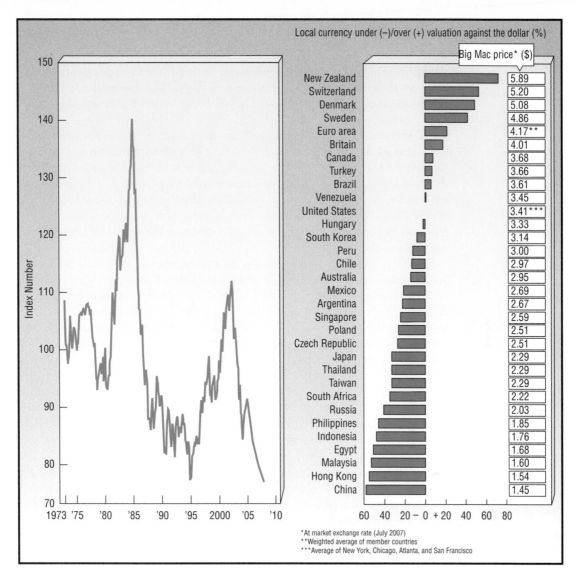

FIGURE 12.1 Calculating the Cost of Goods in the World's Confusing Currency Exchange System

The figure on the left shows the weighted average of the foreign exchange values of the U.S. dollar against a subset of the currencies of a large group of major U.S. trading partners. People from the United States who are traveling abroad use currency exchange rates to convert foreign prices to U.S. dollars. An exchange rate is the price someone must pay in one country's currency to purchase one unit of another country's currency. Economists frequently try to predict the future movement of currency exchange rates by examining purchasing power parity (PPP), which holds that in the long run exchange rates should adjust to equalize the cost of an identical basket of goods and services in any two countries. The index in the figure on the right, formulated by the *Economist*, uses a basket with one item—a McDonald's Big Mac, which is produced in approximately 120 countries around the world. This Big Mac PPP is the exchange rate at which hamburgers would cost the same in America as they would anywhere else in the world. The least expensive burger could be purchased in China for $1.45 (11 yuan at the July 7, 2007 exchange rate), versus an average price of $3.41 in the United States. To make the two prices equal, would require an exchange rate of 3.23 yuan to the dollar, rather than the market rate of 7.65, which implies that the yuan was 58 percent "undervalued" against the dollar at that point in time. Conversely, the euro was 22 percent overvalued against the dollar and the Swiss franc was 53 percent overvalued.

SOURCE: Major Currencies Index, U.S. Federal Reserve; Big Mac Index, the *Economist*, July 7, 2007, p. 74.

(IMF), to help states maintain equilibrium in their balance of payments and stability in their exchange rates with one another. The International Bank for Reconstruction and Development, known as the World Bank, was also created to aid recovery from the war.

Today the IMF and World Bank are important, if controversial, players in the global monetary and financial systems. Their primary mission is to serve as "lenders of last resort" when its member states face financial crises, providing those seeking assistance meet the often painful conditions requiring domestic adjustments to strengthen their economies. In the period immediately after World War II, these institutions commanded little authority and too few resources to cope with the enormous devastation of the war. The United States stepped into the breach.

The U.S. dollar became the key to the hegemonic role that the United States eagerly assumed as manager of the international monetary system. Backed by a vigorous and healthy economy, a fixed relationship between gold and the dollar (pegged at $35 per ounce of gold), and the U.S. commitment to exchange gold for dollars at any time (known as "dollar convertibility"), the dollar became universally recognized as a "parallel currency," accepted in exchange markets as the reserve used by monetary authorities in most countries and by private banks, corporations, and individuals for international trade and capital transactions.

To maintain the value of their currencies, central banks in other countries either bought or sold their own currencies, using the dollar to raise or depress their value. Thus the Bretton Woods monetary regime was based on fixed exchange rates and ultimately required a measure of government intervention for its preservation.

To get U.S. dollars into the hands of those who needed them most, the Marshall Plan provided Western European states billions of dollars in aid to buy the U.S. goods necessary for rebuilding their war-torn economies. The United States also encouraged deficits in its own balance of payments as a way of providing **international liquidity** in the form of dollars.

international liquidity
reserve assets used to settle international accounts.

In addition to providing liquidity, the United States assumed a disproportionate share of the burden of rejuvenating Western Europe and Japan. It supported European and Japanese trade competitiveness, permitted certain forms of protectionism (such as Japanese restrictions on importing U.S. products), and condoned discrimination against the dollar (as in the European Payments Union, which promoted trade within Europe at the expense of trade with the United States). The United States willingly incurred these leadership costs and others' free riding because subsidizing economic growth in Europe and Japan would widen the U.S. export markets and strengthen the West against communism's possible popular appeal.

Although this system initially worked well with the United States operating as the world's banker, the costs grew as the enormous number of dollars held by others made the U.S. economy increasingly vulnerable to financial shocks from abroad. U.S. leaders found it difficult to devalue the dollar without hurting America's allies; nor could inflationary or deflationary pressures at home be managed without hurting allies abroad. This reduced the United

States' ability to use the normal methods available to other states for dealing with the disruption caused by deficits in a country's **balance of trade**, such as adjusting interest and currency exchange rates.

balance of trade
a calculation based on the value of merchandise goods and services imported and exported. A deficit occurs when a country buys more from abroad than it sells.

The End of Bretton Woods

As early as 1960 it was clear that the dollar's top currency status could not be sustained. After 1971, U.S. president Nixon abruptly announced—without consulting with allies—that the United States would no longer exchange dollars for gold. With the price of gold no longer fixed and dollar convertibility no longer guaranteed, the Bretton Woods system gave way to a substitute system based on **floating exchange rates**. Market forces, rather than government intervention, were expected to determine currency values. A country experiencing adverse economic conditions now saw the value of its currency fall in response to the choices of traders, bankers, and businesspeople. This was expected to make its exports cheaper and its imports more expensive, which in turn would pull its currency's value back toward equilibrium—all without the need for central bankers to support their currencies. In this way, it was hoped that the politically humiliating devaluations of the past could be avoided.

floating exchange rates
an unmanaged process whereby market forces rather than governments influence the relative rate of exchange for currencies between countries.

Those expectations were not met. Beginning in the late 1970s, escalating in the 1980s, and persisting through the 1990s, a rising wave of financial crises, both in currency and banking, occurred. These have been compounded by massive defaults by countries unable to service their debts. About one-fifth of the world's countries currently have foreign debts in excess of $10 billion, and together the low- and middle-income countries of the Global South have over $2,742 billion in external debt. Forty-eight countries have debt service payments that exceed 5 percent of their total GNI, and eighteen are paying for past debts more than 10 percent (WDI 2007, 250–256). This staggering debt load compromises these countries' capabilities to chart their future by themselves and leaves many of them exposed to external economic and political influence.

Financial crises have become increasingly frequent around the world as a result of the inability of states to manage income, debt, and inflation in a monetary system fraught with wild currency exchange rate gyrations. In the past forty years, more than 100 major episodes of banking insolvency occurred in ninety developing and emerging countries. The financial cost of these crises, in terms of the percentage of GDP lost, has been huge. The disastrous debts generated by banking and currency disruptions forced governments to suffer, on average between 1970 and 1997, direct loses of nearly 15 percent of their GDP for each crisis and more than a 5 percent decline in output growth after each crisis (World Bank 1999a, 126).

In response to the growing awareness of the extent to which the health of others' economies depended on the value of the U.S. dollar internationally (which in turn depended on the underlying strength of the U.S. economy), since 1985 the **Group of Five** has adhered to the landmark agreement reached secretly at the Plaza Hotel in New York City, in which they pledged

Group of Five (G-5)
a group of advanced industrialized democracies composed of the United States, Britain, France, Japan, and Germany.

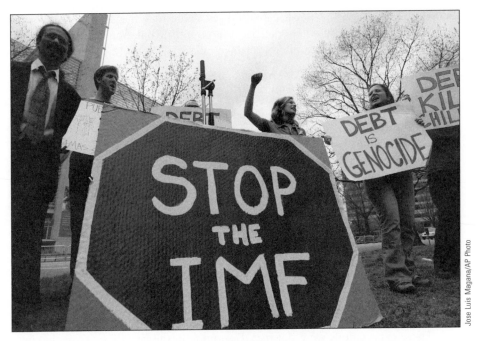

Jose Luis Magana/AP Photo

The Debt Burden Some people believe that the globalization of finance has adversely affected certain countries. Shown is an example of how the policies of the International Monetary Fund sometimes unleash hostile feelings: Protestors at an IMF economic summit call for cancelling the debts owed by many Global South countries.

Group of Seven (G-7)/ Group of Eight (G-8)
the G-5 plus Canada and Italy; since 1997, known as the G-8 with the addition of Russia.

to collectively coordinate their economic policies through management of exchange rates internationally and interest rates domestically.

An expanded **Group of Seven (the G-7)**, and subsequently a **Group of Eight** (the **G-8** with the inclusion of Russia in 1997) have sought to carry out the pledge to coordinate global monetary policy. However, beginning with the G-8 summit in Genoa in July 2001, it became clear that the leading industrial powers were unable to reach consensus about the best way to manage exchange rates, monetary and fiscal policies, and trade relations in order to sustain global economic growth.

In the absence of true collective management of global monetary conditions, it appears likely that the volume of world trade and the activities of currency speculators (who use sophisticated global electronic technologies and rely on about 2,000 "hedge funds" to make profits in currency trading) will increasingly determine national currency values. An average of over $1.5 trillion in currency trading occurs each day—a transfer of capital greater than one-fourth of the world's average *weekly* level of international trade. International sales of stocks and bonds have mushroomed as well and promise to rise through increased investor trading on the Internet. In the volatile world of mobile capital, wide fluctuations in national currencies' exchange rates have become common. The globalization of finance and the removal of barriers to capital flows across borders expose national economies to shocks, with little hope that such volatility will vanish.

Plans for Reforming the International Financial Architecture

No institution currently has global responsibility for the arrangement of capital flows, although there does exists a set of principles and rules of relatively universal scope. Hardly anyone is happy with the prevailing weak and somewhat haphazard global financial architecture, but it appears that only when severe financial crises occur that threaten a global recession that sufficient pressure mounts to engineer new reforms.

Many proposals have been advanced for reforming the international monetary system to help cushion the aftershocks of the rapid movement of investment funds among countries that creates booms and busts, such as the 1980s Latin American debt crisis and the global crisis that followed on the heels of the 1997–1998 flight of capital from Asia. Financial crises swept like an epidemic to fifty-six countries between 1973 and 1997, costing on average 10 percent of each affected state's GNP. The problems that followed—unemployment, rising taxes, crime, and military coups—precipitated numerous calls for reform. Some analysts suggested that a reversion to the pre–World War I gold standard would be preferable to the exchange rates with highly fluctuating currencies. Others recommend something like the Bretton Woods system of fixed but adjustable rates.

What these and other proposals seek is a mechanism for creating the currency stability and flexibility on which prosperity through trade depends and which the current system has failed to achieve. However, there is little agreement on how to bring about reforms. With global democratization, most governments face domestic pressures to sacrifice such goals as exchange rate stability for unemployment reduction, so it seems likely that floating exchange rates, with all their costs and uncertainties, are here to stay. Thus despite a proliferation of schemes for rebuilding the international financial architecture, incremental tinkering is more likely in the years ahead than large-scale restructuring.

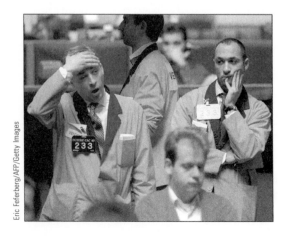

Eric Feferberg/AFP/Getty Images

The Domino Effect in Global Finance When a country's economy collapses, foreign capital flees in panic. No worldwide central bank exists to cushion such crashes. Money problems in one country lead to money problems in others, provoking currency depreciations and plunges in stock prices at home and abroad. Here stunned brokers react to the January 1998 plummet of Hong Kong stocks that caused the key indexes elsewhere in Asia, London, Frankfurt, New York, and Paris to fall.

most-favored-nation (MFN) principle   unconditional nondiscriminatory treatment in trade between contracting parties guaranteed by GATT; in 1997, U.S. senator Daniel Patrick Moynihan introduced legislation to replace the term with "normal trade relations" (NTR) to better reflect its true meaning.

nondiscrimination a principle for trade that proclaims that goods produced at home and abroad are to be treated the same for import and export agreements.

GLOBAL ECONOMIC CONCERNS IN THE TWENTY-FIRST CENTURY

The exponential growth of world trade since 1950 has contributed measurably to the unprecedented rise in global economic prosperity. Reductions in barriers to free trade are expected to accelerate these trends if world trade continues to expand faster than real world output (see Figure 12.2). The anticipated consequence is that countries will be bound ever more tightly in interdependent economic relationships. Indeed, one estimate predicts that by the year 2015 world trade will comprise 40 percent of world GDP (*Global Trends 2015*).

Many states see advantages in accepting the **most-favored-nation (MFN) principle** (which holds that the tariff preferences granted to one state must be granted to all others exporting the same product) and the **nondiscrimination** rule (goods produced at home and abroad are to be treated the same). However,

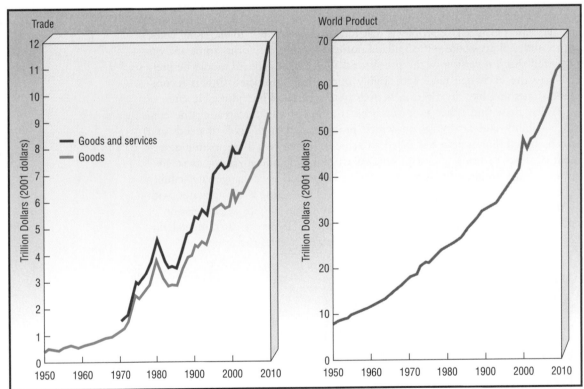

F I G U R E 12.2   The Growth of Global Trade and Wealth

When global trade has risen, almost always so has world wealth. The figure on the left records the rising volume of world trade since 1950, and the figure on the right traces the expansion of the world economy for the same time span. Although trade integration is deepening, the benefits are not evenly distributed, as some countries are not participating at the same levels as others.

SOURCES: Global trade trends WTO, growth of world product from OECD and IMF.

free trade is attractive only if everyone, developed and developing countries alike, can benefit. Today numerous states remain tempted to enhance their domestic well-being by protectionist means. Many of them have retained non-tariff barriers to free trade even as tariff walls have come down. "Trade may be global," warn Ramesh Thakur and Steve Lee (2000), but "politics is still local." If neomercantilism spreads, the preservation of the free-trade regime is unlikely throughout the twenty-first century.

The Fate of Free Trade

Countries differ in their willingness to open their domestic markets. Yet even in many economically open countries, protectionist pressures are increasing. Job losses, attributed by many people to corporate offshore outsourcing, have triggered these calls for protectionism. In hard times, people are tempted to build barriers against foreign competitors. Fifty-eight countries still impose tariffs of 10 percent or more, and the Global South average tariff wall (9.4 percent), and the Global East's (9 percent), remain high in comparison to the Global North's average (3.4 percent). Unfortunately for the fate of the liberal international regime, the threats to global prosperity are multiplying at the same time that the dependency of countries on volatile foreign capital is creating an inherently unstable situation. If global trade experiences anemic growth or worse, declines, this slump will cause the demand for exports to drop, and the world's consumers are likely to respond to the slowdown by turning away from the free-trade regime that engineered their previous period of unprecedented growth.

Given the seemingly clear-cut economic advantages of free trade, commercial liberals find it difficult to understand why many governments resist open markets. The answer lies in the fact that trade can appear in the eye of the beholder to be inherently unfair. Unions in wealthy Global North states complain that the lower wages of the Global South countries give them "unfair" advantages and, for their part, the less-developed Global South states complain that they cannot "fairly" compete against their more productive, technologically advanced Global North counterparts. Given that many people in both wealthy and poor countries think that they are not competing on a level playing field, the age-old debate between free traders and mercantilists is likely to persist as a global issue.

Emerging Regional Trade Policies

For some time, analysts have worried about the possibility that regional trading arrangements will push the open-trading regime, which is central to the Liberal International Economic Order, toward closure. The United States first experimented with creating trade partnerships within particular regions in 1984, with the Caribbean Basin Initiative to reduce tariffs and provide tax incentives to promote industrialization and trade in Central America and the Caribbean. This was soon followed in 1987 with free-trade agreements with Israel and Canada, and in 1989 with the North American Free Trade Agreement (NAFTA) signed by Canada, Mexico, and the United States in 1993 (see Application: NAFTA and

APPLICATION   NAFTA and the Politics of Trade

For over a century, economics and political science developed as separate academic disciplines: the former largely focusing on the production and consumption of goods and services; the latter, on power and influence in policy making. More recently, however, scholars have begun to look at how economics and politics interact. One area where policy makers wrestle with this inter-action is in the creation of regional trade agreements, such as the North American Free Trade Association (NAFTA). In the passage below, James Baker, who served as the U.S. secretary of state for President George H. W. Bush, discusses the political dynamics that preceded NAFTA's birth.

> From the beginning, we all knew that NAFTA would be no cakewalk. Indeed, some of the President's advisers were initially less than enthu-siastic about proceeding. Negotiators would even-tually produce a text that ran to five volumes. It would cover trade, investment, the environment, regulation, standards, and mechanisms to resolve disputes. . . .
>
> We would also have to sell the agreement politically in the United States. Free-trade agree-ments always produce losers in some sectors of the economy. But overall, they always generate greater economic activity, which produces more winners than losers. . . .
>
> The political problems confronting President [Carlos] Salinas [de Gortari] would be even greater. A free trade agreement would demand acceler-ated but painful reform of the Mexican economy. Powerful industrial and agricultural interests would fight tooth and nail against opening their markets. Finally, Salinas would have to overcome a hundred-and-fifty-year tradition of anti-American sentiment. . . .
>
> Salinas's personal commitment proved critical to negotiating NAFTA. Just weeks after George

Bush's election, I had accompanied him to Houston for the traditional get-together between the American President-elect and his Mexican counter-part. This time the meeting was especially oppor-tune: Salinas himself had just been elected. Between them, the two presidents-elect created the "Spirit of Houston" . . . [which] provided the personal foundation for the revolution in bilateral relations that occurred during the next four years.

> For my part, I took the lead in raising the profile of the U.S.-Mexico Binational Commission, a meeting of cabinet members from both nations. . . . The American side developed strong working relationships with key Mexican players. These relationships proved decisive when the two sides, joined by Canada, got down to the difficult business of negotiating NAFTA.
>
> . . . At State and later the White House . . . I always stressed the need for sustained progress, not only to the Mexicans and Canadians, but also to those in our administration who didn't seem to give NAFTA the priority it deserved. Bob Zoellick, my right-hand man on NAFTA, set up an informal channel of communications with José Cordoba de Montoya, Salinas's chief of staff. Through it, the two sides could identify problems and prod our respective bureaucracies (Baker 1995, 607–608).

According to Baker, even though the U.S. economy was inexorably being bound to those of its neighbors, a regional trade agreement would not have materialized without the political groundwork being carefully pre-pared by members of each country's administration. Formal talks between the United States and Mexico began in the summer of 1990, with Canada joining in mid-1991. On December 17, 1992, Presidents Bush, President Salinas, and Canadian Prime Minister Brian Mulroney signed the agreement, which was ratified the following year by the legislatures of the three countries.

the politics of trade). In addition, at their April 2001 Quebec Summit, the United States and thirty-three Western Hemispheric democracies took a bolder step when they pledged to build a Free Trade Area of the Americas (FTAA), creating the world's largest barrier-free trade zone, from the Arctic to Argentina, linking markets to 800 million people. In December 2005, however, negotiations stalled in response to Venezuela's fiery president Hugo Chávez's opposition to an agreement that he claimed would "permanently extend American political domination of the region to the economic realm."

Efforts to link the countries of the Western Hemisphere in an economic partnership are seen by many as a response to European integration. Since the 1950s, European leaders have tried methodically to build a continent-wide economic union. By 2002, they had established a **regional currency union**, with a single currency (the euro) designed to facilitate economic flows among EU members. Although some EU states (Britain, Denmark, and Sweden) have thus far not adopted the euro, its supporters insist that the euro will strengthen European economic consciousness and transform the continent into a single market for business. Indeed, some predict that the euro will replace the dollar as the world's reserve currency. Valued at eighty-six cents when it was introduced, by the summer of 2008 it was worth over $1.50.

The Mercosur free-trade zone in South America is another example of a regional economic regime. Its member countries—Argentina, Brazil, Paraguay, Uruguay, and Venezuela—have expanded trade to $21.1 billion (from only $4.1 billion in 1990). The enlarged ten-member Association of Southeast Asian Nations (ASEAN) free-trade region is representative of yet another among the many multilateral regional trading blocs. Its intra-bloc trade climbed to $143 billion from less than $23.7 billion in 1990 (WDI 2007, 332).

Many people feel that these types of regional trade agreements (RTAs) are consistent with GATT's rules and see regional regimes as vital pieces in the step toward a free-trade agreement for the entire global economy. Others see the division of the globe into competing trade blocs as a danger, fretting that existing regional free-trade zones actually violate the WTO's nondiscrimination principle by moving away from free trade toward inter-bloc competition. In particular, the critics fear that further development of regionalized markets centered on Asia, Europe, and North America has already split globalized trade into competing trade blocs (see Map 12.1). Currently, some three-fifths of exports in Asia go within the APEC region to other Asian countries, two-thirds of European exports go within the European Union, and more than half of exports by North American countries stay within the NAFTA bloc.

The surge in RTAs has continued unabated since the early 1990s, with over 250 in force as of 2008. If the RTAs reportedly planned or already under negotiation are concluded, the total number could reach 300 (World Trade Organization, http://www.wto.org, January 24, 2008). The ultimate impact of this trend toward regionalization of the world political economy remains uncertain. Some analysts are concerned about the prospect of a world divided into separate regional centers that leaves numerous countries outside. Others believe the formation of trade blocs will undermine global free trade and thereby plague world economic growth in the years ahead. If trade-bloc rivalry intensifies, still others warn of a cutthroat mercantile rivalry in which the fear of one another may be the only force binding the regional members together.

Yet, contrary to these fears, there are signs that the international trading system may move toward a complex web of commercial ties due to the growth of cross-regional bilateral agreements that create overlapping RTA memberships for many countries. Mexico, for example, is a member of NAFTA and also has bilateral free trade agreements with Australia, New Zealand, and Japan; the European

regional currency union the pooling of sovereignty to create a common currency (such as the EU's euro) and single monetary system for members in a region, regulated by a regional central bank within the currency bloc to reduce the likelihood of large-scale liquidity crises.

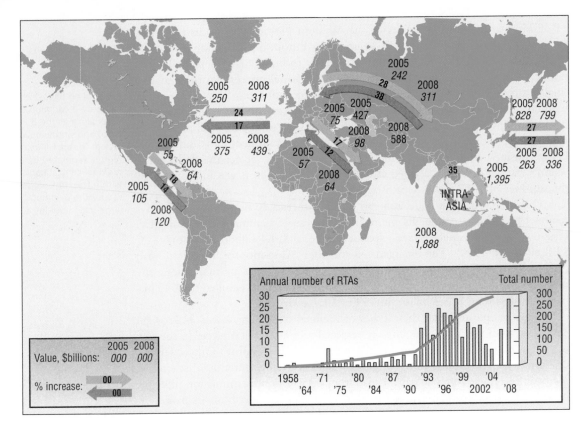

M A P 12.1   Trade Blocs and the Regionalization of Global Trade

A trend shaping the global political economy has been the propensity of trade flows to concentrate *within* regions instead of *between* them. The arrows on this map trace the levels of trade volume and increases between the major regions from 2005 to 2008. Another trend (right) is the growth in regional trade agreements (RTAs).

SOURCES: trade flows, Global Insight; RTAs, WDI 2006, 335

Union has over thirty preferential trade agreements with other states; and the ASEAN countries have individual agreements with China and others are being negotiated with South Korea, Japan, and India. In effect, an intricate network of RTAs and bilateral free-trade agreements currently exists alongside the WTO multilateral trading system.

The Future of Global Economic Governance

Although there are many factors that will define the boundaries within which the global economy is likely to vary in the years ahead, the future will depend heavily on the rules the major economic powers choose to support in trade and monetary policy. Facing the worst financial crisis since the Great Depression, the leaders from twenty of the world's largest economic powers met in Washington,

D.C. in November 2008 to begin discussions on what rules should guide their policies. Possessing the world's largest economy, the United States continues to play a pivotal role; how it makes economic policy will influence the direction in which others are likely to move. But with the federal government spending a staggering amount to rescue financial institutions from Fannie Mae and Freddie Mac to American International Group (AIG), can the United States sustain its ability to maintain global economic order? If the United States falters, how, in an integrated global system can other countries' economies stay upright?

The architecture of the Liberal International Economic Order constructed at Bretton Woods a half-century ago appeared to depend not only on a consensus about the rules governing the world political economy but also on U.S. leadership. The United States is still the dominant economic power and continues to perform many hegemonic functions: It tries to maintain a comparatively open market for others' goods, manage the international monetary system, provide capital to would-be borrowers facing financial stress, and coordinate economic policies among the world's leading economies. Today, however, U.S. willingness to absorb the costs of leadership has waned as Washington increasingly tries to calm economic fears, thaw frozen credit markets, open foreign countries to U.S. exports, and cushion the impact of imports on the domestic economy.

More worrisome still, the collapse of the Doha round of global trade talks in Geneva during the summer of 2008 has raised questions about the future of the WTO as the main forum for crafting rules of world trade. Whereas optimists point to the fits and starts that characterized the earlier Uruguay round to suggest that the suspended talks are merely a temporary interruption within a long-term set of negotiations, pessimists fear that this could spell the end of multilateralism as the organizing principle of global trade. If the Doha round cannot be salvaged, they warn, the WTO will lose its legitimacy as an umpire in trade disputes and fade into irrelevance.

Clearly, the liberal trading agreements so slowly built up over the past five decades remain fragile. The combination of a global recession and financial market volatility could easily bring about a global upsurge in protectionism. Another source of protectionist sentiment comes from worries about the motives driving the investment decisions made by managers of sovereign-wealth funds. Political leaders such as Germany's Angela Merkel and France's Nicolas Sarkozy have voiced suspicions regarding these state-owned funds, the largest of which include the Unite Arab Emirates' Abu Dhabi Investment Authority and Kuwait's Reserve Fund for Future Generations. Projected to have as much as $12 trillion to invest by 2015, the number of sovereign-wealth funds has multiplied in recent years, often due to windfall profits generated by soaring petroleum prices. Because they generally do not disclose their objectives or the range of their investments, sovereign-wealth funds tend to spark interest in protectionist measures, even though they constitute less than 3 percent of global traded securities. Yet, as former U.S. Federal Reserve chairman Alan Greenspan observes, the protectionist cures advanced to address these concerns will make matters worse rather than better. Protectionism will "do little to create jobs and if foreigners retaliate, we will surely lose jobs."

A new wave of mercantilism and trade wars is not preordained, however. A number of other important developments are also likely to influence the future direction of the world political economy, and these, in combination, are likely to sustain and strengthen the liberal free-trade regime that has contributed to global economic growth. World commerce has become globalized, and with the development of more free-trade areas and cross-regional trade agreements, the prospects for commercial liberalism to weather calls for protectionism seem promising.

Some theorists believe that the spread of liberal market philosophies will eliminate the need for new institutions to cope with the changing world political economy. Others, pointing to the global problems emanating in 2008 from highly leveraged securities linked to U.S. mortgages, caution that an unregulated market should not be considered the ideal. The task of reaching agreement about what economic policies countries should adopt is difficult due to the absence of a true consensus about what the world political economy should look like, as the continuing contest between liberalism and mercantilism (as well as the conflict between rich and poor countries) illustrates. Furthermore, the globalization of commerce and finance increasingly seems to shape, rather than be shaped by, states' policies—thus challenging the sovereign prerogatives of states themselves.

The face of the future thus remains uncertain. If liberals are correct, the process of globalization will hasten the trend toward interdependence and integration and, with that, the prospects for economic prosperity and political harmony. If mercantilists are right, however, an emerging era of geoeconomic rivalry will increase states' vulnerability and thus the likelihood of political conflict. Meanwhile, national leaders are struggling with how to reconcile domestic political pressures to protect jobs from overseas outsourcing with external economic forces over which they have little control. In the tug-of-war between the competing values of trade liberalization and protectionism, leaders will constantly face trade-offs as they balance policy initiatives seeking to promote growth with those designed to protect autonomy. How they manage these trade-offs will have profound effects on the global future.

CHAPTER SUMMARY

- World politics and economics are inextricably linked. Whether a state's economic system is open or closed, events in the global political economy have domestic consequences. As a result, policymakers play two-level games. The moves they make on the international level affect what they can do on the domestic level, and vice versa.

- Most debates today in the field of international political economy are ultimately reducible to the competing theories of commercial liberalism and mercantilism. Whereas liberals advocate open markets and free trade, mercantilists call for government regulation of economic endeavors to increase state power and security. Although free trade contributes to economic growth, its benefits are not distributed equally.

- Rules governing international commerce evolve according to the wishes of the powerful. The Bretton Woods agreements of 1944 established a Liberal International Economic Order (LIEO), which rested on three political bases: the concentration of power in the hands of a small number of states, the existence of a cluster of interests shared by those states, and the presence of a hegemonic power (the United States) willing to exercise a leadership role.

- The postwar Liberal International Economic Order led to a dramatic upswing in the exchange of goods and services among states, which brought about an increasingly integrated and prosperous global economy.

- The immediate postwar economic system was a dollar-based system, with the United States operating, in effect, as the world's banker. By the early 1970s, however, U.S. leadership was no longer readily accepted by others or willingly exercised by Washington. Power had become more widely dispersed among states. Where hegemony once reigned, various groups of industrialized nations now participated in a series of quasi-official negotiating forums to deal with monetary issues.

- The simultaneous pursuit of liberalism and mercantilism today shows states' determination to reap the benefits of interdependence while minimizing its costs. It also reveals the tension between the promise that everyone will benefit and the fear that the benefits will not be equally distributed. The absence of world government encourages each state to be more concerned with how it fares competitively in relation to other states—its relative gains—than collectively with its absolute gains. These simple yet powerful ideas shed light on the reasons why the United States, the principal advocate of free trade in the post–World War II era, has increasingly engaged in protectionism.

- Economic nationalism and a retreat from multilateral economic cooperation threaten to undermine the overall prospects for world economic growth. Given the growing regionalization of trade and the formation of competitive trade blocs, the rise of regional neomercantilism is a possibility. However, economic globalization is likely to accelerate, and, as competition expands wealth and reduces the costs of both products and labor, the economic fate of the world's 6.7 billion people will be tied closer together, making the welfare of any one important to the welfare of all.

KEY TERMS

antidumping duties	collective goods	exchange rate
balance of payments	commercial liberalism	export quotas
balance of trade	comparative advantage	fixed exchange rates
beggar-thy-neighbor policies	countervailing duties	floating exchange rates

free riders

Group of Eight (G-8)

Group of Five (G-5)

Group of Seven
(the G-7)

hegemonic stability
theory

import quotas

infant industry

international liquidity

international monetary
system

international political
economy

laissez-faire economics

Liberal International
Economic Order
(LIEO)

mercantilism

money supply

most-favored-nation
(MFN) principle

neomercantilists

nondiscrimination

orderly market
arrangement (OMA)

protectionism

regional currency union

voluntary export
restrictions (VERs)

SUGGESTED READINGS

Bernstein, William J. *A Splendid Exchange: How Trade Shaped the World*. New York: Atlantic Monthly Press, 2008.

Cohn, Theodore H. *Global Political Economy: Theory and Practice*, 4th edition. New York: Pearson Longman, 2008.

Friedman, Benjamin M. *The Moral Consequences of Economic Growth*. New York: Knopf, 2005.

Oatley, Thomas. *International Political Economy: Interests and Institutions in the Global Economy*, 3rd edition. New York: Pearson Longman, 2008.

Prestowitz, Clyde. *Three Billion New Capitalists: The Great Shift of Wealth and Power to the East*. New York: Basic Books, 2005.

CRITICAL THINKING QUESTIONS

On July 26, 1956, Egyptian president Gamal Abdel Nasser announced to a jubilant crowd in Alexandria that he would eradicate the last vestige of Egypt's colonial past by nationalizing the Suez Canal, a vital artery of world commerce linking the Mediterranean to the Red Sea. The canal had been operated by the Universal Suez Canal Company, owned primarily by British and French stockholders. Alarmed that Nasser would now control the waterway through which Britain's oil supply flowed, British Prime Minister Anthony Eden desperately sought a way to oust the charismatic Egyptian president and regain the canal.

Britain's concerns about Nasser were echoed in France and Israel. Political leaders in Paris believed he was helping Algerians resist French colonial rule; those in Tel Aviv grumbled he had closed the Straits of Tiran to Israeli shipping and supported guerrilla attacks against Israel. The United States also found Nasser's behavior deplorable, but insisted on finding a negotiated solution to the dispute. U.S. President Dwight Eisenhower was engaged in a reelection campaign, and the Republican Party had emphasized his contributions to international peace. Unable to secure Washington's backing for a military strike against Nasser, Britain, France, and Israel began planning their next moves in secret.

On October 29, the Israelis attacked the Egyptian army in the Sinai peninsula, and the following day the British and French announced that they would intervene to protect the Suez Canal. British paratroopers landed in Suez and Port Said on November 5, setting off a storm of opposition in the United Nations. Eisenhower was furious with what he saw as British deception on the eve of the American elections. The following day, U.S. Secretary of the Treasury George Humphrey gave the British an ultimatum: Either agree to a cease-fire or the United States would ruin the pound sterling, Britain's currency. Unless the British withdrew, Humphrey threatened to block their drawing rights on the International Monetary Fund, deny credit from the United States Export-Import Bank, and have the American Federal Reserve sell off large quantities of sterling (Neustadt 1970, 26). Faced with a looming monetary crisis, the British capitulated.

Some analysts worry that the United States may someday face pressure similar to that experienced by Great Britain in the Suez crisis. Although America holds unchallenged military might, its economy depends on foreign capital because the country consumes more than it produces and has to borrow at a rate of $2 billion every day to sustain its enormous current account deficit (Foreign Affairs, May/June 2007, 93). Currently, it owes foreign creditors over $12 trillion. This dependence on foreign creditors, these analysts warn, could give other countries leverage over the United States. "Simply by dumping U.S. Treasury bills and other dollar-denominated assets, China—which holds more federal U.S. debt than any other country—could cause the value of the dollar to plummet, leading to a major crisis for the U.S. economy" (Schwenninger 2004, 129). Like Great Britain in 1956, the precarious financial position of United States today could undercut its foreign policy.

Are the fears expressed by these analysts warranted? How much leverage does Beijing have over Washington by holding U.S. debt, given the importance of American consumption of Chinese goods for China's economic growth? What would a steep decline in the dollar do to countries that hold dollar-denominated assets? Is the 1956 Suez analogy helpful in understanding the political economy of U.S.-Chinese relations? What are the key similarities between Great Britain's position in 1956 and that of the United States today? What are the major differences?

13

Human Rights and the Quest for Global Justice

CHAPTER OUTLINE

Evaluating the Human Condition

Communitarian and Cosmopolitan Approaches to Human Rights

Human Development and Human Security

CONTROVERSY: What Is Security?

Human Rights and the Protection of People

The Subordinate Status of Women and Its Consequences

The Precarious Life of Indigenous Peoples

The Global Refugee Crisis

Responding to Human Rights Abuses

Internationally Recognized Human Rights

The Challenge of Enforcement

APPLICATION: Human Rights Start in Small Places, Close to Home

> I have often recalled that the United Nations' Charter begins with
> the words: "We the peoples." What is not always recognized
> is that "we the peoples" are made up of individuals whose claims
> to the most fundamental rights have too often been sacrificed in
> the supposed interests of the state.
>
> KOFI ANNAN
> FORMER UN SECRETARY-GENERAL

On April 29, 2008, the government of Myanmar (formerly known as Burma) announced that rain showers, accompanied by winds reaching forty-five miles an hour, were approaching the country's southern coast. Three days later, Cyclone Nargis made landfall, inundating the Irrawaddy delta in twelve feet of water and pounding the region with winds three times more powerful than predicted. Caught off guard, the population suffered horribly. Estimates placed the number of dead at over 100,000, with more than 1 million people left homeless and vulnerable to infectious waterborne diseases.

For several days after the storm, Myanmar's military government scarcely took any actions to assist the survivors. General Than Shwe, the government's leader, rebuffed attempts by UN Secretary-General Ban Ki-moon to persuade him to allow emergency aid into the country. Although Myanmar was on the verge of a humanitarian catastrophe, the government repeatedly turned away rescue teams from foreign nations as well as offers of relief supplies from U.S. and French naval vessels in the Andaman Sea. According to the World Food Program, only 20 percent of desperately needed food aid was getting to cyclone victims.

Frustrated by the military regime's callous behavior, French Foreign Minister Bernard Kouchner suggested that international aid might have to be imposed on Myanmar. Diego Lopez Garrido, Spain's secretary of state for European affairs, complained that the regime's obstructionism was similar to a crime against humanity. David Miliband, Britain's foreign secretary, added that the world community would be morally justified in using all available instruments to open Myanmar's borders to aid under the doctrine of Responsibility to Protect (*Economist*, May 17, 2008, 73).

At the September 2005 UN World Summit in New York, the "responsibility to protect populations from genocide, war crimes, ethnic cleansing, and crimes against humanity" was unanimously adopted by the assembled heads of state (http://www.un.org/summit2005/). Whereas article 2(7) of the UN Charter proclaims that "nothing should authorize intervention in matters essentially within the domestic jurisdiction of any state," the doctrine of Responsibility to Protect (R2P) holds that outside intervention could be undertaken if national authorities were either unable or unwilling to safeguard their populations and peaceful international engagement proved inadequate for addressing the humanitarian emergency. Calls for applying R2P to Myanmar did not trigger a humanitarian intervention, however. In the first place, natural disasters are not included within the scope of the doctrine. In the second place, many Global South countries worried that any effort to widen its application to situations beyond genocide, war crimes, ethnic cleansing, and crimes against humanity would provide a rationale for powerful, disingenuous states to infringe on the domestic affairs of the weak under the guise of a moral imperative to stop human rights violations.

The intransigence of Myanmar's military government in the aftermath of Cyclone Nargis raises several questions about the role of **human rights** in world

human rights the political and social entitlements recognized by international law as inalienable and valid for individuals in all countries by virtue of their humanity.

politics. What are human rights? When a sovereign state violates them, is it legally permissible for others to intervene on behalf of the victims? Does the world community have a moral responsibility to protect those suffering from egregious human rights violations?

Until relatively recently, the theoretical study of world politics neglected human rights. It pictured the plight of the ordinary people as a matter of domestic politics, shielded from outside scrutiny by a state's sovereignty. Human beings were relegated to the status of "subjects" who rulers could treat as if they were things. This outlook today seems strange, because social scientists can use their humanity as a means of understanding. As the anthropologist Robert Redfield (1962) argued, "The physicist need not sympathize with his atoms, nor the biologist with his fruit flies, but the student of people and institutions must employ [one's] natural sympathies in order to discover what people think or feel." Moreover, understanding how people think and feel has grown in importance as the world community increasingly recognizes the inherent moral status of humans and the concomitant obligation of states to protect that status. Ordinary people are becoming empowered, and should not be seen as "simply hapless victims of fate, devoid of any historical agency" (Saurin 2000).

The purpose of this chapter is to examine the human condition and assess its prospects for the global future. There are now more than 6 billion people on the face of the earth, and the world population is growing. Between 2 and 4 billion more people will be added to the planet's population between now and the last quarter of the twenty-first century. With these numbers comes a concern over how humanity will fare in the decades ahead. To what extent will people around the world have a voice in shaping their destiny?

EVALUATING THE HUMAN CONDITION

"Man is born free, and everywhere he is in chains," the eighteenth-century political philosopher Jean Jacques Rousseau bemoaned in his famous 1762 book, *Social Contract*. Times have since changed, but for some parts of the world Rousseau's characterization of the human condition remains valid. Despite some people enjoying unprecedented standards of living, a daunting scale of poverty is evident throughout the world (see Map 13.1). As measured by the World Bank's common standard of one dollar a day in purchasing power parity (PPP), 1.23 billion people are living in poverty and another 3.2 billion seek to survive on two dollars a day (WDI 2007, 16, 63). The world's most wealthy 500 people have a combined income greater than that of the poorest 416 million, and the richest 10 percent account for 54 percent of global income (UNDP 2005, 4).

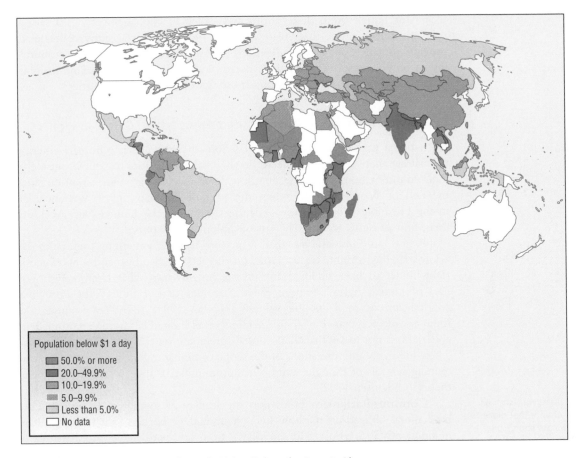

M A P 13.1   The Percentage of People Living Below the Poverty Line

As this map shows, if measured according to the World Bank's standard of one dollar or less a day in purchasing power parity (PPP) terms, 18.4 percent of the world's population live in extreme poverty. Most of these people live in Asia, but Africa has the largest number of high-poverty countries.

SOURCE: World Bank (2007, 20–21)

Another indicator of the state of humanity is the deplorable conditions in which many people live. In the Global South, infant mortality rates are among the highest in the world and less than half of the adult population is literate (a proportion even lower among women). Former World Bank President James Wolfensohn captures the grim realities of global poverty by noting that "120 million children never get a chance to go to school [and] over 40 million people in the developing countries are HIV-positive with little hope of receiving treatment for this dreadful disease." The world is at "a tipping point," he warns. Either the Global North recommits to reducing global poverty, or "the world's poor will be left even further behind—and our children will be left to face the consequences."

Given the serious deprivations facing so many people, there are ample reasons for humanitarian concern. Crushing poverty and lack of opportunity is a recipe for hopelessness, desperation, and violence. Global poverty is a serious problem, but is it one that creates a moral obligation for wealthy countries to provide assistance out of considerations of distributive justice? Or is distributive justice only a matter of domestic concern, with national leaders having no obligation to ameliorate poverty among those who live in other countries?

Communitarian and Cosmopolitan Approaches to Human Rights

Do national leaders have a moral obligation to try to alleviate human suffering no matter where it occurs? Indeed, do they have *any* duties to people outside of their country's borders? These questions have received growing attention since the end of World War II, when the idea of "human rights" was included in the Preamble and in Article 1 of the Charter of the United Nations. Until then, human rights were rarely part of diplomatic discourse.

Rights are entitlements that a person has to something of value. By acknowledging a right, we set limits on the actions of others and empower the right-holder to have nullified any encroachments into what is protected. The idea of human rights has been called "*the* idea of our times," the "principal counter-current to realpolitik values" (Henkin 1991, 187). Yet to note that there is wide acceptance of the principle that all individuals have certain inalienable rights is not to say that there is total agreement on the nature of those rights. There are many interpretations of the scope of human rights; however, two contending schools of thought stand out: communitarian theory and cosmopolitan theory (C. Brown 1992).

communitarianism an ethical theory that places the ultimate source of moral value in political communities.

Communitarianism holds that the leaders of sovereign, territorial states have moral obligations to those living within their borders, not to the welfare of humanity as a whole. Human rights, from this perspective, are a matter of national jurisdiction. Given the diversity of cultures throughout the world, and given that we have no widely accepted basis for choosing among different value systems, communitarian theorists insist that references to universal moral obligations are problematic. A bounded political community, they assert, is necessary for a shared code of morality.

cosmopolitanism an ethical theory that places the ultimate source of moral value in individuals.

In contrast, **cosmopolitanism** emphasizes humankind rather than national communities. It holds that all individuals, solely by virtue of being human, have rights that no state can deny and that warrant global protection. The belief in a transcendent humanitarian imperative—a conviction that human suffering obliges others to respond—has ancient roots. From Zeno (335–263 BCE) and Chrysippus (250–207 BCE) through Seneca (4 BCE–65 CE) and Marcus Aurelius (121–180 CE), Greek and Roman Stoics believed in the equality and unity of humankind. Contemporary cosmopolitans believe that despite the world's division into a welter of separate states, the well-being of people in any one state should not come at the expense of people from different states, because their common humanity entails moral obligations to each other (Linklater 2002; O'Neill 1986). Some argue further that if one has the power to prevent something bad from happening to those living elsewhere, action should be taken as long as it does not sacrifice anything of comparable moral significance (P. Singer 1979).

CONTROVERSY   What Is Security?

How should *security* be defined? Policy makers disagree. Some see it primarily in military terms; others in human welfare terms. Underlying the disagreement are different conceptions of what is most important on the global agenda. One tradition gives states first priority and assumes that protecting their territorial integrity must be foremost in the minds of national leaders. Others challenge this conception and give primacy to the security of individual people, arguing that social and environmental protection must be seen as a global priority, because all people depend on a clean, healthy environment for survival.

What do you think? To what extent should social and environmental protection be defined as security issues? In considering these questions, take into consideration the realist view that national security entails safeguarding the state from external attack. Realists maintain that protecting one's country from existential threats is a political leader's paramount task. For them, national survival overrides all other concerns; thus they define security in military terms, focusing on the state's ability to fend off armed aggression.

In contrast, many liberals contend that "secure states do not automatically mean secure peoples"

(Human Security Centre 2006). Guarding against foreign attacks may be a necessary condition for the security of individuals, but it is not a sufficient one. Proponents of "human security" believe that leaders should also protect individuals from hunger, disease, and natural disasters, since they kill more people than war. From their perspective, the "degradation of natural resources (fresh water, soils, forests, fishery resources, and biological diversity) and vital life-support systems (the ozone layer, climate system, oceans, and atmosphere) ... could have far-reaching effects ... [comparable] to those associated with most military threats that national security establishments prepare for" (Porter 1995). Achieving security, therefore, entails more than generating national military power and employing it in interstate relations.

Which conception of security is more persuasive to you? Is the concept of human security too broad to be useful in policy making? To what extent are the "national security" approach emphasized by realists and the "human security" approach favored by liberals in competition with one another? Might they instead be mutually reinforcing? Can either type of security be achieved in the absence of the other?

While communitarian theories have their adherents, the process of globalization has led many people to gravitate toward the view that all individuals equally hold certain rights simply by sharing a common humanity. Modern telecommunication highlights these commonalities by making us aware that distant strangers often share our everyday hopes and fears. As discussed in Chapter 11, satellites, broadband links, and the Internet have compressed space and time. Of course, not everyone around the world enjoys the human rights that cosmopolitan theories articulate; consequently, officials from IGOs and the members of NGOs have made a significant effort in recent years to promote **human security**, which they believe will enhance development and, in turn, respect for human rights (see Controversy: What is Security?).

human security a concept that refers to the degree to which the welfare of individuals is protected and advanced, in contrast to national security which puts the interests of states first.

Human Development and Human Security

The human dimension of development gained attention in the 1970s when analysts realized the importance of focusing on aspects of human welfare not measured by economic indicators that describe a country's wealth. Beyond looking at indicators such as the average income for each person in a particular country, analysts began devoting attention to noneconomic factors that contributed to living a long, rewarding life.

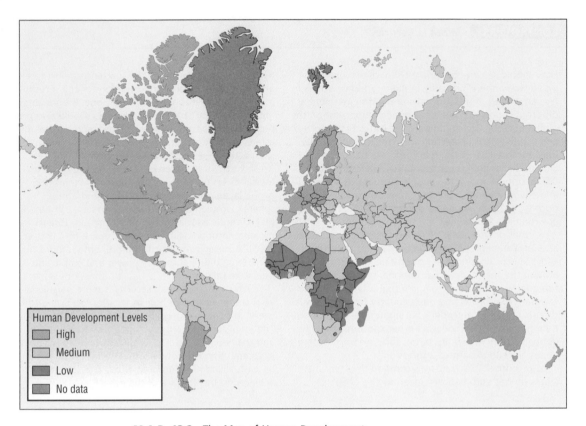

M A P 13.2 The Map of Human Development

This map shows the level of human development in the countries of the world, based on the UN Human Development Index (HDI) that uses life expectancy, literacy, average number of years of schooling, and income to assess a country's performance in providing for its people's welfare and security. Although poorer countries have made big gains in the past quarter century (following political reforms leading to greater democracy and economic reforms leading to free markets), a gap in levels of human development is apparent and parallels to some degree the gap between the Global North and the Global South.

SOURCE: UNDR (2008, 229–232).

Many things affect human development. Among them, political freedom stands out. The degree to which countries rule themselves democratically and protect civil liberties is a potent determinant of human development. Map 13.2 shows the various levels of human development in countries across the globe. One conclusion that the United Nations Development Program has drawn from the data displayed in the map is that human development flourishes where people are free to express their views and participate in the decisions that shape destinies.

For human development goals to be met, prosperity clearly helps, as shown in Figure 13.1. When countries are grouped and ranked according to their

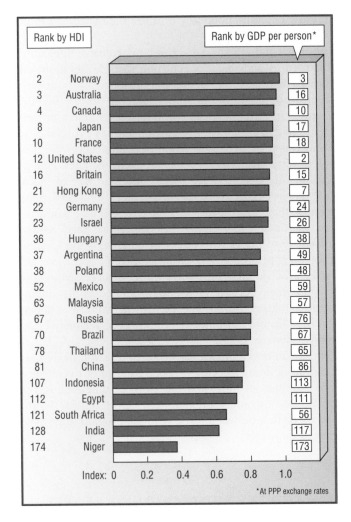

Rank by HDI		Rank by GDP per person*
2	Norway	3
3	Australia	16
4	Canada	10
8	Japan	17
10	France	18
12	United States	2
16	Britain	15
21	Hong Kong	7
22	Germany	24
23	Israel	26
36	Hungary	38
37	Argentina	49
38	Poland	48
52	Mexico	59
63	Malaysia	57
67	Russia	76
70	Brazil	67
78	Thailand	65
81	China	86
107	Indonesia	113
112	Egypt	111
121	South Africa	56
128	India	117
174	Niger	173

Index: 0   0.2   0.4   0.6   0.8   1.0

*At PPP exchange rates

FIGURE 13.1 Measuring Human Development

When using the Human Development Index (HDI) to measure human welfare in different populations, notice how some countries can rank somewhat differently than when using an aggregate measure such as gross domestic product (GDP) per capita. Whereas Norway ranks very high and Niger ranks very low on both measures, South Africa's AIDS epidemic has left it in the 121st position on the HDI index, despite its relatively high income.

SOURCE: UNDP (2008, 230–232).

human development performance, as we might expect, the level of human development is highest in the Global North, where economic prosperity is also highest on average; conversely, it is generally lower in the Global South where per capita economic output is substantially lower. Nevertheless, the link between economic well-being and human development is not automatic. Two countries with similar per capita incomes can have very different levels of human development, because some governments are more effective in converting national wealth into better lives for their people. Equatorial Guinea and the Czech Republic, for example, ranked 38 and 39 out of 173 countries, respectively, on per capita gross domestic product (GDP) in 2002, adjusted for purchasing power parity. When compared on the UN Development Program's Human Development Index (a measure based on life expectancy, literacy, education, and income), Equatorial Guinea ranked 111 and the Czech Republic 33 (*The Economist,* August 3, 2002, 82). In short, income alone is not a good predictor of human development. How countries politically organize themselves is a more important factor.

The rapid transfer of capital and investment across borders that is integrating the world's economies has led to widespread speculation that globalization will provide a cure for the chronic poverty facing the majority of humanity. Impressive gains have been made in various countries. Since 1990, the number of people without access to clean water has been cut in half, the number of children dying before the age of five has fallen by one quarter, and life expectancy in developing countries has increased by two years. Even more impressive, 135 million people have escaped poverty since 1999. At market exchange rates, emerging economies now account for 30 percent of world GDP and half of global GDP growth (*Economist*, January 26, 2008, 27; November 17, 2007, 83). According to global optimists, these gains suggest that poverty can be eradicated.

However, critics complain that while capital may flow more freely around the world, it flows most slowly to places where human suffering is the greatest. The developing countries are a heterogeneous group, and the poorest are not catching up, cautions a skeptical political economist from Mexico. "More and more people across the planet have become increasingly exposed to the amenities of the global marketplace, although mostly as permanent window shoppers and silent spectators. The large majority of humankind, however, is rapidly being left outside and far behind" (Heredia 1999).

Although progress in human development has occurred and will likely persist, so will trends that can erode human security, making the early twenty-first century appear to be both the best of times and the worst of times. Thus, the future of world politics will be not only a struggle between the Global North and Global South but also a contest between those who see progress as possible and those who see regress as inevitable.

HUMAN RIGHTS AND THE PROTECTION OF PEOPLE

As we have seen, human rights are entitlements that a person possesses simply because he or she is a human being. As such, they are held equally by all and cannot be lost or forfeited. Unfortunately, not everyone enjoys all of the human rights recognized by international law. Three major areas where this problem exists are the rights of women, indigenous peoples, and refugees.

The Subordinate Status of Women and Its Consequences

Over the past three decades, the status of women has become a major human rights concern (see Table 13.1). Increasingly people have realized that women have an important influence on human development, and that their treatment is an issue that affects everyone.

T A B L E 13.1   Important Steps on the Path Toward Human Rights and Gender Empowerment

Year	Conference	Key Issue
1968	United Nations International Conference on Human Rights (Teheran)	"Parents have a basic human right to decide freely and responsibly on the number and spacing of their children."
1974	World Population Conference (Bucharest)	"The responsibility of couples and individuals [should take] into account the needs of their living and future children, and their responsibilities toward the community."
1975	International Women's Year Conference (Mexico City)	"The human body, whether that of a woman or man, is inviolable, and respect for it is a fundamental element of human dignity and freedom."
1979	Convention on the Elimination of All Forms of Discrimination Against Women (New York)	Article 12 calls on countries to "take all appropriate measures to eliminate discrimination against women in the field of health care in order to ensure, on a basis of equality of men and women, access to health care services, including those related to family planning."
1984	World Population Conference (Mexico City)	"Governments can do more to assist people in making their reproductive decisions in a responsible way. [Family planning is] a matter of urgency."
1992	United Nations Conference on Environment and Development (Rio de Janeiro)	Agenda 21 calls for "women-centered, women-managed, safe and accessible, responsible planning of family size and service."
1993	United Nations World Conference on Human Rights (Vienna)	The Vienna Declaration includes nine paragraphs on "The Equal Status and Human Rights of Women," and, for the first time recognizes that "violence against women is a human-rights abuse."
1994	International Conference on Population and Development (Cairo)	Program of Action "reaffirms the basic human rights of all couples and individuals to decide freely and responsibly the number and spacing of children and to have the information, education, and means to do so."
1995	United Nations Fourth World Conference on Women (Beijing)	Sets a wide-ranging, ambitious agenda for promoting human development by addressing gender inequality and women's rights.
1999	United Nations Conference on World Population (The Hague)	Drafts recommendations on humane assistance for international family planning programs in the light of the possibility that the global population could start to decline in the late twenty-first century.
2002	World Summit on Sustainable Development (Johannesburg)	Drafts resolutions to combat abject and dehumanizing poverty, stressing the importance of reform to encourage gender equality and the rights of women in order to stimulate sustainable economic growth.
2004	United Nations Conference on the Human Rights Obligations of Multinational Corporations (Geneva)	Opens debate to create a code of human rights and gender equality obligations for businesses.
2005	United Nations Conference on Children (New York)	Creates standards to protect children from exploitation.

As gauged by the UN's Gender Empowerment Measure (GEM), women throughout the world continue to be disadvantaged relative to men in various ways. They have less access to primary education and to advanced training in professional fields, such as science, engineering, law, and business. In addition, within occupational groups, they are almost always in less-prestigious jobs, where they receive less pay than men in comparable positions and they face formidable barriers to advancement. Although these and other gender differences have narrowed in recent years, particularly in Global North countries, gender inequalities remain widespread. Women's share of earned income in developing countries is less than a third of men's. Furthermore, their share of administrative and managerial jobs is minuscule. Only 5 percent of top corporate positions worldwide are held by women. Much the same holds true in politics: Since 1900 only 15 percent of the world's countries have had one or more female heads of state, and many of them came to power as widows of male rulers (*Harper's*, January 2008, 15). In 2007, women accounted for just 19 percent of the seats in parliaments worldwide (HDR 2008, 343-346).

The need to extend women equal rights has been long articulated by feminists and is now widely recognized. "The river of thought on human rights and development runs inexorably toward the emancipation of women everywhere and the equality of men and women," notes one report (*State of the World* 2002), which also warns, "eddies and rivulets carry the water backwards every day—as when pregnant girls are expelled from school, or when the genitals of young women are cut in a ritual destruction of their capacity for sexual pleasure."

Addressing women's rights is difficult because the issues touch deeply entrenched as well as widely divergent religious and cultural beliefs. In certain Islamic countries, for example, women must hide their faces with veils in public, and women and men are often completely separated in social and religious activities. For many in liberal Western countries, these traditions are difficult to understand. On the other hand, various Western ideas about gender roles can be perplexing to people elsewhere. These religious and cultural differences notwithstanding, international progress on securing women's human rights has been slow, with significant gender disparities persisting in Southern Asia, the Middle East, and Sub-Saharan Africa (Coleman 2005).

Gender myopia, denying the existence of the barriers that prevent women from having the same rights and opportunities as enjoyed by men, is pervasive. Much of feminist scholarship seeks to rectify this situation under the conviction that only the realization of the full potential of all people can enable true human development to occur.

The Precarious Life of Indigenous Peoples

indigenous peoples the native ethnic and cultural inhabitant populations within countries ruled by a government controlled by others, often referred to as the "Fourth World."

As noted in Chapter 6, where we first addressed the topic of nonstate actors (NGOs), **indigenous peoples** are members of ethnic groups native to a geographic location now controlled by another state or political group. The planet is populated by an estimated 6,000 separate indigenous "nations," each of which has a unique language, culture, and strong, often spiritual, ties to an ancestral homeland. Estimates suggest there are at least 300 million indigenous peoples comprising more than 5 percent of the world's population living in seventy countries. Recall that this segment of global society is conventionally referred to as the "Fourth World" to heighten awareness of their poverty and lack of self-rule (Wilmer 1993).

Many indigenous peoples feel persecuted because their livelihoods, lands, and cultures are threatened. In part, these fears are inspired by the 130 million indigenous peoples who were slaughtered between 1900 and 1987 by state-sponsored violence in their own countries (Rummel 1994). The mass killing of Armenians by Turks, of Jews (and other groups) by Hitler, of Cambodians by the Khmer Rouge, and of the Tutsi of Rwanda by the Hutu exemplify the atrocities committed during the past century. Responding to the tragedy of the Nazi holocaust, Polish jurist Raphael Lemkin coined the word **genocide** from the Greek word *genos* (race, people) and the Latin *caedere* (to kill), and called for it to be singled out as the gravest violation of human rights, a heinous crime the international community would be morally responsible for punishing (Turk 2001). In his view, genocide has several dimensions, including physical (the annihilation of members of a group), biological (measures taken to reduce the reproductive capacity of a group), and cultural (efforts to eliminate a group's language, literature, art, and other institutions).

genocide the deliberate extermination of an ethnic or minority group.

Various native peoples are now fighting back across the globe against the injustice they perceive states to have perpetrated against them. This is not to suggest that all indigenous minority groups are bent on using violence to attain power. The members of many such nonstate nations are divided about objectives, and militants who are prepared to fight for independence are usually in a minority. In fact, most Fourth World indigenous movements only seek a greater voice in redirecting the policies and allocation of resources within existing states and are eliciting the support of NGOs and IGOs to pressure states to recognize their claims and protect their rights.

A substantial number of indigenous movements in the last decade have successfully negotiated settlements resulting in devolution—the granting of political power to increase local self-governance. Examples include the Miskitos in Nicaragua, the Gagauz in Moldova, and most regional separatists in Ethiopia and in India's Assam region. Yet, as suggested by the hostilities between the Chechens and the Russian Federation, resolving clashes between aspiring peoples and established states can be extremely difficult.

The goal expressed in the UN Charter of promoting "universal respect for, and observance of, human rights and fundamental freedoms" for everyone is a challenge for many nationally diverse countries, because protecting the human rights and civil liberties of minority populations is inherently difficult. The division of these states along ethnic and cultural lines makes them inherently fragile. Consider the degree to which minority groups compose many states: for example, the share of indigenous populations in Bolivia is 70 percent and Peru, 40 percent. Or consider the number of distinct languages spoken in some countries, with Indonesia's 670 languages, Nigeria's 410, India's 380, Australia's 250, and Brazil's 210 being conspicuous examples (Durning 1993, 83, 86).

Racism and intolerance are hothouses for fanaticism and violence. The belief that one's nationality is superior to all others undermines the concept of human rights. Although interethnic competition is a phenomenon that dates back to biblical times, it remains a contemporary plague. According to *The Minorities at Risk Project* (http://www.cidcm.umd.edu/MAR), since 1998, 284 politically active minority groups suffering from organized discrimination have mobilized politically to defend themselves. Some analysts predict that conflict within and between ethnically divided states could become a major axis on which twenty-first-century world politics revolves.

The Global Refugee Crisis

refugees people who flee for safety to another country because of a well-founded fear of persecution.

Nowhere are the problems of human security more evident than in the refugee crisis that now prevails. **Refugees** are individuals whose religion, ethnicity, political opinions, or membership in a particular social group make them targets of persecution in their homelands and who migrate from their country of origin. According to the UN High Commissioner for Refugees (UNHCR), the world's refugee population by 2008 was approximately 9.9 million, or one out of each 360 people throughout the world (see Figure 13.2). The total number of "people of concern" includes some 12.8 internally **displaced people** as well as 5.8 million "stateless" people (though some estimates range as high as 11 million) who, like the Bidoun of the Middle East and the Biharis of South Asia, cannot prove their rights to citizenship anywhere and thus belong to no country.

displaced people people involuntarily uprooted from their homes but still living in their own countries.

Refugees and displaced persons are often the victims of war. For example, the Persian Gulf War in 1991 created a refugee population of 5 million; genocide in Rwanda in 1994 drove more than 1.7 million refugees from their homelands; and the armed conflict between 1991 and 1999 that accompanied the breakup of the former Yugoslavia uprooted nearly 3 million people. More recently, the UN estimates that 3.6 million people have been displaced during the war against Al Qaeda and the Taliban in Afghanistan.

A large proportion of the world's refugees and displaced people flee their homelands when ethnic and religious conflicts weaken the capacity of governments to maintain domestic law and order. As public authority dissolves amid rising civil strife, some people move because they do not receive police protection, cannot expect the prosecution of anyone who violates their rights, nor will they receive legal redress of their grievances.

People also leave home in search of economic opportunity. Legal migrants—particularly young people in the Global South without productive employment—are among those leaving at record rates, mostly to Global North countries, though migration also is occurring *between* developing Global South countries. The World Bank estimates that two in five migrants worldwide did not travel to the Global North, with a majority of migrants from sub-Saharan Africa remaining on their continent (*Economist*, January 5, 2008, 12). Nigeria, for example, attracts workers from Ghana; South Africa, from Tanzania and Zimbabwe. Foreign workers from Global South countries make up over 80 percent of the population of the United Arab Emirates.

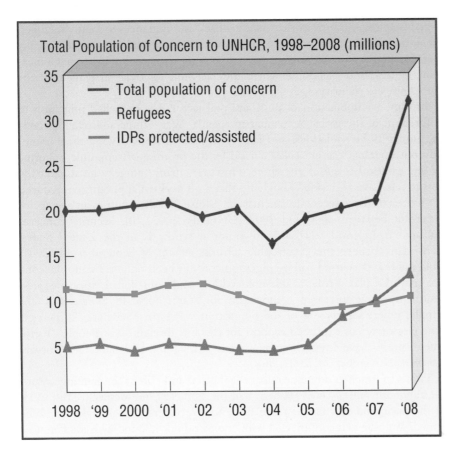

FIGURE 13.2 The World Refugee Crisis

The number of "people of concern" to the UN High Commissioner for Refugees between 1960 and 2008 exceeded 500 million. This figure shows the trends in refugees and internally displaced persons (IDPs) from 1998 to 2008.

SOURCE: UNHCR (2007, 4).

Some leaving their home states are the best educated and most talented, causing a serious **brain drain**. For instance, Moroccan engineers frequently migrate to France, and numerous Malawian nurses have relocated to Great Britain. However, the majority of migrants take low-wage jobs shunned by local inhabitants. Typically this means migrants earn less than the citizens of those states but more than they would earn in their homelands when performing the same tasks. Host countries may admit migrants (as Europe did during the 1970s guest worker era) not only because they accept low wages for undesirable jobs, but also because in many places the host pays little if anything for migrants' health, education, and welfare needs. On the other hand, the home (sending) countries sometimes encourage people to emigrate as a way of exporting unwanted elements of the population, reducing unemployment, or in the expectation that the

brain drain the exodus of the most educated people from their homeland to a more prosperous foreign country where the opportunities for high incomes are better, which deprives their homeland of their ability to contribute to its economic development.

emigrants will send much of their income back as remittances to family members in their homeland. India receives $24 billion a year in remittances, more than any other country, but remittances have a higher proportional impact in Guinea-Bissau, Eritrea, and Tajikistan, where they account for over 35 percent of the GDP (*Economist*, January 5, 2008, 11-12).

In sum, a combination of push and pull factors has propelled migration to the forefront of the global humanitarian agenda. War, ethnic and religious conflict, human rights violations, and famine all *push* millions beyond their homelands; but migrants also are *pulled* abroad by the promise of economic opportunity and political freedom elsewhere. However, many refugees are finding the doors to safe havens closing. Tougher policies on **asylum** applicants has reduced the number of those receiving sanctuary in Global North countries an average of 11 percent between 2006 and 2007 (UNHCR 2007, 10). Security concerns stimulated by terrorist fears are sometimes at work, as in the United States, where many believe the catastrophic terrorist attacks of September 11, 2001, would not have occurred had immigration controls been tighter. Economic concerns may also play a role, as unemployed low and semi-skilled citizens express resentment about increased competition for scarce jobs. In Switzerland, for example, where 24 percent of the population was born elsewhere, 29 percent of the electorate has expressed support for the anti-foreign Swiss People's Party. Similar patterns have emerged among voters in Belgium, Denmark, and Norway (*Economist*, November 24, 2007, 56).

Efforts to toughen domestic refugee legislation and criteria for granting asylum raise important ethical issues. Where will the homeless, the desperate, the weak and the poor find sanctuary—a safe place to live where human rights are safeguarded? Will the rich countries act with compassion or respond with indifference? And more broadly, what is the best way to view human security and reconcile it with national security? These questions may involve irreconcilable values, and will thus make the global refugee crisis a topic of intense debate for years to come.

asylum the provision of sanctuary to safeguard refugees escaping from the threat of persecution in the country where they hold citizenship.

RESPONDING TO HUMAN RIGHTS ABUSES

The idea of human rights has advanced over the past few decades from a mere slogan to a program of action. As the examples of the status of women, indigenous peoples, and refugees illustrate, much work remains to be done on implementing the human rights program. Nevertheless, as former UN Secretary-General Kofi Annan frequently points out, "States are now widely understood to be instruments at the service of their people, and not *vice versa*."

Internationally Recognized Human Rights

The body of legal rules and norms designed to protect individual human beings is anchored in the ethical requirement that every person should be treated with equal concern and respect. The Universal Declaration of Human Rights, unanimously adopted by the UN General Assembly on December 10, 1948, is the most authoritative statement of these norms. It "establishes a broad range of civil and political rights, including freedom of assembly, freedom of thought and expression, and the right to participate in government. The declaration also proclaims that social and economic rights are indispensable, including the right to education, the right to work, and the right to participate in the cultural life of the community. In addition, the preamble boldly asserts that 'it is essential, if man is not to be compelled to have recourse, as a last resort, to rebellion against tyranny and oppression, that human rights should be protected by the rule of law'" (Clapham 2001). These rights have since been codified and extended in a series of treaties, most notably in the International Covenant on Civil and Political Rights, and the International Covenant on Economic, Social, and Cultural Rights (which were both open for signature in 1966 and entered into force a decade later).

There are many ways to classify the rights listed in these treaties. Charles Beitz (2001, 271), an authority on international ethics, groups them into five categories.

1. *Rights of the person:* "Life, liberty, and security of the person; privacy and freedom of movement; ownership of property; freedom of thought, conscience, and religion, including freedom of religious teaching and practice 'in public and private'; and prohibition of slavery, torture, and cruel or degrading punishment."

2. *Rights associated with the rule of law:* "Equal recognition before the law and equal protection of the law; effective legal remedy for violation of legal rights; impartial hearing and trial; presumption of innocence; and prohibition of arbitrary arrest."

3. *Political rights:* "Freedom of expression, assembly, and association; the right to take part in government; and periodic and genuine elections by universal and equal suffrage."

4. *Economic and social rights:* "An adequate standard of living; free choice of employment; protection against unemployment; 'just and favorable remuneration'; the right to join trade unions; 'reasonable limitation of working hours'; free elementary education; social security; and the 'highest attainable standard of physical and mental health.

5. *Rights of communities:* "Self-determination and protection of minority cultures."

Although the multilateral treaties enumerating these rights are legally binding on the states ratifying them, many have either not ratified them or have done so with significant reservations. When states specify reservations, they are expressing agreement with the broad declarations of principle contained in these treaties while indicating that they object to certain specific provisions and elect not to be bound by them. The United States, for example, ratified the International Covenant on Civil and Political Rights with reservations in 1992, but has not ratified the International Covenant on Economic, Social, and Cultural Rights. As this example illustrates, countries who agree with the general principle that all human beings possess certain rights that cannot be withheld may still disagree on the scope

AFP/Getty Images

Human Rights versus States' Rights How a state treats its own citizens was, until very recently, its own business under the nonintervention rule in international law. Now the international community has defined the humane treatment of people as a fundamental human right, and eighty-nine countries have abolished the death penalty because they saw it as a violation of human rights. Other countries do not see the death penalty as a violation of human rights, however. Shown here are a group of alleged criminals who have been sentenced to death in China. The United States, China, Iran, Pakistan, Sudan, and Iraq accounted for nine out of ten known executions worldwide in 2006 (*Economist*, April 28, 2007, 69–70).

of these rights. Thus, some emphasize rights associated with the rule of law and political rights; while others stress the importance of economic and social rights.

The Challenge of Enforcement

Once the content of human rights obligations was enumerated in multilateral treaties, international attention shifted to monitoring their implementation and addressing violations. The policy question now facing the world is what steps can and should be taken to safeguard these rights (see Application: Human Rights Start in Small Places, Close to Home). A consensus has yet to be reached on the extent to which the international community has a responsibility to intervene in order to enforce human rights. As the International Commission on Intervention and State Sovereignty noted in its December 2001 report, *The Responsibility to Protect*, "If intervention for human protection purposes is to be

---

APPLICATION   Human Rights Start in Small Places, Close to Home

---

The failure of the international community to take timely, decisive action in 1994 to stop the genocide in Rwanda prompted many people to ask whether states pick which cases they respond to based on cold calculations of national security interest. Those that do not significantly affect the interests of the permanent members of the UN Security Council, they fear, tend to be ignored. In the following passage, Mary Robinson, who served as the president of Ireland (1990–1997) and as UN High Commissioner for Human Rights (1997–2002), points out that the United Nations is more active in responding to alleged human rights abuses than most people realize.

> Since I was appointed United Nations High Commissioner for Human Rights ..., I have been continuously confronted by the challenge of how human rights can best be secured and defended. Most people know about the gross human rights violations that are all too common in our modern world ... but I would like to draw your attention today to less well-known forms of abuse that are all too prevalent. I refer to the countless individual communications received by my Office each day on behalf of people in detention, women who are victims of violence, children who have been abused and tortured, human rights defenders who are harassed, journalists who have been kidnapped, people who have disappeared, migrant workers who have been victimized, people who have been displaced, refugees and indigenous people who have been intimidated.

> These appeals for help not only come in ever-increasing numbers but also from almost all the countries of the world. Most of the communications are dealt with quietly and do not come to public attention. It can be difficult, therefore, for the public to appreciate the extent and geographic spread of human rights abuses ....

> I see my own challenge in this respect as being to ensure that these allegations are effectively investigated, to redress the wrongs suffered by the victims, and to bring the perpetrators to justice....

> ...Human rights should not be thought of as something for other people or other countries and not for your own country .... Human rights are universal, and, unfortunately, so are human rights abuses. Eleanor Roosevelt, one of the chief architects of the Universal Declaration [of Human Rights], reminds us that "human rights start in small places, close to home" (Robinson 2006, 284–285).

By underscoring the universality of human rights, Robinson counters the argument advanced by former Prime Minister Lee Kuan Yew of Singapore that the prevailing liberal interpretation of rights is not consistent with the culture and political traditions of Asia. Asian values, he contends, emphasize social cohesion and stability over individual freedom and liberty. For Robinson, the yearning for individual rights exists everywhere; it is not a uniquely Western phenomenon.

---

accepted, including the possibility of military action, it remains imperative that the international community develop consistent, credible, and enforceable standards to guide state and intergovernmental practice."

Agreement about the principles that should guide **humanitarian intervention** has proven elusive. The issue is not whether there exists a compelling need to do something about populations at risk of slaughter, starvation, or persecution; the issue is about how to craft a just response, when any response will interfere in the domestic affairs of a sovereign state. The rationale for intervening into the internal affairs of other states has been expressed by William Schulz, the executive director of the NGO Amnesty International. Political realists, he argues, "regard the pursuit of rights as an unnecessary, sometimes even a dangerous extravagance, often at odds with our national interest. What they seem rarely to garner is that in far more cases than they will allow, defending human rights is a prerequisite to *protecting* that interest." Human rights buttress political and

humanitarian intervention the use of peacekeeping forces by foreign states or international organizations to protect endangered people from gross violations of their human rights.

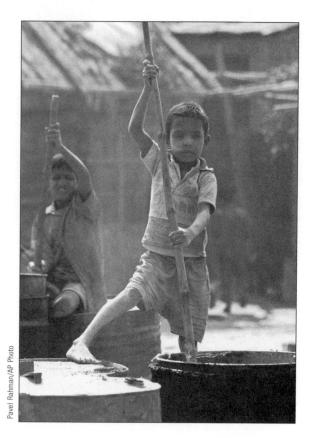

Pavel Rahman/AP Photo

Child Labor in a Global Market Political activists frequently express concern about the human rights of children. The UN Children's Fund estimated in 2005 that some 640 million children worldwide lacked adequate shelter, 270 million were without health care, and 15 million were orphaned because of AIDS. Many are victims of human trafficking, often ending up as soldiers or prostitutes. Although some countries see child labor as exploitative and have laws prohibiting it, others do not. Here children work heating and mixing rubber in a Bangladesh balloon factory, producing goods under conditions that are more hazardous than those where labor laws protect workers.

economic freedom "which in turn tends to bring international trade and prosperity. And governments that treat their own people with tolerance and respect tend to treat their neighbors in the same way" (Schulz 2001, 13, 14).

Humanitarian intervention refers to actions taken by the international community to assist the population of a state experiencing unacceptable, persistent levels of human suffering caused by natural disaster, political collapse, or deliberate government policy (Malaquias 2001). The decision to engage in humanitarian intervention is controversial, because it pits the legal principle of territorial sovereignty against what some see as a moral duty to protect vulnerable populations from egregious violations of human rights. Because concerns for human rights have gained stature under international law and are being monitored more closely by IGOs and NGOs than ever before, we can expect human rights to receive continuing attention, as long as people continue to be in need of help when they are caught in emergency situations such as the threat of famine or genocide.

The global community has expanded its legal protection of human rights significantly over the past fifty years. As Table 13.2 shows, a large number of conventions have been enacted that have steadily endowed individuals with

T A B L E 13.2   Major Conventions in the Development of International Human Rights

1948	Universal Declaration of Human Rights
1949	Convention on the Prevention and the Punishment of the Crime of Genocide
1950	Convention for the Suppression of the Traffic of Persons and the Exploitation of the Prostitution of Others
1951	Convention Relating to the Status of Refugees
1953	Convention on the Political Rights of Women
1959	Declaration of the Rights of the Child
1965	International Convention on the Elimination of All Forms of Racial Discrimination
1966	International Covenant on Civil and Political Rights
1966	International Covenant on Economic, Social, and Cultural Rights
1966	Optional Protocol to the International Covenant on Civil and Political Rights
1967	Declaration of Territorial Asylum
1969	Inter-American Convention on Human Rights
1973	Principles of International Co-Operation in the Punishment of War Crimes and Crimes against Humanity
1977	Protocols on Humanitarian Law for International Armed Conflicts and Noninternational Armed Conflicts
1979	Convention on the Elimination of All Forms of Discrimination Against Women
1981	Declaration on the Elimination of All Forms of Intolerance and of Discrimination Based on Religion or Belief
1984	Convention against Torture and Other Cruel, Inhuman, or Degrading Treatment or Punishment
1989	Second Optional Protocol to the International Covenant on Civil and Political Rights, Aiming at the Abolition of the Death Penalty
1989	Convention on the Rights of the Child
1991	Convention on the Prevention and Suppression of Genocide
1992	Declaration of Principles of International Law on Compensation to Refugees
1993	Vienna Convention on Human Rights
1993	Declaration on the Rights of Persons Belonging to National or Ethnic, Religious, or Linguistic Minorities
1993	Declaration on the Elimination of Violence against Women
1994	African Convention on Human and Peoples' Rights
2000	Convention Prohibiting Trafficking of Women and Children for Prostitution
2000	International Convention for the Suppression of the Financing of Terrorism
2002	Protocol to the Convention against Torture and Other Cruel, Inhuman or Degrading Treatment or Punishment

Note: The International Covenant on Civil and Political Rights, the International Covenant on Economic, Social, and Cultural Rights, and the Optional Protocol were all adopted in 1966 and entered into force in 1976.

rights—asserting that people must be treated as worthy of the freedom and dignity traditionally granted by international law to states and rulers. "The old assumption that national sovereignty trumps all other principles in international relations is under attack as never before" (Rieff 1999, 67). Nevertheless, the persistence of human suffering undermines the standards for a just global society called for by the Universal Declaration of Human Rights. "As with most declarations of faith, their adherents—first and foremost governments—have frequently failed to live up to them [even though] practically all governments say they accept the basic code of conduct these declarations expound. The continuing effort to achieve and maintain those standards is the frontier between civilization and barbarism" (Urquhart 2001).

Promoting the rights and dignity of ordinary people around the world is a formidable challenge. Eleanor Roosevelt was a modern champion of this cosmopolitan ideal, and the energetic leadership she displayed was largely responsible for global acceptance in 1948 of the Universal Declaration of Human Rights. Her noble pursuit shows that one person can make a difference in transforming world politics. When thinking about the human condition in the early twenty-first century, we can profit by the inspiration of her nightly prayer: "Save us from ourselves and show us a vision of a world made new."

CHAPTER SUMMARY

- Although some of humanity enjoys an unprecedented standard of living, a daunting amount of poverty and misery is evident throughout the world. The concept of human security expands the traditional notion of protecting the state from military threats to safeguarding individuals from such threats as poverty and environmental degradation.

- Communitarianism and cosmopolitanism hold different interpretations of human rights: the former anchor them in particularistic moral values held by political communities; the latter, in universalistic moral values that one has simply by being human.

- Women throughout the world continue to be disadvantaged relative to men in various ways.

- Roughly 5 percent of the world's population is composed of indigenous peoples. Many of them feel persecuted because their livelihoods and cultures are threatened by the governments of those states in which they reside; consequently some have joined separatist movements to pursue self-determination, while others have tried to negotiate a measure of local self-governance.

- A combination of push and pull forces have propelled migration to the forefront of population dynamics. Migrants are pushed out of their homelands by war, famine, and human rights violations. They are pulled abroad by the hope of freedom and economic opportunity.

- Over the past fifty years, the United Nations has developed a detailed list of inherent, inalienable rights of all human beings. They can be grouped into five general categories: rights of the person, rights associated with the rule of law, political rights, economic and social rights, and rights of communities.

- Various international treaties and conventions have sought to protect human rights. However, agreement on the principles that should guide states on when humanitarian intervention is justifiable has proven elusive.

KEY TERMS

asylum

brain drain

communitarianism

cosmopolitanism

displaced people

genocide

human rights

human security

humanitarian
  intervention

indigenous peoples

refugees

SUGGESTED READINGS

Alston, Philip, Ryan Goodman, and Henry J. Steiner. *International Human Rights in Context: Law, Politics, Morals*, 3rd edition. New York: Oxford University Press, 2007.

Amstutz, Mark R. International Ethics, 3rd edition. Landham, MD: Rowman & Littlefield, 2008.

Forsythe, David P. *Human Rights in International Relations*, 2nd edition. Cambridge: Cambridge University Press, 2006.

Ishay, Micheline R. *The History of Human Rights: From Ancient Times to the Globalization Era*, 2nd edition. Berkeley: University of California Press, 2008.

Landman, Todd. *Protecting Human Rights*. Washington, DC: Georgetown University Press, 2006.

CRITICAL THINKING QUESTIONS

At 1:00 A.M. on December 20, 1989, U.S. troops supported by stealth aircraft invaded Panama in what President George H. W. Bush called Operation Just Cause. The purpose of the operation was to capture General Manuel Noriega, a military dictator who had gained control over Panama six years earlier. During his time in power, Noriega repressed opposition movements, manipulated elections, and ordered the murder of dissident political leaders. Up to this point, his ruthless behavior had been overlooked because he had previously assisted the United States in its fight against communism in Central America. By 1987, however, Noriega's human rights abuses as well as his involvement in narcotics trafficking and money laundering led Bush's predecessor, Ronald Reagan, to impose economic sanctions on Panama.

Sanctions did little to weaken Noriega's regime. On December 16, 1989, following the murder of an unarmed U.S. marine lieutenant by members of the Panama Defense Forces, the wounding of another American serviceman, and the arrest and brutal interrogation of a U.S. naval officer and his wife, Bush decided to remove Noriega by force. U.S. diplomats Thomas R. Pickering, speaking to the United Nations Security Council on December 20, and Luigi R. Einaudi, speaking to the Organization of American States (OAS) on December 22, justified the intervention by emphasizing America's responsibility to protect the Panamanian people from human rights abuses. Noriega, argued Pickering, "repeatedly obstructed the will of the Panamanian people." Panamanians, added Einaudi, were *"sick of stolen elections, sick of military dictatorships, sick of narco-strongmen, and sick of the likes of Manuel Noriega."* Both diplomats insisted that Washington was supporting the will of the Panamanian people, not simply acting out of its own interests (Panama: A Just Cause 1989, 1–3).

Moral appeals, such as those articulated by Pickering and Einaudi, can be powerful in foreign policy argumentation, swinging the weight of presumption in favor of intervention regardless of the real motives behind the decision to use force. Do you think that there was a moral imperative for the United States to take military action against the Noriega regime? Or do you think that the Bush administration masked its narrow political interests as expansive moral duties? Looking beyond this case to the larger question of international humanitarian engagement, who should have the responsibility to protect the victims of egregious human rights abuses? When is that responsibility acquired? What does it involve? How does the international community know when it is being appropriately discharged?

14

Population Dynamics and Global Environmental Politics

CHAPTER OUTLINE

Global Demographic Patterns

The Demographic Divide between the Global North and South

International Responses to Population Growth

Prospects for a Global Population Implosion

Environmental Security and Sustainable Development

The Ecopolitics of Energy

APPLICATION: Cartels and Commodity Power

The Ecopolitics of the Atmosphere

The Ecopolitics of Land and Water

Future Environmental Policy Choices

CONTROVERSY: How Should the World's Problems be Prioritized?

> Throughout history, humans have lived on the Earth's sustainable yield—the interest from its natural endowment. Now, however, we are consuming the endowment itself.
>
> LESTER BROWN
> PRESIDENT, EARTH POLICY INSTITUTE

According to the folk tales of Central Asia, centuries ago an adviser to a powerful king invented an intriguing game. It was played by moving pieces on a board containing eight columns and eight rows of squares. The king was so delighted with the game that he offered to reward his adviser with gold and jewels. The adviser declined, protesting that he was a humble man with simple tastes. Rather than accept such a lavish reward, he asked that he be given a single grain of rice for the first square of his board game, twice for the second square, twice that for the third, and so on, until each of the 64 squares had their complement of rice. The king quickly agreed to what he believed was a modest request. When the Master of the Royal Granary counted out the grains, the numbers began small enough (1, 2, 4, 8, 16, 32, 64, ...), but before long, he realized the staggering numbers that would soon be involved. For the 64th square alone, 9,223,372,036,854,775,808 grains would be needed to meet the adviser's request. That would amount to roughly 153 billion tons of rice, enough to fill 31 million cargo ships full if each ship held approximately 5,000 tons (Dörner 1996, 111). Of course, that would be merely the amount of rice on the last square of the board game. The next-to-the-last square would take half as much, only 4,611,686,018,427,387,904 grains, the square before it, 2,305,843,009,213,693,952 grains, and so on.

The story of the king's adviser is a fable that reminds us of the consequences of exponential growth. Under certain conditions, amazing configurations can develop over time. Ever since the Reverend Thomas Malthus proposed in 1798 that when unchecked, population increases in a geometric ratio (e.g., 1 to 2, 2 to 4, 4 to 8) while subsistence increases in only an arithmetic ratio (1 to 2, 2 to 3, 3 to 4), demographers have speculated about the long-term consequences of rapid population growth. Earth's population at the beginning of the twentieth century totaled 1.7 billion people; today it has reached 6.7 billion. Every two years, it grows roughly by the size of Russia, with over 200,000 people added to the world total every day. Will these kinds of increases in the world's population continue in the decades ahead? If so, what impact would they have on the planet's **carrying capacity**—the earth's ability to support and sustain life? Will population growth outstrip natural resources? Can enough food be produced to feed the billions who will be born in the future? These concerns have attracted the attention of various scholars and policy makers who are studying how current demographic and environmental trends may affect the global future.

carrying capacity the maximum biomass that can be supported by a given territory.

The **tragedy of the commons** is a metaphor that highlights the potential impact of human behavior on the planet's resources and its delicately balanced ecological systems. First articulated in 1833 by English political economist William Foster Lloyd, the metaphor was later popularized by ecologist Garrett Hardin. It depicts a medieval English village, where the village green was common pasture on which all villagers could graze their cattle. Freedom of access to the commons was a cherished value. Sharing the common grazing area worked well as long as usage by individuals (and their cattle) didn't reduce the land's usefulness to everyone else. Assuming the villagers were driven by the profit motive and no laws existed to restrain their greed, herders had an incentive to increase their stock

tragedy of the commons a metaphor, widely used to explain the impact of human behavior on ecological systems, that explains how rational self-interested behavior by individuals may have a destructive collective impact.

as much as possible. In the short run, the addition of one more animal would produce a personal gain whose feeding costs would be borne by everyone. But if everyone increased their stock of cattle, in the long run the village green would be destroyed by overgrazing. The lesson? "Ruin is the destination toward which all men rush," Hardin (1968) concluded, "each pursuing his own best interest."

This chapter explores the impact of humanity on the natural environment and how it will most likely affect the global future. The chapter opens with an examination of prevailing trends in demography and ecology, and then considers the ways that these trends interact, often creating global environmental problems that can be exacerbated when, like in the tragedy of the commons metaphor, self-interested actors pursue personal, short-run gains without anticipating the side effects and long-term repercussions of their behavior.

GLOBAL DEMOGRAPHIC PATTERNS

How many people can the earth support? This question is almost as old as recorded history. According to demographer Joel Cohen (2005), cuneiform tablets from three and a half millennia ago show that the Babylonians worried that the world already had too many people. Over the last half-century alone, numerous estimates have been made, with some analysts warning about over-population and others concluding that there was little reason to fret about con-tinued population growth. In order to get a better understanding of this issue, it is helpful to trace the global trends in population growth, giving particular atten-tion to changes in fertility and mortality rates (see Figure 14.1).

The story of population growth is told in its statistics: The annual rate of population growth in the twentieth century increased from less than 1 percent in 1900 to a peak of 2.2 percent in 1964. It has since decreased to about 1.2 percent. Despite this recent drop in rate, however, the absolute number of peo-ple *added* each year has been significant, growing from 16 million in 1900 to a peak of 88 million in 1988, and thereafter falling to a current increase of about 74 million annually. Earth is certain to have many more people by the mid-twenty-first century, well beyond the 6.7 billion already on the planet. Yet the feared "population explosion" once believed certain is now unlikely.

If the probability of explosive population growth overwhelming the planet's carrying capacity has decreased, why then do population issues remain so contro-versial in world politics? We can begin to answer that question by exploring how population dynamics are affecting countries in the Global North and South in different ways.

The Demographic Divide between the Global North and South

Population growth rates are not the same throughout the world. They are much higher in the developing Global South countries than in the wealthy countries in

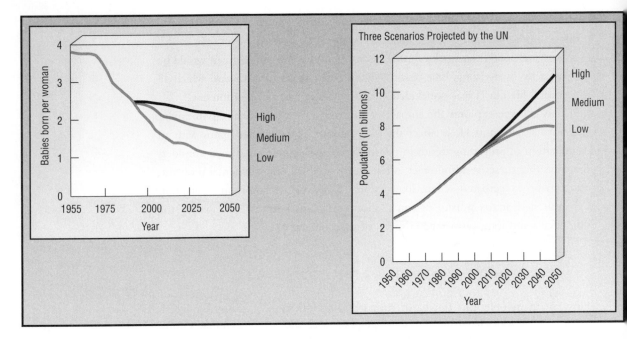

FIGURE 14.1 World Population Growth Projections to the Year 2050

Between 1.2 and 2.4 billion additional people will be living on the earth by the middle of the twenty-first century, depending on how fast fertility rates (the number of babies born for each woman) fall (see figure on left) and life spans increase. The figure on the right sketches three potential scenarios for the future, showing that by 2050 world population is expected to be between 8 billion (low variant) and 11 billion (high variant), with the medium variant producing 9.3 billion.

SOURCE: United Nations Population Division.

the Global North, a trend that is expected to continue. This "demographic divide," as projected in Figure 14.2, suggests why population dynamics have important political and economic ramifications.

Global population cannot be expected to stabilize until it falls below replacement-level fertility in the developing countries. Today the worldwide average number of children born to a woman during her lifetime—the total **fertility rate**—is 2.7. However, projections for the entire globe overlook the different rates for rich and poor countries. Roughly 95 percent of population growth worldwide is centered in the developing Global South, already home to 85 percent of the world's population. Hence, global population growth is the result of new births in the developing Global South, where the fertility rate averaged 3.1 children for each mother (and 5.8 for the least-developed countries). In contrast, the wealthy, developed Global North's fertility rate has actually declined to 1.6 children for each woman, which is below **replacement-level fertility.** Fertility rates around the world must decrease to an average of 2.1 children for each woman in order to fall to replacement level. Yet,

fertility rate the average number of children born to women during their reproductive years.

replacement-level fertility one couple replacing themselves with two children, so that a country's population will remain stable if this rate prevails.

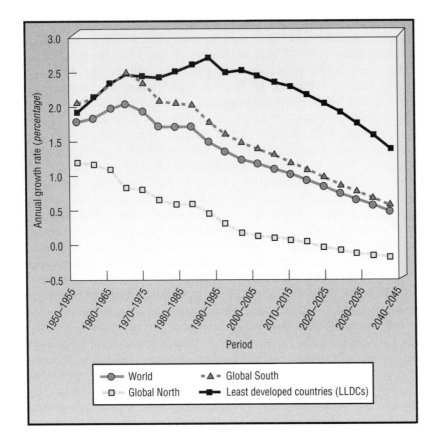

FIGURE 14.2 The Global North—Global South Population Divide

The UN estimates that we can expect a slowing of population growth rates that leads eventually to a reduction in world population. Nearly all the population growth in the twenty-first century will occur in the Global South. Assuming continuing declines in fertility, Global South population is expected to rise to 8.2 billion in 2050 (in the absence of such declining birth rates, the less-developed countries will reach 11.9 billion by 2050).

SOURCE: United Nations Population Division.

throughout much of the Global South, the preferred family size remains far in excess of the replacement level, especially in the poorest countries. Fertility rates in Niger, Guinea-Bissau, and Burundi, for example, are 7.10, 7.07, and 6.80, respectively (*Economist* 2007, 18).

The developing countries' high fertility rates have important economic consequences. Almost all the problems in the North-South dispute can be traced to disparities in income and economic growth that are directly linked to the differentials in population growth rates. A brief look at these dynamics completes the picture of ongoing political conflict between the haves and the have-nots.

Population Momentum. The surge in the Global South's population in the twentieth century is easily explained as a combination of high birthrates and rapidly falling death rates. But to understand the population surge projected throughout the twenty-first century—when birthrates throughout the world will decline—we have to understand the force of population momentum, the continued growth of population for decades into the future because of the large number of women now entering their childbearing years. Like the inertia of a descending airliner when it first touches down on the runway, population growth simply cannot be halted even with an immediate, full application of the brakes. Instead, many years of high fertility mean that more women will be entering their reproductive years than in the past. Not until the size of the generation giving birth to children is no larger than the generation among which deaths are occurring will the population growth come to a halt. Because of population momentum, the number of people is expected to triple by 2050 in Afghanistan, Burkina Faso, Burundi, Chad, Congo, Democratic Republic of Congo, Guinea-Bissau, Liberia, Mali, Niger, and Uganda (J. Cohen 2005, 50).

Sub-Saharan Africa and Western Europe illustrate the force of population momentum. Africa's demographic profile is one of rapid population growth, as each new age group (cohort) contains more people than the one before it. Thus, even if individual African couples choose to have fewer children than their parents, Africa's population will continue to grow because there are now more men and women of childbearing age than ever before. In contrast, Europe's population profile is one of slow growth, as recent cohorts have been smaller than preceding ones. In fact, Europe has moved beyond replacement-level fertility to become a "declining" population, described by low birthrates and a growing number of people who survive middle age. A product of an extended period of low birthrates, low death rates, and increased longevity, Europe is best described as an aging society, where the low birthrates and aging populations have caused alarms that the number of European newborns will not be sufficient to renew populations.

As the Global North generally ages, much of the Global South continues to mirror the sub-Saharan African profile: Because each cohort is typically larger than the one before it, the number of young men and women entering their reproductive years will also continue to grow. The resulting differences in these demographic momentums will produce quite different population profiles in the developed and the developing worlds. The example of Germany illuminates the contrast. Germany has at present a low birthrate of 1.6 per woman and a large number of people who survive middle age; in the year 2030, people over sixty-five will account for almost half the adult population (compared with one-fifth in 2001). The net result will be that Germany's total population of 82.7 million will shrink to about 70 million, and the number of working-age people will fall about 25 percent (from 40 million to 30 million). The figures are similar for most other developed countries: fertility rates in Japan, Greece, and Russia are 1.27, 1.33, and 1.34, respectively (*Economist* 2007, 18). Thus, the population divide will grow; Global North countries will become older and smaller. By 2050, for example, the size of Japan's population will decline 21.6 percent, with almost 36 percent of the population composed of people age sixty-five or older, compared to 21 percent in 2007. If the current retirement and demographic trends continue, Japan at mid-century will have only 1.5 workers for every pensioner. The only Global North country that is an exception to this pattern is the United States, with a fertility rate roughly at replacement level. By the middle of the century, America will be the only developed country among the world's twenty most-populous countries.

The Demographic Transition. High rates of population growth place an enormous burden on a country's economy. The theory of **demographic transition** attempts to explain when population growth in the Global South countries will slow, easing the economic strain on developing countries.

Based on the historical experience of Europe and North America, the theory proposes that countries pass through a series of stages as they modernize. The first stage, traditional society, is characterized by a combination of high birth and death rates, which produce relatively stable populations. Birth rates are high because children provide labor that contributes to family income; death rates, because disease is unchecked by effective, widespread health programs. As societies modernize, they enter a second stage: Birth rates remain high, but improvements in nutrition, medical techniques, and public health facilities reduce death rates, which lead to increased population growth. Once people begin to live longer lives, couples expect more of their children to reach adulthood, and thus they can achieve their desired number of surviving children with fewer births. In this third stage, birth rates decline along with death rates, yielding little or no population growth.

Demographic transition is now under way virtually everywhere in the world, but at much different rates in different countries and regions. Whereas in the Global North, birth and death rates have converged at a low level, in most of the Global South, birth rates have remained high but death rates have declined rapidly due, in part, to more effective public health programs. If these trends continue, Global North countries will possess an increasingly aged world population.

According to the U.S. Census Bureau, the world's senior population over the age of sixty had tripled over the past fifty years, and, at the present rate, in fifty years the number of people older than sixty will again triple. Thus by the middle of the century, the elderly would comprise a third of humanity, outnumbering the world's youths, with two older persons for every child. Furthermore, those eighty years or over are expected to increase even faster, more than fivefold by 2050.

This unprecedented aging of the world could create economic problems of crisis proportions. With the percentage of taxpaying workers shrinking, the budgets of state governments could be overwhelmed by attempts to provide retirement and health benefits for the elderly. In addition, dwindling birthrates, lengthening life spans, and early retirements could spell trouble for a worker-hungry Global North in need of immigrants to supply labor. The graying of world population does not leave the developing countries immune from the challenge faced by the Global North, because in developing countries the pace of aging is even faster, with the proportion of the population over sixty rising from 8 percent in 2002 to 20 percent in 2050. This gives the poorest societies less time to cope as they continue to simultaneously try to confront the scourges of poverty and disease.

Urbanization. When interpreting demographic projections, it is also important to take into account population density. Some states are crowded and others

demographic transition an explanation of population changes that highlights the role of birth and death rates in moving countries from stable to rapidly increasing and finally to declining populations.

are not. For example, Singapore is the most congested, with 6,302 people for each square kilometer; Australia is the most wide open, with only three people per square kilometer (WDI 2007, 16). This difference represents another kind of demographic divide: urban versus rural (see Map 14.1). As of 2005, five mega-cities had populations over 15 million and another fifteen had between 10 and 15 million inhabitants. By 2050, demographers predict that 75 percent of the world's population will live in cities. Already 97.2 percent of Belgians reside in urban areas, as do 93.4 percent of Venezuelans and 90.1 percent of Argentineans. During the next 30 years, more than 80 percent of the planet's urban growth will occur in Africa and Asia, currently home to eighteen of the world's fastest-growing urban areas (*Foreign Policy*, January/February, 2008, 42). This surge in urbanization is likely to aggravate existing environmental problems, straining supplies of energy and resources while complicating efforts to control pollution and provide adequate sanitation.

International Responses to Population Growth

The international community convened its first World Population Conference in Bucharest during 1974 to address policy issues raised by the world's growing population. Many Global South delegates concluded from Europe's and North America's demographic transitions that declining fertility rates flowed more or less automatically from economic growth and proposed policies that focused on economic development rather than population control. They called on the Global North for economic assistance, reasoning that development was the best contraceptive.

M A P 14.1 Global Population Density

Whereas the share of the world's population living in urban areas was nearly 30 percent in 1950, today it stands at about 50 percent. This map shows the clustering of people in the world's urban areas.

SOURCE: *Atlantic Monthly*, October 2005, 48–49.

A decade later, a second World Population Conference was held in Mexico City. By then, a new consensus had converged around the critical importance of family planning. However, the United States, previously a major advocate of this viewpoint, argued that free-market principles ought to take precedence over government intervention in population matters. Markets, asserted the U.S. delegation, effectively maintain a balance among population, resources, and the environment.

However, market mechanisms did not solve the population problem. In 1994 the UN-convened International Conference on Population and Development in Cairo concluded that population stabilization could be achieved only in conjunction with efforts to promote sustainable economic growth, supported by increases in foreign aid. This conclusion was reaffirmed at the August 2002 Johannesburg World Conference on Sustainable Development. Specific goals were set at both conferences, which included improving access to family planning services, health care, and primary education, as well as lowering the rates of infant, child, and maternal mortality. Because the goals emanating from these conferences were only recommendations, few countries acted on them over the ensuing years. Moreover, since domestic political support for foreign aid has declined among donor countries, large subsidies for family planning programs in the Global South are unlikely.

Prospects for a Global Population Implosion

The discussions at Cairo and Johannesburg assumed that population growth would continue in the Global South. It is worth bearing in mind that population projections can be misleading, because natural or human-made events may overturn the conditions that produced today's trends. For example, current projections could be invalidated overnight by a nuclear war or a terrorist act of mass destruction with biological weapons. Other threats also could produce a **population implosion**—a severe reduction in world population. We take a brief look at two possible sources of implosion: **pandemics** and famine.

population implosion a rapid reduction of population that reverses a previous trend toward progressively larger populations.

pandemic a disease that spreads throughout one or more continents.

The Threat of Contagious Diseases   On a global level, life expectancy at birth has increased each year since 1950, climbing to 64.3 years by 2007. However, this trend could be reversed if globally transmittable diseases cut into the extension of life spans made possible by improvements in health care, nutrition, water quality, and public sanitation. For example, drug-resistant strains of tuberculosis (TB) have developed recently, and they can be passed from one country to the next by a sneeze on an international flight. Preventing the outbreak of a highly contagious disease within any region of the world is virtually impossible in an age of globalization.

The grim possibility that virulent disease will reduce the world's population is evident from the spread of the human immunodeficiency virus (HIV) that causes AIDS (acquired immune deficiency syndrome). According to data from the World Health Organization, AIDS has killed over 25 million people worldwide since 1981. In 2007, about 33 million people were living with HIV and, on average, every day almost 5,500 died of AIDS. Every hour more than 300 people become infected, including forty-two children. Antiretroviral treatment can help manage the disease, but patients in the Global South typically lack access to treatment.

Most health experts agree that at the current pace, some countries could lose one-fifth of their gross domestic product due to the effects of AIDS on their workforce. Sub-Saharan Africa has suffered the most, accounting for two-thirds of all HIV cases, with only 11 percent receiving treatment with antiretroviral drugs. Eastern Europe and Central Asia also face serious problems. Because infectious diseases respect no borders, nearly 30 million people worldwide could die from AIDS over the next two decades.

The Threat of Famine.   At the same time that medical experts worry that death rates due to tuberculosis, AIDS, Ebola, and other diseases could take a horrific toll on humanity, agricultural specialists shudder at the possibility of food shortages. If Earth's population grows to 9 billion, will food production keep pace? Whereas pessimists warn of mass starvation, optimists claim these fears are unwarranted, arguing that technological breakthroughs in the field of genetic engineering will revolutionize farming and feed future generations.

Genetically engineered crops are created to develop a desired trait, such as herbicide tolerance or increased oil content. Unlike crop varieties developed through traditional plant breeding, **transgenic crops** often contain genes from unrelated species—of plant, animal, bacteria, or other origin—with which the crop could not reproduce naturally. Despite lingering consumer unease, genetically engineered crops are gaining ground. In 2005, over 820 million hectares were planted with transgenic crops, primarily soybeans, corn, and cotton. The United States accounts for three-fourths of global production, with Argentina, Brazil, Canada, and China included among the world's major producers. Moreover, as the risk of plant and animal extinction escalates, some scientists have tried to replicate certain species through cloning—an approach that has met with considerable opposition from groups who feel that tampering with life is immoral.

Geneticists could revolutionize agriculture and transform the capability of the planet to feed the world's growing population. However, the increasing availability of commercially produced and globally marketed genetically engineered agricultural products is a growing controversy. Should scientists manipulate nature for human needs? Are gene-spliced plants and hormone-treated meat safe? Do crops created through genetic engineering contain allergens that may cause serious allergic reactions and endanger public health?

Mounting a sustained effort to address the consequences of world population growth remains a formidable challenge. An interdependent and rapidly globalizing world promises that none will be immune to population trends, especially those that strain the natural environment on which we depend. Population politics are linked directly to the issue of protecting the planet's ecology, which we now examine.

---

transgenic crops new crops with improved characteristics created artificially through genetic engineering, which combines genes from species that would not naturally interbreed.

ENVIRONMENTAL SECURITY AND SUSTAINABLE DEVELOPMENT

When U.S. astronauts first viewed Earth from the Apollo spacecraft, they described how the clouds and continents flowed into one another without regard to the political boundaries humans had drawn across the planet. Improvement in space technology since the 1960s has enabled the world to see a different set of images—of atmospheric pollution that encircles the globe, of violent storms pounding coastlines with relentless fury, of massive holes in the ozone shield that protects humans from dangerous ultraviolet rays, and of vanishing forests and widening deserts.

To explore the linkage between population pressures and global environmental challenges, we need to examine *ecopolitics*—how political actors influence perceptions of, and policy responses to, managing the impact of human behavior on their environments. By taking an ecopolitical perspective, we can broaden our conception of security, pushing it to include processes that may imperil our ecological niche on the planet.

One of the key concepts embraced by those who look at security from ecopolitical perspectives is **sustainable development.** The level of international attention given to environmental issues increased significantly in 1972, when the United Nations convened the first UN Conference of the Human Environment in Stockholm. Conferences have since been held on a wide range of environmental topics, with scores of treaties negotiated and new international agencies put into place to promote cooperation and monitor environmental developments. The concept of sustainable development entered into popular discourse during the 1980s and today enjoys widespread support among governments and a broad range of NGOs that are active in shaping the global environmental agenda. According to the 1987 report of the World Commission on Environment and Development—popularly known as the "Brundtland Commission" after the Norwegian prime minister who chaired it—a "sustainable society" is one that "meets the needs of the present without compromising the ability of future generations to meet their own needs."

sustainable development improving the quality of life by reconciling economic needs with environmental protection.

Another milestone in the movement to foster sustainable development was the Earth Summit, which took place in Rio de Janeiro in 1992. Formally known as the UN Conference on Environment and Development, the meeting brought together more than 150 states, 1,400 nongovernmental organizations, and 8,000 journalists. Prior to the Earth Summit, environment and economic development had been treated separately—and often regarded as being in conflict with each other. In Rio, the concept of sustainability galvanized a simultaneous treatment of environmental and development issues, and paved the way for the UN World Summit on Sustainable Development that concluded in early September 2002 in Johannesburg. These and other international conferences have stressed that what happens anywhere ultimately affects conditions everywhere, and therefore protecting the global environment is a security issue.

Sustainability cannot be realized without dramatic changes in the social, economic, and political practices of an increasingly interconnected world. But is that possible? The metaphor of the tragedy of the commons provides little basis for optimism, whether applied to individuals or states. When rational, self-interested actors strive for relative gains in the absence of strong international regulation, everyone's well-being may plummet.

To better understand the multiple tensions that global environmental problems pose in an anarchical world, we turn next to consider three interrelated clusters of issues on the global ecopolitical agenda: (1) oil and energy, (2) climate change and ozone depletion, and (3) biodiversity and deforestation. The clusters illustrate the problems and pitfalls that states and nonstate actors (IGOs and NGOs) face as they seek environmental security and sustainable development.

The Ecopolitics of Energy

In April 1990, the average price for a barrel of internationally traded crude oil was less than $15. Five months later—stimulated by Iraq's invasion of the tiny oil sheikdom of Kuwait—it rose to more than $40. For the third time in less than two decades, the world suffered an "oil shock" when the price paid for the most widely used commercial energy source skyrocketed.

The 1990 Persian Gulf War was precipitated by Iraq's attempt to subjugate Kuwait and acquire its oil. Pointing to America's enormous thirst for petroleum, some critics of U.S. president George W. Bush maintained that his decision to go to war against Iraq in 2003 was influenced by economic considerations involving oil. While the president's supporters vigorously denied this charge, ensuring access to the region's oil is nonetheless critical to the economic fortunes of the Global North, because almost all the oil that is inexpensive to extract lies within the borders of a handful of countries around the Persian Gulf.

Global Patterns of Oil Consumption.   The importance of oil to the Global North generally and the United States in particular is evident from their disproportionate share of energy consumption. The average person living in Europe uses more than twice as much energy as people in the Global South, while the United States uses more than six times as much.

Oil consumption has been spiraling upward for decades. The International Energy Agency predicts that by 2030 the world will be using 50 percent more oil than today and warns that $3 trillion will need to be spent over the next two decades to meet the soaring global demand.

The industrialization of many emerging Global South economies has contributed to the growing demand, and the global shift to oil has been propelled by the aggressive production and promotion of a small group of multinational corporations (MNCs). Their operations encompass every aspect of the business, from exploration to the retail sale of products at their gas stations. For decades, their search for, production of, and marketing of low-cost oil was largely unhindered. Concessions from the oil-rich Middle East were easy to obtain, which reduced incentives for developing technologies for alternative energy sources.

Eventually, many of the world's major oil-producing states were able to wrest control from the oil companies, and they formed a **cartel** known as the Organization of Petroleum Exporting Countries (OPEC) in an effort to maximize profits. Because the resources OPEC controls cannot be easily replaced, it has been able to use oil as an instrument of coercive diplomacy (see Application: Cartels and Commodity Power). By cutting production to limit world supplies, OPEC can trigger sharp price increases to exert pressure on countries that rely on oil as their primary source of energy.

cartel an organization of the producers of a commodity that seeks to regulate the pricing and production of that commodity to increase revenue.

APPLICATION   Cartels and Commodity Power

Little more than a century ago, fuelwood was the world's primary energy source. As the mechanical revolution altered the nature of transportation, work, and leisure, coal began replacing fuelwood. New technological developments, particularly the internal combustion engine, then spurred the shift away from coal to oil. OPEC's emergence as a successful oil cartel in the 1970s derived from several factors. One was its ability to take control of production and pricing policies from multinational oil companies. A second factor was the growing dependence of much of the world on Middle Eastern oil. The third factor that contributed to OPEC's success was the absence of inexpensive energy alternatives in the face of growing worldwide demand for oil.

As OPEC began to realize the potential leverage that it had over oil-consuming countries, the possibility of using oil as a political weapon to affect the outcome of the unsettled Arab-Israeli dispute intrigued the organization's Arab members. Their common desire to defeat Israel was a principal element uniting them. Thus, when the Yom Kippur War broke out on October 6, 1973, the stage for using the oil weapon was set. In the passage below, Henry Kissinger, who served as secretary of state in the Nixon and Ford administrations, describes how OPEC's use of commodity power had an enormous psychological impact on policy makers in Global North countries.

> No crisis in the second half of the twentieth century fell on a world less prepared than the one triggered by the quadrupling of oil prices in the fall of 1973. Within the space of three months the global political and economic system found itself faced with a series of stark challenges threatening its very foundations.
>
> ... It was the Middle East War of 1973 that gave the oil-producing countries the pretext for unleashing their new bargaining power to its full extent. On October 16, 1973, OPEC raised the price of oil by 70 percent. ... On October 17 the Arab OPEC oil ministers ... agreed to reduce OPEC production by 5 percent in order to sustain the higher

oil price. On October 18, Saudi Arabia ... cut its production by 10 percent. On October 20, to protest the American airlift to Israel, Saudi Arabia announced a total embargo of oil exports to the United States and also to the Netherlands, which was deemed too supportive of Israel.

> The combined impact of these decisions precipitated an energy crisis lasting well over a decade. Because the principal Western policymakers lacked sufficient understanding of the oil market, their initial reactions made matters worse. Regulatory blunders at home exacerbated short-term shortages. In addition, the urgency and frequency of ... appeals to remove the embargo probably convinced the oil producers that they had discovered a marvelous new lever for extorting concessions.
>
> ... Soon other dangers loomed. Spurred by OPEC's success, producers of other commodities began exploring the prospects of organizing cartels of their own. ... Never before had nations so weak militarily ... been able to impose such strains on the international system (Kissinger 1999, 664, 666–667).

In Kissinger's (1982, 873) opinion, "The true impact of the embargo was psychological." Policy makers in oil-consuming countries feared further production cutbacks were on the horizon, "triggered a wave of panic buying by Europe and Japan, which constricted supplies and drove prices up even more." In the aftermath of this "oil shock" several lessons were drawn about cartels and commodity power. One was that the oil weapon could be used again. The inability of the major multinational oil companies to control the situation, as they had done for decades, was a second. Finally, with American oil production peaking two years before the onset of the Yom Kippur War, the events showed that even the world's foremost power had become vulnerable to foreign economic pressures as it lost energy self-sufficiency and imported over a third of the oil that it consumed.

Is Energy Security an Elusive Goal? The question of oil supplies has great importance to world politics, because petroleum is not a renewable resource and for every two barrels pumped out of the ground, the oil companies discover less than one new barrel. Production in the United States peaked thirty years ago, Russia peaked in 1987, and North Sea production appears to have peaked. Meanwhile, demand for oil keeps rising.

With somewhere between 1.2 and 3.7 trillion barrels of proven reserves that can supply the global market (depending on which estimates one accepts), the era of cheap, abundant oil is ending. One of the major problems the world faces with regard to these reserves is that they are concentrated in a small number of countries, many of which are politically unstable. Because OPEC members, who control approximately half of the world's oil reserves, are drawing down their reserves at half the average global rate, it seems almost inevitable that OPEC's share of the world oil market will grow. This means that OPEC is critical to global oil supply, the Middle East is critical to OPEC, and countries that depend on oil imports from this volatile source are highly vulnerable to disruptions. By 2025, world energy consumption is likely to double, and oil production may be approaching its peak. China, the world's second-largest consumer of oil after the United States, is expected to see its demand rise by 119 percent, accelerating the drain on diminishing oil supplies.

Owing to the vulnerability of oil-consuming Global North countries to economic pressure from oil-producing states, efforts are underway to transform the global energy system. Humans only became dependent on nonrenewable finite stocks of fossilized fuel when Europeans began mining coal in the seventeenth century. Looking back from a century or so in the future, today's hydrocarbon-based economy may be seen as only a brief interlude in history. The primary energy resources in the years ahead may be solar, wind, geothermal, biomass, and other renewable power sources.

The impact of such a global transformation would be huge, overturning the past 125-year pattern in world energy development and consumption. A number of energy analysts and industry officials suggest that in the process we can expect a gradual shift from petroleum to nuclear power and oil derived from unconventional sources (such as tar sands and shale) before relying heavily on renewable sources of energy. As Figure 14.3 shows, these analysts and officials picture a radically changing twenty-first century. They urge immediate planning for a new global "eco-economy, one that satisfies today's need without jeopardizing the prospects of future generations to meet theirs by altering how we light our homes, what we eat, where we live, how we use our leisure time, and how many children we have" (L. Brown 2002). Many people remain skeptical of their vision, but if alternatives to oil become technologically and economically viable, their development would reduce dependence on oil from the volatile Middle East.

In a world in which population growth and industrialization in Global South and East countries means an increasing global demand for energy, how states address their future energy needs will affect the global environment. As biologist E.O. Wilson describes it, we are entering a "bottleneck," a period of

Yanin Arthus Bertrand/CORBIS

The Nuclear Power Debate As of 2007, nuclear power supplied about 15 percent of the world's electricity. Its supporters call for expanding the use of nuclear power because it is reliable, cost-efficient, and does not emit significant amounts of greenhouse gases. Its detractors worry about the risk of nuclear weapons proliferation, the problem of disposing of toxic waste, and the possibility of an accident at a commercial reactor. Shown here is the town of Pripyat, Ukraine, that was abandoned after the Chernobyl accident, in which thousands died; hundreds of thousands were forced to evacuate their homes. New reactor designs, retort supporters, reduce the odds of such accidents.

time that will put enormous stress on the planet's ecology and natural resources. To illustrate his concerns, let us begin by considering the problem of protecting airsheds and other common-pool resources.

The Ecopolitics of the Atmosphere

For years, scientists have warned that global warming—the gradual rise in world temperature—would cause destructive changes in climatological patterns, resulting in rising sea levels and powerful storms. Evidence of global warming abounds. Consider the world's glaciers: only 27 glaciers are left of the 150 estimated to have existed in Glacier National Park in the United States; the

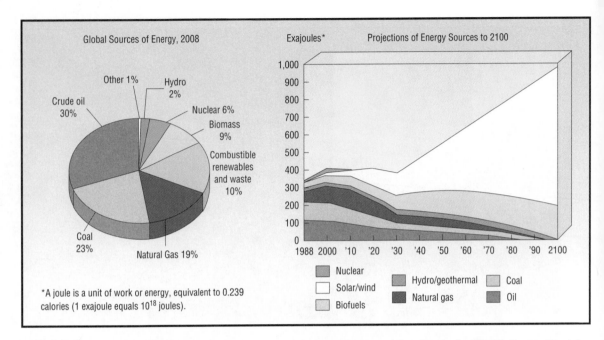

FIGURE 14.3 Phasing Out Fossil Fuels? The Potential for Renewable Energy to Supply the World's Energy Needs by the Year 2100

The global economy's need for energy continues to increase, requiring more energy than is ultimately available from nonrenewable resources. Thus rising demand is likely to change the current distribution of sources on which the world relies to meet its energy needs (left), because 70 percent of the world's energy supply presently comes from fossil fuels, whose global production some analysts expect to peak within a quarter century. As the Fossil Free Energy Scenario prediction (right) suggests, it might be possible to tap renewable sources to meet the world's entire energy needs by the end of the twenty-first century.

Note: Percentages do not equal 100 due to rounding errors.

SOURCE: Global energy supplied by source (left) from International Energy Agency; projections (right) from Crump (1998, 323).

Himalayan glaciers, which provide water to seven of Asia's major river systems, have been receding at an average rate of seventy-five feet per year; Andean glacial runoff, which feeds the rivers that provide 70 percent of Peru's hydroelectric power, is expected to fall significantly after 2020; the snowcap on the summit of 19,340-foot Mount Kilimanjaro in Africa is predicted to disappear in just over a decade; and workers now use reflective sheets to cover parts of the Gurschen glacier above the Swiss ski resort of Andermatt to protect it from melting during the summer. The scientific consensus today is that (1) Earth is warming, (2) human activities are the principal cause, (3) it is affecting the planet's climate, and (4) the impact is substantial and threatening (see Oreskes 2004). Concerned that the earth may be approaching a "tipping point," where small increases in temperature could suddenly cause catastrophic effects, many scientists have called upon the international community to reduce emissions of carbon dioxide and other gases, which they blame for global warming.

Climate Change.   Scientists believe that the gradual rise in the earth's temperature—especially evident since the late eighteenth century when the invention of power-driven machinery produced the Industrial Revolution—is caused by an increase in human-made gases that alter the atmosphere's insulating effects. The gas molecules, primarily carbon dioxide (CO_2) and chlorofluorocarbons (CFCs), trap heat emitted from Earth that would otherwise escape into outer space. As these gases are released into the atmosphere they create a **greenhouse effect** that has caused the global temperature to rise. As shown in Figure 14.4 , the temperature on the earth's surface has increased nearly a half degree since 1950. According to the U.S. National Climatic Data Center, fourteen of the hottest years since record-keeping began over a century ago have occurred since 1987, with the six hottest occurring since 1997. NASA scientist Jim Hansen (2006, 12) suggests one way to visualize how the odds of having unusually hot summers have increased in recent years is to imagine a die with some of its six sides colored red to represent blistering weather. Between 1951 and 1980, two sides would have been red to approximate the odds of a very hot summer. Today, four sides would be red.

> **greenhouse effect** the phenomenon producing planetary warming when gases released by burning fossil fuels act as a blanket in the atmosphere, thereby increasing temperatures.

The earth's average surface temperature has climbed 1.4 degrees Fahrenheit since the early twentieth century and is projected to increase anywhere from 2.7 to 10.7 degrees Fahrenheit over the next 100 years if preventive action is not taken (*U.S. News & World Report*, April 10, 2006, 35). Although CO_2 is the principal greenhouse gas, concentrations of methane in the atmosphere are growing more rapidly. Methane gas emissions arise from livestock populations, rice cultivation, and the production and transportation of natural gas. To many scientists' alarm, the largest concentrations of methane are not in the atmosphere, but are locked in ice and permafrost, which raises the probability that warming will cause more methane to be released into the atmosphere, therein accelerating the process because of methane's strong warming potential.

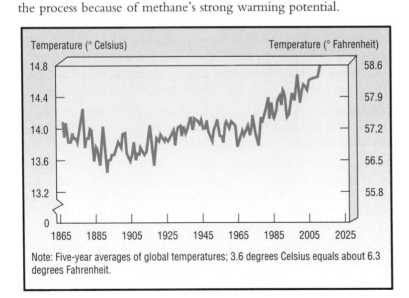

Note: Five-year averages of global temperatures; 3.6 degrees Celsius equals about 6.3 degrees Fahrenheit.

FIGURE 14.4 Rising Average Global Temperatures at the Earth's Surface since 1867

The World Meteorological Organization (WMO) monitors average global surface temperatures at thousands of sites around the world, and its records show that global warming is real. Analysts disagree on the economic impact of climate change, with predictions ranging from a 3 to 20 percent drop in global output by the century's end. As a result, the policy debate has shifted from whether global warming is occurring to how to reduce greenhouse gas concentrations in the atmosphere and at what cost.

SOURCE: Intergovernmental Panel on Climate Change.

While some people believe that the rise in global temperature is primarily due to cyclical changes that the world has experienced for tens of thousands of years, this view has been steadily discredited by scientific research. Since 1988, more than 2,500 scientists from 113 countries have joined forces to study global climate change under the auspices of the UN's Intergovernmental Panel on Climate Change (IPCC). The panel has issued several major assessments. Its 2007 report concluded that human action, not natural cycles, is the dominant source of global warming. Moreover, global temperature will continue to rise throughout the remainder of this century even if greenhouse gasses are curbed tomorrow because the CO_2 being emitted now will stay in the atmosphere long into the future.

Thus, the world has already entered a period of climatic instability likely to cause widespread economic, social, and environmental dislocation over the twenty-first century. The effects of continued temperature rises could be both dramatic and devastating. Africa and Asia are likely to be the hardest-hit, but the IPCC warns that no continent will be spared.

- Sea levels could rise up to two feet, mostly because of melting glaciers and the expansion of water as it warms up. That will inundate vast areas of low-lying coastal land, including major cities, river deltas, and islands throughout the world. More than 100 million people would be put at risk by rising seas and floods.

- Winters will get warmer and warm-weather hot spells more frequent. Droughts and wildfires would be more severe. Because water evaporates more easily in a warmer world, drought-prone regions would become dryer. As oceans heat, hurricanes, which draw their energy from warm oceans, would become even stronger. For every one degree Celsius rise in Atlantic Ocean surface temperature, rainfall from tropical storms increase 6 to 18 percent and wind speed increases up to 8 percent (*Newsweek*, July 7, 2008, 53).

- Entire ecosystems would vanish from the planet, and a hotter earth would drive some plants to higher latitudes and altitudes and require farmers to irrigate and change their crops and agriculture practices. Some species, such as polar bears and walruses, could lose their habitat and become extinct.

- The combination of flooding and droughts would cause tropical diseases such as malaria and dengue fever to flourish in previously temperate regions and at elevations that were formerly too cold for their insect carriers.

- As oceans absorb carbon dioxide, they will become more acidic. By the beginning of the next century, they could be 150 percent more acidic than they were at the onset of the Industrial Revolution, which would endanger plankton and shellfish therein reducing the food supply for larger sea creatures.

- Crop production in high-latitude regions would increase as the growing season lengthened. Formerly icebound shipping lanes would become navigable, and previously inaccessible resources beneath the Arctic Ocean would be easier to obtain.

CO_2 emissions from the burning of fossil fuels have climbed steadily, rising fourfold since 1950. The industrial Global North states are the principal sources, accounting for three-fourths of global CO_2 emissions. The United States emits more CO_2 into the atmosphere that any other state. Due to its big buildings, millions of cars, and relatively inefficient industries, the U.S. CO_2 emissions for each person are five times the world average. Elsewhere, the Global East dynamos China and India have rapidly increased emissions as their economies have grown. The International Energy Agency forecasts that the rise in greenhouse gases from China alone by 2030 will nearly equal the increase from the entire industrial world. India could see its emissions rise 70 percent (Walsh 2006, 61).

Coal, which China relies upon for three-fourths of its energy, is a major source of atmospheric sulfur and nitrogen oxides. These pollutants return to Earth, typically after traveling long distances, in the form of **acid rain,** which adds to the acidification of lakes, the corrosion of materials and structures, and the impairment of ecosystems. Acid rain is a serious problem in much of China. Because the oxides that cause it are also transboundary pollutants, China's domestic energy policies have become a major irritant in its relations with its neighbors, particularly South Korea and Japan. Nonetheless, China plans to increase the amount of coal it burns by nearly 900 million tons a year by 2010. Other Asian states are following in its path, including India which, like China, has sizable coal deposits.

acid rain precipitation that has been made acidic through contact with sulfur dioxide and nitrogen oxides.

To combat the danger of accelerating global warming, the 1997 Kyoto Protocol to the UN Framework Convention on Climate Change called upon industrial countries to reduce their greenhouse gas emissions on average 5.2 percent below 1990 levels by the year 2012. Developing countries were not required to reduce emissions. The Protocol entered into force in 2005, making its emissions targets binding on those that ratified it. As of April 2008, 178 states and regional organizations had ratified the agreement, accounting for over 60 percent of global greenhouse emissions. The United States is the only major industrial power that has not ratified the Protocol. Though signed by the Clinton administration, it was not submitted for ratification because of what then-Vice President Al Gore (2006, 8) called fierce resistance by members of the Senate, who complained about the negative impact that achieving the emissions-reduction targets set by the Protocol might have on the U.S. economy. Nevertheless, three-fifths of American states have taken initiatives to cut greenhouse gas emissions, and 850 U.S. mayors have signed a Climate Protection Agreement to meet or exceed the Kyoto Protocol targets within their cities.

In December 2007, officials from nearly 190 countries met in Bali, Indonesia under the auspices of the United Nations Framework Convention on Climate Change (UNFCCC) to launch the negotiations on an agreement to replace the Kyoto Protocol when it expires in 2012. Little of substance was achieved during the contentious two-week meeting, however. As UN Secretary-General Ban Ki-moon explained, "We will have to engage in more complex, long and difficult negotiations" to reach an accord on cutting greenhouse gas emissions.

ozone layer the protective layer of the upper atmosphere over the earth's surface that shields the planet from the sun's harmful impact on living organisms on the planet.

Ozone Depletion.   The story of climate change is similar to states' efforts to cope with depletion of the atmosphere's protective **ozone layer.** In this case, however, an international regime has emerged, progressively strengthened by mounting scientific evidence that environmental damage was directly caused by human activity.

Ozone is a pollutant in the lower atmosphere, but in the upper atmosphere it provides the earth with a critical layer of protection against the sun's harmful ultraviolet radiation. Scientists have discovered a marked depletion of the ozone layer—most notably an "ozone hole" over Antarctica that has grown larger than the continental United States, and they have linked the thinning of the layer to chlorofluorocarbons (CFCs). Depletion of the ozone layer exposes humans to health hazards of various sorts, particularly skin cancer, and threatens other forms of marine and terrestrial life.

Scientists began to link CFCs to ozone depletion in the early 1970s. This research motivated the United Nations Environment Program (UNEP) to seek some form of regulatory action. The 1987 landmark Montreal Protocol on Substances That Deplete the Ozone Layer treaty was signed by 146 countries and led to a 90 percent reduction since the late 1980s in global atmospheric concentrations of CFCs. Although production of CFCs in the Global North declined sharply, production in the Global South continued, and increased demand for refrigerators, air conditioners, and other products using CFCs is offsetting the gains realized by stopping production in the Global North. Developed countries agreed to provide aid to help the developing countries adopt CFC alternatives, but have failed to provide all of the resources promised. Without this support, many in the Global South may not be able to construct plants to produce CFC alternatives. Meanwhile, an illegal trade in both virgin and recycled CFCs has emerged, threatening to further undermine the positive effects of the ozone regime.

Having clear, persuasive scientific evidence, many believe, is what made the ozone initiative successful. Other factors contributing to its success included precise targets and timetables, verification mechanisms, the existence of economically viable substitutes for CFCs, and a mechanism for financial and technology transfers to assist Global South countries in assuming specific obligations (Simonis and Brühl 2002). Can the ozone regime serve as a model for breakthroughs on other global environmental issues? To explore this question, we turn finally to the problems facing the world's biological heritage.

The Ecopolitics of Land and Water

biodiversity the variety of life on earth.

Forests are critical in preserving the earth's **biodiversity** and to protecting the atmosphere and land resources. For these reasons they have been a rising ecological issue on the global agenda. Some rules have emerged to guide international behavior in the preservation of biodiversity, but issues concerning forests have proven much more difficult to address.

Deforestation.   Destruction of the world's forests contributes to climate change through global warming and threatens the planet's biodiversity and genetic heritage. Currently, about 30 percent of Earth's total landmass is classified as forests, with three-fourths located in the Global South (WDI 2007, 140). Destruction of tropical rain forests in such places as Brazil, Indonesia, and Malaysia is a matter of special concern, since much of the world's genetic heritage is found there.

The representatives sent to the 1992 Earth Summit hoped to secure an easy victory on a statement of principle for global forest conservation. But opposition quickly developed to the notion that the global interest makes all countries responsible for protecting national forests. The Global South—led by Malaysia, a principal exporter of tropical wood products—objected to the view that the world's forests were a "common heritage of mankind," fearing that accepting this view would enable the Global North to interfere with the local management of their tropical forest resources. In the end, the Earth Summit backed away from the goal of establishing international guidelines for trade in "sustainably managed" forest products. The situation today remains largely unchanged, even though the International Tropical Timber Organization (ITTO) exists as a forum for addressing the issue of trade in timber products and the 2007 Bali conference agreed to establish a program to study how tropical deforestation could be reduced.

Desertification.   Meanwhile, high population growth rates, industrialization, and urbanization increase pressure to divert rivers for irrigating marginal land and to clear forests for farming land that might not be well suited for cultivation. This has led to **desertification,** which makes an increasing portion of the earth's landmass useless for agricultural productivity or wildlife habitats. The Aral Sea in Central Asia exemplifies the problem. Because water from the Amu Darya and Syr Darya Rivers was diverted to irrigate cotton fields, this once-vast body of water has shrunk by 75 percent. Villages that once survived on fishing are now forty miles from the coastline and salt from the exposed seabed has blown across nearby pastures and croplands causing ecological damage.

> **desertification** the creation of deserts due to soil erosion, over-farming, and deforestation, which converts cropland to nonproductive, arid sand.

Freshwater supplies are being depleted across the planet. "There's water everywhere, of course, but less than three percent of it is fresh, and most of that is locked up in polar ice caps and glaciers, unrecoverable for practical purposes. Lakes, rivers, marshes, aquifers, and atmospheric vapor make up less than one percent of the earth's total water, and people are already using more than half of the accessible runoff. Water demand, on the other hand, has been growing rapidly—it tripled worldwide between 1950 and 1990—and water use in many areas already exceeds nature's ability to recharge supplies. By 2025, the demand for water around the world is expected to exceed supply by 56 percent" (Finnegan 2002, 44). Already over a billion people lack access to safe drinking water. By 2050, fully two-thirds of the world's population could be living in regions with chronic, widespread water shortages (Cetron and Davies 2005, 15). With roughly 40 percent of the world's population depending on water from river systems that are shared by at least two states, access to water will likely become a growing source of international conflict in the decades ahead. In Africa, for example, the Niger, Nile, Volta, and Zambezi basins are all considered potential flashpoints (Postel 1999).

Soil degradation has stripped billions of acres of the earth's surface from productive farming. Soil erosion and pollution are problems both in densely populated developing countries and in the more highly developed regions of mechanized industrial agriculture. "Since 1950, 11 percent of the planet's vegetation (approximately [2.9 billion acres]), has suffered land degradation" (Crump 1998, 78). Based on previous trends, it has been estimated that an area of one-fourth to one-half of an American football field is deforested each time another person is added to the world population (J. Cohen 1995, 338). This means that the addition of another billion people will require as much as 2.5 million square kilometers of additional land for food production and other uses.

Biodiversity. A term that refers to the earth's variety of life, biodiversity encompasses three basic levels of organization in living systems: genetic diversity,

Arko Datta/AFP/Getty Images

From Farmland to Dust Bowl Desertification is a global phenomenon. Worldwide, each year some 26 billion tons of topsoil are lost to erosion and more than 10 million acres of farmland are becoming deserts. The 1994 UN Convention to Combat Desertification (CCD) has sought to stop the spread of deserts, which now cover 2 million square miles inhabited by one-third of the world's population.

species diversity, and ecosystem diversity. Until recently, public attention has been focused almost exclusively on preserving species diversity, including old growth forests, tall grass prairies, wetlands, coastal habitats, and coral reefs.

Forests, especially tropical forests, are important to preserving biodiversity because they are home to countless species of animals and plants, many of them still unknown. Scientists believe that the global habitat contains between 8 and 10 million species. Of these, only about 1.5 million have been named, and most of them are in the temperate regions of North America, Europe, Russia, and Australia. Destruction of tropical forests, where two-thirds to three-fourths of all species are believed to live, thus threatens the destruction of much of the world's undiscovered biological diversity and genetic heritage.

Many experts worry that the planet is heading toward major species extinction. In 2008, German Environment Minister Sigmar Gabriel estimated that "up to 150 species become extinct every day." Some are lost due to competition from nonnative species entering their habitats through cross-border transportation facilitated by globalization; others die out from poaching, unregulated hunting, and overfishing; and still others become extinct as a result of clearing land for housing, roads, and industries. The latter is particularly troubling given the fact that clearing of tropical rain forests with slash-and-burn techniques to make room for farms and ranches is doubly destructive. On the one hand, fewer trees are able to remove CO_2 from the atmosphere during photosynthesis when forests are cut down, and, on the other, forests are burned for clearing, the amount of CO_2 discharged into the atmosphere increases.

Biodiversity's distributional characteristics also make it unique. Because so much of the earth's biological heritage is concentrated in the tropics, the Global South has a growing concern about protecting its interest in the face of the recent claims that the genetic character of the many species of plants and animals should be considered a part of the global commons and therefore available for commercial use by all, for their medical benefit. Pharmaceutical companies in particular have tried to lay claim to Global South resources. They actively explore plants, microbes, and other living organisms in tropical forests for possible use in prescription drugs. Ten of the world's 25 top-selling drugs are derived from "natural biological sources," and roughly 25 percent of the prescription drugs used in the United States have active ingredients extracted or derived from plants (UNEP, http://www.un.org). At the 1992 Earth Summit in Rio de Janeiro, a convention on biodiversity was adopted that called on signatories to protect habitats and preserve endangered species. In 2004, the International Treaty on Plant Genetic Resources for Food and Agriculture went into effect after seven years of negotiations. Among other things, it created the Global Crop Diversity Trust to coordinate the approximately 1,500 gene banks scattered throughout more than 100 countries that together now store over 600,000 genetically distinct seed samples (Raloff 2006). Still, much more needs to be done. As ecologists Stuart Pimn and Clinton Jenkins (2005, 66) remind us, we do not live in Jurassic Park: once they are gone, nothing can bring extinct species back.

FUTURE ENVIRONMENTAL POLICY CHOICES

We began our exploration of world politics in Chapter 1 by focusing our attention on the interaction of autonomous, territorial states that have no higher authority governing their behavior. Since the birth of the modern state system some three and a half centuries ago, world population has increased eightfold, fossil fuel consumption has risen from nearly nothing to more than 7 billion metric tons of coal equivalent annually, and the use of nonfuel minerals has skyrocketed. Demographic pressures combined with resource-intensive industrialization have placed enormous stress on the global environment. Earth's atmosphere and oceans are becoming polluted; its natural resources, depleted.

Some of the world's environmental problems are localized and can be addressed through unilateral action. Yet, as we have seen in this chapter, many others span the boundaries between territorial states and require multilateral solutions. The political world may be a checkerboard of sovereign states, but the natural world is a seamless web.

Recognizing that Earth's ecosystem transcends national jurisdictions, the international community has taken various steps to address many environmental threats. The number of international environmental treaties has grown from 84 in the nineteenth century to a total of 2,869 by the start of 2009; however, many ecologists fear that still not enough is being done. Part of the reason is that states differ over global priorities (see Contoversy: How Should the World's Problems Be Prioritized?) In addition, because damage caused by environmental degradation accumulates slowly, is unequally distributed, and remedies remain expensive, many states hesitate to join environmental-preservation efforts unless they are sure that others will act as well. Earth's atmosphere and oceans are common-pool resources: They do not belong to any single state, and everyone can benefit from their use regardless of whether they help pay for the costs of their preservation. As a result, various states are tempted to be free riders, negotiating treaties that minimize their responsibilities but maximize the obligations of others.

CONTROVERSY   How Should the World's Problems Be Prioritized?

Many of the world's humanitarian and environmental problems are projected to become more severe in the decades ahead. Yet even if the international community decides not to follow a business-as-usual course and chooses instead to tackle pressing world problems, which ones should it take on, in what order? Arresting global climate change, preserving biodiversity, combating communicable diseases, providing clean water, alleviating poverty, fighting malnutrition and hunger, and restoring forests, fisheries, and other overexploited renewable resources are just a few of the challenges humanity faces.

Whereas there are numerous global problems, financial resources to deal with them are limited. When it is impossible to address every major need at once, priorities must be set. But how should they be established? Faced with multiple competing demands and complicated tradeoffs, how should the international community determine which problems warrant the most attention?

One approach focuses on cost-benefit ratios. Bjørn Lomborg, a Danish political scientist known for his skepticism about many of the ecological threats emphasized by environmental scientists, adopted this method when he convened a panel of eminent economists during May 2004 in Copenhagen and asked them how they would allocate a hypothetical $50 billion to advance global welfare. The exercise resulted in a consensus on spending funds on projects that would yield high benefits for low costs. For example, the panelists strongly supported spending money on such things as promoting condom use to prevent the spread of HIV and AIDS, distributing vitamin and mineral supplements to reduce malnutrition, and providing chemically-treated mosquito netting for beds to reduce the incidence of malaria. Conversely, steps to avert climate change, such as carbon taxes and mandatory targets for lowering greenhouse gas emissions, were not given high priorities, allegedly because of their enormous expense relative to distant and uncertain benefits. A similar exercise involving UN diplomats from seven non-European countries was directed in 2006 by John Bolton, the U.S. ambassador to the United Nations. Once again, health care and nutrition were given higher priorities over mitigating climate change.

The so-called "Copenhagen Consensus" has been criticized on several grounds. First, critics complained that cost-benefit analysis was an inappropriate method for setting global priorities. Although it may be a valuable instrument for making narrow, technical choices between different ways of achieving an agreed-upon goal (such as whether to build a road along proposed route A or proposed route B), they denied that it could determine what goal should receive the highest priority (such as whether to spend funds on building a road or hiring more teachers for the local school). Second, by giving the panel members a small sum to allocate (roughly one-sixth of the cost of the war in Iraq as of the end of fiscal year 2006), the exercise was biased in favor of low-cost projects, like distributing vitamin A supplements to prevent blindness. Finally, critics charged that the panelists did not receive sufficient background information on the state of scientific knowledge in each problem area they attempted to prioritize, which, in particular, led them to overlook existing, affordable technologies that can help in climate stabilization (see Pacala and Socolow 2004). Operating from the assumption that curbing global climate change was a costly, uncertain venture, they discounted the planet's ecological future in favor of immediate health and nutrition concerns.

To avoid emerging disasters, write organization theorists Max Bazerman and Michael Watkins (2004, 155), it is necessary to set priorities. But how should that be done? Does cost-benefit analysis offer the international community a viable method for establishing global funding priorities? Or are there too many difficulties in calculating and comparing costs and benefits for it to be a useful tool for setting priorities among the world's many problems? What do you think? How should we go about prioritizing the world's pressing humanitarian and environmental challenges?

Through numerous forums organized by the United Nations, concern has been repeatedly voiced about the need to protect the environment. However, pledges about safeguarding the planet's ecology in the face of rising world population have not significantly improved the global environment. Despite expressing concern about the global future, many national leaders have failed to make firm commitments to sustainable development that might reconcile the conflicts between economic growth and environmental protection.

Differences between the rich Global North and the developing Global South will continue to spark controversy about such issues as the transfer of resources and technology needed to deal with climate change, biodiversity, and a host of other problem areas. However, one encouraging trend is that, as Global North countries move into the information age and their economies shift away from "smokestack" industries toward cleaner service-oriented activities, it is likely that the adverse environmental consequences of these advanced countries' economic activities will decline. Trade with other states, nevertheless, will ensure continuing pressures on global resources and the environmental burdens they pose. Wealthy countries that have depleted their resources or passed strict laws to protect them can easily look overseas for desired commodities, in ways that shift the environmental stress of high consumption to someone else's backyard.

We stand at a critical juncture. According to Paul Crutzen, a Nobel Prize-winning atmospheric chemist, we are witnessing the beginning of a new era, a time when human influences on the planet will trump natural climate swings (*U.S. News & World Report,* special edition, 2004). The path humanity takes will affect global welfare far into the future. Yet many people remain complacent; ominous predictions have been made before and have been proven wrong. Moreover, numerous environmental risks are only visible in the long term, while countermeasures are costly in the short term. But evidence of serious ecological problems is getting harder to ignore, and because the stakes are so high, all the pieces in the puzzle—population, natural resources, technology, and preferences in lifestyles—must be worked on simultaneously, through coordinated, multilateral efforts. "All things are connected," Chief Seattle of the Suquamish tribe is said to have told the U.S. government in 1854. "Man did not weave the web of life; he is merely a strand in it. Whatever he does to the web, he does to himself."

CHAPTER SUMMARY

- The global environment is a system of delicately and tightly integrated components that together impose limits on the planet's carrying capacity. If population growth exceeds that carrying capacity, it could result in lost economic opportunities, environmental degradation, and domestic strife. However, analysts disagree over the magnitude of Earth's carrying capacity.

- The planet has become a demographically divided world, with Global North countries experiencing low or declining growth and Global South countries experiencing high levels of growth. Population growth in the Global South will create pressures toward outward movement, and the aging of the industrial societies of the Global North will encourage them to search for new sources of labor. These forces will place migration at the center of national political agendas.

- As trends in births, deaths, and migration unfold worldwide, they will promote significant change in world politics, aggravating some existing problems as valuable resources become increasingly scarce, and creating new challenges as the natural environment experiences greater strain.

- Rapid increases in the rate of energy usage in general and petroleum in particular are primarily post–World War II phenomena. The impact of oil price and production policies on the international political economy derives from the uneven distribution of the demand and supply of oil.

- International efforts to address the problems of global warming and the depletion of the atmosphere's protective ozone layer have yielded mixed results. Attempts to deal with climate change remain confined to voluntary restraints. In contrast, an international regime has emerged to restrict the use of ozone-depleting chemicals.

- Deforestation is a global phenomenon, but its rate is much higher in the Global South than in the Global North. While some norms have emerged to guide states in preserving biodiversity, the world's forests remain at risk of destruction through commercial exploitation and agricultural expansion.

- Differences between the countries of the Global North and South over worldwide ecopolitical issues will continue to spark controversy in the global future. The controversy arises in part from clashing views over the responsibility for causing and solving the environmental problems facing the world today.

KEY TERMS

acid rain	fertility rate	replacement-level
biodiversity	greenhouse effect	fertility
carrying capacity	ozone layer	sustainable development
cartel	pandemic	tragedy of the commons
demographic transition	population implosion	transgenic crops
desertification		

SUGGESTED READINGS

Chasek, Pamela, Janet Welsch Brown, and David Leonard Downie. *Global Environmental Politics*, 4th edition. Boulder:: Westview, 2006.

Haas, Peter M., ed. *International Environmental Governance*. Burlington, VT: Ashgate, 2008.

Klare, Michael T. *Rising Powers, Shrinking Planet: The New Geopolitics of Energy*. New York: Metropolitan Books, 2008.

Mitchell, Ronald. *International Environmental Politics*. Thousand Oaks, CA: Sage, 2008.

Speth, James Gustave, and Peter M. Haas. *Global Environmental Governance*. Washington, DC: Island Press, 2006.

CRITICAL THINKING QUESTIONS

Many people assume that states with shared preferences will coalesce and readily cooperate to advance their collective interests. Yet this doesn't always happen in global environmental politics. Virtually all states have expressed a preference to arrest climate change, but many have failed to limit greenhouse gas emissions that contribute to global warming. The United States, in particular, has resisted the approach taken by many other states under the Kyoto Protocol. Due to Washington's intransigence at the 2007 Bali conference on climate change, a frustrated delegate from Papua New Guinea told the Americans to thunderous applause: "We seek your leadership. But if for some reason you are not willing to lead, leave it to the rest of us. Please get out of the way."

The American argument against the Kyoto Protocol is twofold. First, some key officials in Washington question the causal linkage that has been drawn between increases in greenhouse gas emissions and rising world temperatures. Second, they claim that the Protocol hurts the American economy by imposing costs on the United States while exempting competitors from the developing world (such as China and India) that emit a growing amount of greenhouse gases. The rationale for these exemptions is summarized in the principle of common but differential responsibilities: *climate change is a common concern of everyone, but because the industrialization of Global North countries originally caused the problem, they are responsible for making the initial emission cuts.*

Currently, negotiations are underway on crafting an agreement to replace the Kyoto Protocol when it expires in 2012. How important would it be to have the United States accept the new accord? If you were one of the negotiators trying to secure U.S. cooperation, how would you go about gaining American support while retaining the backing of those countries that had ratified the Kyoto Protocol? Should the principle of "common but differentiated responsibilities" be maintained? Or should the level of a country's emissions cuts be tied to the efficiency of its industry, or perhaps to the size of its population or economy? Does the 1987 Montreal Protocol on ozone depletion offer any clues on how to overcome the political obstacles to an agreement on combating climate change?

Alternative World Futures

Most conjectures about the global future are based on some extrapolation from earlier events and experiences. We generally speculate about future prospects based on our understanding of prevailing trends. What makes this difficult is the sheer complexity of world politics: some trends are linear, others change direction; some trends intersect, others diverge over time; some trends amplify one another, others dampen their joint impact. Our challenge in deciphering the meaning of these diverse trends is two-fold: to distinguish between those that are transient versus those that are likely to have a significant impact on world politics, and to project the configuration of the most important trends rather than become preoccupied with any single trend in isolation.

How will the configuration of major trends in world politics today influence the global future? Will the twenty-first century find previous efforts to construct world order useful, or will it reject past approaches as new issues arise on the global agenda?

Part V presents a set of thought-provoking questions about the prospects for the twenty-first century. When thinking about the issues raised by these questions, ask yourself how they might be addressed to create a more peaceful and just global future.

15

Prospects for a New World Order

CHAPTER OUTLINE

The Global Predicament: Questions for a Turbulent World

Will the State Remain the Primary Actor in World Politics?

Is Economic Globalization Irreversible?

Are Ecopolitical Challenges Reordering the Global Agenda?

Will Technological Innovation Solve Pressing Global Problems?

Are Cultural Differences the New Fault Lines on the Geostrategic Landscape?

Is the World Preparing for the Wrong Kind of Security Threats?

Should the World Brace for a New Cold War?

Human Choice and the Global Future

> The person who does not worry about the future will shortly
> have worries about the present.
>
> CHINESE PROVERB

Long before the first Europeans came to North America, the indigenous nations of the continent were engaged in sustained interaction. Commerce and cultural exchanges, as well as rivalries and military clashes, had been taking place for centuries.

When the English, French, and Dutch first traveled through what today is upstate New York, they encountered the Iroquoian-speaking Hodenosaunee, or "People of the Longhouse." Although once mired in internecine warfare, the five Iroquois nations—the Mohawks, Oneidas, Onondagas, Cayugas, and Senecas—put their differences aside and formed the Great League of Peace. Under the terms of this confederation, the individual nations maintained control over their own internal affairs but regularly met in a grand council to reach consensus on policy proposals for dealing with issues of common concern (Calloway 1999, 44–48). Known as skilled diplomats and formidable warriors, the Hodenosaunee were recognized in a 1987 U.S. Senate resolution "for their demonstrated enlightened, democratic principles of Government and their example of a free association of independent Indian nations."

According to Hodenosaunee Faith Keeper, Chief Oren Lyons, one of the principles that guided decision making within the Great League of Peace was a concern for the "seventh generation yet unborn" (Cornish 2004, 217). Leaders participating in the League's grand council were expected to be men of vision who made decisions with the future in mind. Because the seventh generation would not arrive for approximately 200 years, no leader would meet its members; nevertheless, council decisions could affect their lives. Consequently, the pressing issues of the day were examined in the light of what impact any action might have on the security and welfare of those people coming ahead.

In contrast to the farsightedness of the Hodenosaunee, the original inhabitants of Easter Island, a remote patch of land 2,300 miles off the coast of Chile, showed little appreciation for the future. Although they once lived among the largest species of palm tree in the world, the Easter Islanders eventually cut down all the palms in what has been described as among the most extreme cases of forest destruction in the world. Without the giant palms, the diet of the islanders suffered: land birds disappeared, crop yields declined due to soil erosion, wild fruit withered in the hot sun, and fishing became limited to shallow waters because timber was no longer available to build seagoing canoes. Deforestation also meant the loss of fronds for making thatched goods and bark for manufacturing cloth. By overexploiting their natural resources, primarily so chiefs from competitive clans could quarry, transport, and erect larger stone monuments than their rivals, the Easter Islanders bequeathed a legacy of malnutrition and fratricidal conflict to their heirs (Diamond 2005, 79–119).

The contrasting stories of the Hodenosaunee and the Easter Islanders encourage us to reflect on the world that generations yet unborn will inherit as a result of decisions made today. Will it be the kind of place we would like to inhabit? Chapter 15 draws upon the information presented in earlier chapters about prevailing integrative and disintegrative trends to frame a series of questions about the global future. How these questions ultimately are answered will shape world politics throughout the remainder of the twenty-first century.

THE GLOBAL PREDICAMENT: QUESTIONS FOR A TURBULENT WORLD

Throughout this book, we have argued that world politics is shaped by recurring patterns. Under certain conditions, certain types of international actors respond the same way to the same kinds of stimuli. Yet there are exceptions. Sometimes similar actors in similar situations make different decisions. Thus despite the existence of regularities in world politics, social scientists cannot draw on a body of uniform, deterministic laws to predict the global future precisely. Instead, they make probabilistic forecasts about what is likely to happen, other things being equal (J.D. Singer 2000, 12–13).

Another factor that makes it difficult to make predictions is the role of happenstance in world politics. History is replete with what Aristotle called accidental conjunctions—situations where things come together by chance. Consider, for example, the outbreak of World War I. Recall from Chapter 4 that one of the proximate causes of the war was Austrian archduke Franz Ferdinand's assassination in Sarajevo on June 28, 1914. Earlier that day, several would-be assassins had failed to find an opportunity to kill the archduke and apparently gave up in frustration. When Franz Ferdinand's motorcade made a wrong turn in route to visit patients in a city hospital, it stopped briefly in front of a café where Gavrilo Princip, one of the frustrated assassins, coincidently had gone to get something to eat. Astonished to find the archduke's open-air car just five feet away, Princip fired two shots killing him and his wife. Given the political climate in Europe at the time, if Franz Ferdinand had not been assassinated, something else might have precipitated the war. But as political scientist Stuart Bremer (2000, 35) asks, "Who can say whether a different triggering event, a day, a month, or a year later, would have led to the same chain of events that produced World War I?"

Myriad possible futures lie ahead: some are desirable; others, frightening. Although we cannot predict with certainty which one will materialize, we can narrow the range of possibilities by forecasting how current trends will probably develop and how steps might be taken to channel the course of events toward a global future that we prefer. As illustrated by the example of the Hodenosaunee, thinking in the future tense does not demand prophecy or divination; rather, it requires anticipating how today's actions will most likely affect generations yet unborn. In other words, it is an approach to inquiry that uses forecasts of alternative futures to improve policy decisions in the present.

What follows is a series of questions designed to help you think about the future of world politics. Each question is based on information presented in previous chapters. When pondering the long-term implications of these questions, we encourage you to (1) imagine what conceivable global futures are possible, (2) estimate which are the most probable, and (3) consider what policies would be helpful in bringing about the one you find preferable. Although these questions do not exhaust the concerns that are likely to be priorities in the years ahead, they provide a way to look over the horizon and construct scenarios

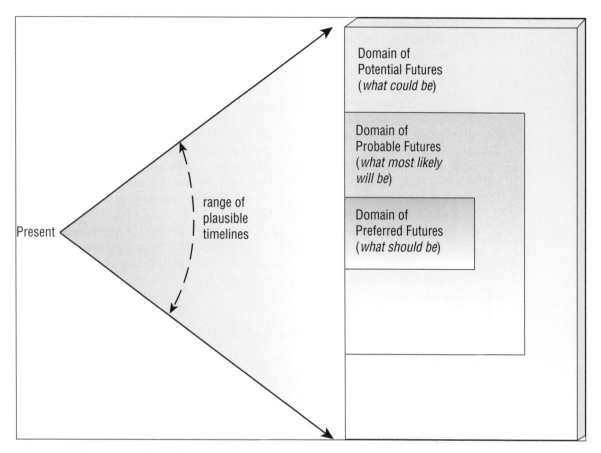

FIGURE 15.1 Forecasting Alternative World Futures

Social scientists frequently construct scenarios that describe what the global future could be, what it is likely to be, and what they believe it should be. These descriptions range from "business-as-usual" scenarios based on simple extrapolations from current conditions to various "wild card" scenarios predicated on sharp discontinuities between the present and the future. Scenario-building helps social scientists clarify their assumptions about global trends and encourages them to consider the long-range consequences of policy decisions made in response to those trends.

about alternative global futures. A **scenario** is a logical, compelling story that traces a timeline of events from the present to some point in the future (see Figure 15.1). How you respond to these questions will suggest which scenarios you find germane for exploring the global future.

scenario a narrative description showing how some hypothetical future state of affairs might evolve out of the present one.

Will the State Remain the Primary Actor in World Politics?

The sovereign, territorial state has been the lead actor on the world stage for nearly four centuries. In some respects it is still flourishing because many people look to the state as a source of security, welfare, and identity. Yet numerous states are failing to fulfill these traditional purposes, leading scholars to ask whether the nation-state will remain capable of addressing issues once considered its sole prerogative. With national boundaries becoming increasingly porous and policy problems transcending political frontiers, the managerial capabilities of states have been severely strained, irrespective of form of government. Auguste Comte, a nineteenth-century French sociologist, argued that human beings create institutions to deal with serious problems. When they are no longer able to perform this vital function, they are replaced by other institutions. Today, as the Westphalian state seems unable to cope with many transnational problems, is there another unit that will replace it as the central actor on the world stage? Is the nation-state becoming obsolete? Will the pace of international integration quicken outside of Europe as the century progresses, leading to the emergence of "regional states" in Africa, Asia, or Latin America to replace the nation-state? Will grassroots NGOs assume more responsibility for responding to transnational problems through global policy networks. If nation-states cannot meet the challenges of the twenty-first century, can the world's people expect a new global architecture to crystallize around some form of supranational global governance?

Is Economic Globalization Irreversible?

Globalization refers to the increasing interconnectedness among societies. It is not a new phenomenon. Two centuries ago, for example, the German philosopher Johann Gottfried von Herder was amazed by the growth of international interdependence in his day. Inventions like the steam engine seemed to be shrinking the world.

Modern technology has reduced geography's constraints on global interaction even further, allowing people to exchange goods and ideas with speed that would have been unimaginable to those living in the eighteenth-century. Although the dramatic decline in worldwide communication and transportation costs has stimulated the economic side of globalization, political globalization lags behind (Stiglitz 2006). Everyone on the planet is now more closely connected than ever before, but on a shaky institutional foundation that remains unprepared to manage the sweeping changes brought on by an expanding global marketplace. As distinctions between what is domestic and what is foreign have become increasingly blurred in the economic arena, multilateral political cooperation among the world's culturally diverse nations has not kept pace. Indeed, some analysts expect political friction to intensify as Asian firms expand in number and reach, giving globalization a non-Western hue.

Can economic globalization be an engine for unity and progress without organized global governance? From one perspective, an awareness of the common destiny of all, alongside the declining ability of many sovereign states to cope with global problems through national means, will energize efforts to put aside political squabbles. Conflict, according to this reasoning, will recede, as states find themselves unable to disentangle themselves from the many economic linkages that bind them together. The emergency financial summit conference held in Washington, D.C. on November 15, 2008 exemplified this vision of the global future. Attended by the leaders of nearly two dozen countries, the meeting culminated with a vow to cooperate closely in reforming international regulatory rules and financial institutions. Drawing attention to how severe financial problems in one part of the world can quickly engulf other regions, Brazilian President Luiz Inácio Lula da Silva warned "No country is safe." Global economic crises require a multilateral response.

From another perspective, however, economic globalization will breed enmity, not amity. Because the world economy is projected to grow substantially over the next two decades but the beneficiaries of that growth will be unevenly distributed, globalization may generate bitter conflicts between winners and losers. Moreover, as the center of gravity of the world economy shifts from the North Atlantic toward Asia, many of these conflicts could involve the world's most powerful states. Without effective international political institutions to mitigate these wrenching economic changes, analysts from this school of thought expect the intricate but fragile tapestry of global economic ties to unravel (Saul 2005).

Charting a Common Course Describing the world's current financial problems as the greatest challenge of our times, U.S. President Barack Obama has acknowledged the need for a coordinated multilateral action to resuscitate the ailing global economy. "No one nation, no matter how large or powerful, can defeat such challenges alone," he told the citizens of Berlin, Germany on July 24, 2008. "Partnership and cooperation among nations is not a choice; it is the one way, the only way, to protect our common security."

Are Ecopolitical Challenges Reordering the Global Agenda?

What goals should states pursue? In earlier times, the answer was easy: the state should provide for defense against external aggression, preserve the nation's values, and promote the welfare of its citizens. Political leaders followed a largely realist script, putting their national interests ahead of wider global interests. This meant competing with other states for power, position, and prestige. Building multilateral institutions that could address transnational problems was secondary—to be considered only after national security was solidified by acquiring military might and political clout.

Most leaders have similar aims today, but their quest for national self-advantage can carry prohibitively high costs. Many of the troubles they face cannot be solved unilaterally. Climate change, the economic fallout from globalization, and the growth of the world's population have expanded the issues states confront. In the words of columnist Thomas Friedman (2008), the world is becoming "hot, flat, and crowded," and it will take concerted action to resolve the problems arising from these conditions.

According to the UN Millennium Project's *2008 State of the Future* report, although important steps have been taken to reduce infant mortality and increase literacy, per capita income, and life expectancy around the world, several ecopolitical challenges cast a shadow over the global future. Even with a decline in fertility rate, the number of inhabitants on Earth will continue to grow due to population momentum, with most of the growth occurring in the poorest countries of the Global South and which are least able to cope with a surge in population. The expected 40 percent increase in the world's inhabitants by mid-century will strain the planet's resources as the demand for water, food, energy, and nonfuel minerals soars. Additional demand will come from the rise in economic activity that accompanies the narrowing gap in average incomes between the Global North and the Global East. Without a resolute international response, the report estimates that roughly half of the world will become vulnerable to social instability and violence attributable to these pressures.

As economist Jeffrey Sachs (2008) summarizes the situation, humanity shares a "common fate on a crowded planet." Business-as-usual policies will yield calamitous results. Ecopolitical issues must move up on the policy agenda, he concludes, and new, robust forms of global cooperation are needed to solve them. "The world has changed in profound ways," laments former UN Secretary-General Kofi Annan, "but I fear our conceptions of national interest have failed to follow suit." A broader definition of global interest is required, "which would induce states to find greater unity in the pursuit of common goods and values." Yet given the planet's political divisions, how will humanity set priorities for action on so many interrelated problems, all of which require attention if peace and prosperity with justice is to prevail?

Will Technological Innovation Solve Pressing Global Problems?

The world today faces a series of difficult and potentially unmanageable challenges. The surge in globalization that followed on the heels of late twentieth-century discoveries in microelectronics and information processing has unleashed revolutionary changes. The consequences, however, are not certain. Technological innovations solve some problems but cause others. "Like any irrepressible force," observes Nobel laureate economist Wassily Leontief, "technology can bestow on us undreamed benefits but also inflict irreparable damage." It can increase productivity and economic output, but it can also displace workers and trigger social unrest.

While acknowledging that there is often a significant time lag between the diffusion of new technology and the adjustment of society to the changes it fosters, some people assert that technological innovation promises humanity a more secure and bountiful future. Indeed, the most optimistic members of this group believe that due to promising developments in such fields as biotechnology and software development, humanity is entering the most innovative period in history. From their perspective, sufficient resources exist to fuel continued progress. With patience, technological solutions eventually will be found to ease the most serious problems facing the world today. Malnutrition and disease, they note as an example, may still exist, but owing to technological advances in agriculture and medicine many people are alive today who might have perished in previous centuries.

In contrast to those who envision technological innovation as a way to increase economic growth and alleviate social welfare problems, others remain concerned that that some proposed technological solutions will compound current problems. Whereas genetically modified crops are seen by members of the former group as a way to reduce famine by developing plants that produce greater yields with more nutrients at lower tillage costs, members of the latter group worry about inadvertent environmental and health consequences, arguing that replacing traditional crops with those that have been genetically modified will reduce genetic diversity and introduce potentially toxic vegetation into the ecosystem. Even the so-called **green revolution** had its drawbacks, they argue. Although fertilizers, pesticides, and herbicides initially increased crop yields in various Global South countries, they eventually spawned new problems, such as contaminated water supplies. Without wise management, technological advances can have detrimental side effects. Consider the case of the world's fisheries. At first, larger ships and improvements in maritime technology resulted in increases in the amount of fish harvested from the world's oceans. Over time, however, many fisheries were depleted. Applying more technology could not increase catches once the ecosystem had collapsed. As one member of this school of thought has put it: "Many of our new technologies confer upon us new power without automatically giving us new wisdom" (Gore 2006, 247).

green revolution the introduction of high-yield seeds, chemical fertilizers, and other agricultural technologies to Global South countries.

Are Cultural Differences the New Fault Lines on the Geostrategic Landscape?

When communism began collapsing throughout Eastern Europe in 1989, former U.S. State Department analyst Francis Fukuyama (1989) suggested that the world

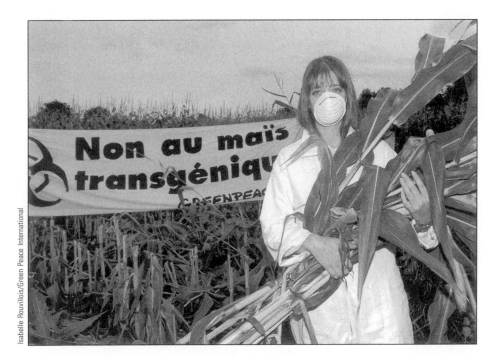

Isabelle Rouvillois/Green Peace International

Genetic Engineering in Agriculture A Greenpeace activist in France protests the import of genetically modified corn, which the United States produces for export around the globe.

end of history the thesis that the demise of communism marked the triumph of Western market democracy and the end of humanity's ideological evolution.

was witnessing the **end of history**. Ideological conflicts were over; democratic capitalism had triumphed. But not everyone was so sure. On the one hand, many of the newly emerging democracies were ruled by individuals who, although elected, disregarded constitutional limits on their power and denied citizens basic political freedoms. On the other hand, political movements that drew inspiration from non-Western belief systems began to challenge liberalism. According to political scientist Samuel Huntington (1996), the most prominent of these appealed to Islamic fundamentalism.

clash of civilizations the thesis that future international conflicts will be based on competing cultural values.

Conflict in the future, Huntington proposed, would involve a **clash of civilizations**, collisions between vast cultural entities holding different views on the relationship between God and humankind as well as different interpretations of the relative importance of equality and hierarchy, liberty and authority. From his vantage point, the world was divided into several major civilizations: Western, Slavic-Orthodox, Islamic, Hindu, Confucian, Japanese, Latin American, and African. Just as when violent geological events occur along the boundaries between tectonic plates, Huntington hypothesized that political friction could be expected where civilizations rubbed against one another. The wars in Chechnya and Bosnia have often been cited as examples that support his contention.

Critics, however, point out that no civilization is homogeneous in beliefs or attitudes. By focusing on civilizations as a whole, they insist that Huntington overlooks salient differences within civilizations, such as those between Sunnis and Shiites within the Islamic world, which are more likely to erupt into violence than clashes between civilizations.

For liberals and constructivists, clashes between civilizations are not inevitable: Common moral values and the growth of global civil society make cooperation across cultural fault lines possible, argue the former; over time, mutually beneficial cross-cultural cooperation can lead people to acquire more open, inclusive identities, add the latter. Many realists retort that clashes of civilizations have occurred throughout history and are likely to continue. Human nature has not changed and anarchy remains a key defining property of the international system. As the realist diplomat and strategic thinker George Kennan once remarked, "Whoever thinks the future is going to be easier than the past is certainly mad."

Is the World Preparing for the Wrong Kind of Security Threats?

The conduct of war has undergone several "generational" changes since the Thirty Years' War drew to a close and gave birth to the modern state system. In what has been called the "first generation of modern warfare," which extended from the Peace of Westphalia to the American Civil War, soldiers armed with smooth-bore muskets were normally deployed in tight linear formations to coordinate volleys from relatively inaccurate weapons. Once weapons with greater accuracy and rates of fire became available, line-and-column tactics on open ground lost their effectiveness, which led to a new generation of tactics that emphasized massive firepower to annihilate fixed-fortification defenses.

The second generation of modern land warfare substituted massed artillery for massed infantry. During the First World War, machine guns, barbed wire, minefields, and entrenched defenses strung along continuous fronts stymied the precise, geometric lines of attack typical of early modern warfare. In response, artillery barrages from the rear were used to breach fortified positions, allowing infantry units to overrun crippled defenses.

Although lengthy preparatory barrages could shatter fixed positions, they alerted the other side to where the subsequent infantry assault would occur. By extending defenses in greater depth and maintaining significant reserve forces, defenders could counterattack before advancing foot soldiers were able to break through. However, improvements in transportation and communication technology provided a way to deal with these tactics. Drawing upon their country's experience of combining suppressive firepower with movement during the spring offenses of 1918, German officers like Heinz Guderian and Erich von Manstein envisioned a third generation of warfare that accentuated speed and surprise rather than firepower and attrition. Tracked-armored vehicles and tactical air power, they reasoned, enabled an attacker to concentrate mobile forces at a decisive point along the front, penetrate deep into enemy territory, and roll the opposition up from the rear in battles of encirclement.

Whereas third-generation thinking has influenced most countries since the Second World War, today the threat of being attacked by the military forces of another nation-state has receded, particularly in the Global North. Instead, a "fourth generation" of warfare has emerged in which nation-states are pitted against nonstate actors in hostilities that lack front lines and clear distinctions between soldiers and civilians (see Hammes 2004). Unable to defeat conventional armies on the field of battle, irregular forces using unconventional tactics focus on their adversary's will, using patience, ingenuity, and gruesome acts of violence to compel their opponent to weigh the mounting costs of continuing a long, drawn-out struggle. Some political and military leaders, however, continue to think of warfare in third-generational terms, dismissing this new face of war as an annoyance that detracts from preparations for decisive, large-scale engagements. Do the wars in Afghanistan and Iraq provide a glimpse into the future? Will most military clashes in the early twenty-first century follow their pattern?

Should the World Brace for a New Cold War?

On August 7, 2008, military units of the Republic of Georgia swarmed into South Ossetia, a secessionist region that had been seeking to withdraw from Georgia and align itself with Russia. The following morning, Russian armored forces launched a counterattack, which compelled the Georgians to retreat and put Russia in control of parts of Georgia. Shortly thereafter, the Kremlin recognized the independence of South Ossetia and Abkhazia, another breakaway region of Georgia. In justifying Russia's actions, President Dmitry Medvedev asserted that Moscow had "privileged interests" in neighboring countries with which it shared "special historical relations." Russia could not idly stand by, he explained, while the Georgians broke a ceasefire with the South Ossetians and endangered Russian citizens in the area.

Many observers in Europe and the United States described Russia's violation of Georgia's territorial integrity as ominous. Swedish Foreign Minister Carl Bildt, for example, likened Russian behavior to that of Nazi Germany in the 1930s. Former U.S. National Security Advisor Zbigniew Brzezinski compared it to Stalin's aggression against Finland in 1939. Other commentators opined that the attack on Georgia was reminiscent of the Soviet Union's invasions of Hungary in 1956 and Czechoslovakia in 1968. Calling Russian action an "affront to civilized standards," the Bush administration offered a $1 billion aid package to Georgia and withdrew a proposed agreement for commercial nuclear cooperation with Russia from consideration.

Signs of friction in U.S.-Russian relations existed prior to the dispute over Georgia. Vladimir Putin, former president and now prime minister, had lashed out at American unilateralism during a February 10, 2007 speech delivered in Munich, Germany. From the Kremlin's vantage point, the United States had been treating Russia in a condescending way since the collapse of communism. From bringing former Soviet republics into NATO to supporting Kosovo's detachment from Serbia to deploying missile defense systems in Poland and the

Czech Republic, Washington seemed unwilling to consider Russian interests and sensibilities in its foreign policy calculations. Yet with vast reserves of oil and natural gas as well as ownership of east-west pipelines, Russia was no longer the chaotic, revenue-strapped country of the 1990s; it was once again an assertive, self-confident great power (Goldman 2008). As President Medvedev declared in the aftermath of the invasion of Georgia, "We are not afraid of anything, including the prospect of a Cold War."

Foreign policy analysts remain divided over the long-term ramifications of the conflict in Georgia. Some worry that with the United States tied down in Iraq and Afghanistan, and with many EU countries dependent on Russia for natural gas, Moscow may try to restore control over Ukraine, the Caucasus, and the Baltic states, thereby sparking future confrontations with the West. Others, believing that Russia has too much at stake in its economic relations with the United States and the European Union to take such actions, contend that the most prudent policy for Washington and Brussels is to remain engaged with Moscow in order to allay fears of encirclement and work constructively on a system of common security.

Inferring from the conflict in Georgia that the world is about to descend into a new cold war is problematic because international politics is a baffling mix of patterned regularities and novel events, deliberate choices and inadvertent accidents. Cognitive psychologists find that we often get blindsided by the way things turn out because of our tendency to imagine that the future can be foreseen simply by extrapolating from the moment. Depicting the global future as a linear extension of the present carries with it the pitfall of focusing on situations, not processes (Dörner 1996). To make useful forecasts about U.S.-Russian relations, we must understand the causal process that produced the situation in Georgia, as well as whether conditions are such that this process will spawn other serious disputes elsewhere. Of course, unraveling complex processes is not easy. Psychological research indicates that most people overlook processes that build slowly; they misjudge the cumulative probability associated with a complicated chain of events; and they underestimate how slow, incremental changes within in a causal chain can give rise to a large, abrupt transformation once some critical threshold is passed. It is for these reasons that Danish physicist and Nobel laureate Niels Bohr once quipped that "prediction is difficult, especially about the future."

HUMAN CHOICE AND THE GLOBAL FUTURE

We have raised the preceding questions to encourage you to think about what alternative global futures are possible, probable, and preferable. Your answers provide the rough outline for a scenario about the global future. Recall from Chapter 1 that system transformation may be said to have occurred when we have a new answer to one of three questions: (1) What are the system's basic units? (2) What are the predominant foreign policy goals that these units seek with respect to one another? and (3) What can these units do to one another with their military and economic capabilities? Does your scenario suggest that the international system will undergo a major transformation? If so, what will be its most likely consequences?

Although we cannot know exactly what the future will hold, exploring different scenarios is valuable because it improves the choices we make here and now. As discussed in earlier chapters of this book, our images of the future—what we expect, what we hope for, and what we fear—all exert an influence on the present. "If our image of the future were different," explains policy analyst Willis Harman (1976, 1), "the decisions of today would be different." An inspiring vision, he adds, "will impel us to action." But "if there is no commonly held image of what is worth striving for, our society will lack both motivation and direction."

Thus the future is not something that just happens; we can shape it with our choices. How, then, should we proceed? Roughly 2,500 years ago, the Greek philosopher Heraclitus of Ephesus observed that nothing about the future is inevitable except change. Rather than fearing change, we should proceed toward the global future by welcoming its opportunities. As U.S. President John F. Kennedy noted in a speech delivered at American University following the Cuban missile crisis, too many of us think "we are gripped by forces we cannot control." But "we need not accept that view," he concluded. "No problem of human destiny is beyond human beings."

CHAPTER SUMMARY

- Social scientists cannot predict the global future with absolute certainty because world politics is a complex mix of chance and human choice.

- The study of the global future entails imagining what is possible, forecasting what is probable, and determining how to attain what is preferable.

- Forecasting what is likely to happen in world politics is difficult because many trends are nonlinear and some display abrupt, discontinuous change. A key task in futures research is to discern which global trends are transient and which will transform the world system.

- Because trends interact, sometimes amplifying and at other times abating one another's impact, it is important to examine the configuration of global trends rather than focus on a single trend in isolation.

KEY TERMS

clash of civilizations   green revolution

end of history   scenario

SUGGESTED READINGS

Cornish, Edward. *Futuring: The Exploration of the Future*. Bethesda, MD: World Future Society, 2004.

Fukuyama, Francis, ed. *Blindside: How to Anticipate Forcing Events and Wild Cards in Global Politics*. Washington, DC: Brookings, 2008.

National Intelligence Council. *Mapping the Global Future: Report of the National Intelligence Council's 2020 Project*. Washington, DC: National Intelligence Council, 2004.

Smil, Vaclav. *Global Catastrophes and Trends: The Next Fifty Years*. Cambridge, MA: The MIT Press, 2008.

Taagepera, Rein. *Making Social Science More Scientific: The Need for Predictive Models*. New York: Oxford University Press, 2008.

CRITICAL THINKING QUESTIONS

What if the terrorists who hijacked United and American Airlines aircraft on September 11, 2001 had been arrested before they could commandeer those flights? Would that have made the war in Iraq less likely? In the absence of Al Qaeda attacks on New York and Washington, would President George W. Bush have committed the U.S. military to a conflict that involved nation-building operations, which he had criticized while debating Al Gore during the 2000 presidential campaign? Or, given Osama bin Laden's desire to strike the United States, is it probable that some other Al Qaeda attack would have occurred, leading Bush to adopt the doctrine of preemption and topple Saddam Hussein's regime even if 9/11 did not happen?

International relations theorists often use counterfactual reasoning *to explore what might have taken place in world politics if some presumed causal factor (X) was changed while all others were held constant. Normally, this entails asking, "If X had not occurred, what would have resulted?" Raising "what if" questions help theorists evaluate their assumptions about why a particular event transpired the way it did, and gauge the importance of the factor they are negating relative to other hypothesized causes. When used judiciously, counterfactuals can mitigate what psychologists call the* hindsight bias*—the tendency to see events that have happened as all but inevitable after they have occurred.*

The challenges of conducting effective counterfactual analyses are considerable. The most persuasive counterfactuals make the case for a different future based on a clear, specific, and plausible change to a single causal factor that is proximate in time to the outcome under investigation. As the sociologist Max Weber once put it, good counterfactual reasoning involves a minimal rewrite of history.

Consider how you could use counterfactual reasoning to explore the global future. Looking back over the last decade, is there some event that you think has moved contemporary history down a particular path, narrowing the probability of certain potential futures while expanding the probability of others? How would the odds of those potential futures change if that event had not occurred? Would a global future that you prefer become more or less likely if something other than that event had happened? Based on what your counterfactual reasoning suggests, are there any foreign policy recommendations that you would make to national leaders about dealing with emerging issues on the international horizon?

Glossary

A

absolute gains conditions in which all participants in exchanges become better off.

acid rain precipitation that has been made acidic through contact with sulfur dioxide and nitrogen oxide.

agenda setting the ability to influence which issues receive attention from governments and international organizations by giving them publicity.

alliance a formal agreement among sovereign states for the purpose of coordinating their behavior to increase mutual security.

antidumping duties tariffs imposed to offset another state's alleged selling of a product at below the cost to produce it.

appeasement a strategy of making concessions to another state in the hope that, satisfied, it will not make additional claims.

arbitrage the selling of one currency (or product) and purchase of another to make a profit on the changing exchange rates; traders ("arbitragers") help to keep states' currencies in balance through their speculative efforts to buy large quantities of devalued currencies and sell them in countries where they are valued more highly.

arms control bilateral or multilateral agreements to contain arms buildups by setting limits on the number and types of weapons that states are permitted.

arms race an action-reaction process in which rival states rapidly increase their military capabilities in response to one another.

asylum the provision of sanctuary to safeguard refugees escaping from the threat of persecution in the country where they hold citizenship.

asymmetric war an armed conflict between belligerents of vastly unequal military strength, in which the weaker side is often a nonstate actor that relies on unconventional tactics.

attribution bias the tendency to emphasize situational factors when explaining one's own behavior while stressing dispositional factors when explaining the same behavior in others.

autocratic rule a governmental system where unlimited power is concentrated in the hands of a single person.

B

balance of payments a calculation summarizing a country's financial transactions with the external world, determined by the level of credits (export earnings, profits from foreign investment, receipts of foreign aid) minus the country's total international debts (imports, interest payments on international debts, foreign direct investments, and the like).

balance of power the theory that national survival in an anarchic world is most likely when military power is distributed to prevent a single hegemon or bloc from dominating the state system.

balance of trade a calculation based on the value of merchandise goods and services imported and exported.

A deficit occurs when a country buys more from abroad than it sells.

balancer an influential global or regional state that throws its support in decisive fashion to the weaker side of the balance of power.

bandwagon the tendency for weak states to seek alliance with the strongest power, irrespective of that power's ideology or form of government, in order to increase security.

barter the exchange of one good for another rather than the use of currency to buy and sell items.

beggar-thy-neighbor politics the attempt to promote trade surpluses through policies that cause other states to suffer trade deficits.

behavioralism an approach to the study of world politics that emphasizes the application of the scientific method.

bilateral relationships or agreements between two states.

biodiversity the variety of life on Earth.

bipolar an international system with two dominant power centers.

brain drain the exodus of the most educated people from their homeland to a more prosperous foreign country where the opportunities for high incomes are better, which deprives their homeland of their ability to contribute to its economic development.

brinkmanship intentionally taking enormous risks in bargaining with an adversary in order to compel submission.

bureaucratic politics a description of decision making that sees foreign policy choices as based on bargaining and compromises among government agencies.

Bush Doctrine a policy that singles out states that support terrorist groups and advocates military strikes against them to prevent a future attack on the United States.

C

capital mobility hypothesis the contention that MNCs' movement of investment capital has led to the globalization of finance.

carrying capacity the maximum biomass that can be supported by a given territory.

cartel an organization of the producers of a commodity that seeks to regulate the pricing and production of that commodity to increase revenue.

civil war armed conflict within a country between the central government and one or more insurgent groups, sometimes referred to as internal war.

clash of civilizations the thesis that future international conflicts will be based on competing cultural values.

coercive diplomacy the use of threats or limited armed force to persuade an adversary to alter its foreign and/or domestic policies.

cognitive dissonance the psychological tendency to deny or rationalize away discrepancies between one's preexisting beliefs and new information.

collective defense a military organization within a specific region created to protect its members from external attack.

collective goods goods from which everyone benefits regardless of their individual contributions.

collective security a security regime based on the principle that an act of aggression by any state will be met by a collective response from the rest.

colonialism the rule of a region by an external sovereign power.

commercial liberalism an economic theory advocating free markets and the removal of barriers to the flow of trade and capital.

communitarianism an ethical theory that places the ultimate source of moral value in political communities.

comparative advantage the concept in liberal economic theory that a state will benefit if it specializes in those goods it can produce comparatively cheaply and acquires through trade goods that it can only produce at a higher cost.

compellence a threat of force aimed at making an adversary grant concessions against its will.

complex interdependence a model of world politics based on the assumptions that states are not the only important actors, security is not the dominant national goal, and military force is not the only significant instrument of foreign policy.

concert a cooperative agreement among great powers to jointly manage international relations.

consequentialism an approach to evaluating moral choices on the basis of the results of the action taken.

constitutional democracy a governmental system in which political leaders' power is limited by a body of fundamental principles, and leaders are held accountable to citizens through regular, fair, and competitive elections.

containment a term coined by U.S. policy maker George Kennan for deterring expansion by the Soviet Union, which has since been used to describe a strategy aimed at preventing a state from using force to increase its territory or sphere of influence.

contingent behavior actions that depend on what others are doing.

cosmopolitanism an ethical theory that places the ultimate source of moral value in individuals.

counterforce targeting strategy targeting nuclear weapons on the military capabilities of an opponent.

countervailing duties tariffs imposed by a government to offset suspected subsidies provided by foreign governments to their producers.

countervalue targeting strategy targeting strategic nuclear weapons against an enemy's most valued non-military resources, such as the people and industries located in its cities (sometimes known as countercity targeting).

covert operations secret activities undertaken by a state outside its borders through clandestine means to achieve specific political or military goals with respect to another state.

crosscutting cleavages a situation where politically relevant divisions between international actors are contradictory, with their interests pulling them together on some issues and separating them on others.

D

decolonization the achievement of independence by countries that were once colonies of other states.

democratic peace the theory that although democratic states sometimes wage wars against other states, they do not fight each other.

demographic transition an explanation of population changes that highlights the role of birth and death rates in moving countries from stable to rapidly increasing and finally to declining populations.

dependency theory a view of development asserting that the leading capitalist states dominate and exploit the poorer countries on the periphery of the world economy.

dependent development the industrialization of areas outside of the leading capitalist states within the confines set by the dominant capitalist states, which enables the poor to become wealthier without ever catching up to the core Global North countries.

desertification the creation of deserts due to soil erosion, overfarming, and deforestation, which converts cropland to nonproductive, arid sand.

détente a strategy of relaxing tensions between adversaries to reduce the possibility of war.

deterrence a strategy designed to dissuade an adversary from doing what it would otherwise do.

development the processes through which a country increases its capacity to meet its citizens' basic human needs and raise their standard of living.

devolution granting political power to ethnopolitical groups within a state under the expectation that greater autonomy for them in particular regions will curtail their quest for independence.

diasporas the migration of religious or ethnic groups to foreign lands despite their continued affiliation with the land and customs of their origin.

digital divide the division between those states that have a high proportion of Internet users and hosts, and those that do not.

diplomatic recognition the formal legal acceptance of a state's official status as an independent country. *De facto* recognition acknowledges the factual existence of another state or government short of full recognition. *De jure* recognition gives a government formal, legal recognition.

disarmament agreements to reduce or eliminate weapons or other means of attack.

displaced people people involuntarily uprooted from their homes but still living in their own countries.

diversionary theory of war the contention that leaders initiate conflict abroad as a way of steering public opinion at home away from controversial domestic issues.

domino theory a metaphor popular during the Cold War which predicted that if one state fell to communism, its neighbors would also fall in a chain reaction, like a row of falling dominoes.

dualism the existence of a rural, impoverished, and neglected sector of society alongside an urban, developing, or modernizing sector, with little interaction between the two.

E

economic sanctions the punitive use of trade or monetary measures, such as an embargo, to harm the economy of an enemy state in order to exercise influence over its policies.

end of history the thesis that the demise of communism marked the triumph of Western market democracy and the end of humanity's ideological evolution.

ethnopolitical group people whose identity is primarily defined by their sense of sharing common ancestral nationality, language, cultural heritage, and kinship ties.

exchange rate the rate at which one state's currency is exchanged for another state's currency in the global marketplace.

export quotas barriers to commerce agreed to by two trading states to protect their domestic producers.

export-led industrialization a growth strategy that concentrates on developing domestic export industries capable of competing in overseas markets.

extended deterrence the use of military threats by a great power to deter an attack on its allies.

externalities the unintended side effects of choices that reduce the true value of the original decision.

F

failed states countries whose governments have little or no control over their territory and population.

failing states states in danger of political collapse due to overwhelming internal strife.

fertility rate the average number of children born to a woman during her lifetime.

firebreak the psychological barrier between conventional and nuclear war.

First World the relatively wealthy industrialized countries that share a commitment to varying forms of democratic political institutions and developed market economies.

fixed exchange rates a system under which states establish the parity of their currencies and commit to keeping fluctuations in their exchange rates within narrow limits.

floating exchange rates an unmanaged process whereby market forces rather than governments influence the relative rate of exchange for currencies between countries.

foreign direct investment (FDI) an investment in a country involving a long-term relationship and control of an enterprise by nonresidents and including equity capital, reinvestment of earnings, other long-term capital, and short-term capital as shown in balance of payments.

free riders those who enjoy the benefits of collective goods but pay little or nothing for them.

functionalism a theory of political integration based on the assumption that technical cooperation among different nationalities in economic and social fields will build communities that transcend sovereign states.

G

genocide the deliberate extermination of an ethnic or minority group.

geopolitics a school of thought claiming that states' foreign policies are determined by their location, natural resources, and physical environment.

Global East the rapidly growing economies of East and South Asia that have made their countries competitors with the traditionally dominant members of the Global North.

Global North a term used to refer to the world's wealthy, industrialized countries located primarily in the Northern Hemisphere.

Global South a term used to designate the less-developed countries located primarily in the Southern Hemisphere.

global village a popular image used to describe the growth of awareness that all people share a common fate, stemming from a view that the world is an integrated and interdependent whole.

globalization a set of processes that are widening, deepening, and accelerating the interconnectedness among societies.

green revolution the introduction of high-yield seeds, chemical fertilizers, and other agricultural technologies to Global South countries.

greenhouse effect the phenomenon producing planetary warming when gases released by burning fossil fuels act as a blanket in the atmosphere, thereby increasing temperatures.

Group of 77 (G-77) the coalition of Third World countries that sponsored the 1963 Joint Declaration of Developing Countries calling for reforms to allow greater equity in North-South trade.

Group of Five (G-5) a group of advanced industrial democracies composed of the United States, Britain, France, Japan, and Germany.

Group of Seven (G-7)/Group of Eight (G-8) a group of advanced industrialized democracies composed of the United States, Britain, France, Japan, Germany, Canada, and Italy that meets in regular economic summit conferences; since 1997, known as the G-8 with the addition of Russia.

groupthink the propensity for members of small, cohesive groups to accept the group's prevailing attitudes in the interest of group harmony, rather than speak out for what they believe.

H

Heavily Indebted Poor Countries (HIPCs) the subset of countries identified by the World Bank's Debtor Reporting System whose ratios of government debt to gross national product are so substantial that they cannot meet their payment obligations without experiencing political instability and economic collapse.

hegemon a single, overwhelmingly powerful state that exercises predominate influence over the global system.

hegemonic stability theory a school of thought that argues free trade and economic order depend on the existence of an overwhelmingly powerful state willing and able to use its strength to open and organize world markets.

high politics the category of global issues related to military and security aspects of relations between governments and peoples.

human rights the political and social entitlements recognized by international law as inalienable and valid for individuals in all countries by virtue of their humanity.

human security a concept that refers to the degree to which the welfare of individuals is protected and advanced, in contrast to national security which puts the interests of states first.

humanitarian intervention the use of peacekeeping forces by foreign states or international organizations to protect endangered people from gross violations of their human rights.

hypotheses conjectural statements that describe the relationship between an independent variable (the presumed cause) and a dependent variable (the effect).

I

imperial overstretch the historical tendency of hegemons to weaken themselves through costly foreign pursuits that drain their resources.

import quotas limits on the quantity of particular products that can be imported.

import-substitution industrialization a strategy for economic development that involves encouraging domestic entrepreneurs to manufacture products traditionally imported from abroad.

indigenous peoples the native ethnic and cultural inhabitant populations within countries ruled by a government controlled by others, often referred to as the "Fourth World."

individual level of analysis an analytical approach to the study of world politics that emphasizes the psychological factors motivating people who make foreign policy decisions on behalf of states and other global actors.

inelastic demand a condition under which the quantity demanded of a good does not decrease as its price increases.

infant industry a newly established industry that is not yet strong enough to compete effectively in the global marketplace.

information warfare attacks on an adversary's telecommunications and computer networks to degrade the technological systems vital to its defense and economic well-being.

intergovernmental organizations (IGOs) institutions created and joined by states' governments, which give them authority to make collective decisions to manage particular problem(s) on the global agenda.

international liquidity reserve assets used to settle international accounts.

international monetary system the financial procedures governing the exchange and conversion of national currencies so that they can be bought and sold for one another to calculate the value of currencies and credits when capital is transferred across borders through trade, investment, and loans.

international political economy the study of the intersection of politics and economics that illuminates the reasons why changes occur in the distribution of states' wealth and power.

international regimes sets of principles, norms, rules, and decision-making procedures agreed to by a group of states to guide their behavior in particular issue areas.

internationalized civil war an armed conflict between the central government of a country and insurgents with outside intervention by at least one other state in support of the insurgents.

interstate war sustained armed combat between two or more sovereign states.

irredentism efforts by an ethnonational or religious group to regain control of territory by force so that existing state boundaries will no longer separate the group.

isolationism a policy of withdrawing from active participation with other actors in world affairs and instead concentrating state efforts on managing internal affairs.

J

just war doctrine a set of criteria that indicate when it is morally justifiable to wage war and how it should be fought once it begins.

L

laissez-faire economics from a French phrase (meaning literally "let do") that Adam Smith and other commercial liberals in the eighteenth century used to describe the advantages of free-wheeling capitalism without government interference in economic affairs.

least developed countries (LDCs) the most impoverished states in the Global South.

Liberal International Economic Order (LIEO) the set of regimes created after World War II, designed to promote monetary stability and reduce barriers to the free flow of trade and capital.

long-cycle theory a theory that focuses on the rise and fall of the leading global power as the central political process of the modern world system.

low politics the category of global issues related to the economic, social, and environmental aspects of relations between governments and people.

M

massive retaliation a policy of responding to any act of aggression with the most destructive capabilities available, including nuclear weapons.

mercantilism the seventeenth-century theory preaching that trading states should increase their wealth and power by expanding exports and protecting their domestic economy from imports.

microfinance providing small loans to poor entrepreneurs, usually to help start or expand a small business.

military intervention overt or covert use of force by one or more countries that cross the border of another country in order to affect the target country's government and policies.

military necessity a legal doctrine asserting that violation of the rules of war may be excused during periods of extreme emergency.

military-industrial complex a term coined by U.S. president Eisenhower to describe the coalition among arms manufacturers, military bureaucracies, and top government officials that promotes defense expenditures for its own profit and power.

mirror images the tendency of people in competitive interaction to perceive each other similarly—to see an adversary the same way as an adversary sees them.

modernization a view of development that argues that self-sustaining economic growth is created through technological innovation, efficient production, and investments from capital accumulation.

money supply the total amount of currency in circulation in a state, calculated to include demand deposits—such as checking accounts—in commercial banks and time deposits—such as savings accounts and bonds—in savings banks.

moral hazard a situation in which international institutions create incentives for states to behave recklessly.

most-favored-nation (MFN) principle unconditional nondiscriminatory treatment in trade between contracting parties guaranteed by GATT; in 1997, U.S. senator Daniel Patrick Moynihan introduced legislation to replace the term with "normal trade relations" (NTR) to better reflect its true meaning.

multinational corporations (MNCs) business enterprises headquartered in one state that invest and operate extensively in other states.

multiple independently targetable reentry vehicles (MIRVs) a technological innovation permitting many nuclear warheads to be delivered from a single missile.

multipolar an international system with more than two dominant power centers.

mutual assured destruction (MAD) a system of deterrence in which both sides possess the ability to survive a first strike and launch a devastating retaliatory attack.

N

nationalism the belief that political loyalty lies with a body of people who share ethnicity, linguistic, or cultural affinity, and perceive themselves to be members of the same group.

neofunctionalism a revised functionalist theory asserting that the IGOs states create to manage common problems provide benefits that exert pressures for further political integration.

neomercantilism a contemporary version of classical mercantilism which advocates promoting domestic production and a balance-of-payment surplus by subsidizing exports and using tariffs and nontariff barriers to reduce imports.

newgroup syndrome the propensity of members of newly formed groups to conform with the opinions expressed by powerful, assertive peers or the group's leader due to a lack of well-developed procedural norms.

New International Economic Order (NIEO) the 1974 policy resolution in the UN that called for a North-South dialogue to open the way for the less-developed countries of the Global South to participate more fully in the making of international economic policy.

newly industrialized countries (NICs) prosperous members of the Global South, which have become important exporters of manufactured goods.

nonalignment a foreign policy posture that rejects participating in military alliances with rival blocs for fear that formal alignment will entangle the state in an unnecessary war.

nondiscrimination a principle for trade that proclaims that goods produced at home and abroad are to be treated the same for import and export agreements.

nongovernmental organizations (NGOs) transnational organizations of private citizens that include foundations, professional associations, multinational corporations, or groups in different countries joined together to work toward common interests.

nonintervention the legal principle prohibiting one state from interfering in another state's internal affairs.

nonstate actors all transnationally active groups other than states, such as international organizations whose members are states (IGOs) and nongovernmental organizations (NGOs) whose members are individuals and private groups from more than one state.

nontariff barrier governmental restrictions not involving a tax or duty that increase the cost of importing goods into a country.

norms generalized standards of behavior that embody collective expectations about appropriate conduct.

Nuclear Nonproliferation Treaty (NPT) an international agreement that seeks to prevent the spread of nuclear weapons by prohibiting further nuclear weapon sales, acquisitions, or production.

nuclear winter the expected freeze that would occur in the earth's climate from the fallout of smoke and dust in the event nuclear weapons were used, blocking out sunlight and destroying plant and animal life that survived the original blast.

O

official development assistance (ODA) grants or loans to countries from other countries, usually channeled through multilateral aid organizations, for the primary purpose of promoting economic development and welfare.

opportunity costs the concept in decision-making theories that when the occasion arises to use resources, what is gained for one purpose is lost for other purposes, so that every choice entails the cost of some lost opportunity.

orderly market arrangements (OMAs) voluntary export restrictions that involve a government-to-government agreement and often specific rules of management.

overlapping cleavages a situation where politically relevant divisions between international actors are complementary; interests pulling them apart on one issue are reinforced by interests that also separate them on other issues.

ozone layer the protective layer of the upper atmosphere over the earth's surface that shields the planet from the sun's harmful impact on living organisms on the planet.

P

pandemic a disease that spreads throughout one or more continents.

peace-building post-conflict actions, predominantly diplomatic and economic, that strengthen and rebuild governmental infrastructure and institutions in order to avoid recourse to armed conflict.

peaceful coexistence Soviet leader Nikita Khrushchev's 1956 doctrine that war between capitalist and communist states is not inevitable and that interbloc competition could be peaceful.

peacemaking peaceful settlement processes such as good offices, conciliation, and mediation, designed to resolve the issues that led to armed conflict.

polarity the degree to which military and economic capabilities are concentrated among the major powers in the state system.

polarization the degree to which states cluster in alliances around the most powerful members of the state system.

political efficacy the extent to which a policymaker believes in his or her ability to control events politically.

political integration the processes and activities by which the populations of two or more states transfer their loyalties to a merged political and economic unit.

politics the exercise of influence to affect the distribution of values, such as power, prestige, and wealth; to Harold Lasswell, the process that determines "who gets what, when, how, and why."

pooled sovereignty legal authority granted to an IGO by its members to make collective decisions regarding specified aspects of public policy heretofore made exclusively by each sovereign government.

population implosion a rapid reduction of population that reverses a previous trend toward progressively larger populations.

power the ability to make someone continue a course of action, change what he or she is doing, or refrain from acting.

power cycle theory the contention that armed conflict is probable when a state passes through certain critical points along a generalized curve of relative power, and wars of enormous magnitude are likely when several great powers pass through critical points at approximately the same time.

power potential the relative capabilities or resources held by a state that are considered necessary to its asserting influence over others.

power transition theory the contention that war is likely when a dominant great power is threatened by the rapid growth of a rival's capabilities, which reduces the difference in their relative power.

preemption a quick first-strike attack that seeks to defeat an adversary before it can organize a retaliatory response.

preventive diplomacy actions taken in advance of a predictable crisis to prevent superpower involvement and limit violence.

preventive war a war undertaken to preclude an adversary from acquiring the capability to attack sometime in the future.

private international law law pertaining to routinized transnational intercourse between or among states as well as nonstate actors.

procedural rationality a method of decision making based on having perfect information with which all possible courses of action are carefully evaluated.

proliferation the spread of weapon capabilities throughout the state system.

prospect theory a behavioral decision theory that contends decision makers assess policy options in comparison to a reference point and that they take greater risks to prevent losses than to achieve gains.

protectionism a policy of creating barriers to foreign trade, such as tariffs and quotas, that protects local industries from competition.

public international law law pertaining to government-to-government relations.

R

rapprochement in diplomacy, a policy seeking to reestablish normal relations between enemies.

rational choice decision-making procedures guided by careful definition of problems, specification of goals, weighing the costs, risks, and benefits of all alternatives, and selection of the optimal alternative.

Reagan Doctrine a pledge of U.S. backing for anti-communist insurgents who sought to overthrow Soviet-supported governments.

refugees people who flee for safety to another country because of a well-founded fear of persecution.

regional currency union the pooling of sovereignty to create a common currency (such as the EU's euro) and single monetary system for members in a region, regulated by a regional central bank within the currency bloc to reduce the likelihood of large-scale liquidity crises.

relative deprivation people's perception that they are unfairly deprived of the wealth and status in comparison to others who are advantaged but not more deserving.

relative gains a measure of how much one side in an agreement benefits in comparison to the other's side.

remittances the money earned by immigrants working in wealthy countries that they send to family members still living in their home country.

replacement-level fertility one couple replacing themselves with two children, so that a country's population will remain stable if this rate prevails.

reprisal a hostile but legal retaliatory act aimed at punishing another state's prior illegal actions.

S

satisficing the tendency for decision makers to choose the first available alternative that meets minimally acceptable standards.

scenario a narrative description showing how some hypothetical future state of affairs might evolve out of the present one.

schematic reasoning the process by which new information is interpreted by comparing it to generic concepts stored in memory about certain stereotypical situations, sequences of events, and characters.

secession the attempt by a religious or ethnic minority to break away from an internationally recognized state.

Second World during the Cold War, the group of countries, including the Soviet Union and its then-Eastern European allies, that shared a commitment to centrally planned economies.

second-strike capability a state's capacity to retaliate after absorbing a first-strike attack with weapons of mass destruction.

security community a group of states whose high level of noninstitutionalized collaboration results in the settlement of disputes by compromise rather than by force.

security dilemma the propensity of armaments undertaken by one state for ostensibly defensive purposes to threaten other states, which arm in reaction, with the result that their national security declines as their arms increase.

self-determination the doctrine that people should be able to determine the government that will manage their affairs.

self-fulfilling prophecies the tendency for one's expectations to evoke behavior that helps to make the expectations become true.

self-help the principle that in anarchy actors must rely on themselves.

smart bombs precision-guided military technology that enables a bomb to search for its target and detonate at the precise time it can do the most damage.

socialization the processes by which people learn the beliefs, values, and behaviors that are acceptable in a given society.

soft power the ability of a country to get what it wants in international affairs through the attractiveness of its culture, political ideals, and policies.

sovereignty under international law, the principle that no higher authority is above the state.

sphere of influence the area dominated by a great power.

spill over the propensity for successful integration across one area of cooperation between states to propel further integration in other areas.

standard operating procedures (SOPs) rules for reaching decisions about particular types of situations.

state an organized political entity with a permanent population, a well-defined territory, and a government.

state level of analysis an analytical approach to the study of world politics that emphasizes how the internal attributes of states influence their foreign policy behavior.

state-sponsored terrorism formal assistance, training, and arming of foreign terrorists by a state in order to achieve foreign policy goals.

strategic corporate alliances cooperation between multinational corporations and foreign companies in the same industry, driven by the movement of MNC manufacturing overseas.

Strategic Defense Initiative (SDI) a plan conceived by the Reagan administration to deploy an antiballistic missile system using space-based lasers that would destroy enemy nuclear missiles.

structural adjustment reforms aimed at reducing the role of the state while increasing the role of the market in Global South countries' economies.

sunk costs a concept that refers to costs that have already been incurred and cannot be recovered.

sustainable development economic growth that does not deplete the resources needed to maintain growth.

system a set of interconnected parts that function as a unitary whole. In world politics, the parts consist primarily of states, corporations, and other organizations that interact in the global arena.

systemic level of analysis an analytical approach to the study of world politics that emphasizes the impact of international structures and processes on the behavior of global actors.

T

tariff a tax imposed by governments on imported goods.

terrorism the premeditated use or threat of violence perpetrated against noncombatants, usually intended to induce fear in a wider audience.

theory a set of interrelated propositions that explains an observed regularity.

Third World a Cold War term to describe the developing countries of Africa, Asia, and Latin America.

trade integration economic globalization measured by the extent to which world trade volume grows faster than the world's combined gross domestic product.

tragedy of the commons a metaphor, widely used to explain the impact of human behavior on ecological systems, that explains how rational self-interested

behavior by individuals may have a destructive collective impact.

transgenic crops new crops with improved characteristics created artificially through genetic engineering, which combines genes from species that would not naturally interbreed.

transnational banks (TNBs) the world's top banking firms, whose financial activities are concentrated in transactions that cross state borders.

transnational relations interactions across state boundaries that involve at least one actor that is not the agent of a government or intergovernmental organization.

triad the combination of ICBMs, SLBMs, and long-range bombers in a second-strike nuclear force.

Truman Doctrine the declaration by President Harry S. Truman that U.S. foreign policy would use intervention to support peoples who allied with the United States against external subjugation.

two-level games a concept that refers to the interaction between international bargaining and domestic politics.

U

ultimatum a demand that contains a time limit for compliance and a threat of punishment for resistance.

unilateral a strategy that relies on independent, self-help behavior in foreign policy.

unipolar an international system with one dominant power center.

unitary actor an agent in world politics (usually a sovereign state) assumed to be internally united, so that changes in its internal circumstances do not influence its foreign policy as much as do the decisions that actor's leaders make to cope with changes in its global environment.

V

voluntary export restrictions (VERs) a protectionist measure popular in the 1980s and early 1990s, in which exporting countries agree to restrict shipments of a particular product to a country to deter it from imposing an even more onerous import quota.

W

war crimes acts performed during war that the international community defines as illegal, such as atrocities committed against enemy civilians and prisoners of war.

Washington consensus the view that Global South countries can best achieve sustained economic growth through democratic governance, fiscal discipline, free markets, a reliance on free enterprise, and trade liberalization.

world federalism a reform movement proposing to combine sovereign states into a single unified federal state.

X

xenophobia a fear of foreigners.

Z

zero-sum game a situation in which what one side wins, the other side loses.

References

Aaronson, Susan Ariel. (2002) *Taking Trade to the Streets: The Lost History of Public Efforts to Shape Globalization.* Ann Arbor: University of Michigan Press.

Abramowitz, Morton. (2002) "The Bush Team Isn't Coping," *International Herald Tribune* (August 20): 6.

Adler, Emanuel. (2002) "Constructivism and International Relations," pp. 95–118 in Walter Carlsnaes, Thomas Risse, and Beth Simons (eds.), *Handbook of International Relations.* London: Sage.

Albright, Madeleine, with Bill Woodward. (2008) *Memo to the President Elect.* New York: HarperCollins.

Aldonsi, Christian. (2006) *Circle in the Sand: Why We Went Back to Iraq.* New York: Doubleday.

Alesina, Alberto, and Enrique Spolaore. (2003) *The Size of Nations.* Cambridge, MA: MIT Press.

Allawi, Ali A. (2007) *The Occupation of Iraq.* New Haven: Yale University Press.

Allen, John L., and Elizabeth J. Leppman. (2004) *Student Atlas of World Politics,* 6th ed. Guilford, CT: Dushkin/McGraw-Hill.

Allen, Susan Hannah. (2005) "The Determinants of Economic Sanctions Success and Failure," *International Interactions* 31 (April/June): 117–138.

Allison, Graham, and Philip Zelikow. (1999) *Essence of Decision: Explaining the Cuban Missile Crisis,* 2nd ed. New York: Longman.

Anderson, John Lee. (2008) "Fidel's Heir: The Influence of Hugo Chávez," *The New Yorker* (June 23): 46–57.

Angell, Norman. (1910) *The Great Illusion: A Study of the Relationship of Military Power in Nations to Their Economic and Social Advantage.* London: Weidenfeld & Nicholson.

Applebaum, Anne. (2005) "The Sources of American Conduct," *The American Interest* 1 (Autumn): 14–16.

Ardrey, Robert. (1966) *The Territorial Imperative: A Personal Inquiry into the Animal Origins of Property and Nations.* New York: Atheneum.

Aron, Raymond. (1965) *The Great Debate: Theories of Nuclear Strategy.* Garden City, NY: Doubleday.

Arreguín-Toft, Ivan. (2005) *How the Weak Win Wars: A Theory of Asymmetric Conflict.* Cambridge, UK: Cambridge University Press.

Art, Robert J. (2005) "Coercive Diplomacy," pp. 163–177 in Robert J. Art and Robert Jervis (eds.), *International Politics,* 7th ed. New York: Pearson Longman.

————. (2003) "Coercive Diplomacy: What Do We Know?" pp. 359–420 in Robert J. Art and Patrick M. Cronin (eds.), *The United States and Coercive Diplomacy.* Washington, DC: United States Institute of Peace Press.

Axworthy, Lloyd. (2008) "Canada and Antipersonnel Landmines: Human Security as a Foreign Policy Priority," pp. 229–249 in Steve Smith, Amelia

Hadfield, and Tim Dunne (eds.), *Foreign Policy: Theories, Actors, Cases.* Oxford, UK: Oxford University Press.

Baker, James A., III, with Thomas M. DeFrank. (1995) *The Politics of Diplomacy.* New York: G. P. Putnam's Sons.

Baldwin, David A. (ed.). (1993) *Neorealism and Neoliberalism: The Contemporary Debate.* New York: Columbia University Press.

————. (1989) *Paradoxes of Power.* New York: Basil Blackwell.

Baratta, Joseph Preston. (2005) *The Politics of World Federation: From World Federalism to Global Governance.* New York: Praeger.

Barber, Benjamin R. (1995) *Jihad vs. McWorld.* New York: Random House.

Barnet, Michael. (2005) "Social Constructivism," pp. 251–270 in John Baylis and Steve Smith (eds.), *The Globalization of World Politics*, 3rd ed. New York: Oxford University Press.

Barnet, Richard J. (1977) *The Giants: Russia and America* New York: Simon & Schuster.

Baron, Samuel H., and Carl Pletsch (eds.). (1985) *Introspection in Biography: The Biographer's Quest for Self-Awareness.* Hillsdale, NJ: Analytic Press.

Bazerman, Max H., and Michael D. Watkins. (2004) *Predictable Surprises.* Boston: Harvard Business School Press.

Beckman, Peter R., and Francine D'Amico (eds.). (1994) *Women, Gender, and World Politics.* Westport, CT: Bergin & Garvey.

Beisner, Robert L. (2006) *Dean Acheson: A Life in the Cold War.* New York: Oxford University Press.

Beitz, Charles R. (2001) "Human Rights as a Common Concern," *American Political Science Review* 95 (June): 269–282.

Bell, Coral. (2005) "The Twilight of the Unipolar World," *American Interest* 1 (Winter): 18–29.

Berger, Peter, and Thomas Luckmann. (1967) *The Social Construction of Reality.* New York: Anchor.

Bergesen, Albert, and Ronald Schoenberg. (1980) "Long Waves of Colonial Expansion and Contraction, 1415 –1969," pp. 231–277 in Albert Bergesen (ed.), *Studies of the Modern World-System.* New York: Academic Press.

Bhagwati, Jagdish. (2004) *In Defense of Globalization.* New York: Oxford University Press.

Bhutto, Benazir. (2008) *Reconciliation: Islam, Democracy, and the West.* New York: HarperCollins.

————. (1988) *Daughter of Destiny: An Autobiography.* New York: Harper.

Blair, Tony. (1999) "Doctrine of International Community," speech delivered at the Economic Club, Chicago, Illinois, April 24.

Blanton, Shannon Lindsey, and Charles W. Kegley, Jr. (1997) "Reconciling U.S. Arms Sales with America's Interests and Ideals," *Futures Research Quarterly* 13 (Spring): 85–101.

Bloom, Mia. (2005) *Dying to Kill: The Allure of Suicide Terror.* New York: Columbia University Press.

Boli, John, Michael A. Elliot, and Franziska Bieri. (2004) "Globalization," pp. 389–415 in George Ritzer (ed.), *Handbook of Social Problems.* London: Sage.

Bork, Robert. (1989/1990) "The Limits of International Law," *The National Interest* (Winter): 3–10.

Brecke, Peter. (1999) "The Characteristics of Violent Conflict since 1400 A.D.," paper presented at the annual meeting of the International Studies Association, Washington, D.C., February 17–20.

Bremer, Stuart A. (2000) "Who Fights Whom, When, Where, and Why?" pp. 23–36 in John A. Vasquez (ed.), *What Do We Know About War?* Lanham, MD: Rowman & Littlefield.

————. (1992) "Dangerous Dyads: Conditions Affecting the Likelihood of Interstate War, 1816–1965," *Journal of Conflict Resolution* 36 (June): 309–341.

Bremmer, Ian. (2007) *The J Curve: A New Way to Understand Why Nations Rise and Fall.* New York: Simon & Schuster.

Broad, Robin (ed.). (2002) *Global Backlash: Citizen Initiatives for a Just World Economy.* Lanham, MD: Rowman and Littlefield.

Broder, David. (2002) "Senator Brings Vietnam Experiences to Bear on Iraq," *The State* (Columbia, S.C.) (September 18): A15.

Bronfenbrenner, Urie. (1961) "The Mirror Image in Soviet-American Relations," *Journal of Social Issues* 17 (No. 3): 45–56.

Brooks, David. (2007) "The Entitlements People," *The State* (Columbia, S.C.) (October 2): A7.

Brooks, Doug, and Gaurav Laroia. (2005) "Privatized Peacekeeping," *The National Interest* 80 (Summer): 121–125.

Brown, Chris. (1992) *International Relations Theory: New Normative Approaches.* New York: Columbia University Press.

Brown, Lester R. (2002) "Planning for the Ecoeconomy," *USA Today* (March): 31–35.

Bueno de Mesquita, Bruce. (1981) "Risk, Power Distributions, and the Likelihood of War," *International Studies Quarterly* 25 (December): 541–568.

Buhaug, Halvard, and Kristian Skrede Gleditsch. (2008) "Contagion or Confusion? Why Conflicts Cluster in Space," *International Studies Quarterly* 52 (June): 215–233.

Bull, Hedley. (1977) *The Anarchical Society: A Study of Order in World Politics.* New York: Columbia University Press.

Bull, Hedley, and Adam Watson (eds.). (1984) *The Expansion of International Society.* Oxford, UK: Oxford University Press.

Bullock, Alan. (1962) *Hitler: A Study in Tyranny.* New York: Harper & Row.

Burns, Arthur Lee. (1968) *Of Powers and Their Politics.* Englewood Cliffs, NJ: Prentice-Hall.

Bussmann, Margit, and Gerald Schneider. (2007) "When Globalization Discontent Turns Violent: Foreign Economic Liberalization and Internal War," *International Studies Quarterly* 51 (March): 79–97.

Caldwell, Dan. (1977) "Bureaucratic Foreign Policy Making," *American Behavioral Scientist* 21 (September–October): 87–110.

Calloway, Colin G. (1999) *First Peoples: A Documentary Survey of American Indian History.* Boston: Bedford/ St. Martin's.

Caporaso, James A. (1993) "Global Political Economy," pp. 451–481 in Ada W. Finifter (ed.), *Political Science: The State of the Discipline II.* Washington, DC: American Political Science Association.

Caporaso, James A., and David P. Levine. (1992). *Theories of Political Economy.* New York: Cambridge University Press.

Caprioli, Mary. (2005) "Primed for Violence: The Role of Gender Inequality in Predicting International Conflict," *International Studies Quarterly* 49 (June): 161–178.

Caprioli, Mary, and Mark Boyer. (2001) "Gender, Violence, and International Crisis," *Journal of Conflict Resolution* 45 (4): 503–518.

Cardoso, Fernando Henrique, and Enzo Faletto. (1979) *Dependency and Development in Latin America.* Berkeley: University of California Press.

Carothers, Thomas. (2008) "A League of Their Own," *Foreign Policy* 167 (July/August): 44–49.

Carr, E. H. (1939) *The Twenty-Years' Crisis, 1919–1939.* London: Macmillan.

Cashman, Greg. (2000) *What Causes War?* 2nd ed. Boston: Lexington Books.

Cashman, Greg, and Leonard C. Robinson. (2007) *An Introduction to the Causes of War.* Lanham, MD: Rowman & Littlefield.

Centron, Martin, and Owen Davies. (2005) *53 Trends Now Shaping the Future.* Bethesda, MD: World Futures Society.

Chase-Dunn, Christopher. (1989) *Global Formation: Structures of the World-Economy.* Oxford: Basil Blackwell.

Chase-Dunn, Christopher, and E. N. Anderson (eds.). (2005) *The Historical Evolution of World-Systems.* London: Palgrave.

Checkel, Jeffrey T. (1998) "The Constructivist Turn in International Relations Theory," *World Politics* 50 (January 1998): 324–348.

Christensen, Thomas J., and Jack Snyder. (1990) "Chain Gangs and Passed Bucks: Predicting Alliance Patterns in Multipolarity," *International Organization* 44 (Spring): 137–168.

Cincotta, Richard P., and Robert Engelman. (2004) "Conflict Thrives Where Young Men Are Many," *International Herald Tribune* (March): 18.

Clapham, Andrew. (2001) "Human Rights," pp. 368–370 in Joel Krieger (ed.), *The Oxford Companion to Politics of the World,* 2nd ed. New York: Oxford University Press.

Claude, Inis L., Jr. (1989) "The Balance of Power Revisited," *Review of International Studies* 15 (January): 77–85.

———. (1971) *Swords into Plowshares,* 4th ed. New York: Random House.

———. (1962) *Power and International Relations.* New York: Random House.

Cohen, Benjamin J. (2000) *The Geography of Money.* Ithaca, NY: Cornell University Press.

————. (1996) "Phoenix Risen: The Resurrection of Global Finance," *World Politics* 48 (January): 268–296.

————. (1973) *The Question of Imperialism.* New York: Basic Books.

Cohen, Daniel. (2006) *Globalization and Its Enemies.* Cambridge, MA: MIT Press.

Cohen, Eliot A. (1998) "A Revolution in Warfare," pp. 34–46 in Charles W. Kegley, Jr. and Eugene R. Wittkopf (eds.), *The Global Agenda,* 4th ed. New York: McGraw-Hill.

Cohen, Joel E. (2005) "Human Population Grows Up," *Scientific American* 293 (September): 48–55.

————. (1995) *How Many People Can the Earth Support?* New York: Norton.

Cohn, Theodore E. (2005) *Global Political Economy: Theory and Practice,* 3rd ed. New York: Pearson Longman.

Cole, Juan. (2006) "9/11," *Foreign Policy* 156 (September/October): 26–32.

Coleman, Isobel. (2005) "The Payoff from Women's Rights," pp. 191–196 in Robert J. Griffiths (ed.), *Developing World 05/06.* Dubuque, IA: Dushkin/McGraw-Hill.

Collier, Paul. (2007) *The Bottom Billion.* New York: Oxford University Press.

————. (2005) "The Market for Civil War," pp. 28–32 in Helen E. Purkitt (ed.), *World Politics 04/05.* Dubuque, IA: Dushkin/McGraw-Hill.

Cornish, Edward. (2004) *Futuring: The Exploration of the Future.* Bethesda, MD: World Future Society.

Cortwright, David, and George A. Lopez (eds.). (2002) *Smart Sanctions: Targeting Economic Statecraft.* Landham, MD: Rowman and Littlefield.

————. (1995) "The Sanctions Era: An Alternative to Military Intervention," *Fletcher Forum of World Affairs* 19 (May): 65–85.

Cox, Robert J., with Timothy J. Sinclair. (1996) *Approaches to World Order.* Cambridge: Cambridge University Press.

Craig, Campbell. (2008) "The Resurgent Idea of World Government," *Ethics & International Affairs* 22 (Summer): 133–142.

Craig, Gordon A., and Alexander L. George. (1990) *Force and Statecraft,* 2nd ed. New York: Oxford University Press.

Crump, Andy. (1998) *The A to Z of World Development.* Oxford, UK: New Internationalist Publications.

D'Amato, Anthony. (1995) *International Law: Process and Prospect.* Irvington, NY: Transnational Publishers.

Davis, Wade. (1999) "Vanishing Cultures," *National Geographic* (August): 62–89.

Dehio, Ludwig. (1962) *The Precarious Balance.* New York: Knopf.

Deibel, Terry. (2007) *Foreign Affairs Strategy: Logic for American Statecraft.* New York: Cambridge University Press.

Dennis, Matthew. (1991) *Cultivating a Landscape of Peace: Iroquois-European Encounters in Seventeenth-Century America.* Ithaca, NY: Cornell University Press.

de Tocqueville, Alexis. (1969 [1835]) *Democracy in America.* New York: Doubleday.

Deudney, Daniel H. (2006) *Bounding Power: Republican Security Theory from the Polis to the Global Village.* Princeton: Princeton University Press.

Deutsch, Karl W. (1974) *Politics and Government.* Boston: Houghton Mifflin.

Deutsch, Karl W., and J. David Singer. (1964) "Multipolar Power Systems and International Stability," *World Politics* 16 (April): 390–406.

Deutsch, Morton. (1986) "Folie à deux: A Psychological Perspective on Soviet-American Relations," pp. 185–196 in Margaret P. Kearns (ed.), *Persistent Pattern and Emerging Structures in a Waning Century.* New York: Praeger.

de Wijk, Rob. (1998) "Towards a New Political Strategy for NATO," *NATO Review* 46: 14–18.

Diamond, Jared. (2005) *Collapse: How Societies Choose to Fail or Succeed.* New York: Viking.

Dickinson, G. Lowes. (1926) *The International Anarchy, 1904–1914.* New York: Century.

DiRenzo, Gordon J. (ed.). (1974) *Personality and Politics.* Garden City, NY: Doubleday-Anchor.

Dixon, William J. (1994) "Democracy and the Peaceful Settlement of International Conflict," *American Political Science Review* 88 (March): 14–32.

Dobbins, James. (2007) "Who Lost Iraq? Lessons from the Debacle," *Foreign Affairs* 86 (September/October): 61–74.

Dobson, William J. (2006) "The Day Nothing Much Changed," *Foreign Policy* 156 (September/October): 22–25.

Doran, Charles F. (2000) "Confronting the Principles of the Power Cycle: Changing Systems Structure, Expectations, and War," pp. 332–368 in Manus I. Midlarsky (ed.), *Handbook of War Studies II*. Ann Arbor: University of Michigan Press.

———. (1989) "Power Cycle Theory of Systems Structure and Stability: Commonalities and Complementarities," pp. 83–110 in Manus I. Midlarsky (ed.), *Handbook of War Studies*. New York: Unwin Hyman.

Doran, Charles F., and Wes Parsons. (1980) "War and the Cycle of Relative Power," *American Political Science Review* 74 (December): 947–965.

Dörner, Dietrich. (1996) *The Logic of Failure*. Reading, MA: Addison-Wesley.

Dos Santos, Theotonio. (1970) "The Structure of Dependence," *American Economic Review* 60 (May): 231–236.

Dougherty, James E., and Robert L. Pfaltzgraff, Jr. (2001) *Contending Theories of International Relations*, 5th ed. New York: Longman.

Downs, George W. (ed.). (1994) *Collective Security beyond the Cold War*. Ann Arbor: University of Michigan Press.

Doyle, Michael W. (1997) *Ways of War and Peace*. New York: Norton.

Drezner, Daniel W. (2004) "The Outsourcing Bogeyman," *Foreign Affairs* 83 (May/June): 22–34.

Durant, Will. (1954) *Our Oriental Heritage*. New York: Simon and Schuster.

Durning, Alan (1993) "Supporting Indigenous Peoples," pp. 80–100 in Lester A. Brown, et al. (eds.), *State of the World 1993*. New York: Norton.

East, Maurice A. (1978) "The International System Perspective and Foreign Policy," pp. 143–160 in Maurice A. East, Stephen A. Salmore, and Charles F. Hermann (eds.), *Why Nations Act: Theoretical Perspectives for Comparative Foreign Policy Studies*. Beverly Hills: Sage.

Easterbrook, Gregg. (2002) "Safe Deposit: The Case for Foreign Aid," *New Republic* (July 29): 16–20.

Eberstadt, Nicholas. (1995) "Population, Food, and Income: Global Trends in the Twentieth Century," pp. 7–47 in Ronald Bailey (ed.), *The True State of the Planet*. New York: Free Press.

Economist. (2007) *Pocket World in Figures*. London: Economist.

Elliott, Kimberly Ann. (1998) "The Sanctions Glass: Half Full or Completely Empty?" *International Security* 23 (Summer): 50–65.

Elrod, Richard. (1976) "The Concert of Europe: A Fresh Look at an International System," *World Politics* 28 (January): 159–174.

Emmanuel, Arghiri. (1972) *Unequal Exchange: An Essay on the Imperialism of Trade*. New York: Monthly Review Press.

Emmott, Bill. (2002) "Present at the Creation: A Survey of America's World Role," *The Economist* (June 29): 1–34.

Enloe, Cynthia H. (2004) *The Curious Feminist*. Berkeley: University of California Press.

———. (2001) "Gender and Politics," pp. 311–315 in Joel Krieger (ed.), *The Oxford Companion to Politics of the World*, 2nd ed. New York: Oxford University Press.

———. (2000) *Maneuvers: The International Politics of Militarizing Women's Lives*. Berkeley: University of California Press.

Etzioni, Amitai. (2005) *From Empire to Community: A New Approach to International Relations*. London: Palgrave Macmillan.

"Failed State Index." (2008) *Foreign Policy* 167 (July/August): 64–73.

Falk, Richard. (2001) "Sovereignty," pp. 789–791 in Joel Krieger (ed.), *The Oxford Companion to World Politics*, 2nd ed. Oxford: Oxford University Press.

Fallows, James. (2002) "The Military-Industrial Complex," *Foreign Policy* 22 (November/December): 46–48.

Fenton, William N. (1998) *The Great Law and the Longhouse: A Political History of the Iroquois Confederacy*. Norman, OK: University of Oklahoma Press.

Ferencz, Benjamin B., and Ken Keyes, Jr. (1991) *Planet-Hood*. Coos Bay, OR: Love Line Books.

Ferguson, Niall. (2004) *Colossus: The Price of America's Empire*. New York: Penguin.

Festinger, Leon. (1957) *A Theory of Cognitive Dissonance*. Evanston, IL: Row, Peterson.

Fieldhouse, D. K. (1973) *Economics and Empire, 1830–1914*. Ithaca, NY: Cornell University Press.

Fields, Lanny B., Russell J. Barber, and Cheryl A. Riggs. (1998) *The Global Past*. Boston: Bedford.

Finnegan, William. (2002) "Leasing the Rain," *The New Yorker* (April 18): 43–53.

Flanagan, Stephen J., Ellen L. Frost, and Richard Kugler. (2001) *Challenges of the Global Century*. Washington, DC: Institute for National Strategic Studies, National Defense University.

Flint, Colin (ed.). (2004) *The Geography of War and Peace*. New York: Oxford University Press.

Frank, André Gunder. (1969) *Latin America: Underdevelopment or Revolution*. New York: Monthly Review Press.

Freedom House. (2006) *Freedom in the World*. Washington, DC: Freedom House.

Freeland, Jonathan. (2007) "Bush's Amazing Achievement," *New York Review of Books* 54 (June 14): 16–20.

Freud, Sigmund. (1968) "Why War," pp. 71–80 in Leon Bramson and George W. Goethals (eds.), *War*. New York: Basic Books.

Friedman, Thomas L. (2008) *Hot, Flat, and Crowded: Why We Need a Green Revolution—And How It Can Renew America*. New York: Farrar, Straus and Giroux.

————. (2006) "The First Law of Petropolitics," *Foreign Policy* 154 (May/June): 28–36.

————. (1999) *The Lexus and the Olive Tree: Understanding Globalization*. New York: Farrar, Straus and Giroux.

Fukuyama, Francis. (1999) *The Great Disruption: Human Nature and the Reconstitution of Social Order*. New York: Free Press.

————. (1989) "The End of History?" *National Interest* 16 (Summer): 3–16.

Gacek, Christopher M. (1994) *The Logic of Force*. New York: Columbia University Press.

Gaddis, John Lewis. (2005) "Grand Strategy in the Second Term," *Foreign Affairs* 84 (January/February): 2–15.

————. (1997) *We Now Know: Rethinking Cold War History*. New York: Oxford University Press.

Galbraith, Peter W. (2006) *The End of Iraq*. New York: Simon & Schuster.

Garrison, Jean. (2007) "From Stop to Go in Foreign Policy," *International Studies Review* 9 (June): 291–293.

————. (1999) *Games Advisers Play*. College Station: Texas A&M University Press.

Gazzaniga, Michael S. (2005) *The Ethical Brain*. New York: Dana Press.

Geller, Daniel S. (2000) "Power and International Conflict," pp. 259–277 in John A. Vasquez (ed.), *What Do We Know About War?* Lanham, MD: Rowman & Littlefield.

Geller, Daniel S., and J. David Singer. (1998) *Nations at War: A Scientific Study of International Conflict*. Cambridge: Cambridge University Press.

George, Alexander L. (2006) *On Foreign Policy*. Boulder, CO: Paradigm.

————. (1993) *Bridging the Gap: Theory and Practice in Foreign Policy*. Washington, DC: United States Institute of Peace Press.

————. (1991) *Forceful Persuasion: Coercive Diplomacy as an Alternative to War*. Washington, DC: United States Institute of Peace Press.

Gershman, Carl. (2005) Democracy as a Policy Goal and Universal Value," *The Whitehead Journal of Diplomacy and International Affairs* (Winter/Spring): 19–38.

Gerson, Michael. (2006) "The View From the Top," *Newsweek* (August 21): 58–60.

Gibler, Douglas M. (2007) "Bordering on Peace," *International Studies Quarterly* 51 (September): 509–532.

Giddens, Anthony. (1984) *The Constitution of Society: Outline of the Theory of Structuration*. Cambridge: Polity.

Gilpin, Robert. (2001) "Three Ideologies of Political Economy," pp. 269–286 in Charles W. Kegley, Jr. and Eugene R. Wittkopf (eds.), *The Global Agenda*, 6th ed. Boston: McGraw-Hill.

————. (1987) *The Political Economy of International Relations*. Princeton, NJ: Princeton University Press.

————. (1981) *War and Change in World Politics*. New York: Cambridge University Press.

Gladwell, Malcom. (2005) *Blink*. New York: Little, Brown.

Gleditsch, Nils Petter, Peter Wallensteen, Mikael Eriksson, Margareta Sollenberg, and Havard Strand. (2002) "Armed Conflict 1946–2001: A New Dataset," *Journal of Peace Research* 39 (September): 615–637.

Global Trends 2015. (2002) Washington, DC: Central Intelligence Agency.

Glynn, Patrick. (1993) "Letter to the Editor," *Foreign Policy* 90 (Spring): 171–174.

Goldman, Marshall I. (2008) *Petrostate: Putin, Power, and the New Russia.* New York: Oxford University Press.

Goldsmith, Jack I., and Eric A. Posner. (2005) *The Limits of International Law.* New York: Oxford University Press.

Goldstein, Joshua. (2002) *War and Gender.* Cambridge: Cambridge University Press.

———. (1988) *Long Cycles: Prosperity and War in the Modern Age.* New Haven: Yale University Press.

Gore, Al. (2006) *An Inconvenient Truth: The Planetary Emergency and What We Can Do About It.* Emmaus, PA: Rodale.

Grant, Rebecca, and Kathleen Newland (eds.). (1991) *Gender and International Relations.* Bloomington: Indiana University Press.

Greenspan, Alan. (2007) *The Age of Turbulence: Adventures in a New World.* New York: Penguin.

———. (2004) "The Critical Role of Education in the Nation's Economy." Speech delivered at the Greater Omaha Chamber of Commerce (February 20). Retrieved at www.federalreserve.gov/boarddocs/speeches/2004/200402202/default.htm.

Greenstein, Fred I. (1987) *Personality and Politics.* Princeton, NJ: Princeton University Press.

Gregor, Thomas, and Clayton A. Robarchek. (1996) "Two Paths to Peace: Semai and Mehinaku Nonviolence, " pp. 159–188 in Thomas Gregor (ed.), *A Natural History of Peace.* Nashville: Vanderbilt University Press.

Grieco, Joseph M. (1995) "Anarchy and the Limits of Cooperation," pp. 151–171 in Charles W. Kegley, Jr. (ed.), *Controversies in International Relations Theory.* New York: St. Martin's.

Grieco, Joseph M., and John I. Ikenberry. (2003) *State Power and World Markets.* New York: Norton.

Grimmett, Richard F. (2007) *Conventional Arms Transfers to Developing Nations, 1999–2006.* Washington, DC: Congressional Research Service.

———. (2006) *Conventional Arms Transfers to Developing Nations, 1998–2005.* Washington, DC: Congressional Research Service.

———. (2005) *Conventional Arms Transfers to Developing Nations, 1997–2004.* Washington, DC: Congressional Research Service.

———. (2004) *Conventional Arms Transfers to Developing Nations, 1997–2003.* Washington, DC: Congressional Research Service.

———. (2002) *Conventional Arms Transfers to Developing Nations, 1994–2001.* Washington, DC: Congressional Research Service.

Grosby, Steven. (2006) *Nationalism.* New York: Oxford University Press.

Gulick, Edward V. (1955) *Europe's Classical Balance of Power.* Ithaca, NY: Cornell University Press.

Gurr, Ted Robert. (2001) "Managing Conflict in Ethnically Divided Societies," pp. 173–186 in Charles W. Kegley, Jr. and Eugene R. Wittkopf (eds.), *The Global Agenda,* 6th ed. Boston: McGraw-Hill.

———. (2000) *Peoples versus States: Minorities at Risk in the New Century.* Washington, DC: United States Institute of Peace Press.

———. (1993) *Minorities at Risk: A Global View of Ethnopolitical Conflicts.* Washington, DC: United States Institute of Peace Press.

———. (1970) *Why Men Rebel.* Princeton, NJ: Princeton University Press.

Gurr, Ted Robert, Monty G. Marshall, and Deepa Khosla. (2001) *Peace and Conflict 2001.* College Park, MD: Integrated Network for Societal Conflict Research, University of Maryland.

Gvosdev, Nikolas K. (2005) "The Value(s) of Realism," *SAIS Review of International Affairs* 25 (Winter/Spring): 17–25.

Haas, Ernst B. (1953) "The Balance of Power: Prescription, Concept, or Propaganda?" *World Politics* 5 (July): 442–477.

Haass, Richard N. (2008) "The Age of Nonpolarity," *Foreign Affairs* 87 (May/June): 44–56.

———. (1997) "Sanctioning Madness," *Foreign Affairs* 76 (December): 74–85.

Habermas, Jürgen. (1984) *The Theory of Communicative Action,* 2 vols. Boston: Beacon Press.

Hacking, Ian. (1999) *The Social Construction of What?* Cambridge, MA: Harvard University Press.

Halperin, Morton, and Priscilla Clapp with Arnold Kanter. (2006) *Bureaucratic Politics and Foreign Policy,* 2nd. Ed. Washington, DC: Brookings.

Hammes, Thomas X. (2004) *The Sling and the Stone: On War in the 21st Century.* St. Paul, MN: Zenith Press.

Handelman, Howard. (2009) *The Challenge of Third World Development*, 5th ed. Upper Saddle River, NJ: Prentice-Hall.

Hansen, Jim. (2006) "The Threat to the Planet," *New York Review of Books* (July 13): 12–16.

Hansenclever, Andreas, Peter Mayer, and Volker Rittberger (1996) "Interests, Power, and Knowledge," *Mershon International Studies Review* 40 (October): 177–228.

Harbom, Lotta, and Peter Wallensteen. (2007) "Armed Conflict, 1989–2006," *Journal of Peace Research* 44 (5): 623–634.

————. (2005) "Patterns of Major Armed Conflicts, 1900–2004," pp. 121–133 in *SIPRI Yearbook 2005.* New York: Oxford University Press.

Hardin, Garrett. (1968) "The Tragedy of the Commons," *Science* 162 (December): 1243–1248.

Harknett, Richard J. (1994) "The Logic of Conventional Deterrence and the End of the Cold War," *Security Studies* 4 (Autumn): 86–114.

Harman, Willis. (1976) *An Incomplete Guide to the Future.* Stanford, CA: Stanford Alumni Association.

Hart, Gary. (2004) *The Fourth Power: A Grand Strategy for the United States in the Twenty-First Century.* New York: Oxford University Press.

Hausmann, Ricardo. (2001) "Prisoners of Geography," *Foreign Policy* 122 (January/February): 45–53.

Haynes, Jeffrey. (2004) "Religion and International Relations," *International Politics* 41 (September): 451–462.

HDI. (2007) *Human Development Indicators.* New York: United Nations Development Programme.

————. (2006) *Human Development Indicators.* New York: United Nations Development Programme.

————. (2005) *Human Development Indicators.* New York: United Nations Development Programme.

HDR. (2008) *Human Development Report.* New York: United Nations Development Programme.

————. (2007) *Human Development Report.* New York: United Nations Development Programme.

————. (2005) *Human Development Report.* New York: United Nations Development Programme.

Hedges, Chris. (2003) "What Every Person Should Know About War," *New York Times* (July 6): www.nytimes.com.

Hegre, Håvard. (2004) "The Duration and Termination of Civil War," *Journal of Peace Research* 41 (May): 243–252.

Heilbroner, Robert L. (1960) *The Future as History.* New York: Grove Press.

Henkin, Louis. (1991) "Law and Politics in International Relations," pp. 163–188 in Robert L. Rothstein (ed.), *The Evolution of Theory in International Relations.* Columbia: University of South Carolina Press.

————. (1979) *How Nations Behave: Law and Foreign Policy.* New York: Columbia University Press.

Hensel, Paul R. (2000) "Theory and Evidence on Geography and Conflict," pp. 57–84 in John A. Vasquez (ed.), *What Do We Know About War?* Lanham, MD: Rowman & Littlefield.

Heredia, Blanca. (1999) "Prosper or Perish? Development in the Age of Global Capital," pp. 93–97 in Robert M. Jackson (ed.), *Global Issues 1999/00,* 15th ed. Guilford, CO: Dushkin/McGraw-Hill.

Hermann, Charles F. (1972) "Some Issues in the Study of International Crisis," pp. 3–17 in Charles F. Hermann (ed.), *International Crises.* New York: Free Press.

Hermann, Margaret G. (1988) "The Role of Leaders and Leadership in the Making of American Foreign Policy," pp. 266–284 in Charles W. Kegley, Jr. and Eugene R. Wittkopf (eds.), *The Domestic Sources of Foreign Policy,* New York: St. Martin's Press.

————. (1976) "When Leader Personality Will Affect Foreign Policy: Some Propositions," pp. 326–333 in James N. Rosenau (ed.), *In Search of Global Patterns.* New York: Free Press.

Hermann, Margaret G., and Joe D. Hagen. (2004) "International Decision Making: Leadership Matters," pp. 182–188 in Karen A. Mingst and Jack L. Snyder (eds.), *Essential Readings in World Politics,* 2nd ed. New York: Norton.

Herz, John H. (1951) *Political Realism and Political Idealism.* Chicago: University of Chicago Press.

Hewitt, J. Joseph, Jonathan Wilkenfeld, and Ted Robert Gurr. (2008) *Peace and Conflict, 2008.* Boulder, CO: Paradigm.

Hilsman, Roger. (1967) *To Move a Nation.* New York: Doubleday.

Hindle, Tim. (2004) "The Third Age of Globalization," pp. 97–98 in the *Economist, The World in 2004.* London: Economist.

Hoffman, Mark. (1987) "Critical Theory and the Inter-Paradigm Debate," *Millennium* 16 (2): 231–249.

Hoffmann, Stanley. (1971) "International Law and the Control of Force," pp. 34–66 in Karl W. Deutsch and Stanley Hoffmann (eds.), *The Relevance of International Law.* Garden City, NY: Doubleday-Anchor.

———. (1961) "International Systems and International Law," pp. 205–237 in Klaus Knorr and Sidney Verba (eds.), *The International System.* Princeton, NJ: Princeton University Press.

Holbrooke, Richard. (1998) *To End a War.* New York: Modern Library.

Hopf, Ted. (1998) "The Promise of Constructivism in International Relations Theory," *International Security* 23 (Summer): 171–200.

Hopkins, Terence K., and Immanuel Wallerstein, (eds.). (1996) *The Age of Transitions: Trajectory of World Systems 1945–2025.* London: Zed Books.

Horkheimer, Max. (1947) *Eclipse of Reason.* New York: Oxford University Press.

Hottelet, Richard C. (1999) "Desertification: Forgotten Threat," *Christian Science Monitor* (December 15): 8.

Howard, Michael E. (1978) *War and the Liberal Conscience.* New York: Oxford University Press.

Hufbauer, Gary Clyde, Jeffrey J. Schott, and Kimberly Ann Elliott. (1990) *Economic Sanctions Reconsidered,* 2nd ed. Washington, DC: Institute for International Economics.

Human Security Centre. (2006) *Human Security Brief.* Vancouver: University of British Columbia.

Hume, David. (1817) *Philosophical Essays on Morals, Literature, and Politics,* vol. 1. Washington, DC: Duffy.

Huntington, Samuel P. (1996) *The Clash of Civilizations and the Remaking of World Order.* New York: Simon & Schuster.

———. (1991) *The Third Wave: Democratization in the Late Twentieth Century.* Norman: University of Oklahoma Presss.

Huth, Paul K., and Todd L. Allee. (2003) *The Democratic Peace and Territorial Conflict in the Twentieth Century.* Cambridge: Cambridge University Press.

IMF (International Monetary Fund). (2007) *World Economic Outlook.* Washington, DC: International Monetary Fund.

James, Barry. (2001) "Mischievous Species Capitalize on Globalization," *International Herald Tribune* (May 21): 1, 9.

Janis, Irving L. (1989) *Crucial Decisions: Leadership in Policymaking and Crisis Management.* New York: Free Press.

———. (1982) *Groupthink: Psychological Studies of Policy Decisions and Fiascoes,* 2nd ed. Boston: Houghton Mifflin.

Jervis, Robert. (2005) *American Foreign Policy in a New Era.* New York: Routledge.

———. (1997) *System Effects: Complexity in Political and Social Life.* Princeton, NJ: Princeton University Press.

———. (1985) "From Balance to Concert: A Study of International Cooperation," *World Politics* 38 (October): 58–79.

———. (1976) *Perception and Misperception in World Politics.* Princeton, NJ: Princeton University Press.

Johnson, Loch K. (2007) *Seven Sins of American Foreign Policy.* New York: Pearson Longman.

Joyner, Christopher C. (2005) *International Law in the 21st Century: Rules for Global Governance.* Lanham, MD: Rowman & Littlefield.

Judah, Tim. (2000) *Kosovo: War and Revenge.* New Haven: Yale University Press.

Juergensmeyer, Mark. (2003) "The Religious Roots of Contemporary Terrorism," pp. 185–193 in Charles W. Kegley, Jr. (ed.), *The New Global Terrorism.* Upper Saddle River, NJ: Prentice Hall.

Kaarbo, Juliet. (2008) "Coalition Cabinet Decision Making: Institutional and Psychological Factors," *International Studies Review* 10 (March): 57–86.

Kagan, Robert. (2008) *The Return of History and the End of Dreams.* New York: Knopf.

Kaplan, Fred. (2008) *Daydream Believers.* Hoboken, NJ: Wiley.

Kaplan, Morton A. (1957) *System and Process in International Politics.* New York: Wiley.

Kearney, A. T. (2007) "The Globalization Index," *Foreign Policy* (November/December): 68–69.

Keck, Margaret E., and Kathryn Sikkink. (2004) "Transnational Advocacy Networks in International Politics," pp. 222–233 in Karen A. Mingst and Jack L. Snyder (eds.), *Essential Readings in World Politics*, 2nd ed. New York: Norton.

Keegan, John. (2005) *The Iraq War*. New York: Vintage.

———. (1999) *The First World War*. New York: Knopf.

———. (1993) *A History of Warfare*. New York: Vintage.

Kegley, Charles W., Jr. (1994) "How Did the Cold War Die? Principles for an Autopsy," *Mershon International Studies Review* 38 (April): 11–41.

Kegley, Charles W., Jr. , and Eugene R. Wittkopf. (2004) *World Politics: Trend and Transformation,* 9th ed. Belmont, CA: Wadsworth.

Kegley, Charles W., Jr. , and Margaret G. Hermann. (2002) "In Pursuit of a Peaceful International System," pp. 15–29 in Peter J. Schraeder (ed.), *Exporting Democracy*. Boulder, CO: Lynne Rienner.

Kegley, Charles W., Jr. , and Gregory A. Raymond. (2007) *After Iraq: The Imperiled American Imperium*. New York: Oxford University Press.

———. (2003) "Preventive War and Permissive Normative Order," *International Studies Perspectives* 4 (November): 385–394.

———. (2002a) *Exorcising the Ghost of Westphalia: Building World Order in the New Millennium*. Upper Saddle River, NJ: Prentice Hall.

———. (2002b) *From War to Peace: Fateful Decisions in World Politics*. Boston: Bedford/St. Martin's, and Belmont, CA: Wadsworth.

———. (1999) *How Nations Make Peace*. Boston: Bedford/St. Martin's.

———. (1994) *A Multipolar Peace? Great-Power Politics in the Twenty-First Century*. New York: St. Martin's.

———. (1990) *When Trust Breaks Down: Alliance Norms and World Politics*. Columbia: University of South Carolina Press.

———. (1982) "Alliance Norms and War: A New Piece in an Old Puzzle," *International Studies Quarterly* 26 (December): 572–595.

Kegley, Charles W., Jr. , Gregory A. Raymond, and Margaret G. Hermann. (1998) "The Rise and Fall of the Nonintervention Norm," *Fletcher Forum of World Affairs* 22 (Winter/Spring): 81–101.

Kelleher, Ann, and Laura Klein. (2006) *Global Perspectives*, 2nd ed. Upper Saddle River, NJ: Prentice-Hall.

Kennan, George F. (1951) *American Diplomacy, 1900–1950*. New York: New American Library.

———. (1985) "Morality and Foreign Policy," *Foreign Affairs* 64 (Winter): 205–218.

———. (1967) *Memoirs*. Boston: Little, Brown.

———["X"]. (1947) "The Sources of Soviet Conduct," *Foreign Affairs* 25 (July): 566–582.

Kennedy, Paul. (2006) "The Perils of Empire," pp. 69–71 in Helen E. Purkitt (ed.), *World Politics 05/06*. Dubuque, IA: Dushkin/McGraw-Hill.

———. (1987) *The Rise and Fall of the Great Powers*. New York: Random House.

Keohane, Robert O., and Joseph S. Nye. (2001a) *Power and Interdependence*, 3rd ed. New York: Addison Wesley-Longman.

———. (2001b) "Power and Interdependence in the Information Age," pp. 26–36 in Charles W. Kegley, Jr. and Eugene R. Wittkopf (eds.), *The Global Agenda,* 6th ed. Boston: McGraw-Hill.

———. (1977) *Power and Interdependence*. Boston: Little, Brown.

———, (eds.). (1971) *Transnational Relations and World Politics*. Cambridge: Harvard University Press.

Kibbe, Jennifer D. (2004) "The Rise of Shadow Warriors," *Foreign Affairs* 83 (March/April): 102–115.

Kim, Dae Jung, and James D. Wolfensohn. (1999) "Economic Growth Requires Good Governance," *International Herald Tribune* (February 26): 6.

Kim, Woosang. (1989) "Power, Alliance, and Major Wars, 1816–1975," *Journal of Conflict Resolution* 32 (3): 255–273.

Kindleberger, Charles P. (1973) *The World in Depression, 1929–1939*. Berkeley: University of California Press.

Kirkpatrick, David D. (2007) "This War Is Not Like the Others—Or Is It?" *New York Times* (August 26): The Week in Review, 1, 4.

Kissinger, Henry A. (2001) *Does America Need a Foreign Policy?* New York: Simon and Schuster.

————. (1999) *Years of Renewal*. New York: Simon and Schuster.

————. (1992) "Balance of Power Sustained," pp. 238–248 in Graham Allison and Gregory F. Treverton (eds.), *Rethinking America's Security*. New York: Norton.

————. (1982) *Years of Upheaval*. Boston: Little, Brown.

Klare, Michael T. (2001) "The New Geography of Conflict," *Foreign Affairs* 80 (May/June): 49–61.

————. (1990) "Wars in the 1990s: Growing Firepower in the Third World," *Bulletin of the Atomic Scientists* 46 (May): 9–13.

Klinghoffer, Arthur Jay. (2006) *The Power of Projections: How Maps Reflect Global Politics and History*. Westport, CT: Praeger.

Kluger, Jeffrey. (2001) "A Climate of Despair," *Time* (April 9): 30–35.

Knorr, Klaus, and James N. Rosenau (eds.). (1969) *Contending Approaches to International Politics*. Princeton, NJ: Princeton University Press.

Korany, Bahgat. (1986) *How Foreign Policy Decisions Are Made in the Third World*. Boulder, CO: Westview Press.

Koslowski, Rey, and Friedrich V. Kratochwil. (1994) "Understanding Change in International Politics: The Soviet Empire's Demise in the International System," *International Organization* 48 (Spring): 215–247.

Krasner, Stephen P. (1993) "International Political Economy," pp. 453–455 in Joel Krieger (ed.), *The Oxford Companion to Politics of the World*. New York: Oxford University Press.

Krauthammer, Charles. (2006) "But Not At the UN," *Time* (October 23): 39.

————. (2004) "Democratic Realism: An American Foreign Policy for a Unipolar World." Speech delivered at the American Enterprise Institute (February 10).

————. (1993) "How Doves Become Hawks," *Time* (May 17): 74.

————. (1991) "The Unipolar Moment," *Foreign Affairs* 70 (Winter): 23–33.

Krueger, Alan B. (2007) *What Makes a Terrorist*. Princeton, NJ: Princeton University Press.

Kugler, Jacek, Ronald Tammen, and Brian Efird. (2004) "Integrating Theory and Policy," *International Studies Review* 6 (December): 163–179.

Kupchan, Charles H., and Clifford A. Kupchan. (1992) "A New Concert for Europe," pp. 249–266 in Graham Allison and Gregory F. Treverton, (eds.), *Rethinking America's Security: Beyond the Cold War to a New World Order*. New York: Norton.

Lake, Anthony. (2000) *Six Nightmares*. Boston: Little, Brown.

Lamy, Steven L. (2008) "Contemporary Mainstream Approaches: Neo-realism and Neo-liberalism," pp. 124–139 in John Baylis, Steve Smith, and Patricia Owens (eds.), *The Globalization of World Politics*, 4th ed. Oxford, UK: Oxford University Press.

Landes, David S. (1998) *The Wealth and Poverty of Nations: Why Are Some So Rich and Some So Poor?* New York: Norton.

Laqueur, Walter. (2001) "Terror's New Face," pp. 82–89 in Charles W. Kegley, Jr. and Eugene R. Wittkopf (eds.), *The Global Agenda*, 6th ed. Boston: McGraw-Hill.

Larson, Deborah Welch. (1994) "The Role of Belief Systems and Schemas in Foreign Policy Decision-Making," *Political Psychology* 15 (March): 17–33.

Lave, Charles A., and James G. March. (1975) *An Introduction to Models in the Social Sciences*. New York: Harper & Row.

Lebow, Richard Ned. (1981) *Between Peace and War*. Baltimore: Johns Hopkins University Press.

Lee, Laura. (2000) *Bad Predictions: 2000 Years of the Best Minds Making the Worst Forecasts*. Roosevelt Hills, MI: Elsewhere Press.

Leffler, Melvyn P. (2007) *For the Soul of Mankind: The United States, the Soviet Union and the Cold War*. New York: Hill and Wang.

Legrain, Philippe. (2003) "Cultural Globalization Is Not Americanization," *Chronicle of Higher Education* (May 9): B7.

Lemke, Douglas. (2003) "Development and War," *International Studies Review* 5 (December): 55–63.

————. (2002) *Regions of War and Peace*. Cambridge, UK: Cambridge University Press.

Lentner, Howard H. (2004) *Power Politics in Globalization: The Indispensable State*. New York: Routledge.

Levy, Jack S. (2003a) "Applications of Prospect Theory to Political Science," *Syntheses* 135 (May): 215–241.

———. (2003b) "Political Psychology and Foreign Policy," pp. 253–284 in David O. Sears, Leonie Huddy, and Robert Jervis (eds.), *Oxford Handbook of Political Psychology.* New York: Oxford University Press.

———. (2001) "War and Its Causes," pp. 47–56 in Charles W. Kegley, Jr. and Eugene Wittkopf (eds.), *The Global Agenda,* 6th edition. Boston: McGraw-Hill.

———. (1998) "The Causes of War and the Conditions of Peace," *American Review of Political Science* 1: 139–165.

———. (1989a) "The Causes of War: A Review of Theories and Evidence," pp. 209–333 in Philip E. Tetlock, Jo L. Husbands, Robert Jervis, Paul C. Stern, and Charles Tilly (eds.), *Behavior, Society, and Nuclear War.* New York: Oxford University Press.

———. (1989b) "The Diversionary Theory of War: A Critique," pp. 259–288 in Manus I. Midlarsky (ed.), *Handbook of War Studies.* Boston: Unwin Hyman.

———. (1985) "The Polarity of the System and International Stability: An Empirical Analysis," pp. 41–66 in Alan Ned Sabrosky (ed.), *Polarity and War.* Boulder, CO: Westview.

Levy, Jack S., and William R. Thompson. (2005) "Hegemonic Threats and Great-Power Balancing in Europe, 1945–1999," *Security Studies* 14 (January-March): 1–30.

Lind, Michael. (1993) "Of Arms and the Woman," *New Republic* (November 15): 36–38.

Lindblom, Charles E. (1979) "Still Muddling, Not Yet Through," *Public Administration Review* 39 (November/December): 517–526.

Lindsay, James M. (1986) "Trade Sanctions as Policy Instruments," *International Studies Quarterly* 30 (June): 153–173.

Linklater, Andrew. (2002) "Cosmopolitan Political Communities in International Relations," *International Relations* 16 (1): 135–150.

Lipson, Charles. (1984) "International Cooperation in Economic and Security Affairs," *World Politics* 37 (October): 1–23.

Little, Richard. (2007) *The Balance of Power in International Relations: Metaphors, Myths and Models.* Cambridge, UK: Cambridge University Press.

Lorenz, Konrad. (1963) *On Aggression.* New York: Harcourt, Brace & World.

Machiavelli, Niccolò. (1950) *The Prince.* New York: New American Library.

Mackinder, Sir Halford. (1919) *Democratic Ideals and Reality.* New York: Holt.

Mahan, Alfred Thayer. (1890) *The Influence of Sea Power in History.* Boston: Little, Brown.

Majeed, Akhtar. (1991) "Has the War System Really Become Obsolete?" *Bulletin of Peace Proposals* 22 (December): 419–425.

Malaquias, Assis V. (2001) "Humanitarian Intervention," pp. 370–374 in Joel Krieger (ed.), *The Oxford Companion to Politics of the World,* 2nd ed. New York: Oxford University Press.

Malešević, Sinisa. (2008) "The Sociology of New Wars?" *International Political Sociology* 2 (June): 97–112.

Mandelbaum, Michael. (2002) *The Ideas That Conquered the World.* New York: Public Affairs/Perseus.

Mansfield, Edward D., and Jack Snyder. (2005) *Electing to Fight.* Cambridge, MA: MIT Press.

Marling, William H. (2006) *How "American" Is Globalization.* Baltimore, MD: Johns Hopkins University Press.

Martin, Lisa L. (2007) "Neoliberalism," pp. 109–126 in Tim Dunne, Milja Kurki, and Steve Smith (eds.), *International Relations Theories.* Oxford, UK: Oxford University Press.

Mastanduno, Michael. (1991) "Do Relative Gains Matter?" *International Security* 16 (Summer): 73–113.

Mathews, Jessica T. (2000) "National Security for the 21st Century," pp. 9–11 in Gary Bertsch and Scott James (eds.), *Russell Symposium Proceedings.* Athens: University of Georgia.

———. (1998) "Are Networks Better than Nations?" pp. 8–11 in James M. Lindsay (ed.), *Perspectives: Global Issues.* Boulder, CO: Coursewise Publishing.

Matlock, Jack. (2004) *Reagan and Gorbachev: How the Cold War Ended.* New York: Random House.

Mazarr, Michael J. (1999) *Global Trends 2005.* London: Palgrave.

McClelland, Scott. (2008) *What Happened: Inside the Bush White House and Washington's Culture of Deception.* New York: PublicAffairs.

Mearsheimer, John J. (2001) *The Tragedy of Great Power Politics.* New York: Norton.

————. (1995) "A Realist Reply," *International Security* 20 (Summer): 82–93.

————. (1994/95) "The False Promise of International Institutions," *International Security* 19 (Winter): 5–49.

Mearsheimer, John J., and Stephen M. Walt. (2003) "An Unnecessary War," 134 *Foreign Policy* (January/February): 50–58.

Melander, Erik. (2005) "Gender Equality and Interstate Armed Conflict," *International Studies Quarterly* 49 (December): 695–714.

Melloan, George. (2002) "Bush's Toughest Struggle Is with His Own Bureaucracy," *Wall Street Journal* (June 25): A19.

Mendelsohn, Jack. (2002) "America and Russia: Make-Believe Arms Control," *Current History 101* (October): 325–329.

Micklethwait, John, and Adrian Wooldridge. (2001) "The Globalization Backlash," *Foreign Policy* (September/October): 16–26.

Midlarsky, Manus I. (ed.). (2000) *Handbook of War Studies II.* Ann Arbor: University of Michigan Press.

————. (1988) *The Onset of World War.* Boston: Unwin Hyman.

Millennium Development Goals Report. (2005) New York: United Nations Department of Public Information.

Mintz, Alex. (2004) "How Do Leaders Make Decisions? A Poliheuristic Perspective," *Journal of Conflict Resolution* 48 (February): 3–13.

Mitrany, David. (1966) *A Working Peace System.* Chicago: Quadrangle.

Modelski, George, and William R. Thompson. (1999) "The Long and the Short of Global Politics in the Twenty-First Century: An Evolutionary Approach," *International Studies Review*, special issue, edited by Davis B. Bobrow: 109–140.

————. (1996) *Leading Sectors and World Powers.* Columbia: University of South Carolina Press.

Mohan, C. Raja. (2006) "India and the Balance of Power," *Foreign Affairs* 85 (July/August): 17–32.

Morgenthau, Hans J. (1948) *Politics Among Nations.* New York: Knopf.

————. (1985) *Politics Among Nations*, 6th ed. Revised by Kenneth W. Thompson. New York: Knopf.

Morris, Desmond. (1969) *The Human Zoo.* New York: Dell.

Mount, Ian, Matthew Maier, and David H. Freeman. (2003) "The New Military-Industrial Complex," *Business* 2 (March): 102–108.

Murdoch, James C., and Todd Sandler. (2004) "Civil Wars and Economic Growth," *American Journal of Political Science* 48 (January): 138–151.

Murray, Williamson, and Allan R. Millett. (2000) *A War to Be Won.* Cambridge, MA: Harvard University Press.

Naím, Moisés. (2007) "The Free-Trade Paradox," *Foreign Policy* 162 (September/October): 95–96.

Nastsios, Andrew S. (2008) "Beyond Darfur: Sudan's Slide Toward Civil War," *Foreign Affairs* 87 (May/June): 77–93.

National Commission on Terrorist Attacks Upon the United States. (2004) *The 9/11 Commission Report.* New York: Norton.

National Intelligence Council (NIC).(2004) *Mapping the Global Future.* Washington, DC: National Intelligence Council.

NCTC (National Counter-Terrorism Center). (2008) *Report on Terrorism.* Washington, DC: National Counter-Terrorism Center.

Neumann, Iver B. (2007) "'A Speech That the Entire Ministry May Stand for,' or: Why Diplomats Never Produce Anything New," *International Political Sociology* 1 (June): 183–200.

Neustadt, Richard E. (1970) *Alliance Politics.* New York: Columbia University Press.

Newland, Kathleen. (1994) "Refugees: The Rising Flood," *World Watch* 7 (May/June): 10–20.

Niebuhr, Reinhold. (1947) *Moral Man and Immoral Society.* New York: Scribner's.

Nuechterlein, Donald E. (2005) *Defiant Superpower.* Washington, DC: Potomac.

Nye, Joseph S., Jr. (2008) "The Costs and Benefits of 'In and Outers'," *International Studies Review* 10 (March): 156–160.

————. (2005) *Understanding International Conflicts*, 5th ed. New York: Pearson Longman.

————. (2004) *Soft Power: The Means to Success in World Politics.* New York: Public Affairs Press.

————. (2002a) "The Dependent Colossus," *Foreign Policy* (March/April): 74–76.

————. (2002b) *The Paradox of American Power.* New York: Oxford University Press.

———. (2001) "The Changing Nature of World Power," pp. 95–107 in Charles W. Kegley, Jr. and Eugene R. Wittkopf (eds.), *The Global Agenda*, 6th ed. Boston: McGraw-Hill.

———. (2000) *Understanding International Conflicts*, 3rd ed. New York: Longman.

———. (1990) *Bound to Lead: The Changing Nature of American Power*. New York: Basic Books.

Oatley, Thomas. (2008) *International Political Economy*, 3rd ed. New York: Pearson Longman.

Obduah, Emmanuel. (2006) "Combating Global Trafficking in Persons," *International Politics* 43 (April): 241–265.

OEDC. (2007) *World Investment Report*. Paris: Organization for Co-operation and Development.

O'Neill, Onora. (1986) *Faces of Hunger: An Essay on Poverty, Justice and Development*. London: Allen and Unwin.

Onuf, Nicholas. (2002) "Worlds of Our Making: The Strange Career of Constructivism in International Relations," pp. 119–141 in Donald J. Puchala (ed.), *Visions of International Relations*. Columbia: University of South Carolina Press.

———. (1989) *World of Our Making: Rules and Rule in Social Theory and International Relations*. Columbia: University of South Carolina Press.

Oreskes, Naomi. (2004) "Beyond the Ivory Tower: The Scientific Consensus on Climate Change," *Science* 306 (December): 1686.

Organski, A. F. K. (1968) *World Politics*. New York: Knopf.

Organski, A. F. K., and Jacek Kugler. (1980) *The War Ledger*. Chicago: University of Chicago Press.

Ostrom, Charles W., Jr. , and John H. Aldrich. (1978) "The Relationship Between Size and Stability in the Major Power International System," *American Journal of Political Science* 22 (November): 743–771.

O'Sullivan, John. (2005) "In Defense of Nationalism," *The National Interest* 78 (Winter): 22–40.

Owen, John M., IV. (2005) "When Do Ideologies Produce Alliances?" *International Studies Quarterly* 49 (March): 73–99.

Pacala, Stephen, and Robert Socolow. (2004) "Stabilization Wedges: Solving the Climate Problem for the Next 50 Years with Current Technologies," *Science* 305 (August): 968–972.

Packenham, Robert. (1992) *The Dependency Movement*. Cambridge, MA: Harvard University Press.

Packer, George. (2005) *The Assassin's Gate: America in Iraq*. New York: Farrar, Straus and Giroux.

Panama: A Just Cause. (1989) Washington, DC: United States Department of State, Bureau of Public Affairs, Current Policy No. 1240.

Pape, Robert A. (2005) *Dying to Win: The Strategic Logic of Suicide Terrorism*. New York: Random House.

———. (1997) "Why Economic Sanctions Do Not Work," *International Security* 22 (Fall): 90–136.

———. (1996) *Bombing to Win: Air Power and Coercion in War*. Ithaca: Cornell University Press.

Paul, T. V., G. John Ikenberry, and John A. Hall (eds.). (2003) *The Nation-State in Question*. Princeton: Princeton University Press.

Peterson, V. Spike, and Anne Sisson Runyan. (1993) *Global Gender Issues*. Boulder, CO: Westview Press.

Pethokoukis, James. (2006) "Multinationals 2.0," *U.S. News & World Report* (July 31): 42–47.

Piasecki, Bruce. (2007) "A Social Responsibility Revolution in the Global Marketplace," *Christian Science Monitor* (August 9): 9.

Pillar, Paul. (2006) "Intelligence, Policy, and the War in Iraq," *Foreign Affairs* 85 (March/April): 15–27.

Pimn, Stuart L., and Clinton Jenkins. (2005) "Sustaining the Variety of Life," *Scientific American* 293 (September): 66–73.

Porter, Gareth. (1995) "Environmental Security as a National Security Issue," *Current History* 94 (May): 218–222.

Postel, Sandra. (1999) *Pillar of Sand: Can the Irrigation Miracle Last?* New York: Norton.

Pound, Edward T., and Danielle Knight. (2006) "Cleaning Up the World Bank," *U.S. News & World Report* (April 3): 40–51.

Powell, Colin L. (2004) "A Strategy of Partnerships," *Foreign Affairs* 83 (January/February): 22–34.

Powell, Colin L., with Joseph E. Persico. (1995) *My American Journey*. New York: Ballantine.

Power, Jonathan. (2004) "United Nations—Much Maligned, But Much Needed," *International Herald Tribune* (February 26): 6.

Preston, Thomas. (2007) *From Lambs to Lions: Future Security Relationships in a World of Biological and*

Nuclear Weapons. Lanham, MD: Rowman and Littlefield.

—————. (2001) *The President and His Inner Circle: Leadership Style and the Advisory Process in Foreign Affairs.* New York: Columbia University Press.

—————. (1997) "Following the Leader: The Impact of U.S. Presidential Style Upon Advisory Group Dynamics, Structure, and Decision," pp. 191–248 in Paul t'Hart, Eric K. Stern, and Bengt Sundelius (eds.), *Beyond Groupthink: Political Group Dynamics and Foreign Policy-Making.* Ann Arbor: University of Michigan Press.

Preston, Thomas, and Margaret G. Hermann. (2004) "Presidential Leadership Style and the Foreign Policy Advisory Process," pp. 363–380 in Eugene R. Wittkopf and James M. McCormick (eds.), *The Domestic Sources of Foreign Policy.* Lanham, MD: Rowman and Littlefield.

Prestowitz, Clyde. (2005) *Three Billion New Capitalists.* New York: Basic Books.

—————. (2003) *Rogue Nation: American Unilateralism and the Failure of Good Intentions.* New York: Basic Books/Perseus.

Price, Richard, and Christian Reus-Smit. (1998) "Dangerous Liaisons? Critical International Theory and Constructivism," *European Journal of International Relations* 4 (3): 259–294.

Puchala, Donald J. (1994) "Some World Order Options for Our Time," *Peace Forum* 11 (November): 17–30.

Putnam, Robert D. (1988) "Diplomacy and Domestic Politics: The Logic of Two-Level Games," *International Organization* 42 (Summer): 427–460.

Quinn, Jane Bryant. (2002) "Iraq: It's the Oil, Stupid," *Newsweek* (September 30): 43.

Raloff, Janet. (2006) "The Ultimate Crop Insurance," pp. 166–168 in Robert J. Griffiths (ed.), *Global Issues 05/06.* Dubuque, IA: Dushkin/McGraw-Hill.

Rasler, Karen, and William R. Thompson. (2005) *Puzzles of the Democratic Peace: Theory, Geopolitics, and the Transformation of World Politics.* London: Palgrave Macmillan.

Ray, James Lee. (1995) *Democracy and International Conflict: An Evaluation of the Democratic Peace Proposition.* Columbia: University of South Carolina Press.

Raymond, Gregory A. (2004) "International Adjudication and Conflict Management," pp. 221–248 in Howard M. Hensel (ed.), *Sovereignty and the Global Community: The Quest for Order in the International System.* Burlington, VT: Ashgate.

—————. (1999) "Necessity in Foreign Policy," *Political Science Quarterly* 113 (Winter): 673–688.

—————. (1997) "Problems and Prospects in the Study of International Norms," *Mershon International Studies Review* 41 (November): 205–245.

—————. (1994) "Democracies, Disputes, and Third-Party Intermediaries," *Journal of Conflict Resolution* 38 (March): 24–42.

Raymond, Gregory A., and Charles W. Kegley, Jr. (1987) "Long Cycles and Internationalized Civil War," *Journal of Politics* 49 (May): 481–99.

Redfield, Robert. (1962) *Human Nature and the Study of Society*, vol. 1. Chicago: University of Illinois Press.

Regan, Patrick M. (1994) *Organizing Societies for War: The Process and Consequences of Societal Militarization.* Westport, CT: Praeger.

Regan, Patrick M., and Aida Paskevicute. (2003) "Women's Access to Politics and Peaceful States," *Journal of Peace Research* 40 (March): 287–302.

Reiter, Dan, and Allan C. Stam. (2002) *Democracies at War.* Princeton: Princeton University Press.

Richburg, Keith B. (1992) "Why Is Africa Eating Asia's Dust?" *Washington Post National Weekly Edition* (July 20–26): 11–12.

Richlieu, Cardinal [Armand Jean du Plessis]. (1961) *The Political Testament of Cardinal Richelieu*, trans. by Henry Bertram Hill, III. Madison: University of Wisconsin Press.

Ricks, Thomas E. (2006) *Fiasco: The American Military Adventure in Iraq.* New York: Penguin.

Rieff, David. (1999) "The Precarious Triumph of Human Rights," *New York Times Magazine* (August 8): 36–41.

Riggs, Robert E., and Jack C. Plano. (1994) *The United Nations*, 2nd ed. Belmont, CA: Wadsworth.

Riker, William H. (1962) *The Theory of Political Coalitions.* New Haven: Yale University Press.

Robinson, Mary, edited by Kevin Boyle. (2006) *A Voice for Human Rights.* Philadelphia: University of Pennsylvania Press.

Rosecrance, Richard. (1999) *The Rise of the Virtual State.* New York: Basic Books.

—————. (1992) "A New Concert of Powers," *Foreign Affairs* 71 (Spring): 64–82.

———. (1986) *The Rise of the Trading State: Commerce and Conquest in the Modern World*. New York: Basic Books.

Rosenau, James N. (1990) *Turbulence in World Politics: A Theory of Change and Continuity*. Princeton: Princeton University Press.

Rosenau, James N., and Mary Durfee. (1995) *Thinking Theory Thoroughly: Coherent Approaches to an Incoherent World*. Boulder, CO: Westview.

Ross, Dennis. (2007) *Statecraft*. New York: Farrar, Straus and Giroux.

Ross, Lee. D. (1977) "The Intuitive Psychologist and His Shortcomings: Distortions in the Attribution Process," pp. 173–220 in Leonard Berkowitz (ed.), *Advances in Experimental Social Psychology*, vol. 10. New York: Academic Press.

Ross, Michael L. (2001) "Does Oil Hinder Democracy?" *World Politics* 53 (April): 325–361.

Rostow, W.W. (1960) *The Stages of Economic Growth*. Cambridge, UK: Cambridge University Press.

Ruggie, John Gerard. (1998) "What Makes the World Hang Together? Neo-Utilitarianism and the Social Constructivist Challenge," *International Organization* 52 (Autumn): 855–885.

Rummel, Rudolph J. (1994) *Death by Government*. New Brunswick, NJ: Transaction Books.

Russett, Bruce. (2001) "How Democracy, Interdependence, and International Organizations Create a System for Peace," pp. 232–242 in Charles W. Kegley, Jr. and Eugene Wittkopf (eds.), *The Global Agenda*, 6th ed. Boston: McGraw-Hill.

Russett, Bruce, and John Oneal. (2001) *Triangulating Peace: Democracy, Interdependence, and International Organizations*. New York: Norton.

Sachs, Jeffrey D. (2008) *Common Wealth: Economics for a Crowded Planet*. New York: Penguin Press.

———. (2002) "A New Global Effort to Control Malaria," *Science* 4 (October): 122–124.

Sagan, Carl, and Richard Turco. (1993) "Nuclear Winter in the Post-Cold War Era," *Journal of Peace Research* 30 (November): 369–373.

Samin, Amir. (1976) *Unequal Development*. New York: Monthly Review Press.

Samuelson, Robert J. (2006) "This Year Could Mark the End of Pax Americana," *The State* (Columbia, S.C.) (December 19): A9.

Sands, Phillippe. (2005) *Lawless World: America and the Making and Breaking of Global Rules*. New York: Viking Penguin.

Saul, John Ralston. (2005) *The Collapse of Globalization and the Reinvention of the World*. London: Atlantic.

———. (2004) "The Collapse of Globalism and the Rebirth of Nationalism," *Harper's* 308 (March): 33–43.

Saurin, Julian. (2000) "Globalization, Poverty, and the Promises of Modernity," pp. 204–229 in Sarah Owen Vandersluis and Paris Yeros (eds.), *Poverty in World Politics*. New York: St. Martin's.

Schelling, Thomas C. (1978) *Micromotives and Macrobehavior*. New York: Norton.

———. (1966) *Arms and Influence*. New Haven: Yale University Press.

Schmookler, Andrew Bard. (1984) *The Parable of the Tribes: The Problem of Power in Social Evolution*. Berkeley: University of California Press.

Schneider, Gerald, Thomas Widmer, and Dieter Ruloff. (1993) "Personality, Unilateralism, or Bullying: What Caused the End of the Cold War?" *International Interactions* 18 (4): 323–342.

Schroeder, Paul W. (1989) "The Nineteenth Century System: Balance of Power or Political Equilibrium?" *Review of International Studies* 15 (April): 135–153.

Schulz, William F. (2001) *In Our Own Best Interest: How Defending Human Rights Benefits Us All*. Boston: Beacon Press.

Schweller, Randall L. (2004) "Unanswered Threats: A Neoclassical Realist Theory of Underbalancing," *International Security* 29 (Fall): 159–201.

Schwenninger, Sherle R. (2004) "America's 'Suez Moment,'" *The Atlantic* 293 (January/February): 129–130.

Sen, Amartya. (2006) *Identity and Violence: The Illusion of Destiny*. New York: Norton.

Shane, Scott. (2005) "The Beast That Feeds on Boxes: Bureaucracy," *New York Times* (April 10): Section 4, 3.

Shannon, Thomas Richard. (1989) *An Introduction to the World-System Perspective*. Boulder, CO: Westview Press.

Shannon, Vaughn. (2005) "Wendt's Violation of the Constructivist Project: Why a World State is Not Inevitable," *European Journal of International Relations* 11 (4): 581–587.

————. (2000) "Norms Are What States Make of Them: The Political Psychology of Norm Violation," *International Studies Quarterly* 44 (June): 293–316.

Shannon, Vaughn, and Jonathan W. Keller (2007) "Leadership Style and International Norm Violation: The Case of the Iraq War," *Foreign Policy Analysis* 3 (January): 79–104.

Shapiro, Ian. (2007) *Containment: Rebuilding a Strategy Against Global Terrorism*. Princeton: Princeton University Press.

Shimko, Keith L. (1995) "Foreign Policy Metaphors: Falling 'Dominoes' and Drug 'Wars'," pp. 71–84 in Laura Neack, Jeanne A. K. Hay, and Patrick J. Haney (eds.), *Foreign Policy Analysis*. Englewood Cliffs, NJ: Prentice-Hall.

Shultz, Richard H., Jr. , and William J. Olson. (1994) *Ethnic and Religious Conflict*. Washington, DC: National Strategy Information Center.

Simon, Herbert A. (1957) *Models of Man*. New York: Wiley.

Simonis, Udo Ernst, and Tanja Brühl. (2002) "World Ecology—Structures and Trends," pp. 97–124 in Paul Kennedy, Dirk Messner, and Franz Nuscheler (eds.), *Global Trends and Global Governance*. London: Pluto Press.

Singer, Hans W., and Javed A. Ansari. (1988) *Rich and Poor Countries*, 4th ed. London: Unwin Hyman.

Singer, J. David. (2000) "The Etiology of Interstate War," pp. 3–21 in John A. Vasquez (ed.), *What Do We Know About War?* Lanham, MD: Rowman & Littlefield.

————. (1991) "Peace in the Global System," pp. 56–84 in Charles W. Kegley, Jr. (ed.), *The Long Postwar Peace*. New York: HarperCollins.

———— (ed.). (1968) *Quantitative International Politics: Insights and Evidence*. New York: Free Press.

Singer, Peter. (2004) *One World: The Ethics of Globalization*, 2nd ed. New Haven: Yale University Press.

————. (1979) *Practical Ethics*. Cambridge, UK: Cambridge University Press.

SIPRI (Stockholm International Peace Research Institute). (2008) *SIPRI Yearbook*. New York: Oxford University Press.

————. (2007) *SIPRI Yearbook*. New York: Oxford University Press.

————. (2006) *SIPRI Yearbook*. New York: Oxford University Press.

Sivard, Ruth Leger. (1996) *World Military and Social Expenditures 1996*. Washington, DC: World Priorities.

————. (1991) *World Military and Social Expenditures 1991*. Washington, DC: World Priorities.

————. (1982) *World Military and Social Expenditures 1982*. Leesburg, VA: World Priorities.

Slaughter, Anne-Marie. (1997) "The Real New World Order," *Foreign Affairs* 76 (September–October): 183–197.

Slomanson, William R. (2003) *Fundamental Perspectives on International Law*, 4th ed. Belmont, CA: Wadsworth.

Small, Melvin, and J. David Singer. (1982) *Resort to Arms: International and Civil Wars, 1816–1980*. Beverly Hills, CA: Sage.

Smith, Jackie, and Timothy Patrick Moran. (2001) "WTO 101: Myths about the World Trade Organization," pp. 68–71 in Robert J. Griffiths (ed.), *Developing World 01/02*, Guilford, CN: Dushkin/McGraw-Hill.

Smith, Steve. (1997) "Bridging the Gap: Social Constructivism," pp. 183–187 in John Baylis and Steve Smith (eds.), *The Globalization of World Politics*. New York: Oxford University Press.

Snyder, Glenn N. (1971) "'Prisoner's Dilemma' and 'Chicken' Models in International Politics," *International Studies Quarterly* 15 (March): 66–103.

Snyder, Jack. (2004) "One World, Rival Theories," *Foreign Policy* 145 (November/December): 53–62.

————. (1984) "The Security Dilemma in Alliances," *World Politics* 36 (July): 461–495.

Snyder, Glenn H., and Paul Diesing. (1977) *Conflict Among Nations*. Princeton, NJ: Princeton University Press.

Sobek, David. (2005) "Machiavelli's Legacy: Domestic Politics and International Conflict," *International Studies Quarterly* 49 (June): 179–204.

Sorensen, Theodore C. (1963) *Decision Making in the White House*. New York: Columbia University Press.

Spero, Joan E., and Jeffrey A. Hart. (1997) *The Politics of International Economic Relations*, 5th ed. New York: St. Martin's.

Sprout, Harold, and Margaret Sprout. (1965) *The Ecological Perspective on Human Affairs*. Princeton: Princeton University Press.

Spykman, Nicholas. (1944) *Geography of Peace*. New York: Harcourt Brace.

Starr, Harvey. (1978) "'Opportunity' and 'Willingness' as Ordering Concepts in the Study of War," *International Interactions* 4: 363–387.

State of Indigenous People. (2002) Olympia, WA: Center for World Indigenous Studies.

State of the World. (2002) Worldwatch Institute. New York: Norton.

Steele, Brent J. (2007) "Liberal-Idealism: A Constructivist Critique," *International Studies Review* 9 (Spring): 23–52.

Steinberg, James B. (2008) "Real Leaders Do Soft Power: Learning the Lessons of Iraq," *Washington Quarterly* 31 (Spring): 155–164.

Steingart, Gabor. (2008) *War for Wealth*. New York: McGraw-Hill.

Stern, Eric K. (1997) "Probing the Plausibility of the Newgroup Syndrome: Kennedy and the Bay of Pigs," pp. 153–189 in Paul 't Hart, Eric K. Stern, and Bengt Sundelius (eds.), *Beyond Groupthink: Political Group Dynamics and Foreign Policy-Making*. Ann Arbor: University of Michigan Press.

Stern, Eric K., and Bengt Sundelius. (1997) "Understanding Small Group Decisions in Foreign Policy: Process Diagnosis and Research Procedure," pp. 123–150 in Paul 't Hart, Eric K. Stern, and Bengt Sundelius (eds.), *Beyond Groupthink: Political Group Dynamics and Foreign Policy-Making*. Ann Arbor: University of Michigan Press.

Stephenson, Carolyn M. (2000) "NGOs and the Principal Organs of the United Nations," pp. 270–294 in Paul Taylor and R. J. Groom (eds.), *The United Nations at the Millennium*. London: Continuum.

Stiglitz, Joseph. (2006) *Making Globalization Work*. New York: Norton.

————. (2003) *Globalization and Its Discontents*. New York: Norton.

Stoessinger, John G. (2005) *Why Nations Go To War*, 9th ed. Belmont, CA: Thomson-Wadsworth.

————. (1993) *Why Nations Go To War*, 6th ed. New York: St. Martin's Press.

Stopford, John. (2001) "Multinational Corporations," pp. 72–77 in Robert J. Griffiths (ed.), *Developing World 01/02*. Guilford, CT: Dushkin/McGraw-Hill.

Stott, Philip. (2002) "Cold Comfort for 'Global Warming,'" *Wall Street Journal* (March 25): A18.

Suskind, Ron. (2006) *The One Percent Doctrine: Deep Inside America's Pursuit of Its Enemies Since 9/11*. New York: Simon & Schuster.

————. (2004) *The Price of Loyalty: George W. Bush, the White House, and the Education of Paul O'Neill*. New York: Simon & Schuster.

Tarrow, Sidney. (2006) *The New Transnational Activism*. New York: Cambridge University Press.

Tessman, Brock, and Steve Chan. (2004) "Power Cycles, Risk Propensity and Great Power Deterrence," *Journal of Conflict Resolution* 48 (April): 131–153.

Tetlock, Philip. (2006) *Expert Political Judgment*. Princeton: Princeton University Press.

Thakur, Ramesh, and Steve Lee. (2000) "Defining New Goals for Diplomacy in the Twenty-First Century," *International Herald Tribune* (January 19): 8.

't Hart, Paul. (1990) *Groupthink in Government: A Study of Small Groups and Policy Failure*. Amsterdam: Swets & Zeitlinger.

Thatcher, Margaret. (2002) *Statecraft: Strategies for a Changing World*. New York: HarperCollins.

Thomas, Daniel C. (2001) *The Helsinki Effect: International Norms, Human Rights, and the Demise of Communism*. Princeton: Princeton University Press.

Thompson, Kenneth W. (1953) "Collective Security Reexamined," *American Political Science Review* 47 (September): 753–772.

Thompson, William R. (1988) *On Global War: Historical-Structural Approaches to World Politics*. Columbia: University of South Carolina Press.

Thurow, Lester C. (1999) *Building Wealth: The New Rules for Individuals, Companies, and Nations in a Knowledge-Based Economy*. New York: Harper-Collins.

————. (1998) "The American Economy in the Next Century," *Harvard International Review* 20 (Winter): 54–59.

Tickner, J. Ann. (2005) "What Is Your Research Program? Some Feminist Answers to International Relations Methodological Questions," *International Studies Quarterly* 49 (March): 1–21.

————. (2002) *Gendering World Politics*. New York: Columbia University Press.

———. (1988) "Hans Morgenthau's Principles of Political Realism: A Feminist Reformulation," *Millennium* 17 (3): 429–440.

Tickner, J. Ann, and Laura Sjoberg (2007) "Feminism," pp. 185–202 in Tim Dunne, Milja Kurki, and Steve Smith (eds.), *International Relations Theories*. Oxford, UK: Oxford University Press.

Tillema, Herbert K. (2006) *Overt Military Intervention in the Cold War Era*. Columba: University of South Carolina Press.

———. (1994) "Cold War Alliance and Overt Military Intervention, 1945–1991," *International Interactions* 20 (No. 3): 249–278.

Timmerman, Kenneth. (1991) *The Death Lobby: How the West Armed Iraq*. Boston: Houghton Mifflin.

Todaro, Michael P. (2000) *Economic Development*, 7th ed. Reading, MA: Addison-Wesley.

Toner, Robin. (2002) "FBI Agent Gives Her Blunt Assessment" (Columbia, S.C.) *The State* (June 7): A5.

Traub, James. (2000) "Holbrooke's Campaign," *New York Times Magazine* (March 26): 41–45, 66, 69, 81.

Tuchman, Barbara W. (1962) *The Guns of August*. New York: Dell.

Turk, Danilo. (2001) "Genocide," p. 316 in Joel Krieger (ed.), *The Oxford Companion to Politics of the World*, 2nd ed. New York: Oxford University Press.

UIA (Union of International Associations). (2006) *Yearbook of International Organizations*. Munich: K. G. Saur.

UNDP (United Nations Development Programme). (2008) *Human Development Report*. New York: United Nations Development Programme.

———. (2007) *Human Development Report*. New York: United Nations Development Programme.

———. (2005) *Human Development Report*. New York: United Nations Development Programme.

UNHCR. (2007) *2006 Global Trends*. Geneva: High Commissioner for Refugees.

United Nations Environment Programme (UNEP). (2004) *State of the Environment and Policy Perspective*. New York: United Nations.

United Nations Population Division (UNPD). (2004) *World Population Prospects*. New York: United Nations.

Urdal, Henrik. (2006) "A Clash of Generations? Youth Bulges and Political Violence," *International Studies Quarterly* 20 (September): 607–629.

Urquhart, Brian. (2001) "Mrs. Roosevelt's Revolution," *New York Review of Books* 49 (April 26): 32–34.

U.S. ACDA (Arms Control and Disarmament Agency). (2002) *World Military Expenditures and Arms Transfers*. Washington, DC: U.S. Government Printing Office.

———. (1998) *World Military Expenditures and Arms Transfers*. Washington, DC: U.S. Government Printing Office.

U.S. Department of State. (2004) *Patterns of Global Terrorism 2004*, rev. ed. Washington, DC: Department of State.

U.S. National Intelligence Council. (2004) *Mapping the Global Future*. Washington, DC: Government Printing Office.

Van Evera, Stephen. (1999) *Causes of War*. Ithaca, NY: Cornell University Press.

———. (1997) *Guide to Methods for Students of Political Science*. Ithaca, NY: Cornell University Press.

———. (1994) "Hypotheses on Nationalism and War," *International Security* 18 (Spring): 5–39.

———. (1990–91) "Primed for Peace: Europe after the Cold War," *International Security* 15 (Winter): 7–57.

Vasquez, John A. (ed.). (2000) *What Do We Know About War?* Lanham, MD: Rowman & Littlefield.

———. (1998) *The Power of Power Politics: From Classical Realism to Neotraditionalism*. Cambridge, UK: Cambridge University Press.

———. (1993) *The War Puzzle*. Cambridge, UK: Cambridge University Press.

———. (1986) "Capability, Types of War, and Peace," *Western Political Quarterly* 39 (June): 313–327.

Vasquez, John A., and Colin Elman (eds.). (2003) *Realism and the Balancing of Power: A New Debate*. Upper Saddle River, NJ: Prentice Hall.

Vital Signs 2006–2007. (2006) New York: Norton, for the Worldwatch Institute.

Vital Signs 2005. (2005) New York: Norton, for the Worldwatch Institute.

Vreeland, James Raymond. (2003) *The IMF and Economic Development*. Cambridge, UK: Cambridge University Press.

Wallace, Michael D. (1973) "Alliance Polarization, Cross-Cutting, and International War, 1815–1964: A Measurement Procedure and Some Preliminary

Evidence," *Journal of Conflict Resolution* 17 (December): 575–604.

Wallensteen, Peter, and Margareta Sollenberg. (2001) "Armed Conflict 1989–2000." *Journal of Peace Research* 38 (September): 629–644.

Wallerstein, Immanuel. (2005) *World-Systems Analysis.* Durham, NC: Duke University Press.

———. (1988) *The Modern World-System III: The Second Era of Great Expansion of the Capitalist World-System, 1730–1840.* San Diego: Academic Press.

Walsh, Brian. (2006) "The Impact of Asia's Giants," *Time* (April 3): 61–62.

Walt, Stephen M. (2005) *Taming American Power.* New York: Norton.

———. (1987) *The Origins of Alliances.* Ithaca, NY: Cornell University Press.

Walter, Barbara F. (2004) "Does Conflict Beget Conflict?" *Journal of Peace Research* 41 (May): 371–388.

Waltz, Kenneth N. (1988) "War in Neorealist Theory," pp. 39–52 in Robert I. Rotberg and Theodore K. Rabb (eds.). *The Origin and Prevention of Major Wars.* New York: Cambridge University Press.

———. (1979) *Theory of International Politics.* Reading, MA: Addison-Wesley.

Watson, Adam. (1992) *The Evolution of International Society.* London: Routledge.

Wayman, Frank. (1985) "Bipolarity, Multipolarity, and the Threat of War," pp. 115–144 in Alan Ned Sabrosky (ed.), *Polarity and War.* Boulder, CO: Westview.

WDI. (2007) *World Development Indicators 2007.* Washington, DC: World Bank.

———. (2006) *World Development Indicators 2006.* Washington, DC: World Bank.

———. (2005) *World Development Indicators 2005.* Washington, DC: World Bank.

WDR. (2008) *World Development Report 2008.* Washington, DC: World Bank.

———. (2007) *World Development Report 2007.* Washington, DC: World Bank.

———. (2006) *World Development Report 2006.* Washington, DC: World Bank.

Weart, Spencer R. (1994) "Peace among Democratic and Oligarchic Republics," *Journal of Peace Research* 31 (August): 299–316.

Weber, Cynthia. (2001) *International Relations Theory: A Critical Introduction.* London: Routledge.

Wedgwood, Ruth. (2002) "Gallant Delusions," *Foreign Policy* 132 (September/October): 44–46.

Weidenbaum, Murray. (2004) "Surveying the Global Marketplace," *USA Today* (January): 26–27.

Wendt, Alexander. (2003) "Why a World State Is Inevitable," *European Journal of International Relations* 9 (4): 491–542.

———. (1999) *Social Theory of International Politics.* Cambridge: Cambridge University Press.

———. (1995) "Constructing International Politics," *International Security* 20 (Summer): 71–81.

———. (1994) "Collective Identity Formation and the International State," *American Political Science Review* 88 (June): 384–396.

Wendzel, Robert L. (1980) *International Relations: A Policymaker Focus.* New York: Wiley.

White, Donald W. (1998) "Mutable Destiny: The End of the American Century?" *Harvard International Review* 20 (Winter): 42–47.

White, Ralph K. (1990) "Why Aggressors Lose," *Political Psychology* 11 (June): 227–242.

———. (1977) "Misperception in the Arab-Israeli Conflict," *Journal of Social Issues* 33 (1): 190–221.

Williamson, Samuel R., Jr. (1988) "The Origins of World War I," pp. 225–248 in Robert I. Rotberg and Theodore K. Rabb (eds.), *The Origins and Prevention of Major Wars.* Cambridge: Cambridge University Press.

Wilmer, Franke. (2000) "Women, the State and War: Feminist Incursions into World Politics," pp. 385–395 in Richard W. Mansbach and Edward Rhodes (eds.), *Global Politics in a Changing World.* Boston: Houghton Mifflin.

———. (1993) *The Indigenous Voice in World Politics.* Newbury Park, CA: Sage.

Wilson, James Q. (1993) *The Moral Sense.* New York: Free Press.

WIR. (2004) *World Investment Report.* New York: United Nations Conference on Trade and Development.

Wittkopf, Eugene R., Charles W. Kegley, Jr., and James M. Scott. (2003) *American Foreign Policy,* 6th ed. Belmont, CA: Wadsworth.

Wohlforth, William C. (1999) "The Stability of a Unipolar World," *International Security* 24 (Summer): 5–41.

Wolf, Martin. (2004) "A Matter More Than Economics," *Financial Times* (April 13): retrieved at yaleglobal.yale.edu/display.article?id=3701.

Wolfensohn, James. (2004) "The Growing Threat of Global Poverty," *International Herald Tribune* (April 24–25): 6.

Wolfers, Arnold. (1962) *Discord and Collaboration.* Baltimore: Johns Hopkins University Press.

Wolfers, Arnold, and Laurence W. Martin (eds.). (1956) *The Anglo-American Tradition in Foreign Affairs.* New York: Oxford University Press.

Woodward, Bob. (2006) *State of Denial.* New York: Simon & Schuster.

————. (2004) *Plan of Attack.* New York: Simon & Schuster.

————. (2002) *Bush At War.* New York: Simon & Schuster.

World Bank. (2007) *Atlas of Global Development.* Washington, DC: World Bank.

World Bank. (2005) *World Bank Atlas.* Washington, DC: World Bank.

————. (1999) *World Bank Atlas.* Washington, DC: World Bank.

WRI (World Resources Institute). (2004) *SDI: Sustainable Development Index.* Washington, DC: World Resources Institute.

Wright, Quincy. (1942) *A Study of War.* Chicago: University of Chicago Press.

Yang, David W. (2005) "In Search of an Effective Democratic Realism," *SAIS Review of International Affairs* 15 (Winter/Spring): 199–205.

Yuan, Jing-dong (2007) "The Dragon and the Elephant: Chinese-Indian Relations in the 21st Century," *Washington Quarterly* 30 (Summer): 131–144.

Yunker, James A. (2007) *Political Globalization: A New Vision of Federal World Government.* Lanham, MD: University Press of America.

Zacher, Mark W., and Richard A. Matthew. (1995) "Liberal International Theory: Common Threads, Divergent Strands," pp. 107–149 in Charles W. Kegley, Jr. (ed.), *Controversies in International Relations Theory.* New York: St. Martin's.

Zakaria, Fareed. (2002a) "Stop the Babel over Babylon," *Newsweek* (October 16): 34.

————. (2002b) "The Trouble with Being the World's Only Superpower," *New Yorker* (October 14 and 21): 72–81.

Index

Abramowitz, Morton, 69
Absolute gains, definition of, 37
Abu Dhabi Investment
    Authority, 335
Abu Ghraib prison-abuse
    scandal, 265
Acid rain, 302, 381
Actors, 22
    identifying, 55
    nation-state, 29–30
    nonstate (*See* Nonstate actors)
    state as primary, 395–396
    use of term, 55
Adjudication, 36, 260
Afghanistan, Soviet invasion of, 97
Afghanistan war, 180–181, 196
Africa, population momentum
    and, 368
Agenda setting, 292
Aging, of world population, 369
Agitational objectives, of
    terrorism, 193
Agriculture, crop yields and,
    372, 399
AIDS (acquired immune deficiency
    syndrome), 303, 371–372
Airplane hijacking, 194
Albanian refugees, 256
al-Bashir, Omar, 177
Albright, Madeleine, 225
Al Jazeera, 294

Alliances, 236
    NATO, 277
    polarization and, 191
Al Qaeda, 99, 195, 196
Amnesty International, 160, 357
Analysis, levels of, 16–18, 21t, 23
    individual, 17, 21t
    state, 17–18, 21t
    systemic, 18, 21t
Analytical framework, 16
Anarchy, 40, 52
Andean Group, 127
Andropov, Yuri, 97
Angell, Norman, 35
Angola, 193
Anheuser-Bush, 320
Annan, Kofi, 244, 340, 398
Anti-Americanism, 248
Antidumping duties, 317
Antipersonnel landmines (APLs),
    244–245
Appeasement, definition of, 89
Applebaum, Anne, 8
Apple iPod, 290, 299
Arab National Congress Party
    (NCP), 177
Aral Sea, 383
Arbatov, Georgi, 19, 98
Arbitrage, 300
Arbitration, 260
Ardrey, Robert, 182

Arias, Oscar, 207
Aristotle, 263, 394
Armed conflict, 176–202. *See also*
    Wars
    causes of, 181–192
    changing frequency of, 180f
    future of, 192–198
    human nature and, 181–183
    internal characteristics of states
        and, 184–189
    system structure/processes and,
        189–192
    trends in, 178–181
Arms control, 240–245. *See also*
    Weapons
    bilateral arms control and disar-
        mament, 241–242
    definition of, 241
    versus disarmament, 241
    multilateral arms control and
        disarmament, 243–244
    patterns of, 245–246
    problematic future of, 244–245
Arms race, 238
Aron, Raymond, 227
"Asian Tigers," 122
Asia-Pacific Economic Cooperation
    (APEC) (1989), 127, 158–159
Association of Southeast Asian
    Nations (ASEAN), 127,
    158, 333

Asylum, 354
Asymmetric warfare, definition of, 192
Attribution biases, definition of, 13
Augustine, Saint, 31
Autocratic rule, definition of, 65
Axis trio, 88

Baker, James, 58, 332
Balance of payments, 324
Balance of power, 234–240, 236
  anti-hegemonic alliance, 238
  arms control and, 240–245
  assumptions of theory of, 235–239
  balancing process, 235–237
  in contemporary international system, 245–252
  difficulties with systems of, 237–239
  future competion in, 247–252
  managing, through concert of great powers, 239–240
Balance of trade, 327
Balancer role, 236
Baldwin, David, 205
Banco del Sur (Bank of the South), 126–127
Bandwagon, definition of, 94
Bandwagoning, 237
Ban Ki-moon, 1, 381
Barter, definition of, 117
Batic, Vladan, 257
Bazerman, Max, 387
Beggar-thy-neighbor policies, 321
Behavioralism, definition of, 50
Behavioral science, 49
Beitz, Charles, 355
Berger, Peter, 40
Berlin Wall, 247
Bevan, Aneurin, 213
Bhagwati, Jagdish, 308
Big Mac PPP, 325
Bilateral, definition of, 151
"Billiard ball model," 160
bin Laden, Osama, 195, 405
Biodiversity, 382, 384–385
Biological weapons, 194, 213–214
Bipolar
  Cold War coalitions, 247
  definition of, 93
  versus multipolar and, 190

Bipolar systems, centers of power and, 190
Bismarck, Otto von, 39
Blair, Tony, 38, 269
Bohr, Niels, 403
Bolívar, Simón, 107
Bolivian Alternative for the Americas (ALBA), 108
Bolton, John, 150, 261
Bonaparte, Napoleon, 81–82
"Bottleneck" period, 376
"Bottom-up" evolutionary strategy, 279
Bourgeoisie, 45
Brain drain, 353
Bremer, Stuart, 394
Bretton Woods monetary system, 324–329
Brezhnev Doctrine, 71
Brinkmanship, 216, 230
Bronfenbenner, Urie, 14
"Brooding shadow of violence," 5
Brown, Lester, 363
Brundtland Commission, 373
Brzezinski, Zbigniew, 68, 402
Buffet, Warren, 111
Bunn, Matthew, 213
Bureaucratic games, 70
Bureaucratic politics, definition of, 68
Bush, George H. W., 19, 183, 361
Bush, George W., 8, 196–197, 374, 405
  arms control and, 242
  India and, 233
Bush Doctrine, 197

Capitalism, 107
  socialist view of, 45
  structural positions of, 45
Capital mobility hypothesis, 300
Caribbean Basin Initiative, 331
Caribbean Community (CARICOM), 158
Carr, E. H., 31
Carrying capacity, 364
Cartel, 375
Carter, Jimmy, 97
Castro, Fidel, 107, 226

Cell phones, 290
Central American Free Trade Agreement (CAFTA) (2005), 127
Central Intelligence Agency (CIA), Sandinista government and, 271–272
Chad, 177–178
Chains of causation, 20
Chamberlain, Neville, 89
Change, constructivism and, 43
Chávez, Hugo, 107, 109, 332
Chemical weapons, 194, 213–214
Chemical Weapons Convention (1993), 213, 244
Cheney, Dick, 57
Chernenko, Konstantin, 97
Children
  child labor, 358
  human rights and, 358
China
  coal use in, 381
  U.S. debt and, 339
  U.S. reaction to growing power of, 248–249
Chlorofluorocarbons (CFCs), 382
Christian Identity Movement, 193
Churchill, Winston, 5, 93, 236, 238
CIA. *See* Central Intelligence Agency (CIA)
Cicero, 263
Civilization, beginnings of, 4
Civil wars
  definition of, 180
  demographic stress and, 184–185
Clarity, of theory, 48
Clash of civilizations, 400
Class divide, 118t
Claude, Inis L., 239
Clemenceau, Georges, 88
Climate change, 1, 379–380
Climate Protection Agreement, 381
Climatological changes, 377–382
Clinton, Bill, 38, 71
Cloning, 372
"CNN-effect," 292
Coal, atmospheric effect of, 381
Cobden, Richard, 34, 35

Coercive diplomacy, 221–227
  definition of, 221
  economic sanctions, 224–227
  effective use of, 223
  persuasive use of military force,
    221–223
Coercive objectives, of terrorism,
  193
Cognitive dissonance, definition of,
  13
Cohen, Joel, 365
Cold War
  bipolarity-associated coalitions of,
    247
  causes and evolutionary course of,
    93–98
  from coexistence to détente, 97
  confrontation, 94–97
  consequences of, 98–99
  direct opposition pattern of,
    246–247
  dismantling of Berlin Wall, 247
  end of, 19–20, 21t, 41, 247
  ideological contest of, 9
  key events in U.S.-Soviet
    relations, 96f
  possibility of "new" Cold War,
    401–403
  from renewed confrontation to
    rapprochement, 97–98
  transformation of world politics
    and, 7
Cole, Juan, 8
Collective defense
  definition of, 277
  regional security organizations
    and, 275–277
Collective goods, 318–319
Collective security
  definition of, 36
  difficulties of, 273
  League of Nations and, 272–273
  logic of, 272–273
"Collective self-regulation," 273
Collier, Paul, 135
Colonialism, 110
Commercial liberalism, 313,
  314–315
Common but differential responsi-
  bilities principle, 390

Common Foreign and Security
  Policy (CFSP), 155, 281
Communications, globalization and,
  289–291
Communist Manifesto (Marx and
  Engels), 45
Communitarianism, 344
Communities, rights of, 355
Comparative advantage, 314
Compellence, 216–217, 230
"Competition" pattern, 246
Complex interdependence,
  definition of, 36
CompuPacific International, 287
Computers, global communication
  and, 290
Comte, Auguste, 396
Concert, definition of, 240
Concert of Europe, 239
Conciliation, 260
Conditionality, 129
Conference of the Human
  Environment (UN), 373
Conflict resolution, in liberal
  theory, 34
Conflict spiral, 243
Congress of Vienna, 81–82, 239
Consequentialism, definition of, 39
Constitutional democracy, defini-
  tion of, 65
Constitutive norms, 41
Constraining norms, 41
Constructivist theory
  constructivist worldview, 40
  critical theory and, 42
  evolution of constructivist
    thought, 40–43
  limitations of constructivism, 43
  realist and liberal theories com-
    pared to, 41
Contagious diseases, 371–372
Containment, definition of,
  20, 95
Contingent behavior, definition of,
  22–23
Conventional Forces in Europe
  Treaty, 98
Convention to Combat
  Desertification, 384
Copenhagen Consensus, 387

Core, in capitalist world economy,
  45–46
Cornish, Edward, 22
Corn Laws, 35
Cosmopolitanism, 344
Council of Arab Economic Unity
  (CAEU), 158
Counterfactual reasoning, 405
Counterforce targeting strategy, 216
Counterterrorism, 194, 196–198
Countervailing duties, 317
Countervalue targeting strategy, 216
Countries, as actors in world
  politics, 55
Covert operations, definition of, 222
Crises, international (frequency of),
  222f
Critical theory, 42
Crop yields, 380, 399
Crosscutting cleavages, definition
  of, 191
Cross-regional bilateral
  agreements, 333
Crutzen, Paul, 388
Cuba, economic sanctions and, 226
Cuban Missile Crisis, 97
Cultural differences, 399–401
Cultural imperialism, 293–294
Currency exchange system, 325f
Cyberterrorism, 194
Cycles, of world leadership, 83
Cyclone Nargis, 341

Dante, 278
Danube River Commission, 279
Da Porto, Luigi, 192
Darfur, 176–177, 179
Darwin, Charles, 182
"Death instinct," 198
"Death of distance," 291
Death penalty, 356
Déby, Idriss, 178
Decatur, Stephen, 186
Decision making. See Foreign policy
Declaration by legitimate authority,
  264
Declaration on the Granting of
  Independence to Colonial
  Countries and Peoples, 116
Decolonization, definition of, 111

Defensive realism, 31–32
Deforestation, 383, 393
de Gaulle, Charles, 213
Deibel, Terry, 254
Del Ponte, Carla, 257, 270
Democracy, location of democratically governed countries, 67m
Democratic peace, definition of, 66
Demographics. *See also* Global demographic patterns
  demographic stress, 184–185
  demographic transition, 369
Dependency theory, 45, 120
Dependent development, definition of, 121
Derivatives, 300
Desertification, 383–384
Détente, 97
Deterrence, 217
Deterrence by denial, 217
Deterrence by punishment, 217
de Tocqueville, Alexis, 93
Deutsch, Karl, 186
Development, definition of, 119
Devolution, 281–282, 351
Diasporas, definition of, 163–164
Dickinson, G. Lowes, 190
Digital divide, 290, 292f
Digital information technology, 165
"Digital war," 4–5
Dingiraddamu, 4
Diplomatic recognition, 260
"Diplomatic Revolution of 1756," 246
Direct deterrence, 217
"Direct opposition" pattern, 245–246
  bipolar system of, 246
  in Cold War, 246–247
Disarmament
  arms control *versus,* 241
  bilateral arms control and, 241–242
  definition of, 241
  multilateral arms control and, 243–244
  problematic future of, 244–245
Discrimination principle, 264
Disintegrative trends, 7, 48

Displaced people, 352
Dispute resolution (legal norms), 260
Diversionary theory of war, definition of, 65
Djindzic, Zoran, 257
Dobson, William, 8
Doha Round, 311
Dollar convertibility, 326
Domestic sources, of foreign policy, 63–69
  economic conditions, 64–65
  military capabilities, 64
  organizational processes and politics, 68–69
  type of government, 65–66
Domino theory, definition of, 94
Doyle, Michael, 246
Dualism, definition of, 121
Dulles, John Foster, 216

Earth Summit, 373, 385
Easter Islanders, 393
Eastern Front, 178
Eban, Abba, 259
Economic and Social Council (UN), 145–146, 148f
Economic Community of West African States (ECOWAS), 158, 159
Economic conditions, and foreign policy, 64–65, 187
Economic hierarchy, 9
Economic nationalists, 316
Economic rights, 355
Economics. *See also* Hegemony
  commercial liberalism, 313
  laissez-faire, 314
  politics and (*See* International political economy)
Economic sanctions, 223, 224–227
Economy
  domino effect in global finance, 329
  global concerns in twenty-first century, 330–336, 396–397
  global economic governance, 334–336
  growth of global trade and wealth, 330f
  of the United States, 320

Ecopolitics, 302, 373
  of the atmosphere, 377–382
  challenges of, and global agenda, 398
  of energy, 374–377
  of land and water, 382–385
Eden, Anthony, 338
Einaudi, Luigi R., 361
Einstein, Albert, 278
Eisenhower, Dwight, 100, 207, 227, 338
Embargo, 224
Emerson, Ralph Waldo, 71
Emigration, 304
Enabling norms, 41
End of history, 400
Energy consumption, 378t
Energy security, 376–377
Engels, Friedrich, 45
"English School" of international relations, 284
Enlightenment, 35
Environmental issues, 302
  policy choices, 386–388
  sustainable development, 373
Eritrea, 178
Estrada, Joseph, 290
"Ethnic cleansing," 256
Ethnopolitical group, definition of, 160
Ethnopolitical movements, 160–161
E-tutoring industry, 287
Euro, as world's reserve currency, 333
Europe, declining population of, 368
European Atomic Energy Community, 155
European Coal and Steel Community, 155
European Constitutional Treaty, 157
European Court of Justice, 157
European Economic Community, 155
European integration, 38
European Payments Union, 326
European Rapid Reaction Force, 281

European Union, 155–158
  as neofunctional approach to
      integration, 280–282
  principal institutions of, 156
  Turkey and, 156
Exchange rates, 300, 323, 325f
  floating exchange rates, 327
  fluctuating currencies and, 329
Executions, 356
Explanatory power, of theory, 48
Explort-led industrialization,
      definition of, 125
Exponential growth, 364
Export quotas, 316
Extended deterrence, 217, 247
Externalities, definition of, 130
External sociocultural constraints, 182
Extinction of species, 385

Failed/failing states
  definition of, 124
  Global South and, 198f
  terrorist groups and, 197–198
"False positives," 220
Falsifiability, of theory, 48
Family planning, 371. *See also*
      Population growth
Famine, 372
Fanaticism, 352
Feminism, 46–47
Fertility rate, 366, 367
Fertilizers, 399
Finance, globalization of, 299–301
Firebreak, 215
First World, 111
Fixed exchange rates, 324
Floating exchange rates, 327
Forced migration, 304–305
Forecasting world futures, 395f
Foreign direct investment (FDI),
      130, 165
Foreign exchange market, 300
Foreign policy, 56–79. *See also*
      Domestic sources, of foreign
      policy
  constraints on process of, 73–77
  decision making theory and
      practice, 76t
  determinants of state choices in,
      60–61

dynamics of, 61f
emerging threats and, 78–79
explaining, 59–61
individual sources of, 70–73
international sources of, 61–63
just war doctrine, 263
liberals and, 38–39
procedural rationality, 76–77
territorial conquest, 9
U.S. economy and, 339
Forests, biodiversity and, 385
Fossil Free Energy Scenario, 378
Fossil fuels, 378t, 381
Franco, Francisco, 89
Frank, André Gunder, 45
Frankfurt School of critical social
      theory, 40, 42
Franklin, Benjamin, 15
Franz Ferdinand Archduke,
      86, 394
Frederick the Great (king of Prussia),
      205
Free market systems, 187
Free ride, 319
Free trade
  fate of, 331
  largest bloc of, 155
  in liberal theory, 35, 315t
Free Trade Area of the Americas
      (FTAA), 108, 332
Freshwater depletion, 383
Freud, Sigmund, 182, 198
Friedman, Thomas, 398
Fukuyama, Francis, 182, 399–400
Functionalism, 279–280

Gabriel, Sigmar, 385
Gaddis, John Lewis, 249
Game theory, 200–202
Garrido, Diego Lopez, 341
Garrison, Jean, 69
Gates, Bill, 111
Gender, and international relations,
      46–47
Gender Empowerment Measure
      (GEM), 350
Gender myopia, 350
General Agreement on Tariffs and
      Trade (GATT), 151, 321
General Assembly (UN), 145, 148f

Genetically engineered crops, 372
Genetically modified crops, 399,
      400
Genetic engineering, 372
Geneva Disarmament Conference
      (1932), 36
Geneval Protocol, 213
Genocide, 351
Geopolitics, definition of, 63
Georgia, Republic of, 402–403
German unification, 203–204
Germany
  occupation zones, after WWII, 92
  in World War II, 19
Gerson, Michael, 33
Giddens, Anthony, 41
Global Crop Diversity Trust, 385
Global demographic patterns,
      365–370, 365–372, 367f
Global East
  definition of, 122
  energy demands of, 376
  map, 110m
Global inequalities, 109–110
Globalization, 289–294
  American media influence and,
      291–294
  changing nature of state power
      and, 206–208
  definition of, 288
  economics of, 294–301
  ecopolitics, 302
  ethical responsibility and,
      308–309
  of finance, 299–301
  global information age, 289–292
  health and, 302–303
  levels of, 297f
  offshore outsourcing, 287
  protests against symbols of, 152
  of trade, 295–299
"Globally integrated
      enterprises," 166
Global North
  arms deliveries to, 210f
  defense spending, 209
  definition of, 109
  demographic divide with Global
      South, 365–370, 367f
  energy consumption of, 374–375

Global North (*continued*)
  global economy and, 187–188
  human development and, 347
  labor needs of, 369
  map of, 110m
  migration to, 352
  military expenditures since 1960,
    209, 209f
  population momentum, 368
  poverty and, 343
  tariffs and, 331
Global security
  politics of, 175 (*See also* Armed
    conflict; Terrorism; Wars)
  preparations for, 401–402
Global South, 106–138
  arms acquisitions and, 124, 188
  arms deliveries to, 210f
  capital investments in, 132f
  colonial experience of, 111–117
  defense spending, 209
  definition of, 109
  deforestation in, 383
  demographic divide with Global
    North, 365–370, 367f
  dependency theory, 120–121
  development goals, 119t
  disparities between Global North
    and, 117–123
  economic development theory,
    120
  energy demands of, 376
  external debt of, 327
  foreign aid, investment, and debt
    relief for, 128–134, 129f
  future of, 135
  human development and, 347
  infant mortality rates, 343
  Internet users in, 290
  map of, 110m
  migration and, 352
  military expenditures since 1960,
    209, 209f
  multinational corporations in, 131
  natural disasters and, 124–125
  in a new international economic
    order, 125–126
  nonalignment and, 123–124
  population growth rates, 365–366
  population momentum, 368

poverty, and imperial past, 112
  regional trade regimes, 127–128
  self-determination and decoloni-
    zation, 116–117
  tariffs and, 331
  terrorist networks and, 197
Global system
  macropolitical persepective of, 22
  micropolitical perspective of, 22
Global terrorism, 194, 195f
Global village, 289
Global warming, 302, 377–382,
    379f
  climate change, 379–380
  deforestation and, 383
  devastating effects of, 380
Goldman Sachs, 287
Gold standard, 329
Good offices, 260
Gorbachev, Mikhail, 20, 41, 73, 98
Gore, Al, 381
Government, type of, and impact on
    foreign policy, 65–66
Greater East Asian Co-Prosperity
    Sphere, 91
"Great Fear" of communism, 95
Great-power politics
  emerging centers of power, 101f
  "just" equilibrium among
    powers, 240
  multipolarity replacement of
    unipolarity, 101–103
  unipolar movement (U.S.),
    99–100
Greek city-states, 65
Greenhouse effect, 379
Greenhouse gases, 381, 389–390
Greenpeace, 160
Green revolution, 399
Greenspan, Alan, 335
Grieco, Joseph, 321
Grotius, Hugo, 263, 264
Group of Eight (G-8), 328
Group of Five, 327–328
Group of 77 (G-77), 126, 147
Group of Seven (G-7), 328
Groupthink, definition of, 75
Gulick, Edward, 237
"Gunboat diplomacy," 221
"Guns *versus* butter," 207

Haass, Richard, 9, 100
Habermas, Jürgen, 42
Hagel, Chuck, 58
Hammarskjöld, Dag, 274
Han Fei, 31
Hansen, Jim, 379
Hardin, Garrett, 364–365
Hard power, 208
Harman, Willis, 1, 404
Hausmann, Ricardo, 118
Havel, Václav, 3, 7
Health, 302–303
Heavily Indebted Poor Countries
    (HIPCs), definition of, 132
Hedge funds, 328
Hegemon
  definition of, 83
  leadership and the collective
    good, 319
Hegemonic core powers, 46
Hegemonic stability theory, 239,
    318
Hegemony, 317–321
  distribution of industrial power
    and, 319–321
  open markets and free trade,
    318–319
  opposition to, 237
Heilbroner, Robert, 6
Helú, Carlos Slim, 111
Henkin, Louis, 262
Heraclitus of Ephesus, 404
Herbicides, 399
Herder, Johann Gottfried von,
    396
Hezbollah, 140–141
Hierarchies, 9
High politics, definition of,
    38
Hilsman, Roger, 56
Hindsight bias, 405
Hiroshima, 92, 211
Hitler, Adolf, 89, 91, 92
HIV (human immunodeficiency
    virus), 303, 371–372
Hobbes, Thomas, 29, 30, 171
Hobson, J. A., 45, 115
Hodenosaunee tribe (North
    America), 392–393
Hoffmann, Stanley, 262

Holbrooke, Richard, 70, 257
Hong Kong, 122
Horkheimer, Max, 42
Hot Line Agreement (1963), 241
Human choice, and global future,
    403–404
Human development
    human security and, 345–348
    map of, 346m
    measuring, 347f
    women and, 348, 350
Human Development Index (HDI),
    346m, 347f
Humanitarian intervention,
    357–358
Human rights and violations of,
    340–362
    approaches to, 344–345
    of children, 358
    classification of, 355
    definition of, 341–342
    displaced people, 352
    enforcement challenges, 356–360
    evaluating the human condition,
        342–348
    gender empowerment and, 349t
    global refugee crisis, 352–354
    indigenous peoples and, 350–352
    internationally recognized,
        354–356
    major conventions in develop-
        ment of, 359t
    Myanmar cyclone catastrophe
        (2008), 340–341
    in Panama, 361–362
    poverty and, 343m
    responding to abuses of,
        354–360
    versus states' rights, 356
    subordinate status of women and,
        348–350
Human security, 285, 345–348
Hume, David, 35
Humphrey, George, 339
Huntington, Samuel, 400
Hussein, Saddam, 4, 57, 64, 211,
    226, 265, 405
Huxley, Aldous, 186
Hydrocarbon-based economy, 376
Hypotheses, definition of, 50

Idealists, 35–36
Ideas, impact of. *See* Constructivist
    theory
Ikenberry, John, 321
Images
    distortion of, 10
    nature and sources of, 10–14
    role of, in world politics, 14–16
Imperialism, 45
    global (1914), 114m
    in Global South, 112–115
*Imperialism, The Highest Stage of
    Capitalism* (Lenin), 115
Imperialism (Hobson), 115
Imperial overstretch, definition of,
    100
Import quotas, 316
Import-substitution industrializa-
    tion, definition of, 125
InBev, 320
India
    China and, 233–234
    economy of, 122
    gross domestic product of, 233
    nuclear power and, 232
    space program and, 232
Indigenous nations and peoples,
    350–351
    as actors in world politics, 55
    definition of, 160–161
    human rights and, 350–352
    map of, 162–163m
    North American, 392–393
Individual level of analysis, 17, 21t
Industrialization
    export-led industrialization, 125
    import-substitution industrializa-
        tion, 125
Industrial Revolution, 294
Inelastic demand, 224
Infant industry, 317
Infant mortality rates, 343
Infectious diseases, 303, 371–372
Influence of Sea Power in History, The
    (Mahan), 63
Information age, globalization and,
    289–291, 293–294
Information warfare, definition of,
    194
Infrastructure investment, 320

"Inherent right" concept, 267
Institute for Social Research, 42
Institutions and regimes, neorealist
    vs. neoliberal views on, 53
Integration
    functionalist approach to,
        279–280
    neofunctional approach to,
        280–282
    political integration, 279
    regional, 279–282
Integrative trends, 7, 48
Intentions *versus* capabilities,
    neorealist and neoliberal views
    on, 53
Inter-American Development Bank,
    118
Inter-bloc trade competition, 333
Intercontinental ballistic missiles,
    247
Interethnic competition, 352
Intergovernmental organizations
    (IGOs)
    classification of, 143t
    definition of, 142–143
    global, 144–154
    International Money Fund, 154
    protests against, 152
    regional, 154–159
    United Nations, 144–151
    World Bank, 152–153
    World Trade Organization, 151
Intergovernmental Panel on Climate
    Change (IPCC), 380
Internalized psychological restraints,
    182
International aid, Myanmar cyclone
    catastrophe and, 340–341
International Atomic Energy
    Agency, 232
International Bank for
    Reconstruction and
    Development. *See* World Bank
International Bill of Human Rights,
    268
International Campaign to Ban
    Landmines, 245
International Commission on
    Intervention and State
    Sovereignty, 356

International community, doctrine of, 269–270
International Conference on Population and Development, 371
International cooperation, neorealist *vs.* neoliberal views on, 52
International Court of Justice (UN), 146, 148f, 270
International Covenant on Civil and Political Rights, 268, 353
International Covenant on Economic, Social, and Cultural Rights, 268, 355
International Criminal Court, 177, 270
International Criminal Tribunal for the former Yugoslavia, 257
International Energy Agency, 374, 381
International institutions, in liberal theory, 35
Internationalized civil wars, definition of, 181
International Labor Organization (ILO), 147, 280
International law, 259–272
    limitations of, 261–263
    preservation of peace and, 263–272
    sovereignty and rules of, 259–261
International liquidity, 326
International Maritime Bureau, 181
International Monetary Fund, 37, 153, 324, 326
    protests against, 328
International Nuclear Fuel Cycle Evaluation (2005), 244
International organizations, as actors in world politics, 55
International Peace Conferences (1899 and 1907), 243
International political economy, 312, 314–317, 336
International regimes, 37, 160
International relations
    feminism and, 46–47
    use of term, 4
    war as feature of, 5

International system transformation, 9
International Telegraphic Union, 279
International Treaty on Plant Genetic Resources for Food and Agriculture, 385
International Tropical Timber Organization, 383
Internet blogs, 2990
Interstate wars, definition of, 179
Intolerance, 352
iPods, 290, 299
Iran, 33
Iraq
    "digital war" in, 4–5
    invasion of Kuwait, 275
    Israel's preventive attack on, 220–221
    U.S. invasion of, 32
    U.S. war in, 25–26, 180–181, 265
Irredentism, definition of, 163
Islamic fundamentalism, 400
Isolationism, definition of, 91
Israel
    Hezbollah concerns of, 140
    Six Day War, 219
Issue advocacy groups, 168–170
Italian Black Order, 193
Italy, invasion of Ethiopia, 36

Janjaweed militia, 177, 179
Japan
    invasion of Manchuria, 36
    UN Security Council and, 150
Japanese Red Army, 193
Jenkins, Clinton, 385
Jervis, Robert, 43, 240
Jiabao, Wen, 234
Jihad, 193
Johannesburg World Conference on Sustainable Development, 371
John Paul II, 20
Jus cogens, 268
Just cause, 263
Justice and Equality Movement, 177
Justice and Homeland Affairs, 155
Just war doctrine, 263–265

Kalma refugee camp, 179
Kant, Immanuel, 33, 34, 66
Kaplan, Morton, 236
Karadzic, Radovan, 270
Kaunitz, Wenzel, 246
Kautilya, 31
Kellogg-Briand Pact, 31
Kennan, George, 20, 39–40, 94–95, 401
Kennedy, John F., 97, 404
Kennedy, Paul, 100
Khrushchev, Nikita, 217, 218
Kindleberger, Charles, 318
King, Martin Luther-Jr., 255
Kissinger, Henry, 68, 76, 97, 375
Kosovo, 256
Kosovo war (1999), 38
Kostunica, Vojislav, 257
Kouchner, Bernard, 341
Krauthammer, Charles, 150, 248
Kuwait, Iraq invasion of, 275
Kyoto Protocol to the UN Framework Convention on Climate Change, 381, 389–390

Laissez-faire economics, 114, 314
Lake, Anthony, 301
Lamy, Pascal, 312
Landmines, 244–245
Larder, Dionysius, 20
Lasswell, Harold, 5
Last resort, 263
Latin American Integration Association (LAIA), 158
Law. *See* International law
Leadership, world. *See* World leadership
"League of Democracies," 173
League of Nations, 36, 272–273
Least-developed countries (LDCs), definition of, 117
Lebanon Hezbollah, 140
Lebow, Richard Ned, 10
Lee, Steve, 331
Lee Kuan Yew, 357
Legal norms. *See* International law
Legrain, Philippe, 294
Leibniz, Gottfried Wilhelm, 6
Lemkin, Raphael, 351

Lenin, Vladimir Ilyich, 45, 95, 115
Leontief, Wassily, 399
Levy, Jack, 185
Lewin, Kurt, 48
Liberal International Economic
    Order (LIEO), 313, 335
Liberalism, commercial liberal
    theory, 314
Liberal theory
    ethical principle of, 33
    evolution of liberal thought, 35–37
    foreign policy as moral crusade,
        38–39
    liberal institutionalism, 38
    liberal worldview, 33–35
    limitations of, 37–40
    neoliberalism, 37
    realist and constructivist theories
        compared to, 41t
    trade and, 315
Lindholm, Charles E., 310, 311
Lloyd, William Foster, 364
Locke, John, 33
Loder, Bernard C. J., 36
Logic of appropriateness, 42
Logic of consequences, 42
Lomborg, Bjørn, 386
Long-cycle theory, definition of, 83
Lorenz, Konrad, 182
Louis XIII, king of France, 220
Louis XIV, king of France, 237
Low politics, definition of, 38
Luckmann, Thomas, 40
Lugal-Zaggisi, King of Umma, 4
Lyons, Oren, 393

Maastricht Treaty, 155
Machiavelli, Niccolò, 29, 30, 220
Mackinder, Sir Halford, 63
Macropolitical perspective, 22
Mahan, Alfred Thayer, 63
Malloch-Brown, Mark, 178
Malthus, Thomas, 364
Manchester School of political
    economy, 35
Mandate system, 116
Map projections, 11–13
Marling, William, 294
Marshall Plan, 326
Marx, Karl, 44–45, 115

Massive retaliation, 216
Mathews, Jessica T., 139
Mazarr, Michael, 296
Mbeki, Thabo, 106
McCarthy, Joseph, 95
McNamara, Robert S., 243
Mearsheimer, John, 32, 80
Media, and globalization, 291–294
Mediation, 260
Medvedev, Dmitry, 402
Mein Kampf (Hitler), 89
Mercantilism, 315–317
    definition of, 112, 314
    liberal *versus* mercantile values,
        314–317, 336
    protectionism and, 316
Mercator projection, 12
Mercosur agreement, 127, 333
Merkel, Angela, 335
Mesopotamia, 4, 5
Methane gas, 379
Microfinance, definition of, 134
Micron Technology Inc., 287
Micropolitical perspective, 22
Middle Eastern oil, 374–375
Migration, brain drain and, 353
Migration, of populations, 303–305
Miliband, David, 341
Military capability
    biological and chemical weapons,
        213–214
    foreign policy and, 64
    pursuit of, 208–215
    trends in military spending,
        208–209, 209f
    trends in weapons technology,
        211–215
    trends in weapons trade, 210–211
Military hierarchy, 9
Military-industrial complex, defini-
    tion of, 210
Military intervention, definition of,
    221–222
Military necessity doctrine, 267
Military proportionality, 264
Military strategy, in nuclear age,
    215–227
    compellence, 216–217
    deterrence, 217
    preemption, 218–220

Military supremacy, as state
    goal, 32
"Millennium+5" reforms, 149
Millennium Round, 322
Milosevic, Slobodan, 38,
    256–258
Minorities at Risk Project, The, 352
Mirror image, definition of, 14
Mishra, Brajesh, 213
Modernization, definition of, 120
Monetary policy
    Bretton Woods monetary system,
        324, 326–329
    coordinating global monetary
        policy, 328
    elements of, 323–324
    reform of global financial
        architecture, 329
Money supply, 323
"Monopoly stage of capitalism," 115
Montesquieu, 35
Montevideo Convention on the
    Rights and Duties of States,
    259
Montreal Protocol on Substances
    That Deplete the Ozone Layer,
    382, 390
Moral hazard, definition of, 37
Morgenthau, Hans J., 31, 246, 262
Most-favored nation (MFN)
    principle, 330
"Most favored" trading partner, 151
Moynihan, Daniel Patrick, 330
Multi-Fiber Arrangement, 316
Multilateralism, 321
Multinational corporations (MNCs),
    164–165
    as actors in world politics, 55
    definition of, 117
    impact of, in Global South, 131
    production facilities of, 298
    strategic corporate alliances and,
        299
Multiple independently targetable
    reentry vehicles (MIRVs)
    definition of, 214
    START agreement and, 242
Multipolar
    and bipolar compared, 190
    definition of, 93

Multipolar (continued)
  systems, power distribution and,
    190
Mutual assured destruction (MAD),
  218
My American Journey (Powell), 58

Nagasaki, 92
Napoleonic Wars, 81–82
Nasrallah, Hassan, 140
Nasser, Gamal Abdel, 219, 338
National Counter-Terrorism
  Center, 192
Nationalism
  conflict and, 185–186, 186
  definition of, 20
Nation-state, use of term, 60
Natural disasters, 124–125
Natural resources, and population
  growth, 364
Nazi Germany, 19, 92
Nazi Party, 89
Nearshoring, 287
Neofunctionalism, 280–282
Neoliberalism, 37
Neomercantilism, 315–316
Neorealism, 31
Newgroup syndrome, definition
  of, 75
New International Economic
  Order (NIEO), definition
  of, 126
Newly industrialized countries
  (NICs), definition of, 121
"New tigers," 122
New World Information and
  Communication Order
  (NWICO), 293
Nicaragua, Marxist regime in, 271
Niebuhr, Reinhold, 31
Nixon, Richard, 97
Nonaligned Movement (NAM),
  123
Nonalignment, definition of, 123
Nondiscrimination trade principle,
  330, 333
Nongovernmental organizations
  (NGOs), 159–170
  as actors in world politics, 55
  definition of, 142, 143

ethnopolitical movements,
    160–161
  issue-advocacy groups and global
    civil society, 168–170
  multinational corporations,
    164–165
  rankings by size of economy/
    revenues, 167–168t
  religious movements, 161–164
  transnational banks, 165
Nonintervention, 260, 269
Nonstate actors. See also
    Intergovernmental organiza-
    tions (IGOs);
    Nongovernmental organiza-
    tions (NGOs)
  definition of, 9
  global diplomacy and, 170–171
  global future and, 170–171
  numbers of, since 1900, 142t
  types of, 141–143
Nontariff barrier, 295, 317
Noriega, Manuel, 361–362
Norms
  definition of, 41
  as sources of action, 41–42
North American Free Trade
    Agreement (NAFTA) (1994),
    127, 331–332
North Atlantic Treaty Organization
    (NATO), 38, 158, 246–247,
    250, 277
  in geostrategic balance of power,
    251m
  as IGO, 142
  U.S. intervention in Iraq
    and, 252
Nuclear arms, 194
Nuclear "club," 212
Nuclear Nonproliferation Treaty
    (NPT), 212–213, 232, 243
Nuclear power debate, 377
Nuclear testing, 212
Nuclear utilization theory (NUTS),
  218
Nuclear weapons, 211–213. See also
    Arms control; Disarmament;
    Military strategy, in nuclear age
  zero-yield nuclear experiments,
    245

Nuclear winter, 215–216
Nye, Joseph, 50, 102, 237

Obama, Barack, 286, 397
Obstructionism, 341
Offensive realism, 32
Official development assistance
    (ODA), definition of, 128, 129f
Offshore outsourcing, 287
Oil consumption, 374–375
Olmert, Ehud, 140
O'Neill, Paul, 58
On the Law of War and Peace
    (Grotius), 264
OPEC (Organization of Petroleum
    Exporting Countries), 375
Operation Desert Storm, 221
Operation Just Cause, 361
Opportunity costs, definition of, 206
Options contracts, 300
Orderly market arrangement
    (OMA), 316
Organizational objectives, of
    terrorism, 193
Organizational processes, and
    foreign policy, 68–69
Organization of American States
    (OAS), 142–143
Organization of Petroleum
    Exporting Countries (OPEC),
    375
Orthographic projection, 13
Outsourcing, offshore, 287
Overlapping cleavages, 191
"Overwhelming necessity," defin-
    ing, 267
Ozone layer, depletion of, 382

Pacta sunt servanda, 260
Pakistan, nuclear power and, 232
Palestinian Jihad, 196
Palestinian Liberation Organization
    (PLO), 140
Palmisano, Samuel, 166
Panama, human rights violations
    and, 361–362
Pan Am flight 103, 226
Pandemics, 304, 371
"Parable of the tribes," 105
Parallel currency, 326

Parsimony, of theory, 48
Partial Test Ban Treaty (1963), 245
Partnership for Peace plan, 250
Patriotism, 186
Peaceful coexistence, 96
Peace/peacekeeping
    free market systems and, 187
    international law and preservation
        of, 263–272
    military and political solutions to,
        278
    peace-building, definition of, 275
    peacemaking, definition of, 275
    United Nations and, 273–275
"Peace through strength" policy, 19,
    227
Peloponnesian War, 28–29, 29, 248
"People of concern," 353
Perceptions, influence on reality,
    10–14
Pérez, Carlos Andrés, 107
Periphery, of capitalist world econ-
    omy, 45
Perle, Richard, 19, 57
Permanent Court of International
    Justice (PCIJ), 36
Perpetual Peace (Kant), 66
Person, rights of the, 355
Pesticides, 399
Peter's projection, 12
Petróleos de Venezuela, 107
Petroleum, 375–376
Pickering, Thomas R., 361
Pimn, Stuart, 385
Piracy, 181
Pirates, 181
Podcasting, 290
Polarity, definition of, 62
Polarization, definition of, 62
Policymakers
    perceptions of, 10–11
    personality and, 72
Political efficacy, definition of, 71
Political hierarchy, 9
Political institutions, war and, 188–
    189
Political integration, 278
Political proportionality, 263
Political protest, Anti-Americanism
    and, 248

Political rights, 355
Political terrorism, 192–193
Politics
    continuity and change in, 5–6
    definition of, 5
    economics and (See International
        political economy)
    foreign policy and, 68–69
Pooled sovereignty, 157
Population growth, 364
    demographic transition, 369
    global population density, 370m
    international responses to,
        370–371
    population momentum, 367–368
    projections to year 2050, 366f
    prospects for global population
        implosion, 371–372
    urbanization and, 369–370
Population implosion, 371
Populations
    global migration, 303–305
    living in poverty, 343m
Powell, Colin, 58, 183, 265
Power. See also State power
    definition of, 30
    distribution of, and war, 190–191
    realism and balancing of, 234–240
Power cycle theory, definition of,
    192
Power potential, definition of, 205
Power transition theory, definition
    of, 191
Prebisch, Raúl, 45
Preemption, 218–220
Preemptive military attack, 219
Prescription drugs, 385
Prescriptive richness, of theory, 48
Prestowitz, Clyde, 100
Preventive diplomacy, 274
Preventive military attack, 219
Preventive war, 219
Princip, Gavrilo, 394
Prioritization, of world problems,
    386–387
Prisoner's Dilemma game, 200–202
Private international law, 259. See
    also International law
Procedural rationality, definition
    of, 74

Procedural rationality, tenets of, 76
Proletariat, 45
Proliferation, definition of, 212
Protectionism, 316, 317, 326
Proximate causes, 18, 21t
Psychological restraints, 182
Public international law, 259. See
    also International law
Purchasing power parities (PPP),
    101, 135, 325f
Putin, Vladimir, 242, 402

Qaddafi, Muammar, 64, 226
"Qualified majority
    voting," 156
Quarterly Review, 20

Racism, 352
Radicalism, 44–46
Radiological weapons, 194
Rapprochement, definition of, 98
Rational choice, definition of, 59
Reagan, Ronald, 19, 69, 97, 361
Reagan Doctrine, definition
    of, 98
Realist theory
    evolution of realist thought,
        31–32
    liberal and constructivist theories
        compared to, 41t
    limitations of, 32–33
    protectionism and, 317
    realist worldview, 29–31
Rebus sic stantibus, 261
Redfield, Robert, 342
Refugees, 179, 256, 352–354
Regional currency union, 333
Regional integration, 279–282
Regional intergovernmental orga-
    nizations, 154–159
Regional security organizations
    collective defense and, 275–277
    examples of, 277
Regional trade agreements, 312,
    333–334, 334m
Regional trade policies, emerging,
    331–334
Relative deprivation, definition
    of, 188
Relative gains, definition of, 30

Relative *versus* absolute gains, neorealist and neoliberal views on, 52
Religious fanaticism, 196
Religious movements, 161–164, 164
Remittances, definition of, 130
Remote causes, 18, 21t
Remote control warfare, 214
Renatus, Flavius Vegetius, 203
Replacement-level fertility, 366
Repressive terror, 193
Reprisal, 266
Republic of Georgia, 402–403
Reserve Fund for Future Generations, 335
Resources
  "resource curse," 137–138
  resource hierarchy, 9
Responsibility to Protect, The, 356
Responsibility to Protect doctrine, 341
Rhine River Commission, 279
Ricardo, David, 314
Richelieu, Cardinal de, 220
Right intention, 263
Robinson, Mary, 357
Roosevelt, Eleanor, 360
Roosevelt, Franklin, 34, 91, 93, 238
Rosecrance, Richard, 206
Rostow, Walt W., 120
Rousseau, Jean-Jacques, 189, 227
Rowley, Coleen, 69
Rule of law, human rights and, 355
Rumsfeld, Donald, 57, 68, 197, 265
Rush-Bagot Agreement (1817), 241
Russia, 402–403

Sachs, Jeffrey, 398
Samin, Amir, 45
Sanctions, economic, 224
Sandinista National Liberation Front, 271
Sarkozy, Nicolas, 335
Satisficing, definition of, 74
Saudi Arabia, oil production and, 375
Sazonov, Sergi, 85
"Scapegoat" phenomenon, 65
Scenario, definition of, 395
Schelling, Thomas, 22

Schematic reasoning, definition of, 11, 13
Schlesinger, James, 68
Schlieffen Plan, 86
Schmookler, Andrew, 105
Schulz, William, 357
Schuman, Robert, 155
Scowcroft, Brent, 58
Seagate Technology, 287
Seattle, Chief of Suquamish tribe, 388
Secession, definition of, 163
Second Lateran Council, 243
Second-strike capability, 217
Second World, definition of, 111
Secretariat (UN), 147, 148t
Security, 401–402. *See also* Regional security organizations
  building world security, 227–228
  energy security, 376–377
  human security, 345–348
  national security as collective good, 319
  social and environmental protection as issues of, 345
Security community, definition of, 155
Security Council (UN), 145, 148f, 270
Security dilemma, 227
Self-determination, definition of, 116
Self-fulfilling prophecies, definition of, 94
Self-help, definition of, 30
Semi-periphery, in capitalist world economy, 45
September 11 terrorist attacks, 7–8, 69, 99, 195–196
"Seventh generation yet unborn," 393
Severe Acute Respiratory Syndrome (SARS), 302
Seville Statement (1986), 182
Shalah, Ramadan, 196
Shanghai Cooperation Organization (SCO), 234
Shang Yang, 31
Shultz, George, 69

Shwe, Than, 341
Silva, Luiz Inácio Lula da, 397
Singapore, 122
Singer, Peter, 308
Singh, Manmohan, 233, 234
Siniora, Fouad, 141
Six Day War, 219
Slavery, 304
Slomanson, William, 262
Smart bombs, 214
Smith, Adam, 33, 35, 113, 314
Snyder, Jack, 43
Socialism, 44, 187
Social rights, 355
Social structure, 40
Sociocultural constraints, 182
Soft power, 208
  definition of, 99
Soil degradation, 384
Solana, Javier, 38
Somoza, Anastasio, 271
South Asian Association for Regional Cooperation (SAARC), 158
Southern African Development Community (SADC), 127, 159
South Korea, 122
South Ossetia, 402
Sovereignty. *See also* Pooled sovereignty
  constitutive and regulative norms of, 42
  definition of, 60
  globalization and, 306
  human rights and, 269
  rules of international law and, 259–261
Sovereign-wealth funds, 335
Soviet Union
  in Cold War, 19
  invasion of Afghanistan, 97
  key events in U.S.-Soviet relations (1948–1991), 96f
Species extinction, 385
Speculators, 324
Spheres of influence, definition of, 115
Spill over, 279–280
Spinoza, Baruch, 31
Spykman, Nicholas, 63

St. Petersburg Declaration (1868), 243
Stages of Economic Growth, The (Rostow), 120
Stalin, Joseph, 90, 93, 238
Standard operating procedures (SOPs), definition of, 68
"Star Wars," 218
State goals, neorealist *vs.* neoliberal views on, 53
State level of analysis, 17–18, 21t
State of the Future report (UN Millennium Project), 398
State power
  elements of, 205–206
  globalization and changing nature of, 205–208
States
  behavior theory, 28
  definition of, 4
  duties of, under international law, 260–261
  foreign policy goals, 9
  future of, as actors in world politics, 395–396
  globalization and sovereignty of, 305–307
  hierarchies of, 9–10
  human rights *versus* states' rights, 356
  influence of institutions on, 38
  nonstate challenges to, 9
  rights of, under international law, 260
State-sponsored terrorism, definition of, 197
Steingart, Gabor, 288
Stiglitz, Joseph, 134, 320
Strategic Arms Limitation Talks (SALT), 97, 241, 244
Strategic Arms Reduction Treaties (START), 98, 241
Strategic corporate alliances
  definition of, 166
  multinationals and, 299
Strategic Defense Initiative (SDI), 218
Strategic Offensive Reductions Treaty (SORT), 242, 242f
Strategic trade policy, 317
Strauss-Kahn, Dominique, 154

Structural adjustment, definition of, 134
Structural realism, 31
Sub-Saharan Africa
  impact of AIDS on, 372
  population momentum and, 368
Subsistence economy, 117
Sudanese Liberation Army, 177
Sudanese violence, 176–177
Sudan People's Liberation Movement (SPLM), 177
Suez Canal crisis, 338–339
Sumeria, 4
Sumner, William Graham, 164
Sunk costs, definition of, 74
Sun Tzu, 176
SuperValu, 287
Sustainable development, 373–385
Sutherland, Peter, 306
System, 6
Systemic level of analysis, 18, 21t
  neorealists and, 31
  "offensive" realism and, 32

Taiwan, 122
Taliban, 196
Tariffs, 295, 316–317
Technology
  globalization and, 396
  global problems and, 398–399
Telecommunications, 289–291
Tennyson, Alfred, 150
Territorial conquest, 9
"Territorial imperative," 182
Territorial issues, 184
Terrorism. *See also* Cyberterrorism; Terrorist attacks of September 11
  Al Qaeda, 195–196
  communication technology and, 196
  counterterrorism, 196–198
  definition of, 192–193
  global terrorism, 195–196
  terrorist objectives, 193–194
Terrorist attacks of September 11, 7–8, 69, 99, 405
  immigration and, 354
  NATO and mutual defense principle, 250

Terrorist networks, as actors in world politics, 55
Text messaging, 290
Thakur, Ramesh, 331
Thatcher, Margaret, 39, 269
Theoretical thinking, 29
Theory, 29
  criteria for judging quality of, 48
  definition of, 29
Third World, definition of, 111
Thirty Years' War, 59–60, 269
Thomson, 165
Thucydides, 28, 29, 248
Time sequences, 18
"Tomahawk diplomacy," 221
"Top-down" peace plan, 279
Trade
  changes in free-trade regime, 321
  commercial liberalism, 313
  Doha Round of trade negotiations, 311
  emerging regional trade policies, 331–334
  fate of free trade, 331
  globalization of, 295–299
  growth of global trade/wealth, 330f
  Liberal International Economic Order and, 313
  open-trading regime, 331
  regional trade regimes, 127–128
  trade blocs and global trade regionalization, 334m
Trade integration, 296–298, 296f
Tragedy of the commons, 364
Transgenic crops, 372
Transnational banks, 165–166
Transnational relations, definition of, 36
Treaty of Brest-Litovsk, 92
Treaty of Utrecht, 237
Trends, 1–2
  complexity of world politics and, 391
  integrative and disintegrative, 7
Triad, 217–218
Triple Alliance, 86
Triple Entente, 86
Tropical forest destruction, 385
Truman, Harry, 93, 95

Truman Doctrine, 95
Trusteeship Council (UN), 146, 148f
Tuberculosis, 371
Turkey, in EU, 156
TWA flight 847 hijacking, 140, 194
Two-level games, definition of, 74

Ultimatum, definition of, 221
UN Educational, Scientific, and Cultural Organization (UNESCO), 147, 280
Unilateral, definition of, 99
Unipolar, definition of, 99
Unipolar movement (United States), 99–100
Unipolar systems, power distribution and, 190
Unitary actors, definition of, 73
United Nations, 144–151
  changing membership of, since 1945, 144f
  headquarters and global network, 146m
  human rights and, 357
  organizational structure, 145–151, 148f
  peace missions since 1948, 276m
  purposes and agenda, 144–145
United Nations Educational, Scientific, and Cultural Organization (UNESCO), 293
United Nations Environment Program (UNEP), 382
United Nations Framework Convention on Climate Change, 381
United States
  ascending powers and, 102
  China and, 248–249
  in Cold War, 19, 93–99 (See also Cold War)
  dollar exchange rate, 326
  economy of, 320, 326–327
  energy consumption and, 374–375
  global economic governance and, 334–335
  investment in public infrastructure, 320

  key events in U.S.-Soviet relations (1948–1991), 96f
  population momentum and, 368
  unipolar movement, 99–100
  war with Iraq, 4, 25–26, 265
Universal Declaration of Human Rights, 268, 354–355, 359
Universal Post Union, 279
Universal Suez Canal Company, 338
Unmanned aerial vehicles (UAVs), 214
Urbanization, demographics and, 369–370
Urquhart, Brian, 150
Uruguay Round agreements, 321

Vance, Cyrus, 69
Vegetius Renatus, Flavius, 203
Venezuela, 107–108
Vigilance, 236
Violence, based on racism and intolerance, 352
Voluntary export restrictions (VERs), 316
von Clausewitz, Karl, 183, 204

Walt, Stephen M., 27, 100, 239
Waltz, Kenneth, 5, 31, 32, 231
War crimes, 269–270
Wars. See also Armed conflict
  diversionary theory of, 188
  ethics and, 264–265
  generational changes in, 401–402
  geographic locations and, 184
  jus ad bellum and jus in bello, 263, 264
  political institutions and, 188–189
  problems in legal control of wars, 265–266
  root causes of great-power war, 105
  transformation of world politics and, 7
Warsaw Pact, 246, 250
Wars of German Unification, 204
Washington consensus, definition of, 134
Water supplies, 383–384
Watkins, Michael, 387

Wealth of Nations, The (Smith), 113
Weapons. See also Arms control
  advanced, 9, 33
  biological and chemical, 213–214
  delivery systems, 214–215
  ethics and, 264–265
  innovations in, and end of Cold War, 247
  of mass destruction, 194, 197–198, 264
  nuclear, 211–213
  trends in technology of, 211–215
  trends in trade of, 210–211
Weber, Cynthia, 43
Weber, Max, 49, 405
Webster, Daniel, 266
Weinberger, Caspar, 69
Welfare, global, 285
Wendt, Alexander, 43, 278
Westphalian system, 59–60
Wiesel, Elie, 269
Wilhelm II (of Germany), 71, 85, 86
Williams, Jody, 244–245
Wilmer, Franke, 47
Wilson, E. O., 376–377
Wilson, James Q., 182
Wilson, Woodrow, 34, 35, 88, 272
Wireless technology, 290
Wolf, Martin, 308–309
Wolfensohn, James, 343
Wolfowitz, Paul, 57
Women
  feminism, 46–47
  human rights and gender empowerment, 349t, 350
  in positions of power, 350
  slavery and, 304–305
  subordinate status of, 348–350
Woodward, Bob, 57
World Bank, 152–153, 326
World Commission on Environment and Development, 373
World federation, 278
World government, 278–279
World Health Organization, 147
World leadership, evolution of great-power rivalry, 84t
World Meteorological Organization (WMO), 379

World order
  international institutions and,
    272–277
  international integration and,
    278–282
  international legal norms and,
    259–272
World politics, 3–26
  behavioral science and, 49
  constructivist theory, 40–43, 41t
  continuity and change in, 6–10
  effect of 9/11 terrorist attacks on,
    8–9
  feminist critique, 46–47
  forecasting global future with
    theories of, 47–50
  future challenges, 20–23
  future of state in, 395–396
  human security and, 285
  international systems and, 284
  levels of analysis, 16–18
  liberal theory, 33–40, 41t
  macro trends in, 22
  metaphorical expressions used
    in, 254
  neorealist/neoliberal debate in,
    52–53

  perceptions influencing reality,
    10–14
  radical critique, 44–46
  realist theory, 29–33, 41t
  recurring patterns, 394
  role of happenstance in, 394
  role of images in, 14–16
  theories of, 27–51 (*See also* specific
    theory)
  time sequences, 18
  as transition period, 7
World Population Conference,
  370
World Summit on Sustainable
  Development, 373
World-system theory, 45–46
World Trade Organization,
  151–152
  controversy, 322
  future legitimacy of, 335
  globalization and, 295m
  protests, 322
World Trade Organization
  (WTO), 321
World War I, 7, 83–85
  causes of, 85–86, 394
  consequences of, 86–88

  evolution of liberal thought and,
    35–36
  territorial changes following, 87m
World War II, 7, 88–93
  causes of, 89–92
  consequences of, 92–93
  events of, leading to Cold
    War, 19
  reconfiguration of Europe
    following, 90m

Xenophobia, 185

Yalta Conference, 93
Yugoslavia, Federal Republic of,
  38–39

Zakaria, Fareed, 58
Zambia, 133
Zero-sum game, 34
Zero-yield nuclear experiments, 245
Zilog Incorporated, 286–287
Zoellick, Robert, 153